BEN TILLMAN

& the Reconstruction of White Supremacy

The FRED W. MORRISON *Series in Southern Studies*

STEPHEN KANTROWITZ

BEN TILLMAN

& the Reconstruction of White Supremacy

The University of North Carolina Press  Chapel Hill and London

Manufactured in the United States of America
Set in New Baskerville and Serifa by Keystone Typesetting, Inc.
The paper in this book meets the guidelines for permanence and durability of the Committee on Production Guidelines for Book Longevity of the Council on Library Resources.
Chapter 5 has been reprinted with permission in revised form from Pieter Spierenburg, ed., *Men and Violence: Gender, Honor, and Rituals in Modern Europe and America* (Columbus: Ohio State University Press, 1998), 213–39.
Library of Congress Cataloging-in-Publication Data
Kantrowitz, Stephen David, 1965–
Ben Tillman and the reconstruction of white supremacy / Stephen Kantrowitz.
p. cm. — (The Fred W. Morrison series in Southern studies)
Includes bibliographical references (p.) and index.
ISBN 0-8078-2530-1 (cloth : alk. paper). — ISBN 0-8078-4839-5 (pbk. : alk. paper)
1. Tillman, Benjamin R. (Benjamin Ryan), 1847–1918. 2. Legislators— United States Biography. 3. United States. Congress. Senate—Biography. 4. White supremacy movements—Southern States—History. 5. White men—Southern States—Political activity—History. 6. Reconstruction—Southern States. 7. Political culture—Southern States. 8. Southern States—Race relations. 9. South Carolina—Politics and government—1865–1950. I. Title. II. Series.
E664.T57K36 2000
975.7'041'092—dc21
[B] 99-032669

04 03 02 01 00 5 4 3 2 1

Contents

Illustrations

BEN TILLMAN

& the Reconstruction of White Supremacy

Introduction: Ben Tillman, Agrarian Rebel

"This is the message I bring to my people," Senator Benjamin Ryan Tillman warned the South Carolina state Democratic convention in 1918: "[T]he world is passing through the greatest crisis in history." In that final year of his life, some of the particulars of the crisis were new, but most, especially the ever-looming "race problem," were not. Tillman's "people" had seemed to stand always on the brink of racial, economic, and political catastrophe. And if the crisis was constant, so was the white citizenry he intended to awaken: more than a generation after the overthrow of Reconstruction, in an industrialized nation poised on the threshold of woman suffrage, Tillman's "people" still consisted of the white farming men he had idealized and derided, represented and misrepresented throughout his adult life.

Ben Tillman defined his world against the revolutions of emancipation and Reconstruction that had overtaken it in his youth. White men were supposed to exercise productive, independent mastery over individual households and Southern society as a whole, but that mastery seemed to face daunting obstacles at every turn. Black laborers aspired to autonomy. Northern corporate interests—the "money power"—strangled the Southern economy. Republicans plotted to reestablish political dominance over the region. Abetted by a handful of traitorous white Southern men, these forces were slowly forcing the region's productive white men—"the farmers," Tillman called them—into "hopeless servitude" or perhaps even bloody revolution. Only by mobilizing beneath the banner of "white supremacy" could these men defeat their foes and create a peaceful and prosperous social order.

The roots of the crisis facing white patriarchy lay far in the past. Long before Tillman's birth in 1847, the region's leaders had warned of a coming struggle against an abolitionist-inspired slave insurrection. Tillman's brothers had stood among the Confederate soldiers who fought unsuccessfully to hold those threats at bay. In the mid-1870s, he himself had taken bloody part in the campaign of terror and fraud that brought down South Carolina's Reconstruction government. But the counterrevolution that the former slaveholders dubbed "Redemption" did not resolve the region's political and economic crises. Tillman continued fighting, first as an insurgent within the state Democratic Party, then as its leader, and finally before a national audience. Throughout his career as planter, terrorist, reformer, governor, senator, and nationally known orator, Tillman struggled to mobilize the farmers—as a constituency and an idea. His vision and his voice shaped the understandings of millions and helped create the violent, repressive world of the Jim Crow South.

Tillman sought to transform the slogan "white supremacy" into a description of social reality, reconstructing white male authority in every sphere from the individual household to national politics. The project was crucial, for in Tillman's world "racial equality" was an oxymoron; one race or another would dominate, and if white men failed to rally together, their households would be invaded or subjugated by hostile forces. Whether white men faced the federal government, African Americans, or furnishing merchants, Tillman wanted them to do so as masters, not slaves. He therefore imagined a world in which the fearsome alliance of racial, financial, and federal corruption had been permanently vanquished. His idealized organic society was an agricultural arcadia in which "the land-owning farmers were the salt of the earth, and called no man master."

"White supremacy," more than a slogan and less than a fact, was a social argument and a political program. It consisted of ideas and practices, promises and threats, oratory and murder. The golden age Tillman imagined had no need for such a slogan, for until Reconstruction, the idea of white supremacy had been implicit in the legal, social, and economic system of slavery and had been enforced and reinforced at every level of society from the plantation to the U.S. Supreme Court. But emancipation, equal protection, and manhood suffrage had destroyed this congruence between the law and the white male monopoly on authority. As a result, white supremacy was anything but a given in the postbellum South. The economic hardships and transformations of the postwar era drove wedges into the historic fissures among white men and created new ones as well. As old arrangements ceased to function, new ones became more and more imaginable. Interracial coalition politics, for example, no longer constituted the capital crime of fomenting insurrection. Whatever basis slavery had created for white unity had been permanently undermined, and thus in the postbellum era, white male solidarity and collective authority would have to be built on a new foundation. As one of the leading proponents of white supremacy, therefore, Tillman had to be many things at once: an ideologue, an organizer, and a terrorist. White supremacy was hard work.[1]

It was one thing to posit white male unity and another thing entirely to create and enforce it. No singular "white mind" existed in the postbellum South, no white "volksgeist," and therefore the reconstruction of white supremacy would require new forms of mastery. Almost from the moment of their military defeat in 1865, Ben Tillman and his colleagues began a war against Reconstruction. They entered the struggle well armed, for as slaveholders and Confederate officers, they had extensive experience mobilizing white men. In the twentieth century, it has become commonplace to explain the violent campaigns they waged against Reconstruction and later insurgent political movements as the product of white Southerners' "racism." But historic prejudices, however powerful and pervasive, do not by themselves do the work of political organization. Black political and economic striving undoubtedly troubled many white men, but paramilitary groups such as the Ku Klux Klan and Tillman's Red-shirts did not simply "rise up." Rather, men of the leadership class forged political arguments and organizations that put white men's expectations of mastery to work. In 1876–77, amid a national political crisis, they succeeded in overthrowing the elected Republican government of South Carolina.[2]

In this and subsequent campaigns, Tillman and his colleagues mobilized not only white men but also ideas about white manhood. Any real analysis of white supremacy cannot limit itself to studying mechanisms of physical violence and economic coercion, institutional effects, and the efforts of critics and opponents; it must also pay close attention to words and ideas. This does not mean simply exploring rhetorical figures or pursuing an intellectual history detached from other realms of human experience; it means confronting the evanescent and the material, the mental and the elemental, all at once—a formidable challenge. A single life, standing at the confluence of these conflicts, can reveal much about their natures and dynamics. Some caution is required: as Barbara Fields has noted, "[T]aking the former slaveholders seriously naturally does not mean taking them literally." Tillman's private thoughts and beliefs remain unknowable, but his words and deeds together allow us to reconstruct the political world of action and argument in which he operated. In this book, I try to take Tillman's words as seriously as his deeds—not because they had precisely the same kinds of effects, but because both words and deeds were planned, shaped, and directed. They were both part of the project of white supremacy.[3]

The reconstruction of white supremacy succeeded in part because it built on words and ideas with deep histories. White Southerners did not respond to postbellum challenges in the light of what might be as much as in the light of what had been. They knew that from slave conspiracies to Reconstruction militias and labor struggles, black men and women had challenged the barriers to their aspirations. Many whites continued to perceive black aspirations as inherently threatening. Rather than interpreting white responses to black striving as "anxieties"—matters of psychology—we must understand that people committed to racial hierarchy had always had a great deal to be anxious about and that whatever insecurities had characterized slaveholders' rule would only be magnified in the postbellum era.[4] But most white Southerners were linked by more than anxiety. They also shared common, if implicit, understandings of the relationship between race, gender, economic position, and social hierarchies–understandings that made white manhood the center around which all else revolved. Tillman made particularly skillful use of the language of "the farmers," who were implicitly white and male. The work required by "farmers" was sometimes performed by "negroes" but often by "laborers" or simply "hands"; "farmers'" helpmeets were "farm wives." Social relations and language did not function with perfect harmony, as indicated by the existence of black proprietors, female-headed households, and dissolute or incompetent white farming men. The meanings of "manhood" and "womanhood" were open to question and contest, as were the meanings of "black" and "white." But the conflict over such meanings took place within the constraints of people's histories, situations, and imaginations, limiting and even undermining radical challenges.[5]

Human beings rarely understand all the ways their history has shaped them, and postbellum Southerners were no exception. Tillman's radical opponents struggled to reconfigure the meanings of race in ways that would bolster their economic and political programs. They failed, in part because they hewed to a notion of producerism that was rooted in a social experience long reserved for white men only, and in part because whenever they attempted to give political life to a different conception of productive labor, men like Tillman took up arms against them. After the failure of biracial agrarianism, other challengers to Tillman's reconstruction of white supremacy—such as black leaders defending manhood suffrage and white women demanding suffrage—often framed their arguments even less expansively, seeking safety in a shared manhood or a shared whiteness. Exploring the history of white manhood thus helps offer a richer explanation of white supremacy and its challengers than do conventional notions that "race" trumped "class."

The reconstruction of white supremacy required vanquishing white foes as well as black ones. Some of Tillman's most fearsome enemies were not Northerners or black Republicans but other white Southern men. In fact, Tillman spent much of his time and energy attacking those who fell outside the boundaries of defiant, agricultural, white Southern manhood, including white men who formed political coalitions with blacks or Republicans. Tillman and his allies understood race to be a biological fact, but they also understood it as something far more subjective; for political purposes, race could be determined by partisan allegiance and behavior as much as by phenotype. The most important negative reference for white manhood was a vision of black manhood that bore slavery's discursive double load of indolent incapacity and insurrectionary intent. But white men who contemplated a biracial political order were denounced as scheming incendiaries, "white negroes" who deserved whatever punishment they got.

White men could also betray white supremacy by asserting unwarranted authority over other white men—in effect, treating these white men not as equals but as slaves. Tillman, like many of his friends and foes, valued only labor that created tangible goods. According to this theory, sometimes called "producerism," merchants and middlemen were dependent for their livelihoods on the efforts of farmers and laborers. But in the post-Reconstruction decades, these unproductive white men rose to positions of great economic and political power. Mill owners, who controlled the work lives of a growing class of white millworkers, presented an even more extreme vision of white men dominating one another. But Tillman reserved his fiercest attacks for the "Redeemer" Democrats he had helped put in power in the 1870s. He claimed that these do-nothing "Bourbons" and "aristocrats" stood by while the mass of white men slid toward dependence. Effete urban dandies and "dudes," they did not understand the need for collective action and treated agricultural white men with derision and disdain.[6]

These "aristocrats'" incompetence and impotence did not make them figuratively female, for in Tillman's producerist vision, white farm women were far superior to many white men. They were not visions of pedestalized purity but productive workers who could help restore the state's white agricultural households. Indeed, Tillman attacked the "aristocrats" for their blindness to women's legitimate roles. But although farmers' wives required respect, they were not actually or even potentially "equal" to white farming men. They did not belong in politics, which Tillman understood in almost military terms. White women had to be protected from threats to their physical safety, and from the 1890s onward—as the region's transformations altered the nature of interracial contact—Tillman would become one of the nation's most notorious advocates of lynching black men who were suspected of raping white women.[7]

Tillman's stinging, provocative attacks on merchants, middlemen, and the Redeemer leadership drew the attention of the state's white Democratic voters and earned him powerful enemies—powerful but not perceptive: when the state leaders responded to his attacks, they focused on Tillman's rough, rude style, denouncing him as a demagogue who was attempting to lead a white mob. Describing Tillman's putative constituency in insulting and belittling terms, these leaders seemed to be precisely the callous aristocrats Tillman had charged them with being.

To those who understood Tillman as he wished to be understood, the nickname "Pitchfork Ben" fit perfectly. The image of the one-eyed farmer poking at his foes before a roaring crowd masks the origins, intentions, and achievements of Tillman's life and career in just the way that Tillman himself desired. His enemies mistook style for substance; we must not repeat that error. Tillman was no radical. He led no mass movement. Although he claimed to represent reform, he had in the past championed policies hostile to poor men's interests; even after his agitation began in the mid-1880s, he offered no substantial programs to address the needs of debt-ridden farmers and ardently opposed programs that might have helped them. In part, this was because he normally refused to admit that federal power might have a legitimate role, tainted as it was by the memory of the Civil War's "coercion" and invasion and Reconstruction's "radical and negro misrule." Tillman claimed to champion the rights and needs of the farmers, but the aspects of his program that one could consider "constructive"—especially his role in founding institutions of higher education for white men and women—remained tightly bound by his fears of racial equality and federal power.

Even legislation aimed specifically at hampering black aspirations revealed the limits of his devotion to white men's collective rights. His efforts to bring state disfranchisement by imposing educational or property qualifications for voting caused many white men to fear that they, like white dissidents and aristocrats, might find themselves read out of the circle of "real" white men. In fact, his successful disfranchisement campaign depressed white turnout for more than a generation. Tillman's career helps explain how white men came to be their own worst enemies—or at least to elect them.[8]

Tillman did not in any literal way "represent" the men he claimed to champion. This is not the story of the white Southern yeomanry feeling its way from the slave South to the twentieth century, for Tillman was not of that class. It is even more emphatically not the story of the poorest Southern whites, landless people who rarely voted and played only a symbolic part in the campaigns of Tillman and his opponents. Instead of being the story of these white Southerners, in fact, it is the story of political and cultural elites manipulating images and ideas about such people. Tillman's political strength did not lie in his ability to preserve most white men's embattled household independence and precarious political authority—he offered them precious little of either. Instead, it lay in his ability to identify and attack the figures who seemed to pose the greatest threat to such men's independence. In the absence of sustained challenges from people offering more substantive remedies—an absence due in large measure to the violent assaults such people faced from Tillman and his allies—Tillman's slashing attacks at least acknowledged the anger, anxiety, and alienation that many white men felt.[9]

Some of Tillman's achievements were much more than symbolic. He did help set profound limits on black attainment in the post-Reconstruction South, presenting the black freedom movement with challenges that it would take more than a generation to overcome. This was no small accomplishment, and Tillman bragged of it constantly. He never hesitated to declare that he and his fellow Red-shirts had gained power through force and fraud in 1876, and he insisted that white men would always violently resist attacks on their power. He called for the nation to follow South Carolina's example and strip black men of the right to vote. But Tillman's victory did not represent the triumph of racial "radicalism" over a "moderate" or "conservative" alternative. Any close inspection of the lives and careers of Tillman's white Democratic opponents will reveal that they set more or less the same limits on black political aspiration as Tillman set. Like Tillman, they had studied political power in slaveholding's school, and if they sometimes made different choices than those made by Tillman, it was a matter of tactics, not a sign that they were less committed than Tillman to mastery by any means necessary. They all agreed on the necessity of a white-dominated, one-party South, and for the most part, they achieved that goal. By the last decade of Tillman's life, national political programs had to submit to the procrustean bed of white-supremacist strictures if they were to have any hope of passage.

This history of a powerful white-supremacist political leader draws much of its inspiration from recent scholarship in the history of race and gender, but it also builds on other legacies. Sixty years ago, C. Vann Woodward published *Tom Watson, Agrarian Rebel*, the story of a wealthy white farmer who fought for a more democratic, egalitarian South, failed, and devolved into a hateful demagogue.[10] Unlike Tom Watson, apostle of Populism, Tillman represented a Democratic Party that steadfastly opposed radical economic and social transformation; despite Tillman's reputation as an insurgent, he was fundamentally a conservative. Like Woodward's story, this one is a tragedy—not because Tillman failed to fulfill his potential but because he succeeded. In keeping with the irony that Woodward made so central to the practice of history in this field, this book suggests that Tillman's empty, symbolic form of "rebellion" triumphed where Watson's radical rebellion failed. It explores the ways Tillman achieved that victory by building on the experiences and expectations of white men, as farmers, soldiers, and formal political equals. It shows how Tillman used the legacies of the past—including racial slavery and white men's assumed monopoly over political and military power—to make radical challenges unbearably costly for their proponents.

It also shows how Tillman shaped the national understanding of the meaning of racial violence. Although Tillman frequently boasted that the Red-shirt campaign of force and fraud had been a concerted effort, he argued that the roots of racial conflict lay not in politics or economics but in racial instinct. When two races lived side by side, one or the other would have to rule, and by the twentieth century, Tillman could point to electoral violence, labor struggles, and widespread lynching as evidence that white men had prevailed. White men were the most civilized race on the planet, responsible for the world's greatest cultural attainments. Their superiority extended to physical courage and strength: when the purity or superiority of the white race was threatened, white men became capable of the most savage violence.

It was the claim of racial instinct, not the admission of a counterrevolutionary conspiracy, that caught the national imagination and gave "Pitchfork Ben" the reputation that has followed him throughout the twentieth century. Tillman seemed to represent the very "white savage" that he described in his speeches. Volatile, uncouth, missing an eye, and clad in unfashionable clothes, Tillman was easily seen as the embodiment of the Southern "poor white," a man with hatred for "the negro" flowing in his veins. To his critics, Tillman represented an ignorant, intolerant white South that had seized the reins of power from a more cautious elite that, whatever its faults, had sought peace through compromise and accommodation. This consensus was a sign of Tillman's victory, not a description of it.

The persistent violence with which Tillman and other white Democrats met their challengers obscured the meaning of their victories. As a result, just as contemporary observers accepted Tillman's self-identification as the champion of the farmers, generations of Americans came to see white-supremacist violence not as a tactic but as a fact of social life, almost a force of nature. As the twentieth century opened, many people began to believe that Tillman was right and that the politics of white men — Southerners and perhaps others as well — followed from racial instinct or a cultural inheritance so deeply ingrained that it might as well be biologically rooted. If that were true, then Reconstruction had indeed been a mistake and biracial politics were foredoomed. If that were true, the nation might have to accept disfranchisement, segregation, and even lynching as the price of sectional reconciliation. If that were true, then perhaps the United States was — or even is — condemned to remain two nations, separate and unequal, and would never be a truly democratic republic. If that were true.

1 Mastery and Its Discontents

Most of the 40,000 people in South Carolina's Edgefield District had been born into slavery. More than half of the rest, white women and a handful of free black people, could never expect to be citizens. But on the eleventh day of August 1847, Benjamin Ryan Tillman entered his world near its apex. He would never be subject to a master's surveillance and coercion, nor, after childhood, would he face legal subordination to a male relation. Like his father, for whom he had been named, he would be free and independent—and rich, for the elder Tillman owned four dozen slaves and 2,500 acres of land, more than most of his neighbors. Ben Tillman would inherit not only the formal citizenship that came with white male adulthood but also the social power that came with wealth.[1]

But wealth based on slavery came at a price, for neither law nor custom could transform people into things. As workers, kinfolk, believers, and rebels, African Americans pitted their wills against their masters', defying their legal status as property and making the practice of slaveholding a constant struggle. Wealthy slaveholders, especially planters (those owning twenty or more slaves), sought to give their regime a human face, claiming that paternalist concern bound owner and owned into a virtual family, each household a peaceable kingdom in which subject and sovereign alike had important roles to play. But any flowers of mutuality that did develop had shallow roots, for they rested on the rock of coercive force. Masters lived in fear of a servile revolution that would destroy their entire society, a fear periodically reinforced by news of insurrection plots and murderous assaults. Slaves did more than fear: they suffered physical and emotional brutalities for which there could be no legal redress, although barns burned with some frequency and white families seemed vulnerable to food-borne ailments that household slaves managed to avoid. These reciprocal terrors—not paternalist myths of reciprocal duties—lay at the heart of antebellum Southern life. Very few masters and even fewer slaves ever forgot that the essence of slavery was physical domination or that a bullwhip carried in a velvet bag was a bullwhip just the same.

South Carolina's planter elite recognized that control of the enslaved majority demanded solidarity among the group that held a collective monopoly on citizenship—the state's white male household heads. These men ranged from the proprietors of modest family farms to wealthy planters heavily invested in slaves, cotton, and the international export market, all sharing common expectations. In theory, no one, outsider or household member, could challenge a master's patriarchal authority over his dependents, male or female, slave or free. That mastery of household and dependents—whether or not these included slaves—in turn entitled a man to participate in the shared arenas of political and civic life. Household and collective sovereignty provided the ideal against which most white men measured their world.[2]

Wherever they turned, planters confronted social realities that contradicted this theory of independent mastery. Inequalities between masters and slaves and between wealthy and less wealthy whites created profound social tensions. Individuals and sometimes groups resisted slaveholders' authority. Patriarchs who violated community norms in the treatment of their dependents might be disciplined by neighbors concerned with preserving the overall legitimacy of patriarchal authority, and legislatures might formally limit masters' power over their slaves. Participation in the international economy made cotton producers vulnerable to forces well beyond their control. By the 1840s, many planters had come to believe that these internal stresses were being exacerbated and exploited by an abolitionist conspiracy "to check, and if possible to exterminate the institution of slavery." Abolitionists, they claimed, sought to close new territories to slavery, distribute insurrectionary materials and ideas throughout the South, and incite the enslaved black workforce to bloody revolution.[3]

At the moment of Ben Tillman's birth, the men of his class had already begun mobilizing a white male army against the threats to slavery. This mobilization was in some respects as delicate a task as slave discipline: the defense of slavery had to be framed as a defense of a society based on white patriarchal privilege rather than a defense of a particular property interest. In the short term, this mobilization succeeded. In slave patrols, antiabolitionist vigilant societies, volunteer militia companies, and finally the Confederate army, white men stood together to defend their households, property, and communities against threats from within and without. Before long, Tillman would be expected to join them—to share in the society's wealth and government, to share in the solidarity and struggles of master-class life. But during the years of his infancy and childhood, his life depended on his class's ability to maintain dominance over millions of slaves and solidarity with millions of nonslaveholding white men. These struggles defined Tillman's early experience. Although he never served in the Confederate army, he became a veteran of the longer, more ambiguous war to make the world safe for mastery.

The Reciprocal Terrors of Slavery

Slaveholders claimed to have paternal feelings for and relations with their slaves, but they also understood that it was crucial that they be feared. In May 1849, the *Edgefield Advertiser* issued an unusually blunt warning to local slaveholders. Alarmed by the recent murder of county resident Michael Long by one of his slaves, the newspaper editor insisted that "rigid discipline" was the only "wise policy and real justice." Those who indulged their slaves, "yielding to the tender and humane emotions of their hearts," violated the most basic precept of mastery: black slaves—a "race of beings naturally ungrateful and treacherous"—could only "be governed by motives of *fear*." The most grievous offense against good discipline, the editor declared, was the practice of allowing slaves to move about freely at night, for this enabled them to trade in stolen property with "wicked white men." Slaves who fell into this practice and under these influences learned to "despise their Master's authority." Before long, "for the smallest offence," these corrupted servants would "inhumanely *murder* him who was their friend and protector." In short, failure to maintain "uniform, vigilant, and rigid control" over their slaves could cost slaveholders their lives.[4]

As Alexis de Tocqueville had noted in *Democracy in America*, although the fear of slave insurrection was "a nightmare constantly haunting the American imagination," white Southerners generally greeted the topic with "frightening . . . silence." But the *Advertiser*'s warning, remarkable only for its lack of euphemism, reflected no merely local, temporary, or peculiar sentiment. Slaves had risen in revolt throughout South Carolina's colonial history. During the War of Independence, many had fought with the British against their revolutionary masters. Countless plots and panics over the next decades reached a climax in 1822, when Denmark Vesey's conspiracy terrified white Charleston. Ben Tillman's father had already reached adulthood when Charleston's authorities hung dozens of slaves implicated in Vesey's abortive rebellion. Events elsewhere, notably Nat Turner's bloody march through Virginia in 1831, made plain the costs of insufficient vigilance. The *Advertiser*'s warning only reminded slaveholders of familiar but unpleasant facts: the people they owned might kill them in pursuit of vengeance or freedom. As the editor pointed out, Michael Long's murder—for which two slaves were finally hung and a dozen others whipped—was "only one of several similar instances in our District within the last two years."[5]

Deterrence, not murder, was the slaveholders' goal, and domination relied on the credibility of each planter's perceived capacity for violence. The hanging of a slave for murdering his or her master represented a failure—for the master, certainly, but for slaveholding society as well. Slaveholders meted out brutal lashings in part to quash real or perceived threats but also to make gruesome examples of the disobedient. Masters' responses to individual acts of disobedience served as a crucial firebreak, for without credible authority on each plantation, the regime would dissolve into economic chaos and perhaps into violence.

As the slaveholders' foremost historian has pointed out, these men knew that resorting to violence in every instance would mean living in a state of war. But just beneath the surface of the late antebellum era's long truce bubbled the knowledge that punishment and retaliation might be only a heartbeat away. The wealthy white men of the Beech Island Farmers' Club, an agricultural society including many Edgefield planters, understood this dynamic. Four days before Ben Tillman's birth, they met to discuss discipline. When slaves became "impatient, unwilling, and rebellious," one declared, masters could not afford to hesitate or negotiate. "It is necessary to whip if your rules are disobeyed," declared another; "enforce your authority, whip if it is necessary to whip, but *do not threaten*." "[I]nstead of perpetual scolding, and threatening," agreed a third, "use the rod." The preservation of a labor system and a way of life demanded vigilance. "[I]t depends entirely on the management of our slaves," one planter warned, "whether this institution shall continue to exist."[6]

Such catastrophes were more likely to affect individual masters than to affect their society as a whole, for slaves as well as masters knew that insurrection plots ended in failure and death. Split up into relatively small groups on separate plantations, living under the watchful eyes of masters, patrollers, and potentially indiscreet fellow bondspeople, black Southerners focused on carving out less dangerous spaces of cultural and social autonomy than those envisioned by Vesey. But slaves never ceased testing the limits of masters' control. Their resistance frequently took place silently, anonymously, and indirectly. They worked more slowly than they could; they "lay out" in the woods to avoid punishment; they stole from the master's stores; and they traded with free people.

Troubled by these signs of individual and collective will, slaveholders sought explanations. Perhaps, they argued, such behavior was the result of racial incapacity: if black people "naturally" malingered and stole, slaveholders reasoned, then no individual master could be blamed if his slaves were less than perfectly reliable. In private correspondence, local agricultural society debates, and regional journals such as *DeBow's Review*, they made an art (and sometimes a science) of parsing the moral and intellectual shortcomings of "the Negro." In addition to arguing that status and behavior followed race, they suggested that inequality was a natural and beneficent aspect of human society. Savannah River planter James Henry Hammond, convener of the Beech Island planters (and later governor and U.S. senator), argued in widely published anti-abolitionist letters and speeches that blacks formed a natural "mudsill" class, freeing white people from society's hardest and dirtiest work. In the North, heartless employers made wage-slaves of white men, and mobs roamed the cities. Racial slavery, by contrast, had made the South a uniquely fortunate and harmonious society.[7]

Hammond's argument for slavery as a just and organic social order appealed to his fellow planters. Masters hoped that if they articulated the rules clearly enough and enforced them reliably, slaves would accept the legitimacy of their masters' authority. As one planter acknowledged, "[S]o long as the slave thinks he is unjustly held in bondage, just so long will he be impatient, unwilling and rebellious." "You must convince them you are not a tyrant but act on the principle of justice," another explained. The plantation, in other words, must become a just and well-ordered world of familial devotion. Nothing captured this ideal more precisely than the slaveowners' language of paternalism. Slaves, essentially childlike, incapable of higher reasoning, and only haltingly responsive to moral tutelage, required the combination of kindness and discipline that only a father could provide. Since no slave parent's authority had any legal standing—slaves' children literally belonged to someone else—paternal responsibility fell to the slaveholder. Like other children, slaves might occasionally require physical correction. A slaveholder representing himself in this way could refer, without apparent irony, to his "family, white and black." He might frame a slave's act of malingering, theft, or insolence as that of a wayward child, not that of a potential revolutionary.[8]

But this paternalism characterized planters' fantasies far better than it did their society, for forbearance and benevolence could exist only in the space created by terror. At the core of paternalism, in other words, lay brutal coercion. Slaves might be part of a figurative "family," but in fact masters frequently threatened slaves with sale away from their actual families as a way of coercing obedience, a practice that exposed the hollowness of paternalist pretensions. Slaves might be described as erring children in need of correction, but few children of the master class were subjected to the kinds of beatings administered to human property on Southern plantations. An individual master and slave might even develop bonds of real affection and shared experience, but a master's death, illness, debt, or whim could in an instant upset what had appeared to be (and even felt like) a system of reciprocal obligations. A master who forbore, who acted with restraint in every extremity, could hardly expect to turn a profit or even to survive. He needed to be able, in the space of a heartbeat, to exchange the paternalist's face for one of savage, violent determination. Planters who surrendered wholly to "tender and humane" feelings, the *Edgefield Advertiser* scoffed, sacrificed the patriarchal authority they most needed, and this left them dangerously vulnerable to the black and white men who would otherwise remain their subordinates. Not long after Ben Tillman's second birthday, a local white man was killed while trying to subdue a shotgun-wielding slave; the killer, the *Advertiser* claimed, "frankly admits that his former master was a kind and indulgent man." Whatever the slave had actually said, however his master had actually behaved, it was impossible to miss the intended point: unchecked leniency had wrought deadly mischief.[9]

For this racial system of labor control to function, slaves had to understand that they had a simple choice: obedience or retribution. The slave who approached a master deferentially to seek a favor might or might not gain it. But the slave who seriously overstepped the bounds of appropriate submission would face no such uncertainty. On an isolated plantation on a hot July afternoon, a master facing a recalcitrant or rebellious slave had only one aim: to make an example of that person by bringing him or her brutally to heel. The slaveholders never forgot for more than passing moments that their dominance—"legitimate" or not—above all required fear.

King Cotton and His Subjects

Participation in the international cotton economy made the Tillmans rich, but it also enmeshed them in financial networks that, like slavery, they could not fully control. Cotton might have been "King," as Hammond insisted on the floor of the U.S. Senate, but not in precisely the way that he meant. Having staked their livelihoods on cotton, planters became less the masters of the staple crop than its subjects. No theory or exhortation could alter large cotton producers' profound dependence (there was no other word for it) on outside capital to produce and market their crop. Fluctuations in the international market created uncertainty even among the very wealthy. At Ben Tillman's birth, South Carolina was in the throes of a long and painful economic depression. The cotton boom of the early nineteenth century had tied the state and its cotton-producing households to the Atlantic economy. When the price of cotton sank to a near-catastrophic low in the late 1830s, it pulled those households down with it.[10]

The depression ruined many fortunes, and it might easily have brought down the Tillmans. The elder Benjamin Tillman died young in 1849, and with cotton prices low and the plantation's longtime manager suddenly absent, the household could easily have fallen from its lofty economic position. But cotton prices rebounded in the 1850s, and families who had retained the land and slaves to capitalize on the recovery could prosper. Sophia Tillman and her older children not only had kept the productive capital the patriarch had left them but had improved on it. During the booming 1850s, the household's wealth in land and slaves nearly doubled. When Tillman was ten, the family's investment in slavery grew to include thirty Africans smuggled to America on the *Wanderer*. Tillman later remembered these recent victims of the middle passage as "the most miserable lot of human beings—the nearest to the missing link with the monkeys."[11]

But the long depression caused some planters to question their way of life, particularly their dependence on cotton. Planter intellectuals such as Edmund Ruffin and James Henry Hammond disapproved of Southerners' single-minded devotion to cotton production at the expense of economic self-sufficiency. Cotton, they feared, not only wore out land but also constrained planter independence. They sought control over their local market centers, employing a proprietary language reflecting slaveholders' expectation of mastery. "We are justly entitled to supply our own market-towns," Hammond declared in 1856; "they are ours Ours [*sic*] they belong to us and we should allow none to compete with us"—especially Northern manufacturers. He and other "reformers" called for diversification, self-sufficiency in grain and meat production, and a host of legal and agricultural reforms that they hoped would improve the productivity and profitability of staple production. They also set in motion the process of industrialization, hoping that factories like Edgefield's Graniteville would both reduce their reliance on Northern manufactured goods and absorb the surplus labor force, both free and slave.[12]

The end of the depression fatally undermined these efforts to diversify the regional economy. As long as slaves constituted planters' primary investment and cotton prices remained high, each planter would seek to gain the maximum possible return, and industrialization, diversification, and soil conservation would attract more pious words than devout deeds. In the short term, slave-produced cotton was simply more profitable than diversification, and with supplies available from producers in other regions, few chose to dedicate land and labor to pursuits other than cotton production. Industry remained an economic sideline, and the Augusta hinterland did not produce enough corn or pork to meet its population's needs. The planter class as a whole entered the 1850s as single-mindedly devoted to cotton production—and as dependent on it—as it had ever been.[13]

White Patriarchal Solidarity and Its Limits

South Carolina's politics fell somewhat short of the Jacksonian ideal of rough parity among adult white men. In most slave states, politics were substantially shaped by rivalries between planter-dominated black belts and yeoman-dominated white belts. After the spread of cotton into the upcountry by the 1820s, however, South Carolina's substantial population of small slaveholders and nonslaveholding white men was overmatched almost everywhere, even in the upcountry. The spread of cotton culture across the state's backcountry created majority or near-majority black populations in nearly every county. Because South Carolina lacked a coherent white belt—elsewhere a counterweight to planter power—the state's political institutions did not democratize as fully as those of other Southern states. Despite a significant expansion of democratic rights among white men during the first decade of the century, the state retained property qualifications for some offices, and the legislature selected or appointed many state and local officers, as well as the state's federal electors.[14]

Although widely distributed slaveholding retarded formal democracy, it encouraged an unusual degree of social consensus among white men. Slaveholding was more widely distributed in South Carolina than almost anywhere else in the South: historian James Oakes estimates that a white man in the antebellum South had about a 50 percent chance of owning a slave sometime during his life, and by 1850 the average white South Carolina man's odds must have been even better. At midcentury, nearly 50 percent of Edgefield's free household heads owned at least one slave, suggesting that in South Carolina, slaveholding was becoming a normal or perhaps even normative part of adult white manhood. At the same time, planters like the elder Benjamin Tillman controlled most of the society's wealth. Although those owning twenty or more slaves made up only the richest 20 percent of Edgefield slaveholders, they owned 60 percent of all the slaves in the district. At any given moment, a majority of white household heads owned no slaves at all, and the number of slaveholding households in Edgefield fell by nearly 100 between 1850 and 1860. Most slaveholders owned no more than five slaves and relied heavily on the labor of white family members. But in 1850, more than half of Edgefield's 22,000 slaves belonged to just 360 planter households, and the wealthiest 10 percent of slaveholders—including the Tillmans—controlled more than half the total wealth.[15]

Wealthy white men sought to limit and defuse the potential conflict between slaveholding and nonslaveholding men by sharing some of the tangible benefits of slavery. A poor white man might be able to borrow or rent a wealthier man's slave for a crucial task or period, and large landowners might allow their less fortunate neighbors to use their lands for hunting, fishing, and foraging. But what a wealthy landowner considered a favor, his resentful "client" might assert as a right. In late 1847, schoolmaster, minister, and proslavery ideologue Iveson Brookes received word from an overseer in Georgia that a "bad neighbour," William Lumpkins, had grown accustomed to farming on some of Brookes's unused acres. Lumpkins "cursed" and "abused" the overseer for ejecting him, then twice burned Brookes's fence, striking at the literal and legal boundaries of Brookes's household. In dealing with white men such as Lumpkins, the least fortunate of the formally enfranchised, the planters walked a tightrope between sacrificing too much of their own autonomy and provoking a rejection of the regime as illegitimate.[16]

These inequalities among white men did not seriously undermine white patriarchal solidarity, for white men's citizenship did not depend on slaveownership but on the control of a household, a more widely distributed form of authority. The right to direct labor inside the household conveyed the right to participate in political and economic life beyond its borders, and under most circumstances, only adult white men had those rights. Children could not be independent social actors, and most white men agreed that black people's "natural" incapacities, like the lesser but still serious ones of white women, relegated them to dependent social roles. The society's laws, restricting political and economic citizenship almost entirely to white men, reflected and reinforced these axioms of white patriarchal republicanism.[17]

The inequalities of slavery and patriarchy likewise reinforced one another. Just as slaveholders likened their authority to that of a father over his children, proslavery ministers and politicians might—carefully—compare a master's authority over his slaves to a husband's authority over his wife. All three were legitimate forms of the mastery that made a white man independent. The point was not to suggest that poor white men's wives were effectively their slaves; indeed, it was bad form to discuss the hard physical labor performed by white women in poor and even middling white households. Rather, white men's legal and customary power over white women within a family characterized the great majority of households, rich and poor. Although a white man's wife and children had rights beyond those of any free or enslaved black person, white husbands and fathers had final legal and social authority in most matters. They could determine when and how their children were educated and what work wives and children did. The patriarch even had the right to deed sons and daughters to a third party away from their mother. Inequality was the rule, not the exception, in social relations, and slavery was not a "peculiar" institution at all but a more absolute form of the same right and proper power God had granted white men over their free wives and children.[18]

A white patriarch's power operated even from beyond the grave. As a wife, Sophia Tillman could not vote or hold office, nor could she engage in economic activity except as her husband's agent. When she became a widow in 1849, she continued to face legal constraints to her autonomy. The land and slaves she inherited at her husband's death were not hers to dispose of as she saw fit: in order to sell some of the land, she had to petition the county Court of Equity. She had to do the same to gain legal guardianship of her own children. Formally entitled to make contracts and hold property, the widow nevertheless remained much less than a full citizen of the white man's republic.[19]

Other laws sought to reconcile the ideal of white patriarchy with uncomfortable racial and sexual realities. Free black men and women who headed households did so under daunting legal and social constraints. Sexual relationships across lines of color and status—a few of which were sanctioned by marriage—had produced many children whose visibly mixed ancestry presented a threat to "commonsense" definitions of whiteness and blackness and to the relationship between race and status. The state legislature, recognizing that many "white" persons had nonwhite antecedents, refused to ban racial intermarriage or even to establish a legal definition of whiteness or blackness. Jurists (including those upper-class white men who felt most intimately implicated in this history) employed a flexible standard in order to avoid confronting the absurdities and contradictions of their notions of "race."[20]

Lawmakers were even more concerned about the immediate threat posed by manumission. Some slaveholders freed slaves who were also their children, and others rewarded those who performed exemplary service—such as betraying insurrection conspiracies—by granting them freedom. Slaves, especially self-hiring skilled workers, could sometimes negotiate to buy their freedom. Statewide, free blacks numbered nearly 10,000 in 1860, including a few who were wealthy but many more who were only somewhat better off than slaves. But all means of achieving freedom had been limited by the 1820 state legislature, which made manumission illegal except by legislative enactment. A truly paternalist elite might have felt compelled to grant the petition of Edgefield slaveholder David Adams, who sought to free the slave who had guarded the dead body of his son on a Mexican battlefield. But lawmakers rejected Adams's petition, as they did most others. The legislators' reasoning was simple: once the moment of paternalist passion had passed, the community would have to deal with one more free black man—in this case, one who had demonstrated his courage under fire. Sever the ties that bound such people to white patriarchal households, allow them to associate freely with one another, and who was to say what they would do? As the *Edgefield Advertiser* warned, "[A] few privileged negroes will instill corruption and disobedience in all the slaves within their reach." By 1850, hemmed in by law and suspicion, fewer than 200 free blacks resided in Edgefield County, making up less than .5 percent of its population. In the world of Ben Tillman's youth, these people who blurred the racial boundary between slavery and freedom were an isolated and increasingly mistrusted minority.[21]

Other blurrings of that important boundary revealed fissures within white patriarchal solidarity itself. Sociability and commerce between slaves and the poorest strata of white society created a biracial underworld in the slave South. Black and white South Carolinians frequently worshiped together, and not always in congregations dominated by whites or neatly divided into masters and slaves. The state's lawmakers, sensitive to the rights of masters who wished to guide the religious lives of their slaves, barred patrollers from breaking up interracial religious meetings—provided that the congregations had white majorities and the meetings took place before 9:00 P.M. Other meetings and assemblies merited no such protection: white violators' names were to be reported to a magistrate, and patrollers could whip nonwhite participants, including free blacks. Whether or not abolitionist propaganda or ideas passed within these black and white circles, their very existence constituted a threat to the proper lines of authority.[22]

Slaveholders knew that their slaves frequently engaged in illegal commerce with white men, a deeply troubling collaboration against slave discipline. Such illegal trade—"traffick"—flew in the face of slaveholders' authority, their property rights, and their insistence on white male solidarity. Masters warned one another about the evil influence of "disorderly, and ill behaved persons, whether white or black." As the *Edgefield Advertiser* had noted in discussing the murder of Michael Long, it was through trading stolen property with wicked free people that slaves learned rebelliousness. The penalties for trafficking were therefore severe. The slaves involved were punished at the master's discretion, and the white men involved faced criminal sanction. Local planters resolved in 1846 to rid their area of the menace, forming the Savannah River Anti-Slave Traffick Association, and in the early 1850s, the Beech Island Farmers' Club reconstituted itself as an "Agricultural and Police Society." Indictments and prosecutions for trafficking filled Edgefield's court dockets, and numerous white Edgefieldians received up to two months in jail and fines of $100, sentences only slightly lighter than those handed down to white men who killed other men's slaves without proper cause. The absolute loss of property in trafficking could not compare to the loss of a major capital asset like a slave, but as the *Advertiser* had suggested, the influence of such white men on slaves constituted a threat to masters' lives and to the system of slavery itself. The defense of planter power required disciplining white people as well as black, but the punishment of white men for interfering with relations of mastery raised the uncomfortable possibility that slaveholders and nonslaveholders had fundamentally different interests.[23]

The Cost of Violence

The violent careers of Ben Tillman's older brothers suggested yet another fissure among white men in this society—the tension between slaveholders' rhetoric of white male equality and their well-learned habit of violently asserting their authority against all challenges. Even proslavery ideologues ostensibly celebrating white male supremacy might describe the virtues of their society in aristocratic terms. Planter-philosopher James Henry Hammond wrote that slavery had created "a large class elevated above the necessity of any kind of labor" who were able to "take enlarged and many views of every thing; to govern masses; to sway, comparatively, a broad expanse of territory; to control and scorn to be controlled, except by kind affection, sound reason, and just laws." The existence of such a class (to which Hammond happened to belong) was "essential" to "a high state of civilization." But what of the majority of white men who did not own slaves, who did in fact have to labor, and who perhaps constituted the "masses" Hammond claimed the authority to govern? Rich men had to tread carefully, a task they found temperamentally difficult. Expectations of mastery were hard to limit or repress, and white male slaveholders frequently trod on the feelings and perceived rights of other white men.[24]

In the 1850s, as Ben Tillman gained a formal education at the hands of country schoolmasters, he also learned from the dramas of white male violence that pervaded his society. His father had left a mixed legacy to Tillman's older brothers, and they in turn instructed their youngest sibling in the rules governing violence among white men. The elder Benjamin Tillman, fond of drinking and gambling, was among a group of nine men convicted for "riot, assault & battery" by an Edgefield jury in 1841.[25] He subsequently sought to cultivate the virtues of restraint, becoming a member of a local temperance society. But his "rehabilitation" would have been swift in any case: physical conflicts such as brawling and assault were common, and county juries included many men who had recently been disciplined by those same bodies. Punishments of white men for violence against one another tended to be light, and offenders who had been duly punished remained full members of the community. In 1843, the elder Tillman served on the grand jury that had punished him two years earlier. The following year, he was foreman of a coroner's jury. The planter continued to oversee the living and the dead.[26]

Not all conflicts were so easily resolved. Large slaveholders, dependent for their survival and prosperity on the credibility of the masks they wore, extended this sensitivity to appearances into other areas of their lives. Young men of the planter class grew up watching their fathers' ease and forbearance give way almost without warning to violent punishment. And they learned to play out the drama of mastery in relation to other white men as well as to slaves. Benjamin Tillman's sons understood from an early age that no slight or suggestion of insincerity would pass unanswered. Their obsession with "honor"—their refusal to let another person question their words, deeds, or appearances—took its urgency from the exigencies of slaveholding.[27]

Benjamin Tillman feared that his teenage son George, having spent a year as an overseer, had learned the lessons of plantation management and white manhood too well. In an 1844 letter to prospective schoolmaster Iveson Brookes, Tillman noted that George might become involved in social "collisions." The teenager's "*disposition* is such not to *submit* to imposition or insult by any," he explained. To "submit," of course, was to act like a slave, not an independent, honorable man, so the father was perhaps boasting as well as warning. But a young man had to learn how to handle his honor. A carefully nuanced negotiation, mediated by mutual acquaintances, might restore social equilibrium; this, and not a potentially deadly duel, was the goal of the "affair of honor." One way or another, however, white men had to maintain both individual images (and self-images) of indomitability and a collective solidarity that transcended their individual squabbles.[28]

Although George became a lawyer and state legislator, his "disposition" eventually proved to be just as dangerous as his father had feared. In July 1856, at a gaming table in an Edgefield hotel, Tillman demanded his winnings on a bet of $10. A local white artisan, J. H. Christian, supported the dealer's contention that Tillman had bet only $5. Tillman called Christian "a damned liar." Christian replied in kind, whereupon Tillman pulled out a pistol and shot his gainsayer dead. This was not a legitimate expression of white male mastery. As one witness opined, "[T]here was nothing said sufficient to provoke the murder, but if there was it was Tilman [*sic*] who gave it." The Edgefield grand jury indicted Tillman for murder, whereupon he fled, joining William Walker's campaign to create a slaveholding republic in Nicaragua.[29]

It was two years before George returned to Edgefield to face justice, but neither his crime nor his flight rendered him anathema to polite society. Convicted of manslaughter, he served his two-year sentence under lenient conditions; he practiced law from within his jail cell, and before his term was over, he had been elected to the state senate. To be sure, he had murdered a respectable white mechanic—"an independent and an honest man," according to the *Edgefield Advertiser*—but his act was hardly unique. The same hotel where he killed Christian had been the scene of another murder of one white man by another only six months before. Furthermore, Tillman's was a crime of passion. Had he committed a different sort of murder—had he, for instance, plotted to murder his wife and then blamed a slave for the crime, as a white Edgefield man had done earlier in 1856—he might have earned the death sentence. George's crime, by contrast, was palliated by its close connection to qualities that his society valued in its leaders—self-assertion and the capacity for explosive violence. After serving his sentence, he was welcomed into the highest levels of his community's civic life.[30]

He returned just in time to save the family household from the ruin of improper governance. In his absence, John (the next oldest son) had run roughshod over the family's feelings and finances. Ben, the youngest, remembered John as a bully, "naturally tyrannical in his disposition," who "lorded over my mother and the other children to his heart's content." John also speculated in slaves, amassing a $20,000 debt that took his mother several years to pay off. His depredations extended beyond the household: at least three times between 1854 and 1860, he was indicted for riot or assault. In 1858, found guilty in two separate cases, he served ten weeks in jail and was fined $80. Even a convicted miscreant could claim gentlemanly status; that year, John also initiated an ominous exchange of letters with a neighbor, asking him to clarify whether or not he had "characterized my conduct as inconsistent with that of a gentleman."[31]

To Ben Tillman, looking back a half-century later, the contrast between George and John was far more stark than their comparably violent careers would suggest. Indeed, he offered George and John as models of legitimate and illegitimate authority, the one "a second father to us all," the other "wild and dissipated." The final confrontation he remembered between them made the contrast clear. When George returned to Edgefield in 1858 and confronted John about his misdeeds, John drew a pistol. George, Ben recalled, "tore his shirt open and said 'shoot, you dam' coward. You are afraid to shoot, for no brave man ever treats widows and orphans as you have done.' After waiting a minute with his bared bosom, he turned and walked up stairs, and John slunk off." John's undisciplined and irresponsible power—potentially the ruin of the Tillmans' fortunes—had been overcome by George's proper understanding of patriarchal responsibilities, which included sound financial practices, proper treatment of dependents, and (not least) physical courage. Christian's loved ones might not have seen George's virtues in the same light, but to ten-year-old Ben, they had embodied proper white manhood. John, by contrast, followed his ruinous course to his own destruction. While under indictment for assault with intent to kill, John was himself murdered in May 1860.[32]

Anti-Antislavery

Slaveholders struggled to contain the paradoxes of white male independence, but they saw abolition and even "Free Soil" as threats of a different order. As the United States expanded across the continent, Southern elites came to see the increasingly determined antislavery movement as a threat to their liberties and lives. Before long, they feared, they would become an insignificant voice, outvoted in the U.S. Senate and overwhelmed in the House of Representatives. In 1820, they drew the line, fighting for the admission of Missouri as a slave state; they ultimately won a compromise that guaranteed slavery's extension into the rich portion of the Louisiana Purchase below 36°30′ north latitude. They also fought to prevent national policy from favoring Northern manufacturing over slaveholding agriculture: South Carolina took the lead in confronting the national government during the nullification crisis a decade later. The cases differed in important respects, but they both revealed the widespread belief of slaveholders that unless they possessed a virtual veto over federal legislation, they and their institution would not long remain safe.[33]

The 1830s witnessed the growth of Northern abolitionism, a biracial movement that denounced slavery as a moral evil. Northern endorsements of Nat Turner's 1831 uprising irrevocably identified abolition with the slaveholders' worst nightmares. By the 1840s, activists on both sides of the slavery debate warned of elaborate plots to subvert the Republic: antislavery activists thought a "slave-power conspiracy" wanted to rule the nation as it ruled black slaves, while proslavery activists feared that a few more free states would tip the national balance, enabling an abolitionist federal government to outlaw slavery throughout the nation and turn the Southern social order on its head. Controversy over the annexation of Texas, followed by war with Mexico, put the question of slavery's westward expansion at the center of national political debate. Most Americans assumed that this war (fought on the U.S. side mainly by troops from Southern states) would result in the annexation of considerable new North American territory by the United States. It was in this context in August 1846 that Pennsylvania's David Wilmot rose in Congress to propose that slavery be prohibited in any territories taken from Mexico. The Wilmot Proviso proved too sharp-edged a weapon for even the well-practiced defenders of sectional compromise to parry with complete success. Wilmot's resolution gained the support of many other Northern Democrats, worrying those who had counted on the national party structure to preserve the peace and suggesting that even a reliably anti-abolitionist party could not hold sectional feelings in check. Even worse, by shifting the debate from abolition to anti-extension, the Wilmot Proviso made antislavery politics central to Northern political debate. Such resistance to the expansion of slavery made it clear to some South Carolina legislators that the "incendiary machinations" of Northern "fanatics" had penetrated the halls of Congress.[34]

In addition to offering the possibility of martial glory, war with Mexico had promised new lands where poor men and younger sons might earn their fortunes. Edgefield's white men had supported the war with gusto. Throughout the conflict, the *Edgefield Advertiser* reported on the Mexican exploits of the Edgefield Hussars, a company that included the Tillman family's eldest son, Thomas. In the summer of 1847, less than two weeks after his brother Ben's birth, Private Thomas Tillman was killed at Churubusco, becoming one of Edgefield's many casualties in the war. Upon receiving this news, a "committee" of local worthies resolved that they "warmly appreciate[d] the courage and spirit" he had displayed. But Thomas's body could not be sent home to receive due honors in South Carolina because he had been buried in Mexico in a mass grave. When Edgefield's slaveholders organized to oppose the Wilmot Proviso, therefore, some of them had already invested their sons' lives in the new territory. At Edgefield's anti–Wilmot Proviso assembly, the outspoken A. P. Aldrich warned of the "controlling power" abolitionists had gained over Northern politicians and of a "design . . . to interfere with the institution of slavery." Such interference, Aldrich and others suggested, should trouble nonslaveholders as well. In theory, slaveholding households were "families," and any interference with their workings constituted interference with a white man's right to govern his household. Challenges to masters' authority therefore constituted threats to husbands' authority, and vice versa. And if such challenges could threaten or undermine the household prerogatives of large slaveholders—the most powerful white men—then less powerful white men could hardly expect their own authority to remain secure.[35]

By 1850, the controversy over slavery in the West had become a national political crisis. To accomplished peacemakers like Henry Clay, the answer lay in a new compromise package, one that would resolve the interwoven issues of slavery and the territories. But to suspicious slaveholder politicians like Clay's old nemesis, South Carolina's John C. Calhoun, no legislative compromise would suffice. Indeed, nothing short of a new constitutional settlement would restore Southern men—and slavery—to their proper place of honor in the nation's councils. Calhoun believed that this, too, would probably fail, and even as he proposed antimajoritarian constitutional remedies, he and his disciples began to lay the organizational groundwork for disunion in the name of "Southern rights."

The language of Southern rights was intended to rally white men against

Northerners who sought to contain slavery. But even as it identified slaveholding as a Southern right worthy of impassioned defense, it did not place slavery itself at the rhetorical heart of its claims. Rather, it appealed to the shared commitment to white manly independence and suggested that by infringing on white Southern men's right to carry their property and way of life into new lands, antislavery forces were relegating the region's white men — "the South," in its revealing shorthand — to the status of subordinates. Indeed, slaveholders had difficulty discussing infringements of a citizen's rights without suggesting that the victim of such affronts had been enslaved. The staunchly pro-extensionist *Edgefield Advertiser*, urging the county's white men to brook no compromise, refused to "so grossly insult their acknowledged bravery and independence as to suppose for a moment that they will *submit* to these wanton infringements of their rights." Submission was for dependents, not for white men. The Reverend Brookes, for his part, demonstrated that he was as committed to protecting Southern white men's collective rights from Northerners' schemes as he was to protecting his own property rights from William Lumpkins's depredations. In 1850, he published a lengthy pamphlet against Northern "reproaches and incroachments" in which he accused abolitionists not only of seeking to unleash a servile rebellion but also of planning to march south and make the slaveholders themselves into slaves. Slavery as political metaphor and slavery as social institution blurred as Brookes interpreted abolitionism for a local audience.[36]

Abolitionists, slaveholders believed, were plotting to foment a bloody slave revolt. Under normal circumstances, proper discipline could catch potential slave rebels early and make examples of them. But how could planters defend themselves if the catalyst for revolt came from outside the system? During the summer of 1849, the arrival of abolitionist pamphlets in the mail alarmed upcountry elites. How, the *Edgefield Advertiser* demanded, had the senders obtained the names of those to whom they addressed the pamphlets? What other information did they have? And what else did these "secret agents" intend? "There are no doubt, men lurking at this time, in our midst," declared the paper. "The community should have an eye upon them. At a time like the present *vigilance* is the sacred duty of every citizen!" That fall, a Spartanburg committee of safety imprisoned a man named Barrett who was purportedly the author or distributor of these pamphlets. Enough confusion and controversy attended his peremptory arrest that the authorities permitted Barrett to leave the state. But the *Advertiser* warned that any future Northern abolitionists found in the South would be "tried, condemned, and hung as spies." Edgefield residents even petitioned the General Assembly to prohibit the importation of slaves or the immigration of free blacks into the state from any point to the north or northwest lest the infection spread. Although the committee voted to reject the petition, recognizing its contradiction of the southern rights claim that slave property was as portable as any other kind of property, a few members understood and sympathized with the petitioners' intent. In a rare minority report, they offered a domino theory of abolitionism: slaves in the border states of the Chesapeake, by virtue of their proximity to free states, had already been "indoctrinated" with "the principles of insubordination, and even of abolitionism." Their movement into South Carolina would do more than "injure and corrupt" South Carolina slaves; the steady drain of slaves from tobacco- to cotton-growing regions would eventually render South Carolina itself a border state, "with Maryland, Virginia, and even North Carolina hostile to our peculiar institution." Isolated and encircled, the state would be helpless against the abolitionists.[37]

In Ben Tillman's world, white men had to take up arms against such threats. In theory, the inculcation of "the sturdy virtues of the soldier" provided "a strong guaranty against the effeminate influences of an easy life, and the erect and manly discipline of military life elevates the character and pride of a man." More practically, threats to slavery itself required an overwhelming and collective military response. Militia and slave-patrol laws made adult white men into a home guard, required by law to cooperate in disciplining the slave labor force. In moments of crisis, moreover, white men frequently organized less formal volunteer companies and vigilance societies to squelch real or perceived threats to local authority. During the spring of 1849, as authorities dealt with the slaves accused of murdering Michael Long, the county's white elite held a series of meetings to establish "committees of safety and vigilance," informal local anti-abolitionist militias.[38]

These unofficial committees drew their authority from the same circumscribed "people" that constituted the region's democratic citizenry. However violent the actions they took in defense of white men's prerogatives, James Henry Hammond explained, they could hardly be considered mobs. Unlike Northern society, with its growing "riot and bloodshed," Southern slave society had no mobs, only the "habitual vigilance" of a citizenry "concerned in the maintenance of order." A band of "the people[,] . . . assemble[d] to chastise" a trespassing abolitionist, "no more [constituted] a mob, than a rally of shepherds to chase a wolf out of their pastures would be one." If abolition were forced on it, that "rally of shepherds" would turn on the blacks so wickedly set free: " '[A]rmed police' . . . would immediately spring into existence," Hammond explained, and before long "the African race would be exterminated, or reduced again to Slavery."[39]

Throughout 1849 and 1850, some of South Carolina's white citizens tried to transform this martial mobilization into secession from the Union. One observer believed that the "military parade of an armed force" he witnessed at an anti–Wilmot Proviso meeting in Charleston was "kept up to scare the Government of the United States as well as the negroes." Those who wanted South Carolina to leave the Union no matter what other states did became known as secessionists. The *Edgefield Advertiser*, placing itself firmly in this camp, solemnly declared in the summer of 1849 that "[w]e now look to disunion as our only hope." Secessionists such as George Tillman contrasted their self-assertion with their opponents' lack of manliness. The Edgefield paper snidely offered space in its columns to "any opponents of resistance, or to speak plainly, *submissionists*, who desire to advocate their cause before the public."[40]

Authority over one's dependents was no more important than equality with one's fellow citizens. When secession met with opposition from men who feared it would disrupt the cotton economy, a writer calling himself "Secession" accused the commercial interests of Charleston and other towns, comprising 50,000 or so white citizens, of attempting to dominate the upcountry's 500,000 white inhabitants. "Secession" urged rural districts to send large delegations to the state's secession convention, hoping that "the sight of an army of sturdy backwoodsmen, may revive the drooping patriotism of Charleston, and reinvigorate the flagging courage of her degenerate sons and perfumed foplings." "Flagging" and "drooping" urban manhood could be invigorated by a manly secessionist stand. A headline in the *Edgefield Advertiser* a few months earlier claimed that by electing secessionist delegates, the counties of Newberry and Laurens had proved themselves "erect." Another writer attempted to persuade slaveholders that men's mastery over human property meant nothing compared to their willingness to resist oppression. "Every cowardly little monster can tyrannize over his slaves," he wrote, but slaveholders who wielded only this kind of power would seem "very ridiculous" if they simultaneously allowed themselves to "endur[e] from the hand of a strong man, the foulest enormities that ever blighted the prosperity of a once free people." If a man's "sovereignty" was the essence of his self-worth, as sacred "as the virgin chastity of your daughters," it could hardly suffice to have the respect and fear of only one's slaves. Proper manhood required defying the strong as well as dominating the weak.[41]

Some white men experienced the secession movement as coercion, an assault on their right to pursue independent thought and action. Out-and-out unionists even wondered whether secessionists saw them as free white men, citizens and equals, or as slaves. In 1849, one Southern unionist claimed to be "a little surprised" that a unionist acquaintance from South Carolina was "suffered to go about Mr. Calhoun's plantation so much *without a pass*." The bitter quip exposed the rigid dichotomies of power and subordination in this society, in which a dissident quickly became an anticitizen—a slave. Likening civil society in South Carolina to a plantation under a despotic leader, this critique suggested that the state's citizens were free to vote on secession only as long as they voted as their masters wished.[42]

For the time being, the secessionists' rhetoric and organization did not carry the day against their somewhat more moderate foes. Cooperationists, despite their name, supported secession as well, but they insisted that South Carolina should only act in concert with other slave states. The divide between factions took place along complex political and economic lines: in general, cooperation gained the support of those with strong commercial ties (who stood to lose the most if South Carolina became isolated) and those yeomen and nonslaveholders least invested in slavery, whereas planters and smaller slaveholders provided the bulk of support for secession. Despite the efforts of George Tillman and other local secession activists, when it came time to elect delegates to the state's special convention on secession in 1851, cooperationists won Edgefield—by a single vote. In the end, nearly 60 percent of South Carolina's voters rejected delegates who favored South Carolina seceding on its own. Most staunch secessionists realized that South Carolina's white men would have to be much more united if they were to lead the region.[43]

Secession

Although secession failed in 1851, the following decade's escalating crisis over slavery strengthened white political solidarity against perceived Northern threats. Still, old intrastate rivalries persisted. Upcountry white men continued to argue that they were dramatically underrepresented in the state legislature, and during the 1850s, George Tillman and other advocates of greater upcountry representation gained election. Lower-house districts were in fact apportioned according to a combination of white population and taxable property, a formula favoring the wealthy coastal producers of rice and long-staple cotton. Meanwhile, the state senate granted additional seats to lowcountry districts (such as Charleston) that consisted of more than one historic "parish." Since South Carolina's constitution gave the legislature the power to choose the state's senators and presidential electors, as well as many local officials, this scheme of apportionment was particularly significant. The development of industries and railroads highlighted the uneven geographical distribution of political power (and state aid) among the state's white men; Edgefield arguably had the most serious grievance against the state leadership in this regard. As a result, men such as George Tillman entered state politics in the late antebellum years with a well-articulated critique of sectional favoritism and the lowcountry "oligarchy," a critique that echoed the eighteenth-century complaints of the backcountry Regulators. But when the sectional crisis heated up, intrastate sectionalism cooled: even as the editorialist "Secession" struck at the manhood of urban commercial interests, he was at pains to distance himself from the struggle between upcountry and lowcountry elites.[44]

By the late 1850s, a shared interest in defending slaveholders' rights united much of the upcountry and lowcountry behind proslavery expansionism. Planters themselves moved outward in many directions. George Tillman, fleeing prosecution for murder, had headed south to join William Walker's proslavery filibuster army in Central America. Another Tillman brother, Oliver, moved to the cotton frontier of Florida in 1858. In the middle years of the decade, Edgefield readers could closely follow the progress of local companies of emigrants sent to Kansas to challenge free-soil settlement. In the 1850s, as Ben Tillman learned to read and interpret developments in the larger world, he saw his society mobilizing its young men in a broad campaign to make the world safe for slavery.[45]

The lessons he learned concerned personal self-assertion as well as collective defiance. Only two months before George Tillman killed J. H. Christian, Edgefield citizens had reacted quite differently to another brutal attack, this one perpetrated by native son U.S. congressman Preston Brooks against antislavery senator Charles Sumner. In a speech on the Kansas question, Sumner had made derisive references to South Carolina's U.S. senator A. P. Butler and his "harlot, slavery." These slights had enraged Brooks, Butler's young relation. The Edgefield representative had fumed, lain in wait, and finally accosted Sumner at his Senate desk, beating him senseless with a cane. Brooks's attack on Sumner (like Tillman's on Christian) certainly did not demonstrate the mutual respect due white male equals. But Brooks, unlike Tillman, required no forgiveness from his fellow South Carolinians: he was defending his relative, his state, and a crucial institution against a man whose commitment to abolition placed him outside the bounds of

Southern white male solidarity. To have challenged Sumner to a duel (which the Northerner would assuredly have refused) would have been to acknowledge him as a social equal; instead, like a rebellious slave, Sumner deserved a beating he would never forget.

Sectional mistrust reached a climax with John Brown's raid at Harpers Ferry in 1859. Brown's attempt to instigate an abolitionist revolution and his contacts with prominent antislavery Northerners confirmed South Carolina planters' worst fears about their opponents. The *Edgefield Advertiser* dubbed the perpetrators "a pack of crazy fanatics and poor deluded slaves," but the newspaper proved only slightly less susceptible to panic than its peers throughout the slave South.[46] At Brown's execution in December, amid widespread fears of militant abolitionist retaliation, the editor felt compelled to dispel rumors that the governor of Virginia had asked South Carolina to furnish "substantial aid to her Northern frontier." The danger, however, might be much closer at hand. Any space not fully under the surveillance and control of the planter class could present a threat, for instance the local market center of Augusta and its concentration of people outside the slaveholders' immediate orbit. James Henry Hammond warned his fellow agricultural reformers at a December 1859 meeting that "there are now more abolitionists in Augusta than took Harpers Ferry. . . . [I]f an inserection should brake out about here Augusta would be the place." The "negro churches" of such cities presented the greatest danger, for they could easily be converted from religious into "military" organizations. He believed slaves could, if they chose, burn Augusta and Savannah within a month, "& if the northern men knew as much as he did it would be done."[47]

Hammond's proposed remedy—a full reorganization of the patrol system—met with wide agreement. From late 1859 onward, a drumbeat of martial mobilization began that would scarcely pause for another five years. In wave after wave of enrollments, volunteer companies—state militia units like the Edgefield Riflemen, as well as local Minute Men's associations—prepared to stand against federal intrusion, abolitionist agents, and the slave revolt abolitionists seemed determined to inspire. The growing support among Northern voters for the party known in South Carolina as the "Black Republicans" suggested that many Northerners intended the violent destruction of Southern civilization. To secessionists, however, the rise of the Republicans had the virtue of clarifying sectional politics: if a Republican became president, surely Southern voters would understand that they were safer out of the Union than in it.[48]

Although South Carolina selected its presidential electors by vote of the

General Assembly, the federal election witnessed popular demonstrations and military mobilization. Secessionists organized militias all through the cotton piedmont. A few weeks after Lincoln's election, the planters of the Saluda region of Edgefield formed their own company of Minute Men, and by their second meeting, they had enrolled nearly fifty members. Ben Tillman watched as several thousand Minute Men, wearing "sashes of red calico torn into strips," paraded in Hamburg. He heard an "impassioned speech" on behalf of secession. He remembered the martial fantasies traded by George Tillman and his friend and fellow lawyer Martin Gary as they brought Ben home from a secession demonstration: "The contempt with which both of them spoke of the Yankees impressed my young mind with the then prevalent opinion amongst the Southern people that all the courage was in the South and all the cowardice in the North."[49]

Moments of crisis and the solidarity they engendered could temporarily obscure slaveholding society's fissures and tensions. Mobilization created a sense of shared struggle, and the white men who served together reinforced their solidarity as the patriarchal rulers of a racially hierarchical society. Tillman "remember[ed] with what ardor and impassioned patriotism the war spirit was fanned into flame." But he also understood the repressive dimension of this mobilization. "There were no Union men at all," he explained; "if there were, they kept silent." Yet support for the Confederacy was shaped by the same competing forces that had defined the antebellum South. Appeals to Southern rights obscured the fact that most supporters of secession understood their interests as essentially local and only secondarily regional. Their loyalties were to their families, their plantations, their communities, and their states, generally in that order. Rhetoric to the contrary, defense of a unitary "South" generally placed a distant fifth. Hence, when the leaders of the Saluda Minute Men proposed on 15 December 1860 that the group offer its services to the governor, only 33 of 74 men assented. A week later, two days after the convention in Charleston had passed the ordinance of secession, just two more Minute Men added their names to that list. The remaining men had signed on in defense of their household authority; it would take more than patriotic speeches to make them march away from that sacred terrain. When the Charleston batteries opened fire on Fort Sumter and Lincoln called for volunteers to put down the rebellion, the call to defend Southern soil against invasion inspired many white men. But even this threat left many others unpersuaded that they should march north to take up the fight. As late as May 1861, many members of the First

South Carolina Volunteers refused to follow their colonel to the camps of Virginia: "[W]e never dreamed of leaving our own state," one explained.[50]

In some parts of the South, such reluctance threatened secession itself. South Carolina's convention voted to leave the Union on 20 December, and by early February, six Lower South states had followed suit. For secessionists in four more slave states, it took Lincoln's call for volunteers after the fall of Fort Sumter to propel their states into the new Confederacy, whereas in the four border slave states, secession faltered. Throughout the South, white-belt unionists demanded that secession follow democratic principles, and secessionist elites resorted to preemptive and often violent coercion. In many areas, secession amounted to a coup d'état against antisecessionist majorities. Throughout the war, white-belt regions of the Confederacy—especially along the slaveholding republic's Appalachian spine—would resist state and national claims on their goods, bodies, and loyalties, making some areas practically ungovernable by Confederate authorities and creating a new free-soil state out of Virginia's western counties. In South Carolina, however, such men found themselves particularly isolated. A decade earlier they had made bitter jokes comparing themselves to slaves, but now unionists were simply bitter. As unionist James Petigru lamented, South Carolina was "too small for a republic, but too large for a lunatic asylum."[51]

Destroying Slavery in Order to Save It

Secession and war in South Carolina revealed the continuing tension between a political culture of white male solidarity and a political economy in which a few men possessed most of the wealth. By the end of the war, well over 2,000 men—more than three-fifths of Edgefield's eligible white male population—would serve. Most of these were volunteers: the *Edgefield Advertiser* had hardly exaggerated when it claimed in early 1861 that "[t]here will be no drafting in Edgefield." Volunteers generally elected their own company officers, in keeping with a long-standing militia practice. But this democratic mass mobilization coexisted with displays of aristocratic power. Since militia men frequently provided their own equipment, at first the burden of equipping a Southern rights army fell to those whose rights had made them the wealthiest. Wade Hampton himself paid for the cannon of the regiment he commanded, which was known as Hampton's Legion. The regiment included the Edgefield Hussars, enlisted as a cavalry company under the well-connected young planter Matthew Butler, as well as an infantry company commanded by George Tillman's friend Martin Gary. The mobilization at least momentarily undid the political rivalries of the previous decade.

Tilman Watson—a former congressman who until recently had been the local cooperationist leader—sponsored Gary's infantry company. George Tillman, although he was Gary's "bosom friend" and fellow secessionist, had recently married and did not immediately enlist. But he, like the others who served, knew that there would be no political future in South Carolina for a white man of fighting age who did not eventually wear the gray.[52]

Ben Tillman, thirteen years old at secession, did not expect to don a uniform for some time, and life continued much as it had for the children of the planter class. During 1861 and 1862, he split his time between living on the family plantation and attending a nearby school. He received news of the Civil War from newspapers, local gossip, and letters from his family. Fears for the health and safety of his brother James, only five years his senior, percolated through his correspondence, and the recent deaths of three of his brothers may have given special charge to his own fantasies about death in battle. Two weeks after his fifteenth birthday, Ben wrote to his sister Anna about Charlie Jackson, a fifteen-year-old Memphis boy who had been mortally wounded at Corinth. Charlie, Tillman wrote, had told his father, "I am not afraid to die. . . . [T]ell the boys when you get back how I died—just as a soldier ought to." This account of a young protagonist bravely mastering war and death, making an exemplary passage into the next world, was exactly the kind of story the men of the planter class loved to tell about themselves. The rhetoric of heroism, like that of paternalism, made brutal realities (in this case, the repeated decimation of a generation of young white men) more bearable. But martial fantasies, like paternalism, played out somewhat less smoothly in practice. As Tillman imagined transcending boyhood by bearing arms in service to his nation, a movement was afoot among the white parents of Edgefield to prevent their sons from carrying concealed weapons to school. Some clearly shared the concerns the elder Benjamin Tillman had articulated years before: if the sons of slaveholders were not denied this "mischievous privilege," the *Edgefield Advertiser* feared, the result would be "rowdyism and bloodshed."[53]

Slaveholders in the infant Confederacy anxiously insisted that slaves would validate their paternalist pretensions. Under the heading "The Faithful Negro," the *Edgefield Advertiser* declared that "the South has no better friend in her troubles than the 'everlasting nigger.' As this wicked war upon us progresses, they catch up more and more of the southern fire, and stand but the more firmly at the posts of duty." A few column inches away, however, the anxieties of the previous decade could be seen creeping back in: was it true, the editor asked cautiously, that local blacks continued to trade in "what is not their own"?[54]

Tillman spent the early years of the war as a schoolboy, but even here the lessons he remembered years later were those that represented proper manly independence. A schoolmistress ordered him to sit on a sooty andiron, and when he refused, she beat him with a switch. He appeased her by appearing to sit, but he did not touch his breeches to the metal—thus submitting "only in appearance." He played games with other boys, fished, swam, and hunted squirrels and rabbits. And he read whatever he could get his hands on: magazines, popular fiction, and especially the novels of Walter Scott.[55]

The absence of so many white men strained the slaveholding order in unexpected ways and revealed that women and slaves had much to teach a young white man. As the oldest white male on the family plantation, Ben had to learn the agricultural skills and negotiations that life as an adult and a slaveholder would require of him. He spent much of 1863 collecting money owed to his mother and paying off debts amassed by his brother John. But Sophia Tillman could not supervise everything, and she appears to have entrusted Tillman's economic education to a slave named Stan. Together, the black man and white boy took butter, eggs, and fruit to market in Augusta and conducted business at grist and textile mills. By law, Stan was in Tillman's charge, but it was the slave, not the master, who knew how to accomplish these tasks. Tillman remembered Stan as "very ambitious," with "far more sense than is usual among negroes," a backhanded acknowledgment that the older man had taught him how to make his way in the marketplace. Unable to admit this inappropriate relation of teacher and student, an older Ben Tillman perhaps felt compelled to minimize how much he had learned from a slave.[56]

Well before the Emancipation Proclamation, slaves took advantage of the war. When the Union occupation of South Carolina's coast began in late 1861, most Union officials had no intention of freeing the slaves they found there. To their surprise and discomfiture, black men and women pressed the issue, forcing Northern soldiers to acknowledge them as human beings with valuable information, crucial skills, and bodies that could work and fight. Hundreds of thousands of black men served by war's end, first as military laborers and then as soldiers, providing myriad tests of Georgia Confederate Howell Cobb's assertion that "[i]f slaves will make good soldiers our whole theory of slavery is wrong." For black South Carolinian men, the war provided an opportunity to demonstrate fitness for citizenship. Robert Smalls, a slave serving aboard a steamboat in Charleston harbor, achieved a small military victory and an enormous propaganda triumph when he and his fellow slave crew members stole their vessel, their families, and themselves. With Smalls impersonating the vessel's white captain, they steamed past the harbor batteries and presented their prize to the Union navy. For Smalls and many others, Union military service would pave the way for a career in politics.[57]

Nothing infuriated the slaveholders more than the Union's enlistment of these black men. The Confederate response to these black Yankees, many of whom had been slaves only months or years before, sometimes resembled the brutal quashing of an insurrection conspiracy. The Confederate leadership often refused to treat captured black soldiers as prisoners of war and threatened to try all such soldiers (and their white officers) for the capital crime of fomenting insurrection. Black soldiers knew that falling into Confederate hands could mean being sent south as plunder, sold as slaves, or slaughtered. Some Confederates took particular satisfaction in killing black troops. "If there was anything that we hated worse than another, it was a negro soldier," declared a cavalry scout serving under Edgefield's Matthew Butler. On an icy Virginia road, two days before Christmas 1864, his men ambushed the black troops of a Union patrol. They took the white officers prisoner but killed all the black soldiers they could chase down. Other units massacred black Union soldiers under circumstances that did not even offer the fig-leaf excuse of military necessity or the heat of battle. But some encounters with black soldiers were less satisfying for Confederates. In the opinion of a captured member of South Carolina's Edisto Rifles, "[T]he most humiliating part of prison life was the fact of being guarded by negro soldiers." Surprised that these guards had displayed no savagery or even malice, he speculated that "many of them had not yet lost that feeling of subserviency to their Southern masters." On the surface, paternalism was proven "true"—former slaves, even after donning a blue uniform, instinctively treated white Southern men with respect. But the fear that this chastening "subserviency" would eventually be "lost" revealed that, beneath it all, the soldier assumed that black people could only be trusted to the extent that they remained cowed by slavery's violent discipline.[58]

From the beginning of the war, Ben Tillman had expressed a blustery Confederate patriotism. In a letter to his sister Anna, he wrote off reports of Confederate defeats as Yankee lies and denounced various Union officials—Pope and McClellan as "lying Gen[erals]," Butler as "an insulter of women," Buell and Johnson as "negro rogues," and "Lincoln, Seward & Co." as "a set of [expletive signs] fools." A career of calumny was off to an auspicious start. He saw the war firsthand in 1863, when he traveled to

Georgia to find his brother James, who had been wounded at the battle of Chickamauga. The trip revealed that even in wartime a young white man had a special place in this society. He had set out to find James with his mother, but at Atlanta she was sent back because no women were allowed to go any further toward the front. Sixteen-year-old Ben, though, was allowed to proceed. He rode atop a boxcar to Marietta, sheltering himself from the rush of chilly air behind a slave accompanying one of the soldiers. "[I]n this way," he recalled, "I became fairly comfortable." One man's mudsill might be another man's windbreak. He finally found James back in Atlanta by searching through makeshift hospitals and becoming "thoroughly familiar with the death scenes and horrors of war." On the way back home, he encountered a line of Union prisoners on their way to the prison at Andersonville and felt a surge of "hatred and intense feeling of animosity toward these invaders of our homes and destroyers of our liberty. I said to myself rather than to anybody else that they all ought to be shot." Tillman was learning the language of defiance.[59]

Tillman had to wait for a chance to shoot someone. He spent early 1864 back in school, as his mother and brothers hoped to give him enough of an education to allow him to enter South Carolina College once the war ended. George was grown, James was wounded, and the rest of the Tillman brothers were dead: in addition to the unlamented John, Ben's brother Henry had died of illness in 1859, and Oliver had been killed in Florida in 1860. Sophia Tillman would not live forever, and she could hardly surrender the household to her married daughter Anna or to either of Ben's older but unmarried sisters Martha and Frances. It made sense to invest the family's resources in Ben, the only male who might realistically take charge of the household. In an 1864 "Essay on Politeness," the youngest son was already clearly trying out the role of paternalist gentleman, imagining how he might acquire the social grace that rendered "a superior amiable, an equal agreeable, and an inferior acceptable." He acknowledged that such an attainment required "many years of study and a strict discipline of the mind."[60]

But there was no time for such study. By the summer of 1864, as the struggling Confederacy reached to the bottom of its pool of potential soldiers, Ben Tillman's two veteran brothers agreed that he should join a coastal artillery unit. The war was going badly enough for the Confederacy: Edgefield officers Martin Gary and Matthew Butler rose to the rank of general, but the typical soldier was not so fortunate. Of the 130 mostly Edgefield men who made up Company K of the Fourteenth South Carolina Volunteers, half were killed or captured, and only 20 still bore arms at the Confederate surrender. These casualty rates represented the kind of catastrophe the war brought to local communities like Tillman's.[61]

The Confederacy's misfortunes demoralized many of its soldiers. Letters from home describing wartime deprivations, as well as fears about the impending Union invasion of the state, caused increasing numbers of enlisted men and officers to desert, Confederate nationalism proving less powerful than the desire to protect their own households. Decades later, even the sentimental memoirs of former Confederate officers would acknowledge that by early 1865 white Southern men of nearly every rank were disappearing from their posts. They had, after all, gone to war in defense of their rights as independent masters of their household arrangements. Now that those households were threatened by actual armies, the relative strengths of their loyalties should have come as no surprise. Elites, although terrified of losing their slave property, hesitated to coerce their poorer white neighbors into continued service. James Henry Hammond had done more than most planters for white people impoverished by the war, providing food at crucial times, but in the waning months of war, he feared that his neighbors would set his property afire if he cooperated with efforts to impose a draft.[62]

Ben Tillman never made it into the increasingly battered and demoralized Confederate army. On 10 July 1864, less than a week after the Confederacy's dramatic defeats at Gettysburg and Vicksburg, a cranial tumor struck him down with fever and convulsions. An army surgeon removed the tumor, but the operation destroyed Tillman's left eye and left him gravely ill. For months, it remained unclear whether he would live or die. He remembered little from this period. To put him out of reach of Sherman's army while he convalesced, Sophia and George sent Ben and his sister Frances to live with relatives in Elberton, Georgia.[63]

Edgefield slaveholders' fervent military commitment expressed itself to the bitter end. Matthew Butler rode with his cavalry for nearly two years after suffering serious injury. At Appomattox, Martin Gary refused to surrender and rode south to join the Confederate cabinet in its flight from Richmond. But the Confederate armies no longer had sufficient men, supplies, or unity of purpose to maintain the struggle. Tillman found the Confederate surrender a "sad & depressing state of affairs." But he was preoccupied with personal concerns not limited to the recovery of his health. In Elberton, he met the woman he would soon court and eventually wed—Sallie Starke, daughter of a wealthy planter. He had never been a soldier and would never be a slaveholder, but he had yet to see what white manhood could offer him as a farmer and husband.[64]

Planters and the "*Gentleman* from Africa"

As he reached eighteen in the summer of 1865, Ben Tillman faced both adulthood and emancipation. Some challenges were private, like his feelings for Sallie Starke, the planter's daughter whom he had met during his convalescence in Georgia. Even in the diary he kept during the first postwar years, she appeared only as the anonymous object of his repeated inscription, "I love you! I adore you!" Although he later remembered having fallen in love with her during the first summer they met, he would not make such a declaration to Sallie herself until early 1867. Material necessity, not lack of ardor, helped explain the delay. Around the same time that he found his future wife, Tillman returned to South Carolina, where he, his mother, and the wounded James attempted to reassemble the broken pieces of the plantation household. For former slaveholders in 1865, the future seemed painfully uncertain, and the available options exasperating. Tillman reached independent manhood in a world where the meanings of those two critical words no longer seemed self-evident.[1]

Between the aspirations of former slaves and those of former masters lay a gap too wide to be bridged. Emancipation and Reconstruction unleashed hopeful strivings among black and white Southerners, but these revolutions also fostered a backlash of devastating ferocity. For more than a decade, former slaves and former slaveholders—one group strong in numbers and long-suppressed ambitions, the other rich in political experience, military capacity, landed wealth, and historic authority—would pursue their very different visions of Southern life and labor. Meanwhile, those Southerners who had been neither masters nor slaves struggled to define and defend their own interests. The struggle began as freedpeople and planters wrestled over the meaning of "free labor," and it gained ferocity in the period after 1868, when the votes of former slaves elected a Republican state government. The black majority's drive for education and landownership threatened to shrink the pool of workers available to men like Tillman, and those workers who remained demanded much higher wages for their labor.

As African Americans moved toward social, political, and economic independence, former slaveholders like Tillman struggled to sustain the antebellum world's hierarchies and habits. They did so in part through electoral democracy, but more and more their campaign unfolded in the realms of collective action, physical intimidation, electoral fraud, and white terrorism. Both Republicans and their opponents deployed economic and physical sanctions against constituents who strayed into the opposing camp; only the foes of Reconstruction, however, with their long experience of violent domination and military mobilization, proved willing to treat the other party as less than human and to make cold-blooded murder a campaign tactic. During the antebellum era, planters had understood that labor control was an essential aspect of "agricultural reform," and even after slavery, they knew that political and economic authority remained linked. Their assault on black autonomy and democratic institutions would have to be as well planned and coordinated as a military campaign if it were to succeed.[2]

In the war over Reconstruction, men did battle, but so did images and ideas flowing from the very different histories of white and black Southern manhood. As Republican militias clashed with Democratic rifle clubs, each group claimed legitimacy: one man's mob was another man's militia. Republicans had allies in the federal government, but they labored against powerful currents of historic hopes and fears. Although Union victory and black citizenship had in theory destroyed (and in practice at least undermined) the white male monopoly on legitimate authority, no defeat could undo white men's expectations. That reconstruction would take time and patience, and former slaveholders and Confederate officers were determined to disrupt it.

White Democrats mobilizing against the Republican government relied on the same strategy of promise and threat, accommodation and violence, that they had employed to govern slaves. This time, they sought to distribute the burden of paternalist protection and violent threat across different parts of their anti-Republican coalition. They used the language of "the mob" to distance themselves from the very acts of violence they promoted, claiming that these assaults were carried out by disreputable white men—"mobs," that is, from which only respectable white men could protect black Southerners. Black and white Republicans, for their part, faced the daunting task of persuading white men that armed black men could represent legitimate order and authority, not a slave insurrection, and that military companies led by former Confederate officers posed the real threat. They also had to contend with allies in the state and federal capitals who made the fatal error of taking the former slaveholders at their word. Amid the turmoil of this revolution and counterrevolution, Ben Tillman rose to the ranks of leadership.

When the War Was Over

At least in terms of relative economic power, emancipation had hardly turned Ben Tillman's world upside down. As wartime visions of confiscation and redistribution faded, former slaves found they had few resources but their labor. Federal officials required them to sign annual labor contracts with former slaveholders, men whose literacy and economic experience gave them the upper hand. These early contracts provided laborers with few rights and little more than a slave's subsistence. At the end of July 1865, James Tillman and his mother Sophia "presented a contract to the Freedmen for their signatures." After two days of deliberation, most signed, although a man named Tucker refused, and by the end of August, Edgefield's federal provost marshal apparently gave his approval. The contract's terms obligated the plantation's laborers to work through the end of the year for the miserly wage of one-tenth of the corn and potatoes and one-twelfth of the peas they produced. "Free labor," it seemed, might mean labor that went virtually unremunerated.[3]

But freedpeople were not slaves, and—at least in theory—they could not be physically forced to labor. Throughout the South, former slaves moved from field to road to town without passes, reconstructing their families, seeking subsistence, and exploring the meanings of freedom. The bounds of the Southern household, once the physical perimeter of a white patriarch's authority, could be crossed and recrossed at will by persons no longer "held to labor." At least four male workers left the Tillmans' fields during a brief period in June; ten days later, James Tillman "sent Amy & child off," probably an act of retaliation against the family of one of those absent men. In early July, four "freedmen"—in his diary, Tillman surrounded the word with skeptical quotation marks—went to Augusta without his permission. One of them was Tucker, the former slave initially reluctant to sign the offered contract, who apparently came and went as he pleased during early August. As planters like the Tillmans struggled to salvage the 1865 season, they seemed not to acknowledge that they had lost legal control of black people's bodies. By November 1865, a fully recovered Ben Tillman noted without further comment, "Mike worked half of today, gave him a whipping."[4]

From the Tillman brothers' perspective, the sources of former slaves' recalcitrance were easy to discern. Part of the explanation for their "misbehavior" was, of course, racial: it was hardly surprising to former slaveholders that black laborers, freed from a master's benevolent coercion, proved fundamentally indolent and unreliable. As under slavery, these natural tendencies were worsened by corrupting influences. In early August, a company of black soldiers from the U.S. Colored Troops briefly camped on the Tillman plantation "near [the] overseer's house" and "rambled all over the place—some of them very bold and impudent." A combination of their color, their uniform, their behavior, and their proximity encouraged one freedman, Henry, to look to them for protection. After Jim Tillman "thrashed" him for having left the plantation "without permission," Henry ran off again—this time to the village of Edgefield, seeking aid from the provost marshal.[5]

Men accustomed to mastery did not easily surrender their expectations of supreme authority over "their" laborers. Although Henry returned from Edgefield having spoken with the federal provost marshal, Tillman whipped him again. But violence was a means of achieving authority more than an end in itself. When another freedman, Thomas, became involved in a dispute with a "Yankee soldier," James Tillman interposed himself between the two men to prevent the soldier from beating the laborer. Authority had to flow in only one direction, but just as important, it also had to flow from only one source. For many planters, this insistence on unrestricted patriarchal authority challenged even the most basic recognition of family ties among the former slaves. That fall, white Edgefield landowner Thomas Price beat a black female employee; when the woman's father refused to assist Price by holding his daughter down, Price beat him as well, breaking the man's arm. Such actions reflected the planters' continued expectation of a patriarchal authority over black people that transcended those people's ties of family and affection. It also served as a grim reminder of their continued readiness to resort to violence.[6]

As the difficult year came to a close, it became apparent that the former slaveholders did not accept the legitimacy of emancipation. South Carolina's 1865 constitutional convention officially accepted the end of slavery, but Edgefield native and secession governor F. W. Pickens warned the new provisional governor not to underestimate the influence of "men taking the ground that slavery was not & could not be abolished & swearing they would never submit to it." Just as the Tillmans put skeptical quotation marks around the word "freedmen," planters throughout the South worked to limit the day-to-day meanings of black freedom. The new legislatures chosen by the old electorate in late 1865 codified this reactionary vision of emancipation. South Carolina's Black Codes, passed in September, placed severe restrictions on black movement, employment, and association, denying black people the right to own land or change employers and providing for punitive whippings and the involuntary "apprenticeship" of black children. Further, planter legislators sought to ensure their collective security against any resistance to this new, old state of affairs. Black laborers' expanded legal autonomy, many planters believed, required expanded monitoring and discipline. No simple patrol system would do, and just as James Henry Hammond had predicted two decades before, white men responded to the end of slavery by organizing "armed police." "We must have mounted Infantry," asserted one planter, "to enforce whatever regulations we can make." Although for the moment the only infantry in place belonged to the U.S. Army, the 1865 legislature did in fact call for dozens of new state militia units.[7] Cooler heads — those who understood the reaction the codes would generate among Northern Republicans — soon prevailed, softening some of the limits on black landownership and other important matters, but moderation only went so far: the legislators almost unanimously rejected the Fourteenth Amendment.

Former slaves as well as former masters could organize themselves to defend their interests. In addition to founding churches and schools, they formed neighborhood associations, political clubs, and other groups to improve their local bargaining power. Some might assemble in reaction to landowners' initiatives, as the Tillmans' former slaves no doubt did in the late summer of 1865. But freedpeople's organizations were much more than discussion groups. Some former slaves banded together in paramilitary units, marching, drilling, and even taking on military titles. They served as self-defense forces for black communities, sometimes seizing white terrorists and handing them over to U.S. authorities. As historian Julie Saville observes, these groups constituted a working-class black male claim to participate in public life, stepping free of antebellum distinctions of race and status and asserting a revolutionary new relationship between black Southerners and the state.[8]

Black men's assumption of the responsibilities of citizenship—from the establishment of individual patriarchal households to collective political and martial action—played havoc with white men's expectations. In the eyes of many white men, black men were inherently unfit for citizenship. They could not constitute a legitimate body of "the people," and they had no place in public meetings, political rallies, or military service. When black men did take on these roles, they were depicted sometimes as comical and ignorant but more often as impudent and riotous—as a mob. For some, black men's mobilizations represented a slave revolt that could not be put down by force of law. Interpreting black self-mobilization as evidence that emancipation would cascade out of control into a Haitian-style revolution, planters feared the worst. As the first Christmas of emancipation approached at the end of 1865, many former slaveholders believed the year would end in the outright revolt that anti-abolitionists had long predicted. James Tillman nervously "turned loose" his "negroes," then watched them "rambling all over the country & running to town." On 30 December, he tersely reported "matters 'in status quo.' " No revolt came. Instead, early January brought a less dramatic but nonetheless unsettling event, as a dozen or more former slaves left the Tillmans forever, to be replaced by hired "negroes" and "freedmen" previously unknown to Sophia, James, and Ben.[9]

Florida

James died of his wounds in 1866, and at the end of that year, Sophia and Ben hit upon a new strategy to recoup the family's fortunes. Following his late brother Oliver's less than successful lead, Tillman departed in December for the cotton lands of Marion County in north central Florida. There he bought land worth $3,500, putting up $100 in earnest money and promising to pay most of the rest by February. After making a brief trip to Edgefield, he returned to Florida with his sister Frances and "several 'persons of color,' all of Edgefield Dist., S.C." It was a decision made by thousands of Georgia and South Carolina planters, and every day brought a new wave of settlers through the junctions of Tallahassee and Jacksonville. As they rebuilt the world of cotton on rich, new soil, they re-created the demographics of their former home counties: by 1867, Marion and seven other Florida counties had black majorities.[10]

As in other land rushes, the inexperienced could become victims, and George Tillman worried that his younger brother had chosen his acres poorly and even that he might have obtained a bad title. "Bennie you are as a lamb among wolves in venturing as you have done about all this land business in Fla.," the grown man lectured the innocent boy. But although it might have been "far better [to] have kept the money in view of the awful times just ahead of us," the deed was done, and George promised to "never more say anything about it." Ben must learn "by experience like myself & all of our various brothers." This might not have been as reassuring to Ben as George intended it to be. But it was independence.[11]

The black men and women who worked for Ben Tillman in Florida in 1867 knew what he expected of them. The contract they signed early that year required them to obey the young white man's orders without discussion or dissent; to show respect for Tillman, his family, and his guests; and to labor from sunup to sundown — or longer when the harvest required. The Florida contract's provisions suggested that the coercions of "free labor" might provide former slaveholders with comforting continuities. A worker who left the fields without permission for even a few days could forfeit the entire season's wage. But the appearance of continuity was deceptive: although Tillman still owned the land and black men and women still labored on it, the terms and texture of those roles had changed forever. The "persons of color" Tillman employed had been free for most of two years, and they no longer accepted the miserly terms offered them in 1865. Tillman's Florida laborers earned a full third of nearly everything they produced — an almost fourfold increase in their wages. Furthermore, landowners' coercive authority no longer rested on the laws of slavery and white patriarchal sovereignty but on a legal agreement subject to review by federal authorities.[12]

Masters had long complained of the shortcomings of "Cuffee" and "Sambo," antebellum archetypes assumed to be childishly mercurial and malleable; now, however, freedpeople's rising expectations produced a new, more defiant figure. Tillman found himself facing "the '*gentleman* from Africa,'" whose grotesque pretensions to manhood and citizenship, supported by a conquering army, thwarted the efforts of landed, white (and therefore real) "gentlemen." "I belong to that class of 'les miserables,'" Tillman complained to his fiancée during the summer of 1867, "who are trying to distill 'green-backs' out of their 'mother-earth' by the 'free-labor process.'" In Florida, Tillman suggested, black workers had become even more "demoralized" by emancipation than they were in Georgia and South Carolina. "Consequently," he delicately explained to Sallie, "what is necessary there, is most especially requisite in Fla." Planters did not stop beating disobedient laborers simply because it was no longer legal. Mastery did not submit so easily.[13]

Commanding free labor in Florida was a grueling, unrewarding experience, but it did allow Tillman to see himself as a household head — not just a master but a potential husband and father as well. By late March 1867, he had found the words to propose marriage to Sallie Starke. Unable either to leave his fields or "to endure the suspense" of waiting until he could see her, he wrote to tell her, "I love you." He had feared to speak, he explained, first because he had not known whether he would recover from his illness and then because of the "convulsions" of the early postwar period. He also acknowledged that he was imperfect: those who knew him well, he told her, called him "passionate, morose, rude, unsocial, obstinate, impulsive, proud; sometimes selfish — which only I utterly deny — and I know that my countenance, originally 'not worth sunburning,' [is] marred by the traces of disease." "*Per contra*," he repeated in conclusion, "I love the truth, and I love you." The letter took weeks to reach Sallie, and she took two more weeks to reply, so her acceptance did not reach Tillman in Florida until the second half of May. Delighted, he immediately began playfully chiding her about having taken so long to write, as he would do during periods of separation over fifty-four years of marriage.[14]

Sallie became his sweetheart — his "Somebody," he called her — and soon his wife. In letters throughout the second half of 1867, he laid out the family's situation, including the necessity of his remaining in Florida. Perhaps as part of negotiations over a wedding date, he asked whether she would return with him to Florida. He did not present a comforting picture of frontier life: in addition to the problem of managing free labor, with which the planter's daughter would have been intimately familiar, Tillman faced a difficult climate. The plantation he had at first grandiloquently dubbed Kenilworth he soon mockingly renamed "Rainy Shanty" or "Mosquito Hall." Still, Sallie assented. Tillman returned north for a series of brief visits early that winter, and the couple married on 8 January 1868 before returning to Florida for the planting season.[15]

The Republicans Come to Power

That year, however, proved to be one of defeat for both Tillman and his class. Farming in Florida grew less and less profitable, culminating in an infestation of caterpillars that wiped out a promising crop. But even before Ben, Sallie, and Frances packed up the household and returned to South Carolina, larger developments rocked the postbellum South. In Washington, D.C., congressional Republicans, enraged by former slaveholders' intransigence and Andrew Johnson's leniency, sought the president's impeachment and took command of Reconstruction. Under the Reconstruction Acts, the new state governments were swept aside and the military took charge of a new voter registration — one that included black men. Confederate general Wade Hampton and a few other wealthy white men tried to hold back the tide, urging former slaves to choose their old masters as their new political leadership, but the elections of 1868 swept them from positions of authority.[16]

Aside from the fact that the old and new leadership classes were composed entirely of men, they had little in common. As freedmen suddenly became a voting majority and began to participate in state politics, a new political coalition of Southerners and Northerners, black and white, slave- and free-born, sought to direct their political energy. Free-born, literate black men like Robert B. Elliott and Benjamin F. Randolph arrived from outside the state to join the Republican Party leadership, and former South Carolina slaves rose to prominence as well, including Union veterans like Lawrence Cain, Prince Rivers, and the intrepid Robert Smalls. Most postbellum black leaders stood unapologetically for manhood suffrage and argued that neither race, nor class, nor education should limit this right. Political judgments, they asserted, were matters of common sense and self-education. "[I]nvestigating and discovering . . . who are his friends and voting for them, and also who are his enemies and refusing to vote for them . . . is a learning easily acquired," declared Randolph in 1867. Many homegrown military companies and neighborhood associations became political clubs of the Union League or Republican Party, and through them, black voters mobilized to register and elect delegates to the constitutional conventions mandated by Congress.[17]

African Americans made up about three-fifths of the state's population, and the delegates they elected wrote a constitution that prohibited slavery, established a nonracial franchise, and for the first time provided for representation by total population rather than by wealth, white population, or the old federal three-fifths ratio. Under that constitution, South Carolina's adult men assembled in June 1868 and elected a Republican government. Black-majority districts like Edgefield not only polled strong Republican majorities but also often elected black men to state and local office. Over the course of Reconstruction, such voters would ultimately put hundreds of black men into state and federal office. More than half of these men had been slaves in 1861.[18]

Freedpeople moved to secure their independence by acquiring land. Against substantial ideological and political obstacles, South Carolina's Reconstruction government went farther than that of any other state in attempting to redistribute land from the former masters to the former slaves. Through a new state agency, the South Carolina Land Commission, Republicans hoped to transfer acreage forfeited for nonpayment of taxes to poor South Carolinians on relatively easy terms.[19] In hindsight, it was an uphill struggle. Even sympathetic Northern Republicans generally endorsed contractual forms of wage labor as a logical first step for freedpeople, and federal proposals to confiscate and redistribute Southern lands encountered widespread opposition from a broad range of Democrats and Republicans. Freedpeople of necessity turned to other arrangements, including sharecropping, in which agricultural households provided a year's labor on land they did not own in exchange for the profits on a fixed proportion of the crop they produced—minus, of course, whatever a landlord or merchant had advanced to them during the year. It was a far cry from independent proprietorship, and it left renters and laborers at the mercy of their creditors.[20]

The Republican revolution did not transform the freedpeople into a black yeomanry, but it did create new institutions and social contexts in which black and white Southerners might learn to see each other as allies or even equals. Manhood suffrage fostered biracial political institutions. Some whites as well as blacks bought land from the state, and other whites became merchants and provided freedpeople with supplies on credit, undercutting planters' economic hold on laborers and renters. Republicans drove more fissures into the edifice of white unity when they stripped prerogatives from the white elite, underlining the fact that not all Southern whites shared the same stake in prior social arrangements. The admission of black students to the state college, for example, mainly offended only those white men who had been privileged enough to attend it.[21]

White Republicans gave the lie to white patriarchal solidarity. Planters dubbed Northern-born white Republicans "carpetbaggers," likening them to the antebellum era's itinerant hawkers of dubious banknotes. The analogy seemed apt, for from a slaveholder's perspective, Northern-born Republicans had in effect created fiat citizens, a worthless majority whose suffrage and officeholding debased the party. As one anti-Reconstruction newspaper protested, these interlopers were "political adventurers, who wish to use the negro to sustain their unlawful and unjust usurpations of power." But the Republican Party nevertheless began to gain support among a wide range of native-born white Southerners. Some elite men joined the party in hopes of moderating its course and serving as its new leadership, among them James L. Orr, who had been elected governor by the state's first postwar legislature in late 1865. Nonelite white Republicanism, however, was an elephant of a different color. Most white Republicans were men who had lacked significant power in the pre-emancipation social order—urban artisans, poor farmers, and dissidents and mavericks of all descriptions. Some seemed to have taken the opportunity to remake themselves completely, like the former slave trader Joe Crews, who became a fiery Republican orator. Their new party allegiance raised troubling possibilities: if poor white men began to see black laborers as political allies rather than potential insurrectionaries, if white male solidarity gave way to divisions of class, the edifice of planter rule might collapse entirely. In black-majority states such as South Carolina, white men's ballots alone could not determine the outcome of elections; if more than a few white men defected, the planter cause would become hopeless.[22]

The Republicans opened up space for the airing of new and long-suppressed social grievances within white society. The white population that had never owned slaves—the poor and middling majority of white South Carolinians—had suffered great hardships over the past half decade, and it was not difficult for them to hold the planter elite responsible. Without regretting that they had once hired or borrowed slaves, white men of limited means could now express animosity toward those slaves' owners, the men who had spearheaded the drive to secession and emerged from the disastrous war with their landholdings largely intact. Challenges to the elite now went beyond individual acts of theft or arson. Calling for debtor-relief legislation, the members of an 1866 meeting in white-majority Pickens County declared "that the people had a right to look for relief to men of place and position, whose influence on their actions had produced such conditions." Poor and middling white men were neither abolitionists nor champions of free-labor ideology, but under the difficult conditions of the postbellum era, they might perhaps be recruited into a Republican coalition that offered them the means to recover their independence.[23]

But the revolution of Reconstruction simultaneously undercut white men's expectations of authority as whites and as men, presenting challenges to those forging new coalitions. Wherever white men turned in the post-1868 South, they found they had lost their long-standing monopoly on political and market relations. With black men an electoral majority and white and black Republican men holding most state and local offices, black men and women gained new civil and criminal protections and began to make use of courts and laws. The lower house of the South Carolina legislature, an institution that had stood near the center of white men's historic authority, even had an outright black majority. This new legislature reshaped the laws governing labor, and for a time, agricultural laborers enjoyed the first legal claim (or "lien") on the crops they helped produce. But the revolution did more than alter the political and economic significance of race. As Republicans expanded married women's rights of property and contract and enacted the state's first divorce law, men's formal authority over women grew less absolute. A local woman suffrage movement emerged, led primarily by black women. And in a step that symbolized the new government's disdain for all barriers of caste, the legislature legalized racial intermarriage. When white opponents referred to these Republicans as "radicals," then, they were correct: for South Carolina society, equal citizenship was truly a radical notion.[24]

Interpreting these changes in the context of postbellum economic hardship, many white men came to understand Reconstruction as a plot against the ordering principles of white patriarchal authority. Many found the influx of black bodies and the recognition of black voices intensely disquieting. The initial shock might appear to have worn off: after seating one "Col'd" juror in late 1868, Edgefield's Court of General Sessions soon ceased noting the race of men called to serve. But the sense that a revolution had taken place was more lasting. A shared investment in whiteness had never fully obscured the class differences among white men or created an unproblematic white unity, but white men had learned to see themselves as the natural ruling group and to define themselves against the inherently unqualified, which mostly meant African Americans. Despite the potential for new alliances and allegiances, Reconstruction Republicanism could not simply erase the "fiction" of racial interest and substitute the "reality" of class solidarity. The expectation of white male privilege survived. Emancipation unshackled blackness from slavery, but it could not erase the centuries of racialized subordination that had made blackness a marker of social inferiority and subjugation.[25]

White Americans' shared understanding of the meanings of whiteness and blackness therefore remained an important cultural resource on which planters could draw in their struggle against Reconstruction. Freedpeople's ascent during the late 1860s created a feeling of wrenching transformation and deep loss among white Southerners that frequently overrode any possible benefits. White men did not have to share the planters' precise understanding of the meaning of "white supremacy" in order to support the return to "normal" rules and roles that such a slogan evoked.[26]

White men's adjustment to black people's new roles would have been traumatic under any circumstances, but freedpeople's rise to citizenship took place in the immediate aftermath of a devastating war and under the administration of the occupying army. Simultaneously, a series of ruinous harvests exacerbated economic difficulties. And although planters had some historical reasons to feel attached (if only economically) to black Southerners, nonslaveholders had few such reasons to form attachments and many more recent ones to see former slaves and former free blacks as the agents and clients of the Yankee invaders and another group of agricultural workers competing for suddenly scarce resources. Furthermore, the expanded state government established by the Republicans was costly compared to the extremely limited governments of the prewar era. The region's historically low tax rates on land soared during Reconstruction, a change that resulted in the forfeiture of some large holdings. Republican tax and land policies infuriated and terrified wealthy families like the Tillmans, who correctly understood them as efforts to split large plantations into small freeholds for poor families and to collect revenue to finance social services that would primarily benefit the freedpeople. Substantial increases in state and local taxation could chip away at large landholdings and the wealth, credit, and power they represented. Increased taxation also created fear and hardship among hard-pressed smaller landowners. Even without burdensome taxes, many white farmers were closer to landless poverty than they had been at any time in recent memory. By 1870, 43 percent of Edgefield households headed by white men owned no real estate. This was slightly higher than the total percentage of landless white households in 1850—a percentage that had also included landless white female-headed households—and it was especially high compared to 1860, when only 25 percent of white households had been landless. The fact that South Carolina's Reconstruction government failed to transcend the rampant venality of its era made these taxes seem even more onerous.[27]

Along with these new sources of fear and anxiety, an old one lived on: the expectation that black freedom was synonymous with slave revolt. The non-uprising of Christmas 1865 did not allay such fears among white Southerners. In the summer of 1866, planters in Orangeburg County pieced together what they believed to be a conspiracy among black military companies to assemble early in September and "kill every white man they could find, and take what they wanted." The political campaign of 1868 raised such fears to a new pitch. From Georgia, Sallie Tillman—a woman with no shortage of plantation experience—urged Ben to take care while he finished packing up the Florida household. "Darling do be very particular and don't get into any difficulty with the negroes," she wrote; "I shall be so uneasy till I hear from you." Insisting that she did not anticipate "anything like an out-break," the lady did perhaps protest too much. She and her new husband had already weathered at least one insurrection scare in Florida earlier that year, during which several blacks had been jailed and Tillman had considered sending her back to the relative safety of South Carolina.[28]

The War against Reconstruction

Leading Edgefield political figures George Tillman and Martin Gary sought to bolster white supremacy against the corrosive forces of change. Believing that the "*land, labor,* and *lives* of the colored races" were "by common consent . . . articles of free trade among Caucasians everywhere," George Tillman warned that black independence spelled the end of white civilization. The pugnacious Gary framed this racial vision in more explicitly militant terms, arguing that where once an "irrepressible conflict between free labor and slave labor" had existed, now there was only "a conflict between the Caucasian and African races." A renewed civil war, presumably, would pit not South against North but white against black. Pulling themselves from the wreck of racial slavery, the planters had begun to articulate a new argument about the continuing significance of race, one that directly challenged the ongoing revolution.[29]

The counterrevolutionary mobilization against Reconstruction emerged piecemeal between 1868 and 1876 as elite white men pursued mutually supporting strategies to regain control of the state government and the labor force. The political efforts of the Union Reform and Democratic Parties and of agricultural reform movements and tax-protest conventions existed side by side—and worked hand in hand—with the violent activities of the Ku Klux Klan, rifle clubs, and other paramilitary organizations. All proceeded from the assumptions that black political activity was inherently corrupt and that black employment should be restricted to agricultural labor under annual contracts. All took as their starting point the hostility and frustration Tillman expressed toward the new status and aspirations of the "*gentleman* from Africa."

In the end, economic resources and the willingness to use them aggressively determined who won each contest. Planters' control of farmland, the state's primary economic resource, gave them power over largely landless and impoverished ex-slaves. By coercive means such as eviction and denial of supplies, as well as outright physical violence, Tillman and his fellow planters attempted to reduce the freedpeople to disfranchised laborers.

The freedpeople fought back, aided, however falteringly, by the legal and military resources of the state and federal governments. In many white-majority Southern states, "Redemption" had triumphed by the early 1870s, but Republicans in black-majority states such as South Carolina did not surrender so quickly. Nor did the freedpeople's own efforts cease with their abandonment by the federal government in 1877.

The resistance to Reconstruction took well-organized, violent form even before the Republican governments came to power. The Tillmans' home county of Edgefield became a center of anti-Reconstruction activism, and George Tillman helped lead local and state efforts to restore planter rule. In the summer of 1868, as Ben Tillman spent his last miserable months in Florida, other white Edgefield men organized to prevent Republicans from taking power and to punish black laborers who voted Republican. Through economic sanctions, intimidation, and murder, white landowners made it economically and physically unhealthy to participate in Republican politics or to seek economic autonomy.[30]

Terror served landowners very well. Masked terrorists known as the Ku Klux Klan punished freedpeople and their allies for acts of political or economic independence. But not all vigilantism was hooded. Abbeville County Democratic leader and planter D. Wyatt Aiken publicly urged the murder of the district's newly elected black Republican state senator. As Aiken had hoped, Benjamin F. Randolph was shot dead soon afterward at the Abbeville train station. As one of the assassins later told investigators, the goals of Klan terror were "to regulate the republican party, break it up if they could, and strengthen the democratic party." Randolph was one of nineteen black Republican and Union League leaders murdered during the 1868 election campaign in the state's third congressional district. White men also mobilized militarily to prevent the November 1868 federal election from taking place in Edgefield County. Some of these men then traveled to neighboring Abbeville County to bolster its Democrats and help them prevent Republicans from voting. As a result, less than 20 percent of Abbeville's black voting majority cast ballots. Abbeville's totals—and the forced silence of Edgefield's active black majority—helped elect a Democratic representative in the upcountry district.[31]

Landowners also attempted to co-opt their Republican foes. By the time the 1870 campaign began, disgruntled combatants in the state's fractious Republican politics joined with planter leaders to form the Union Reform Party, whose statewide ticket included Matthew Butler for lieutenant governor. At the local level, this movement resulted in a brief political peace as black Republican and white Democratic leaders mounted a single compromise ticket for local government. Although Edgefield's biracial "fusion" county ticket was elected in the spring, the statewide Union Reform ticket lost by a substantial margin, roughly equivalent to the state's proportion of black to white voters. Many Republican leaders, as this suggests, remained skeptical of the intentions of such "allies." As a lowcountry Republican paper put it in 1870, "Some of these are good, true men; some only came to us from the most selfish motives. These last so much want place and power that they would be anything . . . to secure it. . . . [W]e must be watchful, and trust no Democrat who joins us till we KNOW him to be an out and out, thorough RADICAL FROM CONVICTION." Edgefield's Republican fusionists would have done well to heed such warnings. Shortly after the 1870 election, Edgefield Union Reform Party chair Lewis Jones, a white landowner, became president of a network of planter paramilitary clubs dubbed the Edgefield County Agricultural and Police Society. The group's name, recalling the slave-control efforts of the antebellum Beech Island planters, reflected the continuing link between political and economic authority.[32]

No man better embodied that linkage than D. Wyatt Aiken, the Abbeville planter who had successfully called for the assassination of Benjamin F. Randolph. As the editor of a planter agricultural journal, the *Rural Carolinian*, Aiken sought to reconstruct the antebellum plantation economy to suit the postemancipation world. He understood, as did many of his readers, that the essential first step in dealing with "free labor" was to place as many limits on its freedom as possible. In the journal, Aiken offered his Abbeville plantation as a model of the postbellum plantation system. Aiken's workers—all black families—had to pay their rent in cotton, which limited the amount of food they could raise and placed them at the mercy of the poor postbellum cotton market.[33] In a gesture toward paternalist ideals, Aiken gave his workers land "on which to erect a church." He most likely provided supplies on credit, for it is difficult to imagine this planter allowing an outside merchant to intrude into the relationship between him and "his" people. This postbellum plantation bore a strong resemblance to the antebellum version: despite evident changes, there were still laborers' cabins for black families, a gin for the obligatory cotton crop, and, at the center, a main house occupied by a single white family. This was what Ben Tillman had tried to achieve in Florida and, despite his failure there, what he ultimately sought throughout his agricultural career.[34]

At least a few readers of the *Rural Carolinian* understood that the adjustment from slave to free labor could not be anything but painful. "[T]he abolition of slavery," declared one, "has affected our social, moral, educational, economical, political, and, to a certain extent, even our religious relations. . . . Slavery so ramified—it was so interlaced throughout the body politic, that we cannot expect the laceration caused by suddenly tearing it out by the roots, can be as suddenly healed." This writer's thoughtful analysis went hand in hand with an affirmation of continuing hierarchies: a few lines later, he proposed "a series of measures" to "place the Southern landholder in a more prosperous condition than he has ever before occupied." Planters must live on their properties to ensure the proper cultivation of the land and oversee "the negro," who "cannot be bound by contracts." Planters and their families must also work, although "[i]t would be wrong to demoralize our sons, by forcing them to work in the fields with the negroes." This last, of course, flew in the face of most white households' reality: even men like Tillman had been working in their own fields throughout Reconstruction; in less prosperous households, white women also worked the fields. But the ideal of keeping black agricultural labor under the supervision of white male landowners retained its force. Sharecropping, to the degree that it fostered black autonomy, was deplored as "an unwilling concession to the freedman's desire to become a proprietor, or [the planters'] inability to make prompt payments of wages in cash."[35]

In the early 1870s, Aiken set about mobilizing his readers for somewhat different efforts on behalf of landholders and white supremacy. As the local agent of the Patrons of Husbandry, better known as the Grange, he initiated a statewide organization to reform agriculture. By the mid-1870s, he had established hundreds of local Granges statewide. The Grange embodied Aiken's desire for unity among planters against both laborers and merchants. Grangers engaged in collective purchasing and worked to establish a common and well-regulated system of labor contracts. Noting that freedmen (like other groups) had "demonstrated to us the power of concert and effect of union" through their political and economic organizations, from the neighborhood to the state level, Aiken urged "profiting by their example."[36]

Grange activities intended to bolster the postbellum plantation system slid naturally—and in South Carolina perhaps inevitably—into the violent enforcement of that system. In the early 1870s, Edgefield's Agricultural and Police Clubs pursued many of the strategies urged by Aiken and other Grange leaders. Led by George Tillman and others, planters agreed to set common wages and contractual terms, to refuse to hire laborers away from other planters, and to ostracize whites who violated these agreements or rented land to blacks. Such plans, of course, were more easily prescribed than enforced: as planters vied for dependable laborers during crucial parts of the growing season, individual and class economic imperatives came into direct conflict. But nearly every planter shared Aiken's avowed commitment to one essential principle: "[I]f any man occup[y] his land as his equal it must be after his death." Militant defiance remained a cardinal planter virtue.[37]

Planter organizations drew strength from this ideological coherence: intellectual, military, economic, and political groups shared overlapping and complementary aims. Agricultural and Police Clubs made the connections explicit, but even where organizations retained apparently discrete identities, their leadership overlapped. In Edgefield and elsewhere, many of the same names appeared on the rosters of Granges, conventions, and later rifle clubs. For example, leaders of Edgefield Granges included two delegates to the 1871 Tax-Payers' Convention, called to protest Republican taxation. When the Tax-Payers' Convention reassembled in 1874, Edgefield was represented by many of the same men who had attended in 1871, including paramilitary leaders Matthew Butler and Martin Gary, as well as by a new generation of Grange masters. Had the Klan kept records, the overlap between Grange and Klan membership would doubtless have been equally significant. The connections were obvious to Republican opponents, who recognized that whatever they called themselves, planter-led organizations shared the same goals.[38]

White elites led the war against Reconstruction just as they had led the militias, the vigilance committees, and the Confederate mobilization. Former Confederate general, Democratic leader, and planter Wade Hampton was "a leading organizer in a statewide movement to raise money and engage lawyers to defend supposed Klansmen." White terrorists, according to their wives, had been "*ordered* off" to one clash with militiamen: the anti-Reconstruction mobilization, reported one observer, was "a complete military organization." Although elite men sometimes portrayed Klan violence as the acts of lower orders of white men, the Klan's membership cut across white society and had allies at its very pinnacle.[39]

When Klan violence surged again in 1870 and 1871, white Republican governor Robert Scott finally armed and mobilized a state militia. This force took its membership from the marching societies and Union League companies that had defended the lives and interests of black South Carolinians since the fall of the Confederacy. Some of these companies had armed themselves and stood their ground during the first wave of Klan violence in 1868. In many areas of the state, militia units patrolled to prevent Klan outrages, sometimes demanding the kinds of explanations from white men that white men historically had demanded from slaves. Although nearly all militia members were black, a few white Republicans, such as Laurens County's Joe Crews, assumed positions of authority.[40]

Black martial mobilization inspired an overwhelming response. Whenever black militia units appeared, their very existence as a body of armed black men provoked the same mass mobilization of white men that rumors of slave revolts had prompted. A great majority of those white men had years of Confederate service; moreover, having been free their entire lives, they had networks throughout the region on which they could draw. This placed serious limits on the militias' ability to retaliate against the Ku Klux Klan, defend the rights of citizens, and sustain the authority of Republican officials. In the winter and spring of 1871, after a militia unit in Chester County fought off Klan attacks, hundreds of white men converged on Chester under the leadership of former Confederate officers. Although the militiamen managed to retreat to safety, a large-scale racial battle could easily have occurred, an outcome the white Republican governor desperately sought to avoid. Militia resistance to the Klan sparked similarly dangerous conflicts in other upcountry counties as well. Crews and his militia had to flee Laurens County when hundreds of armed, mounted white men arrived from Edgefield and elsewhere.[41]

This virtual state of war finally brought federal occupation and trials in several upcountry counties in 1871, teaching the Klan leaders that they needed at least to appear law-abiding. But when congressional investigators called Matthew Butler before them in July 1871, even as he delivered testimony designed to avoid implicating himself, he articulated his assumption that he and his class ought to control the state. Although he denied that he had played any role in the Klan, he emphasized how much influence he had on the white men of his county. Indeed, he suggested that his own authority was more legitimate than that of the state's Republican elected officials. After he had raised a military company and offered its services to the state, he complained, the Republican governor had refused the offer. This suggested to Butler that Governor Scott misunderstood the relationship between the state and men of Butler's class: "[U]ntil [Scott] has treated them with respect," Butler explained, "he cannot expect their cooperation." This was, in essence, the philosophical underpinning of the elite-led rebellion against Reconstruction: certain men were entitled to pass judgment on state policies and unilaterally to veto those of which they disapproved. The owner of 2,200 acres, Butler explained that he represented a group of "men who have a right to know and be heard. . . . [T]here is always a moral power with that class of people which entitles them to respect."[42]

Butler knew better than to claim that he was entitled to establish his own militia. Instead, he focused on the other half of the planter dialectic of authority, emphasizing his capacity for forbearance. Here, as always, the threat of violence was implicit. "Last summer," he told the committee, "I could easily have provoked a riot in ten minutes, but I have taken legal rather than violent means." Although he denied organizing Klan activity, he could not resist asserting once again his capacity to organize and mobilize white men through less formal understandings. He dismissed the Klan raid at Laurens as "a sort of spontaneous thing" but added that he had "advised some young men to go." He denied the existence of an Edgefield Klan but admitted the existence of "informal" organizations, which he described as a "touching of elbows to be ready for any emergency." Pressed by the congressmen as to the intentions of "whites" in South Carolina—for they accepted Butler's neat division of whites and blacks into separate and competing groups—he acknowledged "a very universal determination to overcome the negro majority."[43]

Others offered their Republican opponents the choice between surgical acts of violence against particular individuals and more random and bloodier conflicts with white "mobs." In a speech to the 1874 Tax-Payers' Convention, one delegate defended the Klan's actions as justifiable responses to "outrage[s] against justice" by black criminals that had gone unpunished by the Republican authorities. White men, he explained, had banded together "for mutual protection." But the Republicans had fostered a climate of lawlessness in which such organizations could develop in either of two directions, "according to the relative numbers, intelligence, or morality participating." The choices were "revolution" or "brigandage." When "outrage and abuses" against black South Carolinians occurred, it was the fault of brigands. In those cases, "the Ku-Klux appears to have been mainly a body of ignorant men, and [as] devoid of justice as they were of judgment." When mob ignorance was tempered by the greater "intelligence" of more respectable whites, by contrast, the black pawns of Reconstruction did not suffer. Instead, the revolutionaries "dealt with the white persons that organized the frauds and violence of which they justly complained and made an example in high quarters in Columbia." In other words, lower-class white men could not be expected to know who their real enemies were. They sought justice, but in doing so, they acted like a mob. A better class of white men would have aimed directly at the leaders of the illegitimate party. More than a retrospective apology for some Klan excesses, this was an outline for future assaults on Republican governance.[44]

Butler himself had helped lead the first Tax-Payers' Convention in May 1871. There, the "very best people" had been represented by an array of antebellum and Confederate leaders, and the convention's president had complained that "they who lay the taxes do not pay them, and . . . they who are to pay them have no voice in the laying of them. . . . Can greater wrong or greater tyranny in republican government be well conceived! Less evils than this have produced revolution." Allusions to the republican legacies of the American Revolution coexisted comfortably with attacks on popular democracy. Gary, who chaired the convention's committee on electoral reform, described universal suffrage as an invitation to demagoguery. Another wealthy Edgefieldian urged amending the state constitution so that representation of property might once again restrain popular democracy. Others suggested a cumulative system of voting, which would offer political minorities (in this case, white men) greater opportunities for representation. More concrete proposals for reducing the planters' tax burden were subverted by convention members, including Butler and Gary, who cooperated with anxious bond speculators by declaring the state's existing debt to be legitimate, not the product of Republican frauds.[45]

Rifle Clubs and "Riots"

Despite such pursuits of individual interest, the anti-Republicans did not suffer from division as badly as did the Republicans themselves. More than half of the officials elected during Reconstruction in South Carolina were black, but this group neither spoke with one voice nor wielded power proportionate to its numbers or potential constituency. Many black South Carolinian Reconstruction leaders, born free in the North or South, lacked intuitive understanding of their impoverished constituents' needs. This internally divided black leadership also faced challenges from generally more conservative white Republicans. At the same time, lagging federal prosecutions of accused Klansmen reflected a weakening federal commitment to the state's elected government. National Republican leaders feared the political consequences of using federal power—military rule and the suspension of habeas corpus—against civilians. As bad as it was to be considered the party of the black man, it might be even worse to be seen as the party of federal tyranny.[46]

Still, when faced with a powerful challenge, the fractured party usually managed to rally. In a stinging reply to the accusations of the 1874 Tax-

Payers' Convention, the state Republican Central Committee denied that tax policies were deliberately confiscatory and criticized antebellum undertaxation of landed property for encouraging the formation of "that most dangerous of all oligarchies, a landed aristocracy." "[I]t was from this class," it noted, "that secession and the war sprang." The Republican leadership understood the "Tax-Payers' " efforts as one in a series of political, military, and ideological attempts by the "former ruling element" to regain power: "First, they expected it through the election of Seymour and Blair [the 1868 Democratic presidential ticket]; second, through the midnight murders and assassinations of Ku-Kluxism; and now, thirdly, by the distortion and misrepresentation of facts, in order to create a public sentiment in their favor." Although riven by schisms and class conflict, the Republican leaders could still accurately assess the motives and methods of their opponents.[47]

By 1874, the planters returned to the violent strategies of the Klan and police clubs. New rifle clubs squared off against the state militia, remilitarizing political conflict. Butler and other leaders of earlier movements were prominent in Edgefield's rifle club activity, and local clubs were commanded by men who had attended Tax-Payers' Conventions or had led Granges. The rifle clubs also recruited men who were just becoming old enough to assume leadership roles, including Ben Tillman, who joined the Sweetwater Sabre Club in 1873 and began to take part in the campaign his class had been waging against Reconstruction and the Republican leadership.[48]

Rifle club leaders, Tillman later explained, deliberately sought confrontations with the militia. In 1874, after a local militia regiment showed its strength at a Fourth of July parade in Edgefield, rifle club men responded by firing shots into the house of militia commander Edward "Ned" Tennant. Tennant called out his company, and the rifle clubs also massed. As large numbers of men mobilized on each side, a federal officer acting without orders rushed a small group of soldiers to the scene of the impending conflict. The next day, Tennant dispersed his men, ending what Tillman called the first "Ned Tennant riot." But the federal officer recognized that Tillman and his colleagues effectively had brought matters to the brink of a massacre. The rifle clubs were "perfectly organized," he wrote, "and ready to take the field at any time."[49]

Those troops soon gained an unwitting ally in the governor's mansion. Massachusetts native Daniel Chamberlain had participated in the 1874 Tax-Payers' Convention and in the gubernatorial race received the votes of some conservative Democrats who found the moderate Republican preferable to his radical colleagues. Shortly after Chamberlain's election, Butler traveled to Columbia to meet with him. Upon Butler's return to Edgefield, his house burned down, and some white leaders accused Tennant of instigating an act of arson. In January 1875, rifle club members convinced a sheriff to deputize them, and they set out to arrest Tennant. Again, Tennant sounded the alarm, and rifle clubs and militia companies massed. Butler led the white Democratic forces, numbering as many as a thousand, against Tennant's troops. For several days, the former Confederate general led the search for the militiamen, but Tennant managed to guide his men through and around the rifle club lines. He delivered his company's weapons to his commander, Lawrence Cain, defusing the situation before the rifle club partisans could engineer a direct confrontation that almost certainly would have resulted in a massacre.[50]

Edgefield's militant planter leadership sought to deny black militiamen land and employment, and many Edgefield blacks complained of being driven off lands they had leased or of having their labor contracts broken because they belonged to the state militia or voted Republican. Dissident white men faced similar sanctions. Tillman would later claim that only one local white man had employed militiamen, and he attributed the man's subsequent suicide to the social ostracism that followed his actions. But such "deviance" from white-supremacist orthodoxy was more common than Tillman suggested. A federal officer reported that white terrorists burned the buildings of white people "who had refused to unite with others in the recent proscriptions against the colored people." White men who took a more direct part in the Republican mobilization faced more violent attacks: Democratic partisans assassinated militia leader Joe Crews in 1875.[51]

Chamberlain received reports on the troubling developments in Edgefield from a U.S. officer, Colonel Theodore Parmele, who interpreted the conflict so judiciously that he misunderstood it almost completely. After spending three weeks in the county, Parmele praised the majority of Edgefield's citizens, describing the whites as "a highly cultivated, industrious, law-abiding class" and the blacks as "industrious, respectable, and opposed to any act of lawlessness." He believed the troubles in Edgefield were caused by "a disturbing element in the minority of both races." He did not understand that vigilante violence and rhetorical protest against Reconstruction were often led by the same people or that some whites' refusal to be dictated to by other whites did not necessarily imply that they were satisfied with the Republican government. Furthermore, the conflict Parmele described was tellingly asymmetrical: the white group was "a class of young men who hold human life at little value." These men, "habitually armed and ready to resent any assertion of equality as a citizen when coming from a colored man," probably included Ben Tillman. The black "disturbing element," by contrast, Parmele described as "a class who do not wish to labor and are known as habitual thieves, or disturbers of the peace by making incendiary remarks or suggested threats, in retaliation for acts or language perpetrated or used by white people against them." Unable to fight their foes directly and abandoned or ignored by federal authorities, black activists did indeed resort to stealthier but equally powerful weapons, particularly arson. In a growing number of South Carolina communities, leading Klansmen began to recognize—and fear—the connection between their activities and the fiery loss of their barns and gin houses.[52] But even in Parmele's "balanced" account, the inequality of the two sides' offenses was obvious, as black ne'er-do-wells faced white murderers.

Both Parmele and the governor deplored the actions of the white "disturbing element," but they saw those actions as irrational and incidental. Both failed to see that such conflicts would continue as long as planters were in a position to resist black people's demands for citizenship and autonomy. Parmele believed the rifle clubs would heed the governor's call to disband and opposed stationing U.S. infantry at the Edgefield courthouse. He suggested that "the force of public opinion and the means provided by law will unite to prevent or punish lawlessness hereafter." Even after the struggle had grown far bloodier and more desperate, Chamberlain noted that "daring, lawless, reckless white men, accustomed to arms and deeds of violence . . . are inspired by an intense and brutal hatred of the Negro as a free man, and more particularly as a voter and a republican," but he insisted that "the better and more conservative classes of society" did not approve of their activities. If he truly believed that any substantial segment of Edgefield's "better" white people would openly disapprove of rifle club activities or sought a different end from that sought by men like Tillman, Gary, and Butler, the governor was badly mistaken.[53]

For Tillman and his commanders, such expressions confirmed that the state's Republicans lacked the resources and the desire for armed conflict. Indeed, Parmele's very mission in Edgefield symbolized the Republicans' inefficacy in defending black people's rights. He brought their protests back to the capital, but he also ordered the militia's weapons, black South Carolinians' only defense against the rifle clubs, to be locked in the Edgefield jail, from which they were soon stolen. Nor was disarming the militia Chamberlain's only retreat from confrontation with the planter insurgents. Chamberlain announced a reward for the capture of Joe Crews's assailants, but he vetoed a pointed proposal by Republican legislators Lawrence Cain and Paris Simkins to levy a special tax on areas in which political violence took place.[54]

Parmele's report and Chamberlain's actions foretold how much the planters' ultimate success would depend on the misjudgment and weakness of white Republican leaders. Taking some planters' genteel manners and organic social metaphors at face value, they failed to understand that this way of life and thought relied in the last instance on physical force. As Reconstruction failed to turn out precisely as they had hoped, they lost faith in their black allies and constituents. When the planters mounted their final offensive in 1876 and 1877, they met with far less resistance than they had expected from the federal government and the national Republican leadership.

The Hamburg Massacre

By early 1876, the planters' violent campaign against Republican forces had been quite successful, especially compared to their more peaceful strategies. Many of the state's militia units had disarmed, a moderate white Republican was governor, and the shrunken Republican majority in the state legislature was ever more powerless to pursue its programs. Further, President Ulysses S. Grant's failure to prevent the violent overthrow of Mississippi's Republican government in 1875 indicated that the national party leadership was becoming fatigued and irresolute. Rifle clubs of young white men, including Ben Tillman, operated with relative impunity throughout the upcountry.

But before the old leadership class could regain power, it would have to resolve its own long-standing sectional divisions. In 1865, upcountry activists including George Tillman defeated lowcountry efforts to apportion representation by total population, a formula that would have preserved the disproportionate power of white electorates in areas with large black majorities. But the upcountrymen did not manage to push through their own plan for representation based on white population, which would have guaranteed them a much larger share of state power. Instead, the two sides compromised by apportioning representation by a combination of white population and taxes paid, establishing greater equality among white men while preserving the disproportionate power of wealthy coastal planters.[55]

Once the black majority became an electoral majority in 1868, lowcountry white men found it difficult to retain their accustomed degree of political power. Black political power in the lowcountry operated through well-organized local and county networks, capable of discouraging black men from voting Democratic tickets, although unwilling (unlike their foes) to resort to deadly force. The size and strength of the Republican Party, along with an increasingly militant labor movement among black rice-field workers, encouraged lowcountry elites to compromise. In state contests throughout Reconstruction, lowcountry planters had supported dissident or reform Republicans and sought to attract black voters to the Democratic Party. They pursued state and local "fusion" of the two parties, supporting Republicans—even some black Republicans—in exchange for Republican support for officeholders more friendly to major property owners.[56]

Fusion, whether it consisted of bipartisan endorsements or compromise tickets, was of dubious value to the freedpeople. It had been pioneered in South Carolina by Francis Warrington Dawson, a British citizen who had been so attracted to the secessionist cause that he ran the Union blockade and joined the Confederate military. After the war, he settled in Charleston, where he further strengthened his identification with the antebellum elite and became proprietor of an influential daily paper, the *Charleston News and Courier*. From the beginning, Dawson understood fusion as a way to "overturn our negro governments and re-establish white supremacy." Despite initial hostility, he had developed a personal relationship with Chamberlain, and he believed that support for the Northern Republican could help free South Carolina from Reconstruction without risking massive conflict or subsequent federal intervention.[57]

But fusion was deeply unpopular among the upcountry Democratic forces led by men like Butler and Gary, and in 1876, they provoked a series of violent clashes with state militiamen. A racialized military confrontation, they hoped, would help draw clear lines between the political parties, rallying white men to support a separate Democratic ticket against Chamberlain's government in the November elections. This final military campaign against Reconstruction provoked some of the most serious violence of the period. It also marked a turning point in Ben Tillman's life, establishing him as a member of the political and military leadership.

The first and most crucial of these clashes began, fittingly enough, with a conflict over the right of black men to act as citizens and soldiers. On 4 July 1876, a recently reorganized black militia company led by local Republican activist Dock Adams paraded on a main avenue in Hamburg, a mostly black town just across the river from Augusta and a few miles across the county line from Tillman's Edgefield home. When Henry Getzen and Thomas Butler, two young members of well-to-do local white families, attempted to drive their buggy through the company's ranks, a standoff ensued. After a tense moment in which the company fixed bayonets and the young men brandished their pistols, the militiamen made room for the buggy to pass through their ranks. But Adams and the young men swore out legal complaints against each other, Adams charging the young men with having disturbed his company's drill, and the young men charging Adams with having obstructed a public way.[58]

The two competing narratives of this confrontation revealed that little room existed for compromise between white men who identified with the old planter elite and black men who assumed the roles of citizenship. Getzen and Butler were furious that black men, even a uniformed militia on parade, had failed to move out of their way, but Adams noted that there was ample room on either side of the company for the men to pass. The significance of the town itself became a subject of disagreement. To Adams and his colleagues, Hamburg's largely black population, militia, and government made the town a showcase for black independence. To men like Matthew Butler and Ben Tillman, these same factors made Hamburg a "lawless den." Democratic and oligarchic notions of legitimate authority, citizenship, and public space met head-on: Thomas Butler and his father Robert Butler considered the public road where the clash occurred, which led to their plantation gate, to be their private property. They stressed that it was their wagon, on the way to market in Augusta, that had worn the ruts along the road. Never did they admit the legitimacy of the militia's use of the public way. Although Robert Butler conceded, when pressed, that it was indeed "a common road," his son continued to refer to it as "my father's street." The contest was a microcosm of conflict at the state level, demonstrating that the planter elite did not recognize the legitimacy of either a democratically elected Republican leadership or black citizenship generally.[59]

Some facts were indeed unclear. After the preceding years' conflicts between Ned Tennant's militia unit and Matthew Butler's vigilantes, Chamberlain had pursued a policy of nonconfrontation. But local activists such as Adams rejected disarmament, and his militia may have been more independently organized than state sanctioned. Even Hamburg justice Prince Rivers, the previous commander of the Hamburg militia, denied that Adams's unit was "regularly organized." Rivers, a former slave coachman turned noncommissioned officer in the Union army, had by the mid-1870s become a state and party official and a prosperous businessman. He earnestly sought to forestall the armed confrontation that he knew white elites were seeking. Rivers therefore expressed skepticism about Adams's militia and at the initial hearing ruled Adams himself in contempt of court for using improper language. Adams and his men, for their part, drawing on the physically assertive tradition of the previous decade's marching clubs, may well have seen Rivers's caution as symbolic of the Republican government's weakness in the face of planter arrogance. To planter men, the militia was in fact no militia at all but an illegitimate body of armed men. "We looked upon them as nothing more than a parcel of men—not as militia," explained Robert Butler; "we did not think they had a right to have guns." Hostility to the militia, though, was based not on a deep regard for legal niceties but on former slaveholders' expectations of personal and collective authority. They questioned the validity of Adams's militia charter, but their skepticism ran much deeper: a black militia, they implied, was an oxymoron. An assembly of armed black men could only be a lawless mob.[60]

White Democratic rifle club leaders cared less about such divisions than about the subordination of all blacks and Republicans, and when Rivers scheduled a hearing for 8 July, they knew their moment had come. Tillman later described the premeditation of the violence that followed: "the leading white men of Edgefield," he declared, had determined "to seize the first opportunity that the negroes might offer them to provoke a riot and teach the negroes a lesson . . . [by] having the whites demonstrate their superiority by killing as many of them as was justifiable." The hearing became a pretext for a direct military confrontation with black Republican power. On 8 July, Getzen and Butler arrived in Hamburg accompanied not only by their lawyer, Matthew Butler, but also by at least seventy armed white Democrats from nearby rifle clubs, including Ben Tillman's company, the Sweetwater Sabre Club. The men had fashioned makeshift uniforms from red shirts, and they subsequently became known by that name. But before riding into Hamburg, these first "Red-shirts" had assembled out of uniform and without rifles so as not to raise the alarm prematurely or give Republican and militia officials time to develop a strategy.[61]

The confrontation began immediately. Matthew Butler entered the office of Prince Rivers's clerk, a black man named William Nelson, and demanded that he surrender his seat. When Nelson refused, Butler exploded: "You God damned leather-headed son of a bitch, you, sitting down there fanning yourself, God damn you." Nelson remonstrated with him, declaring that he was "sitting in my own office and 'tending to my own business" and that there was another chair available that was customarily used by visiting lawyers. When he was later interrogated, Butler did not contradict Nelson's description of his demand or his outburst. He did, however, assert that the clerk had been "fanning himself very offensively."[62]

Butler's bellicose manner—to say nothing of the crowd he had brought along with him—convinced Adams and his men that their lives were at risk. They refused to appear in court, instead barricading themselves in their drill room above a Hamburg store. Butler and Rivers then began an uneasy exchange. Butler demanded that the militiamen surrender their arms to him, symbolically asserting his right to control collective martial activity, and he insisted that they apologize for their behavior on 4 July. The demand was militarily real and politically symbolic: it sought to reduce the militia to a counterforce to the Red-shirts while simultaneously placing Butler in a position of almost legal authority—as the representative of a white Democratic shadow-government. However Adams responded, Butler could not lose. If the militiamen acquiesced, they would lose face, and more important, they would lose their arms. The rifle clubs would have won local control without firing a shot. If the men refused, they would provide Butler with the pretext he needed to move against them with armed force.

Would-be mediators discovered that these white men sought neither compromise nor accommodation. Hamburg cotton factor Samuel Spencer, who represented an emerging class of black merchants and professionals, no doubt hoped that his credentials as a man of education and property—a "taxpayer," in the Democratic vernacular—would enable him to mediate between the rival parties. If Democrats truly sought to integrate black citizens into a relatively conservative party, they would have to deal with men like Spencer. But when he politely approached the rifle club leaders to offer his services as a mediator, Butler simply told him, "Sam, there is not any use in parleying any longer. Now, by God, I want [the militia's] guns, and I'll be God damned if I ain't going to have them." As if to underline the point, Tillman's brother-in-law John Swearingen pointed a pistol at Spencer. In a single emblematic moment, the upcountry Democratic leadership informed would-be black allies that their only proper role was as deferential subordinates.[63]

Having created a climate of fear and impending conflict by bringing the Red-shirts to Hamburg, Butler used the massing of armed black men—albeit in small numbers, in an upstairs room, in self-defense—to trigger the martial mobilization of white men. Butler made a brief trip across the river to Augusta, where he told those he met that he "would not be surprised at any time if a riot were to break out" in Hamburg. He did not report saying the more pointed words attributed to him by an Augusta newspaper:

"Things over in Hamburgh [*sic*] look squally; young men, we may want you over there this evening; get yourselves in readiness."[64]

What followed became one of Tillman's proudest memories. Butler's Red-shirts, joined by white Augustans, besieged the militiamen. After one white man was killed, the attackers opened fire with artillery and drove the militiamen from their stronghold. As they attempted to escape, a few were killed or wounded and about thirty were captured. The Democratic guerrillas then had Getzen — a local man, who knew his local enemies — select several captives to be murdered in cold blood. Those who were executed included militia members considered particularly discourteous and a Republican town constable who had frequently fined or arrested white men. The rifle club men called their captives out one by one and shot them through the head. In the midst of these murders, someone in the crowd suggested turning the remaining captives loose, provoking one of the Augusta participants to respond bitterly on behalf of embattled white patriarchal privilege: "[B]y God, if you do that never call the assistance of Georgians any more." After murdering five of those captured, the rifle club men told the others to run, then fired at them as they fled. Before they were through, at least seven of their opponents lay dead. On the way home from Hamburg, Tillman and others stopped at Getzen's house for a celebratory breakfast.[65]

Faced with this murderous challenge to his authority, Governor Chamberlain condemned the massacre's instigators. In letters of protest to the president and the secretary of war, he stated his belief that the violence had been premeditated and that Hamburg was "only the beginning of a series of similar race and party collisions in our State, the deliberate aim of which is . . . the political subjugation and control of this State" through "a campaign conducted on the 'Mississippi Plan.' " Chamberlain asked that federal troops be deployed at the Aiken and Edgefield courthouses. He wrote to one of South Carolina's U.S. senators that "[i]f you can find words to characterize [the massacre's] atrocity of barbarism, the triviality of the causes, the murderous and inhuman spirit which marked it in all its stages, your power of language exceeds mine. . . . Shame and disgust must fill the breast of every man who respects his race or human nature. . . . What hope can we have when such a cruel and blood thirsty spirit waits in our midst for its hour of gratification? Is our civilization so shallow? Is our race so wantonly cruel?"[66]

While Chamberlain lamented the character of his "race" and "civilization," black South Carolinians organized a formal protest. At the Conference of Colored Citizens in late July, the fractured black political leadership was shocked into momentary unity. Three dozen leading black lawmakers declared their belief that the massacre had been "part of a deliberate plan" by Democratic leaders and called for the prosecution of those leaders:

> The late unwarrantable slaughter of our brethren at Hamburg, by the order of General M. C. Butler, of Edgefield County, was an unmitigated and foul murder, premeditated and predetermined, and a sought-for opportunity, by a band of lawless men . . . who are the enemies of the colored race in that county, composed of ex–confederate soldiers, banded together for the purpose of intimidating the colored laborers and voters at elections, and keeping the "negroes in their place," as they say. . . . All the difficulties . . . are instigated and led on by these same men. There is no law or justice . . . because this band of regulators override all law except that of violence. No man's life is safe who does not bow to their wishes.

Appealing to a national audience that had frequently proved unsympathetic to pleas for the protection of black people's rights or lives, the black legislators designed their closing argument to appeal to the entrepreneurial spirit of liberal Republicans and their sympathizers: "We ask that, constituting as we do, a large producing class in our State, contributing what bone and sinew we possess to the development of its industries, we be not hindered by violence in our endeavors to increase the prosperity and material wealth of our commonwealth and in our efforts to advance the commercial interests of our country."[67]

Despite a series of protests and investigations, neither the state nor the federal government punished Tillman and his fellow Red-shirts. Echoing what had become a familiar refrain of wealthy white Democrats, Butler denied that his party of white South Carolinians had been responsible for whatever excesses had taken place. The Red-shirts, he explained, were "generally of a class of people who do not commit outrages of that sort." They had not met in Hamburg by any concerted plan, and once there, they had forborne for hours in the face of outrageous Republican actions. He himself had left Hamburg before the murders took place, he said. Responsibility lay instead with the hundreds of Augustans present, men Butler described as drunken "factory people" and "Irish," who had come across the bridge "for the purpose of plunder." Butler could hardly be blamed for their actions, for "I had no more control over that mob than I would have over a northeast hurricane." Here, Butler (like the Tax-payers' Convention orator of a few years before) was reinventing the complicated game of protection and threat that had undergirded the slave system: black men had to decide whether they preferred to submit to the dictates of genteel, upper-class whites or to become the victims of a bloodthirsty white "mob" over which elites claimed to exercise no control. Denying all, Butler declared that "[i]f I am the red-handed ruffian and bloodhound that I have been accused of being, either [Chamberlain's] government is imbecile and utterly worthless, or I should have been put in the penitentiary long ago." In other words, if Butler had got away with murder, that only demonstrated that black Republicans could not ensure the maintenance of law and order.[68]

From Democrats to "Straightouts"

By mid-August, the Hamburg massacre and other violent episodes had created a coercive political climate in which Democratic leaders found it difficult to continue supporting fusion. White Democrats condemned the violence at Hamburg at their peril. *Charleston News and Courier* editor F. W. Dawson, who saw upcountry extremism as dangerous to Democratic interests, called the massacre "a wholly unjustifiable affray" and the Red-shirts "barbarous in the extreme." But the Edgefield elite soon made it clear that they would not tolerate such opposition from within the ranks of the white Democracy. Antifusionists had already launched a rival Democratic newspaper in Charleston, and Dawson's condemnation of the violence at Hamburg soon brought a boycott of the *News and Courier*. It also earned Dawson a challenge to duel Martin Gary—a challenge delivered to the editor by Matthew Butler. Dawson, long a principled opponent of dueling, refused. But he soon realized that to continue opposing the separate ticket would cost him his influence in the state: by the time the Democrats met at their August convention, Dawson had come around to supporting his fellow Democrats' "efforts" at Hamburg. Fusion gave way to a straight Democratic ticket, led by the planter, general, and guardian of the rights of Klansmen, Wade Hampton III.[69]

This "straightout" (as opposed to fusion or compromise) policy represented a break from the wishes of many lowcountry leaders and a victory for the upcountry forces. It was also presented as a victory for the kind of "reform" previously promoted by the Tax-payers' Conventions and the *Rural Carolinian*. The Democratic platform declared that "substantial and lasting reform is impossible within the ranks of the Republican party of this state" and accused the Republicans of countenancing electoral fraud, accumulating enormous debts, mismanaging the state's finances, injuring its credit, and levying exorbitant taxes and "squandering them when collected," thus "hopelessly involv[ing] in debt a majority of the counties of the state." Black power, it seemed, was inimical to "good government."[70]

Democrats seemed determined to co-opt as well as coerce black voters. In accepting the Democratic nomination, Hampton offered himself as a father to the state's family, black and white. He claimed he would serve as "the Governor of the whole people," promising equal protection under the law, an end to violence, better public schools, and a fair and honest campaign. The Democratic platform encouraged South Carolinians, "irrespective of race or past party affiliation," to join the Democratic campaign, and Hampton spoke to largely black audiences throughout the lowcountry. Some black men undoubtedly did vote Democratic, and for that defection from the Republican Party they often faced ostracism and even violence. Black gentlemen such as Martin Delany took Hampton's promises seriously. But not surprisingly, the racial harmony envisioned by Hampton entailed a rigid political and economic hierarchy. Even Hampton limited his promise of "protection" to "all of your race who choose to vote for democrats." For many white Democrats, promoting black Democratic voting was no more than a tactic. As Gary explained in a widely distributed "plan of campaign," "we ought to begin to organize negro clubs, or pretend that we have organized them. . . . Those who join are to be taken on probation and are not to be taken into full fellowship, until they have proven their sincerity by voting our ticket." Democrats inflated the total number of black Democratic voters in order to make such allegiance seem more acceptable to potential black converts and to disguise blatant Democratic frauds as black crossover voting.[71]

Such Red-shirt Democratic "plans of campaign" also demonstrated the power that property owners could exert over landless people. In the swath of black-majority counties around Edgefield, Democratic club members were urged to "persuade" black voters to vote Democratic or not at all. Since many of these Democrats were also rifle club members or Civil War veterans, persuasion was bound to be physical as well as verbal: as Gary's plan put it, "Every Democrat must feel honor bound to control the vote of at least one negro, by intimidation, purchase, keeping him away [from the polls] or as each individual may determine, how he may best accomplish it." Tenacious black Republicans were not only threatened but also driven off lands they leased or on which they worked under contract.[72]

Where black and white Republican leaders were concerned, Gary believed that economic sanctions and physical threats no longer sufficed. "Never threaten a man individually if he deserves to be threatened," he explained to his troops, for "the necessities of the time require that he should die. A dead Radical is very harmless — a threatened Radical or one driven off by threats from the scene of his operations is often very troublesome, sometimes dangerous, always vindictive." It was a lesson former slaveholders understood implicitly: the man who resorted to threats might leave the impression that he was reluctant to do bodily harm in order to get his way. Republican state legislator Lawrence Cain understood and decided to forgo his annual canvass of Edgefield, having been "warned by a democrat that the subject of his assassination had been discussed in democratic clubs."[73]

Other antebellum lessons proved salient as well, especially the need to enforce white solidarity. When Democratic leaders declared their determination to have "white government," they were not talking about skin color as much as ideology. According to the emerging tenets of white supremacy, only those who supported a return to planter rule under the Democratic Party were truly white. But Democratic leaders knew that their rhetoric of white identity and unanimity did not match reality and that Dawson was not the only white man who needed to be forced into line. At an upcountry rally, former provisional governor Benjamin F. Perry urged Democrats to "stop all social intercourse with any man who is base enough to be a radical. Let him feel by your conduct toward him that the brand of infamy is on him and his children. This is the only way you can reach his black heart." Democratic terrorists singled out white Republican leaders as the first to be punished for the evils of Reconstruction. If the Red-shirt campaign inspired any Republican retaliation, Gary warned, "we will hold the leaders of the Radical Party personally responsible, whether they were present at the time of the commission of the offense or crime or not; beginning first with the white men."[74]

The Democratic straightouts publicly challenged and humiliated white Republicans. Masses of armed Red-shirts arrived at Republican rallies and demanded that their opponents "divide time"; then they "howled down" the Republicans and provoked physical conflicts, breaking up the rallies. In effect, Democrats denied their opponents the right to meet independently, much as slaveholders had formally prohibited slaves from assembling without a white man present. They also transformed peaceful political meetings — assemblies whose legitimacy was difficult to challenge and whose goal was the creation of a unified, energized Republican electorate — into riots. At a Republican political meeting in Edgefield on 12 August 1876, Butler and Gary demanded that they be allowed to speak in response to the governor and other Republicans, and they brought armed partisans to back up their demand with verbal and physical threats. Ultimately, so many Red-shirts forced their way onto the speakers' stand that it collapsed, and Chamberlain and other Republicans beat an undignified retreat. In limiting the right of public debate to those able to coerce their opponents' silence, "dividing time" perfectly represented the white-supremacist conception of democracy. So did Gary's blunt warning from the platform, brutally plausible despite its quotation in a Republican newspaper: "Look here niggers if you don't want trouble at election time, I'll tell you what to do. Go to whoever you work for if he is a white man, and say Mars ——, what ticket must I vote?"[75]

Ben Tillman rode with the Red-shirts throughout the bloody political season of 1876, and by its end, as the white Democratic mobilization reached its climax, he had taken command of his own rifle club. Two months after Hamburg, he played a small part in the worst of the violence. In mid-September, more than a thousand rifle club men attacked a black militia unit in a swampy area near Ellenton in Aiken County, killing at least thirty before a small federal detachment arrived on the scene. The partisans expressed great disappointment that their campaign had been halted so soon. According to a federal officer present, the Red-shirts cursed the federals' arrival and said "they [would] have given five hundred dollars if we had been an hour late." Tillman led fifty Red-shirts thirty miles to Ellenton but arrived too late for the slaughter. However, two men from his unit were detailed to execute an important prisoner, black Republican state senator Simon Coker, who had come to investigate reports of violence. They shot Coker while he knelt in his final prayer.[76]

As Gary had understood, threats might inspire bravery rather than fear, but bullets demonstrated the attackers' sincerity. The bodies of many of the Ellenton victims remained where they fell for days because their friends and families feared to be seen tending to them. Even the white manager of a nearby plantation, who had convinced his workers to remain indoors on the plantation as the fields and swamps around them ran with blood, feared to describe all that he had seen and heard. "I don't feel willing for what I write to you in regard to the riot to be made known," he wrote to the plantation owner. "[N]one of the neighbors will make statements who know all about it. The telegraphic reports don't cover the ground, and many things can be told but not written." Black Republicans bore the brunt of the terror. That fall, twenty or more white men broke down the door of the home of Silas Goodwin, a black Republican activist in Edgefield, and shot him dead. "God damn you," one declared; "you was bragging about how you was going to vote, but now vote if you can."[77]

During the 1876 canvass, reports of Red-shirt attacks reinforced Edgefield's reputation for violence. Native sons cultivated the mystique: at a Barnwell meeting, George Tillman asked, "Why don't you take these carpet-baggers out and hang them to the first tree? . . . If you haven't got moral courage here to do it, we will send a telegram over to Edgefield, and the boys will come over and do it for you." A Republican leader was reported to have nervously asked a Democrat at a campaign meeting, "I observe some Edge-field men here; is there any danger of violence here today?" Even a lowcoun-try Republican paper, observing that a large number of fights had occurred in town, joked that "the wind this last week must have been blowing from Edgefield county." A reputation for violence effectively amplified the mean-ing of every violent act.[78]

At the same time, Democrats in the heavily black and well-organized Republican lowcountry learned a rather different lesson. In the vicinity of Charleston, black Republican activists were frequently a match for white Democratic partisans. As a September labor struggle in the lowcountry rice fields took on a political character, violent conflicts in and around Charles-ton produced more victims among white Democrats than among black Re-publicans. Lowcountry Democrats would remember this for years to come, whereas upcountry white leaders grew increasingly dissatisfied with their party colleagues' apparently inexplicable tendency to compromise and accommodate.[79]

Republicans understood Democrats' intentions. "[T]he entire Demo-cratic party of the State," wrote a Republican editor, "is fully armed and organized and disciplined to carry the State on the Mississippi plan—more dependence is placed in the shotgun than argument." Governor Cham-berlain obtained some federal help and attempted—although too late—to safeguard the lives and voting rights of his citizens. Federal troops were stationed at several courthouses and other polling places, but their presence did little to ensure that votes were cast freely or counted fairly. In October, he formally disbanded all rifle clubs, a gesture that was met with amusement among the upcountry club members. Far from dissolving, the clubs swelled in number to nearly 300, with a total membership estimated at 14,000 or more white men. Edgefield was once again in the vanguard with 35 clubs, one of them Ben Tillman's. He had come of age.[80]

Tillman's conduct in the November election demonstrates how Edge-field polled a Democratic majority and explains why that result was con-tested so heatedly. Tillman was the sole Democratic manager of a local poll, a post he shared with two black Republicans, H. T. Tankersly and Aaron Miles. These two men later testified that when Miles arrived an hour or so after the polls had opened, Tillman questioned his right to serve as manager and remarked that he would have to see what the law said about a late arrival. Miles left before Tillman could demonstrate the finer points of election law, and Democrats soon dispensed with even a show of democratic process. A correspondent had warned President Grant less than a month earlier that "Hampton and Gary and Butler" had been conducting "in every sense a military campaign." Democratic ringleaders threatened to spill blood to assert their right to rule. Tillman harassed black voters as they arrived, declaring that he was manager of the poll and would notice if any Republican votes were cast. Robert Chandler, a black Republican who later testified that he had been driven off his land five weeks earlier, described a "whooping and holloing" group of men, including Tillman, who drew pistols and told Chandler to stay away from the ballot box. They warned him that if he came any closer, he "would come through blood." Chandler said, "Benny Tillman said they had been the rulers of Carolina and they intended to rule it." The final tally at that poll favored the Democrats, 211 to 2. Democratic activists like Tillman could not prevent every Republican from voting, but they effectively neutralized the county's black majority. Edgefield County, with 2,722 white and 4,400 black men of voting age, produced over 5,500 Democratic and fewer than 3,000 Republican votes.[81]

The fraudulent returns from Edgefield and nearby counties ensured that the state totals were inconclusive and hotly contested, and a state and national political crisis ensued. Legal challenges, a constant feature of Reconstruction politics, sprung up immediately. When the legislature met at the end of November, contesting delegations and rival politicians came to the assembly hall with guns and without the inclination to compromise. Bloodshed was averted for the moment when Democrats moved to another hall. Tillman was among the thousands of white Democrats who came to Columbia to protest the exclusion of Edgefield and Laurens Democrats and who rallied around the separate Democratic house. Each partisan house held its own investigation of the election returns, and each returned a majority for its own party's nominees. As a result, the senate (with an uncontested Republican majority) and the Republican house declared Chamberlain governor on 5 December and oversaw his inauguration two days later. The Democratic house, although lacking a quorum, declared Hampton victorious and inaugurated the former Confederate general a week later, giving the state two governments and two governors.[82]

This political stalemate was resolved by the economic inequality of the contending parties and the political capitulation of the national Republican leadership. Hampton's Democratic house called for voluntary tax contributions from its supporters to finance its operations and a refusal to pay taxes to the existing government; this became known as the "starve 'em out" policy. Landowners and laborers negotiated labor contracts early in the year as the landless sought to ensure their subsistence during the winter and spring. For those tenants and croppers who had not done well in the previous year's settling up, the contract and its provision for supplies on credit could mean the difference between eating and starving. The tables would turn as soon as the planting season began in earnest, but in January, the power was in the landowners' hands. Shortly after the November elections, therefore, Democrats called on landowners to evict any of their laborers who had voted Republican. Even after the election, it was possible for voters to switch their allegiance: in mid-January, an editorial presented "Hampton or starvation" as the options available to black laborers in the lowcountry rice fields. Black Republican citizens could withdraw their support from the Chamberlain government and continue to draw supplies from their employers, or they could exercise their right to freedom of political choice—and then also enjoy freedom from food and shelter.[83]

The South's contested electoral votes would resolve the conflict and determine the outcome of the presidential election. In February 1877, Southern Democratic congressmen offered to throw their support to Republican presidential candidate Rutherford B. Hayes in exchange for federal patronage, subsidies, and the withdrawal of federal troops from Southern statehouses. South Carolina's electoral votes allowed Hayes to be inaugurated as president on 4 March 1877, and he soon met with both Chamberlain and Hampton in Washington, D.C. Federal troops departed the South Carolina statehouse on 10 April; the next day, Hampton became the state's undisputed governor. Tillman, Butler, Gary, and their associates were never prosecuted; indeed, the new South Carolina legislature sent Butler to the U.S. Senate. Looking out at the radically altered political landscape, the all-white Edgefield grand jury that met in June 1877 concluded its report with a prayer of thanksgiving: "We humbly thank Almighty God that in his infinite wisdom and mercy He is again allowing old time judicial purity, ability, and courtesy to be exemplified in Edgefield."[84]

Black laborers, making the best of a desperate situation, began signing on for another year's work. To do so, however, they had to do more than acknowledge their defeat: they apparently had to pretend to have participated in it. As a fair-weather white Republican editor cynically reported on 12 April, "It is astonishing how many have just remembered that they voted for Hampton." The victorious Red-shirts had restored planter rule through violence, but proper order could only be reestablished if laborers played their parts correctly, abandoning the self-confident defiance of Republicanism and—if only symbolically and retrospectively—accepting the paternalist promises of white Democratic elites.[85]

But victory brought a struggle among the victors. Some, including Hampton, eventually came to believe their own rhetoric. Upon taking power, Hampton refused to acknowledge that Red-shirt violence had played an important role in the Democratic victory. As governor, Hampton denounced force and fraud and promised black voters "protection," public education, and a safe, subordinate place in a peaceful hierarchy of one-party politics. By contrast, men like Tillman and Gary celebrated the white violence of 1876. As Tillman charged later, Hampton "always maintained that sixteen thousand negroes voted for him in 1876; but every active worker in the cause knew that in this he was woefully mistaken." Gary argued that Hampton had misunderstood the meaning of 1876: politics were essentially "a question of race or struggle for supremacy between the races and not a mere contest for honest government as has been alleged." The Red-shirts understood the lessons of their victory to be the same as those of slave discipline: the only reliable basis for social peace was an underlying climate of terror. In this context, a black man's halfhearted and expedient claim to have voted for Hampton—his apparent submission to the victorious regime—did not represent a victory for the veneer of "paternalism" as much as a victory for the violence that forced the "*gentleman* from Africa" to mouth a master's slogans.[86]

Although men like Hampton and Tillman differed mainly in their interpretations of the victory, the stylistic and rhetorical differences between them have led historians and popular interpreters of Southern history to see them as representing real alternatives. To some, they represent alternate "roads" available to the postbellum generation, one leading to social peace, the other to racial conflict. To others, they represent distinct subcategories of the "white mind," one "radical" in its commitment to the violent racialization of society, the other "conservative," concerned with restoring proper relationships of deference and social place not limited to racial hierarchy. But paternalism and violence were in fact complementary and mutually necessary strategies with common roots in the social and labor system of slavery, where they had functioned as carrot and stick. Hampton might have imagined that he served as the protector of docile blacks against lawless whites, but the upcountry Red-shirts knew how crucial their violent efforts had been to his victory. Veterans of the campaign of 1876 realized that the "force and fraud" Hampton denounced had hardly been the work of lawless mobs. The "shotgun policy" had been no spontaneous eruption of white "radicalism" or violent racial instinct but the work of a well-established leadership class exercising its powers of military mobilization.[87]

Even before the federal government withdrew, an editorial skirmish revealed how weak Hampton's rhetorical position could become. When several upcountry Democratic newspapers tried to lay claim to having been the first to endorse the victorious straightout policy, Dawson's *Charleston News and Courier* mocked them, suggesting that such a search would logically lead them back to 1860 and the signers of the South Carolina ordinance of secession. Dawson's desire to make light of this newspaper war perhaps reflected his own well-founded anxiety over having arrived late in the straightout camp, but he inadvertently made a serious point: he acknowledged that the straightouts—defiant white men asserting themselves militarily against illegitimate authority—had assumed the mantle of the Confederate rebellion. Perhaps without realizing it, the Charleston editor had ceded moral and political advantage to men who had shown an early commitment to conflict over compromise—men like Ben Tillman.[88]

The Shotgun Wedding of White Supremacy and Reform

What Democrats heralded as "Redemption" quickly proved to be a limited victory. Although federal occupation had ended and a Confederate planter sat in the governor's office, slogans such as "good government" and "white supremacy" could not restore the world the slaveholders had lost, and young Democratic militants like Ben Tillman soon discovered that the reconstruction of white patriarchal authority and solidarity remained a complicated task. Everyone understood that the end of slavery had fundamentally changed the agricultural economy, but the events of the past two decades had dramatically altered the parameters of citizenship and of political possibility as well.[1]

Even as Democrats sorted out their winnings, long-simmering conflicts of class and region broke out among white men. The shooting had barely ceased when a factional contest within the Democratic Party recapitulated one set of antebellum struggles. Old political grievances were refracted through contemporary disagreements over the legacy of 1876 and over what constituted proper manly behavior, a struggle that symbolically pitted up-country militants like Martin Gary against lowcountry leaders like Wade Hampton and F. W. Dawson. At the same time, merchant capital emerged as a more dynamic force than landed wealth; this transformation of the economic elite, taking place alongside a revolution in agricultural credit and finance, caused strains within the ranks of white Democrats.

But elites were not the men hardest pressed by the new economy, and an even more serious challenge than Gary's soon emerged from the grass roots. By the late 1870s, the radical change emancipation had wrought in the agricultural economy began to hit home in ways that could no longer be blamed on Reconstruction's "radical misrule." Lacking cash or easy credit, small landowners, renters, and laborers all became dependent on crop liens for agricultural credit. Dependence on merchant capital struck directly at the autonomy white men had long expected; hard times could drive men from landownership to renting or from renting to laboring. For African Americans, sharecropping and other forms of poorly paid labor seemed a paltry reward for years of striving. More and more white men, too, believed their cherished independence to be at risk: as even some white elites felt shortchanged by the victory of 1876, many less wealthy white farmers found themselves slipping into relative or even absolute poverty.

In the early 1880s, preoccupied with the sparring between large landowners and mercantile capitalists, the men who ran Democratic Party clubs and conventions almost overreached. At the instigation of local landholders like Ben Tillman, the legislature altered the state's range laws in ways that provoked heated opposition from some poor men. Simultaneously, they passed restrictive new election laws that threatened the suffrage rights not only of black men but also of already fearful and disgruntled white men. Disaffection with the Redeemers grew so great that some white men began to articulate a producerist critique of the new political-economic order and forge a political coalition with the bloodied but still substantial group of black voters. If these voters could transcend their bitter history, they might bring a Redemption of a very different kind.

Such efforts faced formidable obstacles. Most white men—even those attempting to forge a biracial coalition—continued to understand political and economic independence in terms of white patriarchal authority. Those who moved toward a more expansive conception of male independence did not have time to make their case, for they fell victim to the same forces that had destroyed Reconstruction. Red-shirts like Tillman might have helped create the crisis, but they also did their best to see the party through it, riding against the leaders of the biracial coalition and vanquishing the movement at the hustings and the polls. But all was not well. The new insurgents' calls for "reform" could not be permanently addressed by the Red-shirt slogan "white supremacy." White Democrats could employ violence to limit the parameters of reform, but they would have to follow up that victory with more than slogans and shotguns. If they did not seem to offer any hope of

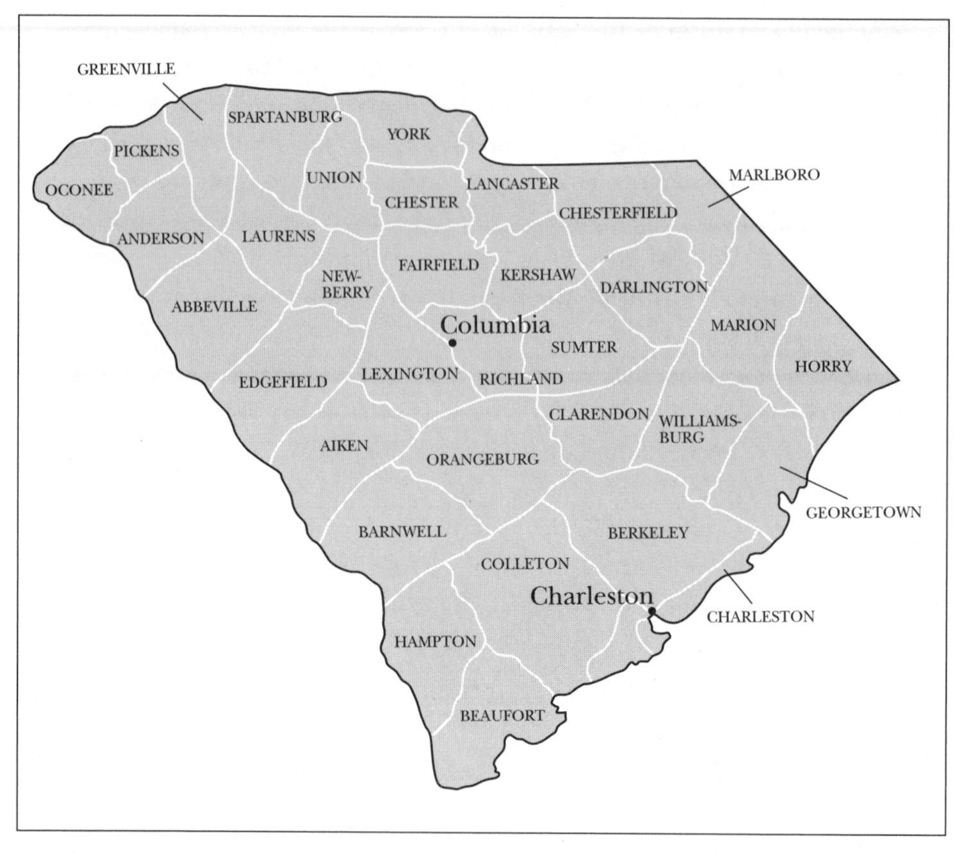

South Carolina in the 1880s

relief to the state's white farming men, it would be only a matter of time before they had to go to war again.[2]

Ben Tillman's Reconstruction

Despite Reconstruction's "radical misrule," Tillman had done well during the 1870s, becoming his township's most substantial landowner. He began the decade with more than 400 acres of land, bought more land in the early 1870s, and inherited 170 acres in 1878 after his mother's death. By 1885, Tillman owned 2,200 acres in several parcels, employed enough laborers to run thirty ploughs, and raised both beef cattle and dairy cows. He was one of postbellum agriculture's success stories.[3]

It was an unpretentious form of prosperity, however. The autobiography of Samuel L. Morris, Edgefield's Presbyterian minister in the years after Reconstruction, provides a rare glimpse of Tillman in the early 1880s. Morris found Tillman both an "uncouth" figure who used "shocking profanity" and "the smartest man I had ever known," who gleefully quoted from the classics. He described Tillman's "tremendous head" covered with "bushy hair, which hung down to his shoulders." The old family home known as "Chester" had apparently burned, and the Tillmans were living in a three-room tenant house in whose front yard "his horses cows and pigs enjoyed social equality." Morris was unable to induce Tillman to join his church, although Tillman attended services and "led the singing as his wife played the organ." By contrast, Sallie Tillman became a member of the Highview Presbyterian Church and appears to have led the way in calling for at least one revival meeting. Ben Tillman's regular church attendance while in Washington, D.C., a decade later—albeit at churches of various denominations—may well have been in response to his wife's urging. But he neither spoke nor wrote much of religion and on occasion expressed impatience, even skepticism, regarding religious disputes. In 1905, during a controversy over the state's hiring of a Catholic as a university instructor, Tillman wrote that he "[did] not see what a man's religion has got to do with our employing him provided he has got any religion at all which you know is a rather scarce article. I mean the genuine."[4]

Tillman's path to prosperity was not open to all the state's residents. Although black South Carolinians continued to pursue their vision of landownership, ever greater numbers reluctantly accepted the limited autonomy of sharecropping. Even this painful compromise left cash-poor planters only half-satisfied, for they would have chosen a system offering "better control" if they had only been able to pay cash wages. Black tenancy and even sharecropping represented a profound loss of authority for landowners. "There was nothing more ruinous or cut-throat to the general welfare," stated an Edgefield planter, declaring "general" his own highly particular interest, "than to have parcels of land here and there rented without the utmost discrimination to laborers—furnishing a mule, supplies &c. on credit, and starting such thriftless people to planting on their own hook." Slaves no more, these "laborers" had the temerity to take more than the traditional Christmas week holiday, returning to their employers' fields only when "starvation drove them out."[5]

In these struggles, Tillman had advantages of which other men merely dreamed. Just as his mother had preserved enough liquidity to purchase land in Florida, Tillman could pay cash wages to many, or perhaps even most, of his workers. In Tillman's expansive dominion, there were few black tenants or sharecroppers. Unsurprisingly, the forms of landowner "control"

Benjamin Ryan Tillman in his thirties. Due to his missing left eye, most photographs were taken in profile or three-quarter view. Special Collections, Clemson University Libraries.

remained strikingly familiar. During the 1880s and 1890s, Tillman's son recalled, the family lands were worked by several gangs of black laborers supervised by a black foreman. Tillman, the "Boss," rode on horseback through his fields, "directing the blacks in what to do and how to do it," or (in a less genteel formulation) "driving the slovenly negroes to their work." Tillman seems to have offered a few families—perhaps especially those working lands not contiguous with his home plantation—other arrangements.[6]

Labor control remained a collective as well as an individual responsibility, although the legal status of the laborers had changed. The Beech Island farmers still met during the 1880s and 1890s, but now they discussed wages more than whippings. Members tried to come to "mutual agreement as [to] the wages to be paid for a certain kind of work . . . not [to] be violated under any circumstances." By colluding with one another in this way, they might well have held down the cost of labor. But here landowners' individual and collective interests diverged. When the labor market grew tight, as it often did during crucial weeks of the growing season, the temptation to break the local wage ceiling was often too great to resist. Advocates of employer collusion complained that others "resort[ed] to what might be termed underhand methods, at the commencement of the year or at seasons when all are pushed to extremities to have certain farm work done." Even landowners like Tillman, who identified himself as an agricultural reformer, understood that plantation agriculture required a pragmatic approach to the labor market. In a "Memorandum about Farm Work," Tillman instructed his wife to have his sons "[h]ire hands at any price they may cost," but "without letting anyone know it so as to cause a row in the neighborhood."[7]

Planters continued to work together to restrict black people's movements and activities. A generation earlier, a black person's body and will were presumed to be subordinate to those of any white man, and black men and women who were suspected of criminal activity could be stopped and questioned by any white man. This was no longer the case under postemancipation law, and black people's freedom to choose destinations, employers, and associates tore the web of scrutiny that had once preserved property owners' peace of mind. In response, employers took both legal and vigilante action against freedpeople and traders who trafficked in stolen cotton. They also weakened Reconstruction-era laws intended to safeguard laborers' interests.[8]

Within the bounds of his plantation, Tillman could sometimes act as though the 1850s had continued without interruption. Indeed, he cultivated a relationship with his dairyman, Joseph Gibson, that resembled the paternalism of a master toward a favored slave. He spoke of "Uncle Joe" with affection and provided for him in his will; when Gibson's death preceded his own, Tillman erected a substantial headstone and paid Gibson's wife a subsidy.[9] In addition to having a job that entailed substantial responsibility, Gibson lived with his wife Kitty in a two-room house in the yard of Tillman's own home. Perhaps Joe and Kitty Gibson shared their private thoughts about Tillman in late-night whispers, or perhaps they silently made their peace with the South Carolina of the post-Reconstruction era. In any case, very few of Tillman's employees appear to have had even the small degree of control over their work lives that Joe Gibson had.

Kitty Gibson was hardly the only black woman working on Tillman's plantation, but her name is one of the few that appears in the surviving records. The documents left by postemancipation plantation owners reflected the changing relationship between black households and the labor force. In annual labor contracts, the head of the household took responsibility for the household's laborers, and across the cotton South, nearly nine out of ten black households were headed by an adult male. Both men and women worked the fields, but in most cases, it was a man who made the formal agreement. On Tillman's acres, black laborers seem to have worked mainly in gangs, a labor arrangement that (unlike sharecropping or tenancy) required no written agreement. The gendered division of labor on the Tillman lands therefore remains a matter of speculation.[10]

Although white as well as black women's labor had always been central to white agricultural households, wealthy and poor white men tacitly agreed not to take public notice of the hard, physical work done by most white women. The dependence of poor and middling white households on the labor of every adult could seem to undermine the independence of the men who formally governed those households. But from small farms to large plantations, the hardships of the Civil War played havoc with such expectations. White women's labor became not only visible but also crucial to the conduct of the Confederate war. Women of the slaveholding class had taken on new, previously inappropriate managerial responsibilities. By the 1880s, these onetime emergency measures had become more or less openly acknowledged elements of postbellum plantation life. Many (although hardly all) white men and women began to recognize white women's physical labor as essential and even honorable. By the mid-1880s, in fact, these daily realities led Tillman to metaphorically exalt these white farm women not as delicate ladies but as "our sun-browned goddess."[11]

Tillman's own success as a planter depended a great deal on one such woman. From their courtship in the 1860s through Tillman's final illnesses in the 1910s, including the births of seven children and the early deaths of two, Ben and Sallie Tillman were devoted familial and agricultural partners. Tillman adored his wife and wrote her teasingly passionate letters: "I had all the bed & all the pillow last night & I rolled all over it many many times looking for my somebody," he flirted after more than thirty years of marriage. But he never put her on a pedestal. He could not afford to, for Sallie Tillman had serious responsibilities on the plantation. The two were not formally equal: Sallie could not vote, and the Redeemer legislature had weakened laws giving married women rights of property and contract. Unlike most black and white farm women, Sallie did not actually tend the crops with her own hands, but she did take on responsibilities unfamiliar to wealthy white women of a generation earlier. She ran the plantation in Ben's absence, and even his love letters frequently doubled as memoranda to his acting plantation manager. When her husband was away, Sallie signed checks with his name, and with a young son sitting behind her, she rode horseback through the family's fields "guiding the business."[12]

Other families' "businesses" did not go nearly so well in the 1880s. African Americans remained the poorest group in the state, and by 1880, Edgefield's whites controlled nearly all the wealth in the county; indeed, over the previous decade, the total wealth of black residents of the county had actually declined. But few white men enjoyed Tillman's level of prosperity, and large numbers of white male household heads found themselves at least periodically without land to call their own.[13] Preoccupied with regaining control over black South Carolinians as an agricultural labor force, the state's new leaders paid little attention to white poverty. But even when they did, they found that the postbellum agricultural economy presented apparently intractable dilemmas. Stripped of slave wealth and labor, postbellum landowners had to offer lenders something else as collateral. Renters and sharecroppers, too, lacked a ready basis for the extension of credit for food and supplies. Local merchants had access to supplies, but they hesitated to extend credit to people who might not be able to make good on their obligations. So before they would advance supplies to credit-hungry farmers, these merchants set two conditions. They insisted first that the farmers plant cotton, for which there would always be a market, and second that the farmers give the merchants a lien on their crops. The farmers got their supplies, and the merchants got their promise of repayment. But the crop lien subjected debtors to everything from the whims of local merchants' interests to the cycles of the international cotton economy. As the price of cotton went into a long decline, laborers, renters, and even landowners found themselves unable to pay off their obligations at the end of the season. Many found themselves falling ever further into debt to the merchants, unable to extricate themselves from the cycle of cotton, credit, and crop lien.[14]

Hostility to merchants grew, not only among debt-ridden tenants and smallholders but also among wealthy landowners, who frequently required merchant capital in order to furnish their laborers with supplies. Of course, no clear line existed between merchant and planter capital: many planters and professionals, once almost entirely invested in land and slaves, provided unprecedented resources for new towns, mills, and railroads. But planting and mercantile interests could easily come into conflict, for merchant credit undercut landlords' control and allowed more freedpeople to farm on their own. As a white political activist complained, "[E]very freedman in the land can pretend to run a farm, and . . . the control of the land and labor passes out of the hands of the owners."[15]

Some agricultural reformers blamed white farmers for their predicament. As early as 1869, the *Rural Carolinian* had called for "diversified agriculture," a refrain that agricultural intellectuals had been singing since the antebellum era. The practice of acquiring credit by producing cotton left farmers "bound hand and foot to the merciless commission Merchant or Middleman, dependent for every pound of food for man and beast." Economic dependence stripped farmers of the autonomy that made them men worthy of citizenship. "[F]orced to give liens on their crops," they became "simply overseers for the Commission men" and had to "do as they dictated" in order to receive supplies. Submission to another's dictation was hardly the independence of a true farmer; such men, critics implied, were no better than black laborers.[16]

Planters complained constantly about the lien system and sought its radical change or abolition. But legislative efforts to abolish the system revealed that the alternative was economic paralysis. Without the crop lien or an alternative source of agricultural credit, the economy would come to a standstill. New laws did give a landlord's interest in a crop higher priority than a laborer's; they also established that landlords' liens for rent did not need to be recorded unless they exceeded one-third of the crop's value, a provision that stripped renters of the legal protection of a written document. But most legislation regarding liens reflected battles among renters, owners, and merchants over issues of priority and did not challenge the lien system itself. Gradually, some came to accept the system as a necessary evil or even (as the *Charleston News and Courier* put it) "the salvation of many of the poorer [white] farmers," who otherwise would not be able to get the credit necessary to plant.[17]

The same wealth that enabled Tillman to pay his laborers in cash and work them in gangs (rather than allow them the autonomy of cultivating household plots) insulated him from this kind of dependence on merchant credit. Free to plant what he chose, Tillman diversified his farming, experimenting with hogs, grapes, and dairy products. As we will see, he showed little sympathy for those among his neighbors who were at greatest risk of losing their economic independence. Tillman would not make common cause with struggling white men until such a posture seemed essential.[18]

Even during the early years of Reconstruction, some white farmers saw other white men as the enemies of widespread white independence. One reader of D. Wyatt Aiken's *Rural Carolinian* suggested that white laborers were leaving the state because the "best lands [were] locked up in the hands of a few men that were once big farmers." According to this skeptical correspondent, such men's cynical response to poor white men's plight was "Bring on your cash." Aiken, for his part, blamed agricultural hardships on a merchant class that profited from planters' lands and laborers and intruded on the relationship between landowners and workers. Under Aiken's leadership, Grange members denounced "monopolies, rings, and middlemen" as forces hostile to "the tillers of the soil."[19]

But Aiken's attempt to deflect hostility away from landowners and toward merchants did not persuade some critics of the new agricultural order. In late 1881, a white Edgefield yeoman wrote a scathing letter to his local newspaper complaining that a white man who employed black agricultural laborers treated his white neighbor—the "honest, hardworking, nothing to do with negro farmer"—with disrespect. "Big Mr. Negro farmer," he wrote, had the gall to complain that poor black and white men conspired to traffic in his seed cotton, but he feared that prosecuting the actual thieves would drive his laborers away. Whereas neighbors ran their farms and businesses on their own labor and credit, this cowardly planter acted selfishly, "always draining some provision store, always twirling and turning and screwing, trying to get out of paying some honest debt that he has contracted." When called to account for an outstanding debt that he could not pay, he took unmanly advantage of the new laws of women's property, shielding resources by placing them in his wife's name—in the words of the angry yeoman, seeking shelter "behind his wife's petticoat." Fearful of offending his black laborers, relying for protection on a white woman, incapable of managing his affairs without taking advantage of other white men, "big Mr. Negro farmer" lacked the honor of a real white man, an honest farmer, or a responsible citizen.[20]

The hostility between white men who were secure in their agricultural independence and those who were not came to a head over changes in the state's range law. Antebellum Southern law had generally recognized an open range: stock owners could let their animals roam free, and farmers had to build substantial fences around their crops if they wished to protect them. Elsewhere in the country, the range had been closed by the time the Civil War began: animals, not crops, had to be fenced in, and stock owners could be held liable for any damage caused by their foraging property. In the late 1870s, Southern agricultural elites and townspeople seeking to protect their urban investments moved to make the law safeguard their property against damage by other men's animals.[21]

Tillman, one of those wealthy landowners, first entered representative politics as a campaigner for the stock-enclosure (or stock) law. In the summer and fall of 1881, local and county assemblies sent him to lobby the legislature in Columbia on behalf of the stock law. Tillman fancied himself a "scientific farmer" who had imposed a carefully diversified order on his growing lands: that year alone, he bought several thousand dollars worth of new farm machinery, going into substantial debt in pursuit of his vision. He and other like-minded landowners argued that unfenced animals imposed undue burdens on farmers, discouraging self-sufficiency and diversification. But despite their claims that stock laws would be "of benefit to all classes of society," wealthy agricultural reformers understood that a law abolishing the open range might well be interpreted as "class legislation . . . against the interests of the poorer class of society."[22]

Indeed, a political response from "the poorer class" was not long in coming. For landless families, a free-ranging hog or two might represent the last shred of self-sufficiency, and by the time fence-law advocates had launched their movement, opponents had organized as well. In Edgefield, many of these opponents were white men whom the *Edgefield Advertiser* carefully described as "of a class that seldom visit the Court House and seldom take part in public meetings." But meet they did. Members of the local Democratic Executive Committee attended the stock-law protest meeting and were allowed to speak on behalf of the law, but for once, a political meeting that included planters was not a planters' meeting. The *Advertiser*, committed to closing the range, struggled to show respect for the forms of white male equality. In the end, the paper praised the stock-law opponents for allowing supporters of the law to speak, explaining that "we know them well, and consequently were not surprised either at their bravery or their honesty." In a patronizing sleight of hand, the editor praised these simple men for respecting democratic principles but did not seriously address their fears and grievances.[23]

Such condescension backfired, revealing that black Republican voters did not constitute the only "sleeping giant" in state politics. When the legislature passed the stock law, some of these frustrated opponents resorted to less civic-minded measures. Militant assertion of white men's rights came home to roost in Richland County—home of the capital, Columbia—as masked "stock-law Ku Klux" burned fences in protest. A state senator from a cattle-rich lowcountry district even threatened to leave the Democratic Party, prompting the *Advertiser* to urge those who had opposed the law to accept its passage and "let the matter entirely alone" rather than continue the dangerous conflict. But those injured by the new law were concerned less with the dangers of division than with the injustices of Democratic rule. Democratic leaders, seeking to blunt the hostility their new policy had engendered and hoping to prevent a protest vote during the party's nomination process, exempted large sections of the state and postponed the law's effects until after the 1882 election. Tillman and the other proponents of the stock law had won a divisive victory.[24]

Martin Gary, Sectional Hostility, and the Coming Class War

Barely a year after Wade Hampton became governor, the *Edgefield Advertiser* already perceived two threats to white unity from within the anti-Reconstruction coalition itself. First, "aristocratic" planters might assume that Hampton's strategy of appealing to black voters could be continued indefinitely; it was but a short step from there to the domination of the party by a coterie of planter bosses manipulating an allegedly purchasable black electorate. Hampton's condemnation of "fraud and intimidation" in the campaign of 1876 struck upcountry Red-shirts as dishearteningly obtuse, perhaps portending an outright betrayal of the straightout legacy. The governor's rhetoric of inclusion and appeasement and his claims that black Democratic votes had made the difference between defeat and victory in 1876 left the *Advertiser*'s editor disgusted: "[R]emember," he warned, "that sentimentality about the negro on paper and in speeches is an exceedingly different thing from a practical application of the negro at the ballot box. The one is pretty; the other is *the devil*!"[25]

The second danger came from below, not above. The *Advertiser* cautioned that white men who owned no land and employed no laborers might come to feel that they had no particular economic stake in the new order. "[P]oor men throughout the country," the editor worried, "unable to control any negroes, because of employing none, and seeing themselves without any voice in the State they helped to save, would leave the Democratic party, reorganize the Republican party, with the assistance of its old leaders, and defeat the land-owners." Disgruntled whites might grow "forgetful of the darkness of radical rule" and "arra[y] themselves against the organization of the party of law and order" as "independents" or a "working-man's party." Drawing comparisons with the recent revolutionary ferment in Europe, the excitable editorialist imagined the establishment of a "southern Commune."[26]

Clearly, something was needed to prevent reckless men—whether oligarchs or communards—from again subjecting South Carolina to "misrule." As an alternative to working-class radicalism or aristocratic tyranny, the *Advertiser* offered Martin Gary and the Red-shirts as a model of white unity, martial manhood, and political virtue. In August 1878, the newspaper commemorated the role of Tillman and other Red-shirts in the Hamburg and Ellenton massacres by publishing a special issue printed in red ink; Gary and McKie Meriwether, the sole white casualty of Hamburg, were held out as emblems of virtuous white manhood, models of an unpretentious and uncompromising militancy that could once again save the day.

The Edgefield paper's choice of local hero Gary as the embodiment of these virtues was not accidental, for the Edgefield lawyer and officer had already set himself in direct opposition to Governor Hampton. Gary made hostility to any black political participation a keynote of his political program as early as the 1878 campaign, arguing that politics "is now and has been a question of race or struggle for supremacy between the races and not a mere contest for honest government as has been alleged." As Edgefield's delegate to the state Democratic convention in 1878, he served on a committee that repudiated all fusion or coalition politics. A Democratic newspaper nervously complained that Gary "held the colored people up in contempt . . . using language which . . . certainly had a tendency to alienate them from the support of Governor Hampton." Gary argued for the repudiation of state debts accumulated under Reconstruction governments. He also objected to a tax for state-funded common schools since some of the proceeds would be used to educate blacks.[27]

For Gary, racial coexistence was a matter of domination and terror, not cooperation. He believed that violence could unseat Republican officials and intimidate black majorities without bringing either unmanageable labor unrest or federal intervention. The opponents of white supremacy deserved humiliation, not debate; he attacked Hampton's conduct during and after the 1876 campaign, alleging that Hampton had offered to withdraw the state's Democratic electors for president in exchange for Republican support for his own election. Hampton denounced Gary's claim as "utterly and absolutely false" and called his views "unwise and dangerous," sealing the enmity between the two former Confederate generals.[28]

Gary's unmoderated posture disturbed powerful interests. Self-consciously genteel elites found his style of manhood crude and ill-mannered, and the state's emerging class of investment-oriented capitalists—championed by newspapers such as the *Charleston News and Courier*—worried that

Gary's insistence on forcible self-assertion would perpetuate the state's reputation for anti-industrial backwardness. This conflict came to a head when Gary publicly defended the conduct of Colonel E. B. C. Cash, a Civil War officer who killed the eminent lawyer Colonel William Shannon in an 1880 duel. Cash had been on cordial terms with the wealthiest and most powerful men in the state, including Hampton. When Shannon became involved in debt proceedings that cast suspicion on Cash's wife, Cash expressed outrage at what he perceived as an attack on his wife's honesty. He challenged Shannon to a duel. The older man refused, but Cash persisted in his attacks until Shannon himself finally issued a challenge.[29]

When the duel ended with Shannon dead, contenders for the leadership of the Democratic Party split over the question of Cash's conduct. Some, inside and outside the state, saw Cash's pursuit of Shannon as a relic of a less-civilized age and believed that Cash should be prosecuted for murder. According to Henry Grady's *Atlanta Constitution*, Cash had hounded a brave man into defying the laws against dueling, making the killing an act of "cold-blooded murder." Newspapers from the *Charleston News and Courier* to the far upcountry weeklies likewise waxed furious over this "chivalric murder." And well they might. Urban and even small-town newspapers represented the interests of local capitalists, who were increasingly likely to be merchants and whose livelihoods depended on their own and their communities' reputations for being safe for investment. But Cash had his allies. A supporter reported a conversation among a "party of gentlemen" to the effect that "if any jury dared convict Col. Cash & he was sentenced for murder," they would "tear down any jail in the State in which he was held."[30]

Economic interest did not mechanically dictate personal loyalties or perceptions of law, custom, and honor, but where one sat did make a difference. Matthew Butler had been a leader in the violent campaign against Reconstruction, but he had since become a U.S. senator and was now allied with the Hampton faction. Butler tried to find a balance between manly self-assertion and a more businesslike personal politics. Although careful to emphasize that dueling could be honorable when the rules of conduct were scrupulously observed, he suggested that Cash's behavior had been dishonorable and that he had "trample[d] the law defiantly under foot."[31]

In letters to Cash, Gary voiced his outrage at such equivocation and described Butler as the worst sort of hypocrite. After all, barely four years earlier, Butler himself had carried a challenge for Gary—the challenge to Dawson after the editor initially condemned the Hamburg massacre. Butler's gift for neat rhetorical footwork no longer seemed as charming as it had when the audience had been Republican congressmen. Butler's new ally, Dawson, was "a bastard," Gary fumed, "a liar, a bribe taker, a coward and a blackguard." In the end, Gary argued, Cash's defense of his wife's honor was justification enough. If Cash's foes saw nothing to admire in the protection of a white woman's good name, Gary exclaimed, "in God's name, what do they regard as sacred and worthy of fighting for?"[32]

Gary's outburst in part reflected his frustrated political ambitions and growing personal enmity for former allies, but it also revealed a mounting struggle over the meaning of manhood in the post-Reconstruction South. Where did propriety lie? Was it a matter of men taking violent responsibility for themselves and their households, as the exigencies of life as a slaveholder had fostered and demanded? Or did manhood require the forbearance that preserved other forms of social peace, notably the need to maintain white supremacy and white male solidarity even at the expense of a given white man's prerogatives? This tension between white men's individual and collective imperatives was not new, but it took on new meaning now that white manhood did not confer an exclusive and virtually automatic citizenship.

More dramatically even than during the secession crisis, the very notion of white patriarchal authority had come under attack, this time not by armies of abolition but by traitors within the ranks. Once, "submissionists" had been a tiny, powerless minority in South Carolina politics; now, it seemed, they governed. Gary understood attacks on Cash, like criticisms of the Hamburg massacre or the "Edgefield policy," as cowardly retreats from the principle that white men ought to use violence to defend their prerogatives. To men who clung to this vision of white patriarchal authority, fulminations against dueling were as ludicrous as new laws imposing the death penalty for rape: no man should allow the state — or its leaders — to tell him when he might or might not exact personal retributive justice.[33]

Gary's unpolished style, coupled with his support for policies such as "usury laws" (which limited the maximum interest rate), earned him a reputation in some quarters as the champion of the white plain folk. One supporter dubbed him the "great 'Commoner,'" leading "the people's battle against the aristocrats and capitalists." This man recognized Gary's wealth but granted him honorary credentials as a representative of the plain folk. His much-discussed volatility and disregard both for convention and for icons like Hampton could strike sympathetic observers as "the violent self-assertion of a proud, brave, free man who will act and cannot be bound." To such devotees, Gary was the architect of Redemption and the defender of ordinary white people's interests; he embodied white manhood unbridled, an alternative to the condescending moderation of the "less worthy sons / Who wear the ermine and the laurel; / . . . 'Christian Statesmen.' "[34]

For a time in 1880, it seemed that Gary might represent not the Edgefield editor's solution but his darkest fears. According to one friendly source, he contemplated an independent challenge to the Democrat leadership on a platform promising homesteads, common schools, and self-sufficiency, all built "on the foundation laid in 1876." In March 1880, Senator Butler warned a confidant of an impending split among white Democrats, claiming to "*know* that certain parties are ready to run independent, and will get the Radical vote and some Democratic following." Butler's warning notwithstanding, however, Gary's bid for the governorship failed in the Democratic nominating convention, where upcountry counties were, as always, underrepresented. Partisans later claimed that the leadership had promised Gary the nomination if he would remain within the party, then betrayed him once he agreed not to bolt. The dominance of local elites in the nominating process makes it nearly impossible for us to gauge the depth of popular support for Gary. But his allies would argue forever after that he had been "stabbed" — cheated and robbed of due political honor.[35]

Even after his untimely death in 1881, Gary's defiance made him an icon for white men disgusted with the arrogance of wealth. The Edgefield farmer who denounced "big Mr. Negro farmer" declared himself to be "on the question of seed cotton traffic, what M. W. Gary was in politics." Although Gary was dead, his combative iconoclasm in the name of white supremacy appealed to men who felt abandoned by their political leaders. Throughout the South, similar strains of class tension opened up space for independent challenges to Democratic rule. Gary's correspondence with Cash during 1880 and 1881 had raised the possibility of a political alliance between the two mavericks, and as the 1882 campaign approached, some disgruntled Democrats turned their eyes to Cash. "[T]he womb of the State is big with revolution," one man declared in a letter to the now-notorious duelist, "and it is a matter for our decision whether we will act as midwives to its birth."[36]

As this discontent brewed within the party's ranks, local Democratic militants like Ben Tillman had been working to consolidate the electoral triumph of 1876. The Republicans had been devastated by their losses in 1876–77, but they were still formally entitled to vote. As the election of 1878 approached, the chairman of the state Democratic Executive Committee urged local leaders to arrive armed and mounted and "divide time" at Republican meetings and to pressure poor blacks to vote the Democratic ticket. In the campaigns of 1878 and 1880, the Red-shirt rifle clubs, many now integrated into the state militia, remained as central to Democratic strategy as they had been in 1876. Throughout the upcountry, Democrats assaulted and murdered their adversaries. In addition to their roles in "witnessing" and harassing Republican assemblies, mounted companies disrupted voting where substantial Republican turnout was rumored or expected. In Oconee County, a Republican convention of less than fifty men was "witnessed" by three times as many mounted and uniformed Democratic partisans. A Democratic mass meeting in the same county drew nine companies of Red-shirts. In some areas, well-organized displays of Red-shirt force became matters of routine; elsewhere, the partisans arrived seeking to make a lasting impression. In Newberry County, "forty mounted horsemen, from parts unknown, came down upon the voters" at one precinct, leaving at least one black man dead.[37]

Despite Red-shirt intimidation, numerous black Republicans voted in the 1878 and 1880 elections. In Beaufort County, black landownership continued to rise throughout the nineteenth century, creating a viable black yeomanry in contradiction to white-supremacist strictures. Robert Smalls led a vibrant Republican Party, but Democrats repeatedly stole elections, gerrymandered the district of which Beaufort was a part, and contested Smalls's victories on the floor of Congress. As a result, the once-enslaved Smalls spent frustratingly little time serving his constituents and much more time defending victories they had already won. These results could be interpreted in several ways. Democrats might relax, satisfied with the overall result, or they might continue to feel anxiety over the more than 15,000 Republican votes cast for the state's leading black politician. George Tillman shouted his party's defiance in the halls of Congress after its members ruled against him in a contested election case in 1882: "[S]ince 1876 . . . the Caucasian has risen in his might [and] asserted his God-given right to rule where any considerable number of his people sojourn among the colored races."[38]

Anxiety about possible federal retaliation persisted, and Democrats sometimes sought to disguise their intentions. "So soon as you read this *Destroy it—Don't fail to do this*," concluded one memorandum on tactics from the state Democratic chairman. Local Democratic officials continued to fear a renewed black Republican mobilization, and in the days before elections, they frequently wrote in panic about surreptitious Republican plans: "[T]he negroes though apparently inactive are working with great energy," a partisan warned Orangeburg Democratic boss Sam Dibble. "I've pried into their camps. . . . *We are in danger.*" This reflected long-standing white fears of collective action by African Americans, but it also worked tactically, helping ensure white Democratic turnout in heavily black districts.[39]

Seeking a surer foundation for Democratic domination, the state legislature crafted election laws designed to minimize black political power in the state. The *Greenville News* frankly described a restrictive registration law as an effort to "keep the State in the hands of white men." The legislature redistricted the state, concentrating as many black voters as possible in a single lowcountry district. The new "eight-box law" specified separate ballots and boxes for eight categories of offices: ballots for each office could list only the candidates for that office, and ballots placed in the wrong box by inattentive or illiterate voters would be discarded. The law required election managers to read the labels on the boxes if asked by voters, a measure designed to allow officials to help like-minded voters overcome barriers of illiteracy.[40]

The legislators intended the law to be applied racially, for by the early 1880s, most white voters supported Democrats and most black voters backed Republicans. Black Democrats hung on in a few lowcountry areas, but their importance was more symbolic than substantive. Similarly, a few white men continued to support the Republican Party: in July 1880, for example, as Republicans crowded the Spartanburg County courthouse to discuss the fall campaign, an upcountry Democratic newspaper acknowledged the presence of "fifty or sixty whites" among the participants. But white Republicans were heavily burdened by the bitter legacy of the federal occupation and the ever-growing legend of Republican corruption, and they remained outliers in a party that was almost entirely black. Such men were unlikely to be disfranchised by a literacy test; they voted openly in the lowcountry, the cities, and apparently in some far upcountry precincts. It may even have served the interests of white Democratic leaders to tolerate a few white Republican voters in some areas since such men would offer constant targets for vilification and negative reference.[41]

But the onerous new voter registration law raised fears that poor white men as well as black men might be disfranchised, and it came within a single vote of defeat in the state legislature. By June, as the 1882 elections approached, Democratic leaders were clearly growing nervous that the law might have backfired. Senator Butler publicly worried that white voters might be disfranchised by the law. "[N]o nervous regard for consistency," fretted the *Charleston News and Courier*, "should prevent the Legislature from abolishing registration, if it can be ascertained that registration will lessen the political power of the white people." The point, after all, was "the maintenance of the supremacy of honesty, intelligence, and capacity," not a foolish consistency that might undermine white Democratic rule. Such fears were apparently well founded: the Democrats' laws and campaign tactics both limited the number of eligible voters and depressed turnout. Between the elections of 1880 and 1882, the number of votes cast for Democratic gubernatorial nominees plummeted from more than 117,000 to just 67,000.[42]

The first sign of mass protest against the Redeemers' stock and election laws came during the season of their passage, the winter of 1881–82, when black farmers and farm laborers began to leave the state in unprecedented numbers. In the last week of 1881 in Edgefield alone, a reported 5,000 blacks departed for points in the Midwest and Southwest; one observer estimated that the migrants made up 20 percent of the local laboring population. Their departure inevitably drove up the price of labor, but Democratic leaders, unwilling to admit that their range policies had negative economic consequences for employers, refused to concede that the stock law might be responsible for the exodus. Their analysis, though, bespoke a deep ambivalence about black South Carolinians generally. As the *Charleston News and Courier* put it, "[P]olitically speaking there are far too many Negroes in South Carolina, but from an industrial standpoint, there is room for many more." This telling contradiction would continue to vex those who, like Tillman, demanded both cheap labor and political hegemony.[43]

South Carolina's Populist Moment

By the time the Democratic leadership pushed through the stock and election laws, some white men had also had enough. The seemingly intractable crisis of the agricultural economy, refracted through the bitter social and economic conflict of the stock law, alienated many poor white men from the Democratic leadership. Some began to consider trading the wages of whiteness for a more tangible, less exclusive prosperity, seeking to forge electoral coalitions with black voters. The most successful of these coalitions was the Readjuster movement, which mobilized black and white Virginia voters behind former Confederate general William Mahone's promise to scale down the payment of the state's debt, secure male suffrage, and protect public education. In 1879, the Readjusters defeated the Democrats at the polls and took power in Virginia; by 1882, it appeared that South Carolina might follow the same path. In early 1882, a Democratic editor in far-upcountry Oconee County acknowledged that the stock law, the election laws, and appropriations for historically upper-class institutions such as

South Carolina College—now the University of South Carolina—and the Citadel might have given some white men cause to "believe and feel that the present government is no better than that of the Radicals." The secretary of the Beech Island Farmers' Club noted that "the passage of the 'Stock Law' by our Legislature is creating much excitement and comment. Threats of a new party are made, and fear is entertained by some that it will unharmonize the Democratic party to such an extent that the state may be easily *Mahone ized* [*sic*]."[44]

A white Fairfield County farmer named J. Hendrix McLane did indeed try to become South Carolina's Mahone. McLane was the same age as Ben Tillman and had shared many of the same experiences: he had lost a brother in the Civil War and had briefly left South Carolina in the 1860s to make a new start. He had become active in Democratic Party politics and had taken part in the straightout movement in 1876. But McLane had quickly become disenchanted with the Redeemer government, and through his Grange, he began organizing local Fairfield farmers behind a third-party alternative, the Greenback-Labor Party. Greenbackers represented the deep-rooted producerist tradition of American radicalism, described by historian Robert McMath as the idea that "the producer deserves the fruits of his or her work." In this vision, money existed only to facilitate the exchange of goods, and the cult of hard currency benefited only nonproducing middlemen and financiers. In an 1879 manifesto, McLane denounced the "money power" and called for greenback dollars and equitable taxation. Like Mahone, McLane sought coalition with black Republicans, demanding free and fair elections and an end to racial and partisan discrimination.[45]

In 1880, McLane's efforts met with little success. But the events of the next two years created an opening for a radical challenge. The stock and election laws angered many black and white men, cotton farmers suffered a particularly harsh year in 1881, and national Republican leaders began seeking to foster alliances with white independents throughout the South. The forces of political resentment, economic hardship, and partisan strategy came together to encourage the development of a grassroots movement. In mass meetings and conventions in 1882, Greenbackers denounced state laws and expenditures that seemed to benefit only an elite few, such as appropriations for the state's colleges.[46]

Greenback state chairman W. W. Russell declared that the party's strategy was to organize "the disaffected throughout the state." But he and other Greenback leaders understood the difficulties inherent in forging an alliance between discontented white Democrats and skeptical black Republicans, and they pursued a flexible strategy. Greenback clubs in some parts of the state included both white and black members. Greenback candidates for the governorship and many congressional seats received the state Republican Party's endorsement, but the two parties retained separate platforms. Greenbackers argued that economic interest, not race, should guide men's political choices, and they attacked "white supremacy" as a blind behind which Democrats passed "class legislation." As Russell put it shortly before the 1882 election, the Democrats' election laws favored the literate and "intelligent classes" over the poor men of either race. "The prejudices that could deprive the colored man of his vote," Russell declared, "cover the contempt of the fortunate classes for those less favored." McLane similarly accused elite Democrats of "foster[ing] prejudice between the two races" so as to be able to "run the state government for their own benefit to the injury of both the white and colored taxpayers of the state."[47]

The critique was persuasive to more than a few hard-pressed white and black men. As Greenback clubs formed throughout the state, even the *Charleston News and Courier* was forced to admit that "some good and intelligent men are joining the Greenback party." But South Carolina's populist moment faced daunting obstacles, for the Greenback-Republican coalition rested on an unstable foundation of disaffection and expediency. Unlike Virginia's Readjusters, who rallied to protect an existing system of public education, South Carolina's Greenbackers and Republicans mainly rallied against policies and leaders they disliked. Furthermore, Greenback leaders seemed willing, even eager, to gain the support of maverick Democrats, often men whose personal ambitions had been stymied in intraparty conflicts. The streams of elite and impoverished discontent came together most remarkably in the Greenback-Labor Party's alliance with Cash, who accepted Greenback support for his bid for the fifth-district congressional seat. Russell even sought to recruit Red-shirt and Grange leader D. Wyatt Aiken, whose attacks on merchants and monopolies made him a lesser but still powerful symbol of the potential for mobilizing white men's discontent. Russell may have hoped that claiming Aiken would help blur the line between dissident Democrats and Greenbackers; unsurprisingly, however, Aiken wanted to have nothing to do with the new party.[48]

As such recruitment efforts suggested, the term "disaffected" took in not only those poor white men who had lost their hogs and votes but also those planters with grievances against merchant capital or the Democratic leadership. The Greenback Party's eagerness to claim such men stemmed in part from its need to attract credible leaders — men whose names, styles, or backgrounds made them reasonable representatives of white discontent. But it also sprang from most Greenbackers' common history as white Democrats and their effort to present their movement as the legitimate inheritor of the Redemption legacy. Thus Greenbackers as well as Democrats invoked the heritage of 1876. One Greenback leader announced his intention to mount "a thorough canvass—a regular 1876 campaign" in which Democrats would have to divide time with his party.[49]

By mid-autumn, Greenback or Greenback-Republican fusion candidates were running in all seven congressional districts, and Republicans had endorsed the Greenback state ticket. This interracial coalition left Democratic conservatives scrambling for explanations. A Democratic paper acknowledged that "the fence law operates hardly on some of our people" but argued that supporting the Greenbackers would bring not relief but ruin, in the form of a renewed and corrupt Republican government. In despair, the editor complained that "the people seem to have forgotten there is any longer danger from misgovernment." *Charleston News and Courier* editor Dawson finally admitted that the stock law had been a hardship in some parts of the state, but he denied that this justified white men's abandonment of the Democratic Party. The Democrats insisted that the only alternative to their "white supremacy" was a return to the evils of "black Reconstruction." Their 1882 campaign against the Greenback-Republican alliance drew heavily on the memory of Reconstruction and argued that white men should not allow their grievances to subvert white-minority rule. "In the South," one editor averred, the alternative to "white government and white supremacy" could only be "ignorance, corruption, and all that works financial and social ruin." The Democrats should not ignore white men's grievances, and "negro rule" would be "worse than anything" and would make all other reform impossible. The only safe course for those who opposed the stock law or other policies such as the registration law was to "hold together . . . for white supremacy and after it is securely won we will fight all our other grievances." An Edgefield newspaper put it rather more emphatically: "If we have family quarrels, for heaven's sake let us fight them out among ourselves, and not go to our enemies for comfort."[50]

These writers were discovering, belatedly, that any credible white supremacy had to mean something more than electing white Democrats to office. Their own platform contained little of interest to white independents and offered black voters only the tired refrain of Hampton's support for public education. Furthermore, it was awkward for lowcountry urban Democrats to criticize the Greenback-Republican alliance. In the coastal towns and counties of Georgetown, Beaufort, and Charleston, Democrats had been running fusion tickets with Republicans, splitting offices among races and parties in order to avoid economically destructive and potentially violent election fights. This strategy looked very similar to that of the interracial movement the Democrats ostensibly reviled.[51]

Philosophical inconsistency did not deter the Democrats from violent action. The Democratic campaign against the Greenbackers utilized the same tactics and the same men as used in previous campaigns, but one man at least took on a new degree of responsibility: in August 1881, Ben Tillman was elected second in command of the Edgefield Hussars, a Red-shirt rifle club that had become a state militia company. This new rank, coming close on the heels of his participation in the stock-law campaign, represented Tillman's coming-of-age as a local leader. In June 1882, he became his township's representative to the County Democratic Executive Committee, and in July, he attended the state Democratic convention. In 1882, Edgefield's rifle clubs, including Tillman's Hussars, turned Democratic rallies into paramilitary events. A local Democratic weekly noted approvingly that Tillman had become "one of the most zealous and useful members" of the partisan militia; it is not hard to imagine what combination of speech making, coercion, and brute force constituted "zealousness" during the campaign of 1882.[52]

Seeking to discredit their opponents in the eyes of both black and white supporters, Democrats accused Greenback leaders of being violent white supremacists but also of being incapable of defending themselves from other white men. As the 1882 election approached, Democratic newspapers distilled hostile accounts of McLane's life into an indictment, headlined "Bully and Braggart," that purported to recount McLane's acts of terrorism as a Democratic vigilante leader in the 1870s. Russell stood accused of having voted for the Black Codes in 1865 and of supporting the stock law—positions with which the ruling Democrats of 1882 could not themselves take issue but through which they hoped to discredit Russell in the eyes of black and poor white constituents. More directly, Democrats attempted to show that McLane and other Greenbackers were incapable of defending themselves—the tactic Gary had pioneered against black and white Republicans in 1876. When confronted by Red-shirt partisans at Winnsboro, they charged, McLane had displayed cowardice. On that occasion, Democrats not only refused to let McLane speak but also collared, pummeled, and kicked him as he turned to leave. McLane, apparently fearing a serious beating, retreated into a hotel parlor. Local Democratic boss Thomas Woodward — under whom McLane had apparently served in 1876 — interceded to prevent the crowd from injuring his former colleague, but the Greenback nominee was foiled in his bid to speak.[53]

As presented to the state's readers in newspaper accounts, McLane's ordeal revealed that white supremacy could discipline whites as well as blacks. It also demonstrated the persistence of the Reconstruction-era rhetoric that contrasted the lawlessness of white mobs with the restraint of white elites. In effect, by playing the master's game of promise and threat, Democrats set the ground rules for McLane's insurgency and established their right to decide when and where he could or could not speak. The Red-shirt rank and file — "some Democrats the worse for drink," according to the paper, a "crowd" of "belligerents" — did the rough work. In this version, to Woodward fell the subtler task of mediating, appearing to stand outside the mob even as it did his party's work. Woodward appeared at a crucial moment, reportedly summoning the sheriff and others to ensure McLane's safety. But Woodward was not an outsider; he was, in fact, the leader of Winnsboro's Democrats. McLane's fate rested, in the end, in the hands of the Democratic Party — the same place it had been when the mob attacked. Less partisan observers might have been harder pressed to distinguish between this "mob," restrained by respectable officers, and the Red-shirt militias performing their accustomed tasks. Newspaper claims that "McLane and his confreres need fear no violence at the hands of our people" could be seen as disingenuous — or as Democrats' declaration of their mastery of the situation. McLane had just experienced that violence, and throughout the campaign, his "confreres" would experience much more.[54]

Such white-on-white violence raised the troubling possibility that conflict among the state's white men might actually become militarized. Although generations of local political leaders had also led the militia, up until 1860, the militia had never played the kind of military role in politics that had become familiar since secession. For most of that time, moreover, the lines between friend and foe had been drawn with relative ease: free versus slave, law and order versus abolition, Confederate versus Yankee, white Democrat versus black Republican. Now both sides — in the leadership as well as the rank and file — included substantial numbers of white Southern men, many of them veterans of the conflicts of the 1860s and the 1870s. In solidarity with one another, these same white men had constituted a formidable enemy against which both the federal army and the black majority had suffered serious losses. But even united, they remained a minority. If the political split now developing within their ranks were to turn bloody — an outcome that recent history made increasingly likely—any victory might also constitute a disastrous, fratricidal defeat for white supremacy.

Violence had its practical uses, but so did restraint. The Democratic leadership was hardly willing to write off McLane's white supporters, and so for Tillman and the Red-shirt leadership, the challenge became to intimidate their white opponents without unleashing a wholesale campaign of terror among white men. Harassment followed well-established patterns. Democrats arrived en masse at Greenback rallies and sought "divisions of time." In Edgefield, they took over such events entirely, slyly promising "safe passage" to white Republican leader Ellery M. Brayton should he choose to attend his own rally. Sometimes the Red-shirts did not stop at threatening or humiliating their white rivals: on 4 July, a Democratic gunman murdered a white independent former congressional candidate at Camden.[55]

But the most serious violence of the campaign followed Cash's efforts to mobilize black supporters in a district outside the traditional Republican lowcountry strongholds. As many as 700 black men and an unspecified number of white men attended Cash's campaign appearance in the town of Lancaster. Members of the audience harassed and perhaps assaulted a Democratic editor who offered a rebuttal; later that day, white terrorists shot six blacks, four fatally. It is difficult to piece together from unfriendly sources just what happened or what it meant. It is quite likely, however, that black voters responded with hostility to the Democratic editor and like-minded spokesmen. The comparative black political freedom of Reconstruction was only a few years past, and black men had often played assertive roles. In murdering four black activists but no white ones, Lancaster's white Democrats apparently chose their targets with care. They might have to negotiate with black power in the lowcountry, but if black men became politically active in other areas, white Democratic rule would truly be in jeopardy. By selectively targeting black voters, Democrats might discourage such a movement without creating irreparable rifts among white men.[56]

Democratic commentators simultaneously blamed Cash for inspiring violence and claimed such violence as a Democratic prerogative. Democratic violence, they suggested, was always a form of self-defense: independent biracial action itself constituted an attack on white supremacy, and retribution needed no further justification. At the same time that they sought to shift the blame for the violence to Cash, Democrats could not resist claiming it as their own particular métier. Republicans, argued Dawson's paper, had realized that the only way to win elections was to have Democrats on their side: the independent coalition knew that Cash stood a chance in the race "because he understands how to handle shot-guns."[57]

The reaction to the Lancaster "riot" followed the model of earlier white panics. Over the next few days, Democratic papers including the *Charleston News and Courier* broadcast rumors that federal troops would garrison Lancaster, that black mobs were planning to burn the town, and even that 1,500 armed black men under the command of a black North Carolinian were poised for invasion. Regardless of whether the *News and Courier*'s staff had made up the rumors out of whole cloth or whether this attempt to play on centuries of accumulated anxiety about a slave revolt seemed credible to most readers, the recourse to the trope of armed black insurrection revealed how readily such images still came to mind.[58]

As in previous campaigns, Democratic newspapers characterized black voters as a hostile bloc of anti-Democratic sentiment, purchasable — by cash or false promises — by whatever enemies the Democrats might have. A group of scheming white men, they claimed, were using a gullible and monolithic black electorate for their own ends. "[T]he strength of the Greenback-Radicals is the strength of the colored vote, as far as the Administration hacks . . . and the local leaders can control and direct it," declared a typical article in the *News and Courier*.[59] The reverse, apparently, was also true: the Republicans would use the Greenback challenge as an opportunity to "Africanize the state."[60] In this reading, the Greenbackers were "for sale, and there is no one to buy them but the Radicals."[61] To be bought was, at the very least, to be another's political creature — that is, to be dependent and therefore less than a real white man. In its most literal reading, the metaphor likened these purchasable white men to slaves.

Democrats sexualized the struggle over political power, suggesting that Greenback leaders were encouraging black men's sexual aspirations toward white women. Most white Southern men understood racial power as a zero-sum problem: in the postbellum South, as in revolutionary Haiti, one race or the other would be in control, and if black men entered politics, their goal must be domination. But since control over a household and its dependents formed the basis of white men's claim to independence and citizenship, domination could not be neatly separated into spheres of "government" and "household." Black men's attempts to enter the white male domain of politics could seem to foreshadow attempts to enter — and therefore dominate — white men's households, particularly their daughters and wives.

This was what white supremacists meant when they declared that political equality was "synonymous with social equality" or when they accused Greenbackers of being "political miscegenationists." Such tortured telescoping seemed implausible and forced to some, but for others, these were potent arguments. The personal or familial shame or anxiety some white men felt regarding the sexual abuse of black women made the prospect of such a reversal deeply troubling. Many more no doubt feared being unable to protect their dependents from the still-powerful stigma of blackness as utter social degradation. South Carolina's independents proved all too vulnerable to such corrosive attacks.[62]

Even as the Greenbackers suffered from their enemies' efforts to sexualize the contest, they also staggered under the burden of their own assumptions about the relationship of race and gender to producerism. In ways they did not fully grasp, the history of white manhood shaped and limited the radicals' producerist critique of Southern society. White Southern men had historically controlled both the region's productive resources and the legitimate use of force. Their ideal of producerist manhood as the basis for legitimate rule was rooted, literally and figuratively, in the history of patriarchal slaveholding republicanism. Even as they sought to forge a coalition of the disaffected that included black men as producers and voters, the history of white solidarity worked against them. An economic critique that equated production with virtue obscured important differences of interest between planters and tenants; and the militant, defiant mobilization they envisioned had historically made black men targets, not allies.[63]

Cash revealed some of these tensions when he spoke to audiences of black and white voters. He protested the "persecution of the negroes by Lynch Law" and their "assassination for political opinion." But the history of race, landownership, and labor relations shaped what followed. Cash appeared to assume that his audience was composed of white employers of black laborers, for his bill of indictment against the Democratic leadership included "[r]unning the negro out of the state & no substitute," a charge that would have resonance mainly for planters. This analytical shortcoming would haunt producerist arguments in South Carolina throughout the 1880s and beyond.[64]

Violence, intimidation, and fraud earned the Democrats a four-to-one victory over the Greenback-Republicans in 1882; in hindsight, Democratic control over the election machinery outside the lowcountry all but precluded the possibility of an upset. Sometimes the electoral wheels turned almost too easily: McLane received not a single vote in the upcountry county of Anderson. But even where election officials counted ballots with some honesty, it was impossible to determine in precisely what ways the campaign of terror had affected participation. McLane's totals reflected the fragmented and unstable basis of his radical challenge: he won only lowcountry Beaufort County, where heavy Republican turnout gave him 80 percent of the vote, and he earned about half that proportion in two other lowcountry counties. He did poorly throughout the piedmont, where white Democratic loyalty, intimidation, and fraud dispatched what little local resistance the Democrats encountered. In Tillman's Edgefield, he earned fewer than 600 votes, or about 15 percent of the total gubernatorial vote — less than half the number the county cast for Republican congressional nominee Ellery Brayton. But two of McLane's five strongest totals came in the white-majority counties of Chesterfield (where Cash actually outpolled his Democratic congressional opponent) and Oconee. In Lancaster, interestingly, McLane won only 22 percent of the vote, but Cash, running on the same ticket, won twice that proportion. Perhaps fraud shaped these unequal totals. Perhaps Cash's manly self-assertion neutralized his biracial alliance in the eyes of otherwise-loyal Democratic voters. Or perhaps some combination of black and white voters in that inland district defiantly resisted the Democrats' brazen attack on their citizenship and suffrage.[65]

The 1882 defeat fractured the Greenback-Republican coalition beyond repair: fusion agreements collapsed, and any trust between the parties evaporated. With the failure of the independent challenge, violence subsided as a concomitant of politics — even in Edgefield. Reporting on an 1884 campaign meeting, a correspondent professed to be "dazed" with shock that "throughout the day I have not seen a pistol and have only seen one drunken man." A well-attended Republican campaign meeting in Edgefield drew Red-shirt observers, but no violence ensued: the local Republicans had become so insignificant that Edgefield Democrats felt that donning their shirts and saddling up sufficed. Ben Tillman was almost certainly one of those observers, for in May 1884 he had been rewarded for his good service in earlier campaigns with a new title: captain of the Edgefield Hussars.[66]

But the Red-shirts' role was about to change. South Carolina Republicans were battered by local losses as well as setbacks in all branches of the federal government: the U.S. Supreme Court effectively overturned the 1875 Civil Rights Act in 1883, and Democrats retook the White House in the election of 1884. After that year, Republicans ceased running statewide tickets. In the absence of a continuing Republican presence in upcountry politics, the rifle-clubs-turned-militia-units became social groups; the Hussars, for example, held a popular annual picnic at their clubhouse. The campaign of 1876 had already begun to glow golden in historical memory: an 1884 Edgefield demonstration featured a "Hampton and Gary" banner from 1876, which had been "faithfully preserved" by a local militia leader "who regards it as a sacred treasure." Even the Hamburg massacre could become the stuff of an advertisement, as a merchant hawking his wares in an Edgefield paper opened with a pitch guaranteed to bring the Red-shirts to mind: "The Greatest Excitement Prevails!" screamed the headline; "Augusta the Scene of the Struggle!" But this struggle concerned his uniquely inexpensive clothing, not the fate of white supremacy.[67]

The history of white manhood had established that no movement for reform could safely look to the black majority for aid. White supremacy had become the sine qua non of statewide political action. But the issues that had threatened to fracture the Democrats in 1882 had not gone away. It remained unclear how the many local and regional splits among white voters could be mended, especially in the absence of a credible Republican opposition. In the lowcountry, accommodationist arrangements only partly neutralized the region's large black majorities. There, Democrats continued to fear the resurgence of black Republican assertiveness, which for them recalled the white victims of lowcountry Reconstruction clashes. In the upcountry, however, where black South Carolinians had relatively little political strength, some white voters had responded to the charge that the state Democratic Party and the government it controlled had not acted in their interests. White political dominance had been only provisionally secured against McLane and Russell's alliance of the "disaffected."[68]

The heart of the problem remained the Redeemers' inability to address the persistent crisis in agriculture. At the end of 1885, as the legislature once again debated repealing the lien law, a correspondent noted with apprehension that the farmers in his area had barely made it through the year and lacked the cash to buy supplies. When the legislature revised the lien law, making liens for supplies inferior to landlords' liens for rent and laborers' liens for wages, Dawson worried publicly that this would "put serious difficulties in the way of the large body of small farmers who rent their farms, and who are not in condition to farm without help until the next crop comes in." His Charleston paper identified with the state's merchants, but its editor understood that the state's fragile political order might be radically imperiled by a wholly alienated yeomanry.[69]

A similar spirit of anxiety led the *Edgefield Advertiser* to publish the bitter complaint of a farmer who excoriated a "class of farmers who want to control the laboring classes and reduce all farming in South Carolina to the boss system of agriculture." In terms recalling other opponents of landed "aristocrats," this man presented himself as the voice of a disfranchised mass whose very freedom was threatened by arrogant elitists whose policies amounted to slavery for the poor:

> The tenant system, according to their gospel, must be broken up, and they propose to accomplish this by impoverishing the small farmers, white and black, and depriving them of the means of getting credit, and starving them into the condition of dependents and hirelings and subjects and slaves. . . . [W]ill the repeal of the lien law bring about the condition of things that the revolutionists hope to accomplish? It ought not to require a moment's reflection to see that it will not. Slavery cannot be re-established. . . . We must build up new systems. . . . [I]T IS NOT STATESMANSHIP TO DEGRADE AND IMPOVERISH THE LABORING CLASSES.[70]

Here, even after the Greenbackers' defeat, were divisions of class that could overshadow differences of race, a call for new approaches to agriculture and labor, an appeal to men's pride in their independence, and suspicion of the motives of the rich and powerful. Here was a hostility to "aristocrats" that offered a potentially powerful weapon against the coastal and urban elite—but also, perhaps, a weapon against local "big" men. It remained unclear, though, what role the political descendants of Gary and McLane would play in shaping and directing these continuing grievances. Gary's assertive white manhood and legislative proposals had generated enthusiasm, but he had failed to break into the party's inner circle; McLane's biracial producerism had run up against the guns of white men and the history of white manhood, but the problems he identified and the economic critique he offered would continue to resonate.

Ben Tillman had been present at each of the major turning points that had created this threatening new white discontent. Between 1876 and 1884, he not only had become a successful planter, militia captain, and local Democratic figure but also had helped officiate at the shotgun wedding of white supremacy and reform, insisting that the pursuit of "good government" must take place only through the channels of the white-only Democratic Party. But he was also heir to the traditions of sectional hostility and Red-shirt rebellion. Beginning in the mid-1880s, he set out to channel his white neighbors' anger into a movement that would protect white supremacy by asserting a particular vision of white male producerism—one that would leave Hampton and his followers almost as helpless as it had left McLane.

Farmers, Dudes, White Negroes, and the Sun-Browned Goddess

Barely a month after Tillman's elevation to the rank of captain of the Edgefield Hussars, he and other local farmers met at the militia unit's pavilion to establish a farmers' club, the Edgefield Agricultural and Mechanical Society. During the summer and fall of 1884, Tillman emerged as the sustaining force behind this effort to organize "the leading agriculturalists, farmers, and business men . . . for the promotion of agriculture, and for the development of the business interests and resources of Edgefield county that are connected with and kindred to agriculture." Tillman helped frame the group's constitution, spoke at its meetings, and in 1885 became its president. That August, he attended the joint convention of the state agricultural society and Grange in Bennettsville, where he gave a provocative speech outlining his vision for the uplift of South Carolina's white farmers.[1]

At Bennettsville and beyond, Tillman posited an identity of interest among "the farmers," by which he meant the state's white male heads of agricultural households. Whiteness, maleness, and productive labor together made these people the state's legitimate citizenry, but in Tillman's view, their prosperity and independence had been jeopardized by the actions of less worthy rivals. White farmers' enemies included black men who aspired to economic or political independence, but the most immediate threat came from powerful white men—the Redeemer leadership Tillman branded an "aristocracy" and the rising mercantile and industrial class. As a slogan, "white supremacy" called for the political unity of white men, but Tillman did not believe that "aristocrats" and "merchants" properly counted as white men, for their personal and economic behavior made them the enemies of "the farmers." Redrawing the circle of legitimate political and economic authority to include the farmers and to exclude all who opposed their interests, Tillman began to argue that only certain white men were truly white and truly men. Many, it seemed, had become so tainted by their association with blacks or their unproductive livelihoods that they had forfeited their right to govern. Yet govern they did, and the farmers paid the price.

Tillman feared that political impotence and economic deprivation would bring another insurgency like the Greenback-Republican challenge, and he sought to forge an alternative. As the *Edgefield Advertiser* had been warning since 1878, grinding poverty and an unresponsive leadership might again drive white men to make alliances with black Republicans, sooner or later returning the state to the horrors of Reconstruction "misrule." "White supremacy" needed to become more than a reactionary slogan. If racial hierarchy and white male independence were to survive, farsighted white men would have to rally the state's authentic citizens around their common interests. The farmers would have to assert their right to act collectively, for only a disciplined martial mobilization like that of 1876 could save them from poverty and subordination to other white men. Together, they could reconstruct their relationship to their party, their government, their lands, and each other and forge a state government that protected white agricultural households rather than colluding in their destruction.

Beginning in the mid-1880s, Tillman sought to reshape the Democratic Party from within, making it the vehicle for rather than the target of white protest. In rhetoric that fused the defiant white male supremacy of Martin Gary with the producerist doctrine of the Greenbackers, he attacked the Democratic Party's leaders as "aristocrats" who were either unwilling or unable to foster agricultural renewal. This assault rallied a broad coalition of agricultural reformers, opponents of state spending, advocates of increased upcountry representation, and the poorly organized legions of those with grievances against the Redeemer government. As they came together to complain and collaborate, first in local clubs and then in county and state conventions, a rebellion coalesced within the Democratic Party known variously as the Farmers' Association, the farmers' movement, or the reform movement. More and more, as Tillman became known as the state's "agricultural Moses," it was simply called the Tillman movement. At the outset, the *Charleston News and Courier* uneasily noted "a nervousness and restlessness in the Democratic party which may become dangerous." But Tillman considered his agitation an act of farsighted statesmanship, a "safety valve so to speak for the Democratic party" that would protect the party of white unity by providing a white-supremacist alternative to class-based interracial radicalism.[2]

Tillman called for a variety of state-level reforms, most notably the creation of a college for white farmers, but he held the attention of the state's voters by making incessant attacks on the Redeemer leadership. These unmanly, unproductive, urban "aristocrats," he charged, hardly embodied the kind of white manhood that could lead the commonwealth through troubled times. They constituted a corrupt "ring" standing between the farmers and prosperity, not so very different from the incompetent black men and nefarious white men who had led during Reconstruction. The victims of these attacks responded that Tillman neither represented the "common man" nor offered him substantive relief, and they were at least partly right. Although Tillman claimed to be the champion and representative of the farmers, his understanding of agricultural poverty was quite limited, and he suspected that most white men—even his farmers—lacked the independence of mind of true citizens. But Tillman's Democratic opponents shared these limitations, and their platform offered disgruntled white farmers even less than Tillman's largely symbolic reforms. In fact, their outraged rebuttals of his attacks backfired, helping distinguish Tillman from the Democratic leadership and substantiating his assertion that they regarded most farming men as their social and political inferiors. Tillman could not have asked for more. In denouncing him as a disreputable demagogue and derisively identifying his speech, dress, and manner as those of a poor white man, Tillman's opponents ironically helped the Edgefield planter establish himself as a representative of the white Southern "common man." In 1890, when Tillman moved to take over the Democratic Party, disgruntled lowcountry leaders mounted an independent challenge and called for black Republican support. Facing opponents who proved to be haughty men and fair-weather white supremacists, Tillman was elected governor by a wide margin.

But Tillman's victory had come in part through the organizational energy of the Farmers' Alliance, which had arrived in the state as Tillman's movement was floundering in the late 1880s. In the early 1890s, Tillman faced a challenge from that group's more radical leaders, who promoted a far more activist agenda, including cooperatives, boycotts, and ultimately political and economic plans of national scope. Tillman feared reforms that went too far, especially those that might require federal intervention or were otherwise reminiscent of Reconstruction. Tillman was instrumental in the defeat of third-party politics in the state, but his victory was not simply a matter of parliamentary or rhetorical tactics. Rather, it represented a strategic victory, the culmination of nearly two decades of political work.

Together, the legacies of 1876 and 1890 help explain why South Carolina, despite its flourishing Farmers' Alliance, produced virtually no Populist movement. Since Reconstruction, men like Tillman had helped establish the limits of insurgent politics. They had read or run white dissidents out of the ranks of "real" white men and had defined federal intervention in local affairs, like biracial politics, as a return to the ever-more-lurid horrors of Reconstruction. By 1890, the Red-shirt campaign of 1876 had become the essence of white Democratic virtue, and Tillman's effort to defuse class conflict among white men through the limited assertion of state power seemed to constitute a reasonable middle ground between the vision of overambitious radicals and the presumption of "Bourbon" aristocrats. Building on the political, military, and rhetorical victories he had won over the previous decade, as well as on the limitations of the radicals' own vision, Tillman managed to defuse this challenge and keep South Carolina safely Democratic. From the perspective of the early 1890s, this might have seemed an almost unaccountable short-circuiting of Populism's radical possibilities. Seen through the wider lens of Tillman's life and career, however, this defeat represented the victory of Tillman's vision of white manhood.

Farmers and Others

In the years after his speech at Bennettsville, Tillman sketched a portrait of conflict between the farmers and their enemies. This juxtaposition of honest citizens and contemptible others usually took the form of an attack, and between 1885 and 1887, Tillman's constant skirmishes with state officials brought him a level of statewide attention that his modest proposals alone would not have received. Before we turn to his organizational practice, therefore, we ought to meet him as most South Carolinians did during this period—as an increasingly skillful rhetorician, deftly playing the expectations of producerism, patriarchy, and white male solidarity against the status quo.

Tillman's farmers were producers, employers, husbands, and fathers; they were "the common people who redeemed the State from Radical rule," the "real Democrats and white men" in whose hands political authority properly belonged. White women and African Americans had legitimate (although quite different) roles to play in this white man's world, whereas white merchants, lawyers, and other urban men owed their livelihoods to the men who produced the society's real wealth. As C. Vann Woodward has noted, "[T]he word 'farmer' is laden with ambiguities that have made it a convenient disguise for a variety of interests." In tying legitimate authority to race, occupation, and gender, Tillman celebrated white farming men's individual and collective mastery while attempting to evade or elide questions of class difference among them. This was not always simple. Before the war, Tillman claimed in an 1886 article, "the land-owning farmers were the salt of the earth and called no man master." As he wrote those words, he himself owned over 1,600 acres, making him a wealthy farmer by any standard.[3] His own activism, he later claimed, had begun after "overextension" and a few "bad years" in the early 1880s left him in debt and forced him to sell several hundred acres. But many white male agricultural workers had never been "land-owning farmers," before the war or since; as tenants or laborers, they had subsisted at the margins of the planters' and yeomen's worlds. As he refined his vision, Tillman sought to muffle or absorb such tensions.[4]

White men's landlessness and indebtedness did not mean that the ideal was faulty but that something had gone seriously awry. He laid blame for white farmers' growing hardship on their granting black laborers too much autonomy, becoming indebted to merchants, and thereby falling under the sway of the corporate and financial "money power." Their fundamental mistake, however, was in allowing themselves to be governed by selfish, incompetent, and corrupt aristocrats. When Tillman began speaking to audiences in 1885 and 1886, he painted a grim picture of the economic state of white farming households. Even "without counting negroes," at least half of the vast agricultural majority had to borrow money to plant, which meant resorting to liens or mortgages. But it was easier to get into debt than to get out of it, and farmers grew dependent on agricultural credit, until "like the opium eater, they cannot quit if they would." Every year, farmers slipped deeper and deeper into debt to predatory merchants and finally into a humiliating "hopeless servitude." Tillman told an upcountry crowd that "we want to get from under the lien law, where it forces men to run to the merchants with their hats in their hands and ask, 'Is the Lien Law opened yet?'" He denounced the "merchants and bankers . . . who have got rich on the poor man." He sought to distinguish between farmers who also acted as merchants and "true" farmers such as himself. Merchants and servants of corporate interests extracted a living from the productive labor of others; they could "make money whether it rains or not." "I had rather a thousand times go down with my brother farmers than fatten at their expense," Tillman declared, allying himself rhetorically with poor white men against other wealthy men.[5]

Tillman's rhetoric notwithstanding, no sharp line separated agricultural and merchant capital: throughout the post-Reconstruction decades, planters became merchants and merchants became planters. During the last decades of the century, men committed to mercantile, industrial, and financial development built mills, stores, and banks. Settlements became villages and towns, and their leading citizens competed with one another to attract railroad lines and investment. Whether they had been planters, yeomen, factors, or Yankees, members of this emerging "town class" saw agriculture as only one among many enterprises. Tillman shared certain goals with such men. Like New South visionaries, he urged farmers to produce more food and less cotton, and he owned a few shares of stock in local banks. But Tillman's orientation remained defiantly agricultural, and he professed enormous skepticism about this rising economic order. He feared a New South in which "half our lands will be owned by aliens and the sons of many old slaveholders will have sunk to the level of their former servants . . . hewers of wood and drawers of water for capitalists and merchants."[6]

White men's hardship, and sometimes their ignorance, allowed those "former servants" to contribute to the agricultural crisis. "[W]e have turned our lands over to the negroes to manage," Tillman complained, "the Anglo-Saxon abdicating in favor of the African, brains and energy giving place to muscle and ignorance." In part, white men were playing out the lessons they had learned during slavery, valuing labor over land and therefore tolerating their workers' destructive farming practices. It was for this reason that Tillman called slaves and slavery "a curse" on the antebellum South. Now that land, not slaves, had become the source of wealth and value in Southern agriculture, he urged farmers to pay more attention to how their tenants and laborers tilled the soil. Freedmen could not farm intelligently on their own account. "Cuff, freed from the dread of a master, does as little as he can," Tillman explained, offering a familiar post-Reconstruction vision of black indolence and incapacity. A white man who rented to "ignorant lazy negroes" was therefore encouraging the "butchery" of his land. Agricultural renewal would be impossible as long as white landowners and tenants took their orders from cotton-obsessed furnishing merchants and landowners allowed black sharecroppers the day-to-day autonomy they so ardently sought.[7]

Whether or not they considered themselves farmers, black South Carolinians lacked the capacity for citizenship that would make them eligible for inclusion in Tillman's farmers' movement. Although it appears that early on black farmers sometimes successfully sought to participate in local reform movement activities, the fact that blacks constituted a majority of the state's farmers did not interest Tillman. "The farmers" were white men. Indeed, Tillman and other "agricultural reformers" sometimes seemed to yearn for a South emptied of African Americans: "[W]e must get rid of the negroes, who are eating up the whites," Tillman told a county fair audience in 1886. But as a large landowner, Tillman would hardly have agreed with the bitter Edgefield farmer who declared in 1889 that planters "who labor with their own hands are independent of the negro, and if those who presume to be our leaders would not retain hundreds upon their plantations we would not be confronted with the 'Southern Problem.' " Tillman might have employed dozens rather than hundreds of black laborers, but he sought to control them, to master them—not to make them disappear. Black labor largely underwrote his kind of "independence."[8]

But when blacks stepped out of white men's fields, Tillman argued, and especially when they entered politics, they threatened to bring back Reconstruction's "radical misrule." Although the Republicans did not seriously contest statewide elections after 1882, they remained locally active. During the 1880s and early 1890s, African Americans continued to vote and hold office, especially in the lowcountry counties constituting the state's vast, gerrymandered "black seventh" congressional district. Despite challenges by white Democrats, black men such as Robert Smalls and George W. Murray periodically represented South Carolina in Congress. The possibility of a political resurgence by the black majority lingered in every development of the early post-Reconstruction decades, threatening at any moment to undo the revolution of 1876. But Tillman believed that "Negro Domination" would not return without aid from villainous white men. Like a writer to the *Charleston News and Courier*, he saw black voters as "credulous, ignorant and suspicious; just the material to be as plastic as putty in the hands of shrewd and ambitious leaders." By the early 1890s, such leaders' reputations for malefaction had transcended the legendary and become more or less occult. To white Democrats, men like Reconstruction governors Franklin Moses, Robert Scott, and Daniel Chamberlain were no longer simply carpetbaggers and scalawags but "vampires" and "phantasmagorical ghosts," so demonized in defeat that only supernatural language could describe their ghastly doings and the horrors that would follow their return.[9]

Tillman also argued that apportionment schemes favoring the lowcountry continued the antebellum tradition of using the black majority against white farmers. In both the state legislature and Democratic Party conventions, methods of apportionment based on total population allowed the lowcountry's tiny white minorities to speak with a louder voice than that of their more numerous upcountry cousins. The current Democratic leaders profited from the status quo and therefore refused either to reapportion the legislature or to modify the convention system of nominating state officers. Continuing Martin Gary and George Tillman's appeal to upcountry sectionalism, Ben Tillman argued that upcountry white men's overthrow of Reconstruction had earned them the right to greater representation. An Edgefield correspondent pointed to the county's large and overwhelmingly Democratic returns in the years since 1876 and asked whether "the very citadel of the Democracy [is] to be denied . . . [just] representation?" Tillman made the charge more racially pointed. He reckoned that a legislator from Edgefield represented 9,000 people, whereas one from Charleston or Richland represented 5,000 or 6,000 people, "mostly negroes." Complaining further that "[o]ne white man in Spartanburg or Edgefield should certainly be equal to one negro in Charleston or Columbia," Tillman made his white urban opponents invisible and the cities they cherished essentially black. He also argued that the convention system was an affront to democracy and an invitation to rule by "a political aristocracy." They "mak[e] us delegate our power to delegates who delegate somebody else," he complained, "so that by the time they reach Columbia they are nothing but office-seeking politicians."[10]

At the 1886 Democratic convention, however, opponents of primaries and reapportionment unself-consciously made arguments that smacked of patrician superiority. If candidates for state offices had to mount popular campaigns seeking support from individual voters across the state, one delegate suggested, men would "get into office simply upon their capital" or be beholden to railroad companies for free passes. Men "without means" would either be denied office or be subject "to corporation influence." Governor John P. Richardson perceived a more practical drawback. Noting that "[e]very dissatisfied element flocks to [Tillman's] standard at once," he feared the Edgefield upstart might actually win the gubernatorial nomination if the party held a primary.[11]

Tillman's main campaign was not for office, however, but for the establishment of a state college for white farmers. Real "agricultural advancement," Tillman argued, could take place only if the state reconsidered its educational priorities and established a freestanding agricultural college, a place where young men could learn progressive, scientific farming. By training a cadre of young white men each year in the latest agricultural methods, the state could exchange the antebellum pattern of "[c]ut down, wear out, and move West" for scientific agriculture and diversification focused on food crops. He contrasted the potential benefits of such a college with the shortcomings of the state's existing institutions for white men, Columbia's South Carolina College and Charleston's Citadel. These were schools for effeminate dandies and parasites, not manly farmers. Echoing both Gary and the Greenbackers, he portrayed South Carolina College—alma mater of half the state leadership—as elitist and ornamental. "[H]aving been taught that labor is degrading," the "liberally educated" graduates of such schools could easily become "helpless beings, . . . 'too proud to beg, too honest to steal, too lazy to work.'" The college's inadequate agricultural "annex," which received the state's Morrill Act money, was "a child [put] to nurse in the house of its enemies."[12]

Defenders of the existing institutions and foes of the agricultural college suggested that collective solutions could not resolve essentially individual problems: farmers' poverty resulted from laziness or incompetence, and those who worked hard would succeed without the state intervention Tillman championed. "If the legislature granted every request made by the farmers, this *alone*, would not materially better their condition," wrote a Charleston planter, rejecting an overture from a Tillman organizer. "The material interest of any class, can only be improved by the individual efforts of the numbers of that class." He therefore opposed "a Farmer's political party." Another foe of the agricultural college put it more succinctly. "The Farmers' Movement is a good thing," he quipped, "if it's a brisk one between the plowhandles."[13]

Such opponents of his efforts, Tillman charged, were effete aristocrats living off of inherited wealth, a corrupt "ring" embodying "all the evils of aristocracy with none of its benefits." The farmer, Tillman said, looked on as his tax money was wasted, and he himself was "contemptuously pushed aside to make room for men who are really his inferiors in intelligence and honesty, and who are selfish in all their aspirations." Their "absurdities, extravagance and folly" recalled the fiscal excesses of "radical misrule." Even the agricultural college would fail unless "real" farmers controlled it, for it could not be entrusted to the current agricultural leadership of "broken-down politicians and old superannuated Bourbon aristocrats, who are thoroughly incompetent, who worship the past, and are incapable of progress of any sort, but who boldly assume to govern us by divine right."

"These men," Tillman explained, "the remnant of the old regime[,] . . . worship the past and are marching backwards when they march at all."[14]

As these attacks suggest, Tillman's understanding of political and economic virtue was sharply gendered, but it was not based on a simple opposition of male independence to female dependence. Rather, it offered a vision of male and female agricultural interdependence, under siege from men whose unproductive and aristocratic ways undercut their claim to leadership and perhaps even to manhood itself. Tillman rooted both masculine and feminine virtue in productive labor. In one of his most provocative attacks, he dubbed the Citadel, a military institution dear to upper-class Charleston, a "military dude factory" and called for its transformation into a college for white women. More than simply derogating the school and its graduates, Tillman implied that such men had less value than the female graduates the new school would produce. But proper education for white women, far more than a slap at urban "dudes," was an essential part of Tillman's vision of a prosperous agricultural commonwealth. A Barnwell newspaper echoed Tillman's analysis when it asserted "that if the funds that have been expended on worthless young men in South Carolina alone since the war had been appropriated to the business education of women, scores of homes would have been spared by mortgages, and ample support made for families who have been dragged down to want." Tillmanite legislators included "schools for our beautiful girls" in the list of changes that would bring "dignity for labor." Tillman spoke in joking but respectful and affectionate terms of his own wife's perspective on his agitation. "[Y]ou don't know how many candle lectures I have received," he told the 1886 farmers' convention, "and I think I will take Mrs. Moses's advice hereafter if I can only get out of this scrimmage without losing my scalp." He claimed that his agitation had initiated conversations between other husbands and wives as well, and "families are split and husbands and wives are in some cases on opposite sides." White farming women clearly had at least a consultative role in the body politic.[15]

By contrast, Tillman suggested, "aristocrats" misunderstood white women's proper roles in predictably haughty ways. The urban Columbia campus of the state university received the state's federal money for agricultural education, but Tillman insisted that although the college subsisted in part on this "stolen 'farmer's money,' " it could never be "a fitting temple for our sun-browned goddess, Agriculture." In its halls, he explained, agriculture occupied "the position of a bond slave . . . only tolerated because of her dower." She was "never . . . made one of the family." Instead of recognizing sun-browned skin as the badge of a white woman's agricultural labor, aristocrats had mistaken her for an African American slave and unfairly appropriated the fruits of her labor. If these men could mistake Ceres for a slave, they could not be relied on to grant white farming women and their labor the respect they deserved.[16]

The rule of the aristocrats had disordered South Carolina's broader "household," for under them the "state has proved a veritable step-mother to her 'agricultural interests,' " Tillman complained, "and they have been neglected or subordinated to everything else." In order to suggest the corrupting influence of nonproducers' rule, Tillman explained that in the years since Redemption, the Democratic Party, "that interesting old lady," had become somewhat "corpulent" and "slouchy." His farmers' movement, however, had stirred her from her lethargy, causing her to recognize "among the farmers who are here this familiar face and that, which she remembered as among the foremost of those who redeemed the state in '76." Moved by that memory, Tillman went on, she resolved to reward the farmers instead of the undeserving offspring who had up until now claimed precedence. "I know who to depend on, and if these boys are going to move I am going to follow them. I can't depend on your city chaps and lawyers any longer." Determining to "move back to the farm," the party/mother explained that "my health has not been good of late, and I am nearly dead for a piece of home-cured bacon and corn bread." But the return to agricultural ways wrought a miraculous transformation. Once she rejoined a farming household, the Democratic mother no longer simply craved homemade provisions but could help produce them, declaring that "[t]hese farmers ought to raise more meat and corn, and I am going to show them how to do it." No longer a weakened, inattentive "step-mother," she had become a nurturing household member with an important role in the process of social and economic regeneration.[17]

But masculine virtues differed from feminine virtues in at least one crucial respect: men were supposed to be soldiers, capable of the kind of collective military action that had produced the victory of 1876. Here again, Tillman argued that the Democratic leadership mistakenly emphasized the honor of individual men rather than understanding martial virtues as essentially collective. Individual "dudes" were nothing; an army of white men was everything.

In the 1880s, when most leading Democrats could point to a Confederate war record, the memory and legacy of 1876 served Tillman extremely well. Tillman's Red-shirt service became evidence of his personal courage, but more important, it became evidence of his boundless commitment to white male authority. In confrontations with lowcountry leaders, he boasted of being "one of the Hamburg rioters who dared even the devil to save the State," and he continually lambasted the *Charleston News and Courier* for its initially critical response to that now-legendary massacre. When an opponent suggested that Tillman had shirked his duty as a white man by failing to serve in the Confederate army, Tillman not only told the story of the loss of his eye but added that instead of a Civil War record, "I have a little record of 1876, and I know something about Ned Tennant and the Ellenton riots, and have had a little to do with managing elections." Anyone who had been with him at Hamburg, he told an upcountry crowd, "would not say that he, Tillman, could split the Democratic party."[18]

When Tillman attacked individual members of the Democratic leadership, these men often responded as though he had provoked them into an affair of honor. But although Tillman delighted in sparking outrage, he showed no interest in giving or demanding "personal satisfaction." In 1885, he sought to make an alliance with Luther Ransom, Columbia correspondent for the *Augusta Chronicle* and secretary to state agricultural commissioner A. P. Butler. Privately, Tillman all but promised Ransom the secretaryship of a proposed farmers' legislature in exchange for favorable newspaper coverage, and he suggested that Ransom could do this without jeopardizing his "bread and butter." But when Tillman publicly charged Butler's agricultural department with wasting money, Ransom defended his employer and attacked Tillman. Tillman responded by writing publicly that Ransom was "trying perhaps to earn his salary and keep his place," "fighting for potatoes" rather than for principles. He warned Ransom to cease his insinuations and "attack me like a man . . . and then I shall know how to answer him." Ransom took what in an earlier decade would have been the only honorable course. Tillman, he wrote, "lied—l-i-e-d. No insinuation about that, I hope, Benjamin?"[19]

But Tillman had no interest in satisfying his own or anyone else's aggrieved sense of honor. He might declare that he could not "now remain silent without being accused of having fled at the first glint of steel," and he sometimes used words such as "insulting" and "resent" that echoed antebellum preliminaries, but he refused to be goaded into a duel. After Ransom's charge, Tillman reminded readers that dueling was now illegal in South Carolina and that if he issued a challenge using weapons "to put us on an equality, if I killed him it would be murder." "A few years ago, my reply would have been a challenge, but it is no longer either safe or honorable to fight duels in South Carolina, and Major Ransom knows it," he explained. In rejecting nonlethal confrontation, he landed another blow: Ransom was not "physically" his "equal," Tillman claimed, and he "would as soon strike a woman." The issue at stake was collective rights, not individual reputations. Ransom's challenge was the act of a "Hessian," a mercenary in the service of the state leadership, and it demanded a collective rather than a personal response. Tillman's "poverty-stricken, debt-enslaved, tax-ridden farmers are organizing . . . [f]rom the mountains to the sea" to take on the "Columbia Ring" that had set Ransom against him. Tillman was interested not in exchanging pistol shots but in defining and mobilizing white manhood.[20]

Organizing the Farmers

Tillman offered the farmers a stark and simple choice: "Organize! Organize! Organize!" or—in language that his audience would have understood in both literal and symbolic terms—"remain slaves." In Tillman's rhetoric, slavery functioned as a present symbol as well as a historical memory. It was time, he said, "for the emancipation of agriculture among us from the shackles of debt and ignorance. Co-operation redeemed us from Radical slavery and co-operation will redeem us from commercial slavery." But Tillman was not entirely convinced that his farmers were capable of such sustained and disciplined effort. Reconstruction rule, he explained to audiences, had deadened white farmers' instincts for citizenship. "[A] more galling slavery was never endured by any people," Tillman explained. "Our bodies were free, but our minds became benumbed, deadened. The disuse of citizenship made us unfit to be citizens, and we farmers, by reason of our volition, have suffered more than all others because of this fatal lethargy. . . . This mental slavery is more hopeless than a merely physical bondage, and unless we throw off these shackles of the mind and become free in truth as well as in name there is no hope for us." Rather than remain dependent on others to serve farmers' interests—a dependence "neither wise nor manly"—farmers should "exert their proper influence."[21]

At times, he seemed to doubt that wisdom and manliness would prevail. He mocked those who lacked the gumption to join the farmers' movement. "My God," he privately exclaimed to a trusted ally, "how pitifully scarce true men are!" Publicly, too, he warned that "if there are any 'Miss Nancys' among you who are afraid to exercise your rights as citizens and taxpayers to discuss these and other questions so vital to our interests you had as well withdraw." Only farmers who saw their interests clearly could be relied on to vote "for measures and not for men." But everywhere, individually and collectively, white farming men seemed all too ready to give up—or, in more directly charged language, to "submit"—and Tillman worried that "the sleepy agricultural giant will sink into quiet submission again soon." All around him, blind and ignorant white men neglected their obligations as agricultural citizens. He confessed to one ally that he felt "sick at heart sometimes when I think of leaving my children among these gullies & surrounded by these dead people, for with one or two exceptions my neighbors are utterly & hopelessly stupid, non progressive." Other farmers, he thought, lacking independence of mind, had been "bamboozled" or "manipulated" into serving the "ring" bosses. Real white men could never accept such a role; in fact, perhaps such men deserved to "remain slaves."[22]

Tillman's goal was to rouse these white men, spurring them to reclaim the Democratic Party and thus the state. And from the moment he rose to speak in Bennettsville in 1885, he attracted the attention of like-minded men throughout South Carolina and even beyond. Some of his earliest allies were former Red-shirts and their sons, men like Martin Gary's nephews Eugene and Frank Gary and John Gary Evans. Tax-cutting upcountry legislators like G. W. Shell wrote to introduce themselves, and local farmers' clubs invited him to speak, giving him the opportunity to meet a variety of men prominent at the county level—from ambitious professionals like John L. McLaurin and J. L. M. Irby to substantial but unpolished farmers like Aaron Cannon and Henry Burn. This emerging "reform" leadership did not represent the revolt of a reactionary Old South. Many leaders of the farmers' movement were what historian Randolph Werner has described as regional capitalists, men invested financially and psychologically in the developing economy. Tillman's disciple John Gary Evans, for example, served as an agent for Northern land and credit interests. Overall, the movement's local leaders represented a wide range of regional and political-economic constituencies, but they all shared a dissatisfaction with the post-Reconstruction order.[23]

In the mid-1880s, Tillman traveled across the state, hoping to knit local and county farmers' clubs into a permanent state farmers' convention—what he called a "farmers' legislature." This "[r]epresentative society would naturally supplant & take the place of the present close corp[oration] known as the State Agl Society—in a few years." He was eagerly received by like-minded local landowners. "The people of Colleton are Lawyer & Merchant ridden," wrote the president of a county agricultural association, "and have been running in the groove so long that I want just such help as you can give me to break their chains. Our people (the farmers) are quite cheered at the

"Leaders of the Farmers' Movement in South Carolina." Tillman is flanked by G. W. Shell, under whose name the Shell Manifesto of 1890 was circulated, and J. L. M. Irby, who became an ally after hosting Tillman during his appearance at Bennettsville in 1885. Special Collections, Clemson University Libraries.

prospect of seeing & hearing you speak." Others wrote to offer support and to mention the names of additional potential allies.[24]

Believing that disgruntled Democrats were desperate for such a movement and knowing that wide publicity was crucial to this effort, Tillman made a critical early alliance with *Charleston News and Courier* editor F. W. Dawson. "[A]n independent movement would have arisen if nothing had been done to provide reform," he told Dawson privately in early 1886. Economic hardship and aristocratic arrogance had strained the bonds of white unity to the breaking point. If the leadership did not reform its ways, "it is only a question of time & not very long off at that when the Democratic party will be broken up," Tillman warned the editor. One ally, he said, had told him that " '[o]ur people are not going to submit to this kind of thing forever. . . . [N]othing but a political earthquake will bring this crowd to its senses.' " "Of course," he went on, "I do not share in any such thoughts, for I would never under any circumstances have anything to do with pulling down our Democratic temple." He shared the same fear articulated by the *Edgefield Advertiser* in 1878: that a calamitous class division among white men would lead both sides to make an expedient alliance with the black majority. "The Devil is always tempting men to use the negro vote . . . to carry their end, and sooner or later it will become the balance of power between the rich-feeling Bourbons and the poor-feeling & more progressive among our people. I fear this—God grant I am mistaken!" In the long letters Dawson subsequently printed, Tillman was equally explicit about the dangers. "[H]e will be a bold man," he wrote in 1887, "who will say that the 'Farmers Movement' has not been a god-send to save the Democratic party from its own incipient rottenness" while presenting "a solid front to all comers on the bond of white supremacy." Dawson printed Tillman's articles and supported the agricultural college plan. In exchange, Tillman ceased his attacks on the Citadel and tried to convince his followers to do so as well. (Tillman also agreed to sell the editor some fancy hams he had produced, beginning a side business as a purveyor of farm goods to the Charleston elite.) This short-term alliance served its purpose by making Tillman's ideas available to a statewide audience.[25]

Like James Henry Hammond two generations before, Tillman claimed to see an "almost spontaneous uprising of the people." "The fire was everywhere smouldering and ready to burst out. I have only fanned it into flame and brought the dissatisfaction, which existed to a head." Such metaphors are convenient for those who fail to see political movements as the products of human agency or for those who wish to make such efforts seem natural. In fact, the movement's early growth had been anything but "spontaneous." Having been immersed throughout his adulthood in South Carolina's militia assemblies, club meetings, and nominating conventions, Tillman understood the principles of practical political organization in the state. "Twenty-five men in each county can b[y] agitating & *work* carry the Legislature provided they don't run for office themselves," he told confidant Charles Crosland.[26]

To pull local movement forces together, Tillman called a statewide meeting in April 1886 in Columbia. The proceedings, needless to say, were anything but "spontaneous." In a caucus on the eve of the convention, Tillman met in his hotel room with members of each county's delegation, seeking to ensure a degree of common understanding and consensus. The convention itself was Tillman's from start to finish: the first day was dominated by his speech, and the second day by the passage of his proposals, including his plans for financial reform in state institutions and an agricultural college. The convention's participants included several hundred white men, representing various factions within the state Democratic Party, but no black delegates or representatives. Leading conservative figures attended and helped ensure that their political leader, Governor Hugh Thompson, would be invited to address the convention. Local bosses such as Milton L. Donaldson of Greenville gained leadership posts. At the other extreme of the white political spectrum, former Greenback leader and sometime Republican W. W. Russell attended as a member of an upcountry delegation; although Tillman and his lieutenants took care to hammer home their commitment to white supremacy and the Democratic Party, no direct objection to Russell's participation was reported.[27]

The purpose of the convention, and of the movement generally, was to control the state Democratic Party from within. Once delegations returned from the 1886 Columbia convention, Tillmanites scheduled farmers' club meetings to precede Democratic club meetings and county farmers' conventions to precede county Democratic assemblies. In Abbeville, for example, the county Farmers' Association met just before the county Democratic convention in order to "suggest" which delegates ought to be sent to the state Democratic convention. Once the farmers' meeting adjourned, "the Democratic county club was immediately called to order," apparently in the same location. The Democratic assembly then elected eleven delegates to the state party convention, including the eight "suggested" by the farmers' convention. Next door in Edgefield, Tillman himself became chairman of the Executive Committee of the county Democratic Party and was a delegate to the 1886 state party convention. For the moment, however, political success for the farmers' movement stopped at the county level. Tillman declined to run for governor, and the movement's alternative candidates for that office failed to achieve nomination. As late as 1888, statewide office eluded the farmers' movement, as legislators denied Tillman the first office he sought beyond the county level—a seat on the board of agriculture. The state party leadership remained in conservative hands.[28]

Tillman's unwillingness to run for governor stemmed in part from the fear he had articulated to Crosland at the outset: if he came to be perceived as a mere office-seeker, his message would lose its power. Indeed, throughout the early phases of the movement, Tillman struggled to strike a balance between presenting himself as the leader of the farmers and claiming to be only their humble servant. The military language with which he described the movement complicated matters. "We are an army of 60,000 white voters, farmers all, against 20,000 of all other classes," he declared. The man some had dubbed "Moses" required his proudly independent farmers to rally as a disciplined army—and to accept that discipline voluntarily. "The way out of this wilderness is very plain. Even I can lead you out, but I cannot either drive or carry you out on my back. 'Who would be free, himself must strike the blow.' . . . [O]ne sharpshooter, no matter how bold, can only annoy our masters. . . . No skirmish line, however, can take this fortress or obtain redress for our grievances." "If you feel incompetent to lead, be ready to follow, and if you can't exactly have your own way don't sulk. Either quit grumbling, or 'fall in,' and having chosen your leaders follow them and obey orders."[29]

But Tillman feared presenting the appearance that he was dictating to other white men. "I trust I am numbered among South Carolina's freemen," declared one white man during the 1890 campaign, "and that I am not anybody's [-]ite." The potential for such protests was never far from Tillman's mind. "I am giving instructions like a general," he explained in early 1886, "but I am ready, willing, and anxious to get in the ranks if others will take the lead." He was at pains to deny that the movement needed his particular leadership and to establish that his role required the consent of the organized. "The pent up indignation of the farmers has found a voice through me, and the masses of our people are ready to follow anyone, however insignificant, who has the boldness to lead. I did not commence this agitation with any such expectation, but I should be a coward to refuse to lead, at least, till we organize." He was right to be anxious. After the April 1886 convention, a hostile Columbia reporter suggested that Tillman had served "as a molder of the action of the convention." In a political culture where men prized their freedom from being "driven" or directed by others, the insinuation was clear: the delegates were Tillman's creatures, not free men.[30]

The Democratic leadership proved resilient enough to withstand Tillman's early challenge, and by the end of 1887, it appeared that the farmers' movement might be disintegrating. At the poorly attended December convention, a dissident faction reportedly even attempted to dislodge Tillman from the organization's leadership. Frustrated by failure, in January 1888 Tillman sent Dawson a bitter "farewell speech" in which he announced his intention to "retire to the shades of private life." His own agricultural undertakings had suffered since he took on the role of agricultural "Moses," he explained, and his wife opposed his continued activism. "I have neglected and sacrificed the interests of my wife and children," he wrote, and "I can't afford the costly luxury of 'reform' any longer."[31]

But a few months later, one "reform" effort suddenly paid off, rescuing Tillman from political obscurity. In the autumn of 1886, Tillman had met with Thomas Green Clemson, heir to John C. Calhoun's upcountry plantation, to ask him to consider endowing an agricultural college. When Clemson died in April 1888, he left a large plantation, $60,000 in cash, and a will laying out the terms under which the state could transform his estate into an agricultural college. Tillman and six other men were to be named life trustees of the college; these men would make up more than half the college's board and would have the power to name their successors. Tillman later stated that this provision was intended to keep any future "radical" government from admitting black students. It also quietly ensured that low-country conservatives would not be able to dismantle the institution by more subtle means. The Clemson bequest reenergized both the movement and its founder. "[O]ld Clemson's expiring spark . . . set the woods on fire," ultimately forcing the state government to found the college for which Tillman had fought.[32]

Simultaneously, a wave of organizational energy from another source revitalized the farmers' movement. Throughout and beyond the South, farmers facing economic hardship had begun to join the Farmers' Alliance. Like Tillman's Farmers' Association, the Alliance was rooted in local chapters (called "sub-Alliances"), but the Alliance's goals were far more ambitious than fiscal reform or the creation of an agricultural college. County and state Alliances founded cooperatives for the purchase and sale of agricultural products and supplies, offering not only a powerful critique of merchants, middlemen, and the "money power" but an alternative as well. Members rallied behind regional and national antimonopoly activities, including national boycotts. Although technically a nonpolitical organization, the Alliance dominated reform politics for a time in many Southern, plains, and mountain states and ultimately spawned the People's Party.[33]

The Alliance overlapped substantially with Tillman's farmers' movement, and its explosive growth offered Tillman a new platform and his constituents new energy. Beginning in 1887, South Carolina farmers organized numerous sub-Alliances, county Alliances, and finally a state Alliance. Men Tillman perceived as close regional allies, notably North Carolina's Leonidas Lafayette Polk, became state and national Alliance leaders. Outsiders routinely conflated Tillman's movement with that of the Alliance, and one correspondent believed that the Farmers' Association might merge with the Alliance, "in which it seems all the farmers have their hearts." The South Carolina Farmers' Alliance did indeed attract the same dissatisfied white owners and renters—primarily the former—who had been drawn to Tillman's Farmers' Association. According to statistics collected by the Alliance's national organ, the *National Economist*, white South Carolina Alliancemen were on the average wealthier than their non-Alliance neighbors. Over half the dues-paying members in the fall of 1888 owned the land they farmed, nearly a third farmed but did not own, and the rest were women and dependent children, doctors, ministers, teachers, and rural mechanics. In Union, an observer approvingly described local white Alliancemen as "the best class of farmers . . . educated men . . . the stanch yeomanry," not men "of a bickering or sorehead sort." The same men who had rallied to Tillman now took their places in the state Alliance leadership. E. T. Stackhouse, who had been a Farmers' Association leader since early 1886, became the state Alliance's first president. The overlaps between the leadership and rank and file of the Alliance and those of the farmers' movement could lead to procedural gymnastics. In 1892, for example, the Anderson County Alliance adjourned its quarterly meeting so that "[d]istinguished gentlemen . . . invited, by the Farmers' Association" might "address the people."[34]

By 1889, the Alliance seemed to be the most dynamic force in state farmers' politics—a paradox of sorts since the Alliance was supposed to be nonpartisan. At the state Alliance meeting in July 1889, Stackhouse reported 20,000 members statewide, including men in nearly every county. Tillman himself joined the organization somewhat belatedly in 1889, immediately taking charge of the Edgefield County organization. But this delayed recognition of the Alliance's importance suggested that Tillman was no longer leading but following. The state's Alliance leaders included foes as well as friends of Tillman's, and he would face challenges both from those who wanted the Alliance to stay out of politics entirely and from those who wanted him to help the Alliance fulfill its radical potential.[35]

Citizens, Soldiers, and "Drunk Driven Cattle"

At the beginning of 1890, under the name of Tillmanite leader G. W. Shell, the *Charleston News and Courier* published a call for a March statewide farmers' convention. The purpose of this convention, explained the Shell Manifesto, was to suggest a "farmers' candidate" for governor, a man who would then have a formidable head start in the race. The author of this effort to preempt the Democratic Party's own processes, as well as the manifesto itself, was obviously Ben Tillman. The Shell Manifesto set off a year-long controversy among the state's Democrats over the fine line between leadership and demagoguery that devolved into harsh words and almost into violence. Tillman and his enemies accused one another of manipulating their followers and leading them down false and even dangerous paths. In a political culture that considered republican independence the essence of responsible citizenship, it was a serious matter to charge that men had allowed themselves to be misled, manipulated, or "driven." Tillman might be vulnerable to many attacks, but his opponents turned out to be even more vulnerable, and their efforts to portray him as a demagogue or dictator backfired, making it appear that they, not he, had little regard for the independence of hard-pressed white men. The Clemson bequest and the emergence of the Farmers' Alliance helped Tillman remain in the spotlight, but only his enemies' attacks enabled him to identify himself as the friend of the ordinary white farmer.

The Shell Manifesto laid out Tillman's vision of South Carolina's history as a tale of two classes. The legitimate citizenry consisted of the farmers, whose devotion to political virtue, household order, and agricultural prosperity had brought them nothing but hardship. Instead, an illegitimate aristocracy governed the state for its own benefit. "South Carolina has never had a real Republican government," the document asserted. "Since the days of the 'Lords Proprietors' it has been an aristocracy under the forms of Democracy." Tillman's campaign of personal insinuation and public attack succeeded in the early 1890s because many of his targets did indeed seem to assume that they represented "the wealth and intelligence" of the state. They did expect to hold the state's top offices, and they did regard men who scratched at the soil and dressed in shapeless clothes as their social inferiors. As Tillman goaded them from the pages of newspapers and the platforms of Democratic stump meetings, he attracted support from the disgruntled rank and file. When his adversaries used his behavior and his followers as proof of Tillman's demagoguery and disreputability, they revealed their own profoundly elitist notions of citizenship and leadership. By attacking Tillman—especially by attacking him as dishonorable or disreputable—they helped him become the symbolic champion of the farmers.[36]

Many of Tillman's enemies believed that the fraudulence of his claim to speak for ordinary white farmers would soon become clear. Tillman's wealth—in 1890, over 1,700 acres of land valued at over $10,000 and forty head of cattle—made him something other than an ordinary "farmer man." More to the point, Tillman often spoke and behaved in ways that threatened to undermine his status as the champion of poor farmers, for his point of reference was always that of a landowning employer. He frequently argued that "[i]mpending bankruptcy stares thousands in the face, while other thousands are overseeing their own plantations for the victuals and clothes," a description of subsistence agriculture that only the wealthiest fraction of white society would have understood as anything out of the ordinary. His attack on the crop-lien system and his call to repeal the lien law brought charges that he and other advocates of repeal sought to "reduce the tenants, the renters and others who are unable to procure supplies except by liens to the level of hired hands for wages" or to "reduce all farming in South Carolina to the boss system of agriculture." During the 1890 campaign, one legislator claimed that several years before, Tillman had asked him to help repeal the lien law. When he had refused on the grounds that it would deprive his poor white constituents of the credit they needed to raise crops, Tillman had supposedly replied, "Well, put them to work for wages, and you can control them." Also, a decade after he helped ensure its passage, the stock law briefly came back to haunt Tillman. During his 1892 reelection campaign, Tillman received an urgent letter asking him to refute rumors, damaging to his cause among poorer white men, that he had "favored and headed the Petition to pass the general stock law." Of course, he could do no such thing since the damaging rumors were entirely true. Pettier allegations, true and false, were brought to bear: by Tillman's second term as governor, hostile commentators would accuse him of turning Clemson into a "dude factory," wearing kid gloves, and dressing in style. Some charges might not have seemed so petty. One neighbor nursed a grievance against Tillman that echoed other white men's outrage at upper-class arrogance. Edgefield farmer J. C. Shaw wrote the new governor in 1891 that for years he had "beged you written you as a friend and gentleman to keep your wagons off my growing crops." Tillman had not complied, and now Shaw was forced to threaten him. "Now Mr. Tillman wil [*sic*] you tell me what do you want is it trouble or what is it? I do not go about you or anything you have. Now if you are a *man* for God Sake let me alone." Here was a Ben Tillman who was conscious of his own class interests and dismissive of a poor white man's prerogatives and even — most disturbing in a self-styled agricultural reformer — his subsistence.[37]

Tillman called himself "a plain, blunt man, who tells his thoughts and views straight at the mark," but he set a low priority on factual accuracy or consistency. Over and over, he charged opponents with conspiracy, corruption, and incompetence, only to retreat when challenged, declaring that he had not meant to impugn any particular individual. After he described the agricultural leadership as "broken-down politicians and old superannuated Bourbon aristocrats, who are thoroughly incompetent," he added that he meant no reflection on the current board of agriculture. When his "dude factory" reference to the Citadel provoked an outcry, Tillman agreed to stop using the phrase, remarking that "although these were his sentiments he didn't want to offend anyone." In the coming months, however, he continued to deploy the phrase in political speeches. After Governor Thompson addressed the April 1886 farmers' convention, despite facing veiled accusations of misappropriating agricultural funds, Tillman first denied that he had accused state officials of robbery and corruption, then immediately made those very charges, accusing the last legislature of "misrule" in rejecting reapportionment and deploring the lien law and the lack of legislation against the manufacture of impure fertilizers as "robbery." When Sumter delegate John J. Dargan, a conservative lawyer skeptical of the movement, protested Tillman's treatment of the governor, Tillman responded that "[h]e had no animosity against any man or class of men, but the lawyers and merchants . . . had dominated the Legislature for the past ten years, and who knew it more than the gentleman from Sumter."[38]

Only repeated insinuations against and confrontations with state officials, he believed, could generate sustained interest. A disillusioned former ally claimed that Tillman had admitted that he had made false accusations "so as to give notoriety to the movement." Another opponent referred to Tillman's attacks—"random shots fired into the multitude that strike innocent parties"—as "audaciously reckless and dangerous to the public welfare, although they may be intended merely as political devices for the attainment of political ends." Even some allies grew uncomfortable with Tillman's tactics, urging him in an 1888 meeting to "be careful in his public utterance" and to "stick to the facts and not make statements he could not prove." Tillman understood both the benefits and potential pitfalls of his tactics: he "struck out some sarcastic allusions" in a letter to the *Charleston News and Courier*, although he wistfully told the editor they had been "spicy, & they would be enjoyed by many of your readers."[39]

Some of Tillman's victims finally began to understand how badly their counterattacks had backfired. From the beginning, the *Edgefield Chronicle* had suggested that "there is a better way of killing Mr. Tillman than by abusing him and his friends and that is to let him alone." Breaking with his former ally over his outrageous attacks, Dawson proposed a "campaign of silence" against Tillman. "Do not allow his name to appear in the *News and Courier* when it is possible to avoid it," he instructed his colleague J. C. Hemphill, who edited the paper after Dawson's death in 1889. But men like Hemphill frequently could not resist. "These gentry regard me as the devil," Tillman gleefully told a confidant. After the Shell Manifesto, of course, the *Charleston News and Courier* could hardly avoid allowing Tillman's name to appear.[40]

Over and over during the early 1890s, however, Tillman's foes could not resist attacking him in ways that identified him with the very men whose support he needed. In part, this was a matter of style rather than wealth. Tillman might have been a wealthy man and a local political leader, but he did not have the polish or bearing of the state's traditional leadership. His plantation house during the 1880s was a simple five-room dwelling. His recreational tastes ran to books rather than elaborate dinners or balls, and in a basically favorable biographical account, the *Edgefield Chronicle* nonetheless described him as "ascetic" and "unsociable." His clothes, some noted, were not well tailored, and his unfashionably shapeless hats in particular came in for satirical commentary. Hostile newspapers advised the women of the state to stay away from campaign meetings at the risk of "having their modesty shocked and their sex insulted" by Tillman's use of profanity. Even Tillman's physical person — his missing eye — could inspire upper-class derision.[41]

In their outrage at Tillman's attacks, his opponents overplayed their hand. Treating the maverick planter with the same elitist disdain they showed for mill-working "tackeys," rough-hewn country folk, and even middling white legislators, Tillman's enemies in Columbia and Charleston handed him a weapon he could never have forged on his own. Tillmanite candidates for the legislature endured derisive descriptions. In private, one opponent portrayed the reform-dominated 1894 legislature as "strangers in a foreign land" — as indeed they were made to feel in Columbia. Tillmanite legislator Josh Ashley, a colorful figure known widely as "Josh," came in for harsh treatment by the anti-Tillman *Columbia State*, which presented his speeches in a nearly impenetrable dialect and mocked him for riding in second-class train cars. *State* editor Narciso Gonzales likened Tillman voters to black men, mockingly pairing the political slogan "1872 — 'Vote for Grant, he 'mancipated you' " with its contemporary equivalent "1892 — 'Vote for Tillman, he emancipated you.' " The substitution of an "e" for an apostrophe would hardly have mollified the white men he compared to freedmen, slavishly casting their ballots for a man who cared nothing about them. Rural whites would have had little trouble decoding the assumptions and prejudices suggested by such portraits. Millworkers, at that time still mostly seasonal laborers or recent refugees from the farm, would have felt the same sting. In private, one woman described Tillman himself as a degraded poor white. She wrote that on a train Tillman had "behaved like a 'tackey,' put his head on the arm of the seat & his feet up in the window & had his mouth open & went fast asleep."[42]

Opponents' undifferentiated disdain for Tillman and "his wool-hats" only bound those unlikely allies closer together. Such opposition "helps us wonderfully," Shell had noted in the early days of the movement, and one opponent suggested to Tillman that demonstrations against the 1890 convention—not the convention itself—had "made him." Tillman denied this but, in discussing a candidate who had been "outspoken in abusing the farmers movement," believed he could "whip him the easier for taking that tack." To be denounced was to join a noble lineage: Thomas Jefferson, noted a leading Tillmanite, "was called a 'rank demagogue' and 'vile agitator.' The Federal press were about as bitter in their denunciation of Mr. Jefferson and his politics as are the Old Liners or ringsters in denouncing Mr. Tillman." "Gov. Tillman lives—yes, lives in the very hearts and souls of his one-gallus boys," declared one Edgefield admirer. "He knows the dear old farmer, raised to toil and hardships, will stick to him, therefore, he does not hesitate to fight for us."[43]

Tillman's claims to be a "backwoods man & farmer only" were indeed laughable. But as opponents attempted to rebut such claims, they often ended up validating Tillman's assertion that "aristocrats" believed that "commoners" were unable to think or act for themselves. L. W. Youmans, a lowcountry conservative and bitter foe, charged that Tillman's "talk about being out at the elbows don't amount to anything when you remember that in 1880 he said that he ran thirty ploughs, and now he comes here and poses as a poor man." But Youmans suggested that Tillman's ploy worked only because farmers could not accurately distinguish between real and fake allies. "If I were to cry 'poor man' and go before the country I, too, could get some votes," he explained, setting himself apart from poor, rural folk in a way that undermined the very point he was trying to make. Less prominent but equally hostile observers unthinkingly betrayed the same distance from poor white men's plight. Tillman, declared a writer to the *Charleston News and Courier*, portrayed himself "as a clodhopper—the poor farmer boy, and the one-gallused boy," but "this is only when he is seeking to get the farmers' vote." Correspondent E. B. Murray warned readers that if Tillman succeeded in repealing the lien law, respectable white men would be forced to hire themselves and their families "as servants to men who had money enough to run without the lien law." But rather than identifying himself as one of those struggling farmers, Murray stood apart. The closest he could come was to reminisce about the bonds forged among white men in 1876, when "the tennant [*sic*] class . . . rode with us on many a night."[44]

Tillman and others portrayed their movement as the literal and metaphorical sequel to the Red-shirt uprising, and they invoked the white solidarity of 1876 without condescending to "the tennant class." To an Edgefield supporter, the 1890 convention's "gathering of the representatives of those who tan their skin and soil their clothes in making bread for the millions" represented a reunion of "the men who wore the red shirts in '76, and saved South Carolina at the ballot box." Edgefield Tillmanite H. H. Townes urged "freeborn white men" to remember the recent past: "[M]en who had to rise at midnight, leave your wives and children exposed to the mercy of brutal negroes whose passion had been excited to the frightful pitch by scalawags and carpet-baggers . . . [D]o you remember?" Tillman lauded members of his political army for asserting themselves and their rights against a haughty foe. "[W]ith the Farmers' Movement to strengthen their backbone [they] have withstood the cajolery, threats, and impotent rage of the old 'ring bosses,' " he declared.[45]

Whereas his foes placed themselves at a social and economic distance from hard-pressed rural whites, Tillman actively identified himself as an ally. Sometimes it even seemed that Tillman was the only "commoner" to be found. A stump-meeting opponent, thinking that no white Democrat would willingly describe himself in the humble terms Tillman employed, asked anyone present who actually considered himself a "common man" to raise his hand. Only Tillman did so—but this gesture was received with what the *Charleston News and Courier* described as "cheering" and "confusion." Tillman's willingness to identify himself in this way, even when others hesitated to make the same claim, may have made his pose even more credible. In this sense, at least, he was accurate in claiming to be "organiz[ing] the common people against the aristocracy." "If you haven't got generals and colonels and captains and gentlemen enough to fill the offices," he told an 1888 meeting, "just pick up some common man and try him." He was willing to be that man and to present himself as the somewhat hapless victim of an overwhelming aristocratic retaliation. The opposition, he said, "having first gently laid Capt. Tillman down, heaps a whole pile of 'Honorables' upon him, topped off with a Governor. . . . How is one poor little farmer, who is only a 'captain in the "melish,"' to get from under such a terrible weight?" The captain of the militia, suitably belittled by disdainful opponents, could indeed seem to be a "poor little farmer."[46]

The attacks on Tillman and his supporters in the 1890 campaign demonstrated that his opponents had learned nothing when it came to political tactics. As white farmers from across the state assembled in Columbia for the March 1890 "Shell Convention," crowds of students from the University of South Carolina greeted them with disdainful jeers and choruses of "We'll

Hang Ben Tillman from a Sour Apple Tree." To Tillman, this proved that the Columbia school "teaches the aristocratic right that those boys are the inheritors of power." Townes agreed that the demonstration was evidence of "the insolence and confidence of long continued power." While the students mocked the hayseeds, the instigators of the demonstration sat "by their comfortable fires in their elegantly furnished rooms, with slippered feet and robed in costly dressing gowns"—this was how "they spend their energies in trying to keep the farmers down."[47]

The "aristocrats" not only refused to acknowledge Tillman's movement as a legitimate successor to the Red-shirts but also depicted it as a dangerous exercise in demagoguery. From the beginning, skeptical observers had worried about Tillman's invocation of the Red-shirt legacy. As Tillman began to make a name for himself in 1886, a Pee Dee newspaper declared that "[t]he time for bulldozing and bluster in South Carolina is passed." The upcoming election would pit "democrat against democrat, white man against white man." Red-shirt force and threat had no place in such a contest, and it would be "foolish [for] any man to think he can carry an election by storm. The people have been taught to think and act for themselves, and we cannot conceive how any white man can be cheated out of their [*sic*] right to vote as they please by blustering people who wish to exhibit what they consider their strength." But such protestations revealed a profound undercurrent of anxiety about the power of "storm" and "bluster" to undermine men's capacity for responsible political action.[48]

To opponents, Tillman's agitation constituted rank demagoguery that threatened to reduce the state to revolution, anarchy, or mob rule. The *Charleston News and Courier* charged that Tillman appealed to "the passions and prejudices of the ignorant." Prominent Democratic leader F. W. McMaster accused Tillmanites of attempting "to incite the poor against the rich to make men believe our State has been governed by a heartless oligarchy and political rings, and if an argument cannot be answered the mob is incited to cry out the opprobrious term 'ringsters' with shameless arrogance and falsehood. . . . Many of our farmers, good, true, and simple-minded men, have been seduced by the wily teachings of this prince of humbugs [and] shut their eyes to argument and blindly follow their leader to their injury." Tillman and Alliance activists set class against class: at every meeting, Tillman opponents claimed, men uttered "base and slanderous sentiments" such as, " 'It is the poor against the rich. Just like it was in the war, the poor men had to do all the fighting and the rich men staid [*sic*] at home.' " Others described Tillman's supporters using the terms of European radicalism. The farmers' movement, complained a former governor, "absorbed and carried along the sans cullots & anarchical element which has always existed." The author of a letter to the *News and Courier* agreed that the reform movement "aims at the destruction of law and order. It is Red Revolution fit for the days of Marat and the Sans-Culottes." Opponents frequently portrayed Tillman's supporters as illiterate rowdies. Barnwell conservative Alfred Aldrich complained of "Tillman toughs (my name for them)." Mobs, blind men, victims of seduction, anarchists—those who followed Tillman deserved to be described in such uncitizenlike terms.[49]

Tillmanites spit the language of their enemies back at them. "By them the farmers are named *sans-culottes*, a term of reproach applied in monarchies to the most abject and degraded people," wrote Townes in a pamphlet pointedly entitled *Don't You Forget It*. "The farmers are called 'deserters' and 'tools of Tillman' and other opprobrious names such as heretofore have only been used by the most vulgar fish woman." "Every farmer and every man in the State who respects honest toil," he said, should "unite as one man to put down this debasing method of political warfare. . . . We trust the day is not distant when the farmer will command as much respect and receive as decent treatment in Columbia as a patent medicine fakir or a circus clown."[50]

The Democratic leadership was not so caught up in its denunciations that its members failed to recognize the Tillmanites' organizational methods. They complained bitterly about the Farmers' Association practice of meeting just prior to Democratic assemblies in order to agree on farmers' candidates. As early as 1886, opponents protested that farmers' movement tickets and resolutions had been "forced upon the Convention by this preconcerted action" of "delegates from the country." Some perceived a "desire on the part of some of the farmers to come in and capture our County Democratic Convention"; in Chesterfield, "the farmers . . . showed no disposition to rule," but in Marlboro "the farmer element prevailed . . . and carried nearly everything in its way."[51]

The farmers' convention of March 1890 represented the culmination of this strategy. The night before it began, Tillman met with a caucus of delegates to plan strategy, and the convention itself started by hitting all the important notes: a pledge to respect "Anglo-Saxon unity," a call for primaries and reapportionment, and invocations of the legacy of 1876. When it came time to "suggest" a nominee for governor, J. L. M. Irby placed Tillman's name in nomination, declaring, "Shame on the party for stabbing Gary, a man who had saved in us in '76. . . . We could now make the amends honorable and choose B. R. Tillman." Opponents had also recognized the potential power of such a "suggestion" and had mobilized to prevent it. Joining local farmers' clubs and finding like-minded skeptics in them, anti-Tillman Democrats almost succeeded in preventing the convention from putting forward a farmers' candidate. Indeed, opponents actually may have won: the vote on whether to make a "suggestion" passed only by a tiny margin and on a recount that may not have been entirely honest. Such a dubious victory, however, was in keeping with the Red-shirt legacy, for since the 1870s, insurgent Democrats had always relied on a combination of careful organizing and brazen fraud.[52]

In the months that followed the March convention, Tillman parlayed his narrow victory into a full-blown campaign for the Democratic nomination. He told his supporters not to organize separate "Tillman clubs" but to "attack the regular forces, the machinery that controls those [Democratic] clubs, and send delegates to the County Convention; then to the Columbia convention, to do your bidding, whether it is for me or for any other man."[53]

Some seemed to believe that only certain men possessed the crucial qualities of leadership and authority. Wounded by the Shell Manifesto's attack on the state's historic leaders, the *Charleston News and Courier* sniffed that "there was and is an aristocracy in South Carolina—an aristocracy of brains and character." The anti-Tillman conservative faction of the Democratic Party, the paper later wrote, "embraces nearly all the wealthiest, best educated and consequently most intelligent people in every county." Conservatives began searching for an alternative candidate. Powerful Democrats such as Johnson Hagood and Governor Richardson (barred by law from a third term), who saw "incipient dissolution & consequent disaster" in a Tillman victory, sought a candidate of "wisdom, conservatism, moderation, & strict equity."[54]

Their efforts were in vain. That summer, as Tillman and two rivals exchanged speeches before crowds throughout the state, local Democratic clubs and county conventions prepared to nominate delegates to the September state nominating convention. But Tillman seemed to have the organizational upper hand. At the end of the canvass, the largely anti-Tillman state Democratic Executive Committee decided that its only hope of preventing a Tillman nomination lay in holding a primary in which anti-Tillman forces would unite behind one candidate. They planned to use the August convention to change the party's rules and call a primary before the September nominating convention. Otherwise, control of the composition of that convention would rest with delegates to the county conventions, who were elected by the local Democratic clubs. Given Tillman's ability to muster support at this level of Democratic politics, retaining the old rules would probably meaning ceding the nomination to him. The *Charleston News and Courier* warned that this would lead to a split in the party, for in its estimation "Regular" Democrats "cannot support Capt. Tillman, if he should be nominated," as long as he let stand his charges against the Democratic Party and its current leaders. The paper also urged the formation of anti-Tillman Democratic clubs in every election district. But as the election drew nearer, a concerned Democrat suggested that "it would be just as well, not to talk of a split, or Seceders, &c: not to assume too much the existence of a condition, which really does not yet exist. Assuming a thing very often forces men to act. . . . [A]ssuming a separation [in the party] may do more to make men feel themselves committed to it, & bring it about than anything else."[55]

As it turned out, the crisis came at the August convention. Tillmanites quickly gained parliamentary control of the body, overrode the Executive Committee, and placed responsibility for selecting nominating-convention delegates in the hands of the county conventions. They elected a new Executive Committee under a new party constitution that called for a statewide primary—beginning in 1892. Outraged anti-Tillmanites from the lowcountry and Columbia left the hall to form a rump convention. Their leader was Richland Democratic boss Alexander Haskell, who had been at the forefront of the anti-Tillman movement since the spring.[56]

Anti-Tillmanites denounced the August convention's adoption of a new party constitution as improper or even illegal. But the pro-Tillman *Greenville News* responded that such protests were as useless as reading "Supreme Court Decisions to a lynching party clamoring furiously at the door of a jail." The Tillmanites' seizure of the party machinery, the *News* suggested, represented the welling up of the spirit of 1876. Once white men had mobilized to seize the day, no force could be expected to stop them. This provided opponents with a rhetorical opening, a way to distinguish between right and might. "It is not only a sensible and timely action to read the law to 'a lynching party,' " responded a *Charleston News and Courier* editorial, "but it is the duty of the respecters and representatives of the law to do so. And unless The [Greenville] News is prepared to maintain that the illegal actions [*sic*] of a lynching party 'is made legal—becomes a law—when done by a power too strong to be resisted' and should not therefore be condemned or criticized afterward, it cannot, we think justify its position relative to the willful and violent course of the wrong doers—the lynching party—in the August Convention." Tillman and his men had lynched democracy.[57]

From "Mahoneism!" to Aristocratic Rebellion

Anti-Tillmanites, often known simply as "antis," continued to insist that they were the legitimate inheritors of the mantle of 1876. Indeed, they had the chutzpah to call themselves "straightouts," and as the 1890 election approached, they even suggested that Tillman's support from Alliancemen and old Greenbackers portended a renewed black and white "independent" coalition like that of William Mahone's Virginia Readjuster Party. According to one hostile observer, "[E]very man in Orangeburg County who ever voted or favored a 'Greenback' or 'Independent' ticket or movement is now a hot Tillman man. . . . '[T]he negroes and Republicans' see 'Mahone and Virginia' in the near future." Some Democrats had long worried that some "bad" or "unprincipled" citizen, "taking hold of some popular movement," would organize an independent challenge that would draw on Republican support. "We should think of the fearsome results that will be sure to follow Mahoneism under whatever name," urged one anti-Tilmanite on the eve of the Shell Convention.[58]

Although these opponents probably did not believe their own charges, it was true that former Greenbackers had nowhere else to turn. Despite Tillman's clear commitment to white supremacy and Democratic rule, his farmers' movement offered Republicans and independents their only hope for a breakup of the Redemption-era Democratic Party. Between 1886 and 1890, W. W. Russell took part in county- and state-level conventions of the movement, and for a time Tillman even captured the imagination of J. Hendrix McLane. In an 1886 speech before his stalwarts at a local Grange, McLane endorsed Tillman as a worthy successor in fighting the Redeemer "Bourbons." "The members of this Grange since 1878 have been where Mr. B. R. Tillman of Edgefield now stands," McLane declared; "he is aiming for the same port for which years ago you set sail." Like Tillman, McLane believed that even "honest farmers" who became legislators could be stymied and corrupted by "Bourbon" institutions. And like Tillman, McLane reached back to the campaign of 1876 as the model for a new farmers' liberation movement. He depicted Reconstruction as a struggle of "the farmers and other honest tax-payers" against "the rule of the 'stranger' " and "bourbo-lawyer" elements that only claimed the name "Democrat." Four short years after his coalition went down in defeat, McLane spoke the Tillmanite vernacular of Redemption, challenging neither its violence and fraud, its implications of racialized manhood, nor its elision of class distinctions among white farmers. McLane's allies likewise sympathetically compared Tillman's and McLane's speeches, suggesting that many former Greenbackers believed Tillman might be a worthy—or at least electable—successor. Clarity would come, though not soon enough. By 1889, McLane himself became a reform Republican and returned to South Carolina several times in an effort to establish the state party on an interracial basis.[59]

McLane's old coalition partners had pursued a variety of political courses since the early 1880s. Some voted for lowcountry fusion tickets, and many continued to imagine a renewed independent coalition. White Republican leader Ellery M. Brayton had prayed in 1889 that someone "among those at heart in the rebellion against the fraud marked, ring ruled and blood stained Bourbon organization" would act "as the bold, brave and wise Mahone did." But especially after the election of Republican Benjamin Harrison to the presidency in 1888, many more placed their hopes in federal action and supported congressional efforts to pass the Lodge Elections Bill. This legislation, which would have allowed local political minorities to call for federal oversight of elections, was referred to by hostile Democrats as the "Force Bill." Although the bill never became law, to Democrats it represented Republicans' continued determination to use federal power to return the South to Reconstruction. In 1891, Tillman warned that the "Force Bill" was an attempt "to Reconstruct us, . . . to make the pyramid stand on its apex and give us back again the negro as a ruler." The defeated Redeemers could not have said it better, and radical Alliancemen who wanted to remain Democrats could not say anything at all.[60]

At the local level, too, black South Carolinians continued to challenge the post-Reconstruction order. In 1886–87, under the auspices of former Knights of Labor leader Hiram Hover (widely misspelled "Hoover"), black farm laborers mobilized as the Cooperative Workers of America in their effort to seek higher wages. Their labor movement elicited a predictably violent response. In the early summer of 1887, white farmers with shotguns forced black laborers in Greenville and other counties to renounce their affiliation with the organization. This did not put a stop to black agricultural protest. As white farmers joined the Farmers' Alliance during the late 1880s, black agricultural workers formed chapters of a parallel organization, the Colored Farmers' Alliance (CFA). We know less about the CFA than about its white counterpart, in part because its members performed much of their work in secret. The CFA shared many of the formal commitments of the Farmers' Alliance and at times took part in national Alliance assemblies; it also supported cooperatives and other moves toward economic independence. But the CFA was primarily made up of black laborers, men whose interest in higher wages could set them directly against white landowners—including many of the leaders of the white Alliance.[61]

Despite the similarity of their organizations' names and constitutions, black and white Alliancemen regarded one another across a chasm of history and of economic circumstance. The CFA's members were primarily laborers and small renters, not owners and large renters as in the white organization. Although both black and white Alliances stressed cooperative economics, black Alliancemen also called for higher wages and lower rents, setting them in direct opposition to many of their white "brethren," their landlords and employers. Moreover, many white Alliancemen feared black political and economic independence as much as Tillman did. Even if their organizations had similar names, black laborers' agenda was quite different from that of white landowners. When an Alliance business agent attacked the lien law, he complained that "[u]nder its pernicious influence every freedman in the land can pretend to run a farm, and consequently the control of the land and labor passes out of the hands of the owners." This argument needed little elaboration for an audience of landowners. When members of a black sub-Alliance boycotted owners who enforced the stock law and threatened black farm workers who continued to work for such men, they were arrested. In Edgefield, a black Alliance was said to have set a wage for cotton picking at 50 cents per 100 pounds and to be planning to fix rents as well. Such grassroots organization for economic betterment did not sit well with white men whose economic aspirations required subordinating both middlemen and laborers. "The Alliance, even among the colored people, is productive of good," noted the article reporting the stock-law opponents' threats, "but boycotting and mob law will not be allowed." White farmers acting collectively might claim the legacy of the Red-shirts, but when black farmers' organizations became mobilizations, they could seem to be part of a heritage that stretched back through the Cooperative Workers of America, the Reconstruction militias, and perhaps even antebellum slave conspiracies.[62]

McLane's efforts, the emergence of the CFA, and the proposed Lodge Bill together led some Democrats to suggest that Tillman planned to mobilize white and black Alliances and create a new biracial independent movement. Tillman had indeed sought to solidify support among white Alliancemen as part of his bid to take over the party. But anti-Tillmanites' accusations went much further than that, blaming any Republican activity, including attempts by black voters to register, on hopes raised by Tillman. They portrayed him as an unwitting tool of scheming Republicans and their "front," the CFA. "In negro-crowded South Carolina," concluded one editorial, "this is certainly not the time for divisions among the white people of the State."[63]

In fact, Tillman's position on black political activity could not have been clearer. Tillman boasted of his participation at Hamburg and Ellenton, and his 1890 running mate, Eugene Gary, made the protection of white prerogative against alleged black depredations the focus of his campaign. Pointing to technical education for blacks at Claflin College, which received $5,000 each year from the state, Gary urged giving "white boys" a comparable education so they could receive the wages earned by black mechanics. Gary also advocated the segregation of railroad cars, presenting black male sexuality as a threat to white women. "What white man," Gary asked, "wants his wife or sister sandwiched between a big bully buck and a saucy wench. I know every [white] woman in South Carolina will endorse [segregated cars]." Tillman's white opponents worried about being outflanked as proponents of this protective, manly white supremacy: an anti-Tillman Columbia audience responded to Gary's speech by shouting, "Come off that Tillman ticket. . . . You ought to be with us." Although Tillman did not make Jim Crow legislation an important element of his campaign in 1890, his explanation for a separate-car bill's defeat was that "somebody got bamboozled" by state railroad boss "Bunch" McBee. Segregation, it appeared, fit neatly into the program of the farmers' movement, and early advocates in the legislature included farmers' movement stalwarts Josh Ashley and Cole Blease.[64]

Despite Tillman's history and Gary's rhetoric, black Alliancemen engaged in heated debate over the proper stance toward Tillman's campaign. One orator responded to Gary's attacks with his own statement of patriarchal authority and protection of black womanhood, declaring that "if his wife was ever subjected to any indignity on the train he would kill the man that attempted it." Others thought that Tillman's fight would ultimately benefit both black and white farmers and that sooner or later the fight within the Democratic Party would make black votes "a factor." The black Alliance's state convention, however, refused to support either Democratic faction, although one black sub-Alliance was reported to have endorsed the Shell Convention's suggestion of Tillman for governor and at least one black Democrat wrote to Tillman claiming to have supported pro-Tillman delegates for the August convention.[65]

Although Tillman never gave any real encouragement to potential black supporters, his coalition was not of one unambiguous mind about black political participation. To be sure, Tillmanites attempted to allay fears that their movement would rally black voters. During the campaign, the Farmers' State Alliance backed a motion by Tillman ally W. J. Talbert that the Lodge Bill should be defeated. But some Tillmanites privately suggested that the campaign attempt to "control the negro vote among alliance negroes for all our congressmen." Alliance president E. T. Stackhouse was confronted in early June with a document purporting to be a Marlboro County black sub-Alliance's endorsement of Tillman. Stackhouse, although uncertain "whether the declaration is honest or not," reportedly commented that "if they are honest . . . and so prove at the November election, if Capt. Tillman should be the nominee, we may hope that the negro is approaching his second emancipation." Stackhouse presumably meant emancipation from the Republican Party, not from the status of laborer, but these were dangerous waters for a white Democrat. The conservatives played this theme for all it was worth. Some black men present at an 1890 campaign meeting were reported to be wearing Tillman badges; when their faces "grew grave" during a vitriolic Gary speech, a conservative shouted, "Better look out, the colored alliances are endorsing you."[66]

Charges that Tillman contemplated a break with Democratic white supremacy proved entirely misplaced, for it was Tillman's opponents who ultimately took that fatal step. Once Tillman gained the Democratic nomination, the hard-line anti-Tillmanites of Columbia and the lowcountry recognized that an independent ticket and an "appeal to the negro vote . . . [were] the only chance of success," and Richland Democratic boss Alexander Haskell led a bolt from the party.[67]

This was a squarely reactionary move, promising not equality or reform but paternalist protection. For some lowcountry elites, the identity of interest between white landowners and black laborers was a better basis for political coalition than the strictures of Tillman's Red-shirt white supremacy. Black Carolinians, gubernatorial aspirant Haskell suggested, should look to white Carolinians of his class for protection, just as they had always done. "We have our own race to preserve," he wrote, and "another race to protect." But the Haskellites—still attempting, against all logic, to claim the name "straightouts"—never presented a serious electoral challenge. If nothing else sufficed to make this clear, an approving letter from Daniel Chamberlain to Haskell should have done the trick.[68]

Letters between Haskellites suggest that they had come to hate Tillman so profoundly that they could only respond to his nomination by committing political suicide. They could not resist making unfavorable comparisons between Tillmanites and African Americans. "[I]t seems to me," wrote one, that "a good, honest negro . . . would be better for Governor than a white Black Guard and his ignorant & malicious followers; who are not farmers but rowdies." Broad democratic participation apparently was no more desirable among white men than it was among black. "Universal suffrage," wrote one Charlestonian, "must prove a failure with an ordinary population of whites . . . but there are some *negroes* better fitted for the exercise of the rights of citizenship than are many whites who actually vote." This was not just a statement of political theory, given the persistence of "fusion" arrangements and black voting in the lowcountry. The *Charleston News and Courier*, covering its first election without Dawson at the helm, predicted that 50,000 qualified black voters would turn out and "vote in a body as they are told to vote." But it required deliberate ignorance of the previous decade's events—or a deeply contrarian spirit—to believe that many whites would support this independent biracial coalition. "[I]f our movement causes this much grief to the Tillmanites it will pay us to have made it," wrote one Haskell supporter to another. Even Haskell knew he would be charged with "folly or madness."[69]

Most anti-Tillman Democrats could not justify voting against the party's nominee. Harry Hammond believed that "a heap of good white folks and good negroes in Carolina" might successfully fight Tillman's "Hamburg Massacre & Ellenton riot government." But he gloomily confided to a conservative Charleston friend that "the go cart of party machinery has dwarfed the moral independence of our citizens," leaving them without the confidence to oppose the party nominee—in this case, tragically, Ben Tillman. If they had more courage, he surmised, they might be willing to abandon the party rather than support such a man. But even nonreformers adopted Gary's language in this moment of apparent white-supremacist crisis. Independent-minded Democratic legislator John Dargan, responding to rumors that he had joined the bolters, wrote that those who appealed to black voters had stepped beyond the pale: "[S]uch men are not to be dealt with by an appeal to the ballot-box or by arguments." Tillman, for his part, fully expected to trounce his opponents, but he remembered to threaten retaliation if something went awry. Should the Haskellites try to count him out, Tillman declared, "we had better have a little war in South Carolina in 1890."[70]

African Americans themselves divided over the proper response to the Haskellite appeal for support. Black Republican leader George Murray thought the Democratic split offered the best opportunity for black voters since 1876, but a Colored Reform Conference in mid-October could not resolve the issue of whether or not to support Haskell. Richard Carroll, a conservative Orangeburg minister, noted that Tillman "put people to thinking on other things than the Negro" — to which outraged opponents replied, "Hamburg! Ellenton!" To some black men, the recent past demanded that black men do more than endorse the bolters. Remembering the violence of 1876, James Robinson defiantly warned that if similar violence were brought to bear in 1890, "Tillman won't have much longer to live." Murray, for his part, mistrusted "the poor whites led on by men like Ben Tillman," but he made no defiant threats. Like another pro-Haskell delegate who would prefer to work with "the best native born element than have the entire federal army for his protection," Murray would not challenge the paternalist language of protection so directly. Some who hoped the conference participants would "stand like men and endorse Haskell" had sought financial support from that faction. The conference ended inconclusively, but at the end of October, the Republican Executive Committee made prior arrangements official by urging Republicans to support Haskell. One reportedly said "that the wealth and intelligence of the country should control, and that the Haskell ticket represents that class."[71]

Running as an independent and seeking Republican support, Haskell won nearly 15,000 votes but gained a majority in only two heavily black low-country counties. Delighted white Democratic voters quickly relegated the bolters to the same dustbin of history occupied by previous enemies. Some Democrats, feeling that the Haskellites had forfeited their racial status, derided them as "*White Negroes*." One supporter asked Tillman, "Don't you think in our next primary all those parties should be delt [*sic*] with as if they were *Black*?" (Tillman even worried privately that white men had proved themselves to be bossable. If they could be "bought like 'drunk driven cattle,' " white men, like black men, became "unworthy to have a 'free vote' & 'fair count.' ") Had South Carolina fallen so far, demanded one newspaper editor, that it would rely on Haskell and his men "as the guardians of our honor, our manhood, our self-respect and our self-defense?" The bolters' "arrogant self-assertion" betrayed the Red-shirt legacy. Haskellites had "no sympathy with the people at large," wrote one Tillman supporter. "A ruling aristocracy — with serfs at command — this is their ideal: and their present attitude shows that they are careless whether their serfs be *white* or *black*, or what befalls the State *if but they may rule*!" Too many of South Carolina's "good men," the *Cotton Plant* reminded voters a few years later, "had rather be controlled by the negro (or as they hope, control white men by the negro) than submit to the votes of the 'white trash,' as they call them."[72]

The bolt solidified the party behind Tillman: as one Democrat put it after the election, "I did not put on very largely of Tillmanism, untill Haskellism took the field. . . . I have never sucked the radical [Republican] paps, nor gloated on Greenback hopes, nor endorsed Haskellism (nor Independantism) [*sic*] and I never will do either because I am a Democrat." The Haskellites had finished the work Tillman's unself-consciously aristocratic critics had begun, and Tillman gloated privately at their generosity in "giving me so good a club to break their heads."[73]

Why There Was No Populism in South Carolina

The Haskellite bolt further solidified Tillman's identification of himself with anti-aristocratic white unity. But even as Haskellites and their sympathizers fumed in defeat, Tillman faced a serious challenge from another quarter. Because he became governor of South Carolina as part of a national wave of agrarian protest and because he drew support from the Farmers' Alliance, Tillman was often mistaken for a Populist. Local as well as national observers counted him as an Alliance governor, and from the third party's inception in 1891, many Alliancemen expected him to support its challenge to both the Democrats and the Republicans.[74]

Tillman refused. Radical Alliance and Populist proposals went far beyond his modest program of reform and college building within a white man's Democratic Party. In particular, he feared the potential for federal control in the Alliance's proposed "subtreasury," a system of government-owned warehouses in which farmers could deposit their crops and receive interest-free loans from the government of up to 80 percent of the crop's market value. The subtreasury's advocates claimed that it would break the crop lien's cycle of credit and debt, turning the federal government into a servant of the producing classes rather than a tool of moneyed interests. As Lawrence Goodwyn has argued, the subtreasury was the heart of the Populist challenge, and struggling white farmers in South Carolina and elsewhere seemed to agree. In many Southern states, white Populist leaders attempted to form political coalitions with black voters, appealing to their common agricultural hardships and offering the subtreasury as an alternative to the crop lien, which oppressed both whites and blacks, owners, renters, and croppers. In nearby states, the leading Democratic insurgents against the Redeemers plunged into these waters, endorsing the subtreasury and seeking alliances with black voters. Georgia's Tom Watson and Alabama's Reuben Kolb stepped across the political color line; in North Carolina, Leonidas Polk seemed ready to do so as well. Yet Tillman demurred. Conservatives accused him of being a Populist, but if "Populism" meant radical economic change through federal intervention, the creation of a third national political party, and an interracial political alliance, Tillman was no Populist. By these standards, in fact, South Carolina's Populists had been the Greenback-Republicans of the early 1880s, and Tillman's position on such a movement had not changed.[75]

Tillman insisted that the war against the "money power" be seen as a continuation of the wars of secession and Redemption. For him, "reform" meant the collective struggle of independent white men against tyrannous federal authority and African American equality. In his view, the Populists had made the critical error of believing that one could fight the "money power" by forming a coalition with its chief allies, black Republicans and the federal government. The subtreasury, Tillman feared, would "concentrate the business of the people in the hands of a centralized power at Washington." Moreover, it would create "an army of political hirelings," guaranteeing "the perpetuation in power of the party by which it was established." As for black political participation, that could only bring back Reconstruction and its concomitant evils. "Negro domination hangs over us," he warned in 1891, "like the sword of Damocles."[76]

Tillman's stand against the subtreasury temporarily reunited him with conservative leaders, including his old commander Matthew Butler. As in 1876, the two men took similar positions on the relationship between federal power and "Negro domination." Butler, debating Populist Tom Watson of Georgia, suggested to an audience of white farmers that "a mulatto would probably govern tyrannically your sub-treasury here," adding parenthetically that he "knew Edgefield's man"—probably a reference to one of the black Republican men who had held office in the county during Reconstruction. But Tillman's opposition to the subtreasury created a deep rift within his coalition. Although he initially said he would submit to the will of an "informed" majority of Alliancemen with regard to the subtreasury, he opposed the subtreasury "in its details" and suggested that a majority of South Carolina Alliancemen did as well. He proposed a safe, state-level alternative: state-chartered banks that could loan paper money based on the value of farmland. But this did not satisfy those with more expansive visions of "reform." Indeed, it offered relief only to landowners—an even narrower definition of "the farmers" than the white male producerism Tillman had generally promoted.[77]

But radical Alliancemen had counted Tillman's victory in 1890 as their own, and they would not willingly defer to him. In 1891, they invited subtreasury advocates to speak, including Watson, who attracted large and enthusiastic Democratic crowds, and national Alliance lecturer Ben Terrell, a gifted orator from Texas who had taken the state by storm less than two years before. Tillman could avoid confronting the Populist Watson, but he could not avoid debating Terrell, still nominally a Democrat. For once, Tillman got the worst of it. The state Alliance convention rebuked him and endorsed the subtreasury over his objections. Reporting on Tillman's debate with Terrell, the Populist-leaning *Cotton Plant* spoke bluntly: "Gov. Tillman opposes the only measure that promises to break the power of a few men to rob the farmer." In Washington, D.C., the Populist *National Economist* was even harsher, accusing Tillman of seeking the Alliance's "destruction."[78]

Tillman's opposition to the subtreasury threatened to cost him his mantle of leadership. Even allies from the early days of the farmers' movement threatened to break with Tillman over the subtreasury, and some seemed ready to support the third-party movement. A fellow subtreasury opponent warned the governor that it was "unwise for you to make an unnecessary issue with the farmers." Since the subtreasury had been endorsed by Alliances all around the country, this reformer did not "see how you can claim that it will be repudiated by the intelligent farmers of the South." His was one of many warnings to Tillman that he dare not alienate the Alliance.[79]

In the case of the subtreasury, Tillman decided that power mattered more than principle. Frightened by the hostile response of his Alliance supporters and the possibility of losing all leverage with them, he first determined "to remain absolutely silent & let things drift." By the time the 1892 campaign began, he went further, making a good show of capitulating to subtreasury advocates. At the May 1892 Democratic convention, the "Alliance governor" accepted the Alliance's national platform, including the subtreasury proposal, and was present when the state Democratic Party adopted it. He did not become a subtreasury advocate, however, and his more or less tacit consent could be interpreted in many ways. Even after the Democratic convention, many were left wondering "what was exactly [his] position" regarding the Alliance's more radical demands. But the many white Alliancemen who had come to see Tillman as their representative welcomed his apparent reversal as the return of the prodigal son. Tillman, after all, had embodied the farmers' movement since before the arrival of the Alliance, and to many, he remained a credible "Moses." The reputation he had built since the mid-1880s stood him in good stead as he faced down this new challenge. As a county Alliance president reassured him during the difficult days of 1891, "We have some complaints in this Co[unty] but . . . will not come up wanting if you do not say too many nice things about those *citadel dudes*."[80]

Tactical capitulation on the subtreasury issue enabled Tillman to prevent state Alliance leaders from taking the far more dangerous step of bolting from the Democratic Party. Tillman implored his more radical allies not to act precipitately. "Above all let me beg you not to join any Third party move this year," he wrote to Alliance Democrat and U.S. congressman A. C. Latimer. "After it is clearly shown that no relief can be expected from the Democratic party as now constituted, we may find it necessary to fight for relief under another name, but for the true principles of Jeffersonian Democracy. The name itself is dear." Although he believed that eventually "self interest might force us" to form a new party in coalition with Midwestern farmers, he insisted that for the time being, white Southerners "had to stand together for God, for home, and for native land" against "the Force Bill and negro domination." "You cannot divide without bringing ruin," he told white audiences, for "division in South Carolina means the negro." In the worst case, "the third party divides the whites & both factions appeal to the negroes, & that means in the long run political debauchery & corruption with a final division of offices between the races & a return to the evils of the reconstruction era." At public occasions such as the July 1891 meeting of the Edgefield County Farmers' Alliance, he made his reform allies swear to fight for Alliance demands within the Democratic Party. This, he later claimed, "tied the hands" of potential third-party leaders in South Carolina. As the 1892 political campaign began, though, several upcountry Democratic county conventions nevertheless seemed poised for a third-party bolt.[81]

In the 1892 election, Tillman once again attacked the conservative leadership of his own party and presented himself as a reformist alternative to Populist radicalism. As luck would have it, an appropriate rallying cry for his middle ground was readily available in the form of "free silver." Insisting that the coinage of silver would expand the circulating medium sufficiently to alleviate the credit crisis, Tillman echoed bimetallists throughout the nation. The rhetoric of silver also suited Tillman's style of attack, for proponents of the white metal charged that the Reconstruction-era demonetization of silver (the "Crime of '73") had been part of a Wall Street conspiracy against producers. Silver was also safe: unlike the subtreasury, it required no extension of federal power into local affairs. For some radicals, this made silver a sham, for it provided the appearance of reform without returning financial control to the producers. Perhaps for this reason, free silver provoked little controversy among even the most conservative South Carolina Democrats.[82]

But free silver's enemies included Grover Cleveland, the likely Democratic nominee for president in 1892 and the man to whom the Populists would point in their campaign to woo South Carolina's Democrats. Advocacy of silver would allow Tillman to distinguish himself from Cleveland and to continue to offer at least the appearance of reform to white Democrats poised on the brink of revolt. Attacking gold Democrat Cleveland as a "bag of beef" and threatening to stick a pitchfork in him — the threat that earned him his ever-after-familiar moniker "Pitchfork Ben" — Tillman attempted to remain the champion of the farmers while muffling more radical alternatives. The tactic worked. Although he continued to oppose any bolt from the party, he volunteered to lead the state against Cleveland's renomination. The delegation he led to the 1892 Democratic National Convention voted almost unanimously against Cleveland, but Cleveland's eventual nomination provoked no mass exodus from the party of white supremacy. Once again, Tillman had used violent attacks on an unworthy white man to establish himself as the spokesman of the farmers.[83]

As the November election approached, Tillman proudly contrasted South Carolina's Democratic orthodoxy with the Populists' inroads in neighboring Georgia and North Carolina. He explained to an admirer that "[w]e have had a hot fight & have been 'between the D——l & the deep sea' " which was to say the "Third Party on one hand & Haskellism on the other. But by good generalship we have kept the party together & are in better shape than any other Southern state." Indeed, South Carolina's Populists fared quite poorly by comparison with their regional counterparts. Alone among the former Confederate states, South Carolina was tardy in selecting representatives to the People's Party's National Committee. The *Cotton Plant*'s editor finally announced a state third-party ticket, including presidential electors, just two weeks before the November election.[84] Nationally, the Populist ticket won over a million votes but no Southern electors, and South Carolina was one of the few Southern states where Populism was reduced to insignificance. "You cannot divide without bringing ruin," Tillman had told audiences of white men, and divide they did not — at least not in the casting and counting of ballots.[85]

Tillman was only correct in boasting that "good generalship" had carried the day if that generalship is understood to have been conducted over most of the preceding two decades. Many of Tillman's critical anti-Populist battles had been won not since 1890 but during the 1870s and 1880s, when he helped bring an end to Reconstruction and establish the white-supremacist limits of state-level reform. By the time he became governor, he had already helped shape a state political culture that severely limited white men's room for maneuver on matters of racial hierarchy and federal power. At the same time, he had crafted an explicitly white-supremacist alternative to producerist radicalism, one that limited legitimate collective action not just to white men but also to white male farmers who forswore interracial political activity. His tactical skills served him well in 1892, but they alone would not have sufficed.

In South Carolina, as throughout the South, no Populist coalition could succeed even momentarily unless it could draw on both black and white support. By the 1890s, however, white radicals' own fear and ambivalence about black political participation, rooted in their experience of the past quarter century, made such a call all but unthinkable. Indeed, even the few white Populists of 1892 made no overt move to attract black support. Some white radicals understood the need to pierce the slogans of white supremacy and expose the racial demagoguery of their enemies, but they did not know how to confront the expectations that gave Tillman's message its potency. Even agrarian radicals who proudly declared themselves opposed to monopoly in all its forms found it difficult to describe democratic citizenship in terms that transcended the particular experiences of white men.

White Populists struggled, mostly without success, to reconcile their economic analyses with their historic and daily experiences of white manhood. The most famous "divided mind" of white Southern Populism belonged to Georgia's Tom Watson, whose intellectual and political biography has been a major historiographical battleground for Populism's analysts. But local, less dramatic cases better explain the structural weaknesses of Populism in South Carolina. Take the case of Alliance leader Colonel Ellison S. Keitt and his son Joseph, who along with *Cotton Plant* editor J. W. Bowden became the state's leading third-party activists. The elder Keitt predicted that a coming revolution would pit "the farmers, mechanics, wage workers and laborers, the wealth producers of the nation" against the "money power." Keitt had fought against Reconstruction, and he understood that Redemption still loomed large in the state's politics, so he boldly attempted to shift the meaning of Redemption's struggle from a conflict over race to one over class and section. "Negro domination we hear so much about is a myth," he declared in 1894. "In the worst days of radicalism the negroes did not control. The carpetbaggers, dominated by Grant's bayonets, dominated." In 1876, "we assaulted their lines and drove them . . . from the State." If the fight had always been a struggle among white men and even an enfranchised black majority could not "dominate," then an opening might exist for a Populist movement. But even this limited retreat from white-supremacist orthodoxy was too much for Bowden, who sought to distance his paper from such sentiments. In the aftermath of the devastating 1892 defeat, Bowden offered an explicitly white-supremacist rationale for allowing those who had supported Populist presidential candidate James Weaver to continue to vote as Democrats in state elections. Haskellites, he pointed out, had continued to vote even after their apostasy, and South Carolina Populists at least had not "appeal[ed] to 'Cuffee' to help them defeat the expressed will of the white people."[86]

Other, more universalistic visions also ran up against the limits of white male producerism. Like many radical Alliancemen, white Abbeville farmer Patrick Henry Adams had understood Ben Tillman's 1890 victory as the prelude to a greater contest against the "money power." At an open meeting of his sub-Alliance, Adams made a bold appeal to "Tillmanite or Anti Tillmanite, . . . Democratic, or Republican, or Third-Partyite, . . . White or Colored," suggesting that he was sympathetic to the possibility of a third party and an interracial coalition. But Adams unwittingly expressed the white supremacy inherent in reform in the world Tillman had helped make. In Adams's analysis, the poverty of "our southern farmers" had begun with emancipation, when they set about planting cotton because "they had labor here trained in the cotton fields." His farmers, like Tillman's, were white landowning employers. It did not occur to Adams that a majority of South Carolina's agricultural workers—"Colored" but by his own reckoning no less a part of "the body politic"—might regard themselves as farmers or understand postemancipation agricultural economics rather differently. Adams also urged his audience to continue resisting the efforts of the "Northern capitalist . . . to crush us to death." Giving up that struggle, he explained, would not "comport well with Southern manhood and Southern heroism." In the sectional context of his remarks, these phrases could only suggest arms-bearing white manhood. They would not have been understood to include black men, whose sectional "heroism" had been almost universally in Northern blue; it certainly seems unlikely that he intended to refer to the black Union soldiers who had made their camps on Edgefield plantations in 1865. Assertive black manhood, far from being understood as "Southern" or "heroic," appeared in white public discourse in the form of the black rapist, the antithesis of white manhood and the enemy of white womanhood. Although Adams's speech was free of overt racial antagonism, when he sought a language of manly resistance adequate to the coming fight, he settled on the idiom of white manhood common to slaveholding, secession, war, and Redemption. Struggling against these self-imposed limits, his envisioned crusade of "our Southern farmers" against the "money power" was doomed to failure.[87]

In winning their struggles from the mid-1870s to 1890, men like Tillman had fatally undermined the possibility of the development of a race-neutral language of manhood and citizenship. What remained was the language of "the farmers," a language common to Democrats and Populists, a language that implied whiteness and masculinity even as it laid claim to universality, a language in which only white men's collective struggle could bring political or economic "redemption." This was not simply a discourse but a powerful political and historical reality, one that overwhelmed the best intentions of those who sought to escape or defeat it. By late 1892, Tillman had done more than convince J. Hendrix McLane that the fight could not be won; he had left McLane without the words to understand his own defeat. For more than a decade, with indisputable courage, McLane had fought against Democratic violence, fraud, and intimidation. Although he had spent time in Boston in self-imposed exile, he had continued to return to South Carolina to seek an alternative to the Democratic Party. As late as the spring of 1892, despite the terror he had encountered in the past, he continued to assert his right to speak publicly as a dissident in his native state, knowing that a man who sought the respect and votes of his fellow citizens could do no less. But McLane's tentative 1886 endorsement of Tillman foreshadowed the disheartening conclusion he reached by late 1892. Although the former Greenbacker believed that black men's rights to vote and hold office would be essential to any agrarian coalition, he now conceded that any attempt to guarantee those rights would backfire. Federal legislative efforts to protect black voting rights, like black officeholding, sustained "the fear of Negro domination" among Southern whites and "help[ed] to make the South more surely solid." For more than ten years, McLane's political work had been based on the principle that this fear and the resulting solidity were anything but natural. But he was left unable to offer any solution at all. His vision of the "political emancipation of both races" would have to wait, he concluded, until Southern whites developed "more kindly" feelings and until "the Negro was at peace with his white neighbor." McLane, reduced to analytically empty pleas for tolerance, gave up. He died in Boston in 1894, shortly before Ben Tillman began the first of his four terms in the U.S. Senate.[88]

Tillman's organization and leadership could not have succeeded without the cooperation of thousands of white voters who shared his concerns about the implications of Populist radicalism and embraced his alternative, albeit almost purely rhetorical, vision of reform. Some Southern radicals may indeed have regarded Tillman, in the words of historian Lawrence Goodwyn, as "a transparent charlatan who was far more dedicated to the building of a personal political career than to leading a party revolution," but clearly many of the men those radicals sought as constituents did not agree. After living with slavery, secession, war, Reconstruction, paramilitary terror, and economic hardship, few white men could articulate a critique of the social order that did not prove vulnerable to co-optation by the state's reigning agrarian rebel, a man who successfully cast the Populists as the latest incarnation of "radical misrule," "Bourbon" incompetence, and "Negro domination." To the extent that Tillman could pass himself off as an authentic representative of white farmers, it was because he understood these men's shared history—and because he had helped shape it. Over the course of the 1890s, as Populists throughout the South struggled vainly to create an alternative political culture in which black and white men could cooperate for mutual benefit, white Democrats mobilized white armies against them. But alongside those armies they also mobilized a common understanding of white manhood, a language and history shaped by men like Ben Tillman.[89]

Even a victorious biracial Populism might not have accomplished the radical transformation its proponents sought. Its programs might have failed to bring the relief they promised, and its coalition might have collapsed because of its own internal divisions. But this is not what happened in the 1880s and 1890s. Rather, during its short life, radical biracial agrarian politics struggled against both the long, deep history of racial hierarchy and the sharp, contemporary reality of Democratic violence, fraud, and legal discrimination. That recent history was not, contra the predictions of James Henry Hammond and the claims of the Red-shirts, virtually "spontaneous." Certainly white-supremacist assumptions and reactions arose unbidden from the minds and hearts of white men. But it took a good deal of strong, often coercive leadership to transform those reactions into collective actions and still more of the same to sustain the project over time. Since Reconstruction, Ben Tillman more and more often had been one of the men providing that leadership, and by 1892, it appeared that he had won. The final victory over the Populists—McLane's own transformation of his hard-fought defeat into a racially determined inevitability—marked yet another defining moment in the reconstruction of white supremacy.

The Mob and the State

In 1892, Governor Ben Tillman became nationally notorious for his "lynching pledge." In cases where a black man was accused of raping a white woman, the governor said, he would himself lead the lynch mob. But this promise, never kept, was not the whole story. In his 1890 inaugural address, Tillman had denounced the lynching of blacks as an "infamous" and "deplorable" crime, and both before and after his 1892 pledge, he backed up his words with state power. The governor corresponded at length with county sheriffs, called out the militia to safeguard prisoners, and demanded that citizens and officials uphold "the majesty of the law." Tillman's foes, focusing on his advocacy of lynching and ignoring his opposition to it, denounced him as the "mob-law governor." But the contradictions revealed more than political expediency or shameful hypocrisy. In juxtaposing Tillman's support for the law with his support for lawlessness, his opponents struck closer to the mark than they understood, for Governor Tillman walked a tightrope between the mob and the state.

Tillman's celebration of the violence at Hamburg and Ellenton established his credentials as a militant white man. It also reinforced the notion that white men had the collective right to define "justice" and mete out punishment. In the antebellum era, white men had constituted the body of citizens who made up juries, patrols, and sheriffs' posses. Even when they acted without formal legal sanction, they claimed the right of local enforcement in more or less formal terms. This was what the Beech Island planters of the 1840s and 1850s and the "Minute Men" of

1860–61 had done; later, the Red-shirts had claimed that kind of legitimacy even while attacking state-sponsored militia units. The Red-shirts' victory, however, neither returned black Southerners to slavery nor fully restored white men's monopoly on legitimate authority. In the postemancipation South, even after 1876, extralegal collective action was still essential. As Red-shirts, "white-caps," or lynchers, white men assaulted those who threatened white-supremacist political, economic, or social strictures. Again, not all of the people they attacked were black: through improper behavior, white men could lose their privileged position and become "white negroes," as vulnerable to violence as any antebellum trader suspected of being a Yankee abolitionist.

Tillman sustained this tradition of violence, but he understood its risks. At campaign meetings throughout the early 1890s, his political tactics encouraged disorderly behavior and brought white men to the verge of rioting against one another. Opponents charged him with being a demagogue and anarchist, and they labeled his followers a "mob." Yet as governor — particularly one whose claim to represent "reform" rested on state-level educational and regulatory programs — Tillman could not simply celebrate extralegal violence. His "lynching pledge" was not the unreflective outburst of a radical Red-shirt but a recognition of the importance many white men placed on the right to define and enforce local "justice." It was an awkward and probably unworkable compromise between the tradition of white-supremacist "justice" and the rule of law. Caught between the history of white men's local authority and the future he envisioned for state power, Tillman sought, rhetorically at least, both to legitimate these "mobs" and to control them through his leadership. In practice, of course, this could not work. No man, not even Ben Tillman, could credibly claim both to suppress mob violence and to be willing to lead a lynch mob.

Tillman was not the only one facing this dilemma. The wealthy men who led the Tillmanite and anti-Tillmanite wings of the Democratic Party feared the consequences of unchecked vigilante violence. A climate of terror would drive black laborers from the state and disorganize the state's agricultural economy. Worse, from the perspective of those building mills and towns, South Carolina's reputation for violence would discourage investment and immigration. To these men, Tillman — the advocate of both mob violence and corporate regulation — appeared to stand squarely between South Carolina and the New South. Put simply, he injured the state's "reputation" as a field for investment. Yet some of these same men also understood and supported the principle of local authority and enforcement. When Tillman's effort to regulate the sale of alcohol seemed to infringe on their "rights," they fought back with the same tactics of local collective defiance that in other contexts had seemed to constitute "mob law."

Tillman welcomed this resistance, for such conflicts enabled him to continue defining himself against powerful enemies. Although Tillman's new relationship to the powers of the state in some ways strained his identification with "the farmers," as governor and head of a powerful legislative coalition he was able to put the state to work—symbolically, at least—against the farmers' enemies. Tillman presented his dispensary system, a state liquor monopoly, as a means of combating the forces that sought to undermine white men's households. His attempts to enforce the law provoked urban opponents to claim that he had overreached and become a tyrant, but Tillman demonstrated once again that he understood the power of martial mobilization to redefine a situation in his favor. In the end, he was able to use his official role to prove that his own forces were simply defending the victory of 1876 against white men who persistently, even perversely, misunderstood its meaning.

The Uses of a Crowd

Tillman provoked conflicts in order to gain attention and rally supporters. Preparing for an 1887 public meeting, he urged a close ally to arrange a joint discussion with opponents "in order to get up a crowd." "If you can have it understood that we are to 'divide time,'" he explained, "you will get a crowd second only to 76." Indeed, at such joint stump appearances, speeches could become secondary. The meeting's real value to the candidate was the opportunity it presented to use his supporters' physical presence in multiple ways: to intimidate his opponents, to demonstrate his own capacity for aggression, and to create a sense of collective identity among his supporters that resembled the solidarity of men in combat. Not surprisingly, intraparty Democratic conflicts soon began to resemble the interparty conflict of "'76." Provocative language from the speaker's platform encouraged verbal and physical aggression in the crowd below. Partisans attempted to drown out the opposition's speakers with hoots and derision—to "howl them down." As supporters of rival factions confronted one another in the close confines of the meeting ground, tempers flared. Men fought with fists, sticks, and knives; they carried guns and sometimes drew them.[1]

Enemies complained that Tillman had created a white mob. The *Edgefield Chronicle* denounced his followers as a "great crowd of men, swept on by a spirit of enthusiasm bordering closely on blind fanaticism, constructed, without mature deliberation, upon a groundless fabric." "Noise, turbulence, and threats of violence characterized the public meetings" of the campaign, complained one anti-Tillmanite, "and converted them into riotous assemblies, where public issues could not be decently and gravely discussed, by which many of our best citizens were practically excluded." Tillman was responsible. When Tillmanites howled down Wade Hampton at an Aiken meeting, opponents blamed Tillman's leadership. A better class of leader, they claimed, would improve the climate for political debate: on occasions when such howling failed to silence anti-Tillmanite speakers, newspapers suggested that the "commanding presence" of a respectable Democratic leader had overawed the mob. The *Charleston News and Courier* lauded such victories of "the irresistible power of intellectual manhood over brute force. It was indeed a sublime sight to see the poor, miserable, illiterate and misguided worshippers of the demagogue cowed into submissive silence." When an evil leader raised up a mob, it fell to the better class of men to subdue these chaotic assemblies.[2]

Whereas anti-Tillmanites described their leaders as exceptional individuals, Tillman identified himself with white voters and asserted that their collective needs outweighed the reputation or "honor" of any individual. During the 1892 Democratic campaign, Tillman faced a nomination challenge from Edgefield lawyer, regional capitalist, and former governor John C. Sheppard. At one stump meeting, longtime Tillman opponent L. W. Youmans spoke on Sheppard's behalf; when Tillman rose to reply, a fight among the factions in the audience seemed imminent. Tillman then left the speaker's stand, and Youmans seized the opportunity to accuse Tillman of cowardice. In a letter to the public, however, an anonymous Tillmanite attempted to reframe this action as responsible leadership. "Tillman's temper is none of the longest," the Tillmanite wrote, and "possibly Youmans' tirades may arouse the Governor to resent them." Had Tillman responded to Youmans's insults with the violence they merited, the result could have been a disastrous bloodbath among the white Democrats at the meeting. This established once again that Tillman was less concerned with his individual "honor" than with safeguarding the interests of his people. And the feelings of solidarity, the writer explained, were mutual: "[M]any staunch, sturdy farmers were present and they felt keenly all insults leveled at Tillman, feeling them to be insults to themselves, viewing Tillman as the representative . . . of the poor but honest tillers of the soil. They would have left but little of Youmans had any trouble occurred." In this context, Tillman's sudden departure when things grew ugly indicated neither cowardice nor self-protection but rather an effort to protect Youmans (and white unity) from Tillman's enraged supporters. By retreating, the writer claimed, Tillman "saved the life of L. W. Youmans" and probably many others.[3]

Manly restraint was, as always, only part of white male authority. On other occasions, Tillman seemed determined to keep men's bodies in violent motion as long as safely possible. During another 1892 confrontation between Tillman and Youmans, this time in Edgefield, Tillman played the possibility of fratricidal violence among about a thousand white Democrats for all it was worth. Jeering and heckling from Tillmanites interrupted Youmans as he spoke, and when fights broke out in the crowd, Tillman declared that the meeting must be halted in order to prevent a "serious riot" from taking place. But this time, Tillman acknowledged the potential for mass violence in order to make direct use of it. He sought to prolong the confrontation, to take the crowd up to the edge of violence, demonstrating his identification with his farmers without quite provoking them to murder.[4]

This balancing act required a careful reading of the crowd. In this case, after having found it possible to make himself heard long enough to urge the meeting's suspension, Tillman instead called for a "hand primary," in which he asked men to raise their hands to show support for one candidate or another. Since Tillman only called for such a showing when he knew he had a majority on his side, these hand primaries had the effect of making his opponents appear marginal. After the hand primary, ostensibly in order to reduce tensions, Tillman and his supporters moved to a nearby building, where the governor continued to speak. His opponents followed, however, and the shouting and fighting continued unabated. In fact, a reporter stated (perhaps overdramatically) that "a pitched battle would have resulted if a single pistol had been drawn." "The madness of the moment was infectious," declared the correspondent; "solid substantial citizens, as well as the most fiery, were thirsting for a fight, and it is a miracle that a regular battle was not fought." But if it was necessary for white men to demonstrate their capacity for violence, it was also essential that they understand its limits. With tensions so high that fratricidal violence among white Democrats seemed inevitable, Tillman once again urged his supporters to move away from their foes, this time to the courthouse. "The Governor's followers were swayed by his coolness and master will and immediately acted upon his suggestion," carrying Tillman inside on their shoulders, reported the friendly local correspondent. In the courthouse, with his opponents excluded, he gave the speech that had been howled down outside.[5]

Such reports solidified Tillman's reputation as the true son of "bloody Edgefield," a county long seen as particularly violent. Writing to an academic colleague, Robert Means Davis of South Carolina College acknowledged that "Edgefield . . . has enjoyed a very unenviable reputation for violence" but blamed that reputation on "lurid reporting" of the events of 1876. Tillman encouraged such coverage. "[I]f we over in Edgefield insult each other," he explained boastfully on another occasion, "there is generally a fight or a funeral afterwards." This reputation was already well developed by the late 1880s. During a Tillman speech in Charleston, someone unexpectedly pounded a bass drum, causing an anxious crowd to flee in panic. When they returned, Tillman twitted them mercilessly: "What were they running like turkeys for? Why in his county, if there was to be a shooting everybody would run to it."[6]

This appetite for violence was only half the story. In order to ensure that an actual riot among white men did not occur, Tillman and his rivals had to avoid losing control of themselves; if the political combat of the 1890s was full of rage, it was a rage well ordered. Despite his heated rhetoric, Tillman remained cool, alternately playing both the bully and the referee as the meeting developed, seeking to heighten partisan identification and an atmosphere of intimidation without quite calling for blood. "To the courage, coolness and magnificent self-control of Tillman is due the fact that the streets of Edgefield are not red to-night with the blood of her sons," declared a friendly newspaper. The capacity for violence had to be balanced by a capacity for restraint.[7]

Tillman, for all his apparent fire, could be cool enough to leave his opponents fuming. His 1894 campaign for the U.S. Senate set him against the incumbent, Matthew Butler. The ex-Confederate general and Red-shirt leader believed he understood the tactics of 1876 as well as any man. In 1890, when Tillman was making his bid for the Democratic nomination for governor, Butler had predicted that Tillman's tactics would recoil on him—invective and bluster "availed its purpose to alarm negroes, but it will not frighten white men. A few rowdys can make a great rumpus and noise, but they do not represent the body of the people." If anyone could neutralize Tillman, it would be Butler, and in the 1894 contest, he took the offensive, playing Tillman's game of accusation and slander. Attempting to undermine Tillman's claim to leadership, Butler presented affidavits from participants stating that when the shooting had started at Hamburg, Tillman was "not to be found." Tillman rebutted the accusation with the reports of his own witnesses and claimed (accurately enough) that Butler had downplayed his role in the violence in his congressional testimony. But Tillman scored his real points against Butler by understanding the difference between public expressions and personal feelings. He emphasized his commitment to white unity, claiming that he had borne Butler's attacks because "as governor of the State, [he] could not afford to create a row at a public gathering and have our people murder each other like dogs." Unable to compete with Tillman in rallying partisans at stump meetings, Butler retreated from the ground rules of 1876. Declaring that "it was not Christian civilization to howl anyone down," he recanted his espousal of that practice. "He was charged with teaching it in 1876. It was wrong and he prayed to change it now."[8]

After he failed to best Tillman in the arena of popular white-supremacist politics, Butler sought to move the conflict back to the more personal ground of the code of honor. After one campaign meeting, he accosted Tillman in his railroad car, called him a liar, and attempted to strike him. But Tillman understood that to establish a claim to leadership in the new era, it was more important to prove one's commitment to collective action than to take part in personal combat. He had no intention of confronting Butler with anything but words. Sallie Tillman, reading reports of Butler's advances, wrote worriedly to her husband. "You *must not* fret & worry about me," Tillman replied; "I pray you have no fear for my safety." "I shall ignore Butler from this on & give no excuse for any more dangerous or exciting scenes." He assured her that his friends at the meetings would warn him of any impending assault and that he himself would remain "cool & watchful."[9]

The Contexts of Lynching

Tillman and Butler were in close agreement on at least one thing, however. Neither man suggested that there had been anything wrong with howling down black Republicans; in fact, their struggle over the legacy of 1876 was in part over who could more legitimately claim to have murdered them. By the 1890s, lethal and nonlethal vigilante violence against African Americans had become a regular feature of Southern life. The causes ranged from violations of political or economic hierarchies to social or sexual transgressions. Bands of armed white men broke up Republican and independent political meetings and black laborers' organizations, and groups known as "white-caps" policed interracial social and sexual boundaries. In May 1891, a couple from Kansas—a white man and a black woman whom the paper identified as "his alleged wife"—were roused from their bed and whipped by white-caps. A few months later, a mob of disguised men destroyed the property of a black man and white woman whom they accused of "improperly living together." Edgefield's white-caps made it a "custom . . . to take out and severely whip disreputable negro women." "Disreputable," unsurprisingly, covered a wide array of activities, ranging from the consensual to the commercial. Tillman recognized the existence of a biracial world of sociability and sexuality; however, he believed that consensual interracial liaisons should be downplayed as much as possible. After investigating one case of a "disorderly house" to which black men came for "criminal intercourse" with white women, a local official wrote to Tillman, acceding to the governor's request that the official reports be suppressed. "The affair is too smutty for publication or of interest to the decent public," he agreed.[10]

White-caps, like other groups of vigilantes, included men from the topmost social strata. In the case of the "disorderly house," the official explained that "the better class of white people [took] steps to run the negro off and break up the nest." Similarly, when black Edgefieldians resisted white-cap attacks, it became obvious that vigilante action had elite sponsors. One night in June 1892, when a white Edgefield man named John Paul mounted the porch of a black man's home and identified himself by name, the people inside shot and killed him. They "had prepared to defend themselves against such depredations, and thought that they were being attacked by the members of the [white-cap] organization," a newspaper explained. That is, they knew Paul by name, believed him to be a white-cap, and shot him. Paul was buried by "his comrades of the Edgefield Rifles," a former Red-shirt unit now integrated into the state militia. Whether the white-caps were a subdivision of the Rifles or had overlapping membership, it is evident that white terror involved white men well outside the putatively degraded "mob element."[11]

During the 1890s, white men more and more often justified their acts of terror by portraying them as efforts to protect white womanhood and by extension the white patriarchal household. White women's sexuality became a crucial defensive perimeter for white supremacy: if black men and white women married or had children together, more than white men's primacy of sexual access to women would be challenged; "whiteness" itself would be undermined. And since few white men would admit that any respectable white woman would voluntarily participate in what they called "mongrelization," they saw such interracial liaisons as necessarily forced. The "black beast rapist," perpetrating what newspapers and politicians called "outrageous assaults" or simply "outrages," emerged as the prime embodiment of the forces threatening white households.[12]

White women's sexuality became an arena — not unlike political or economic relations — in which some men sought dominance over others; murderous spectacles not only terrorized black citizens but also reaffirmed white men's authority over their women, their communities, and the law itself. In one case, after three black South Carolina men were accused of raping a white woman, the lynch mob gave special consideration to the feelings of the "injured husband." After the third accused man was captured, the sheriff waited for the husband's consent before turning the captive over to the mob. With the husband's cooperation, the lynchers tortured the three men before hanging them and repeatedly shooting their dead bodies.[13]

As lynching increased during the 1890s, activists such as Ida B. Wells-Barnett pointed out that only a third of all lynchings were even purportedly in retaliation for acts of rape or attempted rape. She and other critics saw economic conflict as the cause of most lynching and interpreted references to "outrageous assaults" and "brutes in human form" as cynical ploys. Their critique was a well-taken corrective to the mythology of the day, but in focusing on the contradictions and hypocrisies surrounding lynching, it did not fully explain the context and meaning of white-supremacist violence. First, sexual and economic life were not as readily divorced as Victorian proprieties (and analyses of lynching's causes) normally demanded. The separation of public and private spheres, like white supremacy itself, was a social argument, not a social fact. It could therefore be contested and defeated. Many whites accepted the argument that black people's movement into workplaces, political arenas, and public accommodations would logically lead to the "social equality" white supremacists dreaded. Second, the post-Reconstruction Southern economy worked to increase white paranoia about black men's sexual predation of white women and girls. As black men seeking work moved across the South in ever-increasing numbers and the local and personal patron-client relationships born in slavery grew weaker, each black "stranger" moving through the new social and economic landscape became a potential rapist in the eyes of suspicious whites. Simultaneously, many Southern newspapers obsessively repeated reports of rapes and lynchings from all over the region, creating a kind of journalistic feedback loop that distorted social reality. Lynchings that followed rape-related accusations were more likely to draw large carnival-style crowds. Crimes allegedly committed by black men against white women, chiefly rape and attempted rape, were held up as justification for nearly half of all lynchings over most of South Carolina between 1881 and 1895. In sum, a highly disproportionate number of lynchings that white Southerners read about, observed, or participated in followed allegations of rape or attempted rape. Many white men could therefore see lynching as a collective struggle in defense of the sole economic and social resource that most shared: the "sunbrowned goddess," in Tillman's terms, whose productive and reproductive labor made a farm into a household.[14]

Even if lynching made white men into a "mob," it was a label some were prepared to embrace. As historian Drew Gilpin Faust has noted, "Killing is honorable under some circumstances, indictable under others." Just as Tillman's murderous activities in the mid-1870s had been transformed into acts of political courage, many murders in post-Reconstruction South Carolina were transformed into "honorable" deeds through the substitution of white-supremacist justice for the rule of law. As a result, Democratic officials had difficulty preventing or prosecuting lynching. In the last days before Tillman took power in 1890, the Richland County sheriff wrote to Governor John P. Richardson to ask that a prisoner be moved to the state penitentiary before a lynch mob could organize. Otherwise the sheriff anticipated that he would be placed "in a position of being forced to fire on my friends." The governor assented. Richardson frequently corresponded with solicitors and sheriffs regarding potential lynchings, and he offered rewards for the capture of lynchers. He occasionally called out the militia to prevent assaults on prisoners. But lynchings continued, and went unpunished, during his tenure. In communities where lynchings occurred, coroners' juries routinely found that victims had been killed at the hands of "parties unknown." Even papers opposed to lynching, such as the *Edgefield Chronicle*, claimed a suspicious degree of ignorance as to the composition of local lynch mobs.[15]

Just as Tillman became governor in late 1890, the number of lynchings (and the attention paid to them) increased dramatically. Mobs more and more frequently preempted the work of civil authorities, often explicitly claiming the authority of a white-supremacist "higher law": in 1889 and 1890, mobs lynched a total of seventeen South Carolinians. Of 170 lynchings committed in South Carolina in the six decades between 1881 and 1940, nearly a third took place during the 1890s, and during that decade, lynchings in upcountry Edgefield, Abbeville, Laurens, and Newberry Counties actually outnumbered legal executions. As part of a local and regional pattern, lynching cut too close to the heart of white men's expectations and fears for Tillman to ignore it. But now that Tillman was governor, the law might require him, too, to use the militia to prevent lynchings. The former Red-shirt faced the mob as head of state.[16]

Fighting the Mob, Leading the Mob

At first, Tillman presented himself as an outright foe of lynching. The Shell Manifesto's litany of grievances against the Redeemer government had included a complaint about "the continued resurgence of horrible lynchings," which reformers claimed resulted from "bad laws and their inefficient administration." A few months later, an Edgefield grand jury on which Ben Tillman sat blamed lynching on an inefficient and overly lenient Supreme Court. In his inaugural address, Tillman condemned lynching explicitly and at length. "With all the machinery of the law in our hands," he lectured, "it is simply infamous that resort should be had to lynch law, and that prisoners should be murdered because the people have grown weary of the law's delay and its inefficient administration. Negroes have nearly always been the victims; and the confession is a blot on our civilization. Let us see to it that the finger of scorn no longer be pointed at our State because of this deplorable condition of affairs. . . . Let punishment for crime . . . be prompt and sure, and with the removal of the cause the effect will disappear." His inaugural condemnation of lynching concluded with a pious avowal that "every Carolinian worthy the name must long to see the time when law shall reassert its sway."[17]

As governor, though, Tillman found himself in the difficult position of representing both the rule of law and the reconstruction of white supremacy. Tillman had become governor in order to use state power, not to defy it, and a state that could foster agricultural renewal, regulate industry, and defend white men from federal and corporate depredations had to be able to enforce its own laws. But white men's collective action, including violence, had been and continued to be central to his vision of renewal; from 1876 to 1890, such action made his project possible. The clash cut deep. Unlike many of his opponents, who could claim to have been voices for peace, conciliation, and compromise, Tillman risked diluting his appeal if he subordinated "the will of the [white] people" to the "rule of law." He had to continue to wage a struggle against powerful opponents or risk losing his status as iconoclastic champion of the weak. But he also needed to appear to be protecting black South Carolinians against extralegal violence. Shortly after his election, Tillman's secretary conveyed Tillman's views to a black Georgetown resident: "[W]hile . . . white supremacy is best for both races, he believed that the colored people should have the protection of the laws as fully as other citizens." In 1891, he warned a Goldville man who had led a crowd in assaulting a black man "that you will certainly be prosecuted if it [is] not stopped at once." On a more practical level, agricultural employers like Tillman understood that when a climate of terror drove away black Carolinians, it also drove up the price of labor. During a wave of politically inspired violence in 1895, a planter urged Tillman's successor John Gary Evans to restrain local vigilantes: "My farm hands have been driven from plantation by white caps . . . am ruined if my hands dont return I ask for their protection and beg your help."[18]

For over a year, despite these tensions, Ben Tillman continued to oppose lynching and other extralegal violence as attacks on the reputation of the state and the rule of law. In his official letterbooks, he applauded a local sheriff for safeguarding a threatened prisoner and declared that "if all of our peace officers shall act as promptly & decisively, our state will be spared the disgrace of any more lynchings." He corresponded with sheriffs throughout the state, giving and receiving warnings of impending lynchings and ordering investigations when they occurred. He frequently called out local militia units to prevent lynchings. In a lecture to the sheriff of Spartanburg, he displayed his attention to the details of the state's duty to protect its prisoners. "It had just as well be understood that the law in South Carolina must be respected & that Lynch-law will not be tolerated," he wrote. "You will therefore return to Spartanburg tonight & summons a posse of brave & trusty Deputies to be in readiness by Thursday. The prisoner . . . will be sent back to Spartanburg that day. . . . The Morgan Rifles will meet train bearing him at Clifton & escort the prisoner to the jail, after which I shall rely on you & your posse to uphold the majesty of the law & protect the jail against the riot if any assembles. You can if you deem it necessary at any time summon the Morgan Rifles to your assistance, but I rely upon your own loyalty & that of your posse to show that Spartanburg's citizens know their duty & will do it." This commitment seemed to bear fruit. In his first annual address to the legislature in November 1891, Tillman could boast that "during the year the law in the State has been supreme and . . . no person or prisoner has been lynched."[19]

Tillman even asked for the authority to remove sheriffs who did not fulfill their responsibilities, even though this would mean unseating locally elected officials. He justified this unmistakable endorsement of state interference in local affairs—"a last desperate remedy, to be used only when others fail"—by describing it as a necessary compromise between state and local power. He approached the subject gingerly, acknowledging the danger of this sort of executive authority. "The Anglo-Saxon race has ever been jealous of the prerogatives of the King. Their descendants in America are equally watchful against official tyranny, but it is easy to show that there is no possibility of the Executive having the laws 'faithfully executed' unless his hands are strengthened."[20]

A few days after Tillman delivered his 1891 address, however, a black Edgefield man named Dick Lundy was lynched after being charged with murdering the sheriff's son. Tillman immediately alerted the state solicitor, ordering him to go to Edgefield to investigate whether the sheriff had acted appropriately and to "see that the majesty of the law is vindicated." Tillman subsequently held a "crafty leader" responsible, but he also charged local officials with complicity in the lynching. He ridiculed the finding that "parties unknown" had committed the murder, blamed his friend the sheriff for allowing personal tragedy to interfere with upholding the law, and declared that "the law received a wound for every bullet shot into Dick Lundy's body."[21]

Hostile commentators thought the lynching, not the rebuke, represented Tillman's true nature. The *Charleston News and Courier* blamed the "lawless spirit which prevails among the people of Edgefield County." The paper questioned his ability to stop the mob and suggested that had he been present, "with true Edgefield instinct, [Tillman] would probably have been hanging around on the edge of the mob," neither a law-abiding man nor a bold lyncher. Even after Lundy's murder, though, the newspaper praised Tillman for the low incidence of lynching since his inauguration as well as for his public opposition to lynching. "It is to the credit of Governor Tillman that he has lent the whole influence and power of his office to prevent and to discourage such affairs," admitted the normally hostile daily. A mass meeting of black activists protesting the second lynching that occurred during Tillman's administration concurred, commending Tillman for his "efforts . . . to prevent lynchings in this State."[22]

Tillman sought to uphold the law, but he believed that black criminality posed a danger to white society, and he understood the value that white men attached to defending their personal and local prerogatives. As lynchings increased in number and ferocity, he saw his twin commitments to white supremacy and the rule of law come into murderous conflict. At first, he sought to give the law priority: Tillman, his secretary wrote to a constituent, was "in sympathy with and will maintain White Supremacy & will enforce the law in that direction but at the same time justice must not be overridden." But Tillman needed both sets of credentials to carry out his programs, and the conflict was not so easily finessed.[23]

Tillman attempted to reconcile the rule of law and white-supremacist justice by claiming leadership within both systems. At an 1892 stump meeting, he declared that although he opposed lynching, he would himself "willingly lead a mob in lynching a negro who had committed an assault upon a white woman." The authority of his position would render the lynching quasi-official; at the same time, his pledge to *lead* the mob reestablished him as the arbiter of white-supremacist justice. Limiting such legitimation to cases of rape or attempted rape, Tillman was able violently to defend white supremacy but without appearing indiscriminately bloodthirsty. The tactic seemed to meet with his supporters' approval, and at an Abbeville campaign meeting later that summer, supporters presented Tillman with a banner hailing him as the "Champion of White Men's Rule and Woman's Virtue."[24]

Tillman's justification of lynching raised questions about his commitment to equality under the law as well as his commitment to the law itself. The *Charleston News and Courier* began to dub him the state's "mob-law governor," and Tillman soon amended his pledge to justify the lynching of "any man of any color who assaults a virtuous woman of any color." This gesture toward a statesmanlike color blindness fooled no one. Tillman conceivably might have argued that Joe Gibson's wife Kitty deserved his kind of "protection" — but only because she was part of his household, his "family, black and white." In general terms, there was no such thing for Tillman as "virtuous" black womanhood; for him and most whites, the qualifier had a racially restrictive connotation.[25]

For Tillman, the "protection of woman's virtue" did not imply that white women were or should be fragile or helpless. White women could be simultaneously productive and virtuous, and white men ought to foster each attribute in its own way. Even as he suggested that white women needed white men's physical protection, Tillman was working to establish a college that would enable at least some white women to achieve a measure of economic independence. It was true that he believed white women's aspirations ought to have limits: in particular, they had no place in the realm of electoral politics, where white male citizens battled dissidents and interlopers. But this was hardly an exceptional position for a Southern Democratic politician to take. Even white women who vocally disagreed with Tillman about woman suffrage agreed that virtue and utility could go hand in hand. Georgia's Rebecca Latimer Felton, for example, argued that white women should become educated and should exercise considerable economic autonomy; she also made the famous declaration that "if it needs lynching to protect woman's dearest possession from the ravening human beasts — then I say lynch, a thousand times a week, if necessary." Tillman could not have put it better. For him, the reconstruction of the white patriarchal household required fending off intrusions from without and rebuilding economic independence from within. Lynching black men and "uplifting" white women — not onto a pedestal but into productive work roles — could both serve this end.[26]

Lynching did, however, work to establish the boundaries of white female respectability. When Jake Davis, a black man, was lynched for allegedly attempting to rape the wife of a "respectable" white Abbeville man, a reporter noted that Davis had "committed an assault on a white woman in this community a few years ago, but as her character was questionable he was allowed to go unpunished." On another occasion, Tillman pardoned a convicted rapist (race unspecified) "on the ground that the woman in the case was of pronounced questionable character." Like the interracial couples and the "disreputable" black women beaten by white-caps, white women whose "character was questionable" were not protected by white-supremacist justice. Like white men who abandoned the party of Redemption, such women were denied the privileges of whiteness.[27]

The Limits of Opposition

The main opponents of vigilante action were its principal victims, black South Carolinians. They resisted white men's attempts to humiliate, assault, or murder them, as John Paul discovered too late. In sermons, conventions, and antilynching "indignation meetings," preachers and politicians protested that "the rights of the colored people are not respected." In 1885, a group of Charleston ministers asserted that on "[a]ny night a band of desperadoes may ride up to the humble cabin of an inoffensive negro, and for some supposed wrong he may be dragged from his home and be cruelly beaten, and perhaps murdered." Sometimes they took these protests further, seeking to manipulate the discourse of the law and the mob and arguing that this climate of lawlessness reflected poorly on prominent white men's capacity for leadership.[28]

They understood that many white men found vigilante action troubling. In the last days of 1889, a mob of fifty masked white men seized eight black men (four of whom had been accused of murdering whites) from the Barnwell jail and shot them to death; as elsewhere in the post-Reconstruction South, the coroner's jury declared itself utterly ignorant of who might have committed the crime. The *Charleston News and Courier*, struggling to find an editorial line that upheld both white supremacy and regional respectability, ended up simultaneously decrying the lynching as the work of a "mob" who threatened to "disorganize society" and defending Barnwell against outsiders' attacks. The county, it explained, was hardly a place of "lawlessness," as New England newspapers had suggested, for the lynchers numbered no more than fifty, and their work had been done both in disguise and under cover of darkness. "This would scarcely have been necessary in a community where 'the habit of lawlessness' prevails," the editorialist defensively concluded.[29]

Some black South Carolinians attempted to take advantage of this uneasiness about the state's reputation. Seeking "the vindication of law and order," a conference of black ministers suggested that the appearance of a white mob constituted a failure of the "better classes" to assert authority over the "criminal classes of whites." "[I]nfluential leaders among the whites of the State have either directly or indirectly advised or allowed to be taught that any treatment of the negro that would tend to impress him with the white man's superior power in a conflict of force is justifiable. From this irresponsible white men have obtained the notion that there are no rights for the negro which the white man, whether worthy or unworthy, is bound to respect, when the observance of these rights is judged by a white man as in any way contrary to his personal views or prejudices." Understanding that white elites expected to be able to control white men's mobilizations, the ministers concluded that the Barnwell lynching "indicat[ed] the supremacy of the mob element of the Commonwealth over the law-abiding classes." Then, having exposed the failures of their would-be protectors, the ministers let the other shoe drop. They called on "our people to abandon such sections of the State where lawlessness prevails and life is unsafe, and go to sections where life and property are safe." A black citizen who had been badly beaten by whites made the same point to Governor Evans in an anonymous 1895 letter but concluded with the suggestion that there were alternatives to flight. "Some body has to protect the poor nigger," he wrote. "You are the man to do it. If you don't, why we poor devils will be obliged to appeal to those who will. . . . [N]ow we will either have to leave the country or get protection."[30]

As late as 1885, a meeting of black ministers had warned of a revolutionary "outbreak" if black men and women were not treated with respect. But by the end of that decade, an antilynching meeting specifically forswore violent retaliation. Even the mention of retaliation mobilized potentially murderous white anxieties. Next to the *Charleston News and Courier*'s largely approving report on the 1889 declaration of peaceful intentions was a lengthy story (by the same reporter) on a sudden scare among Barnwell whites that local blacks, angry about the lynching, planned to burn the town. The raw materials of such panics had not changed much over the past half-century: a wagon-load of black men seen in one place, a purchase of ammunition in another, a chance remark by "some old trusty colored woman, who had lived with one of the best citizens of the town for years." Together, these rumors were enough to bring scores of armed white men to Barnwell from surrounding towns. It was the postbellum version of an insurrection scare, and it betrayed the same anxiety about black power and black vengeance that slaveholders and other antebellum whites had felt. But such fear was not the exclusive province of a "radical" or a lower-class habit of mind. An employee of one of the town's best citizens had set off the panic, and the men who proceeded to the scene "as private citizens" ranged all the way up the social scale to include colonels of the militia.[31]

Black South Carolinians also sought to protest and refute the emerging rape-lynch complex. "If a colored man is accused, through malice, of an insult to a white lady," protested ministers at the 1885 meeting, "he is likely to be hung, or shot down like a dog." "Outrages are more aggravating," declared an African Methodist Episcopal Zion minister, "when we remember that white men can insult and commit rape upon colored women and very little, if anything, is said about it." Republican leader Robert Smalls urged a black piedmont audience to "make every white man in your town respect your women as they make you respect theirs." In 1888, blacks in white-majority Pickens County lynched a white man accused of the rape and murder of a thirteen-year-old black girl, repulsing white men who came to the lynching victim's aid. Nevertheless, lynching overwhelmingly remained a crime committed by whites against blacks.[32]

White opponents of lynching confronted much the same dilemma that Tillman faced. Under both F. W. Dawson and his successor J. C. Hemphill, the *Charleston News and Courier* took strong stands against dueling, bulldozing, and lynching. But the paper's position on lynching was riddled with ambivalence and contradiction, and the paper subverted its own opposition to "mob rule" in ways both blatant and subtle. It denounced the December 1890 lynching of a black man accused of raping a white woman, but it questioned neither the assumption of guilt nor the sentence of death. Having committed "the unpardonable sin," the lynching victim "richly deserved" his fate, and the paper simply protested that he should "have been put to death by the law." In this case, as in others, it did not expect that "a fair jury" would convict the lynchers.[33] The contradictions multiplied. The *News and Courier* decried "flippant talk" of a "race war," warning that "[t]he strictly material losses through any such conflict would be terrible enough. The cotton would lie unpicked in the fields. The face of the earth would remain unbroken by the plough." The paper approvingly reprinted a Florida story entitled "How Blatant Idiots Get up a War of Races," which described in mocking terms how white men's fears led to rumors of an impending racial conflict, which in turn led black men to organize in defense, culminating in an armed white mob searching the swamps with murderous intent. But the paper continued to use the term, as in a report the following year in which vague rumors from another state appeared under the headline "The Mississippi Race War."[34] The habit of thinking of racial conflict in apocalyptic terms seems to have overridden the editors' rejections of such language. Journalists lent momentum to the mob by reporting that "a crowd of men are now scouring the country . . . and if [the accused criminal] is caught he will no doubt be disposed of." Like South Carolina newspapers on both sides of the Democratic conflict, the Charleston daily obsessively reported lynchings, especially of black men accused of raping or attempting to rape white women. During a period when on average one lynching was being perpetrated every three days in the United States, the *News and Courier* apparently reported as many as it could.[35] When a railroad guard shot an innocent black man, the paper called it a "very deplorable event" but took the occasion to observe that "it is true that the colored population of South Carolina is too large and should be reduced." The ugly joke reflected the white-supremacist conundrum the paper had noted almost a decade before — that wealthy white men's imperatives as employers and Democrats could not easily be reconciled where the state's black majority was concerned.[36]

Some argued that lynching frightened away both immigrant labor and Northern capital. John C. Sheppard, Tillman's opponent for the governorship in 1892, charged that Tillman's espousal of mob violence meant that Northerners "must steer clear of South Carolina for investments and settlement." In early 1893, the editor of the North Carolina *Southern Progress* wrote to ask Tillman for a "brief letter . . . stating that South Carolina is free from influences that cause investments [to be] unsafe." Tillman replied "that vested rights *and* investments, of all kinds are as safe in South Carolina as they are anywhere," that there was "nothing whatever in the bugaboo of a possible race conflict to deter immigrants making homes or those who have money to invest," and that South Carolina was not the lawless place some alleged. "The rights of negroes are respected," he claimed, "and the courts are opened to them for redress the same as to whites." This reply was perhaps too much of a good thing: in outlining all the ways that South Carolina was supposed to be stable and secure, Tillman highlighted Northerners' chief anxieties about investing in Southern states.[37]

Some upper-class white men saw lynching as evidence of other white men's unfitness for democratic self-government. A few tried to impress upon their sons how shamefully many of the state's white people were acting. "[I]t is the hight of folly to try to convict a white man for killing a poor negro," claimed Orangeburg sheriff A. M. Salley in a letter to his son, a student at the Citadel. "A certain class think it is something to be proud of. It was perfectly disgusting to me to see men running after those self-declared murderers. They [the lynchers] had a perfect ovation." Editor J. C. Hemphill's uncle, James Hemphill, complained that lynchings made him doubt "our fitness for government. We should quit boasting that there is no place like South Carolina. We should cover ourselves with sack cloth and ashes."[38]

The state's political factions did not divide neatly into Tillmanite "radicals" espousing violence and anti-Tillmanite "conservatives" demanding law and order. Indeed, even Tillman and Hampton — figures usually offered as archetypes of these positions — took strikingly similar stances on lynching. Tillman, as we have seen, was entirely capable of speaking the language of protection and order. By the late 1880s, Hampton could likewise serve as a model of militant patriarchy. As the former general fought to retain his Senate seat against the Tillmanite onslaught in late 1890, a supporter asked, "[W]hen a political faction at Washington armed and let loose throughout the state a semi-barbarous race, saturated with the brutal lusts of their kind . . . who protected . . . the honor of the farmers' wives and daughters? His name was Wade Hampton." Hampton himself was willing to invoke the possibility of violence when it seemed tactically prudent. Speaking against the passage of the Lodge Bill, he moved from economic concerns to unmistakable warnings. The bill, he said, would "demoralize our labor, shake the confidence of capitalists, retard forever the march of prosperity . . . and lead perhaps to bloodshed." Tillman's assessment of the possible consequences of the Lodge Bill differed from Hampton's only in its bluntness: "I don't doubt if the effort is made to control us by negroes many of them will be buried," he warned. The leaders of both major Democratic factions of the 1890s reminded listeners that South Carolina's white men had gone to war twice in the last generation and would do so again if required.[39]

The Denmark Lynching

Most white South Carolinians who criticized lynching did so because it challenged their notions of social harmony and white civilization. When summary hangings took place at the earliest possible opportunity after the victim had been captured, newspapers praised the calmness of the lynch mob, presenting the action as swift, rational, and just. One lynch mob that transported its victim on a train was praised for behaving so well that white women traveling on the same train had no idea of the group's purpose. At the other end of the spectrum were the mass spectacles described so often in the newspapers then as well as the historiography now, lynchings with elaborate show trials and examinations that culminated in torture, mutilation, burning, shooting, hanging, and the dismemberment of bodies for trophies. In these cases, as a "mob" appropriated state authority and transformed the due process of law into a white-supremacist spectacle, political leaders struggled to retain — or recoup — their authority.[40]

In April 1893, a lynching in the Barnwell County town of Denmark demonstrated the limits both of white opposition to lynching and of Tillman's attempt to reconcile white-supremacist justice with the rule of law. The press reported that Mamie Baxter, a fourteen-year-old from a well-to-do white farm family, had said that a strange black man had attempted to assault her, presumably with intent to rape. Hastily deputized posses brought a score of suspects before her, black men with no immediate alibi or regular local employment. All were exonerated and released. Finally, a black man named Henry Williams was identified by Baxter as somewhat resembling the man who had attacked her. Williams escaped custody, whereupon Tillman offered a $250 reward for his capture and return to the sheriff; white citizens matched that sum, conditional upon only his capture. Williams was caught but not delivered to the sheriff. In the days after Williams's re-apprehension, newspaper accounts depicted Barnwell state senator S. G. Mayfield playing the same role that Tillman had sought — that of the local statesman attempting to guide and thereby legitimate the actions of the crowd. Mayfield was among the "prominent citizens" who initially convinced a crowd of local whites — itself "composed of many of the best citizens of the town and section" — not to lynch Williams on the spot. But Mayfield, like Tillman, understood the terms of the negotiation. As he held Williams under guard in his office, he wrote to Tillman that the crime warranted death and that if Williams was guilty, he should be lynched as soon as possible. Mayfield announced that in response to an ambiguous letter from Tillman, he had told the governor that "Barnwell men would protect their women at all hazards." Local honor and white patriarchy were at stake.[41]

Tillman's letter to Mayfield, written while Williams was still at large, fully expressed the governor's precarious position between the white collective violence on which he had built his career and the state power he now embodied. Tillman had been "hoping to hear that you have caught and lynched" the "would be ravisher." He agreed with Mayfield that the punishment for the "attempt to ravish . . . ought to be death" and that the legal punishment "is inadequate for a case of this kind." But he insisted that he would make good on the promised reward only if Williams was not lynched, for he "would not consider it right to have a man caught by process of law & through the instrumentality of the reward offered by the state, simply to break the law by killing him." Therefore, Tillman thought that any lynching "ought to be before the officers of the law get possession" of the victim. Tillman tried to make his prolynching position clear without appearing to use the law itself to promote a lynching. Although he "[saw] very well what the result will be," he looked to Mayfield "to preserve the proprieties." Mayfield was more concerned with his own version of the same dance. He assured the governor only that "I will do all in my power to *Lynch* the man who did the deed and as much to prevent violence to one who is not guilty."[42]

Elites like Mayfield and Tillman sought to appear gravely law-abiding while they arranged a lynching, but other participants had less power to shape or contest their depictions in the press. According to the *Charleston News and Courier*, unreasonable, violent, disreputable rural whites were the real perpetrators of lynching. White men from the surrounding countryside, it reported, continued to pour into Denmark, gathering "in angry knots . . . armed with every imaginable weapon, from the double-barreled shotgun to the most antiquated make of revolvers." The mayor, sensing danger, ordered the saloons closed, hoping to ensure that the crowd would remain orderly. But the mayor, the senator, and the "fair-minded men" who stood with them reportedly faced a challenge from these new arrivals, men "who would listen to no reason." "The sentiments of this party," explained a correspondent of the state's leading newspaper, were given voice by their leader, "a hard-featured, horny-handed old farmer . . . tall, raw-boned . . . clean-shaven except for a long chin whisker, . . . which he furtively curried from time to time with one bony hand." His position was uncomplicated: "Gentlemen, Barnwell's reputation is at stake, and by —— somebody has got to die."[43]

White-supremacist justice bore the same carnival resemblance to due process that white-supremacist politics bore to democracy. Before a court of the mob, Williams was instructed to prove his innocence or be presumed guilty. As a reporter put it, "[H]e was in the hands of the people, and . . . was above and beyond legal interference" by the governor or militia. Half an hour before Williams was to be killed, however, four white men (including Orangeburg sheriff A. M. Salley, who decried lynching in the letter to his son quoted previously) arrived to corroborate an alibi Williams had been claiming since his capture. Mayfield, playing the role of judge, allowed these respectable white men to make statements and be cross-examined by the crowd. After the men had offered this evidence supporting Williams's story, Mayfield declared, "Gentlemen, you have heard the evidence. The case is in your hands. Is he guilty or not guilty?" Although some members urged that Williams be lynched, others were sobered by the new evidence, and the decision was made to keep Williams locked up while bands of men scoured the countryside for black men fitting Baxter's description of her assailant.[44]

Tillman's involvement in the case became even more direct when a suspect named John Peterson appealed to him for protection. Peterson said that he had an alibi and could prove his innocence, but he feared he would be lynched if he was captured and taken to Denmark by a posse. Tillman sent Peterson to Denmark with a single guard, ostensibly to prove his innocence. When Peterson arrived, however, according to a correspondent, the proceeding was "very similar to that in a trial justice's court. The prisoner was placed upon the stand and made his statement, evidence was taken on both sides and the prisoner permitted to cross examine the witnesses." Neither Peterson's testimony nor the governor's guard saved him: "[T]he jury of public opinion passed upon his case and the verdict was guilty." The mob hung Peterson and shot him to death. The coroner's jury eschewed the customary formulation of "persons unknown," stating simply that Peterson "came to his death at the hands of about 500 citizens who intended to inflict the punishment of death . . . for having assaulted Miss Mamie Baxter . . . with intent to commit rape." At Tillman's request, Mayfield sent him a summary of "the lynching and the verdict." Both men essentially granted the mob the authority of the state.[45]

Black and white spokesmen exploded with outrage at both the lynchers and the governor who seemed to have aided and abetted them. A self-described "mass meeting" of black citizens in Columbia protested the "brutal" acts of "barbarous mobs," as well as the "collusion and sanction" of state officials. The resolutions thanked "the better class of our white citizens" for condemning these acts. But in their deliberations, some black spokesmen took much stronger and more specific positions. "We have nothing more or less in South Carolina than mobocracy," declared Professor J. W. Morris. Some called for a denunciation of Tillman's actions; others went further, suggesting open defiance. "In the present condition," announced Reverend H. M. Rayford, "I don't regard my life as my own. It's better to die plucky than die a coward." A Charleston protest meeting led by black preachers advised black people "to be order-loving and law-abiding citizens" but added that "the time is quite at hand for the men of the negro race to make special provision for the protection of themselves and families against these outrages which may at any time be visited upon them." But black South Carolinians knew that even appearing to mobilize for physical resistance often elicited a massively disproportionate white response. Their experiences both before and after emancipation had taught them that taking up arms collectively without reliable legal and military support was a recipe for massacre. Even Tillman thought this lesson had been sufficiently taught: in the aftermath of the Denmark lynching, he soothed a subordinate's fears by reassuring him that he did "not believe the sensational reports of negroes trying to rescue Rapists."[46]

Indignation meetings of leading black citizens were a part of the political landscape of Columbia and Charleston, but the participation of prominent white citizens struck many as a foolhardy escalation. Among whites, the loudest condemnation of the Denmark lynching came from editor Narciso Gonzales, whose intolerance of vigilante violence reinforced his long hostility toward Tillman. In editorials in his anti-Tillman paper, the *Columbia State*, and at a biracial indignation meeting in Columbia, Gonzales declared that lynching would not end rape or put guards on the roads to protect white women; rather, it would incite black men to express their rage at such injustice—by committing further rapes. In this unforgivingly partisan world, however, prediction was tantamount to advocacy. One newspaper denounced the indignation meeting at which Gonzales spoke as "an exhibition of blind bitter partisan hate and unscrupulous recklessness of consequences the worst that has ever been seen in South Carolina," condemning it for promoting "race antagonism" and "embolden[ing]" black men to perpetrate four subsequent "outrages." This was the white-supremacist argument of the 1870s and 1880s revived in a new context: black men were the brutish tools through which malevolent white men attacked white farmers' households, authority, and independence, and white men who "encouraged" them were accessories to those crimes.[47]

The actions of Gonzales and a few other outspoken contrarians provoked a backlash among some of the white citizens of Barnwell County. Five hundred attended a "mass meeting" in Denmark on 29 April, at which speakers condemned Gonzales and his newspaper for attempting to "besmirch and befoul the people of this community" and incite black men to retaliatory assaults on white women. Gonzales, they resolved, had a heart "blacker than the wretch who assaulted Miss Baxter" and deserved "the same fate as John

Peterson." At another meeting in the town of Barnwell, "three hundred citizens" and "about twenty-five colored men" heard speeches from Mayfield and others before resolving to lynch any future rapists. Stating explicitly the formula of local collective authority, they declared "that the Government was made for the people, and the whole people are a law unto themselves, and that justice is more essential than mere forms of justice, and that the verdict of a jury of five hundred men, the repute of whom was good, if not better, than that of Gonzales, of the State, is entitled to as much respect as a verdict of twelve of the men in a Court room." Black rapists and the white journalists who encouraged them deserved "to fall at the hands of an outraged people." Although many newspapers criticized Tillman's actions, most agreed with the *Edgefield Advertiser* that "the people of Denmark and Barnwell . . . were, by common consent in such cases, the sole judges of [Peterson's] guilt or innocence."[48]

Tillman, for his part, denied bearing any responsibility for Peterson's murder. He declared that had Peterson confessed his guilt to him, he would have sent him under heavier guard or held him in Columbia, but since the man had said he could prove his innocence and the mob had released other innocent men, Tillman had had no reason to expect trouble. Tillman both validated and disavowed the court of Judge Lynch: although his words implied that the mob would not have lynched Peterson if he had been innocent, he declared that the people of Barnwell had "violated his confidence." He had assumed that "they most certainly would not hang a man who said he was innocent and was willing to meet his accusers." Having facilitated a murderous white-supremacist spectacle without unduly dirtying the hands of the state, he went on to defend the state before its Northern critics: when the *Boston Transcript* headlined an article on the Denmark lynching "Brute Rule in the South," Tillman denounced the article as "a tissue of falsehoods." He paid little further attention to South Carolinians who condemned his role in the Denmark lynching.[49]

As lynchings multiplied, the *Charleston News and Courier* continued to denounce "the spirit of lawlessness" and to hope that someone would "make [an] example, for once, of some of the members of a mob." But its writers increasingly seemed to accept the futility of their insistence on "law and order." As a solution, they proposed that special courts be held in areas where lynchings seemed imminent to lend the proceedings a veneer of legality. The question was not the punishment — only death would suffice — but the forms preceding its administration. "[I]f the Legislature will not provide a special Court for the 'prompt' trial and punishment of rapists, the people will," declared the paper, echoing the words of the defenders of the Denmark lynching. After all, "a hasty trial [was] better than none." Adherence to the forms of law, it seemed, might be sufficient to protect the state's reputation, if not its citizens' lives.[50]

By the mid-1890s, "law and order" for blacks accused of serious crimes meant little more than a quiet, orderly mob. "The lynching," began one editorial, "was conducted in a way that reflects great credit on the persons engaged in it." The victim was given time to prepare for his death, with "no bloodthirsty mob crying out for vengeance." In fact, "the crowd was composed of the best men of the community, and was 'orderly to the last.' " If law could not be maintained, order would do. "Savagery does not repress savagery," the paper wrote of another "orderly" lynching that year; "it was a good example for other and all lynchers in the future." Even particularly macabre lynchings — those in which victims were tortured to death or in which trophies or souvenir photos were taken — could seem comparatively "moderate." One victim begged not to be burned alive, reported the *Edgefield Advertiser*, and "some cool heads prevented such a horrible tragedy." His murder nonetheless followed, carried out with what one reporter called "a refinement of cruelty and torture that nearly everyone who witnessed it thought deserved." By the bloody summer of 1893, atrocity had become a relative concept, and black protests soon no longer drew even rhetorical sympathy from white spokesmen. The *Charleston News and Courier* abandoned its support for the protests of black ministers and other citizens. Instead, it characterized such protests as inflammatory and suggested that the ministers' time would be better spent "try[ing] to make the men of the negro race behave themselves. There is evidently a wide field for mission work in the country districts."[51]

Some whites also tried to blunt the brutal racial edge of spectacular lynchings by implicating black South Carolinians. Democratic newspapers took pains to point out the presence of black men and women at several lynchings of black men accused of assaulting white women during the early 1890s. Black women were said to have testified against lynching victims, and black men were spotted in the crowds, among the executioners, and even on the coroner's juries that reached verdicts of "persons unknown." Such reports of black cooperation or participation became relatively common, perhaps revealing the underlying white insecurity manifested in the recurrent fear of an impending "race war." By implicating African Americans in lynchings, these whites sought to reassure themselves that black people were not the monoliths posited by white supremacy, not a New World golem that needed only one more violent provocation to set it in murderous, retaliatory motion. Instead, these black people were a credit to white civilization, accepting the justice of its principles and helping enforce them.[52]

Although lynchings such as Peterson's defined white-supremacist justice, they also revealed the limitations of white supremacy as a mode of governance. Talking out of both sides of his mouth, Tillman had learned to negotiate the conflicting imperatives of lynching and the law. But his tactical successes should not mislead us into thinking that Tillman had found a formula that would reconcile lynching with state building. Judge Lynch's carnivals demonstrated white supremacy's power, but they also made the actual achievement of Tillman's vision more remote by weakening the authority of the state government. In the end, Tillman's attempt to reconcile these gory spectacles with the appearance of state authority left him fatigued and annoyed. Although he continued to assert that accused rapists should be lynched, at the end of 1893, he told reporters that "everybody would have been much better satisfied" if a recent lynching victim could have been "hanged according to [the] law." The tension could not be resolved: as long as a man had to die, Tillman preferred it to be at the hands of the state rather than the mob.[53]

The Dispensary and State Power

Social conflict over alcohol provided Tillman with an opportunity to reconfigure the relationship between the "mob" and the state. When South Carolina's temperance activists advocated the protection of the home against its enemies, they were concerned about matters quite distinct from lynching and rape. But Tillman's effort to address their concerns through state action ended up back on the terrain of state authority and "mob law."

When Tillman was nominated for governor in 1890, state Women's Christian Temperance Union (WCTU) leader Sallie F. Chapin implored him to reveal himself as "the Deliverer for whom we have been praying." Declaring that the WCTU recognized only two political parties, "the party that stands for the Home" and "the party that aims at the destruction of the Home," she tried to work her devout, moral definition of reform into Tillman's political and social reform program. "I pray God," she concluded, "you may have courage to carry your plans for reform into every cranny of the Augean stable, and make us once again a prosperous and a happy people." This was not her first venture into politics: in the early 1880s, Chapin and others had followed the lead of national WCTU leaders in forming a small Prohibition Home Protection Party. Chapin had laid out her position on liquor (as well as tobacco, gambling, extramarital sex, usury, and much else) in her anti-Reconstruction reform novel, *Fitz-Hugh St. Clair, the South Carolina Rebel Boy*. The novel, dedicated to "the children of the Southern Confederacy," attacked racial equality and vicious Union officers, but it blamed the region's continuing economic crisis on white men's moral weakness. Only by giving up expensive and degrading habits such as drinking liquor could white Southern men take their proper places at the head of their households, their society, and their nation. Under Chapin, the state WCTU focused on persuading legislators to provide stronger legal weapons against liquor and its site of distribution, the dreaded saloon.[54]

The social transformation sought by prohibition advocates might appear to offer a moral counterpart to Tillman's political-economic program. Chapin, like Tillman, understood women's and men's roles as complementary but distinct and opposed woman suffrage. "Do we not have three votes now," she asked—"our husband and two sons?" When Tillman came to power, Chapin sent him an inscribed copy of *Fitz-Hugh St. Clair* in hopes that he would adopt its priorities. But Chapin's notions of "reform" and the "home" did not precisely match those of the new governor, for Tillman consistently refused to endorse prohibition. At the April 1886 farmers' convention, Tillman's resolution in favor of a college for white women (on the site of the Citadel) was clearly an attempt to replace white women's political and social activism with a state-aided program of educational and economic self-help. "If they cannot secure that prohibition which would banish alcohol," he suggested, "they can help banish that prohibition, ignorance, which now bars their sex in this State from occupations except sewing, teaching, and working in cotton factories." Despite seeming to applaud temperance advocates, Tillman asserted that outright prohibition could not and should not be achieved. Virginia D. Young, Chapin's rival for leadership of the women's temperance movement, received Tillman's assurance that he was not a habitual drinker and that he favored regulation of the liquor trade. He also gave her the discouraging news that he opposed prohibition on principle, believing that whether or not one drank alcohol was a question of "individual freedom."[55]

Instead, Tillman sought a middle ground with temperance activists. Since white farmers were split over prohibition for personal, philosophical, and religious reasons, temperance politics were a losing proposition for Democrats. Division over alcohol would injure both the farmers' movement and the cause of white unity. Tillman warned that political clashes over liquor would set prohibitionist and antiprohibitionist whites against one another at the polls. Tillmanite reformers thus took pains to avoid what one called the "prohibition vortex, only fit to distract and disturb our social as well as political welfare." In private, Tillman and his supporters were less polite than they were in public about these meddlesome women and sometimes referred to committed temperance activists like Chapin as "cranks."[56]

Temperance politics came to the forefront of state debate in 1892. After legislative failures in previous years, a nonbinding referendum on prohibition passed during the general election. Political good sense demanded that the legislature take some action, and it debated a variety of bills. Tillman's solution was to defuse the issue by offering a state-level reform that he hoped would satisfy both supporters and opponents of prohibition. Through his legislative allies, Tillman sought both to defuse the threat prohibition posed to white supremacy and to expand the authority of the state government by creating a dispensary system, essentially a state monopoly on the sale of liquor. The state would purchase liquor at wholesale prices and distribute it to local retail outlets, known as dispensaries, which would sell sealed packages to be consumed off the premises. A local dispensary would be established only after a majority of a town's freehold voters signed a petition requesting one. The only alternative to a dispensary was local prohibition.[57] Any profits the system generated would be divided between the state and the municipality in which the dispensary was located. The law took effect on 1 July 1893, and constables hired by the governor sought out violators. The dispensary system radically altered the distribution of alcohol throughout much of the state, replacing countless independent proprietors with a single state-run outlet. By September 1893, forty-seven dispensaries were in operation throughout the state. Most counties had only one, but Columbia and Charleston, cities with large populations, were legally entitled to several.[58]

Did the dispensary constitute a moral improvement over the reputedly degraded masculine culture of the saloon? Or would the dispensary corrupt the state itself? Opinion was divided as to whether the whiskey glass was half full or half empty. Supporters of the dispensary, including some prohibitionists, emphasized its wholesome social benefits. Chapin wrote that "[i]f Governor Tillman never does anything but close the barrooms of South Carolina he will have the thanks of thousands of women and children." The *Edgefield Advertiser* crowed, "[T]he gilded bar rooms, pitfalls for the feet of so many boys and young men, will soon be a thing of the past," and "the youth of our state will be saved from the curse of rum." The dispensary struck multiple blows against the saloon, the devil's alternative to the home: it eliminated the "allurements and enticements" of alcoholic sociability and prostitution; it reduced crime and "shooting scrapes"; and it replaced the keepers of bars, men and women of uncertain character, with state officials who could be held accountable for their actions.[59]

But replacing barrooms with dispensaries did not add up to prohibition, and the dispensary system drew criticism from many quarters. Both white WCTU members and a conference of black Methodists in Beaufort condemned the dispensary as too great a compromise of temperance principles. Some prohibitionists even turned to Tillman for aid against his own creation. Invoking Tillman's "well known earnestness in the Temperance cause," the black WCTU chapter of St. Helena Island requested that he refuse any application for a dispensary on the island. Chapin and others in the temperance movement who offered support for the governor's compromise solution were sometimes voted down in their own assemblies.[60] For some prohibitionists, the dispensary added insult to injury by turning a profit. Since dispensary revenues were divided between the state government and the localities, both state and local officials had an incentive to maximize sales. Tillman soon became aware that the appearance that state and local governments were profiting from liquor sales could set prohibitionists firmly against the dispensary. He acknowledged the wisdom of a Georgetown ally's recommendation that he should take "influential temperance people" into account, soft-pedal the revenue-generating feature of the dispensary, and insist that "every official connected with that law (at present) should pose as a conservator of temperance." More significantly, Tillman cautioned allies like Barnwell Democrat S. G. Mayfield (the "judge" in the Denmark lynching) that "you have dispensaries enough in Barnwell county and it is offensive to the Prohibitionists to press things so."[61]

The dispensary gave the governor power to make many local appointments, increasing his influence in county affairs. The governor and two other state officials made up the state board of control, which appointed county boards. These boards selected managers, or "dispensers," who oversaw day-to-day operations and hired additional workers. Tillman was thus in a position to help determine who might or might not gain office, from several high-salaried state officials to a dispenser and a few employees in each county. The law also allowed him to hire a large number of enforcement officers. Dispensary employment was a matter of patronage politics: applicants for dispensary and constabulary posts recited their credentials as Tillmanite reformers. Many opponents feared that the dispensary would ultimately amount to an 800-man patronage machine for the reform faction. Even Alliancemen suspected that the dispensary was essentially a political machine, and some suggested that dispensary officials be barred from politics.[62]

Tillmanites fretted about a possible coalition between frustrated conservatives and disgruntled prohibitionists. But Tillman could not afford to be too careful, for dispensary positions were among the few he had to give. His attacks during the 1892 campaign had permanently alienated Grover Cleveland, the Democrat who was now president. As a result, Tillman had no control over the distribution of federal patronage positions in South Carolina, a loss of boodle one knowledgeable reformer reckoned at $250,000 a year. The disposition of collectorships, post office positions, and Washington, D.C., sinecures ended up in the hands of Senator Butler and other anti-Tillmanites.[63]

The loss of patronage weakened the Tillmanites' political cohesion and power. One man complained that he had lost a federal appointment because Butler had given it to a man he hoped to woo away from the Tillman faction.[64] "The woods are full of traitors," one Tillmanite cautioned another. "The Federal patronage is being used as bait to catch them. It has caught some and will catch a great many others." Ultimately, Tillman feared that it might "catch" the Senate seat he hoped to take in 1894. Squabbling and disorder ensued as factional rivals jockeyed for congressional seats and the opportunity to succeed Tillman as governor. Although liquor helped draw some men closer together, it drove others apart. J. L. M. Irby, who had replaced Hampton in the Senate in 1891, alienated many leading Tillmanites as he descended into an alcoholic confusion and paranoia that reached a climax in the summer of 1893 when he struck another reformer at a leadership meeting.[65]

Personal and political differences threatened to fragment the Tillmanites, but the larger contest against the money power and its servants in Washington, D.C., brought these men back together. Irby's paranoia was less noticeable when he spoke of national politics, for his allegations of persecution hardly differed from Tillman and other reformers' attacks on corporations and the federal government. A conspiracy was at work, Irby declared late in 1893, "a deep laid and desperate game by the money power of New York and the old ring pols in the State to overthrow the rule of the people." Tillman's charges were somewhat more specific, but he envisioned a similar degree of intrigue among corporate and political enemies who schemed against the dispensary. Interstate railroad lines and their federal receivers, federal and state courts, and federal revenue collectors all seemed to Tillman to be collaborating with the "whiskey men," liquor manufacturers and distributors who wanted direct access to the South Carolina market. As usual, Tillman rarely identified these men by name, but he charged that they thwarted the implementation and enforcement of the dispensary law at every turn.[66]

Tillman's efforts to exert power over corporations symbolized the power of the state as an agent of reform, regardless of whether those efforts succeeded. He warned that "if we are to permit capital to shirk taxation and corporations to dictate to the State in order to have money come here for investment, we don't want it." In contrast to investment-oriented capitalists, who believed regulatory legislation would induce the "best citizens" to take their capital elsewhere, Tillman and his supporters sought to demonstrate that a small but assertive state government could improve the lives of all white producers.[67] In fact, Tillman's efforts at state regulation produced mainly symbolic victories. During the late 1880s, he had leveled charges of corruption at the state-chartered monopoly on phosphate mining. As governor, he engaged in a lengthy legal wrangle with the mining company that produced no financial victory for the state but earned him praise for being a foe of corporate greed. When railroad corporations refused to pay state taxes based on new, substantially higher assessments of railroad property, Tillman defied state and federal courts and ordered county sheriffs to impound railroad property. He soon had to back down, but not before symbolically asserting the power of the state government not only over corporations but also over federal judges whose rulings he considered "judicial tyranny." The capital-friendly *Charleston News and Courier* called Tillman's momentary defiance of the courts "states rights run mad." But Tillman understood the political value of defiance of federal authority, even when it failed, and his aggressive style and choice of targets endeared him to those for whom the money power was a palpable enemy. The Farmers' Alliance state newspaper defended Tillman's course as "exactly right," and one reform legislator summed up the relationship between defiance and independence: "We either have to control the railroads or they control us."[68]

Tillman's claim that federal control meant a return to Reconstruction had been bolstered in 1889, when a federal judge appointed Daniel Chamberlain as receiver of the bankrupt South Carolina Railroad. Chamberlain, "who in days past did his utmost to throttle Anglo-Saxon civilization in South Carolina," had returned, Tillman said, "to gloat over [the state's] humiliation at the hands of his obedient instrument," the corrupted judiciary, which "oversaw" his receivership. When Alliancemen and Populists proposed ambitious schemes of federal ownership or regulation, Tillman perceived the threat of a return to Reconstruction: any federal tool powerful enough to benefit Tillman's farmers could also be used against them. In the case of government control of the railroads, Tillman feared that the resulting army of federal railroad employees "would almost inevitably be used as an engine in elections by the use of the employees at the ballot box for the benefit of the party in power."[69]

This "engine" was already at work undermining the dispensary law. Railroads were the chief means of transport for both legal and illegal goods, and barrels of contraband liquor appeared at depots almost immediately after the law went into effect. The laws of federal receivership that Tillman had found so galling in the tax cases continued to outrage him; he complained "that whiskey in the hand of railroads run by receivers cannot be seized and proceeded against without warrant." He pledged to pursue this through the federal courts and lay the blame where it belonged—with the collaborating forces of federal and corporate corruption. The struggle against this conspiracy was enough to fill a reformer's heart. "We may fail," Tillman admitted, "but in contending for right and justice I will never consider either the course or the result."[70]

In 1893, anti-Tillman Wage Workers' Democratic Leagues appeared in Columbia. They declared "the interests of capital and labor to be the same" and denounced "socialism" and "Tillmanism," as well as "Haskellism." Since railroad employees joined the organization, the governor thought he saw Chamberlain's corrupting carpetbag influence at work. The *Edgefield Advertiser* referred to the Wage Workers as the "Wire Workers," implying behind-the-scenes control by Chamberlain. This was Reconstruction corruption redux, for as the *Advertiser* put it, "he's the same old Chamberlain that he ever was." The "Railway Party in Politics" feared by Tillman and others on a national level seemed to be forming in South Carolina, with the added dimension of corruption by antidispensary liquor interests. Before the dispensary law went into effect, an ally had warned Tillman that a local trial justice not only was a member of the Wage Workers—and therefore presumably in the pay of Tillman's corporate and political enemies—but also had gained a primary election victory due to "the free use of whiskey and illegal voters imported here by the Rail Road Company." By the time the 1894 elections approached, Tillman had concluded that "the whiskey ring and the railroads will furnish a large corruption fund to be used in the next campaign." The nexus of corruption included the U.S. Bureau of Internal Revenue, which refused to cooperate with dispensary enforcement efforts and even seized whiskey that state officials had taken from smugglers. Once again, the federal government had proved itself to be a local arm of the money power.[71]

Tillman sometimes tried to reconcile the reality of white industrial wage labor with his ideal of white agricultural patriarchy. When "poor men" were white but not farmers, he turned (as in a speech to Columbia workers) to a broadly defined producerism that championed the rule of "the laboring men" rather than that of "the farmers." He attacked the conservative men who challenged his slate in the 1892 Democratic primary—a mill owner and a banker—as agents of industrial and financial oppression. He implied that the gubernatorial candidate, John C. Sheppard, had used his position as president of an Edgefield bank to extort political support—never mind that Tillman had supported Sheppard in his unsuccessful bid for the governorship only six years before. He accused Sheppard's running mate of earning his $7,000 annual income from "the blood [and] sweat" of women and children who worked thirteen hours a day in his factory and of coercing his employees into supporting conservative candidates.[72]

But in Tillman's republican vision, wage earners dependent on others for their subsistence were inferior precisely because they could be coerced politically in ways that landowning farmers could not. During the 1892 primary campaign, a Tillman organizer in Spartanburg warned that "at the factory towns they arranged it so as to keep the operatives from attending the meetings," and only one mill "held its meeting after night where the hands could vote." In 1886, the *Charleston News and Courier* had warned that "common black agricultural laborers" were "credulous, ignorant and suspicious; just the material to be as plastic as putty in the hands of shrewd and ambitious leaders." Now white laborers were also portrayed as willing or unwilling tools of scheming labor leaders, who "know the precise money value of [the laborer's] vote to either party in any hotly contested election." For his part, Tillman suggested that his opponents—who were themselves "owned" by "the corporations"—had coerced or bought their supporters.[73]

Tillman's ambivalence about wage earners as independent citizens affected his understanding of the national labor struggles of the 1890s. He was no friend of socialist or redistributive programs, and he remained eternally suspicious of labor unions. He did sometimes side rhetorically with white Northern workingmen; when violence erupted in 1892 after the managers of Andrew Carnegie's steel mill at Homestead, Pennsylvania, hired Pinkerton "detectives" to break a strike, Tillman declared that "he would like to see every one of Pinkerton's men hanged." During 1894, in the depths of a national depression, he stated that "Coxey's Army," a band of economic protesters and reformers marching from Ohio to Washington, D.C., had the "full sympathy" of farmers. But Coxey's Army was Northern and economically dispossessed, and it made demands on the federal government. This unbecoming dependence made it an unlikely ally. During his 1894 campaign for the Senate, when Tillman claimed that Butler had hired crowds of men to "boom" him at campaign stops, he likened this disreputable mob to Coxey's Army and called his opponent "Coxey" Butler, a witticism that he reported made the crowd "scream with delight."[74]

In the face of the combined assault from corporate and federal enemies, Tillman sought a degree of control over local affairs that no governor had contemplated since Reconstruction. The centralization represented by the dispensary could be presented as a necessary bulwark against corruption, and Tillman followed suit in his "reform" of county government. Tillman's plan, as introduced in the General Assembly by Evans, gave the governor the authority to appoint the officials who oversaw local finances and construction. The *Charleston News and Courier* called the proposed legislation a "petty system of gubernatorial control of the counties," a means of "making new offices for an army of unemployed Reformers" that would "open the door for fraud in every county and township in the state." Many newspapers condemned such legislation because of "the unbridled power it gave the Governor." Tillman assured the bill's passage by establishing that governors would make appointments in consultation with the county's legislative delegation, thereby giving legislators their own stake in patronage politics. He also recalled the commissions of every notary public in the state on the pretext that some unqualified men (presumably Tillman's black and white political enemies) held the office. A friendly newspaper praised Tillman's "sublime nerve" in "knock[ing] the socks off six thousand office-holders at once." If it did not have precisely this effect, Tillman's action at least reminded local potentates that it paid to be on good terms with the governor. In the absence of federal patronage, Tillman created his own through the control of state jobs and appointments.[75]

The Dispensary and the Mob

The real conflict came when Tillman sought to enforce the dispensary law. The dispensary constables' work against contraband liquor took them to South Carolina's towns and cities, where railroad hubs supplied scores of illicit barrooms known as "blind tigers" and where hostility to Tillman was most pronounced. There, the constables were widely referred to as "spies." As they obtained warrants to search private residences, they encountered massive resistance from urban residents who claimed to be defending their households against outrageous governmental intrusion. The *Charleston News and Courier* declared that "a man's home is his castle" and reported townspeople's "determination . . . that no home shall be invaded."[76]

"Home protection," a rallying cry of prohibitionists and an implicit message of Tillmanism, took on a new meaning in this struggle for power over the public and private spaces of urban South Carolina. Although Tillman himself acknowledged that "Anglo-Saxon blood will not submit" to indiscriminate or warrantless searches, he cautioned that even though " '[a] man's home is his castle,' . . . he has no right to turn it into a saloon." Only guilty men, one commentator suggested, would mind having their houses searched for illegal liquor. And only force could convince such guilty men of the governor's resolve. Assembling the rule of law, the police powers of the state, and his own political machine, Tillman took the battle over state power and the rule of law to his opponents' home field, the cities. Challenging their authority where they appeared strong and he appeared weak, Tillman maneuvered them off the high ground of law and order and onto the streets. There, he proved to be more than a match for them. In the end, the "dispensary war" gave Tillman the opportunity to recast the troubled relationship between white violence and state power.[77]

The dispensary war divided anti-Tillmanites and Tillmanites along familiar, if not impermeable, lines of town and country. Although each side drew some support in every area of the state, Tillman was always at odds with urban leaders, and by the fall of 1893, pro-Tillman newspapers described resistance to the dispensary as urban intransigence. "The country people have cheerfully yielded obedience to the law," declared an upcountry newspaper, "and recalcitrant city liquor dealers should be required to obey it." Those who refused would "sooner or later feel the force of the law." Newspapers drew on this split to make partisan points. When the pro-Tillman *Columbia Register* cheekily suggested that constables' good behavior could be assured by bringing country people into towns to oversee their raids, the *Charleston News and Courier* responded with the complaint that the *Register* was attempting to set town against country. By the mid-1890s, though, few could have been surprised by rural-urban hostility or by its political edge.[78]

The antipathy between Tillmanites and urban Democratic leaders made enforcement of the dispensary law all the more difficult. When Tillman asked the state's mayors to help enforce the law in late 1893, he received a cool response. The mayor of Greenville, for example, replied that he would enforce it as much as he enforced any other law and that he resented

Tillman's implicit questioning of his good faith. The mayor of Yorkville even prosecuted an Edgefield dispensary constable for drunkenness, threatening the man with three years in the penitentiary but ultimately fining him "as if [he] were a negro charged with the same offense."[79]

The racial dimension of the enforcement of the dispensary law was not simply rhetorical. All of Tillman's regular constables were white, which made it difficult to gain information on or entrap black violators of the law. At first, Tillman had his men resort to the laughable expedient of "blacking" themselves like minstrels in order to attempt to purchase illicit liquor. Later, he hired a black detective from Georgia to infiltrate the whiskey ring.[80] But enforcement of the law was mainly intended to demonstrate Tillman's authority over white, urban opponents. He and his supporters generally assumed that black people were paid or otherwise induced to violate the dispensary law. Black men who bought liquor or attacked constables were frequently portrayed as the tools of white men: one Tillmanite warned that "the real guilty parties have some Negro or insignificant white man between them and the law out of whom they are making cat's paws." Tillman's own schedule of rewards for liquor law violation convictions reflected this white-supremacist hierarchy of legal responsibility and criminal importance: convictions of whites brought a bounty of $20 or $25, convictions of blacks only $10. As usual, behind black criminality lay scheming white men.[81]

Sometimes the struggle over the dispensary reframed conflicts that otherwise might easily have been depicted in wholly racial terms. When a group of black men attacked constables at the Spartanburg dispensary, local Alliancemen—rural white citizens—focused their condemnation on the mayor, city council, police force, and unnamed "disreputable white men, actuated by partisan hatred against the Reform Movement," who had "encouraged and instigated" the attack. According to the Alliancemen's version of the story, the real conflict was between rural and urban, reformer and Haskellite, as much as between white and black. The Alliancemen perceived "a strong under-current at work in this city to override our State Laws . . . and wink at the conduct" of "outlaws." Although the Alliancemen declared "a natural pride in the prosperity and upbuilding of our County town," they threatened that "if our laws are to be trodden under foot by ruffians, black or white, and no protection given our farmers when we visit this city, . . . we do not feel encouraged to bring our business here." It was possible, of course, to put a more traditional white-supremacist spin on such reports and accuse the dispensary's opponents of being so reckless in their war against Tillman that they were willing to sanction black attacks on white men. Even dispensary opponents, such arguments ran, must see that the dispensary had become "a race issue with all the rights of law and justice on the side of the white men as against the negro desperadoes and their white sympathizers."[82]

Opponents took up familiar forms of collective action against the dispensary constables. A woman who boarded constables in her house was threatened by white-caps. Attackers in Beaufort broke one constable's nose and showered others with what an elated anti-Tillmanite referred to as "ancient hen-fruit." Tillman complained that especially in Charleston, constables were "treated in an outrageous manner" by "mobs." "Almost all the people of Charleston are in league against the law and determined to overthrow it," he told the legislature. Indeed, following an unruly indignation meeting against dispensary law enforcement in Charleston, a large crowd of opponents marched on a house where three constables were boarding. Tillman's chief constable saw "trouble ahead" and called for more men and heavier guns.[83]

These and other incidents led Tillman to speak of a "dispensary war." In response to assaults on constables during the first month of the dispensary's operation, Tillman warned conservative reporters that he had armed his men and ordered them "to shoot the first man that strikes or interferes with one of them from this [moment] on. I am not going to allow the officers of the State to be made dogs of by a set of barkeepers and roughs. . . . [T]he law is going to be enforced. If it results in killing somebody, it will have to be done, that is all." After constables shot two white men, killing one, while attempting to search for contraband liquor, Tillman grew more strident and seemed to threaten to impose martial law to uphold the dispensary. He reflected aloud that Charleston's own militia companies were "ready to assist in the enforcement of the laws of the State, so I'll not have to send troops there from Edgefield and Aiken and other counties should the occasion for a military force arise." He blamed the *Charleston News and Courier* for "urging resistance to the laws." Given the willful recklessness of the dispensary's opponents in compromising white supremacy and good order, one commentator found the governor justified in "fighting the devil with fire."[84]

When the conflict turned deadly, the *News and Courier* renewed its charge that Tillman was "the mob law Governor" and held him responsible for the "spirit of lawlessness that prevails among his followers." "The Governor," it editorialized, "cannot expect the people to respect [the law] when he does not respect it himself." It contrasted Tillman's aggressive campaign against illegal liquor with his apparent reluctance to prosecute lynch mobs. "Is whiskey thicker than blood in his sight?," asked the Charleston paper. No longer limiting itself to caustic denunciations, the paper warned that Tillman was "challenging mob violence by the very violence of his own conduct." Personal and factional honor were now at stake, and in the affair of honor between the Tillman administration and the urban leadership, the latter refused to back down.[85]

In 1894, the dispensary war came to a violent climax in the town of Darlington. The town was located at a railroad junction in the northeastern section of the state, and its economy depended on interstate traffic, including liquor. During the 1891 legislative debate on a prohibition bill, a Darlington County representative had declared that if prohibition passed, "the flourishing town of Darlington would be utterly destroyed." As early as November 1893, supporters had referred to Darlington as a "*Hell Hole*" of blind tigers and anti-Tillman sentiment, and the town quickly became a center of resistance to the dispensary system. In March 1894, Tillman's supporters in Darlington warned him that "something serious [was] brewing." After receiving reports that illegal liquor traffic in the town was open and pervasive, Tillman warned the mayor that the traffic must be suppressed, and he threatened to take dispensary profits away from the city as of 1 April. Tillman's constables arrived in Darlington, intending to make searches under warrant. Groups described as "[m]en with guns," "mobs," and "crowds" appeared, threatening the small detachment of constables. Tillman sent reinforcements and called out a militia company. Calm was restored until moments before the constables were to leave Darlington by train, when gunfire broke out at the depot between the constables and hostile white Darlingtonians.[86]

After killing a civilian, the constables fled, and suddenly the "mob law Governor" found the tables turned. Angry townspeople fired into the train on which some of the constables sought to flee and chased other constables into the woods. The Darlington dispenser wrote to Tillman that "all the men have left town on horseback to hunt & kill all the constables they can find. They have telegraphed to Sumter & Florence, telling the people there to stop the constables at any cost." Amid conflicting reports of who had fired first, how many on each side had been killed, and the fate of the fleeing agents of state power, Tillman made good on his long-standing threat and mobilized the state militia to put down the Darlington disorder.[87]

Enraged opponents called on the militia to refuse to mobilize for this coercive work, and some did. Tillman, though, had the powers of the state on his side. He took control of the telegraph offices, forbidding the transmission of "any inflammatory telegrams or those calculated to further increase the excitement." He forbade the railroads to provide trains to anyone but officers of the state. He sent loyal militia units to Darlington and Columbia to protect the dispensary, the constables, public order, and the authority of the state. He ordered people "in open rebellion" to disperse, including Columbia citizens who had been reported heading to Darlington to pursue the fleeing constables. He attempted to retrieve the state arms and ammunition belonging to the mutinous militia companies.

With militia companies on the scene and the constables accounted for, order was restored in Darlington and throughout the state. By 6 April, Tillman declared the emergency over. The political and social conflict, however, lasted much longer. The Darlington riot became the polarizing issue of the 1894 political season, drawing the battle lines between reformers and anti-Tillmanites more clearly than ever. In part, these lines followed well-established patterns. One Populist-leaning reform congressman regretted that "feeling between the town folks and country people is so intense," but he pitched his tent with the rural white majority and the governor they supported. The *Edgefield Advertiser* even suggested that the dispensary system itself deserved credit for the speedy and relatively benign resolution of the crisis. "Had barrooms been in existence in S C during the excitement of last week," it explained, "the streets of Col[umbia] would have been full of drunken men, rioting, raging, frenzied citizens and soldiers. Blood would have flowed like water." As it was, Tillman had ordered the dispensaries shut, liquor had dried up, and most white men had apparently behaved reasonably.[88]

In the aftermath of the Darlington riot, both Tillman and his opponents sought to claim the legacy of 1876 and portray themselves as the latter-day Red-shirts. The *Charleston News and Courier* declared that Tillman had destroyed the "harmony" of 1876 by seeking the rule of "his class . . . without regard to the rights of others." Opponents criticized his use of Reconstruction-era emergency powers, calling him "low enough and mean enough to use against the white people a statute passed for the purpose of intimidating the white people by a set of Yankee carpet baggers and niggers." According to a bitter editorialist, Tillman's use of the militia to guard the statehouse and state dispensary in Columbia was "the first time since 1877 [that] a city in South Carolina has hundreds of troops quartered in it under command." One writer privately considered assassinating the governor. Another, former governor Johnson Hagood, best framed the horror Tillman evoked: "With much ability, he combines a disregard of law that looks like incapacity to conceive its obligations, and a recklessness of all save his personal ends that looks like insanity." He called Tillman's course "lawless and tyranous [*sic*]." According to these opponents, Tillman represented the evils of Reconstruction, and the anticonstable "mobs" were liberty-loving white patriots.[89]

Tillman, though, claimed to have protected both the rule of law and the violent victory over Reconstruction. As the crisis ended, he stood in front of the statehouse and, like his adversaries, compared the white unity and harmony of 1876 and 1877 to the chaos of April 1894. "When South Carolina learned [in 1877] that troops had seized this house, within two days' time this whole escarpment back to the monument was black with indignant citizens, (I was among them,) but they were all of one mind," he recalled. The contrast with the present was all too telling. "[T]o-day we find the State divided into two hostile camps . . . because the minority are not willing to let the majority govern." He blamed the conservative press for the division among white men, denouncing the "poison" and "newspaper lies" intended to "keep open the sore" of the fractious 1890 and 1892 campaigns. Indeed, he suggested that the conservatives had sought unsuccessfully to provoke an "explosion," a "civil war." Fortunately, it had not come—it could not—"because the people are in the saddle and will continue to remain there." In quelling the riot, the state militia had recapitulated not the federal occupation but the Red-shirt campaign. Once again, white-supremacist reform, born in 1876, had vanquished its foes. The chastened "whiskey ring," its hirelings the "liquor toughs," and the anticonstable mobs joined blacks, Republicans, carpetbaggers, and goldbugs in the pantheon of white supremacy's enemies.[90]

The two sides traded charges of unmanly cowardice in terms that demonstrated how decisively Tillman had won. "[W]hy didn't [Tillman] go to Darlington himself?," demanded one opponent who hoped to make Tillman's individual actions the issue. "Wade Hampton would have gone, but Tillman, a miserable coward who boasts that he shot down negroes like dogs, stays in his mansion and puts a heavy guard of Edgefield fanatics around the premises to protect his sacred person." Tillman preferred, as usual, to cast the conflict in terms of collective behavior, and he offered an ingeniously double-edged charge against the "mob" that had pursued the constables near Darlington, playing on the tension between vigilante action and legitimate authority. "These men," he told a Columbia audience, "were advertising themselves to the world as lynchers, and . . . they intended to lynch those constables." After defining his opponents as murderous foes of law and order, Tillman shifted position and once more became the authentic voice of violent white supremacy. During the riot, he explained, the mob had caught one of the fleeing constables but had left him unharmed. Tillman therefore mocked the mob for lacking the proper spirit, accusing them of being too cowardly to act on their own violent convictions. "It seems they didn't want to find the constables," he suggested. "If they were lynchers, as they advertised themselves to be, why didn't they lynch the man whom they claimed originated the trouble, and whom they had in their power? They have slandered themselves." These craven white men had challenged Tillman's authority and threatened to murder his agents, but in doing so, they had demonstrated neither a capacity for violence nor a respect for state power. Their threat had proved hollow, an empty hood.[91]

With the glee of one who for the moment had extricated himself from an uncomfortable position astride the fence, Tillman used his control of the government to reinforce his claims. In a move calculated to outrage his urban opponents, he dismissed a Charleston justice who had ruled against his constables, replacing him with the city's former chief constable. More dramatically, Tillman publicly dismissed the militia units that had refused to obey his orders. He compared "the gallant and patriotic soldiers" who had obeyed his orders to the "band-box soldiers" and "disgraced men" who had not. A few weeks later, he disbanded some rebellious units entirely, stripping them of both their military regalia and their martial honor.[92]

Tillman appropriated his opponents' issues as well as their weapons. He claimed that he and his supporters had won a victory not only for violent white supremacy and the rule of law but for the state's economic reputation as well. "If our bonds are at a premium and capital not afraid to seek investment in South Carolina," Tillman told the legislature at the end of 1894, "it is not because the militia of Charleston, Columbia and other towns refused to obey the orders of the Governor" but because loyal upcountry militia units "dropped everything and hastened to the Capital to sustain the Government they had chosen." To ensure such loyalty in future conflicts, Tillman set about commissioning new militia companies whose numbers far exceeded those he had disbanded.[93]

In Tillman's wedding of constitutionalism and coercion, some saw an emerging despotism. During the tumultuous campaign of 1894, some former allies suggested that Tillman sought to make these new forces into a factional army. Tillman's longtime lieutenant Sampson Pope, who split from the Democrats and made an independent run for governor in the fall of 1894, claimed that Tillman had ordered the "bulldozing" of independent voters, not only by reform and Democratic forces but by the dispensary constables and new militia units as well.[94] Others took a more hopeful view of the Darlington riot. Sallie Chapin believed that the dispensary war had demonstrated the ability of the state to "protect the homes" of South Carolinians. "With a man of courage at the head," she wrote to Tillman in the aftermath of the riot, "liquor laws could be enforced, if not absolutely at first, fully as well as laws against burglary, murder, or any other crime." She left lynching off of her list, perhaps recognizing that it might still be a sore point with the governor she was trying so hard to flatter. As it was, she told Tillman exactly what he wanted to hear about the state's role in "home protection."[95]

Others wanted him to go further, extending the principle of state power into areas usually policed more locally. One white woman saw the dispensary constables' investigations as a model for more general state policing on behalf of white purity. In an 1894 letter to Tillman, she suggested that "the Dispensary officers [should] have added to their business that of hunting up all the white men and colored women that are associating together in an unlawful and immoral manner." "The law between white men and colored women," she insisted, "should be just as strict as it is between white women and colored men." But even Tillman was reluctant to make the state responsible for enforcing such prohibitions. He cautiously replied that "if public opinion can be aroused so as to have it proven," white men and black women involved in adulterous liaisons could be punished under existing laws and that some counties did so. He declined, however, to put his constables to work enforcing racial and sexual purity, perhaps recognizing that he had already taken on more responsibility for enforcement than he could comfortably manage. White-supremacist governance had found its limits.[96]

6 Every White Man Who Is Worthy of a Vote

Tillman sought to transform white supremacy into something more than a slogan. He envisioned a structure of state laws and institutions that would nurture and sustain white farming households. But the legacy of Reconstruction thwarted his efforts, raising the possibility not only of resurgent black political participation but of biracial coalitions as well. As long as substantial numbers of black men remained potentially eligible to vote, divisions among white men would continue to imperil Tillman's vision; as in 1880, 1882, 1890, and 1892, dissident white men might appeal to black voters. If they won, they would overturn all the progress made since 1876. Tillman therefore called for a new state constitution, one carefully crafted to exclude most black men and safeguard "Anglo-Saxon supremacy, good government, and . . . our civilization." He and others took their inspiration from the success of white Mississippi Democrats who in 1890 had disfranchised most of the state's black voting majority without prompting a federal response. In the midst of the Haskellite challenge, the *Charleston News and Courier* had looked forward to a time "when white supremacy is not endangered," a time when "like the people of Mississippi, we can devise some modus vivendi between the two races, which will be just to both while securing control to the whites." Following Mississippi's lead, South Carolina's would-be disfranchisers offered poll taxes and literacy or "understanding" tests as effective barriers to black suffrage.[1]

The campaign in support of a constitutional convention and

the debates within the convention itself revealed just how badly the state's white men were divided and how fragile the political-economic basis for white supremacy had become. The Fifteenth Amendment made it difficult to disfranchise blacks without also threatening the suffrage of some whites, but Tillman insisted that he had a plan. Although economic and educational proxies for race would eliminate many black voters, an "understanding" clause would allow even illiterate white men to vote. This plan, Tillman said, would "save the suffrage of every white man who is worthy of a vote, while at the same time reducing the negro voters at least ½, possibly more." Tillman's use of the qualifier "worthy" to describe the white men whose votes would be preserved raised warning flags for many listeners. In the ideal world he envisioned, there would have been no overlap between black and white men along axes of wealth or education. But even after two decades of Redemption and five years of "reform" rule, race did not fully define men's social and economic status in South Carolina, and everyone knew it. Many white men hovered at the same margins of literacy and economic self-sufficiency as their black neighbors, and no one doubted that there were thousands of educated, property-owning black men whose right to vote might in principle be unaffected. Some understood Tillman's use of the word "worthy" as the logical culmination of his effort to define white manhood as a matter of political behavior as much as a matter of color or sex. The debates that followed explored the limits of white supremacy as a coherent program.[2]

However carefully Tillman sailed the white-supremacist ship of state, suffrage restriction proved to be dangerous cargo indeed. The unwieldy vessel groaned under the weight, ominously scraping the barely submerged shoals of protest from dissenting men and women, black and white. As opponents mobilized against the constitutional convention, the campaign of 1894 came closer to splitting the white electorate in two than had any previous conflict. White men who feared a Tillman-dominated convention combined with black voters; together, they gave an insurgent challenger for the governorship—a dissident Tillmanite—the largest vote of any non-Democrat since 1876, and they very nearly prevented the convention from taking place. The statewide referendum calling the convention passed, but only by a tiny and almost certainly fraudulent margin. When the convention finally met, members of this defeated opposition challenged Tillman's claim to be the champion of ordinary white men.

Tillman's growing national ambitions also shaped the new constitution. The hostile *Columbia State* noted in late 1895 that Tillman was "beginning to pose for the national eye." Indeed, Tillman not only sought to replace Matthew Butler in the U.S. Senate but also hoped to forge a new national coalition of white Southern and Western producers. He feared that if white South Carolinians did not appear to abide by national rules of electoral conduct, it would be difficult for them to "retain the sympathy of any class outside the State." The Republicans would then take control of the federal government, pass new election laws akin to the hated Lodge Bill, and "come here and wrest this government from you and you will be as helpless as babes." White-supremacist Democrats must take control of the state government, but they must do so carefully. Tillman explained, "[W]e are being watched from one end of this country to another. We are already twitted with proposing to perpetuate trickery and fraud and to strike down free American voters with our machinations and machinery. We have openly avowed one purpose to do certain things, but we cannot openly avow this purpose. . . . You invite attack from congress, from the supreme court of the United States and from all the enemies of South Carolina and all the enemies of the south and all the friends of the negroes."[3]

The convention itself bore out some of Tillman's anxieties. His fear of external scrutiny, along with divisions among white men, inevitably created openings through which members of the subordinated majority pressed their own claims to citizenship. Before and during the convention, black South Carolinians, white women, and white male dissidents used the debate over "worthiness" to demand a place in the polity. Failing that effort, they used the proceedings to expose the irresolvable contradictions within the racial, martial, and political meanings of "white supremacy." By the time the convention concluded its work, not only Tillman but also a host of his opponents had raised questions about race, gender, and citizenship that would continue to haunt the state, region, and nation. The defeat of Tillman's opponents demonstrated the weakness of their political position, but the debates they provoked revealed that Tillman's project had reached its own limits.

Fraud and the Boundaries of Democracy

Tillman's notion that men had to be "worthy of a vote" had wide currency in the late nineteenth century. In the words of the leading scholar of suffrage restriction, "[C]oncern about the proper extent of the electorate was so widespread in the late nineteenth century that virtually all articulate Southerners and many Northerners felt they had to relate their own political positions to a theory of the franchise." The *Charleston News and Courier* spoke for many conservative white men when it disparaged the postbellum era's "experiments in the science of universal suffrage" and argued that "to the extension of the suffrage is due more than to any other one cause the dangers which now threaten the existence of our present form of government." Most white men would doubtless have agreed with the paper's assertion that black men's "racial peculiarities . . . must continue always to exclude them from recognition as 'Americans' in any other than a forced, artificial, and narrow sense of the term, and from the enjoyment of the most valuable rights and privileges enjoyed by all other Americans." Tillman portrayed black voting as the essential barrier between South Carolina and "good government," and Wade Hampton agreed that black majority rule would bring "total and absolute ruin to the South, and infinite and irreparable loss to the whole country." Debates generally concerned not whether the suffrage ought to be restricted but how far and according to what principles. Republicans like Albion Tourgée and Robert Smalls, who supported universal male suffrage, belonged to a shrinking minority.[4]

To Tillman, the notion that all men were created equal had no legitimate place in discussions of the suffrage. "If you are going to bring the universal brotherhood of man as an argument here," he expostulated, "then are not the blacks as much entitled to that consideration as anybody?" As far as "perfect equality" was concerned, Tillman concluded, "the millennium has not yet come, and I am afraid it will not come in this day and generation, if ever." He knew better than to argue directly against the universal equality of white men, but he clearly believed that whiteness and maleness were not in themselves sufficient. Other wealthy white men agreed. One Charleston aristocrat confided to another that he believed "[u]niversal suffrage must prove a failure with an ordinary population of whites" and that "there are some *negroes* better fitted for the exercise of the rights of citizenship than are many whites who actually vote."[5]

Such men were not speaking entirely theoretically, for black men continued to play a variety of parts in the state's electoral politics. Interracial fusion arrangements flourished in the state's lowcountry. A few black men represented themselves as partisan allies of white Democrats, and some leading Democrats cultivated black informants who kept them posted regarding intraparty Republican rivalries. Even Tillman received declarations of support from a few black voters. But the tide of white sentiment within the party leadership ran against such cooperation. Even in Democratic primaries, where only a few stalwart black Hamptonites were technically entitled to vote, white Democrats threw out black men's ballots.[6]

Meanwhile, most black men continued to identify themselves as Republicans, and black power persisted in the lowcountry. Black majorities of three to one or more had fostered a vibrant although often fractious Republican Party, with as many as three factions of black and white leaders wrestling over offices. Some tried to keep the peace through fusion arrangements with local Democrats, whereas others rejected these alliances as unwarranted capitulations to the small Democratic minority. Beaufort and Georgetown Counties both practiced fusion politics during the 1880s and 1890s. Even in the counties where Red-shirt violence had done its worst, at least a few brave souls turned out for local and federal elections.[7]

Tillman and other Democrats continued to view the black electorate as a "frozen serpent," temporarily rendered impotent but capable of being "warmed into life" to "sting us whenever some more white rascals, native or foreign, come here and mobilize the ignorant blacks." But efforts formally to exclude black men from the national polity came to naught. In Washington, D.C., Butler championed proposals to repeal the Fifteenth Amendment and deport black Americans to another country. Such efforts, however, faced apparently intractable political, demographic, and economic obstacles. So even as the *Charleston News and Courier* denied that blacks could ever be "Americans," it felt obliged to promise that African Americans would "ever be accorded the fullest enjoyment of their political rights as 'citizens.' " A political culture of deception and double-talk was reaching full flower.[8]

Democrats quietly acknowledged that the work of disfranchisement had begun with the registration and eight-box laws of the early 1880s. Although formally neutral, these laws were administered in a discriminatory way. Tillman himself instructed a prospective registration official that "one of the chief requirements of a good supervisor of Registration is not to be particular about the law." But nervous white Democrats knew that these laws had not truly solved the problem of black political participation. Registration lists, for example, made no mention of the voter's race in order to protect officials from potential legal vulnerability. Ironically, this measure left Democrats ignorant of the actual extent of black Republican registration. Despite the policy's apparent success at reducing black participation, therefore, Democratic officials remained fearful and dissatisfied. "I am only surprised," one Democrat wrote the governor in 1886, "at the supineness of the Republican party, in not preparing for future ascendancy through this very Law."[9]

For their part, Republicans complained that these laws and practices made a mockery of democracy. During the 1880s, Democratic governors refused to appoint Republicans to election boards. The resulting system, Republican Party chairman Ellery M. Brayton declared in 1888, did more than political evil; it fostered "a false code of morals." "The despoiler of the ballot box does not hide his crime," Brayton complained, "for it constitutes a claim to preferment." Smalls, addressing a national audience from the pages of the *North American Review*, offered South Carolina's discriminatory laws and fraudulent administration of elections as arguments for passage of the Lodge Bill.[10]

A growing chorus of white Democrats also seemed uncomfortable with the persistence of fraud as a normal part of politics. A supervisor of registration complained that local politicians brought him lists of names to be registered in absentia; he was "willing to bend the law, but not break it like this," but he feared the governor would remove him from office if he refused. A Democratic legislator acknowledged that the presence of a black majority forced Democrats to turn to "wrong and pernicious" means in order to achieve crucial ends; "an era of violence, ballot-box stuffing and fraud . . . while it accomplished the purpose it was intended for, must ever be an era we must deplore."[11]

Some white Democrats believed the solution lay in fusion. In Georgetown and Beaufort, where black and white Republicans and Democrats divided offices, some came to see fusion as a practical, sustainable alternative to the fraud and force of the Red-shirt legacy. Beaufort Democrats referred openly to their coalition partners as "our Republican allies," and archconservative spokesmen such as Narciso Gonzales applauded fusion as an alternative to the distasteful "shotgun policy." "With the ten years' success of 'the Georgetown plan' before us," Gonzales's *Columbia State* declared, "we cannot admit that 'the Edgefield plan' was the only way out of the wilderness." The *State* condemned electoral fraud under any circumstances and explained that Tillmanites sought to "palliate, by associating them with the great victory, the frauds they have, for mere lust of office, been perpetrating upon white men in recent years and which they are planning for the future." Those who cavalierly defrauded or even shot black men, argued fusionists, had no real respect for democracy among white men.[12]

Tillman, whose goal was to "reduce and paralyze" the "remnant of the black cohorts" of Reconstruction, responded to fusion with hostility and impatience. As the 1892 election approached, he declared that he would prefer local defeats to the "trap," "foolishness," and "bad politics" of such arrangements. Nonetheless, leading Georgetown Democrat Walter Hazard sought Tillman's authorization for the usual compromise ticket, which would give Democrats the majority of the offices but require a bipartisan (and biracial) division of commissioners of election. As Tillman resisted, another lowcountry Democrat confirmed that "Democrats can't be elected to an office without keeping good faith with the compromise made with the Republicans." Tillman grew "tired and disgusted" with this "muddle," but he finally appointed black commissioners in order "to pacify them & prevent any independent ticket." Some opponents even charged that Tillman had made his own deal with Republican George W. Murray in order to defeat conservative Democrat William Elliott in the black district.[13]

But debates over fusion did not address the broader crisis in the state's electoral life. If the health of a democracy can be judged by its citizens' rates of participation, neither Redeemers nor reformers had done the state much good, for low turnout had marked South Carolina elections since the 1880s. In 1890, a Kansas newspaper noted critically that 79,000 South Carolina voters elected the same number of congressmen as 334,000 Kansans. By 1894, that charge was echoed by congressmen who placed South Carolina's total population of more than 1 million in awkward contrast with its turnout, which had shrunk to just 70,000. This was not simply a result of the obstacles facing Republicans, for low Democratic turnout began to trouble some local observers as well. In 1892, the *Charleston News and Courier* noted that Tillman's total vote in his 1890 victory had amounted to only one-third of the potential white electorate.[14]

One source of Democratic apathy was the party's own procedures. South Carolina's nomination and election processes had become elaborate, multistage contests favoring early organization over mass participation. Although Tillman had long claimed to champion popular rule, the machinations of convention nominations continued to serve him well. Facing a strong conservative challenge during his first term and in violation of the principles his faction had proposed in 1890, Tillman blocked efforts to call a direct primary in 1892. The call for a primary had been "designed to break up ring rule," the governor explained to white Alliancemen in 1892, and "it was never intended to take any advantage of the brave democrats of the negro counties." A direct primary, he said, would "destroy the political equilibrium of the State"—an equilibrium that, not incidentally, favored the incumbent governor. Tillman had learned that control over a convention's leadership and agenda could guarantee victory. As he acknowledged years later, in conventions "the moving force which dictates the platform and announces the temporary chairmanship sets the machinery in motion."

Having been that "moving force" on many occasions, Tillman knew how often South Carolina's white Democrats' choices had been shaped by organizational forces.[15]

The "machinery" could overwhelm all but the most committed partisans. South Carolina's tradition of Democratic Party discipline made the earliest contest the most important, for voters who participated in any factional or party contest were expected and often required to support the winner at the next stage. As a result, those who attended small, local meetings that took place months before the general election could in effect choose the Democratic nominee and thus the victor in November. The 1894 election, for example, included several "primaries" but hardly any broad-based democracy. In early August of that year, the leadership of Tillman's reform organization called for a "reform primary" to select delegates to a 16 August factional convention. Responding to this call, reform clubs in many counties met on 11 August and selected delegates to county reform conventions. Two days later, while these county assemblies selected delegates to the state reform convention, other counties elected delegates directly in reform primaries—club meetings run by local Tillmanite leaders. The delegates thus selected assembled on 16 August in Columbia, where they continued the tradition of 1890 and "suggested" John Gary Evans as the Democratic candidate for governor. In theory, their "suggested" candidate would be one of many to go before the people in the Democratic primary. Even the Democratic Party's so-called primary, though, was not a direct election. Rather, party members (many of them Tillmanites who had already "voted" for Evans) gathered to elect delegates to a statewide Democratic nominating convention, which also selected the party's nominees for county offices, the state legislature, and the U.S. House.[16]

In theory, Evans still had to run for the Democratic nomination in a statewide party primary on 28 August, but he entered that contest with the enormous head start of a reform endorsement. Reform voters who had taken part in the factional contest were expected to rally around Evans in the Democratic primary and convention, and thus the odds were strongly in his favor long before Democrats voted in their primary. The state's newspapers—even those not allied with Tillman—appeared to understand that a reform "suggestion" was equivalent to the Democratic nomination, almost as surely as that nomination would mean election in November. The day after the reform convention, the *Charleston News and Courier* ran a laudatory biography of Evans, apparently conceding the state election to a man who at that point had only been "suggested" by a party faction.[17]

Tillman's faction had perhaps done its work too well, and skeptical conservatives saw Tillman's reform movement becoming a "political machine." Just four years before, Tillman had complained that party leaders made Democrats "delegate our power to delegates who delegate somebody else, so that by the time they reach Columbia they are nothing but office-seeking politicians." Now the shoe was on the other foot. "Too much power and insatiable ambition coupled together will ruin any government," concluded one observer, who derided the 1894 primary as a "farcical election" without "moral binding force." Turnout in the delegate-selection election for the state Democratic convention totaled just 58,000, a sharp decline from the 88,000 people who cast votes in the 1892 party contest. The *Charleston News and Courier* asked, "[W]hat has become of one-third of Carolina's Democracy?" For his part, Tillman rejected the notion that a light vote in the primary invalidated its result, and he attempted to change the focus of the debate to the preservation of racial hierarchy. He accused his detractors of trying to set the stage for an appeal to black voters. If the primary had no "binding force," did this mean that Democratic voters were free to reject the nominee they had helped choose? He doggedly interpreted procedural objections as preludes to racial and party treason. Retreating to the safety of unassailable slogans, he declared that "[m]y Democracy means white supremacy."[18]

But to more than a few Democrats, Tillman's "Democracy" also smacked of "dictation." Even as the reform primary process unfolded, leading reformer and Allianceman J. William Stokes warned Evans that he feared a rebellion within party ranks unless voters were given another chance to choose among potential candidates. He suggested releasing reformers from their pledges and calling a primary election open to Democrats of all factions. Evans also received troubling news from Greenville, where a reform organizer reported that "a large element of the Reformers" were "dissatisfied with the Reform convention." He reported that the state Alliance secretary had, in a worrying turn of phrase, denounced him as "an 'exponent of Jno. Gary Evans' methods.' "[19]

The Democratic selection process did not directly affect the most significant choice facing voters in November: whether or not to call Tillman's proposed constitutional convention. Evans, like Tillman, supported the convention, but it was impossible to say with certainty how most white men would vote. Black voters, of course, were "bitterly opposed to you on account of the constitutional convention," one correspondent warned Evans, raising—for the third time in as many elections—the possibility of an alliance of interest between disgruntled black and white men.[20]

Democratic unity, strained badly along a multitude of personal and factional lines, did indeed fracture that summer. Tillmanite Sampson Pope, shrugging off the burdensome layers of factional, party, and state contest, withdrew his pledge to abide by the reform primary. At first, Pope declared his intention to enter the Democratic primary whether he was "suggested" or not. After losing the reform primary, however, he left the Democratic Party altogether and ran for governor as an independent. The low turnout in the early contests suggested widespread disaffection; just as important, those who had not voted in earlier contests could not be accused of violating a pledge or "bolting the party" if they now supported one white Democrat over another. Pope therefore asked the 40,000 reformers who had neglected to participate in the reform primary to abstain as well from the 28 August Democratic primary—which would leave them free to vote for Pope in his separate bid for the governorship.[21]

Pope's platform was a medley of familiar dissident tunes. In addition to opposing the constitutional convention as contrary to the interests of poor white men, he called for lower state salaries and a two-year suspension of foreclosures and collections, Garyite and Greenback refrains that Tillman had appropriated a decade before. But the key to Pope's appeal was his opposition to the convention, and he found an audience among voters reluctant to place their suffrage in Tillman's hands. In a "Warning to Poor Whites," one writer argued that a convention would disfranchise poor white men by establishing a high poll tax and an educational qualification. The state's few remaining would-be Populists could not prevent many reformers and Alliancemen from endorsing proconvention Democrats, but they drew support from those who still advocated more radical economic proposals and those who feared disfranchisement. Pope even gained the backing of the *Columbia State*, which attacked the convention on a variety of grounds, including its potential for disfranchising many white voters. But such support for Pope raised new suspicions. The *Cotton Plant*, initially skeptical of the convention, moved gradually toward it during the summer of 1894. By the time Pope received the *State*'s endorsement, the Alliance paper declared the fear of white disfranchisement to be a "political dodge" on the part of those who had always fought against the needs and rights of poor white men.[22]

Tillman won this fight, but only barely. In the gubernatorial election, Evans defeated Pope by the slimmest margin of any Democrat since Reconstruction, with Pope gaining about 30 percent of the vote. But even Democrats who would not support a bolter voted against the convention. Barely a quarter of the potential electorate turned out—38 percent of white men and 17 percent of black men, by one estimation. In total, only 60,000 votes were recorded in the referendum fight, and fewer than 57,000 in the gubernatorial race. In the official count, the convention achieved a majority of less than 2,000 votes statewide, and it seems certain that Democrats engineered its passage through fraud.[23]

Tillman had gone too far, some said, stealing an election from other white men in the name of white supremacy. Conservatives offered evidence of widespread fraud in the counting of independent and anticonvention ballots and proconvention ballot stuffing in the lowcountry. The *Greenville News* wrote bitterly that "[i]t is time to serve and enforce notice that white men are not going to allow their votes to be thrown out because they do not suit managers of election and that the people of this State intend to defend their rights." The *Columbia State* doubted "that the white men of South Carolina will submit to be stripped of their suffrages under the false plea that white supremacy demands it." The men making specific charges of fraud often lacked credibility, for they were known to be enemies of Tillman and the reform faction. The conservative Democratic minority continued to wage its battle against the election, with Butler carrying Pope's petition of protest to the U.S. Senate in early 1895, but Tillman's forces were moving to consolidate their narrow victory. In its postelection session, the state legislature passed a law calling for a new registration of voters before the selection of convention delegates. Butler and others challenged the constitutionality of this law as well, and Pope persuaded a U.S. judge to suspend the law and enjoin Governor Evans from holding the delegate-selection election for the convention.[24]

Republicans, who understood the stakes, seized this moment of crisis to offer aid to white opponents of the convention. Black congressman George Murray threatened a court fight against the 1894 registration law, declaring that "it was no easy job to take the negro's rights away from him if 'they acted as men.'" Fighting "lawfully, not unlawfully, . . . [w]e shall create such conditions that the United States is bound to take a hand." Heartened by the support given to qualified black voting by the *Columbia State* and other papers and by Pope and Butler's efforts against the new registration law, Murray claimed that "white men . . . know that the power used to disfranchise us now will be used hereafter to disfranchise them" and would not be fooled by Tillman's promises.[25]

Tillman's consolidation of the 1894 victory continued apace. Legal challenges to the election and the registration law were ultimately overturned at the circuit level, and the state legislature voted to retire Butler and send Tillman to the U.S. Senate in his place. Preparations began for the constitutional convention, which Tillman looked forward to as "a fitting capstone to the triumphal arch which the common people have erected to liberty, progress and Anglo-Saxon civilization since 1890." But this reconstruction of white supremacy was too important a matter to be placed directly in the apparently unreliable hands of white voters. Many reformers wanted a division of delegates among the Democratic factions before the actual election of delegates, thus avoiding a second bitter electoral battle so soon after the 1894 contest. Tillman told a *Columbia State* reporter that he would not be troubled by a substantial conservative presence at the convention, as long as conservatives subscribed to common principles of white supremacy. Those principles included qualified suffrage, no disfranchisement of white men, and—most telling—no submission of the new constitution to the voters; Tillman explained, "[T]he fight which we are seeking to avoid would be precipitated in such an event." In early 1895, a statewide conference of Democrats resolved to divide county delegations proportionately among the two factions and to secure "the supremacy of Anglo-Saxon civilization . . . by fair and constitutional methods." Conservatives ultimately got almost a third of the convention's seats.[26]

Some black Republicans believed that support for white conservative delegates offered the only possibility of retaining their voting rights. "[T]he Negro . . . must either fight or lamely submit," declared the *New South* in early 1895, as the delegate-selection elections approached. To fight in this case meant to vote for white proxies. "There are thousands of the best white people in South Carolina today who . . . would much prefer Negro rule to the rule of the present tyrannical oligarchy," the Beaufort paper explained; "[t]hose are the men who should be elected delegates." The paper denounced the "conspiracy against the purity of the ballot box" and warned that "[t]here are many more Negroes in South Carolina who are able to read and write and who are free-holders than the casual observer seems to imagine." As they had done in other moments of crisis, black ministers assembled in Columbia to organize against disfranchisement, urging black men to vote for candidates who promised "right and justice to all men." This limited meaning of the word "fight" reflected how restricted black Republicans' room for maneuver had become.[27]

Yet a merger of anti-Tillman forces seemed plausible to at least one white

Democrat. During the 1895 delegate-selection campaign, legislator and longtime Tillman foe John J. Dargan traveled throughout the state calling for the free exercise of black men's suffrage rights. In 1876, such white mavericks had been shot; in 1882, they had been beaten. By 1895, though, the suppression of such dissidents had become a well-ordered process. When Dargan appeared in Edgefield at the end of June, prominent Democrats, including the county sheriff and treasurer, informed him that although he might have the right to speak on universal suffrage, no one would be allowed to hear him. The *Edgefield Advertiser* declared that "Chamberlain was silenced here in seventy-six" and asked whether Dargan should be "entitled to higher consideration in ninety-five?" A Democratic crowd of fifty or more men howled Dargan down, and a "committee of safety" "escorted" him to the train station. The perpetrators justified their "horse-play" and "rough tongue-lashing" by claiming that Dargan's right to free speech did not extend to calling for black political participation since this would inevitably create "friction" between black and white.[28]

While this latter-day vigilance committee carried out its duties, Tillman remained a few miles away at his new plantation in Edgefield's Trenton neighborhood. He had moved to this new property and its attractive frame house shortly after his election to the Senate, and as Dargan was being "escorted" from town, he sat on his porch and gave an impromptu interview to a black visitor, Reverend Richard Carroll. Since 1890, Carroll had sought to become Tillman's intermediary to black South Carolinians. He imagined Tillman as another Hampton who might offer black South Carolinians "protection" and limited political rights within the Democratic Party. Tillman gave Carroll little encouragement. He spurned his invitation to address a conference of black leaders including Booker T. Washington, although Carroll promised to "manage" the meeting. Tillman also refused Carroll's subsequent invitation to speak at the 1908 Colored State Fair or even to send a letter that could be read to the audience. Carroll's persistence in the face of Tillman's refusal to cooperate was remarkable, but by the week before the fair, his frustration had begun to show. "[Y]ou should meet the colored people of your state once in your life," he pleaded vainly with his senator.[29]

Tillman had given Carroll a concise summary of his views on black citizenship on that day in 1895. As Carroll stood at the foot of the steps to the Trenton plantation house, the new senator looked down at him and declared Dargan "a fool." He informed Carroll that "the majority of [blacks] are ignorant and not fit to vote. They can be bought and sold like cattle, and will do whatever their bosses tell them." The Democrats "will carry this election even if all the angels in hell, the devil, all the niggers and Conservatives combine against us." Tillman's invective reflected white Democrats' continuing commitment to a political color line. Despite Democratic warnings that "the negroes . . . are working hard for Dargan," Dargan's campaign to elect antidisfranchisement delegates languished.[30]

In some areas, black political "work" did not mean courting Tillman or voting for men like Dargan. Lowcountry Republicans, accustomed to exercising their right to vote, reportedly responded to Democratic frauds in the delegate-selection elections by breaking up polling places and attempting to force election managers to destroy poll lists and returns. This kind of black Republican self-assertion dated back to the early years of Reconstruction, and it could still bring results. Beaufort elected a straight Republican slate of delegates to the convention, for with political rights themselves at stake, black Republicans were unwilling to fuse with white Democrats and instead exerted their full electoral weight. It turned out to be their last hurrah. In 1896, with new laws in place, Democrats took the county.[31]

At the other end of the state's political spectrum, Edgefield politics had become a white Democrat's game, and Tillman and five other white Democrats were dispatched to Columbia as convention delegates. Reporting results that surpassed even Tillman's impressive performance as an election manager in 1876, the *Edgefield Advertiser* boasted that "[n]ot a Republican vote was cast in the county, nor did a Republican offer to vote!" The generation of Republican challenge had passed and, with it, the days of Democratic mass mobilization.[32]

Education and Citizenship

When the delegates to the constitutional convention assembled in Columbia in late September 1895, all eyes focused on the committee on the suffrage, chaired by U.S. Senator Benjamin Ryan Tillman. The first question on delegates' minds was how to guarantee an electorate that would be "intelligent." Nearly every proposal for suffrage restriction included some form of literacy test, for nearly all agreed that "ignorant" men should not vote. As early as 1888, F. W. Dawson's *Charleston News and Courier* had suggested replacing the eight-box law with a formal, constitutional educational qualification. In the late 1880s, Hampton had described an educational qualification for the suffrage as uniquely fair and objective.[33]

Had Hampton been speaking in the late 1870s, a charitable listener might have been inclined to hear him out, for he had done more than most white men to support education for both black and white children. South

Tillman as a U.S. senator. Special Collections, Clemson University Libraries.

Carolina's first true public schools had emerged during Reconstruction, following the 1868 constitution's mandate for nondiscriminatory public education for children six to sixteen years old. Schools were funded by a dedicated tax of $1 on each citizen. Unlike the poll taxes of the late nineteenth and twentieth centuries, this was not intended as a means of restricting the suffrage; the 1868 constitution specifically forbade using nonpayment of this tax as cause for disfranchisement. School segregation was a fact of life in Hampton's South Carolina, but into the late 1870s, his government had provided roughly equal support for black and white schools and amended the constitution to levy an additional two-mill ($.002 on each dollar) property tax for education. But after the initial flush of Hamptonite paternalism, the allocation of school funds became intensely racially discriminatory. The same 1878 amendment that increased school funding also apportioned the new funds according to school attendance, not school-age population. Since poverty limited many black children's attendance, this sleight of hand channeled disproportionate funds to the white minority. By the mid-1890s, even the veneer of fairness had worn thin. Per-pupil expenditures for white students were hardly generous, but they exceeded annual expenditures for each black student (roughly $1) by a factor of four. Public education was separate, unequal, and inadequate.[34]

Blaming this inadequacy on its poorest victims, white Democrats often alleged that black children received much more in school funding than their parents paid in taxes. The *Charleston News and Courier* offered such arguments in urging the repeal of the two-mill school tax. Tillman suggested that taxpayers should be able to choose the school to which their tax money went, adding caustically that any white men who wanted to subsidize black education would be free to do so. Some white Alliancemen even demanded a constitutional convention for the specific purpose of allocating school funds by race. Evans, in his opening address at the convention, suggested separating white and black school revenues. This, he thought, would bolster white men's support for the public school system since "the great mass of people never complain of taxation for education when they know they derive the direct benefit."[35]

But the search for explanations for education's sorry state sometimes revealed deep cultural grievances among white men. As early as 1882, one self-proclaimed expert offered an elite urban audience one explanation: the "common people," "the 'poor white trash,' " had been "perfectly contented so long as [they] maintained a questionable superiority over the negro, and so long as nature afforded [them] a means of subsistence without toil, without money, and without price." White voices calling for better schools from the benighted countryside reciprocated this hostility. In 1889, an Edgefield editorial demanded a five-month school term across the state, blaming not "poor white trash" but aristocratic villains for impeding such improvements. If public schools had failed to "reach the masses and educate [them] for the duties and responsibilities of citizenship," the responsibility lay with "militia Colonels, oily lawyers, and gentlemen with abnormally developed craniums from Charleston and Columbia."[36]

Tillman had long claimed that education was a top priority of the reform movement. He continued to champion Clemson: during his first summer as governor, he had laid the new school's cornerstone, and his eldest son, B. R., joined the college's first class, graduating in 1896. When the college faced attack at the constitutional convention, Tillman declared, "I will stand by that college if nobody else does." For the rest of his life, he remained deeply involved in Clemson, and not only as a life member of the board of trustees. He concerned himself with the details of construction and hiring practices, and he sometimes seemed to consider himself more superintendent than trustee, lecturing the college's president about such matters as the characteristics of hedge lemon seed and warning him of the worrisome disposition of a particular foreman to "slouch over and do with makeshifts." Although he sometimes fretted about the state of things at Clemson, he considered the school "a fitting monument to myself." This intense identification persisted throughout his life. From his sickbed during the 1910s, he begged President Walter M. Riggs to "write me a long letter and tell me all about the college and its affairs."[37]

But Tillman envisioned Clemson as only the capstone of a system of education for white South Carolinians. He had little patience with those among his allies who saw public primary and secondary schools as unnecessary luxuries, and he continuously bullied voters about school spending. "Let us educate our children," he declared to a crowd at a county fair. "[W]e spend about sixty cents per capita, and there are a great many of you who have spent more than that in whiskey and tobacco since you have been here, and yet you are not willing to go down in your pockets for better schools." He repeatedly called for a $3 poll tax that would simultaneously provide much-needed revenue for education and "make the negroes pay."[38]

The interconnected politics of a poll tax for school funding and the educational qualification to vote brought charges and countercharges. Opponents of the convention repeatedly warned that it would pass such a tax, enact a literacy test, and then sit back as the public schools became too costly to maintain and many white men, unable to read and write, lost their right to vote. The *Charleston News and Courier* in particular warned "country voters" of the dangers of an educational qualification. But Tillmanite and Alliance supporters of the convention regarded such advocacy with suspicion. "[T]hose who claim to fear for the public schools are the folks who always opposed them," declared the *Cotton Plant* as the 1894 election approached; "[t]he cry, 'disfranchisement of the poor white man,' is all a political dodge." But some reformers seemed of two minds. In a convention speech, reformer Henry Burn offered a litany of complaints about the wrongs done to "the laboring white man" that tied school funding to a host of other grievances. Speaking on behalf of the hard-pressed white producer, Burn contrasted demands for white political solidarity with insistence on economic self-reliance. "His vote is relied upon to keep the negro down," Burn argued, "and yet when he asks for work there is none for him, while he sees negroes employed in his stead. When school topics are discussed he is told that it is wrong to take A's money and use it to educate the children of B; and yet it is right to put a musket in the hand of B and, by order of the State, compel him to defend with his life the property of A." If the military responsibility for white supremacy required democratic redistribution, then why should poor men not expect something in return? To Burn, the crowning injustice would be the disfranchisement of such white producers by qualifications that allowed some of those employed "negroes" to vote. "Is it to be that property-owning negroes, educated negroes, can hobnob around politically and educationally with such classes of white men," he demanded, "while 13000 illiterate white men, as good and better, must stand aside, without even a vote to defend their lives?"[39]

Tillman might have sometimes sounded like Burn's ally, but his advocacy of education for poor white men betrayed a deep ambivalence about such men's fitness for citizenship. In the constitutional convention, Tillman offered a plan to rationalize the boundaries of the state's school districts so as to ensure that every white child could reach a classroom. After being informed that some of the existing district lines were irregular because school boosters had been unable to persuade "outlying districts" to join in levying new school taxes, Tillman minced no words. He relied on centralized authority and his own superior understanding of poor white men's true needs. "We'll fix it so that they will have to agree," he explained. "Let us levy the taxes here," in the convention, "and not leave it to any ignoramus or set of ignoramuses who want to breed up ignoramuses." Here Tillman spoke as the contemptuous leader of a wise elite, doing for an ignorant populace what they did not have the sense to do for themselves. The slap at country voters—perhaps the same neighbors Tillman had once described as "utterly & hopelessly stupid"—was echoed a few minutes later by his suggestion that "the outlying country" be made liable for its proportion of school bonds. As the convention concluded its work on the public school system, Tillman insisted that the school tax should be added to the constitution and not left up to the legislature to set. "Statesmen should rise and grasp a duty and send these ignorant boys to school," he said. "I wanted to levy a poll tax of $3. I have been all around through the country and I bamboozled the boys somehow, because all of them voted for me, or nearly all of them, and I wanted to offer the $3 poll tax and I believe I can justify it before the people today." Others present agreed, urging higher levies and larger poll taxes to build up "decent schools" that would foster "wide-awake citizenship" among the farmers and "country people." In the end, Tillman believed he knew what was best for poor white men.[40]

The other danger Burn had noted—black education—was even more troubling. Although Democratic rule ensured inferior education for blacks, it did not eliminate black education entirely. Tillman and many others knew that any formal restriction of black access to public education would bring both local resistance and a Northern outcry and that significant improvements in education for whites could not come entirely at the expense of education for blacks. But black education posed a clear and present danger to white supremacy. As black South Carolinians continued to send their children to school and the overall rate of illiteracy among blacks dropped from nearly 80 percent in 1880 to just over 50 percent in 1900, a rising note of concern appeared in Democratic discourse. Tillman did not "see the good" of educating black children. He declared at an 1886 meeting that "when you educate a negro you educate a candidate for the penitentiary or spoil a good field hand." An editorialist worried that black men were being "educate[d] away from work," becoming urban "swells." But the primary threat was electoral. As early as 1889, one of the state's conservative congressmen had suggested that the state's provision for public schools might give black South Carolinians "an opportunity to take advantage of the school houses, get educations and outvote us." Evans, aware of this trend, told the General Assembly in his 1894 inaugural address that as far as black education was concerned, the state's white Democratic leadership had "performed our duty to the negro possibly too liberally."[41]

Education was not entirely a local matter. Northern philanthropists supported a good deal of black education in the South. Local activists, civic and religious leaders, and a few die-hard missionaries carried on the work of the postemancipation freedom schools. At times, the federal government also became involved. In 1889 and 1890, Southern Democrats anxiously followed the legislative maneuvering over the Blair Federal Education Bill, which would have vastly increased the money available for public education but would also have mandated equal expenditures for white and black children. Although some welcomed the potential infusion of federal dollars, many white Democrats attacked the bill as unwarranted federal interference in local affairs. The *Charleston News and Courier* mocked white supporters of the bill as naive and threatened retaliation if it passed. Arguing that whites provided 90 percent of school revenues and therefore subsidized black public schools, the paper declared that "if it be determined by Congress to fasten a Federal system of education upon the states of the south, the repeal of the two mill tax is inevitable." In other words, they would give up on public education altogether before they would accept any measure of federal oversight. The paper "rejoiced" at the Blair Bill's defeat in the U.S. Senate in 1890. Other federal efforts brought the same warning. If the Lodge Bill had passed, the Charleston paper threatened in 1891, it would have been necessary to cut off support for black education in the state.[42]

Although separate and unequal schools did not come under sustained and successful legal attack for another half-century, the federal government did occasionally try to set limits on discriminatory school funding. Federal land-grant legislation provided substantial aid to state agricultural colleges, aid that was supposed to be divided equitably between white and black institutions—in South Carolina's case, between Clemson and Claflin. Claflin College, which provided industrial education to black men, had been established as part of the state university system in 1872 and received nominal appropriations during the 1880s. By the mid-1890s, it had become essentially an agricultural annex of Claflin University, a private Methodist institution with which it shared faculty and facilities. Still, many reformers believed that Claflin's very existence undermined white supremacy. During the 1890 campaign, Tillman's running mate Eugene Gary pronounced Claflin a threat to white wage earners: its graduates, he said, earned $3–4 a day, wages that ought to go to skilled "white boys." In the 1889 General Assembly, Evans took a page from Tillman's book of symbolic politics and moved to strike out the appropriation for Claflin. The effort failed by a wide margin but earned the praise of the *Edgefield Chronicle*, which explained that educating black people made them "pestiferous."[43]

When the new federal Morrill Act made money available for agricultural colleges in the early 1890s, Tillman proved willing to sacrifice white education to prevent blacks from achieving even a purely symbolic form of "equality." Interior Secretary J. W. Noble explained to Tillman that under the terms of the act, he was to make an "equal division" of federal resources between Clemson and Claflin and that this meant a division proportional to the state's school-age population of whites and blacks. Claflin was therefore entitled to about two-thirds of South Carolina's Morrill Act money. Tillman rejected this attempt to "dictate" the terms of the division, denying that the federal government (perhaps especially under a Republican president) had the right to "determine that Equal is not Equitable and Just in the case of South Carolina." As an Interior Department official pointed out to Tillman, South Carolina's unusual racial demographics did not constitute grounds for special treatment. If "equal" meant "half," most states would spend as much money educating black minorities as they did educating white majorities. Tillman refused to accept this argument. Since Claflin survived primarily on federal aid and philanthropic donations, Tillman's refusal was potentially crippling to public higher education for blacks in the state. Claflin president L. M. Dunton, a white minister, sought to persuade Tillman or the federal authorities to relent. Dunton appealed to Tillman the agrarian reformer, stressing that blacks "must continue to be the practical farmer[s] of the State and of the South" and that education made blacks more law-abiding.[44]

Tillman played the issue for all it was worth before white audiences. "Before I would accept that money and give two-thirds of it to the negroes I will let it stay in the treasury," he defiantly pronounced during the dark days of the subtreasury crisis in 1892. Tillman's assault on Claflin attracted attention from outside the state as well. In an open letter to Tillman during the constitutional convention, Booker T. Washington implored him not to do anything to injure the cause of black education. Like Dunton, Washington argued that ignorance bred poverty and crime. He also suggested that even if Tillman cut off all state money to black education, money would flow in from other regions and other countries and "keep the light of the schoolhouses burning on every hill and in every valley in South Carolina." White South Carolinians, Washington offered, might prefer that black South Carolinians "feel grateful" to their own neighbors for funding their educations "rather than to outside parties wholly." Tillman was not persuaded by such appeals on behalf of black education. In a letter to Dunton, he professed to be "sorry that your school will be crippled," but he brushed all arguments aside. Noble refused to turn over the money on Tillman's terms until South

Carolina's federal representatives — chiefly George Tillman — engineered passage of a bill specifically requiring him to do so.[45]

To the end of his life, Tillman expressed a deep fear of black education. "[I]t is foolish to my mind to disfranchise the negro on account of illiteracy," he wrote an upcountry newspaper in 1913, "and turn right around and compel him to become literate." This lament became a constant refrain of Tillman's lectures, articles, and Senate speeches after 1895. He complained that the Fourteenth and Fifteenth Amendments had "handcuffed" white Southerners — "the Southern people," as he called them — to "the dead carcass of slavery." The only solution, Tillman argued, was to go to the heart of the problem, the federal constitution. Repeal the Fifteenth Amendment and all would be well. Each state should have "the right to say who shall vote in its borders." This was the "natural remedy" to the race problem, and Tillman hoped white men would have "the nerve and the courage" to acknowledge it. Northerners were free to continue experimenting with black suffrage, but white Southerners would prefer to discard their patchwork of suffrage limitations for a more comfortable garment of constitutional white supremacy. "[W]e have made this mistake of enfranchising a race, slaves last week, barbarians three generations ago," Tillman explained. "If it was a mistake, why not say so? And why not retrace our steps?"[46]

Tillman's prognosis for the South if the Fifteenth Amendment was not repealed was grim: "[S]o far from South Carolina being out of the woods . . . the most dreadful crisis which we will have to confront is still ahead rather than behind." In 1911, Tillman was still dreading that future. "I expect to continue the agitation in favor of white supremacy and of making this in law what it is now in fact, a white man's country as far as the South goes. We know how we have kept it a white man's country and the Northern people know how we keep it so." But this determination might not be enough, as more and more black children learned to read and blacks even accumulated property. "Every sensible man in the South who thinks at all must realize," Tillman warned, "that the present anomalous conditions continued must result disastrously for the Southern people. It is only by agitation and discussion that we can hope to create a public sentiment that will bring the necessary changes in our Constitution."[47]

The writing was on the wall — or, more precisely, on the chalkboard: black children outnumbered white children in the state's public schools. If literacy alone stood between those boys and suffrage, then white supremacy would soon collapse, first at the registration office, then at the polls, and quickly transform into the dreaded "social equality." The disease of equality must be denied its pedagogical vectors: black education must be strictly limited, and Northern philanthropists must be made to understand the catastrophe they were inviting. These "fanatics" funded black schools and colleges throughout the South, including Benedict and Allen Universities just a few miles from the South Carolina statehouse. Their purpose was to create literate black adults; sooner or later, the result would be a substantial, educated, property-owning black voting bloc. Renegade (that is, Republican or Populist) white men, perhaps working as the agents of national corporations, would then mobilize that bloc "to participate in the elections and control them." Tillman lambasted those who had encouraged black education and black voting, from Hampton on down, as "the biggest fools alive." Those who were aware of black educational progress but still considered the race problem "settled" were guilty of "besotted ignorance"; those who sought to make black education compulsory were simply "criminal."[48]

Unless the Fifteenth Amendment was repealed, Tillman argued, the nation's sectional divide would persist. The Civil War had settled the question of slavery and nationhood, but the federal government's insistence on enforcing and even extending the Reconstruction amendments left the sword of racial equality hanging over the South. As long as Republicans proposed measures such as the Lodge Bill, the Blair Bill, and the "equal" distribution of federal school funds, white Southerners would have "no conception of the word 'nation' except that it is connected with the word 'nigger.' " Although Tillman did not succeed in convincing his fellow legislators to overturn the Fifteenth Amendment, he accomplished something almost as significant. Tillman's argument against the Fifteenth Amendment reformulated the early-nineteenth-century Southern doctrines of nullification and interposition and solidified the foundation for the twentieth-century language of states' rights. Vilifying federal power as wholly devoted to the cause of black uplift at any cost, Tillman helped shape the language that would echo throughout the twentieth-century nation. His analysis nourished a nascent political culture in which, to paraphrase his own lament, white men used the words "states' rights" as a synonym for "white supremacy."[49]

The rhetoric of "intelligence" and "ignorance" offered some black leaders an opportunity to claim the common ground of citizenship that Henry Burn had feared. In the mid-1880s, D. Augustus Straker, the last black South Carolinian to run for statewide office until the mid-twentieth century, had imagined a South in which equal education drew black and white citizens ever "closer together" in their common fight against "the powers of capital." In 1889, African Methodist Episcopal bishop Benjamin William Arnett took a less ambitious tack, telling a black college audience that "the time is on its way, when the general rule will obtain in this country, that the man of lawful age who cannot read his ballot cannot vote for his fellow man." Unlike Tillman, though, people like Arnett wanted to see all black men both educated and enfranchised. For him and others, the principle of suffrage limitation offered an opportunity for black Americans to demonstrate their capacities on a level playing field.[50]

This vision of equal opportunity proved elusive. By 1895, their idealism curdled by persistent fraud and violence, the six black delegates to the constitutional convention understood that their only hope to shape the new document lay in making use of the rhetorical openings their opponents provided. Black delegates questioned the implicit equation of ignorance with blackness. William Whipper, who had been demanding suffrage rights for almost half a century, conceded that "the negro was unprepared for the ballot when he got it" but asserted that "[t]he white man was equally unfit. One class had been ignorant, the others had been taught to believe the negro the basis of property." Smalls told the white delegates that he was even "willing to accept a scheme that provides that no man who cannot read nor write can vote, if you dare pass it." James Wigg, accepting the principle of an educational or property qualification, suggested that discriminatory laws would lead to "white supremacy with white degradation"; explaining that "the negro does not stand for the rule of ignorance over intelligence, nor of poverty over wealth," he insisted on "the supremacy of law" as well as "of intelligence and property." His proposals were tabled without discussion. When Mary Miller compiled these men's speeches for publication after the convention, she wrote approvingly that their suffrage plans would have "eliminated the ignorant vote, but . . . secured a fair and honest election."[51]

Miller's husband, black Beaufort convention delegate, state representative, and former U.S. congressman Thomas E. Miller, offered a bolder and potentially inflammatory alternative. Like Straker, Miller imagined a coalition of those who feared turning over their government to "the wealthy, to the managers of corporate rights, to the goldbugs, to the whiskey trust." Miller offered a history lesson in which "the common people," European men and women, having been reduced to "white slaves," rose up in justified revolution against their aristocratic oppressors and sought a new life in the New World. Although Miller acknowledged that Africans had been brought to America in chains, he cast the nation's history as a tale of united striving: "Hand in hand, with a united effort, the white man and the black man reclaimed the country and made it the asylum of the oppressed from every clime." In a particularly bold and heterodox conclusion, he presented the Civil War as "the struggle of the common people against the slave-holding class." But Miller's optimistic reimagining of American history was balanced by his attack on the state of "white civilization." In a discussion of public education, Miller applauded any step that would "prevent our white people from remaining isolated and away off in the backwoods. . . . They will be educated by coming into contact with each other. The white people need this education more than any other people in the world. . . . On account of their isolated life, they have remained a lawless people, having little regard for law and order, and at all times ready to take the laws into their own hands."[52]

Property, Virtue, and Independence

Under Tillman's plan, men who could not demonstrate literacy could vote if they owned at least $300 in taxable property. Tillman claimed to represent the interests of ordinary white farmers, and his imagined antebellum arcadia was a Jeffersonian realm of independent proprietorship in which "the land-owning farmers were the salt of the earth, and called no man master." But although the property qualification (like the literacy test) was intended to catch white men while letting black men fall, it too was self-evidently imperfect as a racial filter. By 1900, the U.S. Census found that 40 percent of white and 77 percent of black farm operators in South Carolina were tenants of some kind, figures that did not even include the many of both races counted as "laborers." This persistent white landlessness, along with the growth of the cotton mill economy during the 1890s, threatened the white farm household, the essential building block of Tillman's white republic.[53]

Wealthy Democrats might declare their devotion to poor white men, but Tillmanites and conservatives alike tended to see propertied men as more fit for citizenship. Evans declared matter-of-factly that "the tenant or renter, having no home to love, no castle to defend, no sacred ties to bind him, no vine or fig tree to watch to maturity, cannot nurture patriotism." Tillman thought that a property qualification made intuitive sense. "[T]he very fact that [a man] has a few dollars is a sufficient reason of itself to show that he is probably a better citizen," he explained. Besides, he argued, to deny the suffrage to those who paid taxes—even if they were illiterate—would be "repugnant to American liberty." But the very notion of a property qualification put Tillman in a difficult political position, and he beat a hasty retreat to the high ground of the greater good. He readily "granted" the "perfect equality of white men," from the poor laboring tenant "to the highest man in the state," but he rejected the notion that this equality could stand in the way of ensuring "good government." In an ideal world, no white man's right to vote would be jeopardized, just as no black man's right would be secured, but this was not (he reminded his constituents) an ideal world. The greater good demanded a secure white majority.[54]

Some Democratic members raised the obvious objection that "the poorer a man is the more helpless he is, the more need there is for him to be secure in the protection of his life and property. All that he has in this world is his vote." Tillman found such idealism pointless and even irritating. Some delegates, he complained, believed that "the poor white men must be protected at any and every cost." He himself had "tried to do more" for poor white men than anyone, he insisted. And although his artful combination of tactics would disfranchise a certain number of white men, the proposals of some conservative delegates made Tillman seem relatively sensitive to poor white men's political demands. The conservative minority weighed in over and over with proposals granting or extending the franchise on the basis of wealth. South Carolina had long been governed by a combination of white population and white wealth, and once again, in 1895, some sought to write wealth back into the law. Proposals for property qualifications abounded, some much higher than Tillman's $300, and many included an educational test not as an alternative route to the suffrage but as an additional barrier to it.[55]

If the principle of white landownership was controversial, that of black dependence was not. Black men were never supposed to head fully independent households, and Tillman explicitly denied them the state aid to which he thought poor white men were entitled. This distinction became clear at a moment of economic crisis. A great storm struck South Carolina in August 1893, laying waste to a vast coastal region and leaving most of its population destitute until the following year's growing season. Although Tillman sought to get aid for the white planters whose property had been damaged or ruined by the storm, he insisted that black laborers work for their supplies, for they "cannot be treated as we would treat white people." The correspondence pouring into his office from white allies in Georgetown and Beaufort caught the tune and echoed it in endless, simple variation: "I know great harm will result from giving rations free"; "[E]very precaution has been taken to prevent the abuse of charity." Ordained to occupy different positions in the social and economic order, black and white people could expect dramatically different treatment at the hands of the white-supremacist state.[56]

To protect white men's self-sufficiency, Tillman advocated a strong and unconditional homestead exemption law protecting a certain amount of real and personal property from seizure by creditors. J. William Thurmond of Edgefield, Tillman's lawyer (and soon to be Strom Thurmond's father), wrote that the state's existing homestead exemption law should be preserved in the new constitution. The "manliness, independence and bravery" that he cherished would not survive if the law allowed moneylenders to seize a family's home. Lawmakers, he said, had a duty to protect "orphans, widows and helpless families"; if they chose instead to enrich "the capitalist," society as they knew it could not long survive. Tillman agreed that manliness demanded the protection of white men's dependents against the corrosive forces of capital, but he went much further than Thurmond in asserting an explicitly paternal role for state government. He believed that "capitalists" did not destroy homesteads all by themselves but seduced men into debt through emasculating vices such as liquor and credit. It was the responsibility of the state to step in and ensure that white men did not gamble away, drink up, or mortgage their freeholds. In part, this meant making the homestead exemption inalienable. If an unworthy husband could mortgage his homestead, he might leave a good woman destitute. To those who claimed that poor men could not get credit without signing away their homestead rights, Tillman echoed his argument against the crop lien: "[T]he thrifty man does not need credit." Mortgages must not be allowed to infringe on the homestead exemption, for the essential basis of the white republic had to survive. "A house and a few acres of land," he insisted, "must be saved for the family." Homestead exemptions protected households against the corruption of the financial system in the same way that the dispensary protected them against the moral corruption of the barroom and liquor trust. In both cases, a wise leader would create structures that defended "the mothers and children of the State against the worthless and indifferent and drunken husbands." Many shiftless white men, it seemed, would do better to trust in the protective enactments of a paternalistic state government than to rely on their own ability to manage credit and debt.[57]

Understanding "Understanding"

Given Tillman's skepticism about white men's abilities to act in their own long-term interests, it was no surprise that many voters doubted his promise to preserve the suffrage of landless white illiterates through an "understanding clause." The suffrage plan his committee finally presented to the convention called for purging the voting rolls and starting a new registration limited to adult men who paid taxes on at least $300 worth of property or could read and write any section of the constitution to the satisfaction of a registration official. Until 1898, men would be able to register (albeit on a separate list) if they could satisfactorily "understand" a section chosen by the registrar. After that, the normal provisions would apply—and in fact, anyone who did not register almost as soon as he became eligible would have few future opportunities to do so. It was a highly restrictive system with a specific end in mind. The education and property qualifications would take in most white men but relatively few black men, Tillman argued, and the "understanding" clause would act as a safety net for poor white illiterates. A Democratic election official could continue to register his friends, neighbors, and relations, all good white Democrats who therefore "understood" the constitution. But the great majority of blacks—who did not pay taxes on $300 worth of property and who would not have been able to read, write, or "understand" to the satisfaction of that same official—would slip from the registration books and become forever irrelevant to state politics. Tillman had tried to do his best to safeguard the property and further the education of white men, but the understanding clause was essential. Without it, Tillman admitted, he could not hope to keep his promise to protect white men's suffrage or to lead the state's voters out of the "bog and mire that we have been wallowing in for the last 20 years."[58]

Of course, the understanding clause constituted its own form of "mire," a reality Tillman was willing to acknowledge in all but the most explicit language. When Richard Carroll pressed him on the question of impartial administration, noting that "making laws and enforcing them after they are made is another thing," Tillman did not reply. But at the convention, Tillman acknowledged that the understanding clause both relied on a measure of fraud and placed the rights of the citizen in the hands of a single official. Fraud might be poisonous to democracy, but Tillman archly asserted that "some poisons in small doses are very salutary and valuable medicines." However "nauseous" this particular medicine might seem, Tillman only "swallow[ed] enough of it to preserve the rights of the poor [white] man." Only by this homeopathic theory of justice did his subsequent case for the clause's legality make sense: a registration official, charged with determining whether or not a prospective voter understood the section read to him, would be "responsible to his conscience and his God [and] to nobody else." Therefore, any unfairness was a matter for the official and his maker and no business of the constitution makers—it might easily be a question of "just simply showing partiality, perhaps, or discriminating." This final knowing pun drew appreciative laughter from many in the convention hall.[59]

More often, apologists for this imperfect measure portrayed it as unwelcome but necessary. Upcountry editor A. B. Williams of the *Greenville News* explained in sober terms the hard logic of the understanding clause, fraudulent administration and all. "Some good men believe and say they would rather take their chances and fight the negroes man to man at the polls every two or four years, if necessary, than to put fraud into the Constitution," he wrote. But fraud was hardly the greater of the two evils. Such men, Williams continued, "forget that it is as much violation of law and just as demoralizing to kill and bulldoze people as it is to swindle them."[60]

Sometimes the discussion of the understanding clause made even Tillman nervous. One delegate saw in the understanding clause "the opportunity and possibility of fraud" but "no necessity for fraud" and thus nothing unconstitutional. "My 'understanding' is that this will disfranchise every negro," he joked. Another delegate remarked that "we know that it is the purpose of the proposers of this bill that it shall not be impartially administered." Tillman, mindful of outside reaction, found this "a great deal to say" and, on reflection, "more than any man ought to say." But the speaker did not take the hint. "This is no time for mincing words," he declared in the defiant style Tillman had championed. "The danger that we are in is too great for circumlocution" and "if [the law] is to be enforced honestly I could not vote for it."[61]

Black delegates expressed outrage at these blatant endorsements of fraud. Thomas Miller presented a petition of protest. Smalls pointed out that the proposed qualification was ludicrous: "How can you expect an ordinary man to 'understand and explain' any section of the Constitution, to correspond to the interpretation put upon it by the manager of election, when by a very recent decision of supreme court . . . two of them put one construction upon a section, and the other justice put an entirely different construction upon it." Like the other black delegates, these men spoke earnestly on the rights of suffrage and sought to retain the 1868 constitution's assumption of male voting rights, but their democratic arguments were swept aside by the Democratic majority.[62]

Some white conservatives argued that the codification of fraud—"mere lying devices to enable qualified voters of one color to be disfranchised and a race to which we have pledged protection to be basely swindled"—represented Tillman's general disregard for suffrage rights. They decried the injustice the disfranchisers intended to commit against qualified black voters. "Those who are to administer the law are to administer it unfairly and fraudulently," complained the *Columbia State*; "that is the admitted meaning of the scheme." Gonzales argued that Tillman had made "the negro" into a bogeyman more powerful than any group of real human beings. "It is really strange," agreed a Lexington politician, "that an intelligent community, from fear of negro domination, can run to the other extreme and rob themselves" of political privileges. "Altogether," he concluded, "our 'Reform' friends seem to consider Cuffee an indispensable scarecrow." These white men decried a political order in which "[i]t is necessary to hold the negro down to ensure white supremacy, and it is necessary to hold the whites down to ensure white supremacy."[63]

Butler had made similar arguments during the 1894 Senate campaign. The incumbent, fighting for his political life, declared that the Tillmanites' dictatorial and corrupt ways had fractured white men's social and political relations. White supremacy, he shouted, protesting the convention, the dispensary raids, and the indignities inherent in running against Tillman, "does not mean ring rule and disfranchisement of white tax-paying voters" or "[t]he destruction under the forms of law of their rights and liberties and property!" But Butler took another step. He added, "These wrongs do not acquire sanctity because the perpetrators have white skin." Although he reaffirmed his devotion to white supremacy, he repeated the charge: "[I]f we are to be robbed and plundered as we are now, I do not know that the color of the skin of the robber makes it more bearable." Another Edgefield voice warned voters not to take the rhetoric of white supremacy so seriously that they did themselves harm: "Do not for the sake of a mythical white unity, a unity that cannot from the nature of the case exist, go with a majority that is more completely under the thumb of bosses than the negroes ever were in the days of Radicalism."[64]

Such critics were only echoing distinctions that Tillman had already established. It had of course always been the case that the reconstruction of white supremacy required that certain whites be held down. As many observers had by now discerned, "blackness" had long been nearly as much a political identity as a racial category, and white men could lose their claim to be "worthy of a vote" in any number of ways. Support for qualified suffrage was, according to a letter in the *Edgefield Advertiser*, a way to "put the negro vote out of the way" of "low, unscrupulous demagogues, or 'White Niggers.'" Many Tillmanites argued that Haskellites and even fusionists "should be delt [*sic*] with as if they were *Black*." That is, they should be summarily disfranchised. Tillman himself argued that white men could prove themselves unfit for the privilege of voting, telling a Charlestonian that "many of your people are unworthy to have a 'free vote' & 'fair count' not because they voted against me but because they did not vote at all, & those who did were manipulated or bought." Fools, tools, and fusionists all merited the same derision and disqualification. A decade later, after Beaufort had come under white Democratic control, Tillman continued to define race in terms of political behavior. Referring to the now-defeated fusion officeholders, he noted that "[t]hey had some people of white skin, but I . . . consider that a man with a white skin who consorts with negroes, hugs and kisses them to get votes, is not a genuine white man."[65]

Not every reformer agreed that this fraudulent understanding clause should be written into the constitution. J. L. M. Irby, now thoroughly alienated from his reform compatriots, believed that the disfranchisement proposal discriminated against poor white men. Pointing out that the understanding clause had not yet undergone federal judicial scrutiny, he declared that it was wrong to "build bomb proofs and fortifications for the educated and property owning class" while leaving the "poor white man to risk and endure the tests of a hostile court." Further, the understanding clause would make poor white men "dependent on the grace and favor of supervisors who may be hostile to them from personal reasons, or in the course of local politics may desire their disfranchisement." The *Columbia State* agreed, arguing that a Tillmanite suffrage plan would lead to "the rule of one man through agents of his own choosing, responsible not to the people, but to him . . . putting the suffrages of all South Carolinians at the mercy of the executive." Irby thought the special list for those registered under the understanding clause particularly insulting. He invoked the thousands of boys now nineteen or younger "whose parents are too poor to give them an education or endow them with $300 worth of property." The 1 January 1898 deadline for registration under the understanding clause would, he said, forever deny them the right to vote. "In two years' time you can't educate every white youth in South Carolina both to read and write," he explained, "for the impoverished conditions of thousands of poor white farmers and laborers will not permit them to spare the time for their sons to go to school." As a result, this class of young men "will have no more voice in the government of this State than the mule that they plow or dumb cattle that tread our highways." Worse, they would have less voice than "educated or property-owning negroes, living in our towns or cities," who would "mak[e] laws for those poor white men to live under."[66]

Women and Suffrage

One alternative to the humbug of "understanding" was to overwhelm the black majority with an untapped pool of potentially qualified white voters: the state's white women. Although women's suffrage activism in South Carolina had begun with Reconstruction Republicans, white Democratic women in the state and throughout the region mobilized to take advantage of the disfranchisement movements of the 1890s. Attempts to minimize the number of black voters would inevitably strip many white men of the suffrage, they argued, but extending the franchise to literate or propertied women would provide disproportionate benefits to the forces of white supremacy while swelling the ranks of black voters hardly at all. South Carolina's proponents of suffrage for white women took their lead from Mississippi's 1890 disfranchising convention, which (despite the absence of a statewide woman suffrage movement) had seriously considered qualified female suffrage as a means of swelling the white electorate. After a federal judge ruled against South Carolina's registration law, one suffragist asked the state Democratic Party to let white women help "in this time of dire distress." "Truly the moment has come when its women are needed at the polls for its redemption!," declared another.[67]

Like many white suffrage activists around the nation, these women rooted their arguments in elitist or white-supremacist principles. Viola Neblett, for example, decried a system that made educated white women — "the wives and mothers of the honest, great men that built this republic" — the electoral inferiors of Irish ditchdiggers, illiterate coachmen, and "low-minded criminals." Virginia D. Young, a Women's Christian Temperance Union (WCTU) organizer and the state's sole female newspaper editor, was foremost among the white Democratic women arguing for woman suffrage. Voting was not a matter of physical strength, she held, but a matter of judgment and fairness. If it was true that government derived its just powers from the consent of the governed, she asked, should not South Carolina's women be asked for their consent? At least, she cheekily suggested, they should be allowed to take part in a "hand primary." Otherwise, she argued, women like herself were the victims of taxation without representation. "Who more than we women understand better the bitter mortification of negro rule — the rule of untaxed negroes over white women?" To the objection that woman suffrage would enfranchise black women, Young answered that she was perfectly willing to accept educational or property qualifications. Young understood that if she won her fight, it would not be because of principle. As her longtime rival Sallie Chapin cynically explained, "[O]ur politicians will give woman the ballot as the Republicans did the negro, not from any sense of justice, but for the same reason they have all stuck hayseed in their hair and called themselves farmers."[68]

Just as Chapin had once imagined that Tillman might be her ally on temperance as a matter of reform, Young had some reason to think that Tillman might be sympathetic to her agitation. He had, after all, been the champion of public higher education for the state's white women. For years, some South Carolinians had argued that white women needed an institution of higher education, both to train them for their domestic duties and to give them "every possible opportunity to fit themselves for any business in which they may find it necessary to embark in the bread winning race." As governor, Tillman supported this movement and pushed through legislation establishing a state-funded normal and industrial college for white women, Winthrop College.[69]

Although Tillman believed white women could properly engage in many kinds of "business," voting was not one of them. His speech at the laying of Winthrop's cornerstone in 1894 offered a vision of white women's proper social roles that fell short of suffragists' hopes. He began by praising the white women of South Carolina as models of pluck and resiliency, in terms familiar to those who had been listening over the past decade. "[O]ur wives and daughters," he said, "have met the changed conditions wrought by the emancipation of the slaves with much greater success and fortitude than the men, and . . . they do a much larger proportion of work than we do." Unfortunately, the state had not always recognized the need to cultivate this strength. This was due, he claimed, to the "effects of slavery upon our habits and customs": men had learned to see women as ornaments, and husbands had been reluctant to allow their wives to gain a practical education. Of course, as the celebrator of the "sun-browned goddess" well knew, neither his mother nor his wife—let alone less wealthy white women—had ever been a merely ornamental presence on the farm. The *Charleston News and Courier*, discussing "woman in the Old South," also understood the divergence between myth and reality, concluding that "the Silken Languid Dames of Popular Tradition had no existence." But Tillman, the perpetual critic of the "slaveocracy," could not resist another opportunity to lambaste the state's earlier leadership for its aristocratic pretensions. Normal and industrial education for white women would help rescue white society from the evils of the past as well as those of the present.[70]

Tillman's letters to his wife Sallie reflect the tension between normative notions of male "protection" and the realities of their life together. When

Sallie Starke Tillman. A newspaper noted that "the lines of a strenuous life are as marked in Mrs. Tillman's face as in her husband's" (Wisconsin State Journal, *27 July 1903*). *Special Collections, Clemson University Libraries.*

their oldest son, B. R., was seventeen, Tillman wrote home from Washington, D.C., to reassure his wife that she would not be left helpless should anything happen to him. "B. R. can take care of you if [you] should be left alone," he consoled her. The imperative of male protection was not surprising for a man of his upbringing, class, and era. But having established that patriarchal authority would persist whatever happened to the individual patriarch, Tillman immediately issued directives that told a very different story. "Don't let [B. R.] run wild hunting," he worried, "and make him read some every day or night." Ideology and practicalities did not necessarily have to coincide; they could even contradict one another without causing obvious distress.[71]

Tillman posited limits to women's proper roles, and he particularly opposed woman suffrage as the sort of unwanted reform that would "rub the bloom off of the peach." Higher education was not intended as a steppingstone to gender equality but was part of an effort to protect the material and social bases of the white household. Even if white women were strong and self-confident, they were not and should not be wholly independent; they belonged within men's households, and they required men's physical and economic protection. Although they did not belong on a pedestal so high that it prevented them from doing useful work, white women did still represent purity and had to be protected from dangerous forces. White women, Tillman told the crowd at Winthrop, should be educated to develop self-confidence but should not be "unsexed." Women who sought equality with white men forfeited their respectability, and Tillman derided those who became "strong-minded, bold, brazen, pert, [or] self-asserting," as well as those "prating of 'woman's rights,' 'man's tyranny and selfishness,' the 'degradation of nursing children,' and so on." Such women, he said, would have no place at Winthrop College.[72]

An understanding of women's proper roles, Tillman thought, included an appreciation of sexuality. Tillman was no prude, and he did not idealize white women in such a way as to render them sexually untouchable or sacrosanct. Instead, he understood sexuality as a powerful force with which an intelligent society should deal frankly and pragmatically. "The law of sexuality," he later told the U.S. Senate, "is the most powerful law in nature," the gift of a benevolent God. In private, too, he expressed great enthusiasm. His letters to his wife often included flirtatious but unmistakable references to their sexual relationship. Even when dispensing advice to his daughter Sallie while she was attending Winthrop in the 1910s, his insistence on the value of education included references to sexuality. This, "the most compelling and powerful influence" he knew of, took over women's lives when they were about sixteen. Men and women were often overpowered by it, he wrote, and it was for this reason that both needed education.[73]

But being subject to the same forces did not endow men and women with identical responsibilities. When it came to politics, Tillman saw women playing a figurative role. He hoped that broad white support for Winthrop would heal the political divisions among the state's white men, and he chose a metaphor that offered women a passive and subordinate role in the power struggle among the state's white men. He recalled that "the ancient Sabines were brought to peace with the Romans by the women who had been seized and borne off captives to become the wives of the latter; so may the women of South Carolina become our peacemakers." After being educated at Winthrop, the state's best young women might be able to help their aristocratic-minded husbands see the wisdom of reform. Tillman's conservative social message struck exactly the chord he had sought. The *Edgefield Advertiser* heartily approved of this speech, particularly Tillman's strictures against the "unsexing" of women. It hoped that the widely positive response to the speech would prove a harbinger of "harmony" among the men of South Carolina. Even the unfriendly *Charleston News and Courier* praised Tillman "unreservedly" for "his eloquent and patriotic discourse."[74]

Tillman declared that women were intrinsically unsuited for politics. "[T]he laws of evolution," he argued, "have differentiated the functions of man and woman, and disaster awaits the people which attempts to repeal natural laws." In 1913, Northern senators attacked Tillman when he inserted into the *Congressional Record* a white Southern minister's 1871 critique of Northern feminism, Albert Bledsoe's "Mission of Woman," which presented white Northern women as godless and unnatural. Tillman claimed he had not read the offending passages before endorsing the article, but in typical fashion, he used his "apology" as an opportunity to attack woman suffrage and defend Bledsoe's "warning." For Tillman, opposition to suffrage for white women was a "knightly sword of protection," not a "brutal pike of censure and condemnation." Suffragists might claim that women would purify anything they touched, but he found this view both noble and misguided. White womanhood was indeed "glorious," but it was not so omnipotent that it could withstand the debauchery of politics, "this monstrous and filthy arena." As regrettable as political degradation and corruption might be, they were preferable to degraded and corrupt white womanhood.[75]

Tillman also explained his opposition to women's voting in martial terms. Since violence was a regular feature of the political meetings that constituted the heart of state campaigns, Tillman found the possibility of women's presence at the polls "too horrible to contemplate." As he wrote to Virginia Young in 1890, he had "never given much thought" to woman suffrage but believed that few Southern women would want this "*right* as I suppose you consider it." Those "tempting women to enter into the mire of politics" failed to consider that they might be physically or morally injured. Many agreed, including black political leaders who had experienced such violence from a somewhat different position. Although cautiously in favor of woman suffrage, D. A. Straker admitted being "terribly afraid to see a woman at the polls."[76]

Young articulated a counterargument that turned women's purity into an argument for the safe exercise of their suffrage rights. "You say that politics are 'too corrupt for woman to mix in,' " Young wrote in 1893, "but, my brothers, may not her coming cleanse away the corruption? You know woman's power of putting things to rights." She and Tillman disagreed on this subject, but they understood the history of white womanhood in strikingly similar terms. When Young and a delegation of woman suffrage activists addressed the constitutional convention, the male delegates made a great show of gallantry, escorting the speakers onto the floor and praising them extravagantly. But Virginia Young politely set them straight. Although "it has been customary to set up women on a pedestal to be worshipped," she stated, that custom belonged to the past. "[W]e are very practical these days in this State," she told the convention, "and very few families can afford to have the woman part of it setting up on a pedestal all day doing nothing for self-support and the help of the family." Women often had to deal with men "on a purely business basis," a situation in which men had the advantage because they were voting citizens. Voting was not a matter of physical strength, she argued. "[W]omen will go on being sweethearts, wives and mothers, and loving to dress and enjoying men's attentions just the same when they vote as they do now. I'm not the least afraid that you'll be just as polite to us, too, when we go to the polls as you are now." Indeed, during one of Tillman's confrontations with L. W. Youmans in the 1892 campaign, the white women of Edgefield had been credited with preventing a violent political conflict. The women present "were much calmer than the men," reported the local weekly, "and quietly chatted and smiled and laughed while every one, and they too, knew that the crowd was trembling on the verge of a fearful fight." "Had they not been present at this time," concluded the reporter, "the results might have been far worse." As suffragists had argued in other contexts, women's participation might make politics more civil.[77]

But woman suffrage struck many men as a travesty, a bestowal of citizenship's privileges without requiring its concomitant martial and physical obligations. Suffrage, it seemed, was part of an essentially and incontrovertibly masculine set of civic and social duties. The masculinist opposition to woman suffrage linked the rights of voting and citizenship with the physical responsibilities of roadwork, military service, and electoral violence. The *Anderson Journal* suggested that if women were granted the privilege of voting, they should also be allowed to pay poll taxes and work the roads. Another opponent argued that "[v]oting for a certain law, carries with it the duty of defending that law on the battlefield, if necessary." Men might have to do so, but women would not. Their right to vote, therefore, would not entail the same responsibilities and thus was unfair and illegitimate.[78]

It naturally followed that those who had taken on martial duties could not justly be denied political rights. Irby was one of several delegates to oppose the understanding clause on the grounds that it would strip the franchise from former Confederate soldiers. He estimated that 15,000 illiterate and unpropertied white men had served South Carolina in the Confederate army. No poor white Confederate volunteer had ever been asked if he could read or write before he was enlisted, and to disfranchise such men would be to dishonor the Lost Cause. One black delegate, seeking to take advantage of this argument by extending it to Union veterans, invoked a black military tradition that stretched back to the American Revolution. Both black and white men, declared James Wigg, "have shed their blood in their country's service; and have fought side by side upon an hundred battlefields, from the first skirmish on Boston commons when Crispus Attucks fell, to the battle of New Orleans, when the flower of the English army faded away before the leaden storms from the black battalions of General Jackson." One white delegate even proposed granting suffrage only to those who had served in either of the Civil War armies. In a comment intended to reassure his fellow white delegates that the consequences of such race-neutral enfranchisement would not be too dreadful, he noted that "the negroes who fought on the Federal side have, as a rule, more intelligence than their fellows," undermining more than he may have realized the white-supremacist interpretation of the sectional conflict.[79]

Despite this identification of suffrage with distinctly male obligations, Young and her colleagues met with some initial success. A few delegates, seeking to increase the political power of the wealthy, offered proposals tying woman suffrage to a property qualification. Several suggested that literate, property-holding women should be allowed to vote "by proxy." One delegate even turned this decorous fraud into a straightforward statement of white male upper-class privilege: male voters who paid taxes on at least $200 worth of property "and who represent a family as head thereof" should have the right to cast two votes. But to endorse woman suffrage even on pragmatic grounds required compromising deeply held beliefs. Charleston editor T. D. Jervey could support qualified woman suffrage only as an alternative to fraud and violence. Gonzales's *Columbia State* endorsed qualified female suffrage as a way of securing white dominance but began with the apologetic admission that "[m]anhood suffrage is theoretically the proper form of suffrage for a republic." The *State* argued that women had proved themselves capable of performing all the meaningful tasks of citizenship. Women in Wyoming sat on juries, and the question of women's military service had already been answered: "Didn't she do it in the war just passed," supporting the war effort by nursing, sewing, and shaming reluctant soldiers into service?[80]

A few white men endorsed woman suffrage on principled grounds. During the constitutional convention, the "Men of Lexington" called for "no sex in politics, government or morals" and advocated a qualified female suffrage to that end. Reform-minded legislator and editor Robert R. Hemphill earned the praise of woman suffragists for introducing a woman suffrage bill in the state legislature. Hemphill was the foremost male advocate of white women's suffrage and was a featured speaker at the 1895 National American Woman Suffrage Association Convention in Atlanta.[81]

But manhood, like whiteness, could be forfeited by unacceptable political expressions. To many, men who supported woman suffrage were not real men. Noting the woman suffrage proposals at the 1890 Mississippi convention, the *Cotton Plant* commented that "[i]f the *women* of Mississippi have so much time and talent at their disposal that they must beg to be allowed to do *man's* work, it is to be hoped that the Constitutional Convention of *men* will have enough time and talent to tell these sisters where they belong." The *Charleston News and Courier* suggested that Hemphill sought to postpone votes on such measures until there were "ladies present to hear his speech." This was taking chivalry too far. Edgefield reformer W. J. Talbert offered a less controversial form of solicitude: white women were on a pedestal "so high and grand and great that we might take all of the thrones that have ever been filled by kings and pile them one on another, and top them with the chair of the President of this republic, and they would not reach to her feet."

But women's power was not unlimited, and far from purifying the ballot box, they would be tainted by it. Did his fellow delegates, Talbert demanded, want to drag white womanhood down "and degrade her by putting her at the ballot box? No, no, a thousand times no." D. S. Henderson, a prominent Aiken County lawyer and Red-shirt leader, declared that white-supremacist arguments for woman suffrage were "founded upon pure cowardice." "The idea of saying to the world that the negroes were so numerous that we had to drag the women in the State before us to protect us is pitiful. Before we do that, let us do away with the excellent report of the committee, go back, get our shotguns and stand by the polls, and not in the name of heaven drag our women to the ballot box." The *Cotton Plant* printed approvingly the words of a Seattle correspondent who called woman suffrage an "effeminate movement," championed only by "political amazons on the one hand, and bearded effeminates on the other." Young sought to defuse these attacks by accepting and redeploying their conservative vision of gender roles. She suggested that since women were excellent judges of character, woman suffrage would guarantee the manliness of elected officials. "[N]o Oscar Wildes for us," she promised.[82]

The possibility of black women's political engagement also horrified many white men. For Tillman, black women were in every respect the inferiors of white women. Whereas white women had taken up new responsibilities since the war, "the bulk of labor" in black households was still performed by men. In addition, Tillman was always ready to summon up horrific Reconstruction-era images of black women in politics. "They will make the political night meetings of the colored people more hideous," he offered. Black women would be even harder to manage — even more "pestiferous" — than black men, reason enough to oppose woman suffrage.[83]

Woman suffrage met with a resounding defeat at the constitutional convention, with an amendment granting the vote to women who fulfilled a property qualification losing by a margin of almost five to one. For Tillman, as for most of the 1895 convention's delegates, an appreciation of white women's roles in the household did not suggest that they should be treated as equals outside those bounds. Rather, the state had an obligation to provide white women with educational opportunities and a degree of legal protection against forces that might disorganize a well-functioning household, including not only black rapists but also drunken or dissolute husbands. The symbol of white womanhood retained the tension implicit in the captive "sun-browned goddess" Tillman had praised in the 1880s: she was simultaneously a hard-working, powerful body and an exalted, vulnerable figure. She had a proper and important role to play in many fields of Southern life, but not in the essentially martial domain of politics.[84]

Young and her colleagues did not give up. Speaking before the U.S. Senate Committee on Woman Suffrage just a few months after the 1895 constitutional convention, Young argued that South Carolina's approach to suffrage restriction would not solve the state's deep-seated social crisis. She pointed to electoral fraud as the source of black men's rage, and she warned that the new system would do no better than the old at ensuring white men's and women's safety and security. Indeed, it would ensure the persistence of violent racial hostility. "Rape and murder and houseburning" would continue, provoking the inevitable responses of "lynching and mob rule." The only route to social peace was the implementation of fair and clean elections—and this could be attained by giving literate, propertied women the vote. Then "they will outnumber the negro voters so that these people's ballots can be honestly counted." Eventually, she hoped, white Southern men would come to see that only white women's votes would make democracy safe for white supremacy.[85]

Purity and Its Limits

Suffrage restriction was the convention's main task, but the discussions of education and property ownership inevitably introduced a host of other issues concerning the integrity of white men's households. These discussions were not entirely under Tillman's control. White women and African Americans might have failed to gain or retain suffrage rights, but they had some success pressing other kinds of claims. Tillman and his fellow white Democrats sometimes found themselves having to take positions on issues they would have preferred to leave undiscussed. When it came to matters such as divorce, interracial sex, and the very definitions of whiteness and blackness, even people now excluded from the body politic could force the victors to confront their own contradictions.

Nothing touched the patriarchal household nearer its heart than the question of divorce. By the late nineteenth century, American law was generally moving toward a view of marriage as a contractual relationship that could under certain well-defined circumstances be broken. South Carolina, however, had no divorce law. The state's Reconstruction-era divorce law, its first, had been repealed in 1879, and most Democrats opposed writing a new one into the 1895 constitution. Tillman saw South Carolina's uniquely permanent marriage bond as a heartening example of moral constancy in a world of "legal sophistry" and "false expediency." Marriage was to the spiritual life of the idealized white family what the homestead was to its economic life, and the state was justified in protecting it against men's moral weaknesses. In states where divorce was legal, Tillman noted, a man might marry a woman "in her youth and beauty" but forsake her when she grew old and unattractive in order to gratify his "lustful" desire for "some young and buxom girl." Even worse, a husband would be compelled to treat his wife with disrespect in order to convince her to agree to a divorce. And divorce laws so weakened household relationships that fathers, husbands, and brothers became too demoralized to exercise the "unwritten law" of vengeance against those who debauched their women. Fortunately, South Carolina's men were threatened with no such demoralization. The rule of law might have claimed an ever larger share of the responsibility for maintaining social order, but white men were still required to defend white women from physical harm. In this context, South Carolina's ongoing record of lynching and other vigilante violence testified to white patriarchy's local good health. "The purity and stability of the family has in all ages been the surest bulwark of the State," Tillman wrote; it was surely the state's responsibility to return the favor. Tillman saw the decay of marriage and women's entry into men's sphere as twin warning signs that civilization was about to fall, and he asserted that "the relation between 'votes for women' and divorce, if not one of cause and effect, [was] at least one of mutual acceleration." Not surprisingly, even woman suffragists avoided discussing divorce reform for fear of being dismissed as disreputable "free lovers."[86]

Tillman sought "purity and stability" not only for white households but also for whiteness itself. That meant policing racial boundaries where "purity and stability" seemed most vulnerable—in the realms of law and sex. The framing of a new constitution made the legal definitions of race and the legal consequences of interracial sex a matter of public debate. Whether the delegates decided to accept or to modify historical customs and conventions, they would first have to articulate those customs and conventions in plain language. The ensuing debate gave dissidents and gadflies an opportunity to poke holes in the faulty logic of racial and gender "purity."

Defining race in legal terms was not a simple matter. Many "Negro" or "mulatto" South Carolinians were close kin to "white" South Carolinians, and some well-respected elite white families were known or believed to have recent black ancestry. So the convention unenthusiastically set about the task of deciding how much "negro blood" it took to make a person black. George Tillman, who fancied himself an expert on the subject of racial classification, was the convention's strongest advocate of the "one-eighth rule." He pointed to an antebellum custom by which men with less than one-eighth black ancestry could testify in court and noted that several prominent but unnamed "white" families were known to have black forebears. On the other side of the debate were men who believed that no one with any black ancestry could be considered white, including delegate George Johnstone, who "was opposed to any intermixture." Johnstone was less interested in past instances of racial mixing than in their present and future consequences. He claimed that there were hundreds of undeniably black young men in Charleston and Columbia with less than George Tillman's proposed proportion of "black" blood. "Are you going to turn them loose?," he asked the convention, conjuring up a scenario in which an eighteen-year-old white girl married one of these "white" men, then presented her helpless parents with a grandchild who was unmistakably black. Even if the offspring of such a marriage appeared to be white, this only deferred the calamity to another generation in which the "stain" of blackness might emerge.[87]

While white delegates fretted over the racial purity of white lineages, black delegates attempted to use the rhetoric of purity to protest white men's sexual exploitation of black women. Smalls offered a bitterly double-edged proposal that any white person marrying or cohabiting with a person of one-eighth or more "negro blood" be disqualified from public office. He also suggested that any offspring of such cohabitation be entitled to inherit property from both parents. These proposals did not, needless to say, directly reflect the black leadership's priorities. Smalls, after all, hardly meant to advance the notion that associating with a black woman degraded a white man or made him unsuited for governing. Rather, the former slave and Union veteran sought to take advantage of white men's own rhetorical objections to interracial sex; he described a situation that wealthy and powerful white men claimed to abhor and suggested appropriate deterrents. Daring his white colleagues to vote his proposal down, Smalls stated his hope that "the gentlemen would vote here to purify themselves." He felt sure he would have the support of the white delegates' wives, for such "good and pure" women would want their husbands to be equally respectable. Smalls even taunted the white male delegates with the proposition that "if woman suffrage was allowed the women would pass some such law to purify the men."[88]

Smalls's assault on white supremacy's sexual double standard sent Tillman hurrying for cover. He supported Smalls's proposal, arguing that if the convention was going to make racial intermarriage illegal, it was only "common justice" to make it illegal for white men to "debauch" black women.

But Tillman's notions of "justice" had, as usual, as much to do with political expediency as they had to do with morality. As he put it to his colleagues, half apologetic at his agreement with a longtime Republican nemesis, "We dare not . . . broadcast that after this question has come up we are afraid to act on it."[89]

In fact, Tillman presented his opposition to racial "amalgamation" as evidence that white Southerners were morally (and perhaps racially) superior to white Northerners. He claimed that although Northern white women were marrying black men in ever-increasing numbers, Southern white women would never commit "race suicide" in this way. He never conceded that any Southern white woman would accept a black man as a lover or husband. When a Pennsylvanian wrote to ask him what the child of a black man and a white woman looked like, Tillman responded tersely that he did not know "because I have never seen such a cross." Perhaps, he suggested, the writer would be able to find one in Philadelphia.[90]

Momentary agreement with Smalls did not alter Tillman's view of black women as immoral and degraded. When the opportunity arose, he gave vent to sexual slanders against black women as a group. "[A]s far as sexual relations go," he wrote to a Kansas correspondent, black women "are little better than animals." He believed that they usually did not resist white men's sexual advances. This, he thought, was a result of generations of slavery: having been taught that whites were superior, black women believed that having a child by a white man was a mark of improved status. This explained "the complaisance of the negro women," who, according to Tillman, were "nearly always more than willing" to gratify a white man's lust. This view of black women caused Tillman to balk at raising the state's age of consent. Sallie Chapin denounced the state's current age of consent, ten, as a "foul blot" on the state's reputation, and under her leadership, the state WCTU formally petitioned the convention to raise the age to eighteen. Over the course of discussion and debate, however, the age of consent gradually fell back to 16, then to 15, and finally to 14. White womanhood's rhetorical antipode, black women's "complaisance," was the magnet drawing it down: Tillman was among those who feared that if the age of consent were raised too high, innocent white men might be entrapped and legally ruined by adolescent black seductresses.[91]

In the end, not surprisingly, the convention delegates voted almost entirely along racial lines. Only two white delegates joined the six black delegates in rejecting the constitution, and even these two men agreed to sign the document, an indignity from which the black delegates begged to be excused. The new constitution cut deeply into the remaining Republican electorate. When voters re-registered in 1896, as required by the new constitution, only 5,500 black voters remained, alongside 50,000 whites. The literacy, education, and "understanding" provisions, along with the requirement that voters pay a poll tax six months before voting, dramatically reduced participation in general elections. For the next half-century, the Democratic Party ruled the state through a white primary.[92]

Reducing the numbers of poor voters of both races, the convention thus solidified the rule of the same elites who had first mobilized against Reconstruction a quarter of a century before. Although these men were nearly as politically divided as they had ever been, their collective triumph was nonetheless real, and both reformers and conservatives left the convention generally pleased with how things had turned out. Ben and George Tillman, despite substantial disagreements during the convention, agreed that together they had made a good constitution. At the convention's close, George Tillman formally bade farewell to public life in a speech that looked backward with a mixture of nostalgia and defiance. "We are not a free people," he began, for "[i]f we were free, instead of having negro suffrage, we would have negro slavery. Instead of having the United States government, we would have the Confederate States government." In his telling, white men's recent history took the form of a fall and rise, beginning in the idealized past of the antebellum era, sinking into the trough of Reconstruction, and now soaring again in the wake of the 1895 assemblage. The Tillman who was not a Tillmanite called the convention a "rainbow of hope" and an affirmation of his "faith in the Anglo Saxon race." Loyalty to party and race had overcome black suffrage. White supremacy now had the force of law. White unity had been as nearly reestablished as could be hoped for in a world without slavery. "Nothing can go amiss with us," he concluded in language that celebrated that political and legal reconstruction, "unless we forget that we are white men, Carolinians, and Democrats."[93]

7 The Uses of a Pitchfork

With South Carolina's constitution safely rewritten, Ben Tillman traveled north to take up the fight in the U.S. Senate. Washington, D.C., was where Republicans put forth dangerous proposals such as the Lodge and Blair Bills and where agents of the money power bribed legislators to betray "the people." Senators gave their consent to acts of war and annexation that threatened to overwhelm the nation with new nonwhite citizens and subject it to an imperial presidency. Tillman thought the body needed a man of courage and conviction who would stand up for white producers and fight for a white republic, and he set out to convince the nation that he was that man. Over nearly a quarter of a century in the national spotlight, as a partisan speaker and a paid lecturer on the lyceum and chautauqua circuits, Tillman recapitulated the themes and tactics of his South Carolina campaigns. His three major speeches—against imperial acquisitions, against trusts and monopolies, and on "the race problem"—were less distinct arguments than variations on the same theme he had been articulating since the mid-1880s: white men would lose all they held most dear unless they organized militantly and defiantly against their enemies.

There was one crucial difference between his state and national campaigns. Tillman's mission was no longer to rally an audience of South Carolina's "farmers" against local aristocrats and would-be Populists; now he attempted to set the nation itself on a new course that steered between the looming perils of "industrial slavery" and bloody revolution. To accomplish this, Tillman had to persuade American voters to accept two linked propositions: first, that a producerist coalition required non-Southerners to reconcile themselves to a white-supremacist South, and second, that Tillman both literally and figuratively represented that South. Here, Tillman drew strength from the parts of his and his class's history that had already reached Northern consciousness: abolitionists' views of slaveholders, the caning of Charles Sumner by Preston Brooks, the Confederate rebellion, the white terror of Reconstruction, and the explosion of lynching in the 1890s. Beginning with his first Senate speech in 1896, Tillman cultivated a reputation for violent outbursts. His unrepentant sectionalism and white supremacy established Tillman as the national representative of an angry white South and a fierce, uncompromising crusader, a wild man speaking from his heart.

This was Ben Tillman, agrarian rebel. He lambasted Republicans, boasted of his Red-shirt days, and assaulted a fellow U.S. senator on the floor of the Senate. He warned against imperial ventures that would bring more nonwhites into the body politic, earned the enmity of a powerful president, and demanded the repeal of the Fifteenth Amendment. Although the producerist coalition he imagined went down in defeat in the 1896 election, Tillman himself was victorious, for he came to represent a powerful, violent, intemperate "South." Rough in style, harsh in tone, rhetorically wielding a working man's pitchfork against a host of parasitical enemies, Tillman persuaded many Americans that he embodied the essence of the "revolt" of "the farmers."[1]

He played the part so well that when he finally proved to be a capable legislator, interpreters could only conclude that he was a Jekyll-and-Hyde figure, solon and savage together in one ungainly body. This completed Tillman's victory, for it reproduced the slaveholders' theory and practice of power—paternalist benevolence supported by violent coercion—that he had carried forward into the late nineteenth century. Tillman came to represent both the good master of a peaceful plantation world and a white Southern volk who demanded white supremacy as the price of political peace. He therefore represented a figure with whom Northerners would have to come to terms if they wanted a real "reconciliation" between the sections. As the national press began to echo his argument that white Southern men's racial "instincts" were simply too powerful to be suppressed, racial equality came to seem fundamentally unworkable, and Tillman's violent outbursts became "a very normal expression" of white Southern feeling.[2] By embodying this white-supremacist "South" for the nation, he helped reshape the nation in the interests—and in the image—of that South.

The Silver Crusade and 1896

In Tillman's view, the mid-1890s marked a critical juncture in the history of American freedom. Conspiratorial forces had cast the nation into a great depression, and none of the existing parties offered any hope of relief. Producers everywhere faced betrayal at the hands of antisilver "goldbug" Democrats like Grover Cleveland. Republicans stood for hard money and Reconstruction, Populists for the intrusive subtreasury, and worse yet, in North Carolina, those two groups had combined to form a biracial fusion government. Tillman feared that his producers would not endure this sort of political and economic oppression indefinitely. If their frustration could not find expression through the political process, it would explode in a "bloody revolution."[3]

The times required a new alignment of political forces. Tillman joined the national silver movement, envisioning "free silver" as a bridge between disaffected producers in the Democratic South and their brethren in the Republican West. This realignment, he hoped, would redefine American sectionalism and rally white producers everywhere against their common enemies in the seats of monopoly, finance, and abolition. A silver party, he believed, could play an important role in this effort and perhaps even come to national power in 1896. During 1893 and 1894, he attended national conventions of the growing bimetallic movement. By the time he reached the Senate in 1895, Tillman had become convinced that American politics were about to experience a shift of tectonic proportions. "A new Mason and Dixon's line has been found," he told the members of the Farmers' State Alliance; "[o]n the West of that line are those who plow; on the East are the Capitalists." In this context, loyalty to Cleveland's Democratic Party was worse than foolish; only party labels kept Southern and Western farmers apart. "If you were in a burning house," Tillman asked, "would you refuse to leave it because it was called a Democratic house?"[4]

In correspondence with silver leaders and public speeches, he often spoke of his willingness to abandon the Democratic name if that would help forge a new alliance between South and West. At a meeting in Pickens, an upcountry stronghold of white independents from J. Hendrix McLane to James B. Weaver, Tillman declared his readiness to join the West in a new party. He thought a silver coalition might be able to win control of the House of Representatives in 1894, and then, "if no argument can be had as to a name," a new fourth party would unite the nation's white producers. In 1894 letters to Nebraska Democrat William Jennings Bryan, another leading figure in this growing movement, Tillman wrote that "I am not sure now where South Carolina will be in the next Presidential contest," meaning that he did not know what role the Democratic Party would be able to play. "We will join the West in the fight for the emancipation of the masses from the slavery to gold," he assured the Nebraskan. "What the motto inscribed on our flag will be, depends on circumstances." He even believed that he himself could lead the silver coalition to victory in November 1896. The precedent, he maintained, was the battle he had won in South Carolina. "It is another Farmers Movement on a national scale," he told Irby in 1893, "and the only road to success or relief that I see." Some of his enemies concurred. Harry Hammond thought Tillman's "chances to be [the] next President are as good as his chances to be Governor of South Carolina were a few years ago." Given the hard times faced by many Americans, he gloomily reflected, there was "no telling what may or may not happen."[5]

Southerner and Westerner, Democrat, Republican, and Populist would have to come together, but the sine qua non of Tillman's posited alliance was a shared commitment to white supremacy. As a result, although the *Charleston News and Courier* repeatedly denounced Tillman's silver activities as "incipient Mahoneism," a neutral observer would have seen something rather different. Even at the 1893 silver convention in St. Louis, a gathering intended to demonstrate the collapse of Civil War sectionalism, Tillman presented his credentials as a "Hamburg rioter" who was opposed to both "negro domination" and "Grant's soldiers." He understood that the question of black citizenship presented a "stumbling block" to the alliance he sought but insisted that only the "emancipation of the Anglo-Saxon" would ensure "the preservation of our government."[6]

Tillman's bid for national leadership gained him substantial editorial attention outside South Carolina. Invitations began to arrive in Columbia for Tillman to speak outside the state, and despite his efforts against the Populists in 1892, local as well as national observers continued to depict him as a potential People's Party candidate. Tillman, though, refused to fight under that banner. "[S]o many cranks joined the third party," he told a Texas reformer, "that many Conservative silver men are afraid to join them." Writing to North Carolina Populist leader Marion Butler, he asserted that "a fatal blunder was made by yourself & others in organizing the third party too soon." Tillman believed that by abandoning the Democratic Party before the time was ripe and by resorting to interracial rather than interregional politics, Populists had sacrificed their credibility among white Democrats.[7]

Tillman knew that free silver might not by itself satisfy all currency reformers. As an official of the 1893 St. Louis bimetallist convention, however, he argued that it was "unwise to seek more now, however alluring the prospect." Whereas others saw free silver as a sham reform, Tillman saw it as an entering wedge in the fight against the money power. He noted privately to one South Carolina supporter that "some of the Alliance leaders [are] threatening dire consequences on account of this trying to simplify matters." But silver's weaknesses as an economic panacea were less important than the elaborate and plausible conspiracy theory its advocates wove around its demonetization, first under Republicans during the 1870s, then again under Cleveland in 1893. In widely distributed works such as *Coin's Financial School,* silver advocates persuaded many voters that simply to oppose monometallism was to strike a blow against the money power.[8]

Arriving in Washington, D.C., in late 1895, Tillman settled into temporary lodgings. He urged Sallie to write often to "keep me out of the power of the female seducers here," but his public demeanor was hardly so playful. In his first formal Senate speech, delivered on 29 January 1896, Tillman declared that the nation faced a potentially apocalyptic choice: "bimetallism or industrial slavery." In this speech, Tillman launched a stinging verbal attack on his own party's president and his financial policies; he denounced "sound money" policies as "a damnable scheme of robbery." Echoing attacks made by silverites, Populists, and other critics of the financial system, he declared that agents of the money power—including the "besotted tyrant" Cleveland, high officials dubbed "Judas," and Baron Edmund de Rothschild, the "London Jew"—controlled the nation's political and economic life and threatened the Republic with destruction.[9]

Tillman warned that the economic crisis could lead to a social and political catastrophe. Currency contraction left farmers with no money to buy manufactured goods, and their failure to consume in turn idled the factories. The Civil War, he reminded the Senate, had been fought to emancipate 4 million black slaves, but the current situation was far more grave. "We are fast approaching a condition which will place the collar of industrial bondage around the necks of ten times that many white slaves," he cautioned. "They are burning our candle at both ends, crushing us on the one hand with the tariff and robbing us on the other hand with the gold standard, and they have asked us, like beasts of burden, like dumb driven cattle, to bear these things and say nothing but to vote the party ticket." Tillman's white men had never been willing to submit to such treatment. Faced with "negro domination," they had launched one revolution; enslaved by the money power, they might launch another. The "toiling and now down-trodden masses of the cities and the equally desperate masses of the country"—

including, significantly, the "well-to-do agricultural class"—would ally with one another. If ballots did not bring relief soon, "agrarianism and communism" would join hands and "obtain it by bullets." Although Tillman presented this as a warning, the prospect clearly appealed to the Jeffersonian within him: a successful uprising might leave the Republic "redeemed, regenerated, and disenthralled."[10]

For those seeking a schematic version of his political-economic analysis, Tillman offered a cartoon representation—a pair of "allegorical cows" that he declared would "appeal directly to every farmer in the United States." The first drawing represented Tillman's view of the exploitation of the farmers by Eastern capital. A great cow stood over a map of the country, its hind legs planted in the Northeast and its front legs just west of the Mississippi River. As hardworking farmers of the South and Plains fed the cow their harvests, its udders produced great streams of wealth that a top-hatted man squeezed into a bucket labeled "Wall St." The second drawing represented how the money power had foiled Congress's effort to reverse this inequity. Legislators had attempted to turn the cow around, placing its udders in the hands of the farmers and feeding it an income tax on the Eastern money power, but the corrupted Supreme Court had ruled such a tax unconstitutional, choking off the cow's nourishment. As a result, the Western and Southern farmers were left with empty buckets.[11]

Tillman's rhetorical assault on his own party and his appeal for a new political coalition brought him instant fame. Tillman had "voice[d] my sentiments exactly," wrote a Kansas Democrat, one of thousands who asked for copies of the speech to distribute among friends. Some Populists asserted that Tillman would soon join them; others seemed to assume that he already had. A silver Democrat participating in North Carolina's Republican-Populist fusion movement derived new hope from Tillman's speech. Many correspondents from nonagricultural areas urged Tillman to run for president. Earnest approval came from such diverse auditors as a Spartanburg, South Carolina, newspaper editor who in state matters remained one of Tillman's "bitterest opponents" and a Washington, D.C., leader of the Knights of Labor. A Chicago publisher placed him in the same category as local political and labor heroes, and some of those heroes agreed. From the southern leg of a national speaking tour, pro-Populist railroad labor organizer Eugene V. Debs wrote to congratulate Tillman on his "great speech." "Your fearless and patriotic utterances," declared Debs, "revive the hopes of millions that a government of, by and for the people is to remain with us in spite of the plots and intrigues of the degenerate hirelings of the money power."[12]

"Senator Tillman's Allegorical Cows." These cartoons, drawn to Tillman's specifications and entered into the Congressional Record*, show "his idea of the present American situation." Library of Congress.*

But the tone and content of the speech, especially its vituperative attacks on the president and other leading figures, also drew intense criticism. A Boston newspaper denounced Tillman as "a renegade, violator of law." Closer to home, the *Columbia State* balanced its support for silver with its continued hatred for its new national representative. "So much of his speech as condemns the administration's recent course [on silver] we agree to," wrote editor Narciso Gonzales, but the speech was "vulgar" and "indecent," full of "coarse abuse and gratuitous slander." Others sought to use the rudeness of Tillman's speech to discredit his racial policies. A black newspaper linked Tillman's incivility in the Senate to his part in disfranchising black South Carolinians and concluded that from either perspective, "[h]e is a small man."[13]

Such attacks were music to Tillman's ears. Responding by letter to criticism of his speech in the *New York World*, Tillman accused his attackers of portraying him as "a coarse, brutal, ignorant blackguard" when he only sought to serve as "a sentinel on the watchtower," warning his countrymen of an impending crisis. The editors who so abused him must stand charged with being "reckless partisans or hirelings." Others reached the same conclusion about Tillman's detractors. Joel Chandler Harris, writing in the *Atlanta Constitution*, noted that "[t]here has never arisen a genuine Democrat—a man of the people—of any degree of prominence who has not been denounced by the so-called 'conservatives' as a communist and an anarchist."[14]

"A new party will spring into existence," Tillman told the Senate that spring, "and it will in a short time be able to beat you and your machine." To be sure, "a great army disorganized, without generals, cannot marshal itself like a compact and organized and skilled body," but some seemed already to have selected Tillman as their general—and, best of all, they represented the Western half of the imagined coalition. In Denver, members of Tillman Clubs sported ribbons bearing Tillman's picture, a pitchfork, and silverite slogans such as the proposed silver-to-gold ratio of "sixteen to one." By the late spring and early summer of 1896, correspondents asking Tillman for copies of his now-famous speech were also asking for campaign ribbons. Suddenly, suggestions that he run for president took on new plausibility, and various leaders of the bimetallist movement worked to make Tillman a national candidate.[15]

But bimetallists' plans for a fourth party were overtaken by the transformation of the Democratic Party. By the time the Democrats met at their July 1896 convention, the party of Cleveland and the gold standard had become a silverite party. Tillman's visage and pitchfork had become symbols of this transformation. As the Democratic convention approached, silver men sought Tillman's ear, hoping for "the selection of a nominee . . . who as a candidate can receive the support of all bimetallic forces in the country." Tillman had substantial influence in the selection of South Carolina's delegation to the Chicago convention, where he served as the delegation's chairman and favorite-son candidate and as a member of the convention's Resolutions and Platform Committee. Most important, he followed the reading of the platform on 9 July with a fifty-minute oration of his own.[16]

This speech, Tillman's best opportunity to place himself on a national silver Democratic ticket, effectively destroyed his chances to become a national candidate. As the *Columbia State* scoffed afterward, "Ben Tillman could not miss such an opportunity to advertise himself as 'Pitchfork Ben.' " Indeed, Tillman was simply too much the unreconstructed Confederate to lead a party still trying to shed the "bloody shirt." "I come to you from the South," his speech began, "from the home of secession," and before he could complete this inauspicious first sentence, he was drowned out by the hissing of hundreds of delegates. "Some of my friends from the South and elsewhere," he continued, "have said that this is not a sectional issue. I say it is a sectional issue." Once again, the delegates overwhelmed him with a display of displeasure. Not only did Tillman refuse to retreat from his sectional comparison, but he compounded this indecorousness by attacking the party's sitting president. In order for the coalition to gain electoral victory in the West, he said, the convention would have to do more than endorse free silver: it would have to repudiate goldbug treachery. Tillman therefore offered a resolution to "denounce the administration of Grover Cleveland as undemocratic and tyrannical and as a departure from those principles which are cherished by all liberty-loving Americans." Some delegates cheered, but more were appalled at the violent and sectional tenor of his speech. Although free silver became part of the platform, the resolution condemning Cleveland failed. In the end, only South Carolina's delegates cast their first-ballot votes for Tillman. Instead, William Jennings Bryan gained the nomination with an attack on the gold standard that did not insist on waving a red shirt. Bryan, like Tillman, imagined a war of the producers against the capitalists, and he envisioned the same sectional coalition, but he avoided the charged language of the Civil War. His "cross of gold" speech, a stirring but not divisive exposition of Democratic bimetallism, made Tillman's weaknesses all too plain.[17]

When Tillman returned from Chicago, he put a brave face on his experience. He intimated that he had spoken before Bryan in order to "remove the stumps from his path," articulating a radical message in contrast to which Bryan could appear moderate and conciliatory. Mocking this analysis, the *State* suggested that Tillman himself might have been the biggest "stump" before Bryan and that "the Nebraskan had to pull him up by his sectional roots and cast him aside before he could go on." But many South

Carolinians interpreted Bryan's message as Tillmanism in a form more palatable to non-Southern voters. "To vote for Bryan is to vote for a platform imbued with Populism, Socialism, and Tillmanism," moaned Wade Hampton's personal secretary. But this conservative had learned the lessons of the early 1890s. On reconsideration, he acknowledged that "a young man of the South can't afford to have it appear in his record that he ever faltered in his advocacy of the ticket of his party." Tillman's stumble in 1896 did not undermine his more subtle and enduring success.[18]

Tillman never complained publicly about the convention's result. Perhaps he had never believed he could win national office. More likely, whatever disappointment he felt was overshadowed a week later when his beloved daughter Addie was killed by lightning atop a mountain in North Carolina. Despite his grief, Tillman soldiered on in the service of Bryan and the party. He was particularly active in the Democratic National Committee's efforts to conciliate Georgia Populist Tom Watson. The People's Party's national convention had seconded the Democrats in nominating Bryan for president but, in return, asked that the Democrats accept Watson in place of their own vice presidential nominee, New England gold Democrat Arthur Sewall. The Democrats, however, refused to endorse Watson and instead sought to persuade him to withdraw from the race. After Tillman wrote to Watson in August, he thought the Georgian's response showed that "he is brooding over his wrongs & thinks more of revenge . . . than of national success." In late September, Tillman met with Watson at his home in Thomson, Georgia. The content of their private twelve-hour meeting remains a mystery, but a New York paper might not have been far off when it suggested that Tillman had promised Watson a future cabinet position if he would leave the race and that Watson had refused.[19]

Despite his failures in Chicago and Thomson, the election of 1896 made Tillman a national symbol. In the months between the July convention and the November election, his face and pitchfork graced Northern periodicals such as the *Chicago Tribune* and *Harper's Weekly*. In image after image, hostile commentators made Tillman, Bryan, Debs, and Illinois governor J. P. Altgeld the four horsemen of a nineteenth-century Apocalypse. A gang of them forced an enormous "silver plank" down the throat of a helpless Democratic donkey. A band of pirates, one wielding a pitchfork, made a blindfolded "Labor" walk a free-silver plank. A Constitution-shredding "Populistic" Supreme Court included a glowering Ben Tillman. An anti-American barbershop quartet melded the voice of Tillman's "sectionalism" with Bryan's "repudiation," Altgeld's "anarchy," and Debs's "socialism."[20]

Opponents were not the only ones to blur the lines between Democrats, Populists, socialists, and reformers. Seeking to capitalize on Tillman's fame, an enterprising Atlanta printer exposed the apparent fluidity of radical and reform politics in that tumultuous year. His firm advertised a pitchfork badge on whose tines hung skewered goldbugs and whose handle could be labeled "sixteen to one" or—depending on the purchaser's loyalties—either "Bryan and Sewall or the nominees of the People's Party." After Republican William McKinley defeated Bryan in November, Tillman remained in contact with Altgeld, Bryan, and other leading figures of the 1896 campaign. Even Watson, a man with substantial grounds for bitterness and suspicion, wrote Tillman a gushing letter of praise. "[T]hat the U.S. Senate contains at least one member who does not fear to break through conventionalities, to speak the plain truth as he believes it," declared the Georgian, "is a fact which augurs well for the progress of reform ideas and methods."[21]

Cultivating the Pitchfork

In South Carolina, Tillman's capacity for violent self-assertion had helped establish him as a credible leader, and as he ventured out into the nation, he exhibited the same capacity, becoming the Senate's resident wild man. Much of this reputation for violence was explicitly white supremacist. Newspapers and magazines noted with amazement that he publicly boasted "that in 1876 we shot negroes and stuffed ballot boxes." They also reported his justification of lynching when rape was alleged and his prediction of a coming race war in which black Americans might be exterminated. But Tillman's reputation for political savagery did not rest solely on his grand vision of racial conflict. Instead, as during his post-Reconstruction career in South Carolina, he focused much of his violent energy on the white men who were his immediate political opponents.[22]

His methods remained consistent, and South Carolina conservatives watched in rueful amazement as Tillman deployed his rhetoric of insinuation and denial against his Senate colleagues. "I certainly do not want to attack any member of the committee who does not deserve to be attacked," Tillman explained during a Senate colloquy in 1897, but "nobody denies that there have been rooms occupied for two months by the Republicans on the Senate Finance Committee at the Arlington Hotel, in easy touch with the telephones to New York and elsewhere, and in easy reach of the sugar trust." His offended and outraged colleagues found themselves at the same disadvantage as earlier factional antagonists, damned by the insinuations of an opponent who refused to be pinned down.[23]

But it was physical violence that sealed Tillman's reputation. On 22 February 1902, in Senate debate, he accused his junior colleague and former ally John L. McLaurin of corruption. McLaurin called Tillman a liar, whereupon Tillman rushed across the chamber and punched the onetime reformer in the face. McLaurin struck back, bloodying Tillman's nose before the doorkeeper and several other senators stepped in. Moving immediately into closed session, the Senate unanimously judged both men to be in contempt of that body. Neither man, however, would back down. Offered an opportunity to apologize, Tillman declared that "under the provocation" he "could not have acted otherwise." "I confess I have felt somewhat at a loss," he continued, "how to judge men who in one aspect appeared to be so high and clean and honorable and in another appeared more or less despicable." McLaurin, for his part, had to be urged repeatedly by colleagues not to continue uttering defiant threats against Tillman. The investigating committee found Tillman's verbal and physical conduct "inexcusable," but, despite a minority report urging that McLaurin be suspended for five days and Tillman for twenty, both men ultimately received only a formal censure. Even then, Tillman could not let the matter go. When the roll was called for the vote to censure, both men abstained from voting. But Tillman remained combative, remarking as he announced himself present that "among gentlemen an apology for an offense committed under heat of blood is usually considered sufficient." As he put it a few weeks later in a letter to a South Carolina colleague, "[H]ad I taken the lie my own self respect would have been gone."[24]

It was unusual for Tillman to take politics so personally. Possibly he had decided that a public spectacle would highlight his grievances against McLaurin, whom he saw as a an ally of South Carolina's mill owners and a traitor to the farmers' cause. A lawyer by training, McLaurin had been Tillman's supporter and ally since hosting him at Bennettsville in 1885. McLaurin had served as a reform legislator and as Tillman's attorney general; he had supported both the Clemson fight and the constitutional convention. Elected to the U.S. House and then to the Senate, like any good South Carolina Democrat he had proclaimed himself a supporter of Bryan and silver. But once in national office, McLaurin associated himself more and more with South Carolina's increasingly powerful piedmont cotton mill owners. These men had begun to reshape the state and regional economy, drawing hard-pressed white farmers into the mills. The number of operatives employed in South Carolina mills grew dramatically: whereas in 1890 barely 8,000 white South Carolinians worked in the mills, by 1900 their ranks totaled more than 30,000. As the representative of the men who controlled this increasingly powerful sector of the economy, McLaurin began to outline a political-economic alternative to Tillman's "radical" war against the money power—"industrial Democracy," a vision of prosperity through industrial development and the imperial acquisition of overseas markets.[25]

McLaurin and Tillman quickly became fierce opponents. In May 1901, the two men debated in South Carolina, and their mutual accusations escalated until both agreed to resign from the Senate and put the conflict before the legislature in the form of a special election. Although the governor rejected this proposal, the two continued to regard each other with hostility.[26] While McLaurin denounced Tillman as a "radical," Tillman became convinced that McLaurin's Democracy was not "industrial" but "commercial"—in other words, McLaurin had sold his vote to the money power. In 1899, McLaurin had spoken publicly and privately against the annexation of the Philippines, but he had voted for the administration's treaty and subsequently obtained committee assignments and patronage from the Republican leadership. McLaurin, Tillman told the Senate, had surrendered to "improper influences" and had received these political favors in exchange for his vote. This was the accusation that had led McLaurin to charge Tillman with uttering "a willful, malicious, and deliberate lie," upon which Tillman had attacked him.[27]

Tillman had the last word on McLaurin's fate. The apostate reformer was up for reelection in 1902, and Tillman used his influence with the South Carolina Democratic Party to require that primary candidates sign onto the entire national platform. Tillman himself had helped draft this platform, and McLaurin could not endorse it in full without reversing himself yet again on the question of Philippine annexation; his Senate seat therefore went to a more loyal reformer. Ultimately, Tillman's instincts about McLaurin proved correct. In 1913, a national magazine printed a photograph of a 1901 letter from McLaurin to an agent of Standard Oil in which McLaurin declared that he could "beat Tillman if properly and generously supported." In a 1916 open letter, Tillman reminded his voters that "McLaurin did not hesitate to ask for money to buy South Carolina in 1901, and to ask it from the Arch Trust of them all—the Standard Oil." This "Benedict Arnold" must be forever barred from state politics.[28]

Other incidents reinforced Tillman's reputation for violent self-assertion. In 1903, his erratic nephew Jim Tillman, the sitting lieutenant governor of South Carolina, ended a long feud with Narciso Gonzales by accosting the editor outside the capitol building and shooting him dead. Ben Tillman was not directly implicated, and indeed he described his nephew as in many ways "unspeakable." But he lent his reputation to Jim's defense, sitting at the counsel's table at the trial, and he helped pay his legal costs. The jury acquitted Tillman, confirming to many people that Ben Tillman's South Carolina was a place where public debate was carried on with firearms.[29]

The White Savage

Although Tillman's own pistol-bearing days were over, he continued to be associated directly with acts of violence, especially against black Southerners who remained politically active. He played an especially important symbolic role in the 1898 campaign against North Carolina's Populist-Republican fusion government. In 1894, an alliance between mainly white Populists and the black and white wings of North Carolina's Republican Party had reversed the Redeemers' victory and inaugurated a biracial government that won further victories in 1896. In 1898, the state Democratic Party organized a white-supremacy campaign, attempting to use political violence and intimidation, justified by white men's racial and gender anxieties, to destroy the fusion coalition. Both sides turned for support to their highly successful neighbor to the south.[30]

Marion Butler, national leader of the People's Party and U.S. senator from North Carolina, implored Tillman not to stand with the North Carolina Democratic leadership. He explained, one reformer to another, that these men were the same kind of hidebound Democrats that Tillman had opposed in his own state, "a lot of gold-bug railroad attorneys and hypocrites who are against free silver and every reform that you and I stand for." "I have heard them cussing you," he told Tillman. "Not a single one of the ring leaders in the crowd that invited you to the state and who met you as leaders of the Democratic machine . . . would have met you or heard you speak in 1894, and they would not do it now except they hope by using you in this campaign to embarrass me and demoralize the Populists." The North Carolina Democratic leadership, he concluded, represented "a cause that you despise."[31] Butler failed to recognize that Tillman despised some things even more than goldbug Democrats. In fact, several years earlier, Tillman had warned Butler that he "deprecate[d] dissension among southern white men." Neither agreement over monetary policy nor a shared anti-aristocratic rhetoric could protect his biracial coalition from Red-shirt terror.[32]

To Butler's dismay, Tillman came to the state Democrats' aid. During the late fall of 1898, in speeches at Fayetteville, Red Springs, and elsewhere in southern North Carolina, he opposed Populists, Republicans, and biracial coalition politics and lauded the "shotgun policy." A decade later, Tillman gave a concise summary of his perspective on North Carolina in 1898: "[N]egroes and mountaineers and ultra cranky populists beat the white people who own practically all the property, pay all the taxes, have nearly all of the intelligence, and integrity, and character, and they held the state for four years. Then the banner of white supremacy was thrown to the breeze. The cry was made, 'Rally to your colors. Be a white man or be a nigger. You have got to take your choice.' " Tillman was greeted by audiences wearing red shirts, and in his speeches, he repeatedly invoked the Red-shirt legacy of 1876. North Carolina's 1898 Democratic campaign did not disappoint him. White militias—sometimes uniformed in red shirts—terrorized black and white fusion voters, and in November, the fusion government fell before the white-supremacist assault. The North Carolina silver Democrat who had written so enthusiastically to Tillman in 1896 now found himself forced to choose between supporting the conservative Democrats or becoming their victim; there was, a Democratic paper warned him, "no middle ground upon which white men may stand." Where state Democrats did not win the 1898 elections, they resorted to force. In Wilmington, the state's largest city, white supremacists mobilized two days after the election, destroyed a black newspaper whose editor had challenged white-supremacist rhetoric about black sexuality, murdered at least a dozen black men, and seized the city government. This coup d'état brought down the last major redoubt of biracial Southern politics.[33]

A few days after the overthrow of the fusion government in Wilmington, Red-shirts rode in South Carolina as well. In the town of Phoenix, near Edgefield, the white Republican Tolbert family had attempted to mobilize black voters (including many of their own tenants) to vote in the 1898 election. White Democrats had turned to the familiar forms of force, fraud, and intimidation to defeat them. The Phoenix "riot," like its antecedent in Wilmington, closely followed the Redemption pattern: Democrats provoked an armed conflict at the polls, following which they singled out and murdered Republican activists. Over the next few days and into early 1899, black people were driven or migrated out of the area.[34]

Wilmington and Phoenix gave Tillman an opportunity to underline the lessons of 1876: black political activity brought violent retaliation. But once the immediate threat receded, Tillman sought to focus white Democrats' anger on the white race traitors who had caused the trouble in the first place. The responsibility for the violence lay with South Carolina's Tolberts and North Carolina's white fusionists, who had encouraged blacks to take part in politics. In 1899, as "white-cappers" continued to harass black tenants in the area around Phoenix, Tillman urged white men not to "abuse the poor, innocent black wretches," for such people should not be held accountable. It would be better to "go kill the Tolberts," the men responsible for "the political virus injected into the negroes of that neighborhood." White supremacy required that white men — even more than black men — be brought into line.[35]

After 1898, it became more and more difficult for any American to misunderstand Tillman's fundamental imperatives, for as a speaker on the chautauqua and lyceum circuits, he took his theories of race, politics, and history before audiences in almost every state. Black Americans, Tillman insisted, must never be allowed to forget which race was dominant. In the aftermath of the violence at Phoenix, a black Charleston minister thanked Tillman for condemning the violence against blacks in that neighborhood. Reverend J. L. Dart promised the cooperation of "the better class of colored people" in upholding law and order. The senator, however, flatly rejected his correspondent's implied offer of a cooperative relationship. "[T]he negro," Tillman insisted, "must remain subordinate or be exterminated." These fearsome alternatives — white supremacy or a racial struggle to the death — animated Tillman's public discussion of "the negro problem" from the mid-1890s until the end of his life in 1918.[36]

Tillman believed that "races" instinctively sought to preserve themselves and dominate others, and in thousands of speeches, his depiction of the resulting "race problem" in the United States varied only slightly. Race, he argued, was an essential, irreducible aspect of human society. "The mysterious influence of race antagonism," he wrote, "has always existed; it is ineradicable; and it will continue as a governing factor wherever the races come into contact." But racism was not mere "prejudice." Nor was it particular to Southern whites. Rather, "race preservation" was one of the great motive forces of history, a deep-rooted impulse toward purity and domination. It had justified slavery, and it continued to justify unequal status for blacks and whites, no matter what the Constitution had been amended to say.[37]

Civilization, in Tillman's view, was a product of white, Christian cultural evolution; other races might mimic it, but they could never truly achieve it. Anglo-Saxons were "the superior race on the globe; the flower of humanity; the race responsible for the history of the world; for the achievements of the human family in a large degree." At best, black people might acquire "a little of the veneer of education and civilization," but this only misled and frustrated people who were destined to be laborers. "Whatever of progress the colored race has shown itself capable of achieving," Tillman stated, "has come from slavery." Indeed, Tillman thought that "the restraints and compulsions of slavery" had made barbarian Africans useful, honest, Christian workers. Booker T. Washington's *Up from Slavery* missed the point by its very title, he argued; a more accurate book would be called "Coming up from Barbarism through Slavery."[38]

Their barbarism having been suppressed in slavery's school, Tillman argued, black Southerners had behaved well throughout the sectional crisis and the Civil War. Few had betrayed their masters' trust, let alone attacked white women. But freedom and Reconstruction had placed black men in positions of authority and exposed them to "the virus of equality." Foolish or malicious white men had detached black men from slavery's hierarchical strictures and encouraged them to vote, thereby creating the expectation of "social equality." During Reconstruction, Tillman declared, black men "tasted blood." Given access to white men's institutions of government, black men inevitably sought access to white men's families as well. Since a "respectable" white woman would never voluntarily marry a black man, such efforts met with frustration. Black men then expressed their anger—and their savage natures—by raping white women. Tillman replaced the complexities of Reconstruction's broad, pervasive challenge to white men's monopoly on authority with a simple tale of sexual terror. "[T]he poor African became a fiend," he explained, "a wild beast, seeking whom he may devour, filling our penitentiaries and our jails, lurking around to see if some helpless white woman can be murdered or brutalized." "We realize what it means," he told the Senate, "to allow ever so little a trickle of race equality to break through the dam."[39]

Although the abolitionists and carpetbaggers of Reconstruction had passed from the scene, "false teachers and bad leaders" continued to encourage black men to seek social equality. When Booker T. Washington dined at Theodore Roosevelt's White House, Tillman foresaw dire consequences. "The action of President Roosevelt in entertaining that nigger will necessitate our killing a thousand niggers in the South before they will learn their place again," he predicted. The episode also provided support for Tillman's assertions that even earnest conservatives like Washington aspired to "social equality" and that the Wizard of Tuskegee's gradualism was no better than other men's insistence on political equality. Although Washington had wisely "warned his people against the folly of political office, . . . afar off he sees a vision of equality, and I say that his dream can never come to pass." Mixed-race people, Tillman thought, might have intellectual abilities beyond those of "pure-blooded" blacks and even some of the "lower types of whites"—no small admission—but the widespread and continued mixing of different races would lead to "degeneracy, physical and mental," and the end of American civilization. In Denver, Tillman was heckled by an integrated audience that rejected his characterization of blacks as "brutes" and "savages." When they called out "Booker Washington," Tillman dismissed their counterexample by consigning him to the frustrated and no doubt futureless class of mulattoes. "Booker Washington," he shrugged, "owes his preeminence over his fellow negroes entirely to the proportion of white blood in his veins." Since race was destiny, men like Washington were doomed. "[M]ixed bloods" like "Booker Washington, Dubois [*sic*] and others" saw "amalgamation [as their] dream and hope." Denied that hope, they would become footnotes in racial history, men without a race and therefore without a future.[40]

Black efforts at "amalgamation" activated white men's deepest instincts to protect racial purity and supremacy. Civilization, it turned out, was only one indication of Anglo-Saxon superiority, for the most civilized type of man was also the most fearsome. Anglo-Saxon men would go to any length, even murderous violence, to protect the purity and supremacy of their race. "If you scratch the white man too deep," Tillman warned, "you will find the same savage whose ancestry used to roam wild in Britain when the Danes and Saxons first crossed over." Abolition, emancipation, and Reconstruction had threatened white civilization with "amalgamation," thus forcing the white savage to emerge. (Tillman elided the question of white men's desire for or domination of black women, considering open discussions of such relationships to be highly distasteful.) When black men stood accused of raping white women, the threat of "amalgamation" activated white men's instincts of "race preservation" and revealed the savage beneath the white skin. "I have seen," Tillman said, "the very highest and best men we have lose all semblance of Christian human beings in their anger and frenzy when some female of their acquaintance or one of their daughters had been ravished." Laying civilization aside in defense of the more primal identity of race, the Anglo-Saxon turned his most essential superiority against his racial antagonist. In a sense, black men's resort to violence demonstrated their frustrated inferiority, whereas white men's resort to lynch law demonstrated their racial superiority.[41]

The issue of lynching brought Tillman back to the problems of mob law that had so troubled him in the early 1890s. He believed that the false doctrine of racial equality was "rapidly driving the whites to desperation" and that the South would be pitched into a wholesale conflict—a race war. Black men clearly had not ceased aspiring to equality. In the *Congressional Record*, Tillman quoted at length from a newspaper article in which a black speaker warned that "if this oppression in the South continues the negro must resort to the sword and torch, and that the Southland will become a land of blood and desolation." If this occurred, Tillman warned, lynching would give way to "the massacre of the negroes and to a race war which can have only one result, the destruction of the weaker race." He never tired of reminding his listeners that he had already waged race war during the mid-1870s. "I have nothing to conceal about the Hamburgh [*sic*] riot," he declared in 1909. "[W]e had to shoot negroes to get relief from the galling tyranny to which we had been subjected." But he feared that in a contemporary conflict, "hundreds of good white men and women" would join "thousands" of black victims. At times, the prospect made him deeply pessimistic about the future. "[T]he question is only suspended," he told the *Washington Post* in 1906. "I shudder to think what my children or grandchildren may have to face. More negroes are born every year, and more are learning to read and write. In time, our constitution may not be effective." Nevertheless, he concluded, "you may be sure South Carolina will be ruled by the whites, no matter what occurs."[42]

The new Southern economy was partly to blame, for it removed black men from the immediate supervision of responsible white men. The dregs of the "restless younger generation of negroes," Tillman explained, roamed the Southern roads, traveling from sawmill to turpentine camp to labor gang and posing a constant threat to white women. Tillman estimated that these dangerous men numbered no more than 5 percent of the black population, so it was conceivable that they could be monitored and controlled. But if that proved impossible, "we must hunt these creatures down with the same terrified vigor and perseverance that we would look for tigers and bears. . . . [I]f all of them were shot as ruthlessly as we would shoot wild beasts, the country would be better off."[43]

White Southerners, of course, sought some means of control short of wholesale slaughter. "It would not be right" to shoot all of those young men, Tillman acknowledged, "because we might kill some innocent men, but we can keep them on the chain gang." Contrasting the alleged discernment of Southern lynch mobs with the misdeeds of white Northerners, Tillman pointed delightedly to the New York City draft riots of 1863. In the North, he explained, "white men vent their anger upon the blacks indiscriminately, and their race hatred is so intense that the innocent and unoffending are made to suffer." In the South, by contrast, "the mob hunts down the man who is guilty or supposed to be guilty, and innocent negroes are not molested." Tillman made this argument in late 1906, just a few weeks after white mobs raged through the streets of Atlanta, killing more than a dozen black citizens.[44]

The Empire Strikes Back

Tillman thought that a nation faced with this continuing "race problem" would be mad to take up the burden of a nonwhite overseas empire. As the United States considered annexing territories such as Hawaii, Puerto Rico, Cuba, and the Philippines, Tillman's suspicion of federal and corporate power and his racial antipathies converged. Imperialism, he believed, would inflict "carpetbag government" on the hapless people thus colonized, as monopolistic interests turned the territories into their private reserves and enslaved the native populations in order to exploit their labor and natural resources. Like the carpetbaggers of Reconstruction legend, these men would rule through military force, inflicting hardship and debt on their unfortunate victims. But the impact on the United States would be even worse. The colonized people either would be incorporated into the American body politic, adding millions of nonwhites to white men's already substantial burden, or would become subjects and the United States would be transformed from a republic to an empire.[45]

Tillman had been critical of U.S. intervention overseas as early as 1892, but his main involvement in anti-imperialism began on the eve of the Spanish-American War of 1898. Like many Americans, Tillman understood the Cuban revolt against the Spanish Empire as a heroic struggle, but he suspected that President McKinley was "not a friend to the idea of free Cuba" and that congressional resolutions had been craftily designed to undermine Cuban sovereignty. Tillman believed that American bondholders, fearing the loss of their investments if Cuba gained full independence, wanted the United States to impose an oppressive "reconstruction" government on the island. He explained to the Senate that "we of South Carolina have had so many bonds of that kind foisted on us in the dreary years of the past, during the era of reconstruction," that he could not support any resolution that did not explicitly recognize Cuban sovereignty and limit the American role to "expel[ling] the Spanish robbers and tyrants."[46]

Of course, Tillman did not believe that Cubans or Filipinos, races "of Spaniards and negroes mixed," were capable of self-government. The people in question were mostly nonwhite, "aliens in blood, aliens in language, aliens in thought and feeling." Furthermore, they had the "virus of Spanish misgovernment injected into their blood and bones," making it nearly impossible for them to become "good citizens." But he did not want that incapacity to be used as a pretext for U.S. stewardship. "I do not want to see the American flag floating over a strange people who have to be held down by the bayonet," he declared. Under the best of circumstances—American intervention without annexation—the United States might be able exert a benign influence, "even [on] bandits and mulattoes, and the worst elements of those struggling for liberty." But add to the mix the greedy machinations of the money power—whether in the form of the Spanish bondholders or U.S. congressmen who had invested in Hawaiian sugar plantations—and experiments with nonwhite democracy were certain to fail. Annexation's benefits would fall to a few hundred scheming capitalists, whereas its evils would be borne by the entire country.[47]

Tillman asked whether the Republicans promoting Philippine annexation believed, as Abraham Lincoln had, that the Union could not exist half slave and half free. If they did, how could they propose to make 10 million Filipinos a subject people? Since 1868, Tillman said, South Carolina's "thoughtful" white men had been "lying awake at night" worrying about the corrupting influences of one ill-fated experiment in nonwhite citizenship. He demanded of the proannexation senators, "What do you want to bring in another Pandora's box for and open it?" Colonial expansion would bring 10 million or more nonwhites into the nation, "negroes . . . Malays, Negritos, Japanese and Chinese, [and] mongrels of Spanish blood." To continue on this course would be to "inject this poisoned blood into the body politic." Republicans, in their imperial venture, were using force, fraud, and party discipline "to get these islands incorporated into our territory under conditions which would have made Lincoln blush." Tillman declared that he would only support annexation if the Republican leadership would acknowledge its past errors and declare that participation in government would be limited to whites only. This was, of course, a bluff intended to underline Republican hypocrisy: during the 1900 Senate debates on Hawaiian citizenship, Tillman fought the principle of color-blind citizenship just as fiercely as he fought the economic domination of the new territory by the "sugar trust."[48]

Tillman feared that imperial ventures would teach Americans to be comfortable with "despotic" and "military government." Northerners had never experienced such a regime, but white Southerners had, and this made them uniquely qualified to speak out against it. The need to make the choice between republic and empire overseas would be followed by the need to make the same choice at home. "That party which sneers at and tramples under foot the doctrine of the consent of the governed in the Philippines will soon sneer at that doctrine in the United States," he explained.[49]

As Tillman had warned, the United States soon found itself ruling the Philippines by the bayonet. Tillman had no doubt that the islands could be pacified, but he urged his colleagues to reject what Rudyard Kipling had just dubbed the "white man's burden." Emphasizing the burden of overseeing a subject race, Tillman used the experience of white Southerners since emancipation to argue against bringing still more nonwhite races into uneasy coexistence with whites jealous of their own racial supremacy. "We must turn our faces away from this temptation," Tillman begged the Senate; otherwise, white civilization would either become corrupt or be forced to exterminate another race.[50]

The Limits of White-Supremacist Reform

Tillman was considered not only an anti-imperialist but sometimes a progressive as well. He continued to claim to be the Senate representative of industrial workers and agricultural producers, declaring that "combinations of capital . . . are protected by Congress which has in many cases become the tool and instrument of the capitalistic class." But his commitment to hemming in the money power faltered whenever such regulation might conceivably create a federal government that could challenge white supremacy in the Southern states. Like the slaveholding representatives of a half century before, he argued that the federal government must not be given powers that would enable it to intrude in a state's "domestic affairs." With secession five decades in the past and the backlash against the civil rights movement five decades in the future, Tillman argued for "states' rights" in terms that people at either end of that range would have easily understood. His insistence on white supremacy defined his vision of reform.[51]

Efforts to describe Tillman as a progressive expose the limitations of that concept. In recent years, historians have come to understand progressivism less as a coherent movement than as a term of convenience encompassing a wide variety of reform crusades, organizations, languages, and policies. Tillman might have been described or might have even described himself as a progressive, but the same could be said of some of his fiercest critics—from Theodore Roosevelt to Robert La Follette to the ardent anti-Tillmanites in the leadership of the newly formed National Association for the Advancement of Colored People. Definitions of Southern progressivism range from C. Vann Woodward's conception of "progressivism — for whites only" to Jack Temple Kirby's ironic reflection that "black disfranchisement and segregation" were in essence "the seminal 'progressive' reform of the era." These definitions say as much about the limited explanatory value of the term "progressive" as about the relationship of progressivism to white supremacy. Certainly proponents of disfranchisement and segregation believed that these "reforms" would put better-educated men into office and foster social peace, but by that standard, the members of the 1871 Taxpayers' Convention had been progressives.[52]

Tillman's own progressivism in regulatory matters was shaped by his belief that federal power would have to forswear racial equality and escape the clutches of the money power before it could be trusted. He therefore opposed forms of corporate regulation that other self-styled reformers and progressives found unproblematic. For example, Tillman was deeply suspicious of factory owners, be they from South Carolina or New England. He described lockouts of employees as "cruel and unjustifiable," and he wanted the South Carolina legislature to limit the hours that adults and children could be required to work. But he refused to support federal legislation that would address any of these concerns. "God forbid," he wrote, "that we should ever have to seek relief from Congress, in . . . reform of a local character." The federal government, once it was given power to interfere in state economies, might become a destroyer rather than a protector: if it could limit the working hours of industrial laborers, it could also set limits for agricultural workers. That, Tillman suggested, would cripple Southern agriculture.[53]

Railroads presented the South Carolina "progressive" with a similar dilemma. As governor and senator, Tillman fulminated against collusion between railroads and federal courts. During a 1903 debate, he referred to a court injunction against Debs's railway union a decade earlier as evidence that federal officials helped subordinate the rights of the people to the rights of industrial and financial bosses. All the same, Tillman opposed the federal remedies proposed by Populists and even by Democrats like Bryan. Nationalizing the railroads, he believed, would create a political army to be used by the party in power and would undermine the hard-won political autonomy of the former Confederate states. Although he had been Bryan's ardent supporter for a decade, he suggested that the Nebraskan's support for government ownership of the railroads might cost him the 1908 Democratic nomination.[54]

By the beginning of the twentieth century, no sensible radical would expect Tillman to stand up for economic reform if doing so might conceivably aid blacks or Republicans. Tillman argued that only his version of white-supremacist Democracy was truly progressive. "My definition of a progressive," he explained on one occasion, was "a real Democrat according to the ideas of Thomas Jefferson, and not a hypocrite, or a liar, or a socialist, or 'Bull Moose.' " In 1913, he told the Senate Democratic caucus that since the 1890s he had "preached the true gospel and had as much to do with the success of what is now called 'progressiveness,' I believe, as Bryan himself. The term properly interpreted in its essence is the Chicago platform and nothing else." To the extent that that platform had sought to reconcile outright Democratic white supremacy in the Southern states with a pale reflection of Populist economics, Tillman was correct.[55]

Only under certain limited circumstances would Tillman contemplate the use of federal power. When he first entered the Senate in the 1890s, Tillman argued that the existing navy was adequate to show the flag and to defend the nation's limited overseas interests. To build a larger navy, the federal government would have to issue bonds, which he believed would unjustly enrich wealthy bondholders. "I have denied, and I still deny," he declared in 1896, "the right of the President to issue bonds to carry on the government." Tillman and other inflationists preferred to expand the currency in the belief that this would spread benefits throughout producing society. Government use of bonds to raise revenue, by Tillman's reckoning, created future debts and further consolidated the wealth of the country in a small number of hands. Tillman's stand against the bondholders earned him the approval of Tom Watson, who thought that Tillman "never hit a rottener system than that under which our government constructs its navy."[56]

The longer Tillman sat in the Senate, however, the more willing he became to take advantage of federal resources. From his seat on the Naval Affairs Committee, he was drawn into the sectional politics of military appropriations, and he quickly came to understand that South Carolina could benefit. Beginning in 1900, he steered naval spending toward Charleston. Once the Democrats took control of the Senate in 1913, Tillman became chairman of the Naval Affairs Committee. From that position, during the military buildup of the 1910s, Tillman became an outright champion of naval power. He eventually joined forces with Senator Claude Swanson of Virginia and Navy Secretary Josephus Daniels (a North Carolinian) to ensure that naval spending would be concentrated on the southeast coast. The resulting militarization of the regional economy made the Southeast more dependent on and sympathetic to federal military spending than the one-time Red-shirt could have imagined.[57]

Tillman had always stood against both federal power and corporate capital, but his work against profiteering in military procurement eventually led him to contemplate the usefulness of a limited federal role. When the government solicited bids for armor plate, it became clear that the major suppliers had made a price-fixing arrangement. Tillman suggested that if steel manufacturers would not offer armor plate at a reasonable price and on competitive terms, the government should construct a plant and manufacture the plating itself. Despite being rebuffed by the Senate on several occasions, he held to this position and by the end of his career had gained President Woodrow Wilson's support. This was a remarkable departure from Tillman's opposition to the subtreasury and other large federal programs. But the armor-plate plant had all of the subtreasury's advantages without any of its hazards: it denied government revenues to powerful corporations without entailing federal interference in local affairs — most especially, matters of race. Tillman thought that a single government-owned factory would not corrupt local or national politics nearly as badly as federal-corporate collusion or federal appointees wielding power from county to county.[58]

From Tillman's perspective, only one aspect of life in the Progressive-era United States warranted broad federal intervention in local affairs. Like the slaveholders who demanded the Fugitive Slave Law of 1850, he was willing to sacrifice the principle of local autonomy for the promise of greater control over the black labor force. It was a striking admission. In the early 1890s, the problem of racial control had trapped Tillman between state and local imperatives, but by the turn of the century, even state-level control did not seem adequate to the challenge. Formal segregation, at best a half measure, had proceeded slowly in South Carolina. Railroad officials resisted being forced to provide duplicate facilities, and some representatives believed legal action might be unnecessarily provocative. Although Tillmanites had urged the segregation of railroad cars and other public accommodations, these matters had never been at the top of their political agenda. More to the point, formal segregation of public accommodations could hardly address Tillman's concerns, which were rooted in the autonomy and mobility of the labor force.[59]

By the twentieth century, Tillman's concern for the racial future had become so deep that for the first time he imagined resorting to federal measures. In 1906, he proposed a "passport" system to control the internal movement of the nation's black population. Although all Americans would have to carry identification documents, the purpose of the proposed law was explicitly racial: blacks would be required to have a "fixed domicile," to be registered at a particular workplace, or at least to have the endorsement of a white "sponsor." This system would be enforced in black-majority areas by white men on horseback, who would be empowered to arrest violators on the spot. It would be, in essence, a slave patrol for the postbellum South.[60]

Although Tillman described this system as "a last resort," a "radical departure from all of our ideas of Anglo-Saxon liberty," only his willingness to contemplate federal action made the 1906 plan unusual. Half a century earlier, the Beech Island Agricultural and Police Society had called for "a united and systematic plan with respect to the regulation of our colored population." More recently, as conservative an organ as the *Charleston News and Courier* had suggested something similar. Worriedly noting the ubiquity of black "outcasts," "tramps," and "visitors," especially where "white women and girls are in the habit of going about without guards or protectors," the paper argued that "[t]he time has fully come when every negro tramp in the country should be made to give a sharp account of himself, and if he cannot show papers proving his honesty and respectability should be dealt with as a dangerous character. The chain gang or the county jail is the place for him, not the public highway or the farm. We are coming fast to the point when the old 'patrol' system will have to be revived and enforced, if we have not reached it already. Any orderly system is to be welcomed that will put an end to the frequent lynchings of negro criminals, and to the horrible crimes that render lynchings popular if not necessary." In 1904, North Carolina's Clarence Poe, editor of the widely circulated *Progressive Farmer*, came to the same conclusion, calling for a "rural police force" to protect women "against the reckless, roving elements of blacks." By the twentieth century, Tillman's most radical proposal struck many influential—even "progressive"—white Southerners as simple common sense.[61]

The Gospel of White Supremacy

As Tillman traveled the country in the early twentieth century, he sometimes spoke on "railroads, trusts and monopolies" and on imperialism and annexation. But it was his speech on "the race problem" that made him rich and famous. Lecturing on race, he wrote, had proved to be "the most popular work that I can engage in." In 1906 and 1907, he estimated that he had reached 250 audiences, including as many as 100,000 people during the last four months of 1906 alone. He received $150 to $200 per engagement and sometimes more. In Iowa, Michigan, and elsewhere, he told an enthusiastic South Carolina assembly, he had "preached the gospel of white supremacy straight from the shoulder and had them applaud ten times as much as you have tonight." He also traveled extensively in the West and on the Pacific Coast. But he was particularly determined to drive his message home in the old citadels of abolition and Republicanism. "I want to get into New England and talk on the Race Question and I hope you will push matters in that field," he told his agent in 1901. Indeed, he was convinced that he had a special mission to reach New Englanders; after all, Southern whites were "face to face with the negro," whereas "all the negroes in the North amount to only a million. . . . [W]hat do they know about the negro?" Tillman used "the race problem" and "the negro problem" interchangeably, and he showed little interest in a more expansive conception of race. On a trip to the West Coast, Tillman dismissed white Californians' concerns about Japanese American and Chinese American children in the public schools and contract laborers in the workforce as a "mere side issue." Although he favored Japanese exclusion, for him Asian immigration did not represent the real "race problem." To an audience member who suggested that black laborers were not a serious threat because "the Negro works for American wages," Tillman responded curtly that "it is not a question of wages, God bless and damn you, sir." America was for "white Americans, . . . not for negroes, nor for Mongolians." If Californians really wanted to set their racial house in order, they should eject black students from their schools. Questions of Asian American labor, immigration, and education, he insisted, "sink into insignificance alongside of the greater and more vital question of the relationship of the races in the Southern States of this Union."[62]

As this exchange suggests, Tillman thrived on the rough-and-tumble of angry debate. When challenged by the audience, he responded personally and vituperatively. These colloquies were not distractions from his main point but a crucial part of the show, and Tillman's much-discussed volatility became central to his public image. Just as he enjoyed "having some fun in the Sen[ate] stirring up the animals," he race-baited antagonists around the country. Challenged by an Oregon preacher, Tillman asked, "Are you sure you have no negro blood in your veins?" He told black antagonists that America's black leaders owed their success to white forebears. He boasted that he had educated "all of the North and West" on the race problem, without mincing words "any time or any where."[63]

Some understood Tillman's "act" in just those terms. His public persona, the *Saturday Evening Post* suggested, was a part he had perfected through "long practice." Like any actor, Tillman donned a costume—the unstylish, old-fashioned clothing of a simple man unconcerned with such cosmopolitan matters as the latest fashions. Newspapers contrasted his attire with that of his opponents across the Senate aisle. Nature, listeners agreed, had "made him up well for the part he plays," giving him a harsh voice and style of gesturing, to say nothing of his empty eye socket. Although the famous pitchfork remained figurative, Tillman brought a characteristic set of physical mannerisms to the stage. When he spoke of interracial marriage, sex, or rape, he reached a pitch of emotion he otherwise reserved for personal partisan opponents: he waved his arms, slapped his hands together, and shouted. As Tillman reached the climax of an address to the South Carolina legislature in 1908, he warned of the "ultimate danger" of continuing black advancement in a shouted series of impending calamities: "[T]he traveler in the second century from this will find a breed of mongrels here! Cuba! Mongrelization in full blast! All over the North big buck negroes marrying white women and no law to prevent it!"[64]

He was also quite willing to stage conflicts. In 1903, he signed on for a chautauqua tour in which he debated Republican U.S. senator Joseph Burton of Kansas. These were not Lincoln-Douglas debates, and no great election hung on their outcome. Traveling through the Midwest, Tillman and Burton hammered each other with the same speeches, night after night. The audiences they encountered were mainly Republican, and Tillman's favorite debate proposition—that the Fifteenth Amendment should be repealed—was unlikely to draw broad support in Iowa or Kansas. But Tillman enjoyed himself immensely. He urged Sallie to join him on tour—as he inveigled on another occasion, "I live on love." She boarded a northbound train and met him in the Midwest. In Madison, Wisconsin, where Tillman was "warmly applauded" by 8,000 to 10,000 listeners, the couple toured the university grounds before Tillman continued on the circuit.[65]

Tillman made the transition from regional curiosity to national celebrity in 1906 when Republican senator Nelson Aldrich, attempting to sabotage the Hepburn Bill, a railroad regulation measure favored by President Roosevelt, placed its passage in the South Carolina Democrat's hands. Tillman's reputation was for political bluster rather than legislative achievement. Moreover, Tillman and Roosevelt had been antagonists since the McLaurin episode in 1902. Shortly before the fracas in the Senate, Roosevelt had invited Tillman to a White House reception for a visiting nobleman who was a naval officer. After Tillman struck McLaurin, however, Roosevelt withdrew the invitation. From that point on, Tillman and Roosevelt had regarded each other with contempt. Nor did the Hepburn Bill improve relations between them, for Roosevelt finally betrayed Tillman on the question of judicial review of regulatory decisions; indeed, the legislative process ended with the two on even worse terms than before. But despite being outmaneuvered by the president, Tillman emerged with far more national celebrity than he had ever had. For a moment, he had stood with the leading men of the nation. *Harper's Weekly* caught the striking contrast between this and earlier images of Tillman as the railroad rate bill made its way through Congress: on its cover, a stern Tillman stood in the foreground as a bemused Senator Henry Cabot Lodge asked Roosevelt, "Who's your friend?" Although Tillman declared himself only partly satisfied with the final legislation — since it provided for federal judicial review of regulatory efforts — Tillman had surprised everyone by behaving soberly and defending his views before the nation. Echoing the sentiments of a decade before, correspondents appealed to him as "the representative of the people on the floor of the Senate."[66]

The contrast between the rough-hewn, bitter Tillman whom observers thought they knew and the competent, powerful legislator now before them provoked a moment of reflection. "Deliberately Tillman holds out his worst side to the public," one analyst explained. "Deliberately he paints himself as a savage, wearing a breech-clout and brandishing a spear, and deliberately he shocks and paralyzes decent sentiment in the North and the best part of the South." His Senate speeches "set the whole North raving against this man who ate the flesh and drank the blood of negroes; and what he said well justified the raving. Even his Southern colleagues looked shocked." But the image was apparently just that. "[H]e is as good a fellow, as sensible and decent a citizen, and as wise a man as one could wish to meet with." Tillman's insistence on presenting himself as a "wild man politically" remained an "unsolvable mystery," perhaps even to himself. The writer reported hearing Tillman, stepping off the Senate floor after a characteristically violent speech, rue the inevitable demonization that would come in the morning papers but in the next breath admit that "[i]t's my fault."[67]

Perhaps, reporters suggested, Tillman was the very white man his "race problem" speech described — highly civilized but with a white savage just beneath the surface. Before a Chicago appearance, the *Chicago Daily Tribune* depicted Tillman as a kind of Jekyll-and-Hyde figure. In one drawing, Tillman stood on the stage in angry disarray, scraps of another man's clothing on his stabbing pitchfork, beneath a sign reading, "Back to darkest Africa for the black man." In the other, he faced his audience with a smile, his pitchfork adorned with flowers and bows, beneath a portrait of Lincoln and

"Senator Tillman to tell the difference between black and white in Orchestra Hall tonight. Will he strike D-sharp with a pitchfork or give us soft harmonies with a tuning fork?" Cartoon on the front page of the Chicago Daily Tribune, *27 Nov. 1906.*

a sign reading, "Love one another." The caption of the cartoon explained the contrast: "Senator Tillman to tell the difference between black and white." Press the smiling figure's racial button, and one would quickly see the pitchfork man. Scratch him too deep, and something wildly unexpected would emerge. Tillman had commented that black men's sexual assaults on white women caused "the very highest and best men we have . . . to lose all semblance of Christian human beings in their anger," and some observers came to see him in these very same terms.[68]

After 1906, many white Americans came to regard Tillman as acceptable and even respectable. "People who gauge the South Carolina Senator solely by some of his bursts of rage, and explosive language, misjudge him greatly," wrote one admirer. Unlike other self-styled senatorial champions of "the people" such as Arkansas's Jeff Davis and Mississippi's James K. Vardaman — both judged to be "insincere demagogues" — Tillman was "a man of fine intellect" who "stands for his opinions no matter what the sacrifice." Some asserted that Tillman had once been a wild man but that he had "grown." Tillman's apparent transformation even held out the possibility of redemption for his less worthy colleagues: a Philadelphia newspaper suggested that Jeff Davis "when tamed and domesticated . . . will prove as tolerable as Tillman." By 1918, his sometime antagonist the *New York World* could write that "when he entered the Senate there were grave misgivings because of his extreme views on public questions, but all these were long ago seen to be unwarranted." The *Saturday Evening Post* tried to capture Tillman by comparing him to a coconut, finding under his "[r]ough, hard, shaggy, unprepossessing outside" the "milk of human kindness."[69]

Tillman gloried in his "well deserved" reputation for "being more or less ultra, outspoken, blunt, and frequently frank to a fault," and many praised his refreshing absence of dissimulation. In a 1906 article for *Pearson's Magazine*, journalist James Creelman told Tillman's story to a national audience, keeping his promise to the senator that the character sketch would be "something masculine and telling." In Creelman's portrait, this "honest and outspoken radical" earned the admiration of colleagues by proudly acknowledging his role in "shotgun rule." "His is the fiercest and roughest spirit that has ever found voice" in the Senate, Creelman declared.[70]

The use of such terms as "rough" and "fierce" usually signaled that a writer had accepted Tillman's claim to represent the farmers. As early as 1893, the *St. Louis Republic* declared Tillman to be "worth the keenest watching because he is the sense of an immense body of small farmers in the South who are as hard-headed, independent and determined as any men who tread the soil of America. . . . Mistakes and all, he must be met and met with honesty and reason, for he and his kind are hard to fool and harder to browbeat. . . . Tillman, the spokesman of the Southern small farmer, is a fully accredited agent" of these men. "He enters politics and is one with whom parties must deal." Over and over in the years that followed, interviewers depicted Tillman as a representative of "the honest farmer in revolt." If not exactly a Populist, one writer explained, Tillman was nonetheless "a monument to the Populist uprising."[71]

A photograph dating from the turn of the century repeats this story of Tillman as the champion of the farmers. In this photograph, Tillman, standing on a wagon, is in his element, his face and body articulating severe truths, while his humbly dressed supporters smile in support and admiration, radiating honest, productive whiteness. But even a cursory inspection reveals that this picture is a fake. Its anonymous composer, unable to find an actual photograph that portrayed Tillman as the authentic spokesman for the farmers, created one. In a fit of symbolic manipulation that Tillman would have respected, the creator of this montage cropped the senator from a posed portrait and pasted him onto the wagon, creating an image that was more "true" to the well-developed story of Tillman and Tillmanism than any available photograph.

An actual photograph of Tillman at work before an audience shows a gesticulating Tillman addressing men from an unpretentious platform. But in many respects this image presents a rather different story from that of the montage. A few of the tieless men standing toward the front may perhaps be of modest means, but for the most part, the senator speaks to a well-dressed assemblage. Whereas the montage's smiling farmers live in a world of white agricultural productivity, the audience here is distinctly more urban. Moreover, the white men are joined by a few similarly dressed black men, standing at the edge of the crowd. The presence of these men, however tentative, serves as a reminder that black Southerners' interest in politics did not cease simply because Tillman declared that it must.

The montage symbolized the triumph of Tillman's campaign to represent the farmers. Poor white farmers themselves did not sit in Congress; nor, thanks in some measure to Tillman, did Populists. In the absence of actual poor whites and actual Populists, Tillman could, from a distance, pass muster as the embodiment of either or both. This identification grew more credible as one traveled toward the urban North and East, where Tillman's unfamiliar and unfashionable style took on greater importance than his wealth and policies. Discussions of Tillman's social roots and political base blurred leadership into identity, just as Tillman himself had always done. In a piece entitled "Tillman: A Study of the American from the Soil," *Appleton's Magazine* declared that "[w]ith no experience as a politician, he became at once a political leader. At the head of his fellow farmers, the wool-hats, the one-gallus tillers of the soil, he swept through the State on a political tornado." Here, Tillman's career as a paramilitary leader and political orga-

Montage of Tillman standing in a wagon surrounded by an audience of "farmers." Library of Congress.

Photograph from which the image of Tillman in the montage was cropped. Note that even this photograph does not capture Tillman "in action"; instead, he is posing for the camera, attempting to reproduce a characteristic speaking posture. Library of Congress.

Senator Tillman before an audience. With few exceptions (e.g., the figure at the bottom of the frame, just to the right of the platform), most of the men are wearing town clothes. Behind Tillman and to the left, at the edge of the crowd, stand at least four African American men. Special Collections, Clemson University Libraries.

nizer became a force of nature, and the complex relations of class that had actually characterized Tillmanism in the 1880s and 1890s disappeared entirely. To journalist Zach McGhee, who traveled South to investigate, Tillman embodied "the class struggle in South Carolina." He had risen from his roots as "an uncouth, unknown, uncredited backwoods farmer" to become a much-needed gadfly in the U.S. Senate. McGhee found Tillman's supporters among the "wool-hats" all the more "picturesque" for their calls for "refawm."[72]

Tillman's critics, too, ascribed his boorishness to his assumed origins among the "poor whites." Hostile white South Carolinians commonly remembered Tillman as having sprung from "poor white trash." "He had lost one of his eyes in a common brawl and was without education," recalled a onetime dispensary supplier. Black activist Kelly Miller saw Tillman as the "embodiment and expounder of the rule of the nether whites," who had unseated the complacent aristocrats of the old regime. Writing in the aftermath of the Atlanta riot, Miller argued that Tillman had unleashed lower-class passions that an older generation of aristocratic leaders had held in check. Tillman had been "the first to pitch the poor whites against the Negro in fierce and bitter array. He understood the dynamic power of hatred. . . . Now all factions vie with each other in denunciation of this race." Tillman belonged to the same class of violent racial radicals as Mississippi's Vardaman and Georgia's Watson. Roosevelt concurred. Writing to journalist Ray Stannard Baker, he denounced Tillman, Vardaman, and a few others for their "blatant contempt for the ordinary decencies of civilization," their "readiness violently to champion everything from murder down if the slightest political advantage is to be gained therefrom," and their "homicidal mania against the majority where the majority happens to be black." In his view, Tillman represented the lower order of whites and was "equally hostile to the class above or the class below."[73]

Baker similarly identified Tillman as a "poor white" in his book *Following the Color Line*, a series of essays on the state of black citizenship in early-twentieth-century America. Like Miller and Roosevelt, Baker condemned Tillman's appeal to racial hatred and ascribed it to Tillman's putatively lower-class origins, not to the imperatives and lessons of slaveholding. Yet Baker could not help admiring Tillman for his achievements in "extending popular education, establishing an agricultural college, regulating the liquor traffic." More concerned than either Roosevelt or Miller with the economic and political aspirations of poor white Southerners, Baker allowed himself to be drawn in by Tillman's rhetorical legerdemain. The "average citizen," Baker concluded, was much better off as a result of Tillman's administration. Even in a work remarkable for its focus on the question of black citizenship, Baker seemed to have accepted Tillman's definition of the "citizen" as a white man.[74]

The progressive journalist was not the only opponent who adopted some of Tillman's racial assumptions. When Upton Sinclair dramatized Tillman's 1904 campaign against Chicago socialists in *The Jungle*, he presented Tillman as a tool of the Cook County Democratic machine, which sought to make political capital out of employers' use of black strikebreakers. Sympathetic to the socialists, Sinclair depicted the meeting at which Tillman spoke as a defeat for the South Carolinian. It is worth noting, however, that the same chapter of *The Jungle* that reported Tillman's failure in Chicago also included Sinclair's portrait of the black strikebreakers as lazy, ineducable, and obsessed with white women. Sinclair's harsh vision shared much more with Tillman than it shared with the color-blind class consciousness urged by some socialists. But even the socialists' attacks on Tillman made use of the hostile language of black degradation. In an effort to put Tillman on the defensive, one Chicago socialist demanded, "Whose 'Nigger' are you, anyway?" At least according to the *Chicago Broad Ax*—a black newspaper—that question "floored Senator Tillman," leaving him momentarily speechless. Perhaps Tillman did not exaggerate when he reported to Democratic officials that "there is a marked revolution [in the North] in both feeling and sentiment in regard to the negro" and that race was a "live and burning question" that could be used to advantage with white Northern audiences.[75]

Some critics challenged the myth of Tillman's origins. An occasional article noted that although "it is in many quarters imagined that [Tillman] has worked his way to his present exalted station from the ranks of the 'poor whites,' . . . Tillman is a member of one of the very best families of South Carolina, and the Tillman estate is one of the finest in the South." But Tillman the planter made as good a myth as Tillman the poor white. For some, Tillman even embodied the plantation legend being promoted by writers like Joel Chandler Harris. When journalist Broughton Brandenburg conceived of a series of magazine articles called "At Home with Big Americans" in 1908, the first subject he chose was Ben Tillman, "pictured in the American mind as a man of unbridled speech, soul of steel, and deed of sword and fire." In his profile, Brandenburg deposited himself in a romantic and apparently unreconstructed Edgefield. Arriving at the gate to Tillman's plantation, he noted that "near the unpainted outbuilding, grayed by sun and rain, a good fire was crackling. To my ears there came the voice of an old negress cheerfully uplifted in one of the wailing hymns of her religion. A little black girl with round, wondering eyes ran to open the great barred gate leading to the barnyard lane. The green-wood smoke lifted and I saw the black kettle, the lye jars and the grease keg—they were making soft-soap!" Continuing on through this plantation landscape, he passed a singing work gang of black cotton-pickers and a pair of stubborn mules. The "tall clean-cut young man" riding by with "the incomparable ease of the Southerner" to inspect the cotton was Tillman's eldest son, B. R. Reaching the main house, the writer happily joined the lost world he had miraculously rediscovered. "I threw my bridle to a negro," he wrote, who answered in a plantation dialect that turn-of-the-century readers would have found utterly familiar: "Ya-as, suh. I reckon you fin' Marse Ben on de bench dar by de tree. Walk ri' in suh. Ya-as, suh."[76]

Brandenburg's Tillman was the best the South had to offer: a man of "simplicity," "directness," and "strength," a "mild old gardener" who was nonetheless capable of "attacks on institutions in which the words burned like Greek fire." His much-loved wife was an excellent housekeeper, and his sons had become accomplished scientific farmers. In town, men sought Tillman's opinion as to the state of the cotton market. In his "wonderful mingling of gentleness and ferocity," Tillman had also earned the love and respect of his picturesque black laborers. Brandenburg focused in particular on "Old Joe," Tillman's longtime employee Joseph Gibson, dwelling on his "battered old black hat" and pants with "the weather-worn look of a plank that has been out in the wood-yard for years." Tillman's good stewardship apparently included keeping even his dearest employee in rags. According to Brandenburg, Tillman was "better loved by negroes than any man in Washington," and others agreed that on his plantation he was "the idol of his 'darkies.'" Brandenburg was aware that Tillman had ridden with the rifle clubs (which he identified as the Ku Klux Klan), and he summoned up memories of "the terrifying shouts of the Edgefield Hussars in the dark days of Reconstruction," riding "to intimidate by night the insolent negroes." But the plantation idyll immediately at hand showed no trace of that sort of violence. As Tillman rode over his property, African Americans emerged from their cabins to ask after his health. And when night settled over Edgefield, Brandenburg's "noiseless dark" was punctured only by the sound of a shot "as some planter drives a plundering negro from his melon patch."[77]

Brandenburg's artless white-supremacist romance resembled Tillman's own paternalist pretensions. Tillman did rhapsodize constantly about his relationship with Joe Gibson, whom he had employed since the 1870s. He did so with such regularity that a black Cincinnati newspaper, denouncing the senator as "that foul-mouthed cyclops," remarked on his tendency to "shed a tear o'er the virtues of his humble friend and attendant, 'Old Black Joe.'" Joe, Tillman frequently claimed, did not care about voting or education. He professed their mutual love, interdependence, and obligation. "I would die to protect him from injustice or wrong," he declared. But the language of ownership was never far away, as when he mused, "I do not know whether I belong to Joe or Joe belongs to me." Of course he knew. Joe's place in Tillman's heart was dependent on his place on the farm, for he was a species of subordinate if not in fact a species of property. Creelman's article on Tillman was accompanied by several pictures of Tillman's Trenton estate, including one entitled "The 'Three Joes,'" a photograph of Joe Gibson, "the faithful Negro," holding the reins of "Joe Bailey and Joe Black-

"The 'Three Joes,'" Joe Gibson and two of Tillman's horses, from James Creelman's article "A Defender of the Senate," Pearson's Magazine *(June 1906).*

burn . . . the Senator's favorite horses." All three Joes were faithful; all three Joes were favorites; all three Joes were Tillman's.[78]

The headstone Tillman commissioned for Gibson's grave after his death a few years later reflects the self-consciousness and self-congratulation inherent in Tillman's twentieth-century paternalism. The inscription read: "Erected by Senator B. R. Tillman to the memory of Joseph Gibson, Born a slave about 1845, Died March 1, 1912. He was a loyal friend and faithful servant; the best type of his race, and example of his training." We will never know how Gibson would have felt about such a characterization or the fact that even on the marker for his own grave, his employer's name came first.[79]

The Southernization of American Politics

Tillman had not actually reconstructed the slave South, and in any case, such idealized visions of the plantation represented a paternalist fantasy, not a violently stratified agricultural society where gunshots represented business as usual. African Americans more than a generation removed from slavery regarded Tillman as the enemy of all their aspirations, and in 1906, with

Tillman a national celebrity and the ashes of the Atlanta riot barely cool, black Chicagoans went on the offensive. The philanthropic board of a Chicago hospital association had hired Tillman to speak at a fund-raising event. But by 1906, black Chicagoans numbered in the tens of thousands, and Tillman's impending arrival sparked a militant reaction. At least one death was attributed to conflict over Tillman's upcoming address: a white man who had taunted black Chicagoans with Tillman's views was shot through the head. Hoping to defuse this situation, a trio of black civic leaders — an editor, a minister, and a dentist — offered the head of the hospital association $5,000 (in some reports $10,000) to cancel Tillman's speech. Adele Keeler refused. "O, you colored people are always getting into some brawl," she told the three men. A committee of black ministers then petitioned the city's mayor to declare the advocate of lynching "a menace to public safety and peace" and to ban him from speaking. Although the mayor refused, he also declined to introduce Tillman, describing himself as "not in sympathy with mob-law, lynch law, or assassination." Finally, a group of leading black citizens extracted a vague promise from the hospital association that Tillman would speak not on "the race problem" but on the annexation of Cuba.[80]

Tillman took advantage of the fracas to demonstrate his defiance. Speaking in Michigan and Wisconsin in the days before the Chicago speech, Tillman told worried well-wishers that "[m]y life has been threatened so many times because of my attitude on the race question that I pay no attention now to threats." This bravado provoked admonitions from his worried wife, and two detectives kept close by, as the *Chicago Tribune* put it, to guard him "from any possible outbreak of 'race war.' " Tillman would not promise to discuss only Cuba. "To treat the subject as it should be treated necessitates the introduction of the race question. The annexation of Cuba and the negro situation are so closely linked as to cause me to decline to make any changes in my lecture."[81]

African Americans continued to debate the merits of militant versus peaceful protest. Editor T. Thomas Fortune often "flayed Ben Tillman unmercifully" in his speeches. Responding to a violent Tillman speech in Wisconsin, Fortune was quoted as telling the members of the Afro-American Press Association, "We have cringed and crawled long enough. I don't want any more 'good niggers.' I want 'bad niggers.' It's the 'bad nigger' with a Winchester who can defend his home and children and wife." W. Calvin Chase of the *Washington Bee* forcefully dissented from Fortune's advocacy of armed resistance, fearing that such advice would endanger black Southerners. Julius Taylor, editor of the *Chicago Broad Ax*, spent much of late 1906 and early 1907 denouncing Tillman as "brainless," an "Anarchist," and a "maniac," and he praised black and white ministers and editors who condemned the South Carolinian. Taylor mocked the notion that black men constituted a threat, sexual or otherwise, to white Southerners, and he urged black and white opponents to greet Tillman with demonstrations and hostile questions, not violence.[82]

Verbal attack was the general rule. In *The Souls of Black Folk*, W. E. B. Du Bois declared that it was the "imperative duty of thinking black men" to denounce Ben Tillman. Kelly Miller, despite his misconceptions about Tillman's origins, fulfilled the obligation Du Bois had mandated, describing Tillman as "the guide, philosopher, and friend of those who worship at the shrine of racial narrowness and hate." "The Tillman regime," he explained, "is based upon the fear that, after all, the Negro might not be inferior. He is deprived of his rights lest he develop suspected power." Black ministers, editors, and others worked to combat and neutralize Tillman wherever possible. Two days before Tillman spoke in overwhelmingly white Fond du Lac, Wisconsin, a black minister traveled from Indianapolis to deliver a preemptive rebuttal, "a plea for fairness for the colored man."[83]

Humor could sometimes deflate Tillman's claims to expertise in racial matters. During a speech to the Senate on "the race problem," Tillman asserted that "no man living . . . knows the American negro better than I do," but before he could continue, "a ripple of laughter passed over the chamber and through the galleries, in which many of the colored people in the galleries joined." Lawrence Levine reports a joke, set during the South Carolina constitutional convention, in which Tillman was criticized by a black delegate and responded with the threat, "Why, you dirty black rascal, I'll swallow you alive." The man replied, "If you do, you'll have more brains in your belly than you've got in your head." The rejoinder revealed the deep antipathy Tillman engendered among many black people and the potential for catharsis in direct challenges to his authority. Sometimes the moral point of satirical representations remained ambiguous or grimly ironic: one cartoon entitled "things that might have happened, but won't," showed Tillman inviting Booker T. Washington to lunch.[84]

Some Northern whites lodged protests. In 1907, the *Detroit Free Press* depicted Tillman using his pitchfork to fertilize a plant labeled "race war." A white Midwestern Democrat regretted Tillman's recent local appearance, explaining that he "does not represent the best thought of the South in his discussion of this problem." Tillman was an incendiary, "precipitating a conflagration" from which Midwestern men would have to rescue him, "march[ing] South once more, this time to save Mr. Tillman and his terrified compatriots from a catastrophe which they have recklessly provoked." But more often, white Northerners' responses to black protest foretold the nationalization of white Southern anxieties. The newspaper coverage of Tillman's Chicago appearance persistently depicted African Americans as violent and dangerous. A Wisconsin newspaper reported that "[t]he colored people of Chicago are being aroused to a state of frenzy . . . and the committee has been notified by letter that the senator will be shot on the stage if he attempts to deliver his address." Such threats provoked defiant promises of "[d]etectives, uniformed policemen, . . . and volunteer guards" to escort him from the train station to the hall where he was to speak.[85]

Tillman believed that black in-migration would bring white Northerners around to his point of view. His prediction was given murderous reality in 1908 in Springfield, Illinois. More "riots" followed, in which white mobs attacked black citizens, as in July 1917 in East St. Louis, Illinois. This city, just across the Mississippi River from the old slave markets of St. Louis, was hardly "Northern" enough to expose Yankee hypocrisy. But the year after Tillman's death would bring a wave of antiblack violence that was truly national in scope. The "red summer" of 1919 fulfilled Tillman's prophecy that white Northerners confronting substantial black populations at close quarters would soon resort to murderous violence, as white Chicagoans (among many others) rioted against their black neighbors.[86]

At the same time, Tillman's version of the South's recent history was becoming part of the national consciousness. While Tillman toured the nation as a lecturer, his friend and ally Thomas Dixon Jr. was promoting the same message through more modern media. Dixon, a North Carolinian by birth, had long been an admirer of Tillman's. In the early twentieth century, he published novels such as *The Leopard's Spots: A Romance of the White Man's Burden* (1902) and *The Clansman: An Historical Romance of the Ku Klux Klan* (1905), wildly popular fictions that drew on white-supremacist accounts of the violent overthrow of biracial governments. The hero in Dixon's melodramas was the race-proud white man who mobilized against "Negro domination"; the villain was the frustrated and lustful black rapist. Anyone who had been listening to Tillman during the previous quarter century would have found this story familiar. In fact, Dixon sometimes claimed that Tillman had inspired him to write *The Clansman*. This may simply have been astute marketing: Dixon spread the credit for *The Clansman* wherever he thought it would do the most good, and Tillman was only one of many to whom he attributed it. But the claim was at least credible.[87]

The *Clansman* became an enormously popular stage play, which Tillman praised in the *Augusta Chronicle*. In a note of thanks, Dixon bragged that his work would "probably pay me as much as two millions in the next twenty years," but he claimed to "prize its power & influence in shaping public opinion far above its financial returns." "Public opinion" meant, in part, thought and emotion, and Dixon's work resonated with many white Americans' anxieties and fantasies at the turn of the century. Tillman himself was moved in a profound and particular way. After attending "a war play that stirs the blood like the Clansman," Tillman wrote to his wife, he went to bed and "wanted you with me more than I can tell."[88]

Opponents of Tillman and Dixon understood the power of these men's declarations and representations. As *The Clansman* traveled the country, covering much of the same ground as Tillman's lecture tours, campaigns against the play and the lectures took place side by side. After a white mob attacked blacks in Des Moines, Iowa, a local black leader drew the connections. Such lawlessness, he complained, "was just what may be expected to occur in any community that will patronize such damnable productions as Thos. Dixon's Clansman and such infamous blackguards as the Hon. (?) Sen. Benjamin Ryan Tillman, whose sole purpose is to poison the minds of Northern white men against my people." While black Chicagoans were attempting to stop Tillman's 1906 speech, Philadelphia's black citizens mobilized to protest *The Clansman*. A spokesman described the effects of its depiction of black people: "The respect that we command is destroyed, we are slurred wherever we go; we are pointed out as brutes; our women are sneered at and our children on the streets and in the schools are subjected to indignities." The city's mayor concurred that "the intention of the play is to intensify the racial hatred that existed between our white and Colored citizens in the Southern States during the Reconstruction period, and that the tendency of the play is to produce racial hatred." Promotion of the play deliberately sought to "arous[e] our colored citizens to a state of frenzy. . . . I therefore forbid the play proven [*sic*] as the 'Clansman' to be continued." Some of South Carolina's newspapers denounced the novel and play as racially inflammatory, and a few localities, notably Orangeburg (home of Claflin College), banned the play outright. But *The Clansman* also drew a more pedantic form of criticism in the state whose history it claimed to depict. The *Columbia State* pointed out that the Klan had disappeared in 1871, but Reconstruction had continued in South Carolina for another five years. An authentic representation of Redemption would have included red shirts, not white robes. The film version of *The Clansman*, entitled *The Birth of a Nation*, produced by D. W. Griffith, was released in 1915 to a mixture of enthusiastic praise, bitter condemnation, and local controversy. Kelly Miller, Oswald Garrison Villard, and many others denounced it as a slander against black people. Despite substantial opposition, however, the film gained positive reviews and large audiences. Presidential approval and similar endorsements by congressmen and members of the Supreme Court caused censors to withdraw. The film was immensely popular in South Carolina, where it played to packed houses throughout the 1910s and 1920s.[89]

The wide (if far from unanimous) acclaim for *The Birth of a Nation* represented the triumph of Tillman's evolving vision of Southern history. By the 1910s, Tillman's and Dixon's myths had become the dominant interpretation of Southern history. Through the scholarship of pro-Redemption historians, popular works such as Claude Bowers's *The Tragic Era*, and the repeated assertions of hundreds of politicians, Tillman's version of Reconstruction and Redemption attained broad national acceptance among white Americans. Dissidents such as Du Bois, who outlined a radically different interpretation of Reconstruction, endured generations of neglect. Even after the triumphs of the civil rights movement and the reemergence of a Du Boisian interpretation of Reconstruction, the victory engineered by Tillman and rendered by Dixon and Griffith lived on in American popular culture.[90]

Tillman's white supremacy had reconstructed Reconstruction and, despite opposition, was reconstructing the nation. But as Tillman turned his gaze homeward in the last decade of his life, he found that the foundations he had helped lay in South Carolina did not seem to support the white patriarchal republic he had envisioned.

Demagogues and Disordered Households

In 1908, a stroke temporarily paralyzed Tillman's left side and for a time left him unsteady, weak, and forgetful. In 1910 he fell ill again, collapsing on the steps of the Capitol. For several days, his death was expected, and although he did gradually mend, he never fully regained his strength. Physical weakness took a psychological toll. Although he recognized the figure he saw in the mirror, he admitted that he felt "like I ought to be arrested as a fraud." "I am afraid the days of my fighting are over," he sighed to a supporter; "[t]he spirit is willing but the flesh is weak." But Tillman had known many moments of apparent defeat, and he fought death as determinedly as he had fought emancipation. Applying his eclectic conception of reform to his own body, he became a health faddist and physical culture enthusiast. He turned to a diet of raw onions, spinach, hot water, and an "egg nog" of his own devising; he lifted dumbbells and performed deep-breathing exercises. Thrilled with his recovery, he once again sought to turn his personal experience into a model for social change—this time by reforming the habits of his fellow senators. He deplored the symptoms of "Congressional disease," caused by too much eating, drinking, and smoking and not enough exercise and sleep. He did not claim to have all the answers—"I lament every day of my life the lack of knowledge of my own body," he confessed—but he did want his colleagues to benefit from his experiences and explorations. Among other things, he induced his colleagues to ban smoking in the Senate chamber.[1]

Tillman in his last decade. Special Collections, Clemson University Libraries.

As Tillman struggled against physical debility, the realities of South Carolina politics and his own family life pleased him even less than the mirror by his sickbed. Across the nation, white Americans moved toward accepting Tillman's version of Southern history and racial hierarchy, but Tillman's own son and his most successful political disciple represented failures, perhaps even betrayals, of his efforts. The agricultural renewal that he had sought to nurture and protect seemed less and less plausible. White laborers proved hardly better than black, and an increasing number worked in the mills rather than the fields. Meanwhile, despite his efforts, the "race problem" continued to cast a terrifying shadow over the future of the white republic.

The Decline of Agricultural Patriarchy

Tillman had spent his career trying to reconstruct the world he believed his family and class had lost, a world in which prosperous, independent white men toiled with the aid of sturdy farm wives and grateful black dependents. On paper, he seemed to have achieved at least personal success. By the second decade of the twentieth century, Tillman's primary holdings spread across the upper piedmont: he owned more than 200 acres at his home in Trenton; a parcel of 250 acres near Ninety-Six; about 600 acres at Chester, where he was born and raised; and small holdings of land in Florida, Georgia, and North Carolina. Additional lands in Greenwood County had by 1911 been distributed to his sons. He also owned a growing number of shares of stock, especially in the last years of his life, mainly in agricultural concerns and local banks. The bulk of Tillman's wealth, however, consisted of his earnings as a lecturer. In October 1907, Tillman told his daughter Sophie that his appearances since March of that year would end up netting him "about $25000," which he was "trying to save & invest it wisely" so that his children "may not have to slave & work too hard."[2]

Whenever Tillman was away from Trenton, he wrote a stream of letters to the family members and employees who oversaw his property. Foremost among these was Sallie. Even before he left for the Senate, he wrote to his wife from his desk at the constitutional convention, telling her to notify one tenant "that unless he pays up all rent & advances for the year I cannot let him stay there next year. Cotton has gone down & I urged him to hurry it in & sell early so it is not my fault if he does not pay out. Take corn peas or any cheese but he must pay up & not leave any new debt." He wrote similar letters of direction from the Senate, the road, and his sickbed. Raised during the war and Reconstruction, Sallie Tillman had never expected to live insulated from such practicalities. Responding to her husband in a typical letter, she described hiring women to hoe cotton, putting men to work in the corn and peas, renting a horse, and selling grapes. Without any noticeable change in inflection, she reported having gone "out last night in the back of the garden and shot my pistols several times" to frighten away some "rogue" or "rascal" come to steal grapes or cream. "Your mother says negroes steal more . . . than it takes to feed a family," Ben Tillman casually reported to Sophie. Such confrontations with criminals, whom the Tillmans assumed to be their black laborers, left her annoyed rather than frightened. "I'm so thankful that I'm not afraid," she wrote.[3]

"A good wife was the safest ballast for a man," Tillman thought, and he boasted that Sallie's "petticoat government" had made him "the best henpecked husband in the state, but if he had done any good, she was mainly responsible." When Sallie suffered a partial mental collapse in 1913, Tillman reported to his son that although she was "listless and indifferent," "she still finds fault with me, as is natural." Indeed, Sallie was relentlessly practical. She did not care about fine clothes or expensive possessions. "I do try not to be extravagant," she told her daughter Sophie. "My ring is the most costly thing I've wanted and I'm glad I've got that much safe, for it is an investment." She could become impatient with Tillman about economic matters. "I have been all over the place this morning and the cotton is white I tell you," she wrote testily while he was on tour. Ironically, it was her husband—a longtime proponent of self-sufficiency and diversification—who kept them tied to the cotton economy. She complained that he said he took on speaking engagements because they needed the money for their old age, but then he gambled the money on cotton futures. "When he talks about feeling obliged to do this work for us, I simply wish we could live without spending anything at all."[4]

For this society to perpetuate itself, patriarchs like Tillman had to pass along to their sons their wisdom and virtue—and a stable agricultural order. Tillman kept careful track of the money and land he disbursed to his children, and in his will, he instructed his executors to make sure that each child received an equal amount. Still, he thought that "some work [was] requisite for health & a rational life—self-reliance," so when Sallie made it known that she would not want to stay at Trenton if Tillman died before she did, Tillman considered selling—not giving—the homeplace to his eldest son, B. R.[5]

Tillman worried about his children's futures in the state. "South Carolina," he told B. R. in 1896, "offers less opportunities for men to get rich or comfortable than many others." The commonwealth to which he had dedicated his life remained "the poorest state in some respects east of the Mississippi and its future can never be very great." He became convinced that B. R. and his younger brother Henry should move to Indian Territory (Oklahoma) or the Pacific Northwest. Tillman could invest in land, and the two boys would have "a much better opening there than in S.C." They needed that advantage, he feared, for Henry was "simplehearted & unsophisticated." As it turned out, though, it was the older son, B. R., who gave Tillman cause for concern.[6]

B. R., born in 1878, was hardly the idealized young aristocrat Brandenburg had presented to his readers in 1908. By his twenties, in fact, B. R. had become an alcoholic. For Ben Tillman, architect of the dispensary, this constituted a bitter irony; for Ben and Sallie Tillman, what they saw as their son's weakness and irresolution was a source of constant frustration. "Do you know I've lost all patience with him? He can stop drinking when he wants to," Sallie wrote to her husband, who agreed that "[n]o one can help him if he doesn't leave off drinking." When Tillman was stricken in 1908, B. R. promised to stop drinking while his father was ill, prompting the senator to write that in that case he would almost rather "continue sick." While the family monitored B. R.'s habits, Tillman looked for explanations. He sometimes blamed "bad company" for his son's drinking; if the young man would stay away from the corrupting influence of town folk, Tillman thought, he would be safe from the temptations of alcohol. But if environmental factors were to blame, Tillman knew he could not easily evade responsibility for his son's limitations. An uneven education, he told the young man, had provided him with a "defective foundation." This was a particularly brave admission, for B. R. had been a member of Clemson's first graduating class in 1896. Speaking before a Citadel audience in 1899, Tillman remarked ruefully that "it did not take a military college to make a 'dude,' " for as he had discovered, "even agricultural colleges did the same."[7]

Tillman's direct involvement in his son's affairs did not seem to improve matters. After graduating from Clemson, B. R. had spent several years working on the family farm at Trenton. He had finally left in 1903, when he married aristocratic Lucy Dugas and took over her Edgefield plantation. When their marriage fell apart, B. R. returned to his father's employment as his private secretary, but Tillman finally fired his unreliable son, leaving him "humiliated." In 1909, though, the senator became involved in the battle for custody of his grandchildren. Tillman believed that Lucy was morally and practically unfit to raise the children by herself. B. R. agreed, and the men set in motion a controversy that exposed the twentieth-century limits of patriarchal authority. Under a century-old statute, fathers in South Carolina had the right to deed their children away from mothers. At the end of 1909, B. R., pointing to his estranged wife's "unfitness and inability to raise my two children as they should be raised," deeded his daughters to Ben and Sallie.[8]

Public reaction was swift and harsh. This practice made patriarchy's theory of ownership too explicit, violating many citizens' sense of what constituted a reasonable and proper exercise of paternal power. Hostile politicians jumped on the deed as evidence that Tillman was old and out of touch. Tillman, though, was unapologetic. The law had allowed his son to make the deed, he wrote, and despite "the progress of civilization in emancipating women and giving them more and more rights," he did not think the deed should be retroactively annulled. The case went to the state Supreme Court, which on 15 February 1910 struck down the statute and returned the children to their mother. The very next day, Tillman collapsed on the Capitol steps from his second stroke and entered his long final illness. It was as though he could not tolerate so dense a tangle of personal and philosophical defeat.[9]

B. R. finally gained partial custody of his daughters, but he remained wounded and defensive and resisted his family's suggestions and directives. He retreated to the family home at Trenton, where he worked for, rented from, and finally bought land from his father. But B. R. complained about Tillman's constant criticism and demanded—at the age of thirty-four—to be treated as "a man . . . just as determined as you are [to] receive the deference in my own affairs that you receive in yours." The bluster hardly concealed his shame and diffidence. Even as he demanded autonomy, he continued to rely on Tillman to set the terms of their rental agreement and advise him on agricultural matters.[10]

The management of a free labor force continued to vex the Tillmans. "The great trouble in developing anything in South Carolina is the labor we have had," Ben Tillman sighed. After Joe Gibson's death in 1912, Tillman complained, "My main trouble at Trenton was in having no negro that I could rely on in any way." A half century after emancipation, the "*gentleman* from Africa" continued to leave Tillman dissatisfied. Once workers were hired, he warned, some responsible white person "must stay with them." Given the slightest opportunity, black workers would steal from and otherwise "impose" on a landowner; renters and sharecroppers would "stand back and make the wages negroes do the work"; unsuccessful croppers would do their best to carry crops away if not carefully overseen. Tillman believed he knew individual black men and women well enough to assess their degree of competence and trustworthiness, and he grew irritated with B. R. for renting land to one man instead of another whom Tillman preferred. But Tillman regarded even longtime black employees as unreliable and improvident. The widowed Kitty Gibson "does not attend to her duties as she should when [Sallie] is not there." Another man was "crazy for nineteen dollars," which he said he needed to keep from losing his buggy, but the frugal Sallie had little patience for this seemingly irrational attachment to a luxury item. "I haven't it to let him have and I don't know what he wants with it anyway," Sallie told Tillman.[11]

Tillman constantly worried that his "people" were taking advantage of him. As 1912 drew to a close and it came time to settle up annual rental and sharecropping arrangements, Tillman wrote insistently to B. R. about a small matter that seemed to trouble him a good deal. "I have a mortgage on Ben Lanham's mule," explained the U.S. senator, "and he ought not to be allowed to leave the place and carry the mule or carry any corn away. Let us clean him up before he leaves." Two days later, he reminded his son of the matter, describing the written agreement he had used to ensure "getting the rent and what I advanced him." The master sighed under the burden of such ungrateful servants. "It is very unpleasant to have to deal with negroes and especially when you have known them a long time as I have known Ben: but they have no appreciation of kindness and forbearance, and are ready to 'Do' a white man any time they can get the chance."[12]

Planter paternalism's contradictions continued to bubble up in Tillman's early-twentieth-century letters. Grand statements about "the negro" alternated with highly individualized assessments and reports of privileges offered or withdrawn. Whenever possible, Tillman made arrangements directly with individual African Americans, and like any planter, he sought to control the disposition of the privileges he offered — to be the sole author of any largesse and to grant it to worthy black individuals, not to what seemed to him to be a largely unworthy black community. "About the sweet potatoes," he told B. R., "Mark and Fannie ought to be allowed to eat as many as they can, but not give their friends and neighbors any."[13]

Simply finding enough laborers could be a problem. Some plantation owners reported success: a cousin planting cotton nearby had "more negroes than he wants. He is kind to them, gives them everything they need, and whips them when they do not work to suit him." But others did not fare so well. "I heard at Trenton the usual complaints about some men hav[ing] no hands at all," Tillman reported. It was in such a context that Tillman advised Sallie to "[h]ire hands at any price they may cost"—but to do so without letting other employers know so as to avoid "caus[ing] a row in the neighborhood." Any conflicts arising over such violations of informal wage ceilings went unrecorded. But white landowners like Tillman and his neighbors still feuded over the real and symbolic boundaries of their authority. Tillman might have been the aggressor in such cases: J. C. Shaw's 1891 warning to the governor to "keep your wagons off my growing crops. . . . [I]f you are a *man* for God Sake let me alone" represented a century of ordinary landowners' jealousy of their rights and prerogatives. Tillman himself resented such incursions. For example, a tree on his Trenton property obstructed some right of way, and the local council ordered it removed. Tillman had no objection to this, but he was outraged when the council apparently claimed the right to dispose of the wood from the tree. "I cannot permit any such claim . . . to go unchallenged," Tillman told a white man involved in the proceedings. "I deny the Council's right to give or sell any of my property to anybody, and if it thinks I am wrong, we will settle the matter in the courts." Even if he did not echo Shaw's threat of personal retribution, Tillman remained protective of his property. A few years later, he urged B. R. to keep neighbors' hogs and cows out of his pastures.[14]

By the twentieth century, it was clear that Tillman's real affection was for agrarian politics, not professional agriculture. The institutions that took up Tillman's time were not the farms and households he idealized but the boards, committees, and caucuses of politics and government; he was no longer closely identified with the reform of agricultural methods and economics. Despite his micromanagement of crops and laborers, Tillman was not a great success as a practical farmer and had little useful advice to offer others. The Clemson State Farmers' Institute was just the kind of organization that Tillman had called for during the 1880s, a forum where successful, scientific farmers could dispense their wisdom to an interested audience. But when Tillman appeared on its program in 1906, his topic was the curiously bourgeois "Beautifying the Country House." A few years later, when he did give a somewhat more practical talk on hog raising, he admitted that he had last raised hogs himself fifteen years before. His days as a practical progressive farmer were over.[15]

His detachment from agricultural matters was evident in a 1907 letter from a confidant and protégé. John G. Richards fulminated against the lien law because it allowed black men to act as independent farmers, which he believed they could not do successfully, and because it discouraged them from working for white landowners. Although this was precisely the line

Tillman had taken during the 1880s and 1890s, Richards had to ask Tillman whether the lien law had been an element in his campaigns. Tillman had gained a reputation as an agricultural reformer, but no one seemed to recall any longer precisely what reforms he had endorsed.[16]

The Legacies of Tillmanism

Although the narrative of history had always mattered to Tillman, as a young man he had not worried that others might not be getting his story just right. When a college student wrote to Tillman in 1894 asking for details of the campaign of 1876, Tillman casually put him off. As he grew older, though, Tillman became eager to define his own legacy. In the last decade of his life, it sometimes seemed that the only thing Tillman wanted to talk about were the heroic deeds of his youth. He did extensive research on the campaign of 1876, and he considered writing "a book on the race question" or an autobiography.[17]

Tillman also sought to shape his immediate legacy in South Carolina politics. This was a considerably more difficult task than shaping the past, for it required coming to terms with the political culture he himself had helped create. Tillman had used innuendo and insinuation against his Democratic foes; he had exploded violently against blacks, Republicans, Northerners, and anyone else who had challenged his words or prerogatives. He had controlled political conventions and his own political movement so tightly that, long after he left for Washington, D.C., reformers wrote to him for instructions. "Will you please tell me," wrote one in 1906, "just what we want to fight for in the state convention. . . . Also please tell me what it is that we don't want." Clearly, he had promoted loyalty to his person more than loyalty to a well-defined program. In the 1910s, he began to worry that the style he had nurtured might prove more enduring than the substantive victories.[18]

Illness and distance had diminished Tillman's power in state affairs. Although he won reelection in 1912, after 1910 he would no longer dominate state politics. He remarked matter-of-factly to his friend and lawyer J. William Thurmond in early 1912, "I of course do not know what the feeling in the State is, except from the newspapers." He had spent so long in Washington, D.C., on the road, and recovering from illness that he no longer even claimed to know what "the farmers" were thinking. Men like the urbane Richard Manning, a reform-minded representative of the town classes, won the governorship during the 1910s. But Manning's opponents, the men who followed more closely in Tillman's footsteps, bothered the senator even more.[19]

The most troubling manifestation of the Tillmanite legacy was "Coley"— Coleman Livingston Blease. A Tillmanite legislator in 1890, Blease had subsequently run with mixed success for several offices, including governor. In 1908, he had come in second in the gubernatorial race, and in 1910, with Tillman's support, he was finally elected. But once Blease reached the governorship, Tillman began to doubt the wisdom of his endorsement. Blease's appeal to the state's white male millhands closely followed the pattern Tillman had established a generation before. Claiming to stand up for the disfranchised and dispossessed elements of the state's white population, he leveled baseless charges at his opponents and cast aspersions on their whiteness and manhood. But whereas Tillman had struggled to protect both white men's prerogatives and the rule of law, Blease made no bones about his preference for violent self-assertion. His public persona and policies were wilder and more reckless than Tillman's. Not only did he curse, but he gambled and bragged of drinking bootleg whiskey. He pardoned unprecedented numbers of criminals and used his appointment powers with little regard for appearances or qualifications. He also took Tillman's support for mob violence to new heights. Beyond justifying the lynching of black men accused of raping white women, Blease declared that "[w]hen mobs are no longer possible liberty will be dead." "Sometimes after a lynching," writes his most acute interpreter, "Blease publicly celebrated the savage murder with a bizarre death dance."[20]

Blease's anti-aristocratic rhetoric closely matched Tillman's. In the 1920s, his weekly newspaper urged voters to "save South Carolina from Ring Rule and Corporate Control" and elect the friends of the "Farmers and Laboring Men." His enemies were the state's self-appointed voices of reform and moderation: in Bryant Simon's description, " 'intellectuals,' 'fool theorists,' 'wise-looking old fossils,' and members of the 'holier than thou crowd.' " Like Tillman, too, Blease provided little practical, constructive aid for the men he claimed as constituents. According to Rupert Vance, Blease offered a "class appeal without offering a class program." He opposed legislation that would improve the health of millworkers, denouncing it as a figurative attack on white men's patriarchal prerogatives and a literal attack on the sexual purity of their daughters. Tillman, in Washington, D.C., had long fought federal legislation limiting the hours of work, declaring such regulation to be a "state prerogative." But Blease had no state-level reform to offer. He sometimes supported other people's proposals for protective legislation, but he also argued that millhands "should be left alone . . . and allowed to manage their own affairs." When a plunge in the price of cotton struck the state's farmers in 1911, Blease refused either to endorse the Farmers' Union's proposed warehouse system—a weak state-level echo of the subtreasury plan—or to offer a constructive suggestion of his own.[21]

Blease was another distorted image staring back from Tillman's cloudy mirror, and as both men sought reelection in 1912, the senator vacillated. He knew that various elements of the state Democratic Party would wage a strong fight against Blease, but he could not decide whether he could afford to stand openly against his onetime disciple. In private letters to his close associates, Tillman declared Blease "not fit" for office and a "disgrace" to the state. But he asked them to keep his feelings private. "I know that almost every Blease man is a Tillmanite or was one formerly," he told his nephew. Blease was every bit the stump speaker and organizer that Tillman had been, and Tillman expected the campaign to be as rough as his own reelection fight in 1892. Tillman had always known that hot rhetoric and vehement supporters were the keys to victory and that "the only way to fight the devil was with fire." He thought that "Blease has enough Tillmanism in him to have learned this, if he needed any teaching." Further, Blease's chief opponent in the 1912 race was Ira Jones, chief justice of the state Supreme Court, who had joined the majority in ruling against B. R.'s deed, and Sallie Tillman felt strongly that her husband should give Blease the benefit of the doubt rather than throw his support to Jones.[22]

Blease fulfilled all of Tillman's worst expectations. During the summer stump-meeting campaign, Blease assailed Jones as a "representative of the moneyed interests and the corporations" who had handed down decisions favorable to the railroad that employed his son, a local lawyer. He accused Jones of racial apostasy, pointing to his votes against separate-car legislation, and he publicly aired sexual and racial slanders that Tillman would have left at the level of insinuation. "You people who want social equality vote for Jones," he told one audience. "You men who have nigger children vote for Jones. You who have a nigger wife in your back yard vote for Jones." When a white man interrupted him during a political meeting, Tillman reported, Blease rebuked him by saying, "[W]hen you leave here and it gets dark, you can go around to see your 'nigger' sweetheart." Tillman claimed to be appalled by the indiscriminate use of this charge against a white Democratic opponent. Blease's remark, Tillman thought, violated the rules of decency and decorum and was an offense against "every lady in the audience as well as . . . decent men." It could only injure the state's reputation. A Southern governor might speak of many things, but not white men's sexual liaisons with black women and especially not in mixed and public company.[23]

Tillman admitted that Blease had imitated his practice of reciprocating his enemies' attacks rather than "turn[ing] the other cheek." As a result, he claimed, he would be "surprised, very agreeably so, if some men are not killed" before the end of the Jones-Blease campaign. But Tillman denied that Blease was his political heir and declared that Tillmanism and Blease-ism were "no more alike than day and night." If there was a connection, he thought, it was with Tillman's estranged nephew Jim, not with the senator himself. Tillman believed that he had truly stood for the people against the oligarchs and corporations. But although those battles had been "fought . . . with intense bitterness," they had never caused him to make "indecent" charges against opponents or to be accused of corruption. Although he found Jones unappealing, Tillman ultimately decided that he would rather lose his own race than see Blease reelected. In early August 1912, he made public his negative assessment of the governor, leading to a permanent rift between the two men.[24]

Both men won renomination later that month. But Tillman was not satisfied with the stand he had taken: in an open letter to Blease, Tillman sought to define the differences between them even more explicitly. Tillmanism, he explained, meant "genuine democracy, the rule of the people—of all the white people, rich and poor alike." Bleaseism, by contrast, meant "personal ambition and greed for office . . . for Blease and his friends"; it was "selfish, low, dirty, and revengeful." Tillman noted that both men as governors had earned the enmity of conservatives, but whereas Tillman had gradually begun to earn their support, Blease "deserve[d] the hate and distrust" they evinced.[25]

Rejecting Blease, Tillman denied and disavowed the inflammatory political style he had once championed, including the accusations of dishonesty, fraud, and corruption he had leveled against his white Democratic opponents during the 1880s and 1890s. He found Blease's attacks "discreditable to the state," especially in the eyes of the national audience with which Tillman had become so concerned. There was a quality of pleading to Tillman's repeated claim that his own "bitter" contests with his enemies bore no relation to Blease's "low" tactics. Even more striking, in letters to fellow Southern Democrats, Tillman relied on the moral and historical authority of Northern Republican heroes. Southern Democrats could not afford the division of Blease's dirty electoral fights, he warned, for "a house divided against itself cannot stand." "Let us have peace," he concluded, or at least "decency." In keeping with his quotation of Abraham Lincoln and Ulysses S. Grant, Tillman sought to revise the Democratic political demonology he had once written in stone. Many Haskellites, Tillman said, had voted for him in 1912; therefore, "Haskellite ought not to be an epithet of opprobrium in South Carolina any longer." Astonishingly, he even praised Alexander Haskell himself. Blease, on the other hand, lacked grace or honor and would probably be known as "the very worst native South Carolinian who was ever governor, [Reconstruction Republican Franklin] Moses not excepted."[26]

Tillman's attacks on Blease caused many longtime Tillmanites to feel that their leader had "deserted them and joined their oppressors." Blease himself never forgave Tillman, denouncing him for sending critical letters throughout the state in 1912 after having promised to keep out of the contest. But the greater challenge for Tillman was not Blease's hostility but that of Blease's voters. In a letter to his children, Tillman confessed that he was unable to understand "why so many of these old Tillman-ites should have been misled by a man of the type of Cole L. Blease. . . . [M]any of my old supporters . . . are angry and may scratch me [off the Democratic ticket] in the [primary] election." But he felt that by coming out against Blease he had regained his self-respect: "[S]ick and weak physically, I still have had nerve and brains enough to do a grand thing for the state under very trying conditions." His confusion and ambivalence told the tale of a man increasingly uncomfortable with his emerging legacy.[27]

The election of Woodrow Wilson to the presidency in 1912—the first Democrat since Grover Cleveland and the first Southerner since Andrew Johnson—came late in Tillman's life, but it allowed him to take a few final swings at the legacies of Reconstruction. One among many Republican crimes against white-supremacist order, he believed, was the appointment of black men and women to federal offices, and Tillman worked to cleanse the federal government of this legacy of Reconstruction. For years, Tillman filibustered and protested against President Theodore Roosevelt's nomination of William D. Crum, a black man, as collector of the port of Charleston, a fight that even fostered amicable relations between the senator and *Charleston News and Courier* editor J. C. Hemphill. After the Democrats took over the Senate in 1913, Tillman gained new powers and became more ambitious. He pursued several strategies intended to reduce the number of black federal employees, strip them of authority over whites, and segregate those who remained. As Wilson's cabinet officers pursued this project, Tillman also worked to remove blacks from postmasterships and other appointed positions in the South. This campaign offered a chance to settle old scores once and for all, and Tillman successfully sought to have his longtime nemesis Robert Smalls replaced as the federal collector of customs at Beaufort. Although President William Howard Taft had abolished the office and Smalls was going to retain the position for only another few months, Tillman wrote to a Senate colleague who sat on the appropriate committee, Mississippi's "white chief" James Vardaman, to ask that Smalls be replaced by a white collector. "My reasons are largely sentimental," wrote one white supremacist to another. "[Smalls's] ambition is to be the last collector of the port at Beaufort. . . . I want a white man to supplant him." Vardaman was happy to oblige.[28]

Crum and Smalls made irresistible targets for Tillman's symbolic crusade against black power, but his concerns about the nation's racial destiny made him willing to tolerate exceptions. He thought it appropriate for the United States to appoint black men as ministers to Haiti and Liberia, and he agreed to forward a list of candidates suggested by Reverend Richard Carroll. He saw "no reason why some South Carolina negro should not have one of these places." Tillman also apparently endorsed Carroll as an orator in the Democrats' Midwestern campaign in the 1912 presidential race. Blease, though, seemed blind to the importance of such symbolism. When Blease attacked Wilson for allowing any blacks at all to hold federal positions, Tillman wrote angrily to a South Carolina friend, "President Wilson cannot do more than he is now doing . . . to get rid of the negro. Otherwise he will arouse all the old abolition sentiment throughout the North and all to no purpose."[29]

The Ambivalent Jeffersonian

Tillman's disenchantment with former allies reflected a deeper anxiety about the fate of the nation and even democracy itself. The reconstruction of white supremacy, he realized, might never be completed. Tillman not only had idealized the world of his childhood but also had posited its institutions, anxieties, and imperatives as essential human truths. He had spent most of his adult life seeking to shore up political, economic, and legal foundations that had been catastrophically undermined during his teens and twenties. His successes were obvious: antimonopolism remained a popular political credo; Southern Democrats sat in the White House and at the heads of powerful congressional committees; and racial hierarchy and discrimination were becoming legal and cultural norms of national life. But in important respects, the twentieth-century world seemed to offer only pallid and halfhearted versions of the proud white agricultural patriarchy he had envisioned.

Tillman had built his career on the argument that the solidarity of white male producers as soldiers and citizens was the only proper basis for Southern—or American—government. His white man's democracy, he thought, reflected the best of what Thomas Jefferson had offered the world. He happily cited Jefferson's example as evidence that democracy did not necessarily require black citizenship, but by the last decade of his life, Tillman was no longer sure that even Jefferson's racialized, agrarian democracy could work, and he remained ambivalent about most white men's fitness for self-government. Throughout his career, he claimed that the overthrow of South Carolina's antebellum oligarchy was one of his proudest achievements. But as he saw what his white men did with the democracy he had restored to them, he became less and less confident that he had been on the right side of the fight. "I have come to doubt that the masses of the people have sense enough to govern themselves," he wrote to a colleague in 1916. And lest there be any doubt which "masses" he was referring to, he made his fears explicit: it was South Carolina's white Democratic primary that worried him. Votes for the "demagogue" Blease "haven't strengthened my belief in 'Democracy'—'Jeffersonian' as you call it." When the people got "the mad-dog feeling," as they did during Blease's campaigns, democracy gave way to demagoguery. So almost with one breath he could quote Jefferson on trusting the people but also declare that "a benevolent despotism is the very best form of government."[30]

This ambivalence led him to criticize a primary system that allowed nearly all white men to participate. In the wake of the 1895 constitution, the Democratic primary was the last redoubt of white men's democracy. The Blease-Jones fight in 1912 had drawn nearly 30 percent more voters to the polls than the 1910 primary, but this marked upturn was subject to multiple readings. Rather than interpreting this as evidence of a still-healthy democracy, many Jones supporters believed it meant that Blease had stolen the nomination. Since Jones was backed by longtime conservatives, there was nothing surprising in such suspicion of increased popular participation. But they were seconded in their skepticism by the onetime champion of "the farmers," who joined the chorus of those seeking to "purify" the Democratic primary.[31]

Tillman was deeply troubled by the disparity between the large number of primary voters and the small number eligible to vote in the general election. Whereas the combined 1912 primary vote for Blease and his opponents had exceeded 130,000, the vote in the November election — which included a presidential contest — barely reached 50,000. This reflected the state of general elections in the post-Populist, postdisfranchisement South: between 1904 and 1948, scarcely a third of the much smaller pool of eligible voters made it to the polls for federal elections. Although the explicit intent of his constitutional reforms had been to restrict political power to white men, Tillman now feared that Democratic nominees were being chosen by men who were ineligible to vote in the general election, men who could not help safeguard the state against Republicans and other enemies of white supremacy. He wrote of the need to "cleanse" the primary of men who helped choose a nominee they could not help elect. At first, he spoke only of the need to "save the primary," but over the next year, it became clear that this would involve an entirely new Democratic registration and the party's disfranchisement of those ineligible to vote in the general election.[32]

Tillman's younger allies, sensing grave political danger, tried to persuade him to retreat from this position. John G. Richards, who had gubernatorial aspirations of his own, reminded his mentor that he had given the state its first primary. To take such a "cruel step" as to deprive white Democrats of their votes would only return the state to the conservatives, he argued. Tillman retreated, but his disappointment with the fruits of his constitutional labors did not abate. He spoke disdainfully of those white men who would not "take the trouble" to register. He was, he said, "mortified and disappointed" that the primary system had not made white men better citizens; "the wiles and tricks of demagogues" had taken the place of substantive debate, a "method of campaigning" for which he refused to accept responsibility. Although he still claimed to believe in popular government, his deep misgivings were plain.[33]

Tillman continued to yearn for a white South Carolina in which landowners did not have to rely on free black laborers. He saw a growing labor problem in the South. "[T]he difficulty of getting servants in the houses and . . . efficient labor in the fields grows day by day," he declared in 1908. Even at their best, under the "direct and absolute control" of white overseers, black farm laborers performed inadequately. But the white folk Tillman had claimed to champion seemed scarcely better. The fact that a neighbor's "good new tenant house" had "glass windows and other appliances" still indicated to Tillman that "it is for some white man," but Tillman found the white families he employed barely preferable to black workers. Writing to B. R. in 1916, he described the Berry, Pitts, and McCarty families as "practically worthless." His harsh evaluation of these white households rang with the same grievances he and other planters had long voiced about black laborers: they shirked honest labor, required close supervision, and grew too much cotton and not enough food. The only difference between white and black laborers, Tillman believed, was that the white workers did not steal. Considering the virtues that Tillman's Anglo-Saxons possessed in the abstract, this was a miserably small concession. He continued to seek ways to improve them, regardless of their individual wishes. In 1914, in what turned out to be a premature "farewell to public life," Tillman even pondered the possibilities of a truly compulsory public school system—one that would "force white children into school, and at the same time give the blacks only the kind of training—manual and industrial—which they can assimilate." In correspondence with his nephew John Swearingen, state superintendent of education, however, he indicated that he understood that no coercive system would meet with the approval of the state's suspicious voters.[34]

Perhaps the solution lay in white immigration. Tillman believed that immigrants from favored portions of Europe—Holland, Belgium, Scotland, and Germany—would reclaim lands and establish independent households and that their efforts would "more than double the value of every acre of land in the State." If the state's 800,000 blacks could somehow be exchanged overnight for 800,000 of his chosen Europeans, Tillman imagined, property values would quadruple. Despite this fantasy of wholesale racial translation, though, Tillman recognized that the mass departure of black South Carolinians would create dangers as well as opportunities. Planter wealth continued to rely primarily on arduous, low-wage labor that was hardly likely to attract Tillman's idealized white Europeans. Indeed, during the constitutional convention, Robert Smalls had understood this dependence so well that he had reminded his white colleagues of it: "The negro is needed in the cotton fields and in the low country rice fields, and if you impose too hard conditions upon the negro in this State there will be nothing else for him to do but to leave. . . . I do not believe you want to get rid of the negro, else why did you impose a high tax on immigration agents who might come here to get him to leave?" Although Tillman imagined "millions of thrifty, energetic white homeseekers" tilling the soil with new vigor and industry, he acknowledged that the conditions awaiting new entrants to the state's labor market—who would earn "six, eight, and ten dollars per month, and live in a hut"—would not suffice.[35]

As Tillman's vision of racial purity collided with the realities of agricultural economics, he was forced to consider alternatives. The light-skinned, western Europeans he preferred—"our kith and kin"—were greatly outnumbered by the masses of southern and eastern European immigrants of the early twentieth century. Like many white Americans in every region, he worried that mixing "so much ignorance and filth" with "our American strain of manhood" would undermine American institutions. He believed that Italian immigrants, for example, lowered "the standard of our citizenship." Tillman wondered if the country was becoming "a heterogeneous mass of different nationalities with diverse aims and ideals." These men and women "swarming across the Atlantic" were "not our kind of people," he explained, "except that they are white." But that might be enough. Treated kindly and intelligently, among the "good company" of the state's best white people, these unpromising new arrivals "might be made industrious tenants and good citizens." Just as even the most capable African Americans were doomed by their blackness, these least-promising Europeans might be redeemed by their essential whiteness. It would be a limited victory at best, and it represented an aging Ben Tillman's increasingly pessimistic view of the future of white supremacy.[36]

Whiteness might have lost some of its luster for Tillman, but blackness remained at least as dangerous as it had ever been. Despite Tillman's bold description of the South as "an *imperium in imperio*," the region sometimes seemed to teeter on the edge of his much-feared "race war." During the winter of 1906–7, whites in Beaufort convinced themselves that the black majority intended to rise up against them. In a preemptive strike, a white paramilitary group seized a U.S. military Gatling gun. But the uprising never occurred, and the theft only came to light because the gun was destroyed in a fire. In 1911, a McClellanville man wrote to Tillman to report a series of alleged waylayings and shootings of whites by blacks that he attributed to whites not being "sufficiently armed." Asking Tillman to have the sheriff's weapons released into private hands, he described the situation as "trouble with the 'white man's burden.' "[37]

The specters of "race war" and the "black beast" led Tillman to the painful conclusion that his family would be safer far from South Carolina's black majority. "I never will cease to bless my stars that I have at least two daughters away from the blight of their presence," he wrote to his beloved daughter Sophie in 1916. Sophie, who lived in Oregon with her husband and daughters, had briefly considered returning to South Carolina, but Tillman told her that this would be a mistake. "I cannot get it out of my head that in the future the race problem will cut a great figure in South Carolina," he warned, "and you are away from all this, and your little girls are beyond any possibility of danger on account of it." His defiant bluster about white men ruling South Carolina "no matter what occurs" made good newspaper copy, but his own family required a greater security than the twentieth century's white men could provide.[38]

Familiarity with federal power and naval affairs had weakened Tillman's opposition to overseas intervention, and he became as militant and defiant a war hawk as he had been an anti-imperialist. When William Jennings Bryan, as Wilson's secretary of state, engaged in a policy of international treaty making and conciliation, Tillman turned skeptical and finally disdainful, deriding Bryan as the "evangel of peace at any price." In 1917, he strongly supported Wilson's decision to enter the European war. As head of the Senate Naval Affairs Committee and the representative of a state containing naval facilities, he took a strong interest in naval preparedness. He also saw the fight as a just war, one in which democratic nations fought Germans who had been educated into fatalism—who had become "slaves . . . and not free men at all." The war in Europe became the basis for his 1918 campaign for an unprecedented fifth Senate term. It would be foolish, he told his constituents, to deny the president such a powerful ally in the Senate. He was also determined to prevent Blease from gaining the seat, perhaps agreeing with John Gary Evans's suggestion that "this much you owe to the Movement."[39]

The campaign for a fifth term was under way when Ben Tillman died on 3 July 1918, struck down by a cerebral hemorrhage a month short of his seventy-first birthday. Letters of condolence poured into Trenton, where a distraught Sallie Tillman would not long outlive her beloved husband. The Senate, for its part, produced a volume of memorial addresses that included platitudinous tributes from such unlikely figures as Republican Henry Cabot Lodge. A bitter Cole Blease, fuming that that "Son-of-a-Bitch Tillman" had received such testimonials, could only swear that the old man had not been what he seemed. "Don't believe me," he scrawled on a copy of the Senate's memorial volume, "but look up his life & see."[40]

Epilogue: The Reconstruction of American Democracy

The ensuing decades bore witness to Tillman's reconstruction of white supremacy. South Carolina remained so solidly under white Democratic control that Cole Blease declared himself "astonished" in 1924 to discover that just over a thousand votes had been recorded in the state for Republican Calvin Coolidge, but the victory was broader still. Federal policy and legislation continued to defer to the strictures of Tillman's white supremacy. Until the upheavals of the Second World War altered the regional, national, and international balance of power, regulatory and interventionist federal policies did not simply add white-supremacist codicils to otherwise race-neutral reforms; rather, federal programs and policies had to be refracted through the Southern wing of the Democratic Party.[1]

During the "red summer" of 1919, as white men across the nation lynched scores of black Americans, including veterans of the European war, Tillman's onetime protégé James F. Byrnes rose in Congress to repeat the threat that Tillman had made throughout his life: white men would never accept black men as political or social equals, and any "resort to violence must inevitably bring to the negro the greater suffering." "This is a white man's country and will always remain a white man's country," he declared, repeating as dogma the slogan that Tillman had had to back up with force, fraud, and fear. Despite the countless acts of vigilante terror still faced by black Southerners, Byrnes and his colleagues blocked federal antilynching legislation. When some New Deal policy-makers sought to bring a measure of justice to

Southern agricultural life, they were beaten back by the still-powerful representatives of the Southern planter class, who profited from the policies of the Agricultural Adjustment Administration and insisted that agricultural and domestic employees—the great majority of black Southern workers—be omitted from the wage and Social Security protections enjoyed by other classes of workers.[2]

It was in the context of these crippling limitations that Byrnes, unveiling a statue of Ben Tillman on the grounds of the South Carolina statehouse in 1940, described the planter's son as "the state's 'first New Dealer.'"[3] The statue's inscription would have pleased Tillman even more, for it described him as "the friend and leader of the common people," who had "taught them their political power." Subsequent commentators agreed with this assessment. In 1944, Edgefield native Francis Butler Simkins published a scholarly biography of his former neighbor, concluding that "Pitchfork Ben" had accomplished both good—limited democratization for white men, the establishment of Winthrop and Clemson, and the dispensary system—and evil, especially by encouraging what Simkins—no liberal—saw as increased racial antagonism. Simkins had spent more than twenty years studying Tillman, and he understood the distance between his reputation as a radical and reformer and the reality of his career. But even this acute observer could not help being drawn in: in closing, musing over the statue of Tillman, Simkins found "determination in the expressive face and the rugged strength of a leader of the common people in the lineaments."[4]

The same interpretive trap awaits us today. It is tempting to conclude, remembering the founding of Winthrop or surveying Clemson's Tillman Hall, that Tillman's legacy remains divided, tragically but typically, by race. Perhaps the murderous white supremacist was, just the same, the friend of the white plain folk, and perhaps our assessment of Tillman's legacy must try to "balance" one against the other. Such thoughts would have pleased Ben Tillman, confirming that eighty years after his death, his legacy had the potential to set the descendants of yeomen and slaves (or Yankees and Confederates) against one another.

But people struggling to make a new world from the ashes of Confederate defeat needed a better friend than Ben Tillman. His "love" for his "common people" was mixed with disdain and always limited by his fear of offering black Americans the opportunity to pursue their own visions. If he was able to pose as white men's great protector and ally, it was in large measure because he had so skillfully and insistently made war on the competition. Even the tangible contributions he made to white South Carolinians' welfare—especially Clemson and Winthrop—must be reconsidered in this light. Ben Tillman's legacy cannot include the Clemson that now exists, an integrated and coeducational institution, for through the doors of Tillman Hall now pass men and women whose paths stretch back to many continents, men and women who understand the right to wage political struggles without fear of violent retaliation as a basic element of citizenship. In this, Clemson repudiates rather than represents Tillman's legacy. He would have torn down his beloved "farmers' college" brick by brick before he would have allowed it to foster a world where neither sex nor race defined the limits of a person's attainments.

Moreover, the image of the white savage that Tillman promoted did a graver injury to "his people" than any blow struck by their foes. Since the antebellum era, Northern travelers had frequently perceived the white South as a society composed of two classes: aristocrats and "poor white trash." The Red-shirts' rhetorical tactics had reinforced this notion, holding degraded white men responsible for the worst acts of violence while alternately suggesting that elite whites could control them but would not do so unless their demands were met. Tillman and his ilk did not so much use poor white men to achieve their ends as they used the image of the poor white man, the white savage lurking just beneath respectable restraint.[5]

The consequences for the nation have been profound and tragic. A national discourse of white Southern degradation and poverty continues to persuade many non-Southerners that the white South is America's evil twin. Throughout our popular culture and even in high-budget dramatic works purporting to tell the truth about Southern history, lower-class white Southern men of staggering ignorance and almost primal viciousness *are* the "real" South. Of course, the discourse is not wholly fabricated, and there is no point in evading the many brutalities perpetrated by real white Southerners in the name of "white supremacy." But Tillman's most insidious success is the persuasiveness of this image, a negative reference so potent that it still clouds our vision. It allows white non-Southerners, against all evidence, to blame someone else for the country's continuing struggle over the meaning of race. Worse still, it encourages the belief that the defeat of Birmingham's Bull Connor represented victory over white supremacy itself. At the very least, Tillman's story should remind us that the most earnest advocates of violent white supremacy were actually among the wealthiest white Southerners and that it took all of their historically accumulated skill and dexterity to beat back the challenges that never stopped bubbling up from below.[6]

Some of our forebears' dreams remain nightmares from which we are trying to awake. These include the ruthless greed of Yankee slave traders, the often genocidal expansionism of "manifest destiny," and the vision of violent white manhood that animated Ben Tillman's seventy years. Tillman's true legacy lives on wherever Americans continue to shore up the battered foundations of white supremacy. It lives on wherever dissent is met with violence, wherever white men are the only first-class citizens, wherever "populism" is reduced to what one contemporary called Tillman's "gospel of discontent."[7] To undo Tillman's reconstruction of white supremacy requires us not only to challenge the consequences of his actions but also to understand the words and ideas that he used and the sources of their power. Only that understanding can provide the basis for a real reconstruction of American democracy.

Notes

Abbreviations

The following abbreviations are used in the notes.

BIFCR	Beech Island Farmers' Club Records, 1846–93, South Caroliniana Library, University of South Carolina, Columbia, S.C.
BRT	Benjamin Ryan Tillman (1847–1918).
BRTP-CL	Benjamin Ryan Tillman Papers, Special Collections, Robert Muldrow Cooper Library, Clemson University, Clemson, S.C.
BRTP-SCL	Benjamin Ryan Tillman Papers, South Caroliniana Library, University of South Carolina, Columbia, S.C.
ECA	Edgefield County Archives, Edgefield, S.C.
JCC	Constitutional Convention of the State of South Carolina, *Journal of the Constitutional Convention of the State of South Carolina, Begun to Be Holden at Columbia, S.C., on Tuesday, the Tenth Day of September . . . until Wednesday, the Fourth Day of December [1895] . . . When Finally Adjourned* (Columbia, S.C.: Charles A. Calvo Jr., 1895).
PL	Special Collections, Perkins Library, Duke University, Durham, N.C.
SCDAH	South Carolina Department of Archives and History, Columbia, S.C.
SCHS	South Carolina Historical Society, Charleston, S.C.
SCL	South Caroliniana Library, University of South Carolina, Columbia, S.C.
SHC	Southern Historical Collection, Wilson Library, University of North Carolina, Chapel Hill, N.C.
SL	Manuscripts and Archives, Sterling Library, Yale University, New Haven, Conn.

Introduction

1. Students of U.S. history will recognize in the title of this introduction the allusion to C. Vann Woodward's story of Populist dreams and defeat, *Tom Watson,*

Agrarian Rebel. My purpose in appropriating this phrase is not to suggest that Tillman was actually the spokesman for a radical farmers' movement; on the contrary, as I hope this work makes clear, his "rebellion" was almost wholly symbolic and his definition of "the farmers" was both exclusionary and obfuscatory. Yet I am not simply using the phrase ironically; I am using it in order to suggest two hard truths that emerge from the comparison between the stories of Watson the Populist and Tillman the white supremacist. First, Tillman's empty "agrarian rebellion" triumphed over Watson's more ambitious imaginings. Second, the contradictions and ambivalences within radical Populists' own thinking made them susceptible to the same confused and exclusive version of producerism that Tillman offered—a version that couched its appeals in the language and history of white manhood. A half-century ago, Woodward revolutionized the study of the post–Reconstruction South by placing political divisions among white men at the center of the story. Subsequent generations of scholarship on Populism, labor relations, educational and organizational life, and violence have enhanced and often transformed our understanding of the period, yet they have failed to generate a new, compelling political synthesis of the period. To the extent that we are still working out the full implications of Woodward's insights and arguments, the study of gender may constitute the "missing piece." Recent works on gender and its relations to other aspects of human experience, ranging from Glenda Gilmore's study of black women negotiating the boundaries of white supremacy, to Peter Bardaglio's exploration of the laws governing household relations, to Bryant Simon's investigation of the political world of white male industrial workers, demonstrate the centrality of gender identities, ideologies, relations, and conflicts to political life. See Woodward, *Origins of the New South*; Gilmore, *Gender and Jim Crow*; Bardaglio, *Reconstructing the Household*; and Simon, *Fabric of Defeat.*

2. Cf. Fredrickson, *Black Image*, and Joel Williamson, *Crucible of Race.* The enforcement of a social hierarchy, like the destruction of a people, is first and foremost a matter of political organization, not ethnic chauvinism or cultural pathology. Philip Gourevitch's history of the Rwandan genocide, *We Wish to Inform You That Tomorrow We Will Be Killed with Our Families* (New York: Farrar, Straus, & Giroux, 1998), makes this point with devastating clarity. For a compelling description of the overthrow of Reconstruction as a military campaign, see Zuczek, *State of Rebellion.*
3. Fields, *Slavery and Freedom*, 165. For the most persuasive reading of "white supremacy" as a slogan, see Fields, "Ideology and Race." As Fields correctly observes, white supremacy had to mean different things to upcountry yeomen and black-belt planters. I argue here, however, that those differences were obscured not by the simple substitution of racial identity for economic interest but by the way historical experience had shaped white men's understanding of household authority and productive labor. At the other end of the continuum of "materialist" versus "idealist" understandings of white supremacy lie the works of George Fredrickson (especially *Black Image*) and Joel Williamson (*Crucible of Race*). These historians have informed my understanding of the terms and languages of

white supremacy, but I agree with Thomas Holt ("Marking") that we need to explore "racial thought" in the context of its social relations and practices. An early call for the integration of discourses of gender into such studies, Joan Wallach Scott's "On Language, Gender, and Working Class History" is both foundational to this kind of scholarship and particularly useful in this instance since it concerns the relationship between group consciousness and gender. A helpful example, much closer to home geographically (although focused on the more typically urban and industrial terrain of labor history), is Janiewski, "Southern Honor, Southern Dishonor," which begins with the observation that "Southern employers behaved and spoke in ways designed to enhance awareness of racial and gender differences as they muted the recognition of any possible conflict between their own interests and those of white members of the laboring class" (70).

4. For a recent interpretation emphasizing the reciprocal terrors of racial slavery, see Berlin, *Many Thousands Gone*, esp. 1–14. As I was completing the manuscript for this book, our understanding of the ordinariness of rebellion within the plantation South was enriched by the appearance of Franklin and Schweninger, *Runaway Slaves*.
5. Recent scholarship on "whiteness," rooted in Du Bois's observation that white privilege constituted a "psychological wage" (*Black Reconstruction*, 700–701), explores the relationship of language to social, economic, and political practice—until recently, mainly in the North. See, e.g., Roediger, *Wages of Whiteness*; Ignatiev, *How the Irish Became White*; and Jacobson, *Whiteness of a Different Color*. Hale, *Making Whiteness*, and Simon, *Fabric of Defeat*, explore "whiteness" in the segregated South, paying close attention to the intersections of race and gender.
6. For thoughtful introductions to the meanings of "producerism" in the context of the late-nineteenth-century South, see McMath, *American Populism*; Goodwyn, *Democratic Promise*; and Palmer, *"Man over Money."* On white Southern men's struggles with the transition from agricultural to industrial social and economic relations, see Carlton, *Mill and Town*; MacLean, "Leo Frank Case"; and Simon, *Fabric of Defeat* and "Appeal of Cole Blease."
7. The full story of the evolving discourses of Southern womanhood in this period remains to be written, but recent scholarship has taken us far. Important contributions, centered on the concerns of this work, include Elsa Barkley Brown, "Womanist Consciousness" and "Negotiating and Transforming the Public Sphere"; Schwalm, *Hard Fight*; Hunter, *To 'Joy My Freedom*; Gilmore, *Gender and Jim Crow*; McCurry, *Masters of Small Worlds*; Fox-Genovese, *Within the Plantation Household*; Faust, *Mothers of Invention*; Hodes, *White Women, Black Men*; Whites, "Wife's Farm"; and Laura F. Edwards, *Gendered Strife and Confusion*.
8. Raymond Arsenault argues that "demagogues . . . from Tillman to Helms" caused their supporters "to pay a heavy price for what often turned out to be ephemeral and self-defeating accomplishments." The term itself, however, is so broad as to lack analytical force in describing political behavior or allegiances. "Demagoguery," as Arsenault argues, is better understood as a style not particular to the South; indeed, I would suggest that his use of the term to describe a

largely symbolic politics of resentment, mistrust, and empty "reform" closely resembles what other historians less usefully and less precisely call "populism." See Arsenault, "Folklore of Southern Demagoguery," 131–32.

9. The history of manhood, white or otherwise, frequently seems to be composed of a succession of crises, so much so that one critic has suggested thinking of the history of patriarchy as "crisis studies" (Judith M. Bennett, "Feminism and History"). I would argue that the term "masculinity crisis" gives gender relations and identities a life separate and distinct from other kinds of social, economic, and political experience. White Southern men's power had come from the confluence of race and gender, and (in practice) economic status, as well as other factors. When that power came under sustained attack during the second half of the nineteenth century, these men understood and described their situation in language that focused on both race and gender, for their conceptions of social power and social order did not treat "whiteness" or "manhood" as meaningfully distinct aspects of what it was to be a "real white man." It is worth noting, too, that hierarchies of gender inspire the same kinds of daily challenges, and are thus prone to the same kinds of ongoing "crisis," as other hierarchies—for example, racial slavery.
10. The ensuing debate on the racial ideology of white Populists (including Tom Watson himself) has become a substantial historiography. For an overview, see Rosengarten, " 'I Stand Where My Boyhood Put Me.' " Other scholars have also followed Woodward's lead by writing biographies exploring Southern political leadership at the turn of the century. For the best of these, see Arsenault, *Wild Ass of the Ozarks*, and Holmes, *White Chief*.

Chapter One

1. Over the preceding two decades, Benjamin Tillman had deeded many of his slaves to his wife and children, securing this valuable property against any changes in his personal fortunes; at his death in 1849, therefore, he had only twenty-four slaves to will to his family. See Sophia A. Tillman and Oliver H. Tillman vs. George D. Tillman et al., for the sale of real estate and relief, minutes, Nov. 1860, Edgefield Court of Equity, ECA, and deeds, 31 Mar. 1827, 13 Aug. 1829, BRTP-CL, pt. 12. See also Simkins, *Pitchfork Ben Tillman*, 27–30. On the distribution of wealth among Edgefield heads of household, see Burton, *In My Father's House*, 40–46, and Ford, *Origins of Southern Radicalism*, 76–78.
2. Groundbreaking works on white male solidarity in the antebellum South include Genovese, "Yeoman Farmers," and Fox-Genovese, *Within the Plantation Household*, 37–99. For compelling discussions of the meaning and limits of white male independence and solidarity in the late antebellum decades, see McCurry, *Masters of Small Worlds* and "Two Faces of Republicanism." See also Burton, *In My Father's House*, esp. 44, 99–103, and Bardaglio, *Reconstructing the Household*, esp. 27–28. On deviance and punishment, see Bynum, *Unruly Women*. In 1860, the

Southern planter class numbered about 43,000 household heads, of whom 90 percent were male and almost all were white. See Roark, *Masters without Slaves*, ix.

3. *Edgefield Advertiser*, 14 Feb. 1849.
4. Ibid., 2 May 1849 (emphasis in original).
5. Tocqueville, *Democracy in America*, 358; *Edgefield Advertiser*, 2 May 1849. For a detailed reading of this dynamic among white South Carolinians, see Channing, *Crisis of Fear*. On antebellum slave rebellions, see Egerton, *Gabriel's Rebellion*; Pearson, "From Stono to Vesey"; Oates, *Fires of Jubilee*; and *Edgefield Advertiser*, 25 Apr., 2, 9, 16 May 1849.
6. Minutes, 7 Aug. 1847, BIFCR (emphasis in original). Eugene Genovese offers "paternalism" as an alternative to that "state of war." His *Roll, Jordan, Roll* provides insight into aspects of slave society that otherwise remain inscrutable, especially the powerful ties of loyalty and affection between individual masters and slaves. But his analysis leaves unduly muted the anxiety and violence of a society in which patriarchal authority could be exercised without warning or redress. Ira Berlin has recently captured in metaphor the meaning of masters' not-quite-perfect "monopoly of force" to the ongoing negotiation between master and slave. "Even when their cards were reduced to near worthlessness," he writes, "slaves still held that last card, which, as their owners well understood, they might play at any time" (*Many Thousands Gone*, 2).
7. Faust, *James Henry Hammond*, esp. 346–47.
8. Minutes, 4 Sept., 7 Aug. 1847, BIFCR; Genovese, "'Our Family, White and Black.'"
9. *Edgefield Advertiser*, 5, 12 Sept. 1849. On the coercive power of threats of sale, see Norrece T. Jones Jr., *Born a Child of Freedom*. Works that shed light on the effects of violence and coercion on the lives of enslaved people—and that suggest the further limits of Genovese's vision of paternalism—include Jones, *Born a Child of Freedom*; Stevenson, "Distress and Discord"; Painter, "Soul Murder and Slavery"; and Wyatt-Brown, "Mask of Obedience."
10. Lacy Ford describes planter intellectuals' vision of the world as "a system of commercial and industrial satellites revolving around a staple-producing metropole—the South" (*Origins of Southern Radicalism*, 3). On South Carolina's antebellum economic crises, see Ford, *Origins of Southern Radicalism*, and Burton, *In My Father's House*, 40–44.
11. Ford, *Origins of Southern Radicalism*, chaps. 6–9; BRT, "My Childhood Days," BRTP-SCL; Simkins, *Pitchfork Ben Tillman*, chap. 2; Wells, *Slave Ship Wanderer*, 29, 44, 86; Diane Neal, "Benjamin Ryan Tillman," 6 (quotation). As late as 1880, Tillman's Edgefield household included two African Americans whose birthplace was listed as Africa. See 1880 Manuscript Census, Schedule 1, Meriwether Township, Edgefield County, S.C., p. 17.
12. Minutes, 5 Apr. 1856, BIFCR. Faust, *Sacred Circle*, examines the shared world of five such Southern intellectuals. See also Faust, "The Rhetoric and Ritual of Agriculture," and Ford, *Origins of Southern Radicalism*, 263–75.
13. Faust, *Sacred Circle*, esp. 95–99; Harris, *Plain Folk and Gentry*, 27–29.
14. I follow Lacy Ford's definition of South Carolina's sections: the lowcountry con-

sisted of the state's coastal parishes and some districts immediately inland, with the exception of the less fertile Pee Dee section in the northeast; the upcountry took in most of the remaining districts, from the midland piedmont areas around the fall line all the way to the hilly northwestern border. See Ford, *Origins of Southern Radicalism*, 281. On South Carolina's degree of democracy, see Banner, "Problem of South Carolina," and the compelling rejoinder in Ford, *Origins of Southern Radicalism*, 99–144.

15. Burton, *In My Father's House*, 44–46; Oakes, *Slavery and Freedom*, 92–93.
16. McCurry, *Masters of Small Worlds*, esp. 5–36; R. Ben Brown, "Southern Range"; Scott to Brookes, 19 Nov. 1847, Iveson L. Brookes Papers, PL. Lumpkins's fence burning did not necessarily make him the self-conscious champion of customary rights any more than his alleged theft of two of the overseer's horses made him an advocate of communal stock ownership.
17. To the voters of the antebellum South, "freedom meant a white man's ability to be his own master and to hold dominion over those less powerful—especially the young, the female, and most of all the black" (Stewart, "'Great Talking and Eating Machine,'" 220). The literature on slave-labor republicanism and the "country" ideology from which it developed has become too large to cite. Historians have examined the rise of this ideology, its elaboration by individuals, and its interconnections with political and economic processes. Works specifically focusing on these developments in South Carolina include Klein, *Unification of a Slave State*; Faust, *James Henry Hammond*; Ford, *Origins of Southern Radicalism*; and McCurry, *Masters of Small Worlds*.
18. For discussions of particular forms of patriarchal authority in antebellum South Carolina, see McCurry, *Masters of Small Worlds*, esp. 85–91, and Burton, *In My Father' House*, esp. 99–103.
19. Ex Parte Sophia A. Tillman, 1 June 1863, Edgefield County Court of Equity Records, ECA; 1860 equity ruling, BRTP-CL, pt. 10.
20. Burton, *In My Father's House*, 185–89; Bardaglio, *Reconstructing the Household*, 48–64. On the complexities of race, color, and ancestry, see Hodes, *White Women, Black Men*, 96–122.
21. Burton, *In My Father's House*, 203–24; *Edgefield Advertiser*, 2 May 1849.
22. *The Militia and Patrol Laws of South Carolina to December 1851, Published by Order of the Executive* (Columbia, S.C., 1852), SCL. This biracial world and the legal and social response of "respectable" white society are the subjects of Bynum, *Unruly Women*.
23. Minutes, 7 Aug., 4 Sept. 1847, BIFCR; McCurry, *Masters of Small Worlds*, 120–21. See also, e.g., minutes, spring 1849, spring 1854, spring 1856, spring 1857, Sessions Journal, Edgefield County Judge of Probate Records, typescript, 1848–68, SCDAH, and minutes, Feb. 1849, Edgefield County Coroner Inquisition Books, typescript, 1851–59, pp. 77–79, SCDAH.
24. Quoted in Burton, *In My Father's House*, 38. For an analysis of violent conflict among white men in antebellum South Carolina, see West, "From Yeoman to Redneck," 134–67.
25. Minutes, 1841, Sessions Journal, Edgefield County Judge of Probate Records,

typescript, 1838–47, p. 52, SCDAH. Francis Butler Simkins, citing a record of trial expenses in the Tillman Papers, writes that the elder Ben Tillman killed a man in 1847 (*Pitchfork Ben Tillman*, 29, n. 21). I have not been able to locate the record to which he refers. The Tillman Papers were housed at the University of South Carolina during the period of Simkins's research, but Tillman's son B. R., infuriated by some interpretations in Simkins's *Pitchfork Ben Tillman*, subsequently removed the papers to Clemson University; in the process, at least a few items referred to in Simkins's research notes (in the Francis Butler Simkins Papers, SHC) seem to have disappeared.

26. Benjamin Tillman Sr. to Brookes, 6 Aug. 1844, Iveson L. Brookes Papers, SCL; minutes, fall 1843, Sessions Journal, Edgefield County Judge of Probate Records, typescript, 1838–47, p. 86, SCDAH; minutes, Mar. 1844, Edgefield County Coroner Inquisition Books, typescript, 1844–50, SCDAH.
27. For influential perspectives on "honor," see Stowe, *Intimacy and Power*; Wyatt-Brown, *Southern Honor*; and Greenberg, *Honor and Slavery*.
28. Benjamin Tillman Sr. to Brookes, 6 Aug. 1844, Iveson L. Brookes Papers, SCL (emphasis in original).
29. Minutes, July 1856, Edgefield County Coroner Inquisition Books, typescript, 1851–59, SCDAH.
30. *Edgefield Advertiser*, 23 July 1856; minutes, 14 Feb. 1856, Edgefield County Coroner Inquisition Books, typescript, 1851–59, SCDAH.
31. BRT, "My Childhood Days," BRTP-SCL; John M. Tillman to Meriwether, 27 Aug. 1858, BRTP-CL, pt. 3.
32. BRT, "My Childhood Days," BRTP-SCL.
33. For the connections between nullification and slavery, see Freehling, *Prelude to Civil War*.
34. *Edgefield Advertiser*, 1, 22 Dec. 1847 (quotation). For overviews of these political and ideological developments, see Potter, *Impending Crisis*, and David Brion Davis, *Slave Power Conspiracy*.
35. *Edgefield Advertiser*, 22 Sept., 1 Dec. 1847, 5 Apr. 1848, 8 Sept. 1847 (Aldrich quotation). Stephanie McCurry has offered the useful metaphor of a white man's republicanism with two faces, one directed inward at the household, the other facing out into the realm of interhousehold political and economic relations ("Two Faces of Republicanism" and *Masters of Small Worlds*, esp. 208–38).
36. *Edgefield Advertiser*, 14 Feb. 1849 (emphasis in original); Iveson L. Brookes, *A Defence of the South against the Reproaches and Incroachments of the North* (Hamburg, S.C., 1850), microfilm at State Historical Society of Wisconsin, Madison, Wis.
37. *Edgefield Advertiser*, 6 June ("*vigilance*"; emphasis in original), 7 Nov., 22 Aug. 1849 ("spies"); Report of the Committee on the Colored Population, Dec. 1851, South Carolina General Assembly Records, SCDAH. See the discussions of the Barrett case (and the tensions inherent in vigilantism) in Ford, *Origins of Southern Radicalism*, 188, and West, "From Yeoman to Redneck," 129–34.
38. *Edgefield Advertiser*, 16 May 1849 ("sturdy virtues"); *The Militia and Patrol Laws of South Carolina to December 1851, Published by Order of the Executive* (Columbia, S.C., 1852), SCL; Henry, *Police Control of the Slave*; *Edgefield Advertiser*, 2 May 1849.

39. Hammond, "Letter to an English Abolitionist," 177–79, 201–2.

40. Barnwell, *Love of Order*, 48; *Edgefield Advertiser*, 22 Aug. 1849, 3 Apr. 1851 (emphasis in original). For expressions of anxiety about a slave revolt during secession crises, see Barnwell, *Love of Order*, 82. For George Tillman's secessionism, see Ford, "Origins of the Edgefield Tradition."

41. *Edgefield Advertiser*, 17 Apr., 13 Feb., 8 May 1851.

42. Barnwell, *Love of Order*, 48 (emphasis in original).

43. Ford, *Origins of Southern Radicalism*, 185–213, 293–303.

44. Ibid., 293–303; Banner, "Problem of South Carolina"; Burton, *In My Father's House*, chap. 2; *Edgefield Advertiser*, 17 Apr. 1851. Lacy Ford has suggested that Ben Tillman's "sense of grievance and personal mission plausibly can be traced to Edgefield's late antebellum economic frustrations and sense of political impotence" ("Origins of the Edgefield Tradition," 348). I would argue that Tillman was making use of a tradition that offered him a ready-made language of grievance and discontent; the tradition survived because it continued to be politically useful.

45. BRT, "My Childhood Days," BRTP-SCL; *Edgefield Advertiser*, 6, 20 Feb., 14 May, 23 July 1856. The deaths of John and Oliver followed by one year the death of another brother, Henry, from illness.

46. *Edgefield Advertiser*, 26 Oct. 1859.

47. Ibid., 26 Oct., 7 Dec. 1859; minutes, 3 Dec. 1859, BIFCR. From the porch of his new home at Redcliffe, Hammond would no doubt have seen the fires of Augusta, just across the Savannah River.

48. *Edgefield Advertiser*, 22 Feb. 1860.

49. "Constitution of Minute Men for the Defence of Southern Rights, Adopted at Laurens C.H., Oct. 31, 1860," broadside, SCL; minutes, 24 Nov., 1 Dec. 1860, Minute Men, Saluda Association, SCL; BRT, "My Childhood Days," BRTP-SCL.

50. BRT, "My Childhood Days," BRTP-SCL; minutes, 15, 22 Dec. 1860, Minute Men, Saluda Association, SCL; *Edgefield Advertiser*, 15 May 1861. I am deeply grateful to Orville Vernon Burton for sharing with me his unpublished work on this subject.

51. Petigru in Ford, *Origins of Southern Radicalism*, 371. On resistance to secession, see Bolton, *Poor Whites of the Antebellum South*, esp. 139–80, and Crofts, *Reluctant Confederates*. Discussion of South Carolina's peculiarities can shed light on the state's pivotal role in nineteenth-century American history; it can also lead the unwary to imagine that some other (unnamed) Southern state experienced a "typical" or "normal" history through the period. For an insightful discussion of the "problem" literature, see Ford, *Origins of Southern Radicalism*, 99–144.

52. McArthur and Burton, *A Gentleman and an Officer*, 48–51; *Edgefield Advertiser*, 9 Jan. 1861; BRT, "My Childhood Days," BRTP-SCL. On Watson's earlier activities, see *Edgefield Advertiser*, 28 Aug. 1851.

53. BRT to Anna Swearingen, 25 Aug., 28 Sept. 1862, John Eldred Swearingen Papers, SCL; *Edgefield Advertiser*, 6 Mar. 1861.

54. *Edgefield Advertiser*, 19 June 1861.

55. BRT, "My Childhood Days," BRTP-SCL.

56. Ibid.
57. Rose, *Rehearsal for Reconstruction*; Schwalm, *Hard Fight for We*; Cobb in McPherson, *Battle Cry of Freedom*, 835. On Smalls's career, see Edward A. Miller Jr., *Gullah Statesman*. On other black veterans, see Burton, "Effects of the Civil War."
58. Brooks, *Butler and His Cavalry*, 389–92; McPherson, *Battle Cry of Freedom*, 748, 759–60, 793–95; Izlar, *Sketch of the War Record of the Edisto Rifles*, 125.
59. BRT to Anna Swearingen, 28 Sept. 1862, John Eldred Swearingen Papers, SCL; BRT, "My Childhood Days," BRTP-SCL. James, "much reduced" by injury and illness, died in 1866. See James Tillman Civil War diary, 19 Dec. 1862, 9 Oct. 1864, BRTP-CL, pt. 10.
60. BRT, "Essay on Politeness," 1864, BRTP-CL, pt. 10.
61. Wager, "Strongest Ties," vi. See also Tompkins and Tompkins, *Company K*. The Confederate government refused officially to enlist black men until the last weeks of its existence, but individual black soldiers did fight with Confederate armies, primarily as the body servants of their owners in the Confederate officers corps. It should not surprise us that enslaved Southerners, generally forbidden to organize as a group, pursued their freedom through complex individual calculuses of risk and benefit that occasionally included Confederate military service; nor should this cause us to doubt that a Confederate victory would have kept most Southern blacks in slavery long after 1865.
62. McArthur and Burton, *A Gentleman and an Officer*, 73–75, 277; Hagood, *Memoirs of the War of Secession*, 331–33; Hammond in Burton, "Confederate Homefront." Such fears were common; see Roark, *Masters without Slaves*, 76. Gary Gallagher has recently mounted an impassioned rebuttal to such emphases on the weakness of Confederate commitment. Rightly pointing out that Confederate soldiers continued to fight long after experiencing casualty rates far higher than those of any force of U.S. soldiers before or since, he suggests that historians have failed to explain why the nonslaveholding white majority poured such unprecedented "energy and resources into a fight profoundly tainted by the institution of slavery" (*Confederate War*, 172). The interpretation of secession advanced here (and in McCurry, *Masters of Small Worlds*) may offer a partial answer to Gallagher's challenge: by 1860, the planter class (which, according to Gallagher, provided the most ardent promoters of Confederate nationalism and patriotism) had built a political culture in which slavery was one of many relations of white male authority and in which a challenge to masters' authority could seem to constitute a challenge to the authority of husbands or fathers. The principle of such a subversion of patriarchal household authority, dovetailing neatly with the physical fears evoked by the prospect of black freedom, helped keep Confederate soldiers of all classes in the field—although not in numbers sufficient to counter the combined force of their white and black foes.
63. Only the southern Edgefield village of Aiken saw any military conflict.
64. BRT, "My Childhood Days," BRTP-SCL; Simkins, *Pitchfork Ben Tillman*, chap. 2; BRT diary, 1865, BRTP-CL, pt. 10. See also Burton, "Effects of the Civil War."

Chapter Two

1. BRT to Sophia Tillman, 2 June 1867, BRTP-CL, pt. 10; BRT diary, 1865, pp. 42–46, BRTP-CL, pt. 8. On Reconstruction in South Carolina, see Simkins and Woody, *South Carolina during Reconstruction*; Joel Williamson, *After Slavery*; Abbott, *Freedmen's Bureau*; Burton, "Ungrateful Servants?"; Holt, *Black over White*; Saville, *Work of Reconstruction*; and Zuczek, *State of Rebellion*.
2. Richard Zuczek's important and meticulously researched study, *State of Rebellion*, discusses the campaign against Reconstruction as a continuation of the Confederate military struggle. I am wary of his tendency to use "white" and "conservative" interchangeably, and I believe that antebellum legacies, conflicts, and practices were at least as important as the Civil War in shaping the campaign against Reconstruction. Nonetheless, his work represents a renewed focus on the mechanisms of "Redemption" that historians of Reconstruction will ignore at their peril.
3. James Tillman diary, 31 July, 2, 31 Aug. 1865, BRTP-CL, pt. 8; "Contract," 1 Aug. 1865, "Contract-reckoning," Dec. 1865, BRTP-CL, pt. 10. Such miserly proportions were common to the contracts between former masters and former slaves in 1865; see Ransom and Sutch, *One Kind of Freedom*, 60.
4. James Tillman diary, 31 May, 8, 31 July, 2, 6, 8, 9, 10 Aug. 1865, BRTP-CL, pt. 8; BRT diary, 7 Nov. 1865, BRTP-CL, pt. 8. The standard account of this class in the immediate postwar period is Roark, *Masters without Slaves*.
5. James Tillman diary, 8 Aug., 25, 27 Sept. 1865, BRTP-CL, pt. 8.
6. Ibid., 25, 26, 27 Sept. 1865; Saville, *Work of Reconstruction*, 105.
7. Pickens to Perry, 7 Sept. 1865, B. F. Perry Papers, quoted in Joel Williamson, *After Slavery*, 71; Millikey to Gourdin, 14 Aug. 1865, R. H. Gourdin Papers, quoted in ibid., 74; Simkins and Woody, *South Carolina during Reconstruction*, 50. On the Black Codes, see Joel Williamson, *After Slavery*, 72–79; Lamson, *Glorious Failure*, 35–36; and Simkins and Woody, *South Carolina during Reconstruction*, 48–50. For an insightful discussion of "apprenticeship" laws in another postemancipation polity, see Fields, *Slavery and Freedom*, 139–56.
8. Saville, "Grassroots Reconstruction," 173–82, and *Work of Reconstruction*, esp. 87–95, 143–53.
9. Dan T. Carter, "Anatomy of Fear," 345–64; James Tillman diary, 25, 26, 30 Dec. 1865, 2, 8 Jan. 1866, BRTP-CL, pt. 8; BRT diary, Jan. 1866, BRTP-CL, pt. 8.
10. BRT diary, 14, 31 Dec. 1866, BRTP-CL, pt. 8; "Articles of Agreement," 20 Feb. 1867, BRTP-CL, pt. 10; William Watson Davis, *Civil War*, 88, 450–51, 514, n. 1; Fernald and Purdum, *Atlas of Florida*, 104, 110.
11. George Tillman to BRT, [8] Mar. 1867, BRTP-CL, pt. 3.
12. "Articles of Agreement," 20 Feb. 1867, BRTP-CL, pt. 10; "Accounts, 1867," James Tillman diary, BRTP-CL, pt. 8 (James died in June 1866, and subsequent notations in this diary are probably by Ben Tillman). For an analysis of the development of the idea of "free labor" that speaks directly to this transition, see Steinfeld, *Invention of Free Labor*, esp. 173–84.
13. BRT to Starke, 10 Aug. 1867, BRTP-CL, pt. 10 (emphasis in original). For an

illuminating discussion of the linkage between Tillman's derision of fiat currency and his suggestion that freedmen were fiat citizens (or at least fiat "*gentlemen*"), see O'Malley, "Specie and Species."

14. BRT to Sallie Starke, 30 Mar., 25 May 1867, BRTP-CL, pt. 10.
15. Ibid., 10 Aug., 4 (names for Kenilworth), 7 Oct., 22, 30 Nov., 19, 24 Dec. 1867; George Tillman to BRT, [8] Mar. 1867, BRTP-CL, pt. 3; Bible, Swearingen Family Papers, SCL.
16. On the caterpillar infestation, see BRT in *Congressional Record*, 61st Cong., 1st sess., 1909, 44, pt. 4:3885.
17. Randolph in Saville, *Work of Reconstruction*, 159. On South Carolina's black Reconstruction leaders, see Holt, *Black over White*; Joel Williamson, *After Slavery*; Edward A. Miller Jr., *Gullah Statesman*; Lamson, *Glorious Failure*; Burton, "Black Leadership in Edgefield"; and Higginson, *Army Life in a Black Regiment.*
18. Commonwealth of South Carolina, *Constitution . . . Ratified April 16, 1868*; Burton, "Ungrateful Servants?," 75–124; Holt, *Black over White*, 9–40, 43.
19. Both black and white people bought land through the land commission, but the program's successes remained local. Modest in scope, inefficient, and corrupt, the commission also struggled against the strenuous opposition of large landowners. On the South Carolina Land Commission, see Bleser, *Promised Land.* For the proposition that the failure of land redistribution safeguarded planter power during and after Reconstruction, see Foner, *Reconstruction*, 603.
20. Those profits were frequently insufficient to cover all of the obligations on the crop, and landlords, supply merchants, and sharecroppers each sought "priority"—the right to take their share of the profits first—for their lien. State laws (and judicial rulings) governing the priority of liens and the rights of landlords, merchants, and croppers varied over time, reflecting changes in the relative political influence of each of these groups. In order to ensure that the crops they financed would yield sufficient return, lenders frequently insisted that borrowers plant cotton, for which a market could always be found. For excellent analyses of these developments, see Woodman, *New South—New Law*, and Ford, "Labor and Ideology," 25–42. For more general discussion of the transition to free labor and the development of sharecropping, see Ransom and Sutch, *One Kind of Freedom*; Jaynes, *Branches without Roots*; Wiener, "Class Structure"; and Glymph and Kushma, *Essays on the Postbellum Southern Economy.*
21. Ford, "Rednecks and Merchants"; Joel Williamson, *After Slavery*, esp. 126–63; Woodman, *New South—New Law*, 78–80.
22. Unidentified article from *Gleaner and Advocate*, 24 Sept. 1874, typescript in Richard Lathers Papers, Manuscript Division, Library of Congress, Washington, D.C. On carpetbaggers, see O'Malley, "Specie and Species." On Crews, see Simkins and Woody, *South Carolina during Reconstruction*, 128, and Leland, *Voice from South Carolina*, 51–67, 134.
23. *Keowee Courier*, 11 Aug. 1866, paraphrased in Woody, "Economic Condition of South Carolina," 360.
24. On Reconstruction-era woman suffrage activities, see Gatewood, " 'Remarkable Misses Rollin,' " and Smedley, "Martha Schofield."

25. Sessions Journal, Edgefield County Judge of Probate Records, typescript, 1868–79, pp. 39, 62–63, SCDAH. On public space, race, and authority, see Dailey, "Deference and Violence." Crucial interpretations of the historical meanings of whiteness include Du Bois, *Black Reconstruction*, 700–701; Morgan, *American Slavery, American Freedom*, esp. 295–362; and Roediger, *Wages of Whiteness*. For recent scholarship that links emancipation and Reconstruction's revolution in the meaning of race to the simultaneous challenge it presented to ideologies and practices of gender, see Laura F. Edwards, *Gendered Strife and Confusion*; Whites, *Civil War as a Crisis in Gender*; and Bardaglio, *Reconstructing the Household*. Recent work by Scott Nelson, "Livestock, Boundaries, and Public Space," offers a dramatic South Carolina example of the practical implications of these simultaneous revolutions both for white men's authority and for other Southerners' autonomy.
26. On class-specific understandings of "white supremacy," see Fields, "Ideology and Race."
27. Percentages calculated from Burton, *In My Father's House*, 264–65, 113. On taxation, see Thornton, "Fiscal Policy." Landlessness did not necessarily imply wage labor or poverty; some white men who did not own real estate had artisanal skills or worked successfully in other nonagricultural occupations. But in an overwhelmingly agricultural county, state, and region, landownership remained a reasonable proxy for the economic self-sufficiency that was the sine qua non of independent patriarchal authority.
28. Affidavit of J. D. Palmer, quoted in Saville, *Work of Reconstruction*, 144; Sallie Tillman to BRT, 2 Nov. 1868, BRTP-CL, pt. 3; BRT to Sophia Tillman, fragment, [1868], BRTP-CL, pt. 10.
29. *Edgefield Advertiser*, 10, 24 June, 1 July 1868, quoted in Burton, "Ungrateful Servants?," 101–2 (emphasis in original).
30. Burton, "Ungrateful Servants?," 59–60, 99–103, and "Race and Reconstruction"; Stagg, "Problem of Klan Violence," 316. For a recent historiographical summary that emphasizes the centrality of organized violence to the collapse of Reconstruction, see Perman, "Counter Reconstruction," which nonetheless stops short of calling the campaign a "counterrevolution." For the specifics of the anti-Reconstruction military-political campaign, see Zuczek, *State of Rebellion*.
31. On Randolph, see Trelease, *White Terror*, 116, and William Tolbert in Zuczek, *State of Rebellion*, 57–58. On the 1868 election, see *U.S. House Misc. Doc.* no. 18, 41st Cong., 1st sess., 42, 2–8, 34. On the Klan more generally, see Stagg, "Problem of Klan Violence," esp. 312–16, and Trelease, *White Terror*, 65–73, 115–17, 349–80, 398–417.
32. Werner, "Hegemony and Conflict," 79–80; Simkins and Woody, *South Carolina during Reconstruction*, 453; *Beaufort Republican and Sea Island Chronicle*, 21 May 1870; Burton, "Ungrateful Servants?," 104–5.
33. *Rural Carolinian* 3 (Dec. 1871).
34. Ibid., 3 (Jan. 1872).
35. Ibid., 6 (Oct. 1874), 1 (June 1870).
36. Easterby, "Granger Movement," 26; *Rural Carolinian* 3 (Dec. 1871).

37. Burton, "Ungrateful Servants?," 104–6; Aiken in *Beaufort Republican and Sea Island Chronicle*, 21 May 1870.

38. Convention delegates listed in Tax-Payers' Convention, *Proceedings of the Tax-Payers' Convention . . . 1874*, 11–17, 22–23, 44–46; Grange officers listed in *Rural Carolinian* 4 (Aug.–Sept. 1873); 5 (Oct., Dec. 1873–Apr., June 1874); 6 (Nov.–Dec. 1874, Feb.–Mar., June–July, Sept. 1875). For Republican comment, see *Port Royal Standard and Commercial*, 23 Dec. 1875.

39. Joel Williamson, *After Slavery*, 264–65 and n. 78; Zuczek, *State of Rebellion*, 80–81 (emphasis in original). See also the discussion in Trelease, *White Terror*, 51.

40. Zuczek, *State of Rebellion*, 59; Simkins and Woody, *South Carolina during Reconstruction*, 451; Singletary, *Negro Militia and Reconstruction*, 123–24.

41. Trelease, *White Terror*, 355–56; Zuczek, *State of Rebellion*, 80–81.

42. *U.S. Senate Rep.* no. 41, 42d Cong., 2d sess., 4:1208, 1203–4.

43. Ibid., 4:1204–18.

44. Tax-Payers' Convention, *Proceedings of the Tax-Payers' Convention . . . 1874*, 95. Historians, too, have found "mobs" and "riots" to be troubling concepts, in part because of the inherently subjective (or partisan) nature of such judgments. For an outline of the conceptual problems limited to North American history, see Gilje, *Rioting in America*, 1–11. The rich literature on European "mobs" is too large to cite here, but to begin with, see E. P. Thompson, *Customs in Common*, chaps. 4–5.

45. Tax-Payers' Convention, *Proceedings of the Tax-Payers' Convention . . . 1871*, 17–18, 57–58, 66–67. For details regarding the debt, see Joel Williamson, *After Slavery*, 383–85.

46. Holt, *Black over White*, 95–207; Trelease, *White Terror*, 415–18.

47. "Counterstatement and Reply of the Republican Central Committee," *U.S. House Misc. Doc.* no. 234, 43d Cong., 1st sess., 4–7.

48. Simkins, *Pitchfork Ben Tillman*, 58. For lists of officers of rifle clubs, see *U.S. Senate Misc. Doc.* no. 48, 44th Cong., 2d sess., 3:499–509. Black militia leaders such as Republican state senator Lawrence Cain understood the stakes. Cain knew that rifle club leaders wanted his seat in the legislature; the members of Cain's militia units knew that planters wanted to return them to the status of disfranchised agricultural laborers. See Burton, "Race and Reconstruction," 40, n. 25, and "Effects of the Civil War," 204–24.

49. BRT, "My Childhood Days," BRTP-SCL, and *Struggles of 1876*; Zuczek, *State of Rebellion*, 139–48, quotation on 142. See also the narrative of these events in Simkins, *Pitchfork Ben Tillman*, 58–61.

50. BRT, *Struggles of 1876*.

51. Ibid.; Zuczek, *State of Rebellion*, 139–48; Parmele to Chamberlain, 21–23 Feb. 1875, Governor Chamberlain Papers, SCDAH; Simkins and Woody, *South Carolina during Reconstruction*, 128, 451; Singletary, *Negro Militia and Reconstruction*, 123–24.

52. Parmele to Chamberlain, 21–23 Feb. 1875, Governor Chamberlain Papers, SCDAH; Trelease, *White Terror*, 364–65.

53. Parmele to Chamberlain, 23 Feb. 1875, Governor Chamberlain Papers, SCDAH; *U.S. Senate Ex. Doc.*, no. 85, 44th Cong., 1st sess., 3.
54. BRT, "My Childhood Days," BRTP-SCL; Singletary, *Negro Militia and Reconstruction*, 124; Burton, "Ungrateful Servants?," 110–11. Such thefts occurred frequently; see Trelease, *White Terror*, 365.
55. Chapman, *History of Edgefield County*, 256; Simkins and Woody, *South Carolina during Reconstruction*, 39–41.
56. On the nature and limits of Republican efforts to enforce political unanimity, see Saville, *Work of Reconstruction*, 169–77, 186–88.
57. Clark, *Francis Warrington Dawson*, 9–23; Dawson in Joel Williamson, *After Slavery*, 354; Holt, *Black over White*, 181–85.
58. BRT, "My Childhood Days," BRTP-SCL, and *Struggles of 1876*.
59. BRT, *Struggles of 1876*; *U.S. Senate Misc. Doc.* no. 48, 44th Cong., 2d sess., 1:1051–57, 2:309 (quotations). For various perspectives on the events in Hamburg between 4 and 8 July 1876, see also BRT, "My Childhood Days," BRTP-SCL; untitled notebook, [1876], Martin Witherspoon Gary Papers, SCL; *U.S. Senate Ex. Doc.* no. 85, 44th Cong., 1st sess., reprinted as U.S. Congress, Senate, *South Carolina in 1876*; *Centennial Fourth of July Democratic Celebration*; Joel Williamson, *After Slavery*, 266–71; and Zuczek, *State of Rebellion*, 163–65. For a broader perspective on questions of public and private space in the context of Reconstruction conflict, see Dailey, "Deference and Violence."
60. Deposition of Prince Rivers, [July 1876], reprinted in *Augusta (Ga.) Chronicle and Sentinel*, 12 Aug. 1876; Robert Butler in *U.S. Senate Misc. Doc.* no. 48, 44th Cong., 2d sess., 1:1057. For information on Rivers's life and career, I am indebted to Isabel Vandervelde, chief researcher, Aiken County Historical Museum.
61. BRT, *Struggles of 1876* and "My Childhood Days," BRTP-SCL.
62. *U.S. Senate Misc. Doc.* no. 48, 44th Cong., 2d sess., 2:603 (Nelson), 2:240 (Butler).
63. Ibid., 1:710.
64. Ibid., 2:240–41; *Centennial Fourth of July Democratic Celebration*, 4.
65. BRT, "My Childhood Days," BRTP-SCL; deposition of Butler Edwards, [1876], untitled notebook, Martin Witherspoon Gary Papers, SCL; BRT, *Struggles of 1876*.
66. Chamberlain to Grant, 22 July 1876, in *U.S. Senate Ex. Doc.* no. 85, 44th Cong., 1st sess., 2–5; Chamberlain to Cameron, 12 July 1876, Chamberlain to Robertson, 13 July 1876, Governor Chamberlain Letterbooks, SCDAH.
67. Conference of Colored Citizens, *Address to the People of the United States*.
68. *U.S. Senate Misc. Doc.* no. 48, 44th Cong., 2d sess., 2:243–47.
69. *Charleston News and Courier*, 10, 11 July 1876; Clark, *Francis Warrington Dawson*, 60–68. For documents regarding the challenge, see scrapbooks, Francis Warrington Dawson Papers, PL. Dawson's opposition to a separate or "straightout" Democratic ticket had been essentially demographic. But Dawson underestimated the power of the "shot-gun policy" he derided, just as he overestimated the severity of the federal response to it. As a sympathetic commentator put it a decade later, "it had not occurred to [Dawson] that 4,000 Democrats in Edge-

field could cast 6,000 votes" ("South Carolina in 1886, and Tillman Downed," typescript, [1886], in Robert Means Davis Papers, SCL).

70. *Charleston News and Courier*, 18 Aug. 1876.

71. Hampton, *Free Men! Free Ballots!! Free Schools!!!*; Simkins and Woody, *South Carolina during Reconstruction*, 488–90; Joel Williamson, *After Slavery*, 407; Painter, "Martin Delany"; Hampton in *Port Royal Standard and Commercial*, 19 Oct. 1876; "plan of campaign" reprinted in Simkins and Woody, *South Carolina during Reconstruction*, 564–69. Tillman himself later claimed to have carried word of the nomination to Hampton; see *Edgefield Chronicle*, 17 Sept. 1890. Congressional Democrats on investigating subcommittees used examples of Republican coercion to muddy the waters and conceal the overwhelmingly Democratic character of fraud, violence, and intimidation; see testimony in U.S. Congress, Senate, *South Carolina in 1876*.

72. Simkins and Woody, *South Carolina during Reconstruction*, 568–69; *Charleston News and Courier*, 29 Aug. 1876; Matthew Butler in *U.S. House Rep.* no. 175, 44th Cong., 2d sess., 2:38–39.

73. Simkins and Woody, *South Carolina during Reconstruction*, 568–69; U.S. Congress, Senate, *South Carolina in 1876*, 310.

74. U.S. Congress, Senate, *South Carolina in 1876*, 286; Simkins and Woody, *South Carolina during Reconstruction*, 568–69.

75. Simkins and Woody, *South Carolina during Reconstruction*, 492–94; *Port Royal Standard and Commercial*, 17 Aug. 1876.

76. U.S. Congress, Senate, *South Carolina in 1876*, 205; Chamberlain in *New York Tribune*, 25 Oct. 1876, quoted in Allen, *Governor Chamberlain's Administration*, 414; BRT, *Struggles of 1876* (murder of Coker); Simkins, *Pitchfork Ben Tillman*, 66.

77. "F" to Aycock, 21, 22 Sept. 1876, J. H. Aycock Papers, SCL; *U.S. Senate Misc. Doc.* no. 48, 44th Cong., 2d sess., 1:719–23.

78. *U.S. Senate Misc. Doc.* no. 48, 44th Cong., 2d sess., 1:680–81, 567–68; *Port Royal Standard and Commercial*, 27 July 1876.

79. Joel Williamson, *After Slavery*, 271–73.

80. *Port Royal Standard and Commercial*, 5 Oct. 1876; Simkins, *Pitchfork Ben Tillman*, 66–67; *U.S. House Rep.* no. 175, 44th Cong., 2d sess., 1:77. The ineffectuality of federal peacekeepers was crucial. As Eric Foner has observed, "the abandonment of Reconstruction was as much a cause of the crisis of 1876–77 as a consequence, for had Republicans still been willing to intervene in defense of black rights, Tilden would never have come close to carrying the entire South" (*Reconstruction*, 582).

81. Winsmith to Grant, 14 Oct. 1876, quoted in Zuczek, *State of Rebellion*, 177; "Tillman vs. Smalls," in *U.S. House Misc. Doc.* no. 11, 45th Cong., 1st sess., testimony of H. T. Tankersly (Tanksly), 332–36, testimony of Robert Chandler, 336–40; *U.S. House Misc. Doc.* no. 31, 44th Cong., 2d sess., 1:61–64, 10, 25; *U.S. Senate Misc. Doc.* no. 48, 44th Cong., 2d sess., 1:ii–iii (map).

82. *Edgefield Chronicle*, 17 Sept. 1890; Simkins and Woody, *South Carolina during Reconstruction*, 514–41.

83. D. Wyatt Aiken in *Charleston News and Courier*, 5 Jan. 1877; Bailey to McKie,

24 Jan. 1877, Thomas Jefferson McKie Papers, PL; Zuczek, *State of Rebellion*, 198–99; *Charleston News and Courier*, 17 Jan. 1877. The economic crisis starved the Republican Party apparatus, including its newspapers. The *Port Royal Standard and Commercial* soon fell victim to the forces it had earlier described: by January 1877, it had been absorbed into the *Beaufort Tribune and Port Royal Commercial*, which quickly cast its lot with the Democrats and derided Republican newspapers as "parasitical sheets." See *Beaufort Tribune and Port Royal Commercial*, 4 Jan., 21 June 1877.

84. Minutes, 26 June 1877, Sessions Journal, Edgefield County Judge of Probate Records, typescript, 1868–79, p. 369, SCDAH.
85. *Beaufort Tribune and Port Royal Commercial*, 12 Apr. 1877.
86. BRT, *Struggles of 1876*; "Saxon," "The Philosophy of Straightout Democracy," *Abbeville Medium*, [1880–82], clipping in Fitz William McMaster and Mary Jane Macfie McMaster Papers, SCL.
87. South Carolina's historiography is particularly rich in "roads"; see especially Jarrell, *Wade Hampton and the Negro*, and Lewis Pinckney Jones, *Stormy Petrel* and "Two Roads Tried." On racial radicalism and conservatism as "mentalities," see Joel Williamson, *Crucible of Race*, or the abridged version, *Rage for Order*. Williamson's effort to embody distinct "white minds" in the persons of particular historical figures—including Tillman—offers some compelling insights, but it amplifies the underlying methodological problems of works such as Fredrickson, *Black Image*. We need an intellectual and cultural history of racial ideology that assumes such ideology to be related closely (although usually in complicated ways) to the political and economic structures of racial power. Closer investigation of the biographies of men such as Tillman and Hampton, the supposedly emblematic racial ideologues these historians discuss, suggests that their differences were more tactical than substantive. Although Tillman favored the language of threat and Hampton the language of compromise, each could and did use both languages. See chapter 5 for further discussion of this question.
88. *Charleston News and Courier*, 23 Jan. 1877.

Chapter Three

1. The rule and collapse of South Carolina's "Redeemers" are described in Cooper, *Conservative Regime*.
2. For another use of the "shotgun marriage" metaphor, see Rogers M. Smith, *Civic Ideals*, 200.
3. 1880 Manuscript Census, Schedule 1, Meriwether Township, Edgefield County, S.C., p. 17; notes on 1880 agricultural schedule in Francis Butler Simkins Papers, SHC; BRT to McKie, 21, 28 Aug. 1873, Thomas Jefferson McKie Papers, PL; "The Sins of the Senate," *Charleston News and Courier*, 30 Mar. 1887.
4. Morris, *Autobiography*, 64–66; *Edgefield Chronicle*, 6 Aug. 1890; BRT to Sallie Tillman, 8 Dec. 1895, BRT to Mell, 11 Jan. 1905, BRTP-CL, pt. 1. I am grateful to Bettis Rainsford for bringing Morris's *Autobiography* to my attention.

5. Minutes, 3 Nov. 1883, 1 Jan. 1881, BIFCR. For an analysis of the world of post-Reconstruction black farmers, see Painter, *Exodusters.*
6. Burton, *In My Father's House,* 269–72; Benjamin Ryan Tillman Jr., typescript biography of BRT, chap. 4, BRTP-CL, pt. 7. In 1879, Frank Thomas gave a lien on 800 pounds of lint cotton, apparently for rent, to Edgefield planter John R. Talbert. During much of the 1880s, a Frank Thomas received annual advances ranging from $25 to $70 while working at "Benj. Tillman's place." By 1891, Thomas appeared to have moved to the land of a person named Prescott, to whom he gave a lien for rent on 1,000 pounds of lint cotton. See 1 May 1879, 8 May 1883, 2 Feb. 1884, 9 Mar., 16 June 1886, 29 Jan. 1887, 13 Feb. 1888, 16 Feb. 1891, Index to Liens, ECA. A white Aiken County man named DeMedicis who wrote Tillman seeking farmwork received a cordial but unambiguous response from the governor's secretary: "Governor Tillman directs me to ask if you will work on shares or not. He doesn't want a man for wages at all" (Tompkins to DeMedicis, 13 Oct. 1891, Governor BRT Letterbooks, SCDAH). DeMedicis, who wrote from the mill town of Graniteville, may have been a recent Italian immigrant, some of whom were employed in phosphate mining and other low-wage, low-status activities. There is no evidence that DeMedicis accepted Tillman's offer. For reasons discussed in n. 17 below, the surviving records cannot portray the number or kind of rental arrangements or the informal transactions that took place between Tillman and agricultural workers. In the 1910s, Tillman experimented with hiring white farm families, but the results did not satisfy him, as we will see in chapter 8.
7. Minutes, 3 Nov. 1883, BIFCR; BRT, "Memorandum about Farm Work," [1895], BRTP-CL, pt. 1.
8. On laws restricting the sale of cotton, see Jaynes, *Branches without Roots,* 299–300. On labor law, see Woodman, *New South—New Law,* 78–79.
9. BRT will, 2 Dec. 1911, BRTP-CL, pt. 3 (box 18). Tillman discussed Joe Gibson in many speeches, including *Race Problem.*
10. On black women's experience of work and family during the early postbellum years, see Schwalm, *Hard Fight for We,* 147–268.
11. Follow this transition through McCurry, *Masters of Small Worlds,* 78–85; Faust, *Mothers of Invention,* 53–79; and Laura F. Edwards, *Gendered Strife and Confusion,* 145–83. For some white women's postbellum claims based on this experience, see Whites, *Civil War as a Crisis in Gender,* 132–98. See also the discussion in chapter 4.
12. BRT to Sallie Tillman, 21 Oct. 1900, BRTP-CL, pt. 1; Lebsock, "Radical Reconstruction"; Benjamin Ryan Tillman Jr., typescript biography of BRT, chap. 4, BRTP-CL, pt. 7. On plantation management, see, e.g., BRT to Sallie Tillman, 12 Sept., 1, 2, 13, 17, 22, 24 Oct., 6 Nov. 1895, BRTP-CL, pt. 1. In 1891, a local black man cashed a check forged in Tillman's name. The storekeeper cashing the check noted a "feminine style of handwriting" but "suspected nothing wrong . . . as . . . Mrs. Tillman frequently signs the Governor's name when he is away from home" (*Charleston News and Courier,* 1 Sept. 1891).
13. Burton, "Ungrateful Servants?," 244–46, 264–65.

14. On postbellum economic transformations, see Woodman, *New South—New Law*; Ford, "Rednecks and Merchants"; Carlton, *Mill and Town*, esp. 13–39; and Werner, "Hegemony and Conflict." Steven Hahn describes the cycle of liens and debts as "the vortex of the cotton economy" (*Roots of Southern Populism*).
15. *Charleston News and Courier*, 26 Aug. 1889. For complaints about freedpeople's independent access to credit, see *Keowee Courier*, 23 Jan., 6 Feb. 1879.
16. *Rural Carolinian* 1 (Oct. 1869); minutes, 7 Oct. 1882, 3 Jan. 1885 (quotation), BIFCR.
17. *Charleston News and Courier*, 25 Feb. 1885, 6 Dec. 1886. The contours of elite debate on liens can be studied in State Grange and Agricultural and Mechanical Society, *Proceedings of the Joint Summer Meeting . . . 1881*, esp. 82–84, SCL, and minutes, BIFCR. The 1877 legislature repealed the state's Reconstruction-era lien laws but, fearing economic disaster if crops could not be planted, reenacted the laws before the repeal paralyzed the state's agriculture. See Woodman, *New South—New Law*, 50, 78–79. During this period, only two forms of liens had to be recorded officially: liens for rent exceeding one-third of the crop's value and liens for supplies, which could be enforced only after any landlord's lien had been satisfied. Other liens did not have to be recorded, making it difficult to reconstruct the details of agricultural arrangements. On the nature and evolution of the lien system in South Carolina, see ibid., 48–51.
18. It appears that Frank Thomas worked some of Tillman's acres during the 1880s using supplies obtained from the firm of Durst & Andrews. It also appears likely that Tillman, like many other wealthy landowners, sometimes relied on merchant credit for at least a portion of his planting costs. See advance of $198, 25 May 1887, Index to Liens, ECA. On Tillman's experiments, see *Edgefield Chronicle*, 24 July 1880, and minutes, 6 Jan. 1883, BIFCR.
19. *Rural Carolinian* 1 (May 1870); letter from "Granger," *Barnwell Sentinel*, 21 May 1875. For Aiken's hostility to merchants, see *Rural Carolinian* 3 (Sept. 1872).
20. *Edgefield Advertiser*, 20 Oct. 1881.
21. R. Ben Brown, "Southern Range," esp. 247–72.
22. *Charleston News and Courier*, 30 Mar. 1887; *Edgefield Chronicle*, 17, 31 Aug., 7 Sept., 5 Oct. 1881; minutes, 7 July 1877, BIFCR (quotation).
23. *Edgefield Chronicle*, 14 Sept., 19, 26 Oct. 1881, 4, 11, 18 Jan. 1882; *Edgefield Advertiser*, 20 Oct. 1881 (quotation). The classic account of the struggle over the fence as a class conflict is Hahn, *Roots of Southern Populism*. In a debate that highlights (and perhaps caricatures) the divide between humanistic and social science models of political history, critics call into question Hahn's interpretation of the struggle over the fence and offer sophisticated statistical interpretations of election results that suggest a less dramatic set of social cleavages among white men than those Hahn depicts. See Kantor and Kousser, "Common Sense or Commonwealth?" and "Rejoinder." But the dynamic Hahn is investigating—a political culture in transition, refracting antebellum expectations through the lens of tumultuous economic hardship and electoral conflict—cannot be captured in the snapshots represented by election results, no matter how carefully those data are interpreted.

24. *Edgefield Advertiser*, 12 Jan. 1882; *Edgefield Chronicle*, 29 Mar. 1882; *Charleston News and Courier*, 28, 31 Mar. 1882.
25. *Edgefield Advertiser*, 18 July 1878 (quotations); Cooper, *Conservative Regime*, chap. 3; Tindall, *South Carolina Negroes*, 41–67.
26. *Edgefield Advertiser*, 18 July 1878.
27. "Saxon," "The Philosophy of Straightout Democracy," *Abbeville Medium*, [1880–82], clipping in Fitz William McMaster and Mary Jane Macfie McMaster Papers, SCL; *Greenville Enterprise and Mountaineer*, quoted in *Keowee Courier*, 29 Aug. 1878. Gary had been a "man on the make" since before the Civil War, jockeying for position even within the Confederate army. See McArthur and Burton, *A Gentleman and an Officer*, 58–62.
28. *Keowee Courier*, 25 Dec. 1879; *Sumter True Southron*, 23 Dec. 1879, typescript in Martin Witherspoon Gary Papers, PL (quotations).
29. Hampton to Cash, 10 Jan. 1877, 13 Nov. 1880, 29 Jan. 1881, 10 Mar. 1887, Ellerbe Broggan Crawford Cash Papers, SCL. For an account of the Cash-Shannon affair that reaches similar conclusions, see West, "From Yeoman to Redneck," 378–81.
30. Newspapers quoted in *Keowee Courier*, 15 July 1880; Werner, "Hegemony and Conflict"; Wilkins [?] to Cash, 12 Feb. 1881, Ellerbe Broggan Crawford Cash Papers, SCL.
31. *Charleston News and Courier*, reprinted in *Keowee Courier*, 13 July 1880.
32. Gary to Cash, 3 Aug. 1880, Ellerbe Broggan Crawford Cash Papers, SCL. See also ibid., 16 Dec. 1880, 28 Jan., 19 Mar. 1881.
33. The prosecution of Cash ended in a mistrial, but the debate did not end there, nor did it end with Gary's death: in 1883, the South Carolina secretary of state would come within a hair's breadth of a duel with the capitol's leading reporter—a fracas prevented only by the personal intervention of the governor himself. See Gary to Cash, 19 Mar. 1881, Ellerbe Broggan Crawford Cash Papers, SCL, and *Keowee Courier*, 20 Sept. 1883.
34. Letter from "Freeman," *Abbeville Medium*, quoted in *Beaufort Crescent*, 11 Sept. 1879; "Saxon," eulogy for Gary in unidentified newspaper, clipping in John Gary Evans Papers, SCL (quotation). On the tension this implies between evangelical and nonevangelical men, see Ownby, *Subduing Satan*.
35. Gaines to BRT, 11 Sept. 1890, BRTP-CL, pt. 3; Butler to Dargan, 24 Mar. 1880, John Julius Dargan Papers, SCL (emphasis in original); "Some Unwritten History in South Carolina, 1880–1890," *Lyceum* 1 (Oct. 1890), 2 (Nov. 1890).
36. *Edgefield Advertiser*, 20 Oct. 1881 (quotation); Gary to Cash, 16 Dec. 1880, 28 Jan., 19 Mar. 1881, Hyler to Cash, 28 Sept. 1881, Ellerbe Broggan Crawford Cash Papers, SCL.
37. Kennedy to McCall, 23 Aug. 1878, Charles Spencer McCall Papers, SCL; Williams to Hampton, 23 Feb. 1877, Benjamin S. Williams Papers, PL; "Smalls vs. Tillman," in *U.S. House Rep.* no. 1525, 47th Cong., 1st sess.; State Executive Committee of the Union Republican Party of South Carolina, *Election of 1880*, SCL; *Keowee Courier*, 26 Sept., 10 Oct. 1878 (Oconee meetings), 4 Nov. 1880 (Newberry).

38. "Smalls vs. Tillman," in *U.S. House Rep.* no. 1525, 47th Cong., 1st sess.; "Tillman vs. Smalls," in *U.S. House Rep.* no. 916, 45th Cong., 2d sess.; Edward A. Miller Jr., *Gullah Statesman*; George Tillman in *Charleston News and Courier*, 22 July 1882. In 1878, Republicans did not put up a state ticket, but they did contest most congressional seats; over 50,000 votes were counted for black and white Republican candidates. In 1880, Republican presidential electors received about 58,000 votes. Although these figures represented substantial declines from the heights of Reconstruction Republican voting, they made up about one-third of all votes cast in each of those years. See South Carolina General Assembly, *Reports and Resolutions*, 1878, 440–44; 1880, 549–51.
39. Kennedy to McCall, 23 Aug. 1878 (emphasis in original), Gary to McCall, 16 Sept. 1878, Charles Spencer McCall Papers, SCL; Snider to Dibble, 22 Oct. 1880, Samuel Dibble Papers, PL (emphasis in original).
40. *Greenville News*, quoted in *Edgefield Chronicle*, 29 Mar. 1882; text of election law in South Carolina General Assembly, *Acts and Joint Resolutions*, 1881–82, 1110–22; Cooper, *Conservative Regime*, 103–5; *Charleston News and Courier*, 26 May, 14 June, 4 July 1882; *Edgefield Chronicle*, 12 Apr., 21 June 1882.
41. *Keowee Courier*, 29 July (Spartanburg), 12 Aug. (Oconee), 2 Sept. (Abbeville) 1880.
42. *Edgefield Chronicle*, 18 Jan. 1882; *Charleston News and Courier*, 22 June 1882; South Carolina General Assembly, *Reports and Resolutions*, 1880, 560; 1882, 1719.
43. *Charleston News and Courier*, 2 Jan. 1882, quoted in Tindall, *South Carolina Negroes*, 177. On the regional causes and contexts of this migration, see Painter, *Exodusters*. For the South Carolina exodus of 1881– 82, see Devlin, *South Carolina and Black Migration*; *Charleston News and Courier*, Dec. 1881–Feb. 1882; and *Edgefield Chronicle*, 14 Sept. 1881, 22 Feb. 1882.
44. Dailey, "Race, Sex, and Citizenship" (Virginia); *Keowee Courier*, 18 Apr., 11 May 1882 (first quotation); minutes, 1 Jan. 1882, BIFCR (second quotation; emphasis in original). On white Republicans and independents in this period, see Hyman, *Anti-Redeemers*, and De Santis, *Republicans Face the Southern Question*, 133–78.
45. Seligmann, "South Carolina Independent"; McMath, *American Populism*, esp. 50–82, quotation on 51; J. Hendrix McLane, "Labor and Finance," 1879, John Augustus Hendrix McLane Papers, SL.
46. Werner, "Hegemony and Conflict," 112–13; De Santis, *Republicans Face the Southern Question*, 133–78; *Charleston News and Courier*, 5, 14, 18 Aug., 5, 27 Sept. 1882.
47. Russell in *Keowee Courier*, 30 Aug. 1882; *Charleston News and Courier*, 27 July, 12, 13 Sept., 2, 3 Oct. 1882; Russell in *National View* (Washington, D.C.), 28 Oct. 1882, McLane in ibid., 14 Oct. 1882, typescripts in John Augustus Hendrix McLane Papers, SL.
48. *Charleston News and Courier*, 27 July, 14 Aug. (quotation) 1882. See also *Keowee Courier*, 14 Sept. 1882. On Aiken, see ibid., 30 Aug. 1882, and *Charleston News and Courier*, 25 Nov. 1882.
49. *Charleston News and Courier*, 22 Aug. 1882.

50. Ibid., 12, 13 Sept., 2, 3 Oct. 1882; *Keowee Courier*, 3 Aug. 1882; Dawson in *Charleston News and Courier*, 10 Oct. 1882; *Keowee Courier*, 27 July 1882 ("hold together"); *Edgefield Chronicle*, 26 Oct. 1882.
51. South Carolina Democratic platform broadside, 2 Aug. 1882, scrapbooks, Francis Warrington Dawson Papers, PL; *Charleston News and Courier*, 1 Aug. 1882. See also "reasons why all colored citizens who are at all interested in obtaining for themselves or their children a good education, should support the candidates of the Democratic party in the coming election," 10 Sept. 1880, Samuel Dibble Papers, PL. On fusion, see *Charleston News and Courier*, 4 Apr., 15 July, 10, 16 Aug. 1882, and *Edgefield Chronicle*, 30 Aug. 1882.
52. *Edgefield Chronicle*, 10 Aug. 1881, 21 June, 26 July, 25 Oct. 1882, 7 May 1884.
53. *Keowee Courier*, 12 Oct., 10 Aug., 5 Oct. (Winnsboro) 1882. The irony was that although there could easily have been some truth to the accusations, Democrats lied about their opponents so artlessly and consistently that it is doubtful that their charges would have been granted much credibility. Little information is available about either man's activities during the postwar decade. McLane's papers contain no pertinent information other than notes on a newspaper clipping in which he admitted being a Redeemer Democratic partisan but denied having shot anyone—a claim Tillman himself could have made had he desired to frame his activities in the negative. See typescript of press clippings, *Boston Herald*, [1892], John Augustus Hendrix McLane Papers, SL. Russell does not appear to have left papers at all. In any case, at some point during the previous generation, most adult white Southern men had participated in some activity that could be construed as antiblack. The question was not whether a given white independent had always stood with the angels but whether (or to what extent) he had come to a different understanding of the proper relationship of race to citizenship. Absolute purity of personal history or political motive mattered less than the possibility that new circumstances might lead substantial numbers of white men to conceive of their interests in terms not totally racialized.
54. *Keowee Courier*, 5 Oct. 1882.
55. *Charleston News and Courier*, 18 Aug. 1882; *Edgefield Chronicle*, 1 Nov. 1882; *National View* (Washington, D.C.), 7 Oct. 1882, typescript in John Augustus Hendrix McLane Papers, SL.
56. *Yorkville Enquirer*, 5 Oct. 1882.
57. *Charleston News and Courier*, 5 Aug., 26 Sept. (quotation), 4 Nov. 1882.
58. Ibid., 4 Oct. 1882; *Keowee Courier*, 5 Oct. 1882.
59. *Charleston News and Courier*, 28 Sept. 1882.
60. Ibid., 2 Oct. 1882.
61. Ibid., 5 Sept. 1882.
62. "Saxon," "The Philosophy of Straightout Democracy," *Abbeville Medium*, [1880–82], clipping in Fitz William McMaster and Mary Jane Macfie McMaster Papers, SCL; *Charleston News and Courier*, 25 Sept. 1882. See also ibid., 22 Sept. 1884. On "social equality," see Painter, "'Social Equality,' Miscegenation, Labor, and Power," and Dailey, "Deference and Violence" and "Race, Sex, and Citizenship."
63. Analyses of Southern agrarianism have paid scant attention to gender; more

surprising, they have only rarely investigated the roles of women. See Jeffrey, "Women in the Southern Farmers' Alliance." For an investigation of white-supremacist agrarianism, see Whites, "Wife's Farm." Of related interest is MacLean, "Leo Frank Case."

64. E. B. C. Cash, "Preliminary Remarks" and "1876–1882," [1882], Ellerbe Broggan Crawford Cash Papers, SCL.
65. *Charleston News and Courier*, 25 Nov. 1882; South Carolina General Assembly, *Reports and Resolutions*, 1882, 1719–22.
66. *Charleston News and Courier*, 5, 10 (quotation) Oct. 1884; *Edgefield Chronicle*, 7 May 1884.
67. BRT to McKie, 19 Nov. 1884, Thomas Jefferson McKie Papers, PL; *Charleston News and Courier*, 17 Oct. 1884; *Edgefield Advertiser*, 4 Jan. 1883, clipping in BRTP-CL, pt. 12.
68. On the Georgetown compromise ticket, see *Charleston News and Courier*, 10, 16 Aug. 1882. On Democrats' fears, see *Sea Island News*, 15 Nov. 1884.
69. *Charleston News and Courier*, 30, 21 Dec. (quotation) 1885. See also, e.g., ibid., 11, 14 Dec. 1885.
70. Ibid., 14 Dec. 1885.

Chapter Four

1. *Edgefield Chronicle*, 11 June, 23 July, 6 Aug., 3, 17 Sept., 8 Oct. 1884, 24 June, 1 July 1885; *Edgefield Advertiser*, 9 July 1885, clipping in BRTP-CL, pt. 5.
2. *Charleston News and Courier*, 20, 21 Aug., 9 Sept. 1885 ("nervousness"), 18 Jan. 1886 ("Moses"); BRT to Dawson, 23 Dec. 1886, Francis Warrington Dawson Papers, PL.
3. *Charleston News and Courier*, 23 Jan. 1890; Woodward, *Origins of the New South*, 192; BRT in *Charleston News and Courier*, 18 Jan., 30 Apr. 1886, 30 Mar. 1887; Simkins, *Pitchfork Ben Tillman*, 88–90. When Tillman ran for governor in 1890, he owned 1,702 acres. See *Charleston News and Courier*, 6 July 1890. For antebellum planter-reformers' similar vision, see Ford, *Origins of Southern Radicalism*, 3. For earlier efforts at agricultural reform in Tillman's area, see Faust, *James Henry Hammond*, 274–75, 349, 367. McLane's political start also had come through agricultural reform, via a local Grange. See McLane, *Labor and Finance* and *Speech Delivered before Feasterville Grange*. For evidence that the latter speech was McLane's, see McCrory to McLane, 10 Aug. 1886, John Augustus Hendrix McLane Papers, SL.
4. BRT deed to Whitney, 1887, Index to Deeds, book 10, p. 33, ECA.
5. BRT Bennettsville speech, 5 Aug. 1885, clipping in BRTP-CL, pt. 5; *Edgefield Advertiser*, 26 Aug. 1886; *Edgefield Chronicle*, 21 Oct. 1885; *Charleston News and Courier*, 9 June 1892, 9 Sept. 1891, 6 Jan., 30 Mar. 1887. On credit as an addiction, see West, "From Yeoman to Redneck," 324–25.
6. BRT in "The Farmers Aroused," *Charleston News and Courier*, 30 Apr. 1886. On the post-Reconstruction economic transformation of the state, see Carlton, *Mill*

and Town; Ford, "Rednecks and Merchants"; Werner, "Hegemony and Conflict"; and Gaston, *New South Creed*, 65–68. As an upcountry weekly noted, Tillman's agitation had raised the question of "who is a farmer": "Is a man who rents land and gives a lien a farmer, or only men who own and operate their own farms? Is a farmer who is interested in merchandising entitled to a hearing? or is a merchant who runs a farm of his own to be considered a farmer? Is a farmer who is also a preacher to be recognized, and a lawyer who runs a farm to be ignored? Where is the line to be drawn, and who is to draw the line?" (*Anderson Journal*, quoted in *Charleston News and Courier*, 31 Mar. 1886).

7. *Charleston News and Courier*, 18 Jan. 1886; BRT, speech to the Edgefield Agricultural Society, *Edgefield Chronicle*, 24 June, 1 July 1885; *Edgefield Advertiser*, 9 July 1885, clipping in BRTP-CL, pt. 5.
8. *Charleston News and Courier*, 6, 8 Apr., 22 Mar., 1 Nov. (county fair) 1886; *Edgefield Chronicle*, 26 June 1889. For comparably dismissive expressions of frustration, see *Cotton Plant*, Mar. 1885.
9. *Charleston News and Courier*, 18 Dec. 1886; Wolfe to Hemphill, 18 July 1892, Hemphill Family Papers, PL.
10. Editorial against the "Greenville Idea" for reapportionment, *Charleston News and Courier*, 21 July 1886; *Edgefield Advertiser*, 22 July 1886; *Charleston News and Courier*, 5 May 1890. By 1892, however, Tillman had made a complete about-face and adopted Dawson's line on representation. The call for a primary "was designed to break up ring rule," the governor explained to white Alliancemen in 1892; "it was never intended to take any advantage of the brave democrats of the negro counties" (ibid., 25 Mar. 1892). A direct primary, he said, would "destroy the political equilibrium of the State"—not incidentally an equilibrium that favored the incumbent governor (*Columbia Daily Register*, 24 Mar. 189[2], clipping in BRTP-CL, pt. 8).
11. *Charleston News and Courier*, 6 Aug. 1886; Begley, "Governor Richardson Faces the Tillman Challenge."
12. BRT Bennettsville speech, 5 Aug. 1885, clipping in BRTP-CL, pt. 5; *Charleston News and Courier*, 11 Jan. 1886. On alumni, see Cooper, *Conservative Regime*, table 6, p. 213, and Hollis, *College to University*.
13. Rivers to Crosland, 19 July 1887, Elias S. Rivers Papers, SCL (emphasis in original); *Edgefield Advertiser*, 25 Nov. 1886.
14. BRT in *Charleston News and Courier*, 5 May 1890, 30 Nov. 1885, 10 Nov. 1886, 3 Dec. 1885.
15. *Barnwell Sentinel*, quoted in *Charleston News and Courier*, 15 Oct. 1889; BRT to Waddill, 30 May 1892, "Measure for Measure," n.d., Burn Family Papers, SCL; *Charleston News and Courier*, 30 Apr. 1886; unidentified newspaper, 23 Apr. 1892, clipping in BRTP-CL, pt. 5, vol. 2 ("split").
16. BRT in *Charleston News and Courier*, 3 Dec. 1885. On farm women as productive laborers in another late-nineteenth-century context, see Goldberg, *Army of Women*, esp. 26–27. For a similar protest against the dismissive treatment of farm women by urbanites in the context of Texas Populism, see Turner, "Understanding the Populists," 371.

17. *Charleston News and Courier*, 28, 11 Jan., 30 Apr. 1886.
18. Ibid., 4, 29 Aug., 26 Jan. 1888, 28 June, 12 May 1890; Simkins, *Pitchfork Ben Tillman*, 130.
19. Tillman to Ransom, 11 Aug., 2 Sept., 9 Oct., 11 Nov. 1885, typescript in BRTP-CL (originals in Littlejohn Clemson History File IB8, Robert Muldrow Cooper Library, Clemson University, Clemson, S.C.). Ransom was present at the April 1886 farmers' convention. See *Charleston News and Courier*, 30 Apr. 1886. Their falling-out begins in ibid., 16, 20 Sept. 1886.
20. BRT in *Charleston News and Courier*, 1, 7 Dec. 1885; Howard to BRT, 25 May 1890, BRTP-CL, pt. 3; BRT to Barnwell, 17, 23 July 1890, BRTP-CL, pt. 2; BRT in *Charleston News and Courier*, 28 Sept. 1886; Ransom in ibid., 4 Oct. 1886.
21. *Charleston News and Courier*, 18 Jan. 1886; BRT speech to Edgefield Agricultural Society, quoted in *Edgefield Chronicle*, 1 July 1885; "The Farmers Aroused," *Charleston News and Courier*, 30 Apr., 11 Aug. 1886.
22. BRT to Crosland, 14 Jan. 1885 [1886?], BRTP-CL, pt. 3; "The Farmers Aroused," *Charleston News and Courier*, 30 Apr. 1886; report on meeting of Farmers' Association Executive Committee, *Charleston News and Courier*, 11 Aug. 1886; BRT to Crosland, 31 Dec. 1885, 19 May 1887, BRTP-CL, pt. 3; "The Fight of the Farmers," *Charleston News and Courier*, 28, 18 Jan. 1886.
23. On Tillman's lieutenants, see Stroup, "John L. McLaurin," 11–13; Hendrick, "John Gary Evans"; Slaunwhite, "John L. M. Irby"; Burn Family Papers and Aaron Cannon Diaries, SCL; and Werner, "Hegemony and Conflict," 177. Although many of Tillman's allies lived in towns—as indeed Gary had—the "anti-Tillman" faction of the Democratic Party was popularly identified with the town classes, so much so that a candidate for sheriff in Laurens County felt compelled to issue a public statement denouncing reports "that I am an anti in town and Tillmanite in the country" as the work of his enemies ("A Card" from G. S. McGravy, *Laurensville Herald*, 10 June 1892). Werner, "Hegemony and Conflict," describes the conflicts of the 1880s and 1890s as taking place between three groups of white men: two factions of bourgeois "capitalists" (oriented toward either state or national capital) and reactionary "plantation survivors." Werner's exhaustive research and healthy iconoclasm usefully shatter the romantic conception of the Alliance (and Tillmanism) as a class-based uprising either of "sturdy yeomen" or of the dispossessed. But it forces South Carolina's white men too neatly into a few well-defined categories and detaches them too easily from the complexities of their histories and identities as whites, men, and farmers. For example, Werner identifies George Tillman as a plantation survivor and Gary as bourgeois, minimizing the importance of their personal ties to their political loyalties and choices and to the state's political development. Similarly, Werner argues that South Carolina's extended Reconstruction "clouded" the development of this new, bourgeois consciousness (70), reducing one of the formative events in the state's recent past to an inconvenient detour from a predetermined path. He is at least partly correct that for most Southerners, ideological alternatives to a New South vision "were rigidly circumscribed by the success of the regional bourgeoisies in defining the issues and questions of public life" (192).

But these "issues and questions" did not fall neatly into what Werner portrays as a single New South ideology. Radical Republicans had sought progress through federal intervention and authority, later taken up by South Carolina's Republican state government, however inadequately, in public schools and land sales. Greenbackers and poorer whites sought a revitalized yeomanry and denounced both "capitalists" and "plantation survivors." And scores of local, sectional, and generational grievances shaped political belief and behavior beyond the capacity of Werner's model to explain.

24. BRT to Crosland, 31 Dec. 1885, BRTP-CL, pt. 3; Bidon to BRT, 17 Jan. 1887, BRTP-CL, pt. 2. For other support, see Donaldson to BRT, 9, 20 Feb. 1886, Ellerbe to BRT, 6 July 1886, Norris to BRT, 7 Oct. 1887, BRTP-CL, pt. 2.
25. BRT to Dawson, 17 May, 23 Dec. 1886, Francis Warrington Dawson Papers, PL; BRT in *Charleston News and Courier*, 30 Mar. 1887; BRT to Crosland, 14 June 1886, BRTP-CL, pt. 3; BRT to Dawson, 22 June 1886, Francis Warrington Dawson Papers, PL.
26. "The Farmers Aroused," *Charleston News and Courier*, 30 Apr. 1886; BRT to Crosland, 14 Jan. 1885 [1886?], BRTP-CL, pt. 3 (emphasis in original).
27. *Charleston News and Courier*, 29, 30 Apr., 1 May 1886; Donaldson to BRT, 9, 20 Feb. 1886, and n.d., BRTP-CL, pt. 2.
28. *Charleston News and Courier*, 6, 10, 19, 21 July, 3, 5 Aug. 1886; *Edgefield Advertiser*, 8, 22 July 1886; BRT to Crosland, 15, 25 July 1886, BRTP-CL, pt. 3; South Carolina General Assembly, Senate, *Journal*, 1888; *Charleston News and Courier*, 12, 13, 14 Dec. 1888.
29. *Charleston News and Courier*, 18, 28 Jan. 1886.
30. Ibid., 16 Apr. 1890, 28 Jan., 10 May 1886 ("molder"). This last hostile analysis came from Narciso G. Gonzales, who made opposition to Tillman one of the central themes of his journalistic career until he was murdered by Tillman's nephew. See Lewis Pinckney Jones, *Stormy Petrel.*
31. BRT to Crosland, 11 Feb., 19 May, 29 Aug. 1887, BRTP-CL, pt. 3; *Charleston News and Courier*, 2 Dec. 1887; BRT to Dawson, 12 Dec. 1887, 20 Jan. 1888, Francis Warrington Dawson Papers, PL; *Charleston News and Courier*, 26 Jan. 1888. See also BRT to Crosland, 14 May 1886, BRTP-CL, pt. 3.
32. BRT, "The Origins of Clemson College," 18 Jan. 1912, BRTP-CL. On the final battle for Clemson, see BRT to Dawson, 24 Apr., 5 May 1888, F. W. Dawson Papers, SCHS; notes on Manifesto of Farmers' Association Executive Committee, 21 Apr. 1888, in Francis Butler Simkins Papers, SHC; Bratton to Davis, 2 May 1888, Robert Means Davis Papers, SCL; and *Charleston News and Courier*, 26–28 Nov. 1889.
33. On the Alliance generally, see Goodwyn, *Democratic Promise*, and McMath, *Populist Vanguard*. On the movement in South Carolina, see Church, "Farmers' Alliance." Manuscript sources include Edgefield County Farmers' Alliance Minutes; South Carolina Farmers' State Alliance Minutes; South Carolina Farmers' State Alliance, Kershaw County Records; South Carolina Farmers' State Alliance Exchange Papers; and South Carolina Farmers' State Alliance Rejection Book,

all at SCL; and Anderson County Farmers' Alliance Minutes and South Carolina Farmers' State Alliance, list of sub-Alliances, typescript, 1936, SCDAH.

34. Telegram from Arkansas Farmers' State Alliance convention, in Farmers' State Alliance of South Carolina, *Proceedings of the . . . Third Annual Meeting*, 12, SCL (conflation); *Charleston News and Courier*, 4 July 1889; *National Economist*, 25 May 1889 (Alliance membership); *Charleston News and Courier*, 12 Oct. 1889; and Anderson County Farmers' Alliance Minutes, 5 Apr. 1892, SCDAH ("gentlemen"). In July 1888, the State Alliance claimed 3,000 members; a year later, it had 20,000. This growth continued into the first half of 1890, when the annual convention reported gaining 17,500 new members over the previous twelve months. See South Carolina Farmers' State Alliance Minutes, 24 July 1889, 23 July 1890, SCL. For interstate contacts, see BRT to Polk, 1 June 1886, 28 Feb. 1887, Leonidas Lafayette Polk Papers, SHC. For other Alliance activity on Tillman's behalf during the early stages of the 1890 campaign, see *Charleston News and Courier*, 17, 18, 28 Apr., 5, 7 May 1890; unidentified letter, 27 May 1890, James F. Sloan Papers, SCL; McCormick to Meares, 21 Apr. 1890, Shell to Meares, 24 Apr. 1890, Richard Ashe Meares Papers, SCL; and Anderson County Farmers' Alliance Minutes, 2 May 1890, SCDAH.

35. South Carolina Farmers' State Alliance Minutes, 11, 24 July 1889, SCL; *National Economist*, 25 May 1889; BRT to Polk, 1 June 1886, 28 Feb. 1887, Leonidas Lafayette Polk Papers, SHC; *Charleston News and Courier*, 8, 12 July, 29 Aug., 8 Oct. 1889; Edgefield County Farmers' Alliance Minutes, 26 Aug. 1889, SCL.

36. Shell Manifesto quoted in *Charleston News and Courier*, 23 Jan. 1890.

37. Richardson to Courtenay, 12 May 1890, William Ashmead Courtenay Papers, SCL; Sawyer to Morgan, 28 Apr., 25 June 1890, Alexander Samuel Salley Jr. Papers, SCL; *Charleston News and Courier*, 12, 15, 17, 22, 28 May 1890, coverage of campaign meetings throughout June and July 1890; *Charleston News and Courier*, 6 July 1890 (BRT's wealth), 9 Mar. 1886 ("bankruptcy"), 20 June 1890 ("wages"); *Edgefield Chronicle*, 14 Dec. 1885 ("boss system"); *Charleston News and Courier*, 13 July 1890 ("control"); Barnhill to BRT, 9 Aug. 1892, Governor BRT Letters, SCDAH (stock law); *Columbia State*, 6 Mar. 1891 (gloves); Shaw to BRT, 17 July 1891, BRTP-CL, pt. 10 (emphasis in original). Tillman waffled on the subject of stock laws, declaring them "a blessing if properly used" but fearing that they discouraged stock raising and therefore self-sufficiency (*Charleston News and Courier*, 29 Feb. 1892). During his first term as governor, Tillman accepted a railroad pass, although he had frequently criticized legislators and others who received such suspicious favors. Claiming that he rode as the governor and not as an individual, he saw such passes as "compliments," not bribes. See Simkins, *Pitchfork Ben Tillman*, 190–94; BRT to McBee, 23 Jan. 1891, Governor BRT Letterbooks, SCDAH; BRT to Ward, 20 Feb. 1891, BRT to Moore, 27 June 1891, BRTP-CL; Richardson to BRT, 7 Apr. 1892, Governor BRT Letters, SCDAH; and *Charleston News and Courier*, 22 June 1891. Both friends and foes protested Tillman's use of such passes; see Richardson to BRT, 7 Apr. 1892, Governor BRT Letters, SCDAH, and BRT to Moore, 27 June 1891, BRTP-CL, pt. 1.

38. *Charleston News and Courier*, 21 Oct., 1 May 1886; BRT speech quoted in *Edgefield*

Advertiser, 26 Aug. 1886 ("dude factory"); *Charleston News and Courier*, 30 Apr., 1 May 1886 (Thompson incident).

39. BRT to Crosland, 13 Mar. 1886, BRTP-CL, pt. 3; "Farmer Ancrum on B. R. Tillman," 12 July 1890, broadside, Alexander Samuel Salley Jr. Papers, SCL; *Charleston News and Courier*, 11 June 1890; *Edgefield Chronicle*, 18 July 1888; BRT to Dawson, 17 May 1886, Francis Warrington Dawson Papers, PL.
40. Butler to *Charleston News and Courier*, 25 Nov. 1886, quoted in *Edgefield Advertiser*, 2 Dec. 1886; *Edgefield Chronicle*, 17 Mar. 1887; Dawson to Hemphill, 11 Sept. 1888, Hemphill Family Papers, PL; BRT to Crosland, 22 May 1886, BRTP-CL, pt. 3.
41. *Edgefield Chronicle*, 17 Sept. 1890; *Edgefield Advertiser*, 16 June 1892; Chapin to Hemphill, 29 Mar. 1890, Hemphill Family Papers, PL (profanity); *Greenville News*, 11 June 1890, quoted in notes in Francis Butler Simkins Papers, SHC; *Charleston News and Courier*, 16 June 1890. See also E. B. Murray, *Read and Learn*, and Ownby, *Subduing Satan*, 49–50. On Tillman's appearance, see *Edgefield Advertiser*, 16 June 1892. *Columbia State* editor Narciso Gonzales could never resist pointing out a wool hat, even after 1895, when Tillman had left the state for Washington, D.C. At an 1895 Alliance meeting in the capital, "[t]here were some fine specimens of 'wool hats.' . . . Two were seen which were larger and broader-brimmed than any sighted hereabouts" since 1890 (*Columbia State*, 20 Feb. 1895).
42. Izlar to Courtenay, 28 Aug. 1888, William Ashmead Courtenay Papers, SCL; Aldrich to Hemphill, 29 June 1890, Francis Warrington Dawson Papers, SCL; Dawson to Hemphill, 11 Sept. 1888, Hemphill Family Papers, PL; Thompson to Dawson, 9 Aug. 1888, F. W. Dawson Papers, SCHS; Butler to Dawson, 17 Aug. 1888, Francis Warrington Dawson Papers, PL; F. W. McMaster to G. McMaster, 26 Dec. 1894, Fitz William McMaster and Mary Jane Macfie McMaster Papers, SCL; *Columbia State*, 13 Dec. 1894, 27 Aug. 1892; Lucas to Lucas, 9 July 1894, James Jonathan Lucas Papers, SCL. For more on town folk's belittling usages, see West, "From Yeoman to Redneck," 350–51.
43. Shell to BRT, 5 Mar. 1887, BRTP-CL, pt. 2; *Charleston News and Courier*, 12 May 1890; BRT to Crosland, 14 June 1886, BRTP-CL, pt. 3; *Charleston News and Courier*, 6 May 1890; "Mine Creek Dots," *Edgefield Advertiser*, 30 June 1892.
44. BRT to Dawson, 17 May 1886, Francis Warrington Dawson Papers, PL; *Charleston News and Courier*, 5 May, 20 June 1890; E. B. Murray, *Read and Learn*.
45. W. T. Walton in *Edgefield Chronicle*, 23 Apr. 1890; H. H. Towns [*sic*], "A Voice from Poverty Hill," broadside, SCL; BRT in *Charleston News and Courier*, 23 Jan. 1890.
46. BRT in *Charleston News and Courier*, 4 July, 1 Apr. 1890, 29 Aug. 1888, 7 Dec. 1885.
47. Ibid., 12 May 1890; H. H. Towns [*sic*], "Don't You Forget It," broadside, Apr. 1890, filed with "Voice from Poverty Hill," SCL.
48. *Marlboro Chronicle* (Bennettsville, S.C.), 21 Aug. 1886.
49. Editorial, *Charleston News and Courier*, 22 May 1890 ("passions"); ibid., 21 July 1890 ("injury"); ibid., 16 Aug. 1892 ("staid at home"); Hagood to McCall, 8 Apr. 1894, Charles Spencer McCall Papers, SCL ("anarchical element"); Or-

angeburg letter, *Charleston News and Courier*, 14 July 1890; ibid., 7 July 1890; Aldrich to Hemphill, 29 June 1890, Francis Warrington Dawson Papers, SCL.

50. Towns [*sic*], "Don't You Forget It," SCL.
51. *Charleston News and Courier*, 23, 21, 27 July 1886.
52. Ibid., 27, 28 Mar. 1890.
53. Ibid., 5 May 1890.
54. Ibid., 31 Mar. 1890, 1 Jan. 1894; Hemphill to BRT, 28 Mar. 1890, BRTP-CL, pt. 3; Richardson to Courtenay, 12 May 1890, William Ashmead Courtenay Papers, SCL.
55. *Charleston News and Courier*, 24 June, 12, 14 July 1890; "Primary or Split," ibid., 9, 14 July 1890; "Hopewell Township Democratic Club No. 2 (Anti-Tillman)," [5 July 1890], Alexander Samuel Salley Jr. Papers, SCL; Smythe to Courtenay, 20 Aug. 1890, William Ashmead Courtenay Papers, SCL.
56. *Charleston News and Courier*, 14, 15 Aug. 1890; circular letter, 30 June 1890, Joseph Walker Barnwell Papers, SCHS.
57. *Charleston News and Courier*, 22 Aug. 1890.
58. Ibid., 26 June 1890; Parker to Sheppard, 21 Sept. 1886, Governor Sheppard Letters, SCDAH; *Charleston News and Courier*, 21 Mar. 1890. For a similar comparison to Mahone, see "Sand-lotism in Carolina," ibid., 11 Apr. 1890.
59. Russell at an Anderson County meeting, reported in *Charleston News and Courier*, 8 Apr. 1886; McLane, *Speech Delivered before Feasterville Grange*; McCrory to J. H. McLane, 10 Aug. 1886, James McLane to J. H. McLane, 18 Aug. 1886, Russell to J. H. McLane, 19 Nov. 1887, J. H. McLane diary, July–Sept. 1888, Jan.–Mar. 1889, 29 Mar., 12 Apr., 7 May, 13 Oct., 9 Nov. 1892, Duncan to J. H. McLane, 21 Aug. 1887, J. H. McLane to Capen, 18, 23 Nov. 1887, John Augustus Hendrix McLane Papers, SL.
60. Brayton, *Address upon the Election Law*; BRT in *Charleston News and Courier*, 17 Aug. 1891. The Lodge Bill's one-vote defeat in the Senate the following month was hardly reassuring to white supremacists. See Woodward, *Origins of the New South*, 254–55, and Crofts, "Blair Bill," esp. 333–36.
61. *Charleston News and Courier*, 23 June, 6 July 1887; Kremm and Neal, "Clandestine Black Labor Societies"; Bruce Baker, "The 'Hoover Scare' in South Carolina, 1887: An Attempt to Organize Black Farm Labor," *Labor History* 40, no. 3 (1999): 261–82.
62. *Charleston News and Courier*, 26 Aug. (Alliance agent), 23, 25 Mar. (stock law), 16 Sept. 1889 (wages). In 1891, the latent tension between black laborers and white owners exploded when the Colored Alliance called for a national cotton pickers' strike for higher wages. A bloody massacre of Arkansas strikers effectively shut down the black Alliance as a national organization. See Holmes, "Arkansas Cotton Pickers' Strike" and "Demise of the Colored Farmers' Alliance." The *Charleston News and Courier*, 8, 10, 16 Sept. 1891, minimized the importance of strike activity in South Carolina. South Carolina's black labor force, nearly 300,000 strong in 1890, was 75 percent agricultural, yet fewer than 10 percent of black agricultural laborers owned the land they farmed, and only about 33 percent rented. In the lowcountry, especially Beaufort County, many

black farmers owned their land, but few black farmers could realistically expect to become owners, and most were wage laborers or sharecroppers. See U.S. Bureau of the Census, *Eleventh Census of the United States, 1890: Report on Farms and Homes* and *Compendium.*

63. *Charleston News and Courier,* 23, 25 Mar., 11, 25 Apr., 10 Nov. 1889, 21, 22, 28 Mar., 6, 23, 24 Aug., 3, 8 Dec. 1890; Shell to BRT, 14 Oct. 1889, BRTP-CL, pt. 2; *Charleston News and Courier,* 19 Mar. 1890 (quotation).
64. *Charleston News and Courier,* 26 June, 5 July 1890. On segregation, see ibid., 9 Dec. 1893. White women sometimes encouraged this form of "protection." Describing a trip by train, a white woman complained that a nonwhite man had taken the last available first-class seat, forcing her to journey in the "colored people's car." She protested the impropriety of forcing "a delicate, refined woman to sit, shoulder to shoulder" with a black male laborer. "Oh, men," she concluded, "call to life some of the spirit of your brave forefathers and think what it will be for your fair young daughters if you do not rouse yourselves" (ibid., 14 Oct. 1889). On "protection" as a resurgent element of late-nineteenth-century discourse between white men and white women, see Whites, "De Graffenreid Controversy" and "Wife's Farm."
65. *Charleston News and Courier,* 6, 24 Aug., 27 June 1890; Davis to BRT, 4 Aug. 1890, BRTP-CL, pt. 3. See also Diane Neal, "Benjamin Ryan Tillman," 199–200.
66. South Carolina Farmers' State Alliance Minutes, July 1890, SCL; Crosland to BRT, 7 Oct. 1890, BRTP-CL, pt. 3; Stackhouse in *Charleston News and Courier,* 27 June, 17 July 1890; ibid., 28 June, 3, 11 July 1890. On Tillman's continuing commitment to white-only politics, see *Charleston News and Courier,* 27, 28 June, 3, 9, 11, 17 July 1890.
67. Smythe to Courtenay, 23 Aug. 1890, William Ashmead Courtenay Papers, SCL; *Charleston News and Courier,* 14 Aug. 1890; circular letter, 30 June 1890, Joseph Walker Barnwell Papers, SCHS.
68. *Charleston News and Courier,* 1 Oct. 1890; Harllee to Barnwell, 1, 7 Oct. 1890, Chamberlain to Barnwell, 4 Oct. 1890, Fordham to Barnwell, 10 Oct. 1890, Lyles to Barnwell, 20, 21, 22, 28 Oct. 1890, Hazzard to Barnwell, 25 Oct. 1890, Hammond to Barnwell, 25 Oct. 1890, Featherstone to Barnwell, 22 Oct. 1890, Chamberlain to Haskell, 4 Oct. 1890, Joseph Walker Barnwell Papers, SCHS.
69. Hanckel to Barnwell, 9 Aug. 1890, Joseph Walker Barnwell Papers, SCHS; Earle to Courtenay, 1 Nov. 1890, William Ashmead Courtenay Papers, SCL (emphasis in original); *Charleston News and Courier,* 2 Aug. 1890; Aldrich to Barnwell, 12 Oct. 1890, Joseph Walker Barnwell Papers, SCHS; *Columbia Register,* 1 Oct. 1890; *Charleston News and Courier,* 12, 15 Sept., 1 Oct. 1890; "Beware of Frauds at the Polls," broadside, 1890, William Haynesworth Lyles Papers, SCL.
70. Hammond to "Katharine," 13 Apr. 1894, Hammond, Bryan, and Cummings Families Papers, SCL; Hammond to Barnwell, 25 Oct. 1890, Hanckel to Barnwell, 9 Aug. 1890, Joseph Walker Barnwell Papers, SCHS; Dargan in *Charleston News and Courier,* 11 Sept. 1890; BRT in *Columbia Register,* 31 Oct. 1890, clipping in Yates Snowden Papers, SCL. Tillman believed that few men would be found

willing to count him out. See BRT to Courtenay, 20 Oct. 1890, William Ashmead Courtenay Papers, SCL.

71. *Charleston News and Courier*, 20 Sept., 17 Oct. 1890; Fordham to Barnwell, 10 Oct. 1890, Joseph Walker Barnwell Papers, SCHS; *Charleston News and Courier*, 15, 17, 27, 28 ("wealth and intelligence"; 3d ed.) Oct. 1890.

72. Daggett to BRT, 21 Dec. 1890, Governor BRT Letters, SCDAH; BRT to Jervey, 21 Sept. 1892, Theodore Dehon Jervey Jr. Papers, SCHS; Willoughby to BRT, 16 Nov. 1892, Governor BRT Papers, SCDAH (emphasis in original); "That 'Ugly Question,'" unidentified newspaper, 25 Oct. 1890, clipping in Yates Snowden Papers, SCL; Joynes to Courtenay, 22 Oct. 1890, William Ashmead Courtenay Papers, SCL (emphasis in original); "Fifth Congressional District," *Cotton Plant*, 6 Oct. 1894. The final tally was Tillman, 59,159, Haskell, 14,828. See South Carolina General Assembly, *Reports and Resolutions*, 1890, 604. Cooper, "Economics or Race," 209–19, concludes that the evidence "strongly suggests that the bulk of Haskell votes came from Negro citizens" (218).

73. Kemmershin to BRT, 29 Nov. 1890, Governor BRT Papers, SCDAH; BRT to Irby, 8 Feb. 1892, BRTP-CL, pt. 1.

74. *National Economist*, 15 Nov. 1890.

75. For the subtreasury proposal, see Tindall, *Populist Reader*, 80–87. For a discussion of its economics, see Goodwyn, *Democratic Promise*, 571–81.

76. *Charleston News and Courier*, 25 July 1892 (2d ed.); *Atlanta Journal*, 30 Apr. 1891, quoted in *Charleston News and Courier*, 5 May 1891.

77. Butler in *Charleston News and Courier*, 31 July 1891; BRT to Elder, 8 June 1891, BRTP-CL ("details"); BRT interview in *Cotton Plant*, n.d., reprinted in *Spartanburg Herald*, 30 May 1891, clipping in BRTP-CL, pt. 5; BRT to Wilson, 18 June 1891, BRTP-CL; *Atlanta Journal*, 30 Apr. 1891, quoted in *Charleston News and Courier*, 5 May 1891; ibid., 12 May (BRT's alternative), 9 June (rebuttal noting many defects of proposal) 1891. Butler also feared that South Carolina's congressional delegation would lose stature within the Democratic Party if it came to Congress "asking impossible and impracticable things like the sub Treasury scheme, the Government ownership of railroads &c." (Butler to Pope, 11 Jan. 1891, Governor BRT Letters, SCDAH).

78. *National Economist*, 15 Nov. 1890; Wolfe to BRT, 7 July 1891, Governor BRT Letters, SCDAH; *Charleston News and Courier*, 11 Sept. 1891; Watson to Charles, 11 June 1892, Charles Family Papers, SCL; Edgefield County Farmers' Alliance Minutes, 2 Oct. 1891, SCL; *Cotton Plant*, 11 Apr. 1891; *National Economist*, 1, 8 Aug. 1891.

79. Elder to BRT, 2 June 1891, Pope to BRT, 24 Jan. 1891, Governor BRT Papers, SCDAH; *Charleston News and Courier*, 12 May, 11, 14 July 1891; Neal to BRT, 15, 24 Apr. 1891, Governor BRT Letters, SCDAH.

80. BRT to Stokes, 30 May 1892, BRT to Crosland, 26 Aug. 1891, BRTP-CL, pt. 1; Irby to Evans, 8 Feb. 1892, John Gary Evans Papers, SCL; *Charleston News and Courier*, 20 May 1892; Barber to BRT, 4 June 1892, Governor BRT Letters, SCDAH ("position"); BRT to Stokes, 30 May 1892, BRTP-CL, pt. 1; Harvey to BRT, 27 July 1891, Governor BRT Letters, SCDAH ("*dudes*"; emphasis in original).

81. BRT to Latimer, 2 Mar. 1892, BRTP-CL, pt. 1; *Charleston News and Courier*, 29 Feb. 1892, 9 Sept. 1891, 25 July 1892 (2d ed.); BRT to Cartledge, 17 Sept. 1892, Governor BRT Letterbooks, SCDAH; BRT to *Augusta Chronicle*, 13 Feb. 1893, BRTP-CL; *Cotton Plant*, 19 May 1894; *Charleston News and Courier*, 28 June 1894; third-party efforts in ibid., 4 (Anderson), 20 (Oconee) May 1892.

82. On silver, see Silverman, "Silver Movement," and Ritter, *Goldbugs and Greenbacks*.

83. *Charleston News and Courier*, 29 Feb. 1892, 27 Dec. 1885 (silver), 27 June 1890, 19 May, 24, 25 June 1892. Tillman had used the figure of the pitchfork before this: e.g., "He didn't object to fair criticism and analysis, but when they attacked him he also attacked them with the pitchfork end" (*Charleston News and Courier*, 4 Aug. 1889).

84. BRT to Moore, 5 Oct. 1892, Governor BRT Letterbooks, SCDAH; *Charleston News and Courier*, 5 July 1892; *Columbia State*, 20 Oct. 1892; *Charleston News and Courier*, 21 Oct. 1892. At the last moment, the party reportedly received and rejected offers of cooperation from the Republican Party, which had mobilized for the federal election. See *Charleston News and Courier*, 30, 31 Oct. 1892.

85. *Charleston News and Courier*, 9 Sept. 1891, 25 July 1892 (2d ed.); BRT to Latimer, 2 Mar., 1 Sept. 1892, Tompkins to McLaurin, 1 Nov. 1892, BRTP-CL, pt. 1. Unlike earlier independent movements, the Populists appear to have drawn mainly white voters. Thirty-six percent of the total Populist presidential vote came from two white-majority upcountry counties, Pickens and Oconee. The voting record in the latter is particularly interesting, for during the post-Reconstruction period, up to 200 voters regularly turned out against Democrats in federal elections, with the exception of the election of 1882, when about 600 voted for Greenback gubernatorial and congressional nominees. In 1892, Oconee's pattern of casting about 200 Republican votes (in this case for presidential electors) persisted, but although a total of 1,258 votes were counted for incumbent governor Ben Tillman, only 909 were cast for Cleveland electors. Weaver electors earned 428 votes. It is reasonable to infer that Weaver's votes came from disaffected white Democrats, and (given that the total of Populist and Democratic presidential votes exceeded the gubernatorial vote) that more than 100 of these white Democrats refused to vote for Tillman. The lowcountry counties that had turned out strongly for McLane in 1882 and against Tillman in 1890 together provided only a few dozen votes for Populist presidential electors in 1892. Substantial numbers of voters were reported only for Republican congressional candidates. Cleveland, with 54,692 votes counted, handily defeated Republican Benjamin Harrison, with 13,345. Those Republican votes elected George Murray to Congress, the last black South Carolinian to represent the state for almost a century. See South Carolina General Assembly, *Reports and Resolutions*, 1878, 442; 1880, 554; 1882, 1716–19; 1884, 834; 1888, 556–60; 1890, 604–10; 1892, 546–55; *Charleston News and Courier*, 10, 11, 21 Nov. 1892, 11 Jan. 1893; and *Columbia State*, 9 Nov. 1892.

86. *Charleston News and Courier*, 19 May 1892; list of Populist electors-at-large in *Columbia State*, 20 Oct. 1892; Keitt in *Charleston News and Courier*, 5 Aug. 1890; *Cotton Plant*, 10 Mar. ("myth"), 26 May, 1 Sept. 1894 ("Cuffee"). The debate

over the Democratic credentials of onetime Haskell and Weaver voters continued among the members of the state Democratic Executive Committee. See *Charleston News and Courier*, 8 June 1894. As one historian notes, "None of the Southern Populists escaped their history" (Palmer, *"Man over Money,"* 50). For dramatic efforts to do so, see Goodwyn, "Populist Dreams," and Cantrell, *Kenneth and John B. Rayner*. Watson could declare to white and black farmers that "[y]ou are kept apart that you may be separately fleeced of your earnings. You are made to hate each other because upon that hatred is rested the keystone of the arch of financial despotism which enslaves you both" (*Arena* 6 [1892], quoted in Woodward, *Tom Watson*, 220). But he could also, before a white South Carolina audience, call the Lodge Elections Bill the "Force Bill" and claim that it had been defeated through the efforts of the national Alliance. See *Charleston News and Courier*, 11 Sept. 1891. For critical perspectives on Watson and Georgia Populists' biracialism, see Crowe, "Tom Watson," and Shaw, *Wool-Hat Boys*.

87. Untitled manuscript, [1890–92], Patrick Henry Adams Papers, SCL.
88. J. H. McLane diary, 7 May, 13 Oct. 1892, John Augustus Hendrix McLane Papers, SL.
89. Goodwyn, *Democratic Promise*, 248.

Chapter Five

1. BRT to Crosland, 29 Aug. 1887, BRTP-CL, pt. 3.
2. *Edgefield Chronicle*, 2 July 1890; *Charleston News and Courier*, 11 Oct. ("noise"), 30 June (Hampton), 7 July 1890 ("silence").
3. *Edgefield Advertiser*, 23 June 1892.
4. Ibid., 14 July 1892.
5. Ibid.
6. Davis to Laughlin, 21 Mar. 1887, Robert Means Davis Papers, SCL; *Charleston News and Courier*, 22 June 1894 ("funeral"), 4 Aug. 1889 ("turkeys").
7. Quoted in *Edgefield Advertiser*, 14 July 1892.
8. Butler to Hemphill, 16 June 1890, Hemphill Family Papers, PL; *Charleston News and Courier*, 21 (Butler's charge), 22 June 1894 (BRT's rebuttal); *U.S. Senate Misc. Doc.* no. 48, 44th Cong., 2d sess., 1:1051–57, 2:309; *Charleston News and Courier*, 24 June 1894 (Butler's retreat).
9. *Charleston News and Courier*, 1 Aug. 1894; BRT to Sallie Tillman, 3 Aug. 1894, BRTP-CL, pt. 1 (emphasis in original).
10. *Charleston News and Courier*, 31 May, 26 July 1891, 15 June 1892; Haumans [?] to BRT, 19 Apr. 1892, Governor BRT Letters, SCDAH.
11. Haumans [?] to BRT, 19 Apr. 1892, Governor BRT Letters, SCDAH; *Charleston News and Courier*, 15–16 June 1892; *Edgefield Advertiser*, 16 June 1892. In a nearby Georgia community, the nine white men sentenced to a chain gang for participating in "white-capping" included a "prominent farmer" and a "prominent physician" (*Charleston News and Courier*, 23 Apr. 1893).
12. The emergence of this dynamic has become one of the chief subjects of scholar-

ship on gender, race, and violence in the Southern United States. Scholarly discussion of these questions often takes the writing of earlier social commentators and critics as its point of departure; key texts include Wells-Barnett, "Southern Horrors" and "Red Record"; Cash, *Mind of the South*; and Lillian Smith, *Killers of the Dream.* Groundbreaking scholarship from the 1970s including Hall, " 'The Mind That Burns' " and *Revolt against Chivalry*, has paved the way for an extensive literature. Some works have focused on the "psychosexual" dynamics of lynching and other violence, notably Joel Williamson, *Crucible of Race.* Others have sought to understand the sexual dimensions of violence—in both its alleged causes and its brutal practice—in relation to the problem of postemancipation labor and law and to show how lynching functioned to discipline white women as well as African Americans; important contributions include Painter, " 'Social Equality' "; Hodes, *White Women, Black Men*; Laura F. Edwards, *Gendered Strife and Confusion*; Bederman, *Manliness and Civilization*; Gilmore, "Flight of the Incubus"; and MacLean, *Behind the Mask of Chivalry* and "Leo Frank Case." This section and the next draw on the insights of these authors. One historian has proposed a four-part "taxonomy of mob violence" to describe lynching: small "private" mobs, larger "terrorist" mobs, posses, and mass mobs of more than fifty people (Brundage, *Lynching in the New South*, 18–19).

13. *Charleston News and Courier*, 1 Aug. 1893.
14. Wells-Barnett, "Southern Horrors" and "Red Record"; Bederman, *Manliness and Civilization*, 45–76; Dailey, "Deference and Violence" (public and private); Ayers, *Vengeance and Justice*, 238–55, and *Promise of the New South*, 156–57 ("stranger"); Finnegan, " 'At the Hands of Parties Unknown,' " 168, 319 (justification for lynching in South Carolina).
15. Faust, "Southern Violence Revisited," 205–10; Roman to Richardson, 17 Nov. 1890, Governor Richardson Letters, SCDAH; *Charleston News and Courier*, 3 Jan. 1890 (juries); Richardson to McDonald, 13 Mar. 1890, Roman to Richardson, 17 Nov. 1890, Governor Richardson Letters, SCDAH; *Edgefield Chronicle*, 16 Dec. 1891. Although its own list of those investigated by the circuit solicitor included many prominent white Edgefield Democrats, the paper professed ignorance of the identities of the actual participants.
16. Figures in Diane Neal, "Benjamin Ryan Tillman," 307, and Finnegan, " 'At the Hands of Parties Unknown,' " 11, 15, 61.
17. *Charleston News and Courier*, 23 Jan. 1890; *Edgefield Chronicle*, 12 Mar. 1890; BRT, *Inaugural Address . . . 1890* and *Message to the General Assembly, 1891.*
18. Bean to Herriot, [9] Dec. 1890, Governor BRT Letterbooks (labeled Richardson "G"), SCDAH; Tompkins to Hanston [?], 1 Sept. 1891, Governor BRT Letterbooks, SCDAH; telegram, Nevils to Evans, 15 Aug. 1895, Governor Evans Papers, SCDAH.
19. BRT to Lenore, 17 Dec. 1890, Governor BRT Letterbooks, SCDAH; telegrams to sheriffs and militias, 12 Feb., 23 Oct., 7 Dec. 1891, 7, 30 Nov., 17 Dec. 1892, Governor BRT Telegrams, SCDAH; BRT to Nichols, 29 Sept. 1891, Governor BRT Letterbooks, SCDAH (Spartanburg); BRT, *Message to the General Assembly, 1891*, 29 ("no person").

20. BRT, *Inaugural Address . . . 1890* and *Message to the General Assembly, 1891*, 22.
21. BRT to Nelson, 7 Dec. 1891, Governor BRT Letterbooks, SCDAH; *Charleston News and Courier*, 15 Dec. 1891.
22. *Charleston News and Courier*, 15 Dec. 1891, 25 May, 1 June 1892.
23. Tompkins to Heyward, 27 May 1892, Governor BRT Letterbooks, SCDAH.
24. BRT speech at Barnwell campaign meeting, 7 June 1892, quoted in *Edgefield Advertiser*, 16 June 1892; *Charleston News and Courier*, 18 Aug. 1892 (Abbeville).
25. *Charleston News and Courier*, 27 July 1892; McPherson to BRT, 29 June 1892, Tompkins to McPherson, 1 July 1892, Governor BRT Letters, SCDAH.
26. On Felton, see Whites, "Love, Hate, Rape, Lynching" and "Wife's Farm." Whites argues that for Felton, both positions arose ultimately from her horror over miscegenation. Tillman shared these feelings, but for him miscegenation was only one of many forces threatening the white farming household.
27. *Edgefield Advertiser*, 24 Aug. 1893; *Charleston News and Courier*, 14 June 1894. Tillman's defense of lynching was not the most uncompromising position put forward during the 1890s. One writer suggested repealing both "mob violence" and rape laws in Georgia, the effect of which would be to deny accused rapists the protection of the law and weaken the ability of the state to punish their lynchers. This proposal demonstrated how earnestly some white supremacists believed that black-on-white rape should be regarded less as a violation of law than as a blow against white civilization. See Townsend to BRT, 18 Oct. 1894, Sundberg to BRT, 13 Aug. 1894, Hall to BRT, 29 May 1894, Governor BRT Letters, SCDAH.
28. *Charleston News and Courier*, 25 Nov. 1885.
29. Ibid., 30 Dec. 1889, 4 Jan. 1890.
30. *Charleston News and Courier*, 3 Jan. 1890; anonymous to Evans, 19 Aug. 1895, Governor Evans Papers, SCDAH.
31. *Charleston News and Courier*, 25 Nov. 1885, 3 Jan. 1890.
32. Ibid., 25 Nov. 1885; *Star of Zion*, 4 Oct. 1894; Smalls in *Charleston News and Courier*, 25 Sept. 1891; ibid., 3, 6 Jan. 1888 (Pickens County). The suggestion that consensual sexual relationships, not rapes, were the basis for lynching was a persistent, albeit dangerous, theme in black critiques. An incautiously worded but basically similar charge in 1898 by black Wilmington, North Carolina, editor Alexander Manly became the rhetorical foundation for a white-supremacist newspaper campaign that helped destroy Populist-Republican fusion in that state. See Prather, "We Have Taken a City."
33. *Charleston News and Courier*, 16 Dec. 1890.
34. Ibid., 19 Dec. 1888, 15 Sept. 1889.
35. During one five-week period in early 1892, the paper recorded six incidents of lynching in five states that claimed nine black victims. See ibid., 13, 14, 17, 22 Feb., 10, 22 Mar. 1892. Weekly papers such as the *Edgefield Advertiser* often reported at least one lynching in each issue for long stretches during the early 1890s. Some white readers may have come to see these reports, like sermons or campaign meetings, as unexceptional features of the social landscape.
36. *Charleston News and Courier*, 24 July 1889.
37. Ibid., 1, 6 July 1892; Lyles to BRT, 4 Apr. 1893, Governor BRT Letters, SCDAH;

BRT to Lyles, 16 May 1893, Governor BRT Letterbooks, SCDAH (emphasis in original).

38. A. M. Salley to A. S. Salley, 26 Jan. 1889, Alexander Samuel Salley Jr. Papers, SCL; James Hemphill to "Calvin," 24 Jan. 1890, Hemphill Family Papers, PL.
39. *Charleston News and Courier*, 10 Dec. 1890, 28 Jan. 1891 (Hampton), 14 July 1892 (BRT). Reconsideration of the so-called moderates is badly needed; for a beginning, see Gergel, "Wade Hampton."
40. See, e.g., reports and comments in *Edgefield Advertiser*, 3, 24 Aug. 1893, and *Charleston News and Courier*, 16 Dec. 1890, 25 May 1892, 1 Aug. 1893. For more discussion of spectacular lynchings, see Finnegan, " 'At the Hands of Parties Unknown' "; Brundage, *Lynching in the New South*; Joel Williamson, *Crucible of Race*; and Hale, *Making Whiteness*.
41. *Charleston News and Courier*, 20, 22, 23 Apr. 1893. In addition to the sources cited here and below, this narrative of the Denmark lynching draws on Finnegan, " 'At the Hands of Parties Unknown,' " 131–35.
42. Tompkins to Mayfield, 18 Apr. 1893, BRTP-CL, pt. 1; Mayfield to BRT, 22 Apr. 1893, Governor BRT Letters, SCDAH (emphasis in original).
43. *Charleston News and Courier*, 23 Apr. 1893. On the social tensions generated even under ordinary circumstances when rural whites massed in Southern towns, see Ownby, *Subduing Satan*, esp. 38–55.
44. *Charleston News and Courier*, 23 Apr. 1893.
45. *Augusta Chronicle*, reprinted in *Edgefield Advertiser*, 4 May 1893; *Charleston News and Courier*, 26–28 Apr. 1893.
46. *Charleston News and Courier*, 28 Apr., 13 May 1893; telegram, BRT to Farley, 28 July 1893, Governor BRT Telegrams, SCDAH.
47. *Charleston News and Courier*, 2 May 1893; *Cotton Plant*, 20 May 1893.
48. *Charleston News and Courier*, 30 Apr., 2 May 1893; *Edgefield Advertiser*, 4 May 1893.
49. *Charleston News and Courier*, 26–27 Apr. 1893; BRT to *Boston Transcript*, 20 May 1893, BRTP-CL; *Charleston News and Courier*, 2 May 1893.
50. *Charleston News and Courier*, 29 Sept. ("spirit"), 12 May 1893 (courts); *Edgefield Advertiser*, 18 May 1893; *Charleston News and Courier*, 10, 18 July 1893. These special courts were never created, but that fall, some members of the house supported public executions as a means of deterring violent offenders (ibid., 16 Dec. 1893). Stephen West concludes that "white critics of lynching were . . . primarily concerned with the injustice mobs did to the state, not to the victims they killed" ("From Yeoman to Redneck," 461).
51. *Charleston News and Courier*, 2, 3, 4 Oct., 23 Aug. 1893 ("savagery"); *Edgefield Advertiser*, 3 Aug. 1893; *Charleston News and Courier*, 1 Aug., 13 May 1893 ("mission work").
52. *Edgefield Advertiser*, 4 May, 24 Aug. 1893; *Charleston News and Courier*, 12 May 1893.
53. *Charleston News and Courier*, 3 Oct. 1893.
54. Chapin to BRT, 21 July 1890, BRTP-CL, pt. 3; Mims, *(Un)Recorded History*; Chapin, *Fitz-Hugh St. Clair*. For a portrait of the affective and institutional world

of male sociability that Chapin sought to reform, see Ownby, *Subduing Satan*, 21–66, 167–77.

55. Mims, *(Un)Recorded History*; Chapin, *Fitz-Hugh St. Clair*, inscribed copy, SCL; *Charleston News and Courier*, 1 May 1886; BRT to Young, 23 Sept. 1890, BRTP-CL; Young to BRT, Dec. 1891, 15 Jan. 1892, Governor BRT Letters, SCDAH.
56. Shell to BRT, 24 Jan. 1887, BRTP-CL, pt. 3. For fears that temperance politics would divide Democrats, see Congdon to BRT, 14 Dec. 1892, Governor BRT Letters, SCDAH, and minutes, 7 Mar. 1885, BIFCR.
57. Tillman subsequently sought to amend the bill, removing the provision that allowed local majorities to decide whether or not to establish a dispensary and instead allowing the (appointed) county boards to decide (BRT, *Message to the General Assembly, 1893*).
58. *Edgefield Advertiser*, 3, 31 Aug., 14 Sept. 1893; *Charleston News and Courier*, 15 Dec. 1893. On the law and its contexts, see South Carolina General Assembly, *Dispensary Law*, SCL; Eubanks, *Ben Tillman's Baby*; and Hamm, *Shaping the Eighteenth Amendment*.
59. Minutes, 12 May 1893, Women's Christian Temperance Union of South Carolina Records, SCL; *Colleton Courier*, quoted in *Edgefield Advertiser*, 21 Mar. 1894; ibid., 14 Feb. 1894, 4, 12 Jan. 1893; *Abbeville Press and Banner*, quoted in *Edgefield Advertiser*, 21 Feb. 1894.
60. *Charleston News and Courier*, 10 Aug. 1893; Colored Women's Christian Temperance Union to BRT, 4 Dec. 1894, Governor BRT Letters, SCDAH. See also "Secret Sub-Committee of Temperance Society" to BRT, n.d., Governor BRT Letters, box 34, SCDAH, and *Charleston News and Courier*, 8 May 1893.
61. Donaldson to BRT, 12 July 1893, Gowdy to BRT, 22 July 1893, Governor BRT Letters, SCDAH; Tompkins to Mayfield, 23 Sept. 1893, Governor BRT Letterbooks, SCDAH.
62. Kelly to BRT, 3 July 1893, Harper to BRT, 26 Dec. 1892, Behie to Tompkins, 21 Apr. 1893, Governor BRT Letters, SCDAH; Tompkins to Townes, 18 July 1893, Governor BRT Letterbooks, SCDAH. Even the "nonpartisan" Alliance thought it appropriate to make recommendations regarding dispensary appointments. See Williamsburg Alliance to BRT, 15 Feb. 1893, Governor BRT Letters, SCDAH; *Charleston News and Courier*, 15 Jan. 1894; and *Cotton Plant*, 11 Aug. 1894. The dispensary law combined the traditional patronage practices of employment and treating: it rewarded political supporters with jobs serving drinks.
63. Cook to BRT, 20 Apr. 1893, [?] to BRT, 16 June 1893, Marshall to BRT, 24 June 1893, Governor BRT Letters, SCDAH; *Columbia State*, 4 Oct. 1892; BRT to Latimer, 1 Sept. 1892, BRTP-CL; BRT to Latimer, 22 Nov. 1892, Governor BRT Letterbooks, SCDAH.
64. McMaster to "George," 6 Aug. 1893, Fitz William McMaster and Mary Jane Macfie McMaster Papers, SCL.
65. Irby to Evans, 21 June 1893, John Gary Evans Papers, SCL; typed transcript of meeting, 5 Apr. 1893, Hemphill Family Papers, PL. On Irby, see Breazeale to BRT, 24 June 1893, Governor BRT Letters, SCDAH; Irby to BRT, 25 July 1893,

BRT to Irby, 2 Aug. 1893, BRTP-CL; Irby to Evans, 3 Jan., 3 Feb. 1894, BRT to Evans, 2 Feb. 1894, John Gary Evans Papers, SCL; *Charleston News and Courier*, 8 July 1893; and Slaunwhite, "John L. M. Irby."

66. *Edgefield Advertiser*, 16 Nov. 1893; BRT to Purcell, 25 Jan. 1893, Governor BRT Letterbooks, SCDAH; Metts to BRT, 13, 25 July 189[3], Governor BRT Letters, SCDAH.
67. *Charleston News and Courier*, 29 May 1893.
68. On the phosphate monopoly, see *Edgefield Advertiser*, 13 Jan. 1887; *Charleston News and Courier*, 10 Nov. 1886, 6 Jan. 1887, 2 Aug. 1890, 7 Mar., 20 Dec. 1891; [?] to BRT, 16 Apr. 1891, Governor BRT Letters, SCDAH; and BRT, *Message to the General Assembly, 1891*. In the meantime, richer phosphate beds were discovered in Florida, and the state's mining industry gradually declined. On railroads, see BRT, *Message to the General Assembly, 1892*; BRT to sheriffs (form letter), 28 Jan. 1893, Governor BRT Letterbooks, SCDAH; Skinner to BRT, 28 Jan. 1893, Harrell et al. to BRT, 2–4 Apr. 1892, Governor BRT Letters, SCDAH; *Charleston News and Courier*, 6, 8 ("states rights"), 9, 10, 17 Feb., 25 Apr. 1893; *Edgefield Advertiser*, 4 May 1893; BRT, *Message to the General Assembly, 1893*; *Cotton Plant*, 18 Feb. 1893 ("exactly right"); and *Charleston News and Courier*, 22 Dec. 1892 ("control"). See also N. B. Ashby, "The Riddle of the Sphinx," in Tindall, *Populist Reader*, 26–36.
69. BRT, *Message to the General Assembly, 1893*.
70. *Charleston News and Courier*, 5 July 1893; Bloyd to BRT, 21 Sept. 1893, Governor BRT Letters, SCDAH; *Charleston News and Courier*, 11 Aug., 9 Sept. 1893 ("result").
71. *Charleston News and Courier*, 12 Jan. ("interests"), 11, 21 Apr., 21 May 1893 ("socialism"); *Edgefield Advertiser*, 27 Apr., 18 May 1893; Dukes to BRT, 21 June 1893, Governor BRT Letters, SCDAH; *Edgefield Advertiser*, 14 Mar. 1894. See also Robinson, "Railway Party." On federal collusion, see Hamm, "Southern States' Liquor Policies"; Wilbur R. Miller, *Revenuers and Moonshiners*, esp. 165–88; Collector of Internal Revenue to BRT, 19 June 1893, Governor BRT Letters, SCDAH; BRT to Miller, 6, 20 Feb. 1894, Governor BRT Letterbooks, SCDAH; and Scruggs to Evans, 31 Aug. 1894, John Gary Evans Papers, SCL. Federal revenue officials had already gained a reputation in some upcountry counties for invading white men's homes; see, e.g., *Keowee Courier*, 4 July 1878. Thomas Dixon Jr., a popular New York preacher soon to become a literary celebrity as the author of white-supremacist novels about the postbellum South, pointed out that since the dispensary would undoubtedly supplant the saloon, "the liquor men, not only of that State, but of New York as well, are arrayed in deadly opposition to a fearless, just, and honest governor" (*Edgefield Advertiser*, 18 Apr. 1894).
72. *Charleston News and Courier*, 9 Sept. 1891, 25 Apr., 15 Aug. 1892.
73. Hailey [?] to BRT, 12 Apr. 1892, Governor BRT Letters, SCDAH; *Charleston News and Courier*, 18 Dec. 1886, 2 Sept. 1890, 28 July 1892 ("owned").
74. *Charleston News and Courier*, 8 July 1892 (Pinkertons), 22 June 1894 (Coxey); BRT to Sallie Tillman, 22 June 1894, BRTP-CL, pt. 1.
75. *Charleston News and Courier*, 25 Dec. 1893, 1 Jan. 1894; South Carolina General

Assembly, *Acts and Joint Resolutions*, 1893, p. 481; *Anderson Intelligencer*, 23 Nov. 1892; *Edgefield Chronicle*, 23 Dec. 1891; *Edgefield Advertiser*, 9 Nov. 1893.

76. *Edgefield Advertiser*, 20 July 1893; *Charleston News and Courier*, 29 Mar. 1894. By the end of 1894, the state employed sixty-five constables and detectives (BRT, *Message to the General Assembly, 1894*, 21).
77. BRT, "Our Whiskey Rebellion"; *Edgefield Advertiser*, 4 Apr. ("saloon"), 18 Jan. 1894.
78. Pope to BRT, 24 Jan. 1891, Governor BRT Letters, SCDAH (hostility of cities and towns); *Abbeville Press and Banner*, quoted in *Edgefield Advertiser*, 12 Oct. 1893 ("the law"); *Charleston News and Courier*, 7 Aug. 1893.
79. Williams to BRT, 8 Jan. 1894, James Thomas Williams Papers, SCL; Ficken to BRT, 11 Aug. 1893, Governor BRT Letters, SCDAH; Tompkins to "Mayor," 1 Jan. 1894, Governor BRT Letterbooks, SCDAH; *Edgefield Advertiser*, 28 Feb. 1894.
80. BRT to Brunson, 11 Aug. 1893, notes in Francis Butler Simkins Papers, SHC ("blacking"); Bruce to BRT, 28 June 1893, Graves to Bruce, 28 June 1893, Black to BRT, 28 June 1893 (black detective), Governor BRT Letters, SCDAH.
81. Smith to BRT, 12 Mar. ("cat's paws"), 3 Oct. 1894, Carson to BRT, 13 Apr. 1894 (bounties), Governor BRT Letters, SCDAH.
82. Resolutions of Spartanburg County Alliance, 12 Jan. 1894, BRTP-CL, pt. 3; *Charleston Sun*, reprinted in *Edgefield Advertiser*, 4 Jan. 1894.
83. Newsom to BRT, 12 Feb. 1894, Governor BRT Letters, SCDAH; Lucas to "Mother," 25 Nov. 1893, James Jonathan Lucas Papers, SCL; BRT, *Message to the General Assembly, 1893*; Fanisberg to BRT, 25 Jan. 1894, Governor BRT Letters, SCDAH (march); telegram, Gaillard to BRT, 27 Jan. 1894, Governor BRT Telegrams, SCDAH (guns).
84. BRT to Miller, 6 Feb. 1894, Governor BRT Letterbooks, SCDAH; *Edgefield Advertiser*, 10 Aug. 1893 (arming); *Charleston News and Courier*, 29 Jan. 1894; *Edgefield Advertiser*, 14 Feb. 1894.
85. *Charleston News and Courier*, 27, 29 Jan., 6, 7 Feb. 1894.
86. Unidentified newspaper, [Dec. 1891], clipping in Lysander D. Childs Papers, SCL ("utterly destroyed"); Early to BRT, 20 Nov. 1893 ("*Hell Hole*"; emphasis in original), Parrott to Tompkins, 12 Dec. 1893, Johnson to Tompkins, 13 Jan. 1894, Governor BRT Letters, SCDAH; *Charleston News and Courier*, 28, 29 Mar. 1894. The account of the Darlington riot in the following paragraphs draws primarily on Tillman's papers in Governors Letters, Letterbooks, and Telegrams, SCDAH, and *Charleston News and Courier*, 30 Mar.–6 Apr. 1894; *Edgefield Advertiser*, 4, 11 Apr. 1894; and BRT, *Message to the General Assembly, 1894*.
87. Bloyd to BRT, 31 Mar. 1894, Governor BRT Letters, SCDAH.
88. A. C. Latimer in *Charleston News and Courier*, 18 Apr. 1894; *Edgefield Advertiser*, 11 Apr. 1894.
89. *Charleston News and Courier*, 4, 6 Apr. 1894; "Bay" to Bettie Aycock, 4 Apr. 1894, Aycock Family Papers, SCL; *Charleston News and Courier*, 2 Apr. 1894; Lucas to "Mother," 7 Apr. 1894, James Jonathan Lucas Papers, SCL; Hagood to McCall, 8 Apr. 1894, Hagood to Hoyt, 7 Apr. 1894, Charles Spencer McCall Papers, SCL.

90. *Edgefield Advertiser*, 4 Apr. 1894; *Charleston News and Courier*, 21 June 1894. Dispensary foes gained a brief victory when the state Supreme Court declared the dispensary law unconstitutional (ibid., 20 Apr. 1894). But soon Tillman was able to appoint Lieutenant Governor Gary to the three-justice Supreme Court, which promptly overturned its earlier ruling. The dispensary's success became a point of pride with Tillman, who continued to brag about it into the twentieth century. See BRT, "Dispensary Law," 323–28.
91. "Bay" to Bettie Aycock, 4 Apr. 1894, Aycock Family Papers, SCL; *Edgefield Advertiser*, 11 Apr. 1894.
92. *Charleston News and Courier*, 1 June, 4, 11 Apr. 1894 ("band-box soldiers"); BRT, "Our Whiskey Rebellion"; *Charleston News and Courier*, 17 Apr. 1894; BRT, *Message to the General Assembly, 1894*. See also BRT and Dargan, "Last Word," 46–60.
93. BRT, *Message to the General Assembly, 1894*; *Charleston News and Courier*, 5 May 1894. The riot provided the impetus for more conservative, investment-oriented reformers to break with the governor. Reform Congressman John L. McLaurin, for example, regretted that the important issues of finance and "ring-smashing" had been sidetracked by "whiskey supplying and despotism" and urged the election of a "good, conservative, business-like Governor" (J. L. McLaurin in *Charleston News and Courier*, 23 Apr. 1894).
94. *Charleston News and Courier*, 2 Nov. 1894.
95. *Columbia Register*, 30 May 1894, quoted in Women's Christian Temperance Union of South Carolina Records, 75–76, SCL.
96. Garner to BRT, 6 Mar. 1894, and BRT notes on envelope, Governor BRT Letters, SCDAH. A few decades later, the members of the Ku Klux Klan in Georgia took it upon themselves to enforce racial purity, and in the mid-twentieth century, the Mississippi State Sovereignty Commission investigated cases of white women bearing nonwhite children. See MacLean, *Behind the Mask of Chivalry*, and Trillin, "State Secrets."

Chapter Six

1. BRT speech in *JCC*, 443–72; Commonwealth of South Carolina, *Constitution . . . Ratified April 16, 1868*, art. 8, sec. 8, as amended 21 Dec. 1882; *Charleston News and Courier*, 17 Oct., 8, 21 Aug. 1890; *Cotton Plant*, 4 Oct. 1890. On the Mississippi convention, see Bond, *Political Culture*, 245–50. Like all students of Southern disfranchisement, I am indebted to J. Morgan Kousser for his painstaking work and penetrating insights. See Kousser, *Shaping of Southern Politics*, 145–50.
2. *Charleston News and Courier*, 30 Oct. 1894.
3. *Columbia State*, 28 Sept., 9 Nov. 1895. For outside comment on suffrage in South Carolina, see ibid., 18 Nov. 1895.
4. Kousser, *Shaping of Southern Politics*, 256, n. 18; *Charleston News and Courier*, 11, 13 Sept. 1890, 31 July 1894; Hampton, "What Negro Supremacy Means," 383–95. In "Shall White Minorities Rule?," 144, Tourgée declared that "the rule of the

majority is the fundamental principle of our government," a right, not a "privilege." Smalls, writing in 1890, supported the Lodge Elections Bill and protested against Democratic electoral frauds ("Election Methods in the South").

5. *JCC*, 443–72; Earle to Courtenay, 1 Nov. 1890, William Ashmead Courtenay Papers, SCL (emphasis in original).
6. For an informant, see Butler to Dibble, 29 Oct. 1888, Samuel Dibble Papers, SCL. For black support for Tillman, see Crigler to BRT, 8 Mar. 1893, Blackshear to BRT, 24 Apr. 1893, Byshewood [?] to BRT, 21 June 1893, Governor BRT Letters, SCDAH, and Lazenberry to Evans, 27 Aug. 1894, John Gary Evans Papers, SCL. When Richard Carroll pointed to an Aiken lawyer as evidence that black men supported Tillman's faction of the party, a Tillmanite demanded, "How many more can you name?" Carroll wrote that after this he "declined to speak further." See *Columbia State*, 13 Oct. 1895. On throwing out black men's ballots, see 30 Aug., 29 Nov. 1894, J. W. Moore Papers, SCL.
7. Patton, "Republican Party," 91–111; Tindall, *South Carolina Negroes*, 61–64; Rogers, *History of Georgetown County*, 474–77. In the 1892 congressional elections, Republicans contested four of the six seats outside the lowcountry "black district." Running both black and white men for federal office, the party earned between 8 and 20 percent of the vote in these districts, meaning that nearly 6,500 Republican votes were cast (and counted) outside the areas of persistent Republican strength. See *Congressional Quarterly's Guide to U.S. Elections*, 1068. When one considers figures like those posted by Edgefield, where a total of twenty-six votes were counted for Republican presidential electors that year, it is hard to know whose audacity merits more astonishment—that of the Democrats who all but shut down democracy or that of the handful of Republicans who nevertheless risked depositing their ballots. See South Carolina General Assembly, *Reports and Resolutions*, 1892, 546–49.
8. BRT in *Edgefield Advertiser*, 30 June 1892; Burn to BRT, 8 Nov. 1892, Governor BRT Letters, SCDAH; *JCC*, 463 ("warmed"); *Charleston News and Courier*, 24 Dec. 1890 (Butler); ibid., 11 Sept. 1890. For a black colonizationist's response to Butler's efforts, see Turner to Butler, 10 Apr. 1890, Matthew Calbraith Butler Papers, SCL.
9. Tompkins to Congdon, 15 Nov. 1893, Governor BRT Letterbooks, SCDAH; Parker to Sheppard, 21 Sept. 1886, Governor Sheppard Letters, SCDAH. Republicans in the lowcountry "black district" sometimes took Democratic supervisors to court; see *Charleston News and Courier*, 5 June 1890. Tillman took a personal interest when supervisors of registration ran into legal trouble for discriminatory practices; see *Columbia State*, 9 Nov. 1894, and Bedenbaugh to BRT, 17 Nov. 1894, and reply noted on envelope, Governor BRT Letters, SCDAH. For fears of Democratic officials, see Richland to Dibble, 23 July 1888, Samuel Dibble Papers, SCL, and Hoyt to McCall (form letter), 13 May 1890, Charles Spencer McCall Papers, SCL.
10. Wheeler to Sheppard, 28 Aug. 1886, Governor Sheppard Papers, SCDAH; Brayton, *Address upon the Election Law*; Smalls, "Election Methods in the South."

11. Rouquie to Sheppard, 4 Oct. 1886, Governor Sheppard Letters, SCDAH; *Charleston News and Courier*, 22 Nov. 1893.
12. Beaufort County Democratic Convention Minutes, 6 Aug. 1894, Governor BRT Letters, SCDAH; *Columbia State*, 1, 8 Nov. 1895.
13. *JCC*, 443–72. On the Georgetown "muddle," see Hazard to BRT, 8, 9, 13 Sept. 1892, Congdon to BRT, 26 Sept. 1892, 14 July 1894, petition to BRT, 31 July 1894, Doar to BRT, 10, 21 Sept. 1892, Governor BRT Letters, SCDAH, and BRT to Detyens, 12 Apr. 1892, Tompkins to Donaldson, 11 Oct. 1894, BRTP-CL, pt. 1. This did not mean that Tillman would give ground to Republicans acting alone. In 1894, coastal Republicans asked Tillman to appoint one Republican supervisor for the federal election. Tillman refused, leading Republicans to sue in federal court. See Webster to BRT, 10 Sept. 1894, Brayton to BRT, 28 Sept. 1894, Bedenbaugh to BRT, 17 Nov. 1894, Governor BRT Letters, SCDAH. On Murray, see *Charleston News and Courier*, 3, 4 Nov. 1894. Tillman denied any alliance with Murray or other Republicans against his Democratic rivals, but he had sought to meet with Murray the previous year for purposes he did not discuss in his brusque letter of invitation. See Tompkins to Murray, 31 July 1893, Governor BRT Letterbooks, SCDAH.
14. *Charleston News and Courier*, 20 July 1890, 14 Mar., 3 Apr. 1894, 25 Apr. 1892.
15. Ibid., 23, 24 Jan., 25 Mar. 1892 ("ring rule"); *Columbia Daily Register*, 24 Mar. 189[2], clipping in BRTP-CL, pt. 8 ("equilibrium"); BRT, *Annexation of Hawaii*, 3 ("moving force").
16. For detailed accounts of each stage of this contest, see *Charleston News and Courier*, Aug. 1894.
17. Ibid., 17 Aug. 1894.
18. Irby to Hemphill, 5 Feb. 1894, Hemphill Family Papers, PL; *Charleston News and Courier*, 5 May 1890; *Edgefield Advertiser*, 22 Aug. 1894; *Charleston News and Courier*, 1 Sept. (turnout), 30 Aug. 1894 (BRT).
19. Stokes to Evans, 13 Aug. 1894, Scruggs to Evans, 31 Aug. 1894, John Gary Evans Papers, SCL.
20. Patterson to Evans, 10 Aug. 1894, John Gary Evans Papers, SCL.
21. Stokes to Evans, 8 Oct. 1894, John Gary Evans Papers, SCL; *Charleston News and Courier*, 24 Aug., 8 Sept. 1894; *Edgefield Advertiser*, 1 Aug. 1894; *Columbia State*, 8 Sept. 1894.
22. *Charleston News and Courier*, 4 Oct. 1894 ("Warning"); *Columbia State*, 5 Nov. 1894; *Cotton Plant*, 10, 17 Feb., 17 Mar., 25 Aug., 29 Sept., 6, 27 Oct., 3 Nov. 1894.
23. Kousser, *Shaping of Southern Politics*, 145–50; South Carolina General Assembly, *Reports and Resolutions*, 1894, 470–72. Frauds are recounted in *Columbia State*, 8–11 Nov. 1894. Based on an analysis of the official returns, Kousser concludes that "[n]early a third of those who supported Tillman in 1892 and voted in the referendum split with their leader," voting against the convention; Evans did somewhat better but still lost a quarter of Tillman's 1892 voters to Pope (*Shaping of Southern Politics*, 149–50).
24. *Greenville News*, reprinted in *Columbia State*, 8 Nov. 1894; ibid., 11 Nov. 1894

("stripped"); Pope's petition in *Edgefield Advertiser*, 30 Jan., 20 Feb. 1895; *Charleston News and Courier*, 21, 27 Nov., 12 Dec. 1894. For protests against this law and its administration, see *Columbia State*, 5 Mar. 1895, and *Edgefield Advertiser*, 19 Dec. 1894, 24 Apr., 15 May 1895.

25. *Columbia State*, 23 Mar. 1895.
26. BRT, *Message to the General Assembly, 1894*; BRT in *Columbia State*, 22 Feb. 1895; *Edgefield Advertiser*, 5 Dec. 1894, 27 Mar., 3 Apr. 1895.
27. *New South*, 7 Mar. 1895; ministers in *Columbia State*, 15 Feb. 1895. Some of the men at this conference did indeed seem ready to "submit," like the black minister who opposed organizing against disfranchisement and later promised Evans that if he protected black suffrage in the convention, "the negro will no mor[e] look to the north but to the south." See ibid. and Rice to Evans, 27 Sept. 1895, Governor Evans Letters, SCDAH.
28. *Edgefield Advertiser*, 26 June, 3, 10 July 1895.
29. Carroll to BRT, 16 Jan. 1907, 26, 31 Oct., 2 Nov. 1908, BRTP-CL, pt. 2. Tillman apparently did write at least one letter of recommendation for Carroll; see Carroll to BRT, 1 Dec. 1908, BRTP-CL, pt. 2. Tillman also may have suggested Carroll as a Democratic speaker in the Midwest during the 1912 presidential campaign; see unidentified newspaper, 29 Oct. 1912, clipping in BRTP-CL, pt. 5, vol. 10. For a brief biography of Carroll, see John Hammond Moore, *Columbia and Richland County*, 372–79.
30. *Columbia State*, 3 July 1895; James to Evans, 1 Aug. 1895, Governor Evans Letters, SCDAH.
31. Sunny to Evans, 2 Sept. 1895, Governor Evans Letters, SCDAH; Saville, *Work of Reconstruction*, 172–75; Tindall, *South Carolina Negroes*, 61–63.
32. *Edgefield Advertiser*, 7, 28 Aug. 1895.
33. *Charleston News and Courier*, 17 Dec. 1888; Hampton, "What Negro Supremacy Means."
34. Commonwealth of South Carolina, *Constitution . . . Ratified April 16, 1868*, art. 10, secs. 3, 4, 5, 10; Hampton, *Free Men! Free Ballots!! Free Schools!!!*; Commonwealth of South Carolina, *Constitution . . . Ratified April 16, 1868*, art. 10, secs. 4, 5, as amended 22 Jan. 1878; Margo, *Disenfranchisement, School Finance, and the Economics of Segregated Schools*, 41, 47; Tindall, *South Carolina Negroes*, 216–17; Lott, "Development of Education in Edgefield County," 56. For an admission that the 1878 provision was intended to fool "Yankees," see *Cotton Plant*, 3 Nov. 1894. Although the 1895 constitution provided for a minimum expenditure of $3 per enrolled student and empowered the state comptroller-general to levy and redistribute a special tax if other assessments failed to provide the necessary funds, state officials appear to have ignored this constitutional mandate until well into the twentieth century. See Wingard Williams Carter, "State Support for Public Schools in South Carolina," 3–5. At the turn of the century, public schools in Edgefield offered twenty weeks of instruction for white students and twelve weeks for black students. See *Charleston News and Courier*, 23 Dec. 1900.
35. *Charleston News and Courier*, 23 Jan. 1889; *Columbia State*, 3 July 1895; South Carolina Farmers' State Alliance Minutes, 28 Aug. 1895, SCL; resolution, 3 Oct.

1890, South Carolina Farmers' State Alliance, Kershaw County Records, SCL; Evans in *JCC*, 12.

36. Ramage, "Local Government and Free Schools," 31; *Edgefield Chronicle*, 30 Oct. 1889.

37. *Charleston News and Courier*, 28 July 1891; *Columbia State*, 16, 17 ("nobody else") Nov. 1895; BRT to Riggs, 6 Jan. 1910, Walter M. Riggs Presidential Records, Special Collections, Robert Muldrow Cooper Library, Clemson University, Clemson, S.C. ("makeshifts"); BRT to Richards, 3 Dec. 1908, 12, 19 Jan. 1910, John G. Richards Papers, SCL; BRT to Riggs, 10 Sept. 1910, 12 Feb., 14 Mar. 1911, BRTP-CL, pt. 1; BRT to Riggs, 14 Mar. 1911 ("monument"), 15 July 1912 ("affairs"), BRTP-CL, pt. 1.

38. *Charleston News and Courier*, 17 Aug. 1891, 17 Apr. 1892.

39. Ibid., 11 Oct. 1894; *Cotton Plant*, 27 Oct. 1894; Burn in *Columbia State*, 29 Oct. 1895.

40. BRT in *Columbia State*, 14, 15 Nov. 1895; BRT to Crosland, 19 May 1887, BRTP-CL, pt. 3.

41. Tindall, *South Carolina Negroes*, 223 (literacy figures); BRT in *Columbia State*, 3 July 1895; *Yorkville Enquirer*, 28 July 1886, clipping in BRTP-CL, pt. 5, vol. 18; *Edgefield Chronicle*, 30 Oct. 1889 ("swells"); *Washington Post*, 25 Nov. 1889, reprinted in *Charleston News and Courier*, 4 Dec. 1889; Evans in Tindall, *South Carolina Negroes*, 221.

42. Crofts, "Blair Bill," iii–iv; *Charleston News and Courier*, 23 Jan., 21 Nov. 1889 (quotation), 21 Mar. 1890, 20 May 1891. On the regional experience, see Link, *Paradox of Southern Progressivism*, esp. 124–34. In the 1890s, Martha Schofield's Aiken school continued to serve hundreds of black students each term in a county where free schools existed only for whites. See *Schofield School Bulletin* 4, no. 2 (Nov. 1893), 5, no. 5 (Feb. 1895), and Smedley, *Martha Schofield*, esp. 180–95. For an editorial supporting the Blair Bill, see *Edgefield Chronicle*, 4 Sept. 1889; see also Sallie Chapin's support in *Charleston News and Courier*, 22 June 1889.

43. Gary in *Charleston News and Courier*, 26 June 1890; *Edgefield Chronicle*, 25 Dec. 1889. On Claflin, see Gore, *On a Hilltop High*, and McMillan, *Founding of South Carolina's State College for Negroes*, SCL. See also Jenkins, *Steps along the Way*.

44. Noble to BRT, 31 Jan., 2 Feb. 1891, Dunton to BRT, 18, 24 Feb., 20 Apr., 29 Oct., 16 Nov., 12, 14 Dec. 1891, Chandler to BRT, 1 July 1891, Governor BRT Letters, SCDAH; BRT to Noble, 17 Apr. 1891, Bean to Dunton, 25 Mar. 1891, Tompkins to Dunton, 12, 14 Dec. 1891, BRT to Chandler, 6 Apr. 1891, BRT to Northen, 8 Feb. 1892, Tompkins to Lee, 4 Nov. 1892, Governor BRT Letterbooks, SCDAH.

45. *Charleston News and Courier*, 25 Apr. 1892; Washington to BRT, n.d., in Harlan, *Booker T. Washington Papers*, 1:85–87; BRT to Dunton, 25 Mar. 1891, Governor BRT Letterbooks, SCDAH. For George Tillman's speech in Congress, see *Edgefield Advertiser*, 14 July 1892. After the controversy died down, Tillman found another way to turn federal dollars for black education into political capital. Referring to federal land-grant money in an 1894 address, he remarked that "[a]s Claflin . . . gets each year a larger and larger amount from the Morrill fund, its appropriation from the State can be diminished without injury" (BRT, *Mes-*

sage to the General Assembly, 1894). But as George Tillman, having tested the waters in Congress, warned the constitutional convention, the federal government could recall its appropriations: "[L]et us dare not to be liberal with Claflin and see what will happen" (*Columbia State*, 16 Nov. 1895).

46. BRT to *Greenville News*, 16 Sept. 1913, BRTP-CL, pt. 5, box 3; BRT, *Negro Problem and Immigration*, 8, 20–21, and *Brownsville Raid*, 7.
47. BRT, *Negro Problem and Immigration*, 5; BRT to Taylor, 22 May 1911, BRTP-CL, pt. 1.
48. BRT, *Negro Problem and Immigration*, 8–9, and *Struggles of 1876*, 7–8. Tillman would modify his position on compulsory education only if black students received carefully limited manual and industrial training "which they can assimilate"—presumably without danger either to themselves or to white supremacy. See BRT, "Farewell to Public Life," 6.
49. BRT, *Brownsville Raid*, 4.
50. Straker, *New South Investigated*, 151–52, 184; Arnett, *Annual Address*.
51. *Columbia State*, 27, 26 Oct. 1895; Mary J. Miller, *Suffrage*.
52. Mary J. Miller, *Suffrage*; *Columbia State*, 26 Oct. 1895.
53. U.S. Bureau of the Census, *Twelfth Census of the United States, 1900: Report on Agriculture*, vol. 5, pt. 1, 4–12.
54. *JCC*, 11–12, 470.
55. *Columbia State*, 31 Oct. 1895; *JCC*, 110, 152 (proposals).
56. BRT to Russell, 12 Sept. 1893, BRT to Holmes, 9 Sept. 1893, Governor BRT Letterbooks, SCDAH; Babcock to BRT, 4, 5 Sept. 1893, Hazzard to BRT, 23 Dec. 1893, Governor BRT Letters, SCDAH. Half a century later, Mississippi planter William Alexander Percy expressed a similar attitude toward relief for black flood victims in *Lanterns on the Levee: Recollections of a Planter's Son* (1941).
57. *Edgefield Advertiser*, 26 June (Thurmond), 23 Oct. 1895 (BRT); *Columbia State*, 27 Nov. 1895. For a discussion of homestead exemptions in the postbellum South, see Hyman, *Anti-Redeemers*, chap. 2, and Hahn, *Roots of Southern Populism*, 193–97.
58. *JCC*, 297–99; *Columbia State*, 31 Oct. 1895.
59. Carroll in *Columbia State*, 3 July 1895; BRT in *JCC*, 469; *Columbia State*, 30 Oct. 1895.
60. *Columbia State*, 27 Oct. 1895.
61. Ibid., 30 Oct., 2 Nov. 1895.
62. Ibid., 24 Sept., 27 Oct. 1895.
63. Ibid., 6 Nov. ("swindled"), 7 Dec. 1894 ("admitted meaning"), 25 Jan. ("scarecrow"), 19 Feb. 1895 ("necessary").
64. Butler in *Edgefield Advertiser*, 27 June, 25 July, 8 Aug., 19 Sept. 1894; *Edgefield Chronicle*, quoted in *Edgefield Advertiser*, 24 July 1895.
65. *Edgefield Advertiser*, 2 Jan. 1895; Willoughby to BRT, 16 Nov. 1892, Governor BRT Letters, SCDAH (emphasis in original); BRT to Jervey, 21 Sept. 1892, Theodore Dehon Jervey Jr. Papers, SCHS; BRT, *Negro Problem and Immigration*, 5.
66. Irby in *Columbia State*, 10, 23 Oct., 1 Nov. 1895; editorials in ibid., 7 Dec. 1894, 25 Sept. 1895; Irby in ibid., 10 Oct. 1895.

67. Joel Williamson, *After Slavery*, 338; *Edgefield Advertiser*, 22 May 1895 ("distress"); unidentified newspaper, [1895], clipping in Floride Cunningham Papers, SCL ("moment"). See also *Charleston News and Courier*, 15 July 1894; *JCC*, 343; and Bailey to Evans, 1 Oct. 1895, Campbell to Evans, 9 Oct. 1895, Governor Evans Letters, SCDAH. On woman suffrage in the South generally, see Elna C. Green, *Southern Strategies*, and Marjorie Spruill Wheeler, *New Women*. On woman suffrage in South Carolina, see Ulmer, "Virginia Durant Young," and Antoinette Elizabeth Taylor, "South Carolina and the Enfranchisement of Women."
68. Marjorie Spruill Wheeler, *New Women*, 74; Young in *Columbia State*, 18, 28 Sept. 1895; Young in *Cotton Plant*, 20 July 1895; Young, "Star in the West," 2 ("hand primary," qualifications); Young in *Charleston News and Courier*, 4 Apr. 1894 ("mortification"); Chapin in ibid., 9 Mar. 1891. On Chapin's opposition to woman suffrage, see Ulmer, "Virginia Durant Young," 18–20. On taxation without representation, see Buckner to Evans, 2 Sept. 1895, Governor Evans Papers, SCDAH; *Columbia State*, 14, 18 Sept. 1895; and *JCC*, 371–72, 420.
69. *Charleston News and Courier*, 15 Oct. 1889, 15, 23 Dec. 1888, 26 Jan. 1891; McCandless, *Past in the Present*, 25–27; Peggy Diane Neal, "Benjamin Ryan Tillman," SCL; Holleman, "Contributions of Benjamin Ryan Tillman to Higher Education." See also Mary Little Yeargin Papers, SCL, for the efforts of one young white feminist.
70. *Charleston News and Courier*, 20 Feb. 1893; BRT, *Laying of the Corner-Stone*, 14–29.
71. BRT to Sallie Tillman, 7 Dec. 1895, BRTP-CL, pt. 1.
72. BRT, *Laying of the Corner-Stone*.
73. BRT, *Dr. Bledsoe's "Mission of Woman,"* 9; BRT to Sallie Tillman, 21 Oct. 1900, BRT to Sophie Tillman, 4 Mar. 1912, BRTP-CL.
74. BRT, *Laying of the Corner-Stone*; *Edgefield Advertiser*, 16 May 1894; *Charleston News and Courier*, 14 May 1894.
75. BRT to Duncan, 17 Mar. 1916, Mr. and Mrs. Walter E. Duncan Papers, SCL; BRT, *Dr. Bledsoe's "Mission of Woman,"* 5, 7. On Bledsoe, see Marjorie Spruill Wheeler, *New Women*, 7.
76. BRT to Young, 23 Sept. 1890, Governor BRT Letterbooks, SCDAH (emphasis in original); Straker, *New South Investigated*, 123–24.
77. Young, "Star in the West," 1 ("corruption"); *Columbia State*, 18 Sept. 1895; *Edgefield Advertiser*, 14 July 1892.
78. *Edgefield Advertiser*, 17 Apr. (*Anderson Journal*), 8 May 1895 ("battlefield").
79. *Columbia State*, 31 Oct., 1 Nov., 10 Oct. 1895 (Irby), 26 (Wigg), 30 Oct. 1895 ("intelligence").
80. *JCC*, 110 (proxy), 151 (two votes); Jervey in *Cotton Plant*, 13 Apr. 1895; *Columbia State*, 27, 29 Oct. 1895.
81. *Columbia State*, 29 Oct. 1895; Young, Yeargin, et al. to Hemphill, 1892–93, Hemphill Family Papers, PL; *JCC*, 414–15; Marjorie Spruill Wheeler, *New Women*, 116.
82. *Cotton Plant*, 4 Oct. 1890 (sisters; emphasis in original); *Charleston News and Courier*, 21 Dec. 1893; *Columbia State*, 30 (Talbert), 29 Oct. 1895 (Henderson); *Cotton Plant*, 10 Aug. 1895; Young in *Charleston News and Courier*, 4 May 1895, quoted in Ulmer, "Virginia Durant Young," 54–63.

83. BRT, *Laying of the Corner-Stone*; *Macon Telegraph*, 19 Apr. 1918, clipping in BRTP-CL, pt. 5, vol. 14.
84. *JCC*, 422–23 (vote); *Columbia State*, 30 Oct. 1895.
85. *U.S. Sen. Misc. Doc.* no. 157, 54th Cong., 1st sess.
86. Bardaglio, *Reconstructing the Household*, 134–75; BRT, *Dr. Bledsoe's "Mission of Woman,"* 8–9, 11–12; Marjorie Spruill Wheeler, *New Women*, 88.
87. *Columbia State*, 4, 17 Oct. 1895.
88. Ibid., 3, 4 Oct. 1895.
89. Ibid., 4 Oct. 1895.
90. BRT, *Negro Problem and Immigration*, 11; BRT to Keboch, 23 Feb. 1911, BRTP-CL, pt. 1.
91. BRT to Barber, 5 Aug. 1912 ("animals"), BRT to Keboch, 23 Feb. 1911 ("willing"), BRTP-CL, pt. 1. On the age of consent, see Chapin to Evans, 19 Oct. 1895, Governor Evans Letters, SCDAH; *JCC*, 172–73, 218–19, 236, 343, 369, 607; and "A Personal Letter from Senator Tillman to the Editor of the *Maryland Suffrage News*," 27 Nov. 1914, BRT to Mary Bartlett Dixon, Woman Suffrage Files, box 389, group 1, Administrative Files, National Association for the Advancement of Colored People Papers, Manuscript Division, Library of Congress, Washington, D.C. (I am grateful to Dolores Janiewski for this reference). On age-of-consent campaigns in the South, see Dunlap, "Reform of Rape Law."
92. *JCC*, 725–27 (vote); Rogers, *Georgetown County*, 480–81; Newby, *Black Carolinians*, 43; Key, *Southern Politics*, 146.
93. *JCC*, 731–34.

Chapter Seven

1. On Tillman as an "agrarian rebel," see the introduction, esp. n. 1.
2. Avery O. Craven, quoted on the back cover of Simkins, *Pitchfork Ben Tillman*.
3. BRT to Barker, 3 May 1894, BRTP-CL, pt. 1.
4. BRT to Fisk, 23 Oct. 1893, BRT to Irby, 26 Oct. 1893, BRTP-CL, pt. 1; Latimer to BRT, 7 Sept. 1893, Governor BRT Letters, SCDAH; BRT in *Cotton Plant*, 3 Aug. 1895. See also BRT typescript, with note from Kohn to Hemphill, 16 June 1894, Hemphill Family Papers, PL.
5. *Charleston News and Courier*, 5 Aug. 1894 (Pickens); BRT to Irby, 26 Oct. 1893, BRTP-CL, pt. 1; BRT to Bryan, 23 July 1894, BRTP-CL, pt. 1; Hammond to "Katharine," 13 Apr. 1894, Hammond, Bryan, and Cummings Families Papers, SCL. See also Bryan to Jervey, 26 Nov. 1893 [1894], Theodore Dehon Jervey Jr. Papers, SCHS.
6. *Charleston News and Courier*, 5 Aug. 1894; *Atlanta Constitution*, 10 Oct. 1893, clipping in BRTP-CL, pt. 5.
7. Fragment, BRT to unidentified Texas writer, 4 May 1894, BRT to Marion Butler, 8 May 1894, BRTP-CL, pt. 1. For outside attention, see James to BRT, 27 Mar. 1891, Skipworth to BRT, 13 Mar. 1893, Governor BRT Letters, SCDAH, and *Baltimore Mirror*, quoted in *Edgefield Advertiser*, 14 Dec. 1893. On Tillman as a

potential Populist, see "That Populist President," *Newberry Herald and News,* quoted in *Charleston News and Courier,* 10 Oct. 1893, and "A Real Populist," *Columbia State,* 22 Feb. 1895.

8. *Charleston News and Courier,* 7 Oct. 1893; BRT, note on envelope of Wade to BRT, 12 June 1894, Governor BRT Letters, SCDAH. On Populist debates over free silver, see Goodwyn, *Democratic Promise,* and Palmer, *"Man over Money."*
9. BRT to Sallie Tillman, 6 Dec. 1895, BRTP-CL, pt. 1; BRT, *Bimetallism or Industrial Slavery.* These references, typical of the financial-conspiracy theories of the 1890s and beyond, were hardly the exclusive property of the Populists—or of Tillman.
10. BRT, *Bimetallism or Industrial Slavery.*
11. BRT in *New York World,* 1 Mar. 1896, reprinted in *Minneapolis and St. Paul Representative,* 8 Apr. 1896. I am grateful to Rebecca Edwards for this and other items from Populist newspapers. Tillman entered these cartoons into the *Congressional Record.*
12. Letters of reaction to Tillman's speech take up several linear feet of archive space in the BRTP-CL. See, e.g., the letters of two Alabama Populists, DuBose to BRT, 12 Feb. 1896, and Waugh to BRT, 12 Feb. 1896, BRTP-CL, pt. 5; Keith to BRT, 30 Jan. 1896 (North Carolina), Anthony to BRT, 30 Jan. 1896, Hayes to BRT, 30 Jan. 1896 (Knights), Garlington to BRT, 1 Feb. 1896 (Spartanburg), Conger to BRT, 30 Jan. 1896, Lowers to BRT, 30 Jan. 1896, BRTP-CL, pt. 3; and Debs to BRT, 13 [Feb.] 1896, BRTP-CL, pt. 3. For Debs's ideas and activities during this period, see Salvatore, *Eugene V. Debs,* 147–69.
13. *Boston Journal,* 30 Jan. 1896, clipping in BRTP-CL, pt. 3; *Columbia State,* 1 Feb. 1896; *Christian Index,* 8 Feb. 1896 (I am grateful to John Giggie for this reference).
14. BRT to *New York World,* 14 Feb. 1896, BRTP-CL, pt. 1; Harris in *Atlanta Constitution,* reprinted in *Cotton Plant,* 28 May 1896, clipping in BRTP-CL, pt. 5, vol. 6.
15. BRT, *Naval Appropriation Bill,* 15; campaign ribbon and clipping from *Denver Post,* [1896], BRTP-CL, pt. 5, vol. 13. See also, e.g., Brown to BRT, 4 June 1896, BRTP-CL, pt. 3. On the presidency, see, e.g., Keeney to BRT, 9 May 1896, Ladd-Davis to BRT, 22, 27 May, 1 June 1896, Flowers to BRT, 5 May 1896, and Keeney to Stackhouse, 18 May, 6 June 1896, BRTP-CL, pt. 3.
16. Hartman and [Bowen] to BRT, 6 July 1896, BRTP-CL, pt. 3.
17. *Columbia State,* 9, 10, 11 July 1896; National Democratic Convention, *Official Proceedings . . . 1896,* 198–209 (BRT), 226–34 (Bryan).
18. *Columbia State,* 14 July 1896; C. E. Thomas to "Mother," 30 Sept., 20 Oct. 1896, Thomas Family Papers, SCL.
19. Telegram to BRT, 15 July 1896, BRTP-CL (Addie); BRT to Jervey, 6 Aug. 1896, Theodore Dehon Jervey Jr. Papers, SCHS; Woodward, *Tom Watson,* 324–26.
20. "The Crime of '96," *Chicago Tribune,* 10 July 1896; "The Ship of State if Bryan Should Win," ibid., 24 Oct. 1896; "On a Populistic Basis," *Harper's Weekly,* 12 Sept. 1896; "Campaign Music," *Chicago Inter-Ocean,* reprinted in *Boston Globe,* 25 Oct. 1896.
21. "That Silver Pitchfork," *American Nonconformist,* 13 Aug. 1896; Altgeld to BRT,

25 Apr. 1897, BRTP-CL, pt. 3; BRT to Bryan, 7 Jan. 1898, Hemphill Family Papers, PL; Watson to BRT, 3 Mar. 1897, BRTP-CL, pt. 3.

22. BRT in *Washington Post*, 18 Nov. 1906, clipping in BRTP-CL, pt. 5, vol. 6.
23. BRT, *Senatorial Corruption*, 6.
24. "The Senators from South Carolina," *U.S. Senate Doc.* no. 228, 57th Cong., 1st sess., 5–10; BRT to Magill, 3 Mar. 1902, BRTP-CL, pt. 1.
25. Stroup, "John L. McLaurin," 97–101, 105; Hearden, *Independence and Empire*, 135–36. On the industrial transformation of the state, see Carlton and Coclanis, "Capital Mobilization and Southern Industry," and Carlton, *Mill and Town*, esp. 127, 134.
26. McLaurin to BRT, 25 May 1901, John Lowndes McLaurin Papers, SCL; BRT to Richards, 13 June 1901, John G. Richards Papers, SCL; BRT and McLaurin resignations, 25 May 1901, BRTP-CL, pt. 3. For a pro-McLaurin Northern comment on this quarrel, see *World's Work* 2 (July 1901): 910–11.
27. Stroup, "John L. McLaurin," 105–6; "The Senators from South Carolina," *U.S. Senate Doc.* no. 228, 57th Cong., 1st sess., 2–3.
28. Stroup, "John L. McLaurin," 113; BRT, *Free Panama Canal Tolls*, 6; *Hearst's Magazine*, Jan. 1913, cited in Simkins, *Pitchfork Ben Tillman*, 389, n. 59; BRT to "People of South Carolina," 9 Sept. 1916, John Patrick Grace Papers, PL; BRT, *Struggles of 1876*, 5–6.
29. Simkins, *Pitchfork Ben Tillman*, 380–85; BRT to John P. Tillman, 12 Sept. 1909, BRTP-CL, pt. 1. For outside comment, see "The Matter with South Carolina," *World's Work* 3 (Mar. 1903): 3153. On turn-of-the-century debates on violence among white men, see West, "From Yeoman to Redneck," esp. 425–67.
30. On the 1898 campaign, see Prather, "We Have Taken a City."
31. Butler to BRT, 5 Nov. 1898, BRTP-CL, pt. 3.
32. BRT to Butler, 8 May 1894, BRTP-CL, pt. 1.
33. *Chicago Tribune*, 28 Nov. 1906; *Fayetteville Observer*, 11 Aug., 13, 20, 27 Oct., 17 Nov. 1898; *Wilmington Messenger*, 7 Sept. 1898. See also Keith to Butler, 14, 28 Nov. 1898, Marion Butler Papers, SHC. On the Wilmington "riot," see Cecelski and Tyson, *Democracy Betrayed*.
34. Prather, "Origins of the Phoenix Racial Massacre."
35. *Charleston News and Courier*, 13 Nov. 1898, 17 Aug. 1899.
36. Dart to BRT, 19 Aug. 1899, BRTP-CL, pt. 2; BRT to Dart, 26 Aug. 1899, BRTP-CL, pt. 1.
37. BRT, "Causes of Southern Opposition to Imperialism," 443 ("mysterious influence"). See also BRT, *Race Problem* and "Race Question"; *Chicago Tribune*, 28 Nov. 1906; and *Lake Geneva News*, 6 Dec. 1906.
38. BRT, *Negro Problem and Immigration*, 4; *Race Problem*, 30; and "Race Question," 28 (Washington).
39. BRT, *Race Problem*, 28–29, 10.
40. *Augusta Chronicle*, 7 Oct. 1906, clipping in BRTP-CL, pt. 5, vol. 6; Dewey Grantham Jr., "Dinner at the White House: Theodore Roosevelt, Booker T. Washington, and the South," *Tennessee Historical Quarterly* 17 (1958): 117, quoted in Clayton, *Savage Ideal*, 186; BRT, *Race Problem*, 11, 23–24 (Washington), and

"Race Question," 28 (mixed-race people); *Denver Times*, 26 Oct. 1907, clipping in BRTP-CL, pt. 5.

41. BRT, *Race Problem*, 25–26, and "Race Question," 26.
42. *Augusta Chronicle*, 7 Oct. 1906, clipping in BRTP-CL, pt. 5, vol. 6 ("desperation"); BRT, *Race Problem*, 26–27 ("oppression"); *Augusta Chronicle*, 7 Oct. 1906, clipping in BRTP-CL, pt. 5, vol. 6 ("massacre"); BRT, *Struggles of 1876*, 14 (Hamburg), and *Negro Problem and Immigration*, 22 ("hundreds"); *Washington Post*, 18 Nov. 1906, clipping in BRTP-CL, pt. 5, vol. 6.
43. *Augusta Chronicle*, 7 Oct. 1906, clipping in BRTP-CL, pt. 5, vol. 6.
44. Ibid.; BRT, "Causes of Southern Opposition to Imperialism," 443.
45. For Tillman's description of U.S. imperial profiteers as "carpetbaggers," see, e.g., BRT, *Massachusetts and South Carolina in the Revolution*, 4, 16, SCL. For an overview of U.S. imperialism in the context of American ideologies and practices of race, see Painter, *Standing at Armageddon*, 141–69.
46. BRT to *New York World*, 26 Jan. 1892, Governor BRT Letterbooks, SCDAH; BRT, *Independence of Cuba*, 8, 12–15.
47. BRT, *Annexation of Hawaii*, 3–4, 14; Jamie W. Moore, "Ben Tillman and Government for Hawaii," 5–19.
48. BRT, *Philippines*, 4–6, 12–13; Moore, "Ben Tillman and Government for Hawaii," 12–13.
49. BRT, *Philippines*, 15; "Causes of Southern Opposition to Imperialism," 440.
50. BRT, *Annexation of the Philippine Islands*, 7, 11–13. American responses to Kipling's 1899 poem, "The White Man's Burden," during this period are discussed in Painter, *Standing at Armageddon*, 153–62, and Gilmore, *Gender and Jim Crow*, 61.
51. BRT to Heald, 17 May 1902, BRTP-CL, pt. 1. See also his insinuations in BRT, *Senatorial Corruption*.
52. Woodward, *Origins of the New South*, 369–428; Kirby, *Darkness at the Dawning*, 4. For various perspectives on Southern progressivism focusing primarily on regional life and institutions, see Link, *Paradox of Southern Progressivism*; Grantham, *Southern Progressivism*; and Kirby, *Darkness at the Dawning*. For a critical approach to the category itself, see Rodgers, "In Search of Progressivism."
53. BRT to Walsh, 14 May 1902, BRT to Hoyt, 17 May 1902, BRTP-CL, pt. 1.
54. BRT, *Coal Famine*, 31–32; *Harper's Weekly*, 6 Oct. 1906, p. 1411.
55. "Sen. Tillman's Definition of a Progressive," unidentified newspaper, n.d., clipping in BRTP-CL, pt. 5, vol. 8; BRT, *Chairmanship of the Committee on Appropriations: Speech . . . in the Democratic Caucus, 15 March 1913* (Washington, D.C., 1913), in Rare Book Collection, Wilson Library, University of North Carolina, Chapel Hill, N.C.
56. BRT, *Naval Appropriation Bill*, 5; Watson to BRT, 3, 11 Mar. 1897, BRTP-CL, pt. 3.
57. For buildup, see BRT to Smyth, 22 May 1900, BRT to J. C. Hemphill, 16, 23 Apr., 4, 5 June 1906, Hemphill Family Papers, PL; Elliott to Elliott Jr., 19, 20 Feb., 26, 28 May 1900, W. E. Elliott Jr. Papers, SCL; BRT, *Pork or Preparedness*; and Ferrell, "Regional Rivalries" and *Claude A. Swanson*, 105–22.
58. Simkins, *Pitchfork Ben Tillman*, 346–51; Wilson to BRT, 6 Jan., 14 Feb. 1916, BRTP-CL, pt. 2; BRT, *Free Panama Canal Tolls*, 4.

59. Although legal segregation came relatively late to South Carolina, customary segregation had been interrupted only fitfully during Reconstruction. State and national forces made it risky for white supremacists to propose legal racial segregation during the late nineteenth century, and railroad companies in particular, their eyes on the bottom line in an era of federal receivership, did not want to spend money duplicating facilities. See Matthews, "Keeping Down Jim Crow." For white people whose standpoint was fundamentally rural and agricultural, questions of segregation in "public accommodations" such as railroads, restaurants, hotels, and entertainment facilities were part of a larger complex of dangers and anxieties associated with the dynamics of the "urban" South.
60. On the passport system, see *Augusta Chronicle*, 7 Oct. 1906, clipping in BRTP-CL, pt. 5, vol. 6.
61. Ibid. See also ibid., 1 Nov. 1906, clipping in BRTP-CL, pt. 5, vol. 6; minutes, 28 June 1851, BIFCR; *Charleston News and Courier*, 4 Oct. 1893; Poe in Crow, "Apartheid for the South," 220.
62. BRT to Hershey, 14 Sept. 1901, BRTP-CL, pt. 1 ("most popular," $150, "New England"); BRT, *Negro Problem and Immigration*, 18 (250 audiences), 20 ("gospel"), 22 ("million"), and *Brownsville Raid*, 4 (100,000 people), 7 ("face to face"), 5 ("insignificance"); *San Francisco Examiner*, n.d., and unidentified San Francisco newspaper, n.d., clippings in BRTP-CL, pt. 5, vol. 18.
63. BRT to Sophie Tillman, 16 Jan. 1906, BRTP-CL, pt. 9 ("animals"); "You Yellow Cur!," unidentified newspaper, [1906–7], clipping in BRTP-CL, pt. 5, vol. 6; BRT to Taylor, 22 May 1911, BRTP-CL, pt. 1.
64. *Saturday Evening Post*, 7 Apr. 1906, clipping in BRTP-CL, pt. 5, vol. 6; *Wisconsin State Journal*, 27 July 1903; *Chicago Tribune*, 28 Nov. 1906; BRT, *Negro Problem and Immigration*, 23 ("no law").
65. BRT to Sallie Tillman, 10 June 1906, BRTP-CL, pt. 1; *Wisconsin State Journal*, 27 July 1903.
66. *Harper's Weekly*, 7 Apr. 1906; Thayer to BRT, 29 Mar. 1906, BRTP-CL ("representative"). For the hostility between BRT and Roosevelt, see Simkins, *Pitchfork Ben Tillman*, 408–18. On the Hepburn Bill itself, see ibid., 419–40, and Kolko, *Railroads and Regulation*, 136–46. A cartoon in the *New York World* depicted Roosevelt—with his big stick, riding a donkey—alongside Tillman, pitchfork in hand, riding an elephant, charging a line of locomotives ("Up to Date," *New York World*, 1 Apr. 1906, clipping in BRTP-CL, pt. 5, vol. 6). For BRT's experience of the legislative process, see BRT to Sallie Tillman, 28 Mar., 4, 6 Apr., 13, 14 May, 1, 3 June 1906, BRTP-CL, pt. 1, and Keith to BRT, 6 June 1906, BRTP-CL, pt. 2. See also Roosevelt to Lodge, 19 May 1906, in Morison, *Letters of Theodore Roosevelt*, 5:270–75.
67. Charles Willis Thompson, *Party Leaders*, 132–35. See also Creelman, "Defender of the Senate," and McGhee, "Tillman, Smasher of Traditions."
68. *Chicago Daily Tribune*, 27 Nov. 1906; BRT, *Race Problem*, 25.
69. *Morning Star*, 24 Dec. 1906 ("people who gauge"), and *Jacksonville Sun*, 24 Mar. 1906 ("grown"), clippings in BRTP-CL, pt. 5, vol. 6; Arsenault, *Wild Ass of the Ozarks*, 232 ("when tamed"); *New York World*, [1918], clipping in BRTP-CL, pt. 5,

vol. 14 ("unwarranted"); *Saturday Evening Post,* 7 Apr. 1906, clipping in BRTP-CL, pt. 5, vol. 6 ("rough"). See also Tillman's report of his reception on the Senate floor in BRT to Sallie Tillman, 28 May 1906, BRTP-CL, pt. 1. On Vardaman, see Holmes, *White Chief*; on Davis, see Arsenault, *Wild Ass of the Ozarks.*

70. BRT, *Negro Problem and Immigration,* 3; Creelman to BRT, 26 Mar. 1906, BRTP-CL, pt. 2; Creelman, "Defender of the Senate," 622–29.
71. *St. Louis Republic,* reprinted in *Charleston News and Courier,* 11 Oct. 1893; *Independent,* 12 July 1906, clipping in BRTP-CL, pt. 5.
72. Clifford Howard, "Tillman: A Study of the American from the Soil," *Appleton's Magazine,* n.d., clipping in BRTP-CL, pt. 5; McGhee, "Tillman, Smasher of Traditions."
73. Untitled manuscript, n.d., 77, Paul Garrett Papers, PL; Kelly Miller, *Race Adjustment,* 63–64, 30; Roosevelt to Baker, 3 June 1908, in Morison, *Letters of Theodore Roosevelt,* 6:1046–49.
74. Baker, *Following the Color Line,* 236–39. See the analysis of Baker in Godshalk, "In the Wake of Riot," 362–72.
75. Sinclair, *The Jungle,* chap. 30; *Chicago Broad-Ax,* 24 Nov. 1906; BRT to McCarville, 16 Oct. 1904, BRTP-SCL.
76. *Johnson News Monitor,* 26 June 1907, clipping in BRTP-CL, pt. 5, box 2; Broughton Brandenburg, "With 'Pitchfork' Ben Tillman in Edgefield, South Carolina," *Delineator* (Feb. [1908]), clipping in BRTP-CL, pt. 5, box 2.
77. Brandenburg, "With 'Pitchfork' Ben Tillman"; Charles Willis Thompson, *Party Leaders,* 136.
78. "Choose between Manhood and Serfdom," *Ohio Enterprise,* 4 Apr. 1903; BRT, *Race Problem,* 31 ("belong"); Creelman, "Defender of the Senate," 627.
79. Gravestone at Shaw's Creek Church, Edgefield, S.C., visited by the author in March 1997.
80. *Platteville (Wisc.) Journal,* 28 Nov. 1906; *Chicago Tribune,* 27 Nov. 1906; *Chicago Chronicle* and *Chicago Inter-Ocean,* [27–28 Nov. 1906], clippings in BRTP-CL, pt. 5, vol. 16; *Chicago Broad-Ax,* 15 Dec. 1906.
81. Sallie Tillman to BRT, 24, 26, 27 Nov. 1906, BRTP-CL, pt. 2; *Chicago Tribune,* 28 Nov. 1906; *Fond du Lac Daily Commonwealth,* 26 Nov. 1906.
82. *Colored American,* 20 Oct. 1900, quoted in Thornbrough, *T. Thomas Fortune,* 197; Fortune and Chase in *Washington Bee,* 10 Aug. 1901; *Chicago Broad-Ax,* 24 Nov., 1, 8, 15, 22, 29 Dec. 1906, 12, 26 Jan., 2 Feb. 1907.
83. Du Bois, *Souls of Black Folk,* 47; Kelly Miller, *Race Adjustment,* 62; *Fond du Lac Daily Commonwealth,* 27 Nov. 1906.
84. *Washington Post,* 13 Jan. 1907, clipping in BRTP-CL, pt. 5, vol. 6; Levine, *Black Culture and Black Consciousness,* 307; unidentified newspaper, 1 Apr. 1906 and n.d., clippings in BRTP-CL, pt. 5.
85. *Detroit Free Press,* 14 Jan. 1907; *Lake Geneva News,* 13 Dec., 22 Nov. 1906.
86. BRT, "Race Question," 24–25; Tuttle, *Race Riot.*
87. Dixon to BRT, 2, 22 Mar. 1897, BRTP-CL, pt. 3; Clayton, *W. J. Cash,* 17; John Hammond Moore, "South Carolina's Reaction," 34. On Dixon's novels, see Gilmore, *Gender and Jim Crow,* 66–68, 135–38.

88. Dixon to BRT, 5 Nov. 1905, BRTP-CL, pt. 2; BRT to Sallie Tillman, 23 Nov. 1905, BRTP-CL, pt. 1.

89. Franklin, "*Birth of a Nation*," 12–13, 15–18; unidentified Des Moines newspaper, [1912], clipping in BRTP-CL, pt. 5, vol. 8; *Philadelphia Citizen*, quoted in *Chicago Broad-Ax*, 10 Nov. 1906; John Hammond Moore, "South Carolina's Reaction," 30–40 (bans). See also Rogin " 'Sword Became a Flashing Vision.' " A year after the film was released, Dixon was still complaining of attempts to censor it; in a telegram to Tillman, he claimed to have spent $75,000 fighting censorship and asked for the senator's help in "reaffirm[ing] the principles of free speech in America" (telegram, Dixon to BRT, 17 Jan. 1916, BRTP-CL, pt. 2).

90. Du Bois, *Souls of Black Folk*, 16–35. This chapter became the basis of his *Black Reconstruction in America*. One scholar concludes that *The Birth of a Nation* "illustrated in graphic fashion [Woodrow] Wilson's own vision of national reunion" (Gaughan, "Woodrow Wilson," 237). That legacy persisted: at least as late as the 1980s, the packaging of videocassettes of *The Birth of a Nation* included uncritical summaries of Dixon's version of Southern history, and the University Press of Kentucky continued to sell a 1970 edition of *The Clansman* with copy on the back cover describing the Klan as "an organization formed with the intention of restoring the pride and prosperity of the South" and praising the novel for "offer[ing] a greater understanding of the social and political turmoil in the Klan's early years."

Chapter Eight

1. BRT to Richards, 5 May 1908, John G. Richards Papers, SCL; BRT to J. P. Tillman, 12 Sept. 1909, BRT to Abney, 21 Feb. 1911, BRT to Wilson, 28 June 1911, BRTP-CL, pt. 1; BRT, "How I Restored My Health and Vigor," 7–15; Eugene Christian, "How to Eat and Enjoy Life," unidentified magazine, [1912], clipping in BRTP-SCL; BRT to Richards, 15 June 1912, John G. Richards Papers, SCL; BRT, *Prohibition of Smoking*.

2. For details on Tillman's holdings, see BRT wills, 2 Dec. 1911, 30 Jan. 1914, codicil, Jan. 1918, BRTP-CL, pt. 3, box 18, folder 249; Treasurer's Tax Duplicate Books, Edgefield County, 1903, 1907, ECA; BRT to Sophie Tillman, 20 Oct. 1907, BRTP-CL, pt. 9.

3. BRT to Sallie Tillman, 21 Nov. 1895, BRTP-CL, pt. 1; Sallie Tillman to BRT, 13 July 1909, BRT to Sophie Tillman, 4 May 1916, Sallie Tillman to BRT, 11 Oct. 1906, BRTP-CL, pt. 9. See also BRT to Sallie Tillman, Sept.–Nov. 1895, BRTP-CL, pt. 1.

4. BRT, *Commencement Exercises*, 25; BRT to Henry Tillman, 25 Apr. 1913, Sallie Tillman to Sophie Tillman, 22 June 1906 ("my ring," "feeling obliged"), Sallie Tillman to BRT, 11 Oct. 1906, BRTP-CL, pt. 9.

5. BRT to Sophie Tillman, 20 Oct. 1907, BRTP-CL, pt. 9.

6. BRT to B. R. Tillman, 28 Oct. 1896, BRTP-CL, pt. 1; BRT to Sophie Tillman, 28 Oct. 1906, BRTP-CL, pt. 9. Tillman's efforts to purchase Western lands led to

a widely publicized scandal in which Roosevelt and others accused him of taking advantage of his office for personal gain. See Simkins, *Pitchfork Ben Tillman*, 445–54.

7. Sallie Tillman to BRT, 20 July 1907, BRT to Sophie Tillman, 29 June 1908, BRTP-CL, pt. 9; BRT to B. R. Tillman, 16 Apr. 1908, BRTP-CL, pt. 2; BRT to Sallie Tillman, 3 Apr. 1906, BRT to B. R. Tillman, 28 Oct. 1896, BRTP-CL, pt. 1; BRT, *Commencement Exercises*, 23.
8. Rental accounts in Benjamin Ryan Tillman Jr., notebook, [1905], BRTP-CL, pt. 8, envelope 10; B. R. Tillman to Sophie Tillman, 25 May 1909, BRTP-CL, pt. 9; Titles to Real Estate, 1 Dec. 1909, Edgefield Deed Book 21, p. 517, ECA.
9. BRT to Richards, 8, 14 Feb. 1910, John G. Richards Papers, SCL; Simkins, *Pitchfork Ben Tillman*, 483.
10. B. R. Tillman to BRT, 13 Dec. 1912, BRTP-CL, pt. 2.
11. BRT to Sophie Tillman, 11 Jan. 1914, BRTP-CL, pt. 9; BRT, "Memorandum about farm work," [1895], BRTP-CL, pt. 1, box 1, folder 1; BRT to B. R. Tillman, 9, 7 Dec. 1912, BRTP-CL, pt. 1; BRT to Sophie Tillman, 11 Jan. 1914, BRTP-CL, pt. 9 (Kitty Gibson); Sallie Tillman to BRT, 17 Oct. 1906, BRTP-CL, pt. 9.
12. BRT to B. R. Tillman, 10, 12 Dec. 1912, BRTP-CL, pt. 1.
13. Ibid., 8 Feb. 1913. "I wrote those negroes to come see me when I get home," Tillman told his son (ibid., 7 Dec. 1912).
14. BRT to Sophie Tillman, 11 Jan. 1914, BRTP-CL, pt. 9; "Memorandum about farm work," [1895], BRTP-CL, pt. 1, box 1, folder 1; Shaw to BRT, 17 July 1891, BRTP-CL, (emphasis in original); BRT to Wise, 30 Aug. 1899, BRT to B. R. Tillman, 19 Feb. 1913, BRTP-CL, pt. 1.
15. Simkins, *Pitchfork Ben Tillman*, 474–80; State Farmers' Institute schedule, Clemson College, 7–10 Aug. 1906, BRTP-CL, pt. 2, box 9; BRT, "Hog Raising in South Carolina," in BRTP-CL, pt. 5, vol. 4.
16. Richards to BRT, 9 Dec. 1907, BRTP-CL, pt. 2.
17. Duncan to BRT, 15 Feb. 1894, and reply on envelope, Governor BRT Letters, SCDAH; BRT to Page, 7 Feb. 1900, Thomas Nelson Page Papers, PL; BRT, *Struggles of 1876*; Kohn to BRT, 27 Sept., 4 Oct. 1909, BRTP-CL, pt. 2; BRT to Jervey, 14 Nov. 1908, 24 Mar. 1914, Theodore Dehon Jervey Jr. Papers, SCHS; BRT, "My Childhood Days," BRTP-SCL. Tillman wrote neither proposed book, although the manuscript "My Childhood Days" and the speech *Struggles of 1876* provide revealing beginnings.
18. Harris to BRT, 3 May 1906, BRTP-CL, pt. 2.
19. BRT to Thurmond, 19 Feb. 1912, BRTP-CL; Grantham, *Southern Progressivism*, 59–60 (Manning).
20. Simon, *Fabric of Defeat*, 11–35, quotation on 32; Simkins, *Pitchfork Ben Tillman*, 485–504.
21. *Blease's Weekly*, 9 Sept. 1926; Simon, *Fabric of Defeat*, 27–28; Vance in West, "From Yeoman to Redneck," 579; BRT in *Charleston News and Courier*, 14 May 1902, clipping in BRTP-CL, pt. 1, box 26; Burnside, "Coleman Livingston Blease," 239–47, 255, 259–60.
22. BRT to Richards, 12 Feb. 1912, BRT to J. E. Swearingen, 17 Feb. 1912, BRT to

Thurmond, 19 Feb. 1912, BRTP-CL; BRT to Richards, 17 Nov. 1913, John G. Richards Papers, SCL.

23. Burnside, "Coleman Livingston Blease," 147–48; *Newberry Herald and News*, 16 July 1912, quoted in Burnside, "Coleman Livingston Blease," 153–54 ("back yard"); BRT to Ferguson, 9 Aug. 1912 ("sweetheart"), BRT to Bowie, 5 Aug. 1912, BRTP-CL. For keen analyses of the sexual stresses within white mill society in the early decades of the century, see MacLean, "Leo Frank Case," and Simon, *Fabric of Defeat* and "Appeal of Cole Blease."

24. Untitled manuscript, 9 Aug. 1912, BRT to Thurmond, 19 Feb. 1912, BRT to Crosland, 7 Aug. 1912, BRT to Ferguson, 9 Aug. 1912, BRTP-CL.

25. BRT, open letter to Blease, Aug. 1912, BRTP-CL.

26. BRT to Bowie, 5 Aug. 1912, BRT, open letter to Blease, Aug. 1912, untitled manuscript, 9 Aug. 1912, BRTP-CL. Arsenault, "Folklore of Southern Demagoguery," puts Blease in the "first wave" of demagogues that began with Tillman, Georgia's Tom Watson, Texas's James Hogg, and Tennessee's "Fiddlin' Bob" Taylor.

27. BRT to family, 24 Aug. 1912, BRTP-CL, pt. 10; Blease, *Message of Governor Cole L. Blease to the General Assembly . . . January 1913*; BRT to Richards, 8, 17 Nov. 1913, John G. Richards Papers, SCL. The political genealogy of Tillmanism and Bleaseism was analyzed in detail by a close observer, Tillman's onetime shill George R. Koester. In 1916, as editor of the *Greenville Piedmont*, he published a multipart essay entitled "Bleaseism" containing many plausible "revelations" about South Carolina politics during the 1890s and 1900s. He concluded that "its daddy was the Reform movement" and that Blease represented "a class vote . . . a hope planted by Tillman, . . . fostered by Jim Tillman . . . [and] blown to white heat by Cole. Blease" (*Greenville Piedmont*, 16, 23 Sept. 1916, clippings in BRTP-CL, pt. 5, vol. 17). When Blease was defeated in his bid for a Senate seat in 1914, Tillman gloated. In a short, scathing telegram, he offered his defeated former protégé a biblical quotation: "The heathen are still raging, but the people rejoice. See Deuteronomy Thirty-Two Fifteen. Goodbye." In that verse, Moses describes how Israel "grew fat and . . . abandoned the God who made him and rejected the Rock his Savior" and suffered the consequences (telegram, BRT to Blease, 26 Aug. 1914, BRTP-CL, pt. 1).

28. BRT to J. C. Hemphill, 6 Feb. 1903, Hemphill Family Papers, PL; BRT to Vardaman, 3 May 1913, BRTP-CL; Vardaman to BRT, 5 May 1913, BRTP-CL, pt. 2; press release, 11 Dec. 1912, BRTP-CL. On the Crum fight, see also Simkins, *Pitchfork Ben Tillman*, 416–18. See also Roosevelt to Aldrich, 16 Apr. 1904, and Roosevelt to Pritchett, 14 Dec. 1904, in Morison, *Letters of Theodore Roosevelt*, 4:774, 1066–72. On appointments and segregation, see Joel Williamson, *Crucible of Race*, 364–89, and Clements, *Presidency of Woodrow Wilson*, 45–46.

29. BRT to Carroll, 10 Feb. 1913, BRTP-CL, pt. 1; Carroll to BRT, 6 Feb., 8 Mar. 1913, BRTP-CL, pt. 2; "Bull Moosers in South Carolina," unidentified newspaper, 29 Oct. 1912, clipping in BRTP-CL, pt. 5, vol. 10; BRT to Richards, 2 Dec. 1913, John G. Richards Papers, SCL.

30. BRT, "Causes of Southern Opposition to Imperialism," 443 (Jefferson); BRT to

Richards, 12 Feb. 1912, John G. Richards Papers, SCL ("taught"); BRT to Rice, 8 Mar. 1916, James Henry Rice Jr. Papers, PL ("demagogue"); BRT to McMahan, 13 Aug. 1912, BRTP-CL, pt. 1 ("mad-dog"); BRT to J. E. Swearingen, 3 Feb. 1912, BRTP-CL ("despotism"). In 1906, Tillman described the U.S. Senate approvingly as a "bulwark against revolution" (BRT, "Is the Senate Honest?," *Sunday Magazine*, 29 Apr. 1906, clipping in BRTP-CL, pt. 5, vol. 6).

31. Burnside, "Coleman Livingston Blease," 165–68. The primary had not failed Tillman: in his 1912 fight, he had beaten back two opponents and earned more than 50 percent of the total Democratic vote (Frank E. Jordan Jr., *Primary State*, 63).
32. Frank E. Jordan Jr., *Primary State*, 63; Grantham, *Life and Death of the Solid South*, 65; BRT to Crosland, 5 Sept. 1912, BRTP-CL, pt. 1 ("cleanse"); BRT to Richards, 12 Sept. 1912, 3 Nov. 1913, John G. Richards Papers, SCL. Tillman also opposed a federal amendment providing for the direct election of U.S. senators because it called for federal control of state electoral affairs. Tillman argued that "an unscrupulous President would not hesitate even to use troops at the polls" (BRT to Bacon, 3 June 1911, BRTP-CL, pt. 1).
33. Richards to BRT, 18 Nov. 1913, BRTP-CL; Richards to BRT, 27 May 1914, BRT to Richards, 30 May 1914, John G. Richards Papers, SCL; BRT, "Farewell to Public Life," 4–5. Richards disappointed Tillman by refusing to join in condemning Blease (BRT to Hammett, 15 Aug. 1914, John G. Richards Papers, SCL). After Tillman's death, Richards gained Blease's support for governor in terms that Tillman would have found disquietingly familiar: in 1926, Blease's newspaper ran a pro-Richards banner reading, "Vote for John G. Richards and save South Carolina from Ring Rule and Corporate Control. . . . A vote for Richards is a vote for a friend of the Farmers and Laboring Men" (*Blease's Weekly*, 9 Sept. 1926).
34. BRT, *Negro Problem and Immigration*, 15; BRT, "Race Question," 25; BRT to Sophie Tillman, 11 Jan. 1914, BRTP-CL, pt. 9 ("white man"); BRT to B. R. Tillman, 23 Mar. 1916, BRTP-CL; BRT, "Farewell to Public Life," 6; BRT to Swearingen, 3 Feb. 1912, BRTP-CL.
35. BRT, *Negro Problem and Immigration*, 15–17 ("double"); Smalls in *Columbia State*, 27 Oct. 1895; BRT, "Race Question," 24 ("millions"), and *Negro Problem and Immigration*, 15–17 ("hut").
36. BRT, *Negro Problem and Immigration*, 16–17 ("kith and kin"); BRT to Wilson, 28 June 1911, BRTP-CL, pt. 1 ("standard"); BRT to Christie, 24 Feb. 1917, BRTP-SCL ("heterogeneous"); BRT, *Negro Problem and Immigration*, 16–17 ("good citizens"). Tillman, true to his belief in corporate conspiracies against the Republic, was convinced that large steamship companies were behind the mass immigration of these undesirables (BRT to Wilson, 28 June 1911, BRTP-CL, pt. 1).
37. BRT, "Race Question," 23 ("*imperio*"); Smalls to Secretary of the Navy, 28 Jan. 1907, Wieland to BRT, 7 Dec. 1911, BRTP-CL, pt. 2. It is worth considering whether the fire that destroyed the gun might have been set intentionally by black activists determined to prevent fearful whites from taking their preemptive actions a bloody step farther against a black majority, as they had less than a decade before in Wilmington, North Carolina.

38. BRT to Sophie Tillman, 4 May 1916, 25 Jan. 1915, BRTP-CL, pt. 9. Cf. BRT in *Washington Post,* 18 Nov. 1906, clipping in BRTP-CL, pt. 5, vol. 6.
39. BRT to Rice, 3 Feb., 8 Mar. 1916, James Henry Rice Jr. Papers, PL (Bryan); unidentified newspaper, [1914–16], clipping in BRTP-CL, pt. 5, vol. 12 ("evangel"); BRT to Rice, 28 Mar. 1918, James Henry Rice Jr. Papers, PL ("slaves"); BRT to Maxwell, 18 Aug. 1917, BRTP-SCL; BRT to Dixon, 27 Apr. 1917, BRTP-CL; BRT, *Speech . . . Delivered before the State Democratic Convention . . . May 15, 1918,* 1; Evans to BRT, 26 Nov. 1917, BRTP-CL, pt. 2; BRT to Woodward, 25 June 1918, William Watts Ball Papers, PL. For a close analysis of Bryan's own transformation during this period, see Levine, *Defender of the Faith.*
40. Handwritten annotation by Cole L. Blease on frontispiece of *Benjamin Ryan Tillman (Late a Senator from South Carolina): Memorial Addresses Delivered in the Senate and House of Representatives, Sixty-fifth Congress . . . December 15, 1918* (Washington, D.C., 1919), Augustus Tompkins Graydon Collection, subject file I-6-1, Governors and Lieutenant Governors Letters, Letterbooks, and Telegrams, SCDAH.

Epilogue

1. Quoted in Bailey, "Only Game in Town," 76.
2. Winfred Bobo Moore Jr., " 'Unrewarding Stone,' " 13. See also Winfred Bobo Moore Jr., "New South Statesman."
3. *Columbia Record,* 1 May 1940, clipping in BRTP-CL, pt. 5, unmarked folder. Tillman's legacy also took the form of the naval destroyer USS *Tillman,* launched in December 1941 (unidentified newspaper, 21 Dec. 1941, clipping in BRTP-CL, pt. 5, unmarked folder).
4. Simkins, *Pitchfork Ben Tillman,* 555. After his father's death, B. R. attempted to take custody of his father's legacy. He was outraged by the "slander" and "falsehoods" he saw in Simkins's work, and after moving the Tillman Papers from the University of South Carolina to Clemson University, B. R. set about writing a corrective biography. This manuscript, incomplete and unpublished at B. R.'s death in 1950, remains—along with his hostile comments regarding Simkins—in the BRTP-CL, pt. 7.
5. In the twentieth century, even Southern observers as astute as Lillian Smith have fallen back on this two-class model of Mr. Rich White and Mr. Poor White, substituting a discourse for social analysis (Lillian Smith, *Killers of the Dream,* 175–90). For an acute interpretation of the "fall" of white Southern men from respectability to ignominy in the late nineteenth century, see West, "From Yeoman to Redneck."
6. As Charles Payne notes, "[G]iving racism the face of the ignorant, the potbellied, the tobacco-chewing . . . easily supplants more complex and realistic images of racism" and makes it harder to tell the story of the black freedom movement itself (*I've Got the Light,* 418–19).
7. George R. Koester, "Bleaseism," *Greenville Piedmont,* 28 Sept. 1916, in BRTP-CL, pt. 5, vol. 17.

Bibliography

Primary Sources

MANUSCRIPT COLLECTIONS

Chapel Hill, N.C.
  Southern Historical Collection, Wilson Library, University of North Carolina
    Marion Butler Papers
    Elliott and Gonzales Family Papers
    Alexander Cheves Haskell Papers
    Meares-DeRosset Family Papers
    Leonidas Lafayette Polk Papers
    Francis Butler Simkins Papers
    William Francis Stevenson Papers
    Marguerite Tolbert interview, Southern Oral History Project
    Daniel Augustus Tompkins Papers
    Alfred Moore Waddell Papers
    John Blake White Papers
    Benjamin C. Yancey Papers
Charleston, S.C.
  South Carolina Historical Society
    Joseph Walker Barnwell Papers
    F. W. Dawson Papers
    Theodore Dehon Jervey Jr. Papers
Clemson, S.C.
  Special Collections, Robert Muldrow Cooper Library, Clemson University
    Asbury Francis Lever Papers
    Quattlebaum Family Papers
    Walter M. Riggs Presidential Records
    Benjamin Ryan Tillman Papers
Columbia, S.C.
  South Carolina Department of Archives and History
    Anderson County Farmers' Alliance Minutes

Edgefield County Coroner Inquisition Books
Edgefield County Court of Equity Records
Edgefield County Judge of Probate Records
Governors and Lieutenant Governors Letters, Letterbooks, and Telegrams
Augustus Tompkins Graydon Collection
South Carolina Election Commission Records
South Carolina General Assembly Records
South Caroliniana Library, University of South Carolina
Eugene Avery Adams Papers
Patrick Henry Adams Papers
J. H. Aycock Papers
Aycock Family Papers
Beech Island Farmers' Club Records, 1846–93
W. B. Boyle Papers
Iveson L. Brookes Papers
Burn Family Papers
Francis Wilkinson Pickens Butler Papers
Matthew Calbraith Butler Papers
James Butler Campbell Papers
Aaron Cannon Diaries
Ellerbe Broggan Crawford Cash Papers
Charles Family Papers
Lysander D. Childs Papers
William Ashmead Courtenay Papers
Floride Cunningham Papers
Eugene W. Dabbs Papers
John Julius Dargan Papers
Robert Means Davis Papers
Francis Warrington Dawson Papers
Samuel Dibble Papers
Mr. and Mrs. Walter E. Duncan Papers
Edgefield County Farmers' Alliance Minutes
W. E. Elliott Jr. Papers
John Gary Evans Papers
Florence County Papers
Martin Witherspoon Gary Papers
Narciso Gener Gonzales Papers
Edwin Luther Green Papers
David Jefferson Griffith Papers
Hammond, Bryan, and Cummings Families Papers
Edward Spann Hammond Papers
Hampton Family Papers
Walter Hazard Papers
Horse Range Democratic Club Book
James A. Hoyt Papers

John L. M. Irby Papers
Andrew Johnstone Papers
August Philip Kohn Papers
James Jonathan Lucas Papers
William Haynesworth Lyles Papers
Charles Spencer McCall Papers
McKissick Family Papers
Edward Perrin McKissick Papers
James Rion McKissick Papers
John Lowndes McLaurin Papers
Fitz William McMaster and Mary Jane Macfie McMaster Papers
Richard Ashe Meares Papers
Minute Men (Laurens County)
Minute Men, Saluda Association
J. W. Moore Papers
Thomas J. Moore Papers
Young John Pope Papers
John G. Richards Papers
Elias S. Rivers Papers
Alexander Samuel Salley Jr. Papers
James F. Sloan Papers
Yates Snowden Papers
South Carolina Farmers' State Alliance, Kershaw County Records
South Carolina Farmers' State Alliance Exchange Papers
South Carolina Farmers' State Alliance Minutes
South Carolina Farmers' State Alliance Rejection Book
South Carolina Industrial Home for Colored Children Papers
John Eldred Swearingen Papers
Swearingen Family Papers
Thomas Family Papers
John Peyre Thomas Papers
Benjamin Ryan Tillman Papers
Samuel P. Verner Papers
Thomas J. Warren Papers
James Thomas Williams Papers
Simon Peter Wingard Papers
Women's Christian Temperance Union of South Carolina Records
Mary Little Yeargin Papers

Durham, N.C.

Special Collections, Perkins Library, Duke University

William Watts Ball Papers
Iveson L. Brookes Papers
Matthew Calbraith Butler Papers
Francis Warrington Dawson Papers
Samuel Dibble Papers

Paul Garrett Papers
Martin Witherspoon Gary Papers
John Patrick Grace Papers
Hemphill Family Papers
Joseph Travis Johnson Papers
Thomas Jefferson McKie Papers
Thomas John Moore Papers
Thomas Nelson Page Papers
James Henry Rice Jr. Papers
Benjamin S. Williams Papers
Edgefield, S.C.
Edgefield County Archives
Index to Deeds
Index to Liens
Court of Common Pleas Records
Probate Court Records
Treasurer's Tax Duplicate Books
Wills
New Haven, Conn.
Manuscripts and Archives, Sterling Library, Yale University
John Augustus Hendrix McLane Papers
Washington, D.C.
Manuscript Division, Library of Congress
Richard Lathers Papers
National Association for the Advancement of Colored People Papers
Benjamin Ryan Tillman Papers

NEWSPAPERS

Georgia
Augusta Chronicle
Illinois
Chicago Broad-Ax
Chicago Tribune
North Carolina
Fayetteville Observer
Star of Zion (Salisbury)
Ohio
Cleveland Gazette
Ohio Enterprise (Cleveland)
South Carolina
Aiken Times
Anderson Intelligencer
Barnwell People
Barnwell Sentinel

Beaufort Crescent
Beaufort Republican and Sea Island Chronicle
Beaufort Tribune and Port Royal Commercial
Blease's Weekly (Anderson)
Charleston Advocate
Charleston News and Courier
Charleston World
Christian Soldier (Columbia)
Columbia Register
Columbia State
Cotton Plant (Marion)
Easley Messenger
Edgefield Advertiser
Edgefield Chronicle
Georgetown Planet
Keowee Courier
Marlboro Chronicle
New South (Beaufort)
Palmetto Post (Port Royal)
Pee Dee Educator (Bennettsville)
Port Royal Standard and Commercial
Sea Island News (Beaufort)
Williamsburg Republican
Yorkville Enquirer

Washington, D.C.
National Economist

Wisconsin
Fond du Lac Daily Commonwealth
Lake Geneva News
Marinette Daily Eagle
Wisconsin State Journal (Madison)

BOOKS AND ARTICLES

Allen, Walter. *Governor Chamberlain's Administration in South Carolina.* 1888. Reprint, New York: Negro Universities Press, 1969.

Baker, Ray Stannard. *Following the Color Line: An Account of Negro Citizenship in the American Democracy.* 1908. Reprint, New York: Harper & Row, 1964.

Ball, William Watts. *The State That Forgot: South Carolina's Surrender to Democracy.* Indianapolis: Bobbs-Merrill, 1932.

Brooks, U. R. *Butler and His Cavalry in the War of Secession, 1861–1865.* Columbia, S.C., 1909.

Bryan, William Jennings, ed. *Republic or Empire.* Chicago: Independence, 1899.

Calhoun, William Patrick. *The Caucasian and the Negro in the United States: They Must*

Be Separate, If Not, Then Extermination; A Proposed Solution — Colonization. Columbia, S.C.: R. L. Bryan, 1902.
Cash, W. J. *The Mind of the South.* New York: Knopf, 1941.
Chapin, Sallie F. *Fitz-Hugh St. Clair, the South Carolina Rebel Boy; or, It Is No Crime to Be Born a Gentleman.* Philadelphia: Claxton, Remsen, & Haffelfinger, 1873.
Chapman, John A. *History of Edgefield County from the Earliest Settlements to 1897.* Newberry, S.C.: Elbert H. Aull, 1897.
Creelman, James. "A Defender of the Senate." *Pearson's Magazine* (June 1906): 622–29.
Du Bois, W. E. B. *The Souls of Black Folk.* 1903. Reprint, New York: Vintage, 1990.
Evans, Maurice S. *Black and White in the Southern States: A Study of the Race Problem in the United States from a South African Point of View.* London: Longmans, Green, 1915.
Hagood, Johnson. *Memoirs of the War of Secession from the Original Manuscripts of Johnson Hagood, Brigadier-General, C.S.A.* Edited by U. R. Brooks. Columbia, S.C., 1910.
Hampton, Wade. "What Negro Supremacy Means." *Forum* 5 (June 1888): 383–95.
Higginson, Thomas Wentworth. *Army Life in a Black Regiment.* 1869. Reprint, New York: Norton, 1962.
Izlar, William Valmore. *A Sketch of the War Record of the Edisto Rifles, 1861–1865.* Columbia, S.C.: A. Kohn, 1914.
Leland, John A. *A Voice from South Carolina.* 1879. Reprint, Freeport, N.Y.: Books for Libraries Press, 1971.
McGhee, Zach. "Tillman, Smasher of Traditions." *World's Work* (Sept. 1906): 8013–20.
McKinley, Carlyle. *An Appeal to Pharaoh: The Negro Problem and Its Radical Solution.* 3d ed. Columbia, S.C., 1907.
McMillan, Lewis K. *The Founding of South Carolina's State College for Negroes.* Rowesville, S.C.: A. L. Bonnett & Son, [1952].
Miller, Kelly. *Race Adjustment and the Everlasting Stain.* Reprint, 2 vols. in 1, New York: Arno, 1968.
Morris, Samuel Leslie. *An Autobiography.* Richmond: Presbyterian Committee of Publication, 1932.
Poe, Clarence. "Suffrage Restriction in the South: Its Causes and Consequences." *North American Review* 175 (Oct. 1902): 534–43.
Redkey, Edwin S., ed. *Respect Black: The Writings and Speeches of Henry McNeal Turner.* New York: Arno, 1971.
Robinson, Harry P. "A Railway Party in Politics." *North American Review* 156 (May 1893): 552–60.
Sheppard, William Arthur. *Red Shirts Remembered: Southern Brigadiers of the Reconstruction Period.* Atlanta: Ruralist Press, 1940.
Sinclair, Upton. *The Jungle.* 1906. Reprint, New York: Heritage, 1965.
Smalls, Robert. "Election Methods in the South." *North American Review* 151 (Nov. 1890): 593–600.
Smith, Lillian. *Killers of the Dream.* 1961. Rev. ed., New York: Norton, 1978.

Southern Society for the Promotion of the Study of Race Conditions and Problems in the South. *Race Problems of the South.* 1900. Reprint, New York: Negro Universities Press, 1969.
Stone, Hon. J. M. "The Suppression of Lawlessness in the South." *North American Review* 158 (Apr. 1894): 500–506.
Straker, David Augustus. *The New South Investigated.* Detroit: Ferguson, 1888.
Thompson, Charles Willis. *Party Leaders of the Time.* New York: G. W. Dillingham, 1906.
Tillman, Benjamin Ryan. "Causes of Southern Opposition to Imperialism." *North American Review* 171 (Oct. 1900): 439–46.
———. "The Dispensary Law of South Carolina as a Working Success." *Frank Leslie's Popular Monthly* 53 (Jan. 1902): 323–28.
———. "Hog Raising in South Carolina." *Clemson Agricultural College Extension Work* 5 (Oct. 1909).
———. "How I Restored My Health and Vigor." *Physical Culture* 37 (Apr. 1917): 7–15.
———. "Is the Senate Honest?" *Sunday Magazine,* 29 Apr. 1906.
———. "Our Whiskey Rebellion." *North American Review* 158 (May 1894): 513–19.
———. "The Race Question." *Van Norden Magazine* (Apr. 1907): 19–28.
———. "The South Carolina Liquor Law." *North American Review* 158 (Feb. 1894): 141–49.
Tillman, Benjamin Ryan, and Hon. W. F. Dargan, Mayor of Darlington. "A Last Word on the South Carolina Liquor Law." *North American Review* 159 (July 1894): 46–60.
Tompkins, D. A., and A. S. Tompkins. *Company K, 14th South Carolina Volunteers.* Charlotte, N.C.: Observer, 1897.
Tourgée, Albion. "Shall White Minorities Rule?" *Forum* 7 (1889): 143–55.
Williams, Alfred B. *Wade Hampton and His Red Shirts: South Carolina's Deliverance.* Charleston: Walker, Evans, and Cogswell, 1935.
Young, Virginia Durant. "The Star in the West." *Woman Suffrage Leaflet* 4, no. 1 (Jan. 1893): 1–4.

PROCEEDINGS AND CONSTITUTIONS

Commonwealth of South Carolina. *Constitution . . . Ratified April 16, 1868.* Columbia, S.C.: Charles A. Calvo Jr., 1883.
Constitutional Convention of the State of South Carolina. *Journal of the Constitutional Convention of the State of South Carolina, Begun to Be Holden at Columbia, S.C., on Tuesday, the Tenth Day of September . . . until Wednesday, the Fourth Day of December [1895] . . . When Finally Adjourned.* Columbia, S.C.: Charles A. Calvo Jr., 1895.
Democratic National Convention. *Official Proceedings of the Democratic National Convention Held in Kansas City, Mo., July 4th, 5th and 6th, 1900.* Chicago: McLellan, 1900.
Farmers' State Alliance of South Carolina. *Constitution . . . Adopted at Florence, S.C., July 12, 1888.* Greenville, S.C.: Hoyt & Keys, 1889.

———. *Constitution . . . Adopted at Spartanburg, July 23, 1891*. Washington, D.C.: National Economist, 1891.
———. *Proceedings of the . . . Third Annual Meeting, Greenville, . . . July 23rd and 24th, 1890*. Greenville, S.C.: Shannon, [1890].
National Democratic Convention. *Official Proceedings of the National Democratic Convention, Held in Chicago, Ill., June 21st, 22nd and 23rd, 1892*. Chicago: Cameron, Amberg, 1892.
———. *Official Proceedings of the Democratic National Convention . . . 1896*. Logansport, Ind.: Wilson, Humphreys, 1896.
National Democratic Party. *Proceedings of the Convention of the National Democratic Party, Held at Indianapolis, Indiana, September 2 and 3, 1896*. N.p., 1896.
South Carolina Democratic Party. *Constitution of the Democratic Party of South Carolina, As Amended in State Convention at Columbia, Sept. 6, 1888*. N.p., [1888].
———. *Constitution of the Democratic Party of South Carolina, Adopted in State Convention at Columbia, S.C., September 10, 1890*. N.p., [1890].
———. *Constitution of the Democratic Party of South Carolina, Amended at State Convention in Columbia, September 21, 1892*. N.p., [1892].
———. *Constitution of the Democratic Party of South Carolina, Adopted in State Convention at Columbia, S.C., September 19, 1894*. N.p., [1894].
South Carolina Democratic Party Executive Committee. *Rules for Governing the Membership of Democratic Clubs, the Qualification of Voters, and the Conduct of Primary Elections of the Democratic Party of South Carolina, Amended July 26, 1892*. N.p., [1892].
———. *Rules for Governing the Membership of Democratic Clubs, the Qualification of Voters, and the Conduct of Primary Elections of the Democratic Party of South Carolina, Adopted June 5, 1896*. N.p., [1896].
State Executive Committee of the Union Republican Party of South Carolina. *The Election of 1880 in South Carolina . . . Detailing the Frauds, Violence, and Intimidation, by Which South Carolina Was Carried for Hancock*. Charleston: J. W. Hammond, 1880.
State Farmers' Institute of South Carolina. *Proceedings of the State Farmers' Institute of South Carolina . . . Held at Spartanburg, August 9th and 10th, 1888*. N.p., [1888].
State Grange and Agricultural and Mechanical Society. *Essays Read . . . at Anderson, S.C., on the 8th, 9th, and 10th of August, 1877, Together with the Proceedings of the State Grange and the State Agricultural and Mechanical Society*. Columbia, S.C.: Hoyt, Emly, & McDaniel, 1877.
———. *Proceedings of the Joint Summer Meeting of the State Agricultural and Mechanical Society of So. Ca., and the State Grange P[atrons] of H[usbandry], Held at Greenville, S.C., July 26th and 27th, 1881*. Charleston: Lucas & Richardson, 1881.
Tax-Payers' Convention. *Proceedings of the Tax-Payers' Convention . . . 1871*. Charleston: Edward Perry, 1871.
———. *Proceedings of the Tax-Payers' Convention . . . 1874*. Charleston: News and Courier Job Presses, 1874.

PAMPHLETS AND SPEECHES

Unless otherwise noted, the following documents can be found at the South Caroliniana Library, University of South Carolina, Columbia, S.C.

Arnett, Rt. Rev. Benjamin William. *The Annual Address, Delivered before the Faculty, Students, and Friends of Claflin University and the Claflin College of Agriculture and Mechanical Institute, May 22nd 1889*. Columbia, S.C.: Wm. Sloane, 1889.

Blease, Coleman L. *Message of Governor Cole L. Blease to the General Assembly . . . January 1913*. Columbia, S.C.: Gonzales and Bryan, 1913.

Brayton, Ellery M. *An Address upon the Election Law of South Carolina and the Methods Employed to Suppress the Republican Vote*. Columbia, S.C.: Wm. Sloane, 1889.

Butler, Matthew Calbraith. *Speech Delivered by Hon. M. C. Butler at Gaffney, S.C., July 4th, 1899*. N.p., n.d.

A Centennial Fourth of July Democratic Celebration: The Massacre of Six Colored Citizens of the United States at Hamburg, S.C., on July 4, 1876; Debate on the Hamburg Massacre, in the U.S. House of Representatives, July 15th and 18th, 1876. N.p., n.d.

Conference of Colored Citizens. *An Address to the People of the United States, Adopted at a Conference of Colored Citizens, Held at Columbia, S.C., July 20 and 21st, 1876*. Columbia, S.C.: Republican, 1876.

Hampton, Wade. *Free Men! Free Ballots!! Free Schools!!!: The Pledges of Gen. Wade Hampton, Democratic Candidate for Governor, to the Colored People of South Carolina, 1865–1876*. N.p., n.d.

Hemphill, John J. *Smalls vs. Elliott: Speech of Hon. John J. Hemphill of South Carolina, in the House of Representatives, Wednesday, February 13, 1889*. Washington, D.C., 1889.

Henderson, Daniel S. *The White Man's Revolution in South Carolina: Address of Hon. D. S. Henderson, Delivered at the Unveiling of the McKie Merriweather Monument, North Augusta, South Carolina, 16th February, 1916*. N.p., n.d.

Johnson, William E. *Government Liquor Monopoly, As Demonstrated by the South Carolina Liquor Dispensary*. Washington, D.C., n.d.

McLane, John Augustus Hendrix. *Labor and Finance: Address to the People of South Carolina by J. H. McLane, Nov. 30, 1879*. N.p., n.d. John Augustus Hendrix McLane Papers, Manuscripts and Archives, Sterling Library, Yale University, New Haven, Conn.

———. *Speech Delivered before Feasterville Grange by One of Its Members upon the Condition of the State, February 13th, 1886*. Charlotte, N.C.: Hirst, 1886.

Miller, Mary J., ed. *The Suffrage: Speeches by Negroes in the Constitutional Convention—The Part Taken by Colored Orators in Their Fight for a Fair and Impartial Ballot Being Provided for in the Fundamental Law*. N.p., n.d.

Mims, Mrs. J. L. *(Un)Recorded History of South Carolina's Women's Christian Temperance Union from 1881–1901*. [Edgefield, S.C., 1944].

Murray, E. B. *Read and Learn: Speech . . . at Abbeville on July 18th, 1892*. N.p., n.d.

Murray, George W. *An Oration Delivered in the City of Charleston on the Twenty-Seventh Anniversary of the Emancipation Proclamation*. Charleston: Walker, Evans, and Cogswell, 1890.

Nicholson, Alfred W. *Brief Sketch of the Life and Labors of Rev. Alexander Bettis*. Trenton, S.C., 1913.

Ramage, B. James. "Local Government and Free Schools in South Carolina (First Part Read before the Historical Society of South Carolina, Dec. 15, 1882)." *Johns Hopkins University Studies in Historical and Political Science* 12 (1883): 1–39.

Taylor, B. F. *The Darlington Riot: Paper Read before the Kosmos Club . . . January 22nd, 1910*. Columbia, S.C.: University Press, [1910].

Tillman, Benjamin Ryan. *Annexation of Hawaii*. Speech in the U.S. Senate, 30 June 1898.

——. *Annexation of the Philippine Islands*. Speech in the U.S. Senate, 7 Feb. 1899.

——. *Bimetallism or Industrial Slavery*. Speech in the U.S. Senate, 29 Jan. 1896.

——. *Bounty on Agricultural Exports*. Speech in the U.S. Senate, 10 June 1897.

——. *The Brownsville Raid*. Speech in the U.S. Senate, 12 Jan. 1907.

——. *The Coal Famine — Who Is Responsible for It?* Speech in the U.S. Senate, 14–15 Jan. 1903.

——. *Commencement Exercises of the South Carolina Military Academy: Address by the Honorable B. R. Tillman, June 30, 1899*. Charleston: Walker, Evans, and Cogswell, 1899.

——. *Dr. Bledsoe's "Mission of Woman" and Woman Suffrage*. Speech in the U.S. Senate, 18 Aug. 1913.

——. *Executive Usurpation in Santo Domingo*. Speech in the U.S. Senate, 17 Jan. 1906.

——. "Farewell to Public Life." *Congressional Record*, 27 Feb. 1915.

——. *Free Panama Canal Tolls*. Speech in the U.S. Senate, 9 June 1914.

——. *Inaugural Address . . . 1890*. Columbia, S.C., 1890.

——. *Independence of Cuba*. Speech in the U.S. Senate, 15 Apr. 1898.

——. *Laying of the Corner-Stone of the Winthrop Normal and Industrial College of South Carolina at Rock Hill, S.C., May 12, 1894*. Lancaster, S.C., 1894.

——. *Massachusetts and South Carolina in the Revolution*. Speech in the U.S. Senate, 30 Jan. 1902.

——. *Message to the General Assembly, 1891*. Columbia, S.C., 1891.

——. *Message to the General Assembly, 1892*. Columbia, S.C., 1892.

——. *Message to the General Assembly, 1893*. Columbia, S.C., 1893.

——. *Message to the General Assembly, 1894*. Columbia, S.C., 1894.

——. *Naval Appropriation Bill*. Speech in the U.S. Senate, 1 May 1896.

——. *The Negro Problem and Immigration*. Speech in the South Carolina House of Representatives, 24 Jan. 1908.

——. *The Philippines*. Speech in the U.S. Senate, 29 Jan. 1900.

——. *Pork or Preparedness*. Speech in the U.S. Senate, 20 May 1916.

——. *Prohibition of Smoking in the Senate Chamber—Physical Culture*. Speech in the U.S. Senate, 9 Mar. 1914.

——. *The Race Problem*. Speech in the U.S. Senate, 23–24 Feb. 1903.

——. *Senatorial Corruption and the Sugar Trust Investigation*. Speech in the U.S. Senate, 28 May, 3 June 1897.

——. *Speech . . . Delivered before the State Democratic Convention . . . May 15, 1918*. N.p., n.d.

——. *The Struggles of 1876—How South Carolina Was Delivered from Carpet-bag and Negro Rule: Speech at the Red-Shirt Re-Union at Anderson [25 Aug. 1909]; Personal Reminiscences and Incidents by Senator B. R. Tillman*. N.p., [1909].

Wells-Barnett, Ida B. "Southern Horrors" and "A Red Record." In *On Lynchings*. Reprint, Salem, N.H., 1991.

Wheeler, Thos. H. *Thomas E. Miller, Contestant, vs. William Elliott, Contestee: Contested Election from the Seventh Congressional District of South Carolina . . . 51st Congress*. Washington, D.C.: Rufus H. Darby, [1891].

———. *Thomas E. Miller, Contestant, vs. William Elliott, Contestee: Contested Election from the Seventh Congressional District of South Carolina . . . 52d Congress*. Washington, D.C., [1892].

GOVERNMENT DOCUMENTS

Congressional Quarterly's Guide to U.S. Elections. 3d ed. Washington, D.C., 1994.

Congressional Record. Washington, D.C., 1870–1918.

South Carolina General Assembly. *The Dispensary Law*. Sumter, S.C., 1893.

———. *Reports and Resolutions*.

South Carolina General Assembly. House of Representatives. *Acts and Joint Resolutions of the General Assembly of the State of South Carolina*. Columbia, S.C.

South Carolina General Assembly. House of Representatives. *Journal of the House of Representatives of the General Assembly of the State of South Carolina*.

South Carolina General Assembly. Senate. *Journal of the Senate of the General Assembly of the State of South Carolina*.

U.S. Bureau of the Census. *Ninth Census of the United States, 1870: Wealth and Industry and Population*. Washington, D.C., 1882.

———. *Tenth Census of the United States, 1880: Agriculture and Population*. Washington, D.C., 1883.

———. *Eleventh Census of the United States, 1890: Report on Farms and Homes and Compendium*. Washington, D.C., 1893.

———. *Twelfth Census of the United States, 1900: Report on Agriculture*. 2 vols. Washington, D.C., 1903.

U.S. Congress. Senate. *The Condition of Affairs in the Late Insurrectionary States*. [Ku Klux Klan hearings.] 42d Cong., 2d sess., 1871, S. Rep. 41, pt. 4.

———. *The Senators from South Carolina*. 57th Cong., 1st sess., 1902, S. Doc. 228.

———. *South Carolina in 1876: Report on the Denial of the Elective Franchise . . . by the United States Senate . . . to Accompany Senate Miscellaneous Document No. 48, 44th Congress, 2d Session*. Washington, D.C., 1877.

Secondary Sources

BOOKS

Abbott, Martin. *The Freedmen's Bureau in South Carolina, 1865–1872*. Chapel Hill: University of North Carolina Press, 1967.

Anderson, James D. *The Education of Blacks in the South*. Chapel Hill: University of North Carolina Press, 1988.

Arsenault, Raymond. *The Wild Ass of the Ozarks: Jeff Davis and the Social Bases of Southern Politics*. Philadelphia: Temple University Press, 1984.

Ayers, Edward L. *The Promise of the New South: Life after Reconstruction*. New York: Oxford University Press, 1992.

———. *Vengeance and Justice: Crime and Punishment in the Nineteenth-Century American South*. New York: Oxford University Press, 1984.

Bardaglio, Peter W. *Reconstructing the Household: Families, Sex, and the Law in the Nineteenth-Century South*. Chapel Hill: University of North Carolina Press, 1995.

Barnwell, John. *Love of Order: South Carolina's First Secession Crisis*. Chapel Hill: University of North Carolina Press, 1982.

Bederman, Gail. *Manliness and Civilization: A Cultural History of Gender and Race in the United States, 1880–1917*. Chicago: University of Chicago Press, 1995.

Bennett, David Harry. *The Party of Fear: From Nativist Movements to the New Right in American History*. Chapel Hill: University of North Carolina Press, 1988.

Berlin, Ira. *Many Thousands Gone: The First Two Centuries of Slavery in North America*. Cambridge: Harvard Belknap, 1998.

Bethel, Elizabeth K. *Promiseland*. Philadelphia: Temple University Press, 1981.

Blakey, Leonard Stott. *The Sale of Liquor in the South: The Development of a Normal Social Restraint in the Southern Commonwealths*. New York: Columbia University, Longmans, Green, 1912.

Bleser, Carol K. Rothrock. *The Promised Land: The History of the South Carolina Land Commission, 1869–1890*. Columbia: University of South Carolina Press, 1969.

Bolton, Charles C. *Poor Whites of the Antebellum South: Tenants and Laborers in Central North Carolina and Northeast Mississippi*. Durham: Duke University Press, 1994.

Bond, Bradley G. *Political Culture in the Nineteenth-Century South: Mississippi, 1830–1900*. Baton Rouge: Louisiana State University Press, 1995.

Bordin, Ruth. *Woman and Temperance: The Quest for Power and Liberty, 1873–1900*. Philadelphia: Temple University Press, 1981.

Boydston, Jeanne. *Home and Work: Housework, Wages, and the Ideology of Labor in the Early Republic*. New York: Oxford University Press, 1990.

Brown, Richard Maxwell. *Strain of Violence: Historical Studies of American Violence and Vigilantism*. New York: Oxford University Press, 1975.

Brundage, W. Fitzhugh. *Lynching in the New South: Georgia and Virginia, 1880–1930*. Urbana: University of Illinois Press, 1993.

Bryant, Lawrence C., ed. *Negro Senators and Representatives in the South Carolina Legislature, 1868–1902*. Orangeburg, S.C., 1968.

Buck, Solon J. *The Granger Movement*. Cambridge: Harvard University Press, 1913.

Burton, Orville Vernon. *In My Father's House Are Many Mansions: Family and Community in Edgefield, South Carolina*. Chapel Hill: University of North Carolina Press, 1985.

Bynum, Victoria. *Unruly Women: The Politics of Social and Sexual Control in the Old South*. Chapel Hill: University of North Carolina Press, 1992.

Cantrell, Gregg. *Kenneth and John B. Rayner and the Limits of Southern Dissent*. Urbana: University of Illinois Press, 1993.

Carlton, David L. *Mill and Town in South Carolina, 1880–1920*. Baton Rouge: Louisiana State University Press, 1982.

Cecelski, David S., and Timothy B. Tyson, eds. *Democracy Betrayed: The Wilmington Race Riot of 1898 and Its Legacy*. Chapel Hill: University of North Carolina Press, 1998.

Cell, John W. *The Highest Stage of White Supremacy: The Origins of Segregation in South Africa and the American South*. Cambridge: Cambridge University Press, 1982.

Chalmers, David M. *Neither Socialism nor Monopoly: Theodore Roosevelt and the Decision to Regulate the Railroads*. Philadelphia: Lippincott, 1976.

Channing, Steven A. *Crisis of Fear: Secession in South Carolina*. New York: Norton, 1974.

Clark, E. Culpepper. *Francis Warrington Dawson and the Politics of Restoration: South Carolina, 1874–1889*. Tuscaloosa: University of Alabama Press, 1980.

Clayton, Bruce. *The Savage Ideal: Intolerance and Intellectual Leadership in the South, 1890–1914*. Baltimore: Johns Hopkins University Press, 1972.

——. *W. J. Cash: A Life*. Baton Rouge: Louisiana State University Press, 1991.

Clements, Kendrick. *The Presidency of Woodrow Wilson*. Lawrence: University Press of Kansas, 1992.

Coclanis, Peter A. *The Shadow of a Dream: Economic Life and Death in the South Carolina Low Country, 1670–1920*. New York: Oxford University Press, 1988.

Cook, Raymond Allen. *Fire from the Flint: The Amazing Careers of Thomas Dixon*. Winston-Salem, N.C.: J. F. Blair, 1968.

Cooper, William J., Jr. *The Conservative Regime: South Carolina, 1877–1890*. Baltimore: Johns Hopkins University Press, 1968. Reprint, Baton Rouge: Louisiana State University Press, 1991.

Cox, LaWanda. *Lincoln and Black Freedom*. Columbia: University of South Carolina Press, 1981.

Crofts, Daniel. *Reluctant Confederates: Upper South Unionists in the Secession Crisis*. Chapel Hill: University of North Carolina Press, 1989.

Crow, Jeffrey J., Paul D. Escott, and Charles L. Flynn Jr., eds. *Race, Class, and Politics in Southern History: Essays in Honor of Robert F. Durden*. Baton Rouge: Louisiana State University Press, 1989.

Davis, David Brion. *The Problem of Slavery in the Age of Revolution, 1770–1823*. Ithaca, N.Y.: Cornell University Press, 1975.

——. *The Slave Power Conspiracy and the Paranoid Style*. Baton Rouge: Louisiana State University Press, 1969.

Davis, William Watson. *The Civil War and Reconstruction in Florida*. New York: Columbia University Press, 1913.

De Santis, Vincent P. *Republicans Face the Southern Question: The New Departure Years, 1877–1897*. Baltimore: Johns Hopkins University Press, 1959.

Devlin, George A. *South Carolina and Black Migration, 1865–1940: In Search of the Promised Land*. New York: Garland, 1990.

Du Bois, W. E. B. *Black Reconstruction in America, 1860–1880*. New York: Atheneum, 1935.

Durden, Robert F. *The Climax of Populism: The Election of 1896*. Lexington: University Press of Kentucky, 1965.

Dyer, Thomas G. *Theodore Roosevelt and the Idea of Race*. Baton Rouge: Louisiana State University Press, 1980.

Edgar, Walter. *South Carolina: A History*. Columbia: University of South Carolina Press, 1998.

Edmonds, Helen G. *The Negro and Fusion Politics in North Carolina, 1894–1901*. Chapel Hill: University of North Carolina Press, 1951.

Edwards, Laura F. *Gendered Strife and Confusion: The Political Culture of Reconstruction*. Urbana: University of Illinois Press, 1997.

Edwards, Rebecca. *Angels in the Machinery: Gender in American Party Politics from the Civil War to the Progressive Era*. New York: Oxford University Press, 1997.

Egerton, Douglas R. *Gabriel's Rebellion: The Virginia Slave Conspiracies of 1800 and 1802*. Chapel Hill: University of North Carolina Press, 1993.

Eubanks, John Evans. *Ben Tillman's Baby: The Dispensary System of South Carolina, 1892–1915*. Augusta, Ga.: Tidwell, [1950].

Faust, Drew Gilpin. *James Henry Hammond and the Old South: A Design for Mastery*. Baton Rouge: Louisiana State University Press, 1982.

———. *Mothers of Invention: Women of the Slaveholding South in the American Civil War*. Chapel Hill: University of North Carolina Press, 1996.

———. *A Sacred Circle: The Dilemma of the Intellectual in the Old South, 1840–1860*. Philadelphia: University of Pennsylvania Press, 1977.

Fernald, Edward A., and Elizabeth D. Purdum, eds. *Atlas of Florida*. Gainesville: University of Florida Press, 1992.

Ferrell, Henry C., Jr. *Claude A. Swanson: A Political Biography*. Lexington: University Press of Kentucky, 1985.

Fields, Barbara J. *Slavery and Freedom on the Middle Ground: Maryland during the Nineteenth Century*. New Haven: Yale University Press, 1985.

Flynn, Charles L. *White Land, Black Labor: Caste and Class in Late Nineteenth-Century Georgia*. Baton Rouge: Louisiana State University Press, 1983.

Foner, Eric. *Reconstruction: America's Unfinished Revolution, 1863–1877*. New York: Harper & Row, 1988.

Ford, Lacy K., Jr. *Origins of Southern Radicalism: The South Carolina Up-Country, 1800–1860*. New York: Oxford University Press, 1988.

Foster, Gaines. *Ghosts of the Confederacy: Defeat, the Lost Cause, and the Emergence of the New South, 1865–1913*. New York: Oxford University Press, 1987.

Fox-Genovese, Elizabeth. *Within the Plantation Household: Black and White Women of the Old South*. Chapel Hill: University of North Carolina Press, 1988.

Fox-Genovese, Elizabeth, and Eugene D. Genovese. *Fruits of Merchant Capital: Slavery and Bourgeois Property in the Rise and Expansion of Capitalism*. New York: Oxford University Press, 1983.

Franklin, John Hope. *The Militant South, 1800–1861*. Cambridge: Harvard University Press, 1956.

Franklin, John Hope, and Loren Schweninger. *Runaway Slaves: Rebels on the Plantation*. New York: Oxford University Press, 1999.

Fraser, Walter J., Jr. *Charleston! Charleston!: The History of a Southern City.* Columbia: University of South Carolina Press, 1989.

Fredrickson, George M. *The Arrogance of Race: Historical Perspectives on Slavery, Racism, and Social Inequality.* Middletown, Conn.: Wesleyan University Press, 1988.

———. *The Black Image in the White Mind: The Debate on Afro-American Character and Destiny, 1817–1914.* New York: Harper & Row, 1971.

———. *White Supremacy: A Comparative Study in American and South African History.* New York: Oxford University Press, 1981.

Freehling, William W. *Prelude to Civil War: The Nullification Controversy in South Carolina, 1816–1836.* New York: Harper & Row, 1968.

Friedman, Lawrence J. *The White Savage: Racial Fantasies in the Postbellum South.* Englewood Cliffs, N.J.: Prentice-Hall, 1970.

Gaither, Gerald H. *Blacks and the Populist Revolt: Ballots and Bigotry in the "New South."* Tuscaloosa: University of Alabama Press, 1977.

Gallagher, Gary W. *The Confederate War.* Cambridge: Harvard University Press, 1997.

Gaston, Paul M. *The New South Creed: A Study in Southern Myth-Making.* Baton Rouge: Louisiana State University Press, 1976.

Genovese, Eugene D. *Roll, Jordan, Roll: The World the Slaves Made.* New York: Pantheon, 1974.

Gilje, Paul A. *Rioting in America.* Bloomington: University of Indiana Press, 1996.

Gilmore, Glenda E. *Gender and Jim Crow: Women and the Politics of White Supremacy in North Carolina, 1896–1920.* Chapel Hill: University of North Carolina Press, 1996.

Glymph, Thavolia, and John J. Kushma, eds. *Essays on the Postbellum Southern Economy.* College Station: Texas A & M Press for University of Texas at Arlington, 1985.

Goldberg, Michael. *An Army of Women: Gender and Politics in Gilded Age Kansas.* Baltimore: Johns Hopkins University Press, 1997.

Goodwyn, Lawrence. *Democratic Promise: The Populist Moment in America.* New York: Oxford University Press, 1976.

Gore, Blinzy L. *On a Hilltop High: The Origin and History of Claflin College to 1894.* Spartanburg, S.C.: Reprint Company, 1994.

Gossett, Thomas F. *Race: The History of an Idea in America.* New York: Schocken, 1965.

Gould, Lewis L. *The Presidency of Theodore Roosevelt.* Lawrence: University Press of Kansas, 1991.

Gould, Stephen Jay. *The Mismeasure of Man.* New York: Oxford University Press, 1981.

Grantham, Dewey W. *The Life and Death of the Solid South: A Political History.* Lexington: University Press of Kentucky, 1988.

———. *Southern Progressivism: The Reconciliation of Progress and Tradition.* Knoxville: University of Tennessee Press, 1983.

Green, Elna C. *Southern Strategies: Southern Women and the Woman Suffrage Question.* Chapel Hill: University of North Carolina Press, 1997.

Green, Fletcher M., ed. *Essays in Southern History Presented to Joseph Gregoire de Roulhac Hamilton.* Chapel Hill: University of North Carolina Press, 1949.

Greenberg, Kenneth. *Honor and Slavery: Lies, Duels, Noses, Masks, Dressing as a*

Woman, Gifts, Strangers, Humanitarianism, Death, Slave Rebellions, the Proslavery Argument, Baseball, Hunting, and Gambling in the Old South. Princeton: Princeton University Press, 1996.

Hackney, Sheldon. *Populism to Progressivism in Alabama*. Princeton: Princeton University Press, 1969.

Hahn, Steven. *The Roots of Southern Populism: Yeoman Farmers and the Transformation of the Georgia Upcountry, 1850–1890*. New York: Oxford University Press, 1983.

Hale, Grace Elizabeth. *Making Whiteness: The Culture of Segregation in the South, 1890–1940*. New York: Pantheon, 1998.

Hall, Jacquelyn Dowd. *Revolt against Chivalry: Jesse Daniel Ames and the Women's Campaign against Lynching*. Rev. ed. New York: Columbia University Press, 1993.

Hamm, Richard F. *Shaping the Eighteenth Amendment*. Chapel Hill: University of North Carolina Press, 1995.

Harlan, Louis, ed. *The Booker T. Washington Papers*. 14 vols. Urbana: University of Illinois Press, 1972–89.

Harris, J. William. *Plain Folk and Gentry in a Slave Society: White Liberty and Black Slavery in Augusta's Hinterlands*. Middletown, Conn: Wesleyan University Press, 1985.

Hearden, Patrick J. *Independence and Empire: The New South's Cotton Mill Campaign, 1865–1901*. DeKalb: Northern Illinois University Press, 1982.

Hennig, Helen K. *August Kohn, Versatile South Carolinian*. Columbia: University of South Carolina Press, 1949.

Henry, H. M. *Police Control of the Slave in South Carolina*. Emory, Va., 1914.

Hicks, John D. *The Populist Revolt: A History of the Farmers' Alliance and the People's Party*. Lincoln: University of Nebraska Press, 1931. Reprint, Minneapolis: University of Minnesota Press, 1955.

Hindus, Michael S. *Prison and Plantation: Crime, Justice, and Authority in Massachusetts and South Carolina*. Chapel Hill: University of North Carolina Press, 1980.

Hodes, Martha. *White Women, Black Men: Illicit Sex in the Nineteenth-Century South*. New Haven: Yale University Press, 1997.

——, ed. *Sex, Love, Race: Crossing Boundaries in North American History*. New York: New York University Press, 1999.

Hofstadter, Richard. *The Age of Reform: From Bryan to F. D. R.* New York: Vintage, 1955.

Hollis, Daniel Walker. *College to University*. Vol. 2 of *University of South Carolina*. Columbia: University of South Carolina Press, 1956.

Holmes, William F. *The White Chief: James Kimble Vardaman*. Baton Rouge: Louisiana State University Press, 1970.

Holt, Thomas. *Black over White: Negro Political Leadership in South Carolina during Reconstruction*. Urbana: University of Illinois Press, 1977.

Hunter, Tera. *To 'Joy My Freedom: Southern Black Women's Lives and Labors after the Civil War*. Cambridge: Harvard University Press, 1997.

Hyman, Michael R. *The Anti-Redeemers: Hill-Country Political Dissidents in the Lower South from Redemption to Populism*. Baton Rouge: Louisiana State University Press, 1990.

Ignatiev, Noel. *How the Irish Became White*. New York: Routledge, 1995.

Jacobson, Matthew Frye. *Whiteness of a Different Color: European Immigrants and the Alchemy of Race.* Cambridge: Harvard University Press, 1998.

Jarrell, Hampton M. *Wade Hampton and the Negro: The Road Not Taken.* Columbia: University of South Carolina Press, 1950.

Jaynes, Gerald David. *Branches without Roots: Genesis of the Black Working Class in the American South, 1862–1882.* New York: Oxford University Press, 1986.

Jefferson, Thomas. *Notes on the State of Virginia.* Edited by William Peden. New York: Norton, 1972.

Jenkins, Warren M. *Steps along the Way: The Origin and Development of the South Carolina Conference of the Central Jurisdiction of the Methodist Church.* Columbia: University of South Carolina Press, 1967.

Jervey, Theodore D. *The Slave Trade: Slavery and Color.* Columbia: University of South Carolina Press, 1925.

Jones, Lewis Pinckney. *Stormy Petrel: N. G. Gonzales and His State.* Columbia: University of South Carolina Press, 1973.

Jones, Norrece T., Jr. *Born a Child of Freedom, yet a Slave: Mechanisms of Control and Strategies of Resistance in Antebellum South Carolina.* Hanover, N.H.: Wesleyan University Press and University Press of New England, 1990.

Jordan, Ervin. *Black Confederates and Afro-Yankees in Civil War Virginia.* Charlottesville: University Press of Virginia, 1995.

Jordan, Frank E., Jr. *The Primary State: A History of the Democratic Party in South Carolina, 1876–1962.* N.p., n.d.

Kazin, Michael. *The Populist Persuasion: An American History.* New York: Basic Books, 1995.

Kerber, Linda K. *Women of the Republic: Intellect and Ideology in Revolutionary America.* Chapel Hill: University of North Carolina Press, 1980.

Key, V. O., Jr. *Southern Politics in State and Nation.* New York: Vintage, 1949.

Kirby, Jack Temple. *Darkness at the Dawning: Race and Reform in the Progressive South.* Philadelphia: Lippincott, 1972.

Kirwan, Albert D. *Revolt of the Rednecks: Mississippi Politics, 1876–1925.* New York: Harper & Row, 1965.

Klein, Rachel. *Unification of a Slave State: The Rise of the Planter Class in the South Carolina Backcountry, 1760–1808.* Chapel Hill: University of North Carolina Press, 1990.

Kolko, Gabriel. *Railroads and Regulation, 1877–1916.* Princeton: Princeton University Press, 1965.

Kousser, J. Morgan. *The Shaping of Southern Politics: Suffrage Restriction and the Establishment of the One-Party South, 1880–1910.* New Haven: Yale University Press, 1974.

Lamson, Peggy. *The Glorious Failure: Black Congressman Robert B. Elliott and the Reconstruction in South Carolina.* New York: Norton, 1973.

Levine, Lawrence. *Black Culture and Black Consciousness: Afro-American Folk Thought from Slavery to Freedom.* New York: Oxford University Press, 1977.

———. *Defender of the Faith: William Jennings Bryan, the Last Decade, 1915–1925.* Cambridge: Harvard University Press, 1965.

——. *The Unpredictable Past: Explorations in American Cultural History*. New York: Oxford University Press, 1993.

Lewontin, R. C., Steven Rose, and Leon J. Kamin. *Not in Our Genes: Biology, Ideology, and Human Nature*. New York: Pantheon, 1984.

Link, William A. *The Paradox of Southern Progressivism*. Chapel Hill: University of North Carolina Press, 1992.

Litwack, Leon. *Trouble in Mind: Black Southerners in the Jim Crow South*. New York: Knopf, 1998.

Litwack, Leon, and August Meier, eds. *Black Leaders of the Nineteenth Century*. Urbana: University of Illinois Press, 1988.

Logue, Cal M., and Howard Dorgan, eds. *The Oratory of Southern Demagogues*. Baton Rouge: Louisiana State University Press, 1981.

Luker, Ralph. *The Social Gospel in Black and White: American Racial Reform, 1885–1912*. Chapel Hill: University of North Carolina Press, 1991.

Luthin, Reinhard H. *American Demagogues: Twentieth Century*. Boston: Beacon, 1954.

McArthur, Judith N., and Orville Vernon Burton. *A Gentleman and an Officer: A Military and Social History of James B. Griffin's Civil War*. New York: Oxford University Press, 1996.

McCandless, Amy Thompson. *The Past in the Present: Women's Higher Education in the Twentieth-Century American South*. Tuscaloosa: University of Alabama Press, 1999.

McCoy, Drew R. *The Elusive Republic: Political Economy in Jeffersonian America*. Chapel Hill: University of North Carolina Press, 1980.

McCurry, Stephanie. *Masters of Small Worlds: Yeoman Households, Gender Relations, and the Political Culture of the Antebellum South Carolina Low Country*. New York: Oxford University Press, 1995.

McGerr, Michael E. *The Decline of Popular Politics: The American North, 1865–1928*. New York: Oxford University Press, 1986.

McLaurin, Melton A. *Paternalism and Protest: Southern Cotton Mill Workers and Organized Labor, 1875–1905*. Westport, Conn.: Greenwood, 1971.

MacLean, Nancy. *Behind the Mask of Chivalry: The Making of the Second Ku Klux Klan*. New York: Oxford University Press, 1994.

McMath, Robert C., Jr. *American Populism: A Social History, 1877–1898*. New York: Hill & Wang, 1993.

——. *Populist Vanguard: A History of the Southern Farmers' Alliance*. Chapel Hill: University of North Carolina Press, 1975.

McPherson, James M. *Battle Cry of Freedom*. New York: Oxford University Press, 1988.

Margo, Robert A. *Disenfranchisement, School Finance, and the Economics of Segregated Schools in the United States South, 1890–1910*. New York: Garland, 1985.

——. *Race and Schooling in the South, 1880–1950*. Chicago: University of Chicago Press, 1990.

Miller, Edward A., Jr. *Gullah Statesman: Robert Smalls from Slavery to Congress, 1839–1915*. Columbia: University of South Carolina Press, 1995.

Miller, Wilbur R. *Revenuers and Moonshiners: Enforcing Federal Liquor Law in the Mountain South, 1865–1900*. Chapel Hill: University of North Carolina Press, 1991.

Moore, John Hammond. *Columbia and Richland County: A South Carolina Community, 1740–1990.* Columbia: University of South Carolina Press, 1993.

Moore, Winfred B., Jr., Joseph F. Tripp, and Lyon G. Tyler Jr., eds. *Developing Dixie: Modernization in a Traditional Society.* New York: Greenwood, 1988.

Morgan, Edmund M. *American Slavery, American Freedom: The Ordeal of Colonial Virginia.* New York: Norton, 1975.

Morison, Elting E., et al., eds. *The Letters of Theodore Roosevelt.* 8 vols. Cambridge: Harvard University Press, 1951–54.

National Association for the Advancement of Colored People. *Thirty Years of Lynching in the United States, 1889–1918.* New York: The Association, 1919.

Newby, I. A. *Black Carolinians: A History of Blacks in South Carolina from 1895 to 1968.* Columbia: University of South Carolina Press, 1973.

———. *Jim Crow's Defense: Anti-Negro Thought in America, 1900–1930.* Baton Rouge: Louisiana State University Press, 1965.

———, ed. *The Development of Segregationist Thought.* Homewood, Ill.: Dorsey, 1968.

Nolen, Claude H. *The Negro's Image in the South: The Anatomy of White Supremacy.* Lexington: University Press of Kentucky, 1968.

Oakes, James. *Slavery and Freedom: An Interpretation of the Old South.* New York: Knopf, 1990.

Oates, Stephen. *Fires of Jubilee: Nat Turner's Fierce Rebellion.* New York: Harper & Row, 1975.

Ownby, Ted. *Subduing Satan: Religion, Recreation, and Manhood in the Rural South, 1865–1920.* Chapel Hill: University of North Carolina Press, 1990.

Painter, Nell Irvin. *Exodusters: Black Migration to Kansas after Reconstruction.* New York: Knopf, 1976.

———. *Standing at Armageddon: The United States, 1877–1919.* New York: Norton, 1987.

Palmer, Bruce. *"Man over Money": The Southern Populist Critique of American Capitalism.* Chapel Hill: University of North Carolina Press, 1980.

Payne, Charles M. *I've Got the Light of Freedom: The Organizing Tradition and the Mississippi Freedom Struggle.* Berkeley: University of California Press, 1995.

Poe, Clarence. *My First 80 Years.* Chapel Hill: University of North Carolina Press, 1963.

Pollack, Norman. *The Just Polity: Populism, Law, and Human Welfare.* Urbana: University of Illinois Press, 1987.

———. *The Populist Response to Industrial America.* New York: Norton, 1962.

Potter, David M. *The Impending Crisis, 1848–1861.* New York: Harper, 1976.

Prather, H. Leon. *We Have Taken a City: Wilmington Racial Massacre and Coup of 1898.* Rutherford, N.J.: Fairleigh Dickinson University Press, 1984.

Pritchard, C. H. *Col. D. Wyatt Aiken, South Carolina's Militant Agrarian.* N.p., 1970.

Rabinowitz, Howard. *Race Relations in the Urban South, 1865–1900.* New York: Oxford University Press, 1978.

Ransom, Roger L., and Richard Sutch. *One Kind of Freedom: The Economic Consequences of Emancipation.* New York: Cambridge University Press, 1977.

Ritter, Gretchen. *Goldbugs and Greenbacks: The Antimonopoly Tradition and the Politics of Finance in America, 1865–1896*. New York: Cambridge University Press, 1997.

Roark, James L. *Masters without Slaves: Southern Planters in the Civil War and Reconstruction*. New York: Norton, 1977.

Roediger, David. *The Wages of Whiteness: Race and the Making of the American Working Class*. New York: Verso, 1991.

Rogers, George C., Jr. *The History of Georgetown County, South Carolina*. Columbia: University of South Carolina Press, 1970.

Rose, Willie Lee. *Rehearsal for Reconstruction: The Port Royal Experiment*. New York: Oxford University Press, 1976.

Salvatore, Nick. *Eugene V. Debs: Citizen and Socialist*. Urbana: University of Illinois Press, 1982.

Saville, Julie. *The Work of Reconstruction: From Slave to Wage Laborer in South Carolina, 1860–1870*. Cambridge: Cambridge University Press, 1995.

Saxton, Alexander. *The Rise and Fall of the White Republic: Class Politics and Mass Culture in Nineteenth-Century America*. New York: Verso, 1990.

Schwalm, Leslie. *A Hard Fight for We: Women's Transition from Slavery to Freedom in South Carolina*. Urbana: University of Illinois Press, 1997.

Scott, Joan Wallach. *Gender and the Politics of History*. New York: Columbia University Press, 1988.

Shaw, Barton C. *The Wool-Hat Boys: Georgia's Populist Party*. Baton Rouge: Louisiana State University Press, 1984.

Simkins, Francis Butler. *Pitchfork Ben Tillman—South Carolinian*. Baton Rouge: Louisiana State University Press, 1944. Reprint, Baton Rouge: Louisiana State University Press, 1967.

———. *The Tillman Movement in South Carolina*. Durham: Duke University Press, 1926. Reprint, Gloucester, Mass.: Peter Smith, 1964.

Simkins, Francis Butler, and Robert Hilliard Woody. *South Carolina during Reconstruction*. Chapel Hill: University of North Carolina Press, 1932.

Simon, Bryant. *A Fabric of Defeat: The Politics of South Carolina Millhands, 1910–1948*. Chapel Hill: University of North Carolina Press, 1998.

Singletary, Otis A. *Negro Militia and Reconstruction*. New York: McGraw-Hill, 1963.

Smedley, Katherine. *Martha Schofield and the Re-Education of the South, 1839–1916*. Lewiston, N.Y.: E. Mellen Press, 1987.

Smith, Rogers M. *Civic Ideals: Conflicting Visions of Citizenship in U.S. History*. New Haven: Yale University Press, 1997.

Spear, Alan. *Black Chicago: Making of a Negro Ghetto, 1890–1920*. Chicago: University of Chicago Press, 1967.

Stark, John D. *Damned Upcountryman: William Watts Ball, a Study in American Conservatism*. Durham: Duke University Press, 1968.

Steinfeld, Robert J. *The Invention of Free Labor: The Employment Relation in English and American Law and Culture, 1350–1870*. Chapel Hill: University of North Carolina Press, 1991.

Stowe, Steven. *Intimacy and Power in the Old South: Ritual in the Lives of the Planters*. Baltimore: Johns Hopkins University Press, 1987.

Stowell, Jay S. *Methodist Adventures in Negro Education.* New York: Methodist Book Concern, 1922.
Thompson, E. P. *Customs in Common: Studies in Traditional Popular Culture.* New York: New Press, 1993.
Thornbrough, Emma Lou. *T. Thomas Fortune, Militant Journalist.* Chicago: University of Chicago Press, 1972.
Tindall, George Brown. *The Persistent Tradition in New South Politics.* Baton Rouge: Louisiana State University Press, 1975.
———. *South Carolina Negroes, 1877–1900.* Columbia: University of South Carolina Press, 1952. Reprint, Baton Rouge: Louisiana State University Press, 1966.
———, ed. *A Populist Reader.* New York: Harper & Row, 1966. Reprint, Gloucester, Mass.: Peter Smith, 1976.
Tocqueville, Alexis de. *Democracy in America.* Translated by George Lawrence; edited by J. P. Mayer. New York: Harper, 1988.
Trelease, Allen W. *White Terror: The Ku Klux Klan Conspiracy and Southern Reconstruction.* Baton Rouge: Louisiana State University Press, 1995.
Tuttle, William. *Race Riot: Chicago in the Red Summer of 1919.* New York: Atheneum, 1970.
Tyson, Timothy B. *Radio Free Dixie: Robert F. Williams and the Roots of Black Power.* Chapel Hill: University of North Carolina Press, 1999.
Underwood, James Lowell. *The Constitution of South Carolina.* Vol. 2, *The Journey toward Local Self-Government.* Columbia: University of South Carolina Press, 1989.
Unger, Irwin. *The Greenback Era: A Social and Political History of American Finance, 1865–1879.* Princeton: Princeton University Press, 1964.
Uya, Okon Edet. *From Slavery to Public Service: Robert Smalls, 1839–1915.* New York: Oxford University Press, 1971.
Wallace, David Duncan. *The History of South Carolina.* 4 vols. New York: American Historical Society, 1934.
———. *The South Carolina Constitution of 1895.* Columbia: University of South Carolina Press, 1927.
Wang, Xi. *The Trial of Democracy: Black Suffrage and Northern Republicans, 1860–1910.* Athens: University of Georgia Press, 1997.
Wells, Tom Henderson. *The Slave Ship Wanderer.* Athens: University of Georgia Press, 1967.
Wheeler, Marjorie Spruill. *New Women of the New South: The Leaders of the Woman Suffrage Movement in the Southern States.* New York: Oxford University Press, 1993.
Whites, LeeAnn. *The Civil War as a Crisis in Gender: Augusta, Georgia, 1860–1890.* Athens: University of Georgia Press, 1995.
Williamson, Joel. *After Slavery: The Negro in South Carolina during Reconstruction, 1861–1877.* Chapel Hill: University of North Carolina Press, 1965. Reprint, New York: Norton, 1975.
———. *The Crucible of Race: Black-White Relations in the American South since Emancipation.* New York: Oxford University Press, 1984.
———. *A Rage for Order: Black-White Relations in the American South since Emancipation.* New York: Oxford University Press, 1986.

Woodman, Harold D. *King Cotton and His Retainers: Financing and Marketing the Cotton Crop of the South, 1800–1925*. Lexington: University Press of Kentucky, 1968.

———. *New South—New Law: The Legal Foundations of Credit and Labor Relations in the Postbellum Agricultural South*. Baton Rouge: Louisiana State University Press, 1995.

Woodward, C. Vann. *Origins of the New South, 1877–1913*. Baton Rouge: Louisiana State University Press, 1951.

———. *The Strange Career of Jim Crow*. 3d ed. New York: Galaxy, 1974.

———. *Tom Watson, Agrarian Rebel*. New York: Macmillan, 1938. Reprint, New York: Oxford University Press, 1963.

Wyatt-Brown, Bertram. *Southern Honor: Ethics and Behavior in the Old South*. New York: Oxford University Press, 1982.

Wynne, Lewis N. *The Continuity of Cotton: Planter Politics in Georgia, 1865–1892*. Macon, Ga.: Mercer University Press, 1986.

Zuczek, Richard. *State of Rebellion: Reconstruction in South Carolina*. Columbia: University of South Carolina Press, 1996.

ARTICLES, DISSERTATIONS, THESES, AND PAPERS

Abramowitz, Jack. "The Negro in the Populist Movement." *Journal of Negro History* 38 (July 1953): 257–89.

Arsenault, Ray. "The Folklore of Southern Demagoguery." In *Is There a Southern Political Tradition?*, edited by Charles Eagles, 79–132. Jackson: University Press of Mississippi, 1996.

Bailey, Harris M., Jr. "The Only Game in Town: The South Carolina Republican Party in the Post-Reconstruction Era." *Proceedings of the South Carolina Historical Association* (1992): 76–86.

Baker, Bruce E. "The 'Hoover Scare' in South Carolina, 1887: An Attempt to Organize Black Farm Labor." *Labor History* 40, no. 3 (1999): 261–82.

Banner, James. "The Problem of South Carolina." In *The Hofstadter Aegis: A Memorial*, edited by Stanley Elkins and Eric McKitrick, 60–93. New York: Knopf, 1974.

Bartley, Numan V. "Another New South?" *Georgia Historical Quarterly* 65 (Summer 1981): 121–37.

Begley, Paul R. "Governor Richardson Faces the Tillman Challenge." *South Carolina Historical Magazine* 89, no. 2 (1988): 119–26.

Bennett, Judith M. "Feminism and History." *Gender and History* 1 (1989): 251–72.

Boggs, Doyle W. "Charleston Politics, 1900–1930." In *Proceedings of the South Carolina Historical Association* (1979): 1–13.

———. "John Patrick Grace and the Politics of Reform in South Carolina, 1900–1931." Ph.D. dissertation, University of South Carolina, 1977.

Brown, Elsa Barkley. "Negotiating and Transforming the Public Sphere: African American Political Life in the Transition from Slavery to Freedom." *Public Culture* 7 (1994): 107–46.

———. "Womanist Consciousness: Maggie Lena Walker and the Independent Order of St. Luke." *Signs* 14 (Spring 1989): 610–33.

Brown, R. Ben. "The Southern Range: A Study in Nineteenth Century Law and Society." Ph.D. dissertation, University of Michigan, 1993.

Burnside, Ronald Dantan. "The Governorship of Coleman Livingston Blease of South Carolina." Ph.D. dissertation, Indiana University, 1963.

Burton, Orville Vernon. "Black Leadership in Edgefield." *Proceedings of the South Carolina Historical Association* (1988): 27–38.

——. "The Effects of the Civil War and Reconstruction on the Coming of Age of Southern Males, Edgefield County, South Carolina." In *The Web of Southern Social Relations: Women, Family, and Education*, edited by Walter J. Fraser Jr., R. Frank Saunders Jr., and Jon L. Wakelyn, 204–24. Athens: University of Georgia Press, 1985.

——. "On the Confederate Homefront: The Transformation of Values from Community to Nation in Edgefield, South Carolina." Paper presented at the Woodrow Wilson Center for Scholars, 19 July 1989; in possession of author.

——. "Race and Reconstruction: Edgefield County, South Carolina." *Journal of Social History* 12 (Fall 1978): 31–56.

——. "The Rise and Fall of Afro-American Town Life." In *Toward a New South?*, edited by Orville Vernon Burton and Robert C. McMath, 152–92. Westport, Conn.: Greenwood, 1988.

——. "Ungrateful Servants?: Edgefield's Black Reconstruction; Part 1 of the Total History of Edgefield County, South Carolina." Ph.D. dissertation, Princeton University, 1976.

Carlton, David L., and Peter A. Coclanis. "Capital Mobilization and Southern Industry, 1880–1905: The Case of the Carolina Piedmont." *Journal of Economic History* 49 (Mar. 1989): 73–94.

Carter, Dan T. "The Anatomy of Fear: The Christmas Day Insurrection Scare of 1865." *Journal of Southern History* 42 (Aug. 1976): 345–64.

Carter, Wingard Williams. "State Support for Public Schools in South Carolina since 1895." M.A. thesis, University of South Carolina, 1936.

Church, Joseph. "The Farmers' Alliance and the Populist Movement in South Carolina, 1887–1896." M.A. thesis, University of South Carolina, 1953.

Clark, E. Culpepper. "Pitchfork Ben Tillman and the Emergence of Southern Demagoguery." *Quarterly Journal of Speech* 69 (1983): 423–33.

Cooper, William J., Jr. "Economics or Race: An Analysis of the Gubernatorial Election of 1890 in South Carolina." *South Carolina Historical Magazine* 73 (Oct. 1972): 209–19.

Crofts, Daniel W. "The Blair Bill and the Elections Bill: The Congressional Aftermath to Reconstruction." Ph.D. dissertation, Yale University, 1968.

Crow, Jeffrey J. "An Apartheid for the South." In *Race, Class, and Politics in Southern History: Essays in Honor of Robert F. Durden*, edited by Jeffrey J. Crow, Paul D. Escott, and Charles L. Flynn Jr., 216–59. Baton Rouge: Louisiana State University Press, 1989.

Crowe, Charles. "Tom Watson, Populists, and Blacks Reconsidered." *Journal of Negro History* 55 (1970): 99–116.

Dailey, Jane. "Deference and Violence in the Postbellum Urban South: Manners

and Massacres in Danville, Virginia." *Journal of Southern History* 63 (Aug. 1997): 553–90.
———. "Race, Sex, and Citizenship: Biracial Democracy in Readjuster Virginia, 1879–1883." Ph.D. dissertation, Princeton University, 1995.
Dubbert, Joe. "Progressivism and the Masculinity Crisis." *Psychohistory Review* 61 (1974): 443–55.
Duffy, John Joseph. "Charleston Politics in the Progressive Era." Ph.D. dissertation, University of South Carolina, 1963.
Dunlap, Leslie K. "The Reform of Rape Law and the Problem of White Men: Age-of-Consent Campaigns in the South, 1885–1910." In *Sex, Love, Race: Crossing Boundaries in North American History*, edited by Martha Hodes, 352–72. New York: New York University Press, 1999.
Easterby, J. H. "The Granger Movement in South Carolina." *Proceedings of the South Carolina Historical Association* (1931): 21–32.
Everett, Robert Burke. "Race Relations in South Carolina, 1900–1932." Ph.D. dissertation, University of Georgia, 1969.
Faust, Drew Gilpin. "The Rhetoric and Ritual of Agriculture in Antebellum South Carolina." *Journal of Southern History* 45 (Nov. 1979): 541–68.
———. "Southern Violence Revisited." *Reviews in American History* 13 (June 1985): 205–10.
Ferrell, Henry C., Jr. "Regional Rivalries, Congress, and MIC: The Norfolk and Charleston Navy Yards, 1913–1920." In *War, Business, and American Society: Historical Perspectives on the Military-Industrial Complex*, edited by B. F. Cooling, 59–72. Port Washington, N.Y.: Kennikat, 1977.
Fields, Barbara J. "Ideology and Race in American History." In *Region, Race, and Reconstruction: Essays in Honor of C. Vann Woodward*, edited by J. Morgan Kousser and James M. McPherson, 143–77. New York: Oxford University Press, 1982.
———. "Slavery, Race, and Ideology in the United States of America." *New Left Review* 181 (May/June 1990): 95–118.
Finnegan, Terence Robert. " 'At the Hands of Parties Unknown': Lynching in Mississippi and South Carolina, 1881–1940." Ph.D. dissertation, University of Illinois at Urbana–Champaign, 1992.
Ford, Lacy K., Jr. "Labor and Ideology in the Southern Upcountry: The Transition to Free-Labor Agriculture." In *The Southern Enigma: Essays on Race, Class, and Folk Culture*, edited by Walter J. Fraser and Winfred B. Moore, 25–41. Westport, Conn.: Greenwood, 1982.
———. "Origins of the Edgefield Tradition: The Late Antebellum Experience and the Roots of Political Insurgency." *South Carolina Historical Magazine* 98 (Oct. 1997): 328–48.
———. "Rednecks and Merchants: Economic Development and Social Tensions in the South Carolina Upcountry, 1865–1900." *Journal of American History* 71 (Sept. 1984): 294–318.
Franklin, John Hope. "*The Birth of a Nation*: Propaganda as History." In *Race and History: Selected Essays, 1938–1988*. Baton Rouge: Louisiana State University Press, 1989.

Fredrickson, George M. "The South and South Africa: Political Foundations of White Supremacy." In *The Evolution of Southern Culture*, edited by Numan V. Bartley, 68–86. Athens: University of Georgia Press, 1988.

Gatewood, Willard B. " 'The Remarkable Misses Rollin': Black Women in Reconstruction South Carolina." *South Carolina Historical Magazine* 92 (July 1991): 172–88.

———. "Theodore Roosevelt and the Southern Republicans: The Case of South Carolina, 1901–1904." *South Carolina Historical Magazine* 70 (Oct. 1969): 251–66.

Gaughan, Anthony. "Woodrow Wilson and the Legacy of the Civil War." *Civil War History* 43 (1997): 225–42.

Genovese, Eugene D. " 'Our Family, White and Black': Family and Household in the Southern Slaveholders' World View." In *In Joy and in Sorrow: Women, Family, and Marriage in the Victorian South, 1830–1900*, edited by Carol Bleser, 69–87. New York: Oxford University Press, 1991.

———. "Yeoman Farmers in a Slaveholders' Democracy." *Agricultural History* 49 (Apr. 1975): 331–42.

Gergel, Richard Mark. "Wade Hampton and the Rise of One Party Racial Orthodoxy in South Carolina." *Proceedings of the South Carolina Historical Association* (1977): 5–16.

Gilmore, Glenda E. "Murder, Memory, and the Flight of the Incubus." In *Democracy Betrayed: The Wilmington Race Riot of 1898 and Its Legacy*, edited by David S. Cecelski and Timothy B. Tyson, 73–94. Chapel Hill: University of North Carolina Press, 1998.

Godshalk, David Fort. "In the Wake of Riot: Atlanta's Struggle for Order, 1899–1919." Ph.D. dissertation, Yale University, 1992.

Goodwyn, Lawrence. "Populist Dreams and Negro Rights: East Texas as a Case Study." *American Historical Review* 76 (Dec. 1971): 1435–56.

Hackney, Sheldon. "Southern Violence." *American Historical Review* 74 (Feb. 1969): 906–25.

Hahn, Steven. "Class and State in Postemancipation Societies: Southern Planters in Comparative Perspective." *American Historical Review* 95 (Feb. 1990): 75–98.

———. "A Response: Common Cents or Historical Sense?" *Journal of Southern History* 59 (May 1993): 243–58.

Hall, Jacquelyn Dowd. " 'The Mind That Burns in Each Body': Women, Rape, and Racial Violence." In *Powers of Desire: The Politics of Sexuality*, edited by Anne Snitow, Christine Stansell, and Sharon Thompson, 328–49. New York: Monthly Review Press, 1983.

Hamm, Richard F. "Southern States' Liquor Policies and the Federal Tax System, 1880–1920." Paper presented at the annual meeting of the Southern Historical Association, Norfolk, Va., Nov. 1988.

Hammond, James Henry. "Letter to an English Abolitionist." In *Ideology of Slavery: Proslavery Thought in the Antebellum South, 1830–1860*, edited by Drew Gilpin Faust, 170–205. Baton Rouge: Louisiana State University Press, 1981.

Heath, Frederick M., and Harriet H. Kinard. "Prohibition in South Carolina, 1880–

1940: An Overview." *Proceedings of the South Carolina Historical Association* (1980): 118–32.

Hendrick, Carlanna Lindamood. "John Gary Evans: A Political Biography." Ph.D. dissertation, University of South Carolina, 1966.

Hodes, Martha. "The Sexualization of Reconstruction Politics: White Women and Black Men in the South after the Civil War." *Journal of the History of Sexuality* 3 (1993): 402–17.

Holleman, Sarah Edna. "Contributions of Benjamin Ryan Tillman to Higher Education for White Men of South Carolina from 1885 to 1895." M.A. thesis, Clemson University, 1952.

Holmes, William F. "The Arkansas Cotton Pickers' Strike of 1891 and the Demise of the Colored Farmers' Alliance." *Arkansas Historical Quarterly* 32 (Summer 1973): 107–19.

——. "The Demise of the Colored Farmers' Alliance." *Journal of Southern History* 41 (May 1975): 187–200.

——. "The Southern Farmers' Alliance and the Jute Cartel." *Journal of Southern History* 60 (Feb. 1994): 59–80.

Holt, Thomas. "Marking: Race, Race-Making, and the Writing of History." *American Historical Review* 100 (Feb. 1995): 1–20.

Janiewski, Dolores. "Southern Honor, Southern Dishonor: Managerial Ideology and the Construction of Gender, Race, and Class Relations in Southern Industry." In *Work Engendered: Toward a New History of American Labor*, edited by Ava Baron, 70–91. Ithaca, N.Y.: Cornell University Press, 1991.

Jeffrey, Julie Roy. "Women in the Southern Farmers' Alliance: A Reconsideration of the Role and Status of Women in the Late Nineteenth Century South." *Feminist Studies* 3 (1975): 72–91.

Johnson, Guion Griffis. "The Ideology of White Supremacy, 1876–1910." In *Essays in Southern History*, edited by Fletcher M. Green, 124–56. Chapel Hill: University of North Carolina Press, 1949.

Jones, Lewis Pinckney. "Two Roads Tried—And One Detour." *South Carolina Historical Magazine* 79 (July 1978): 207–18.

Kantor, Shawn Everett, and J. Morgan Kousser. "Common Sense or Commonwealth?: The Fence Law and Institutional Change in the Postbellum South." *Journal of Southern History* 59 (May 1993): 201–42.

——. "A Rejoinder: Two Visions of History." *Journal of Southern History* 59 (May 1993): 259–66.

Kantrowitz, Stephen. "The Two Faces of Domination in North Carolina, 1800–1898." In *Democracy Betrayed: The Wilmington Race Riot of 1898 and Its Legacy*, edited by David S. Cecelski and Timothy B. Tyson, 95–112. Chapel Hill: University of North Carolina Press, 1998.

Kremm, Thomas W., and Diane Neal. "Clandestine Black Labor Societies and White Fear: Hiram F. Hoover and the 'Cooperative Workers of America' in the South." *Labor History* 19, no. 2 (Spring 1978): 226–37.

Lebsock, Suzanne D. "Radical Reconstruction and the Property Rights of Southern Women." *Journal of Southern History* 43 (May 1977): 195–216.

Lott, Stanton Norris. "The Development of Education in Edgefield County, S.C., 1748–1930." M.A. thesis, University of South Carolina, 1930.
Mabry, William Alexander. "Ben Tillman Disfranchised the Negro." *South Atlantic Quarterly* 37 (Apr. 1938): 170–83.
McCurry, Stephanie. "The Politics of Yeoman Households in South Carolina." In *Divided Houses: Gender and the Civil War*, edited by Catherine Clinton and Nina Silber, 22–38. New York: Oxford University Press, 1992.
——. "The Two Faces of Republicanism: Gender and Proslavery Politics in Antebellum South Carolina." *Journal of American History* 78 (Mar. 1992): 1245–64.
McLaurin, Melton A. "Early Labor Union Organizational Efforts in South Carolina Cotton Mills, 1880–1905." *South Carolina Historical Magazine* 72 (Jan. 1971): 44–59.
MacLean, Nancy. "The Leo Frank Case Reconsidered: Gender and Sexual Politics in the Making of Reactionary Populism." *Journal of American History* 78 (Dec. 1991): 917–48.
Matthews, Linda M. "Keeping Down Jim Crow: The Railroads and the Separate Coach Bill in South Carolina." *South Atlantic Quarterly* 73 (Winter 1974): 117–29.
Mellen, Katherine M. "From Silence to Voice: Septima P. Clark and the African American Freedom Struggle." M.A. thesis, University of Wisconsin–Madison, 1997.
Mitchell, W. "The County Legislative Delegation in South Carolina County Government." M.A. thesis, University of North Carolina at Chapel Hill, 1940.
Moore, Jamie W. "Ben Tillman and Government for Hawaii." *Proceedings of the South Carolina Historical Association* (1973): 5–19.
Moore, John Hammond. "The Negro and Prohibition in Atlanta, 1885–1887." *South Atlantic Quarterly* 69 (Winter 1970): 38–57.
——. "South Carolina's Reaction to the Photoplay, *The Birth of a Nation*." *Proceedings of the South Carolina Historical Association* (1963): 30–40.
Moore, Winfred Bobo, Jr. "New South Statesman: The Political Career of James Francis Byrnes, 1911–1941." Ph.D. dissertation, Duke University, 1975.
——. "The 'Unrewarding Stone': James F. Byrnes and the Burden of Race, 1908–1944." In *The South Is Another Land*, edited by Bruce L. Clayton and John A. Salmond, 3–27. Westport, Conn.: Greenwood, 1987.
Neal, Diane. "Agrarian Reform versus Bourbon Democracy: The South Carolina Gubernatorial Campaign of 1890." *Proceedings of the South Carolina Historical Association* (1983): 5–14.
——. "Benjamin Ryan Tillman: The South Carolina Years, 1847–1894." Ph.D. dissertation, Kent State University, 1976.
——. " 'What Have They Done for Our Women?': The Impact of the Tillman Movement upon Higher Education for Women in South Carolina." *Proceedings of the South Carolina Historical Association* (1986): 8–16.
Neal, Peggy Diane. "Benjamin Ryan Tillman: His Role in the Founding and Early History of Winthrop College." Senior honors thesis, Winthrop College, 1970.

Nelson, Scott. "Livestock, Boundaries, and Public Space in Spartanburg: African American Men, Elite White Women, and the Spectacle of Conjugal Relations." In *Sex, Love, Race: Crossing Boundaries in North American History*, edited by Martha Hodes, 313–27. New York: New York University Press, 1999.

O'Malley, Michael. "Specie and Species: Race and the Money Question in Nineteenth Century America." *American Historical Review* 99 (Apr. 1994): 369–408.

Painter, Nell Irvin. "Martin Delany and Elitist Black Nationalism." In *Black Leaders of the Nineteenth Century*, edited by August Meier and Leon Litwack, 149–71. Urbana: University of Illinois Press, 1988.

———. " 'Social Equality,' Miscegenation, Labor, and Power." In *The Evolution of Southern Culture*, edited by Numan V. Bartley, 47–67. Athens: University of Georgia Press, 1988.

———. "Soul Murder and Slavery: Toward a Fully Loaded Cost Accounting." In *U.S. History as Women's History: New Feminist Essays*, edited by Linda K. Kerber, Alice Kessler-Harris, and Kathryn Kish Sklar, 125–46. Chapel Hill: University of North Carolina Press, 1995.

———. "Thinking about the Languages of Money and Race: A Response to Michael O'Malley, 'Specie and Species.' " *American Historical Review* 99 (Apr. 1994): 396–404.

Patton, James Welch. "The Republican Party in South Carolina, 1876–1895." In *Essays in Southern History*, edited by Fletcher M. Green, 91–111. Chapel Hill: University of North Carolina Press, 1949.

Pearson, Edward. "From Stono to Vesey: Slavery, Resistance, and Ideology in South Carolina, 1739–1822." Ph.D. dissertation, University of Wisconsin–Madison, 1992.

Perkins, Lindsey Saunders. "The Oratory of Benjamin Ryan Tillman." Ph.D. dissertation, Northwestern University, 1945.

Perman, Michael. "Counter Reconstruction: The Role of Violence in Southern Redemption." In *The Facts of Reconstruction: Essays in Honor of John Hope Franklin*, edited by Eric Anderson and Alfred A. Moss Jr., 121–40. Baton Rouge: Louisiana State University Press, 1991.

Prather, H. Leon. "The Origins of the Phoenix Racial Massacre of 1898." In *Developing Dixie: Modernization in a Traditional Society*, edited by Winfred B. Moore Jr., Joseph F. Tripp, and Lyon G. Tyler Jr., 59–72. New York: Greenwood, 1988.

———. "We Have Taken a City: A Centennial Essay." In *Democracy Betrayed: The Wilmington Race Riot of 1898 and Its Legacy*, edited by David S. Cecelski and Timothy B. Tyson, 15–41. Chapel Hill: University of North Carolina Press, 1998.

Robison, Daniel M. "From Tillman to Long: Some Striking Leaders of the Rural South." *Journal of Southern History* 3 (Aug. 1937): 289–310.

Rodgers, Daniel T. "In Search of Progressivism." *Reviews in American History* 10 (Dec. 1982): 113–32.

Rogin, Michael. " 'The Sword Became a Flashing Vision': D. W. Griffith's *The Birth of a Nation*." *Representations* 9 (Winter 1985): 150–95.

Rosengarten, Theodore. " 'I Stand Where My Boyhood Put Me': Reconsidering Woodward's *Tom Watson.*" *Georgia Historical Quarterly* 72 (Winter 1988): 684–97.

Saunders, Robert. "Southern Populists and the Negro, 1893–1895." *Journal of Negro History* 54 (July 1969): 240–61.

———. "The Transformation of Tom Watson, 1894–1895." *Georgia Historical Quarterly* 54 (Fall 1970): 339–56.

Saville, Julie. "Grassroots Reconstruction: Agricultural Labour and Collective Action in South Carolina, 1860–1868." *Slavery and Abolition* 12 (Dec. 1991): 173–82.

Seligmann, Herbert. "A South Carolina Independent of the 1880s: J. Hendrix McLane." N.p., 1965. John Augustus Hendrix McLane Papers, Manuscripts and Archives, Sterling Library, Yale University, New Haven, Conn.

Silverman, Max. "A Political and Intellectual History of the Silver Movement in the United States, 1888–1896." Ph.D. dissertation, New York University, 1986.

Simkins, Francis Butler. "The Election of 1876 in South Carolina." *South Atlantic Quarterly* 21 (July–Oct. 1922): 225–40, 335–51.

———. "Race Legislation in South Carolina since 1865." *South Atlantic Quarterly* 20 (Jan.–Apr. 1921): 61–71, 165–77.

Simon, Bryant. "The Appeal of Cole Blease: Race, Class, and Sex in the New South." *Journal of Southern History* 62 (Feb. 1996): 57–86.

Slaunwhite, Jerry L. "John L. M. Irby: The Creation of a Crisis." Ph.D. dissertation, University of South Carolina, 1973.

Smedley, Katherine. "Martha Schofield and the Rights of Women." *South Carolina Historical Magazine* 85 (July 1984): 195–210.

Stagg, J. C. A. "The Problem of Klan Violence: The South Carolina Up-Country, 1868–1871." *Journal of American Studies* 8 (1974): 303–18.

Stevenson, Brenda. "Distress and Discord in Virginia Slave Families, 1830–1860." In *In Joy and in Sorrow: Women, Family, and Marriage in the Victorian South, 1830–1900*, edited by Carol Bleser, 103–24. New York: Oxford University Press, 1991.

Stewart, James Brewer. " 'A Great Talking and Eating Machine': Patriarchy, Mobilization, and the Dynamics of Nullification in South Carolina." *Civil War History* 27 (1981): 197–220.

Stokes, Allen Heath. "Black and White Labor and the Development of the Southern Textile Industry, 1800–1920." Ph.D. dissertation, University of South Carolina, 1977.

Stone, Clarence. "Bleaseism and the 1912 Election in South Carolina." *North Carolina Historical Review* 40 (Winter 1963): 54–74.

Stroup, Rodger Emerson. "John L. McLaurin: A Political Biography." Ph.D. dissertation, University of South Carolina, 1980.

Taylor, Antoinette Elizabeth. "South Carolina and the Enfranchisement of Women: The Early Years." *South Carolina Historical Magazine* 77 (Apr. 1976): 115–26.

Thornton, J. Mills, III. "Fiscal Policy and the Failure of Radical Reconstruction in the Lower South." In *Region, Race, and Reconstruction: Essays in Honor of C. Vann Woodward*, edited by J. Morgan Kousser and James M. McPherson, 349–94. New York: Oxford University Press, 1982.

Tindall, George Brown. "The Campaign for the Disfranchisement of Negroes in South Carolina." *Journal of Southern History* 15 (May 1949): 212–34.

———. "The Question of Race in the South Carolina Constitutional Convention of 1895." *Journal of Negro History* 37 (July 1952): 277–303.

Trillin, Calvin. "State Secrets." *New Yorker*, 29 May 1995, 54–64.

Turner, James. "Understanding the Populists." *Journal of American History* 67 (Sept. 1980): 354–73.

Ulmer, Barbara Bellows. "Virginia Durant Young: New South Suffragist." M.A. thesis, University of South Carolina, 1979.

VanderZanden, James W. "The Ideology of White Supremacy." *Journal of the History of Ideas* 20 (June/Sept. 1959): 385–402.

Vandiver, Frank. "The Southerner as Extremist." In *The Idea of the South*, edited by Frank Vandiver, 43–56. Chicago: University of Chicago Press, 1964.

Wager, Daniel Hunt. "The Strongest Ties of Blood and Friendship: Company K, Fourteenth South Carolina Volunteer Infantry." M.A. thesis, Clemson University, 1996.

Weir, Robert M. "The South Carolinian as Extremist." *South Atlantic Quarterly* 74 (Winter 1975): 86–103.

Werner, Randolph Dennis. "Hegemony and Conflict: The Political Economy of a Southern Region, Augusta, Georgia, 1865–1895." Ph.D. dissertation, University of Virginia, 1977.

———. " 'New South' Carolina: Ben Tillman and the Rise of Bourgeois Politics, 1880–1893." In *Developing Dixie: Modernization in a Traditional Society*, edited by Winifred B. Moore, Joseph F. Tripp, and Lyon G. Tyler Jr., 149–65. Westport, Conn.: Greenwood, 1988.

West, Stephen A. "From Yeoman to Redneck in Upstate South Carolina, 1850–1915." Ph.D. dissertation, Columbia University, 1998.

Whites, LeeAnn. "The De Graffenreid Controversy: Class, Race, and Gender in the New South." *Journal of Southern History* 54 (Aug. 1988): 449–78.

———. "Love, Hate, Rape, Lynching: Rebecca Latimer Felton and the Gender Politics of Racial Violence." In *Democracy Betrayed: The Wilmington Race Riot of 1898 and Its Legacy*, edited by David S. Cecelski and Timothy B. Tyson, 143–62. Chapel Hill: University of North Carolina Press, 1998.

———. "Rebecca Latimer Felton and the Wife's Farm: The Class and Racial Politics of Gender Reform." *Georgia Historical Quarterly* 76 (Summer 1992): 354–72.

Wiener, Jonathan. "Class Structure and Economic Development in the American South, 1865–1955." *American Historical Review* 84 (Oct. 1979): 970–92.

Williamson, Gustavus G., Jr. "South Carolina Cotton Mills and the Tillman Movement." *Proceedings of the South Carolina Historical Association* (1949): 36–49.

Woodman, Harold D. "Sequel to Slavery: The New History Views the Post-Bellum South." *Journal of Southern History* 43 (Nov. 1977): 523–54.

Woody, Robert H. "Some Aspects of the Economic Condition of South Carolina after the Civil War." *North Carolina Historical Review* 7 (July 1930): 346–64.

Wyatt-Brown, Bertram. "The Mask of Obedience: Male Slave Psychology in the Old South." *American Historical Review* 93 (Dec. 1988): 1228–52.

Acknowledgments

I have spent much of the last decade in the company of Ben Tillman. During that time, countless people have asked me how I could stand it. The question still seems reasonable. The normal perils of the biographer do not apply in this case: unlike those writers who over time become disillusioned with their protagonists, I had no expectation at the outset that I would ever admire Ben Tillman. Nor, following another typical scenario, did I grow more fond of him along the way, although my respect for the power of his poisonous legacy has only increased with my understanding of it.

The raw materials were strange and at first unfamiliar, for my roots in the United States are in the deep North. My ancestors did not set foot on these shores until late in Ben Tillman's life. Yet in some way, I always knew that this story, or one like it, would eventually draw me in. I grew up in a comfortable world of assimilated, suburban Jewry, a world whose calm concealed a more perilous history. I now know that our unproblematic whiteness and the safety that came with it were only a generation old; as I look at that moment in time with a historian's eye, it no longer seems odd that I was always conscious of the death camps, barely twenty years gone when I was born. From that awareness came a terrified fascination with stories of men who mobilized fear into atrocity. From it, too, came a sense of urgency about the fears and violence troubling our own society—but not a real understanding of what had brought us all to that cold new world just past the assassinations and the riots. As Boston's struggles over bussing took place almost within earshot and as I sat by the radio with my father, watching the intensity of his attention to voices from Phnom Penh, what filtered through did not seem to match the complexities of reality, not even the protected reality I knew. I turned to history to find out why the world I lived in worked the way it did and how it might work differently. And once I turned to our past, I had to study the history of racial hierarchy, political violence, and coercive authority. My fears demanded it, and my hopes insisted on it.

I have been blessed with extraordinary fellow travelers on this road. They opened their doors, handed me books, shared their dinner, poured me drinks, played me records, brought me pie, heard me out, spoke their minds, helped me with my writing, and trusted me with their own. They offered insightful readings of papers, chapters, and even the whole manuscript. They leaned across tables from Nassau Street to Five Points to the corner of Atwood and Dunning, pushing me to think harder about my corner of the past. They brightened the corridors and conference rooms of this profession with their questions, quarrels, and conversation. I am deeply grateful to them all.

For four years, Tim Tyson has believed in this book and its author. I hesitate to remind him how many drafts of these chapters he has read along the way, and his own race to complete his first book provided much-needed proof that the job could not only be done but be done with grace and care. Despite his bullheaded insistence on studying the wrong century, his gifts as a historian, teacher, reader, and critic are matched only by his generosity of spirit. He is somehow always able to remind me why we do what we do—and why it matters. He and Perri, Hope, and Sam have offered me a warm, welcoming world to which I could always turn. They know how much this means to me.

I especially want to thank five people whose comments on the manuscript helped me pull it all together. For ten years, Walter Johnson has been a boon companion, a friend whose intellectual journey has enriched me and helped me make sense of my own. For almost as long, Vernon Burton and Glenda Gilmore have served as models of the kind of scholar and teacher I hope to be; when push came to shove, they gave this work the readings it needed. Ray Arsenault and Laura Edwards stepped in later, offering serious intellectual engagement and affirmation and showing me things about the work I had not yet seen.

Some of my most important teachers have been, well, my teachers. More than ten years ago, Susan Johnson suggested that I think about taking this path. Since my first days in graduate school, Nell Painter's questions and insights have helped me cut far more deeply into the material of Southern history and white supremacy than I could otherwise have done; as a mentor, critic, and ally, she gave me faith in my ability to shape this material and sustained my confidence as I acquired the critical and analytical tools with which to work it. My historical thinking and writing were also profoundly shaped at the outset by Dan Rodgers, John Murrin, and Jim McPherson, historians whose complementary gifts and insights made my graduate education rich and challenging.

I owe a great deal to other friends and colleagues, for help, advice, criticism, and encouragement: Steve Aron, who showed me how to make the transition from graduate student to faculty member; Bruce Baker; Jeanne Boydston, who has shared her critical intellect and sly wit; Ben Brown; David Cecelski, who wrote less of this book than he remembers; Jacob Cogan; Chuck Cohen; John Cooper; Bill Cronon; Jane Dailey; Leslie Dunlap; Rebecca Edwards; Bill Evans; Drew Faust; Lacy Ford; Tony Gaughan; Jess Gilbert; Lawrence Goodwyn; Linda Gordon; Steven Hahn; Grace Hale; Jacquelyn Hall; James Hill; Nancy Langston; Jean Lee; Grazia Lolla; Nancy MacLean; Florencia Mallon; Tony Michels; Cynthia Milton; John Hammond Moore; Ted Ownby; Ron Radano; David Roediger; Eden Rosenbush; Francisco Scarano; Diana Selig; Dick Sewell; Bryant Simon; Steve Stern; Steve Stowe; Harry Watson;

Craig Werner; Steve West; and several anonymous readers. Students in my graduate seminars offered challenging questions and helpful suggestions. To the extraordinary students Tim Tyson and I shared in "Southern Slavery, Southern Freedom"—especially Jay Driskell, Michael Kwas, Danielle McGuire, and Alison Stocking—I offer warm thanks. Every teacher should be so lucky.

On my travels, dear friends lit a burner on the stove. I was welcomed by Lesley Williams, the Burton family, Rob Smith, James Hill, Carol Guedalia, Alan and Maxine Stern, Renée Schwalberg and John Anton, and John and Glenda Wertheimer. In Princeton, Maribel Dietz reminded me that hilarity is essential to perseverance, and Gary Hewitt quietly showed me how to think an idea through. And "Garden State" lost its farcical quality once New Jersey brought me everyday people like Maureen Waller, Sumaiya Hamdani, Annie Reinhardt, Vince DiGirolamo, April Masten, Michael Joyce, Uli Scheven, Jennifer Delton, Jennifer Baszile, Ronit Arié, Sally Gordon, Barbara Gershen, Gayle Pemberton, Amy Randall, Nervous Rex, and the Revolting Masses. And so on and so on, and scooby dooby dooby. Some of our roads have diverged, but I think of these folks often. Others kept me rooted in my own history: Jeff Lowenstein; Pete D'Angelo and Sarah Moseley; Hisao, Karen, and Kate Kushi; David and Jody Kris; Evan Notman and Ana Cristina Villegas; and Andrew Lichtenstein. They understand what it means to me still to be part of this tribe. Other folks have helped make Madison feel like home: Suzanne Desan; Barbara Forrest; Laird Boswell; Florence Bernault; Joy Newmann; Colleen Dunlavy; Seth Pollack; Jenny Saffran; Nina Hasen; the queen herself, Miss Alison Mader, who saved my first paragraph from shipwreck; and the brave souls of book club #6, Mike Weiden, Tim Size, Tom Leiterman, Dick Cates, and John Frey, this work's first voluntary lay readers. The only really bad thing about college towns is that the truly irreplaceable people sometimes can't help leaving; there will always be a place at the bar and a song on the jukebox for Kat Charron and Allyson Goldin.

Academic historians are profoundly dependent on the librarians and archivists who make their work possible, and along the way I have met some of the best. The folks at the South Carolina Department of Archives and History cheerfully pulled hundreds of boxes for me and gently pointed me in important directions. I trust that Mike Kohl and others in Special Collections of the Robert Muldrow Cooper Library at Clemson University (housed in the Strom Thurmond Institute, where a larger-than-life bust of Tillman stared directly at me as I worked) will forgive my iconoclasm. I had wonderful days at Duke University's Perkins Library; the Library of Congress; the South Carolina Historical Society in Charleston; and the Southern Historical Collection at the University of North Carolina, Chapel Hill. In Edgefield, Bettis Rainsford and Carrie Clarke graciously helped a stranger find his way through their files, vaults, and attics. And at the South Caroliniana Library at the University of South Carolina in Columbia, this son of Massachusetts felt completely at home despite daily confrontations with the headstone of Preston Brooks.

There is more. Neal Basen, Rebecca Edwards, Harold Forsythe, Ted Frantz, John Giggie, James Hogue, Dolores Janiewski, Bettis Rainsford, and Isabel Vandervelde all provided me with important material drawn from their own research. My time in graduate school was made substantially less stressful by fellowships from the Mellon

Foundation and Princeton University. Grants from the Research Committee of the Graduate School of the University of Wisconsin facilitated my work; the greatest luxury these grants afforded me was a semester of research assistance from Lisa Tetrault, one of the many gifted Wisconsin graduate students to have enriched this project. At the University of North Carolina Press, Lewis Bateman has been consistently encouraging, and Paula Wald's copyediting was a thing of beauty. David Perry's gifts clearly do not stop at shucking oysters.

Even before I imagined becoming a historian, four people—Stuart Coonin, Margaret Metzger, Janet Papale, and J. D. McClatchy—set examples of unflinching honesty in writing and teaching and introduced me to literature that has helped in unexpected ways. Primo Levi's *The Periodic Table* and W. H. Auden's "The Shield of Achilles" showed me what it means to bear witness to our shared past and its long, sometimes deadly reverberations and reminded me that even these terrors can produce moments of unexpected beauty. A world rich enough to hold all these things is a world worth fighting for.

Finally, the love and encouragement of my parents, Paul and Judy; my sister, Amy; my brother, Jeff; and my grandmother, Sophia, have made all the difference.

Index